From the reviews of Tudor Ireland *(1985), the first version*

'*Tudor Ireland* is a stimulating and valuable book, and it makes an important contribution not just to sixteenth-century Irish studies but to Irish historiography in general.'

Mary O'Dowd, Irish Literary Supplement

'The first comprehensive survey of the period since Bagwell's three-volume work a century ago, it is an impressive achievement and should enjoy a long life as one of the standard guides to the Tudor period in Ireland.'

Art Cosgrove, Irish Independent

'All students of the history of Britain and Ireland will welcome this learned and readable synthesis of scholarship on the subject. Viewpoints apart, all will also recognise the work of a sober, industrious master. In a sense, Steven G. Ellis does for Ireland what G.R. Elton has done for Tudor England.'

M.R. Powicke, American Historical Review

'the volume is mandatory reading for anyone who seeks to understand the means by which the Tudors drew Ireland firmly into the orbit of crown government.'

Hans S. Pawlisch, Journal of Modern History

'In fine, this interesting and persuasive book well repays study by those whose interest is usually confined to this side of the Irish sea.' *Margaret Condon*, Parliamentary History

'Nothing that could facilitate investigation of Tudor Ireland has been omitted, and the result is an ideal companion and reference work.' *Karl S. Bottigheimer*, Albion

'Ellis's massive learning in a neglected but crucial area of Tudor Ireland's history is most impressive; and his informed speculation as to the likely cause of religious change . . . is a delight to read. Taken as a whole, his book is a signal achievement.'

Thomas Bartlett, Linen Hall Review, Belfast

'The ambitious scope of this study, coupled with its author's proper wish to stimulate as well as to inform, makes it inevitable that it should provoke some disagreement. . . . Yet, putting aside these regrets, we should not stint our praise and gratitude to the publisher and author for making so much so readily (and so cheaply) available.' *T.C. Barnard*, English Historical Review

'an excellent study of the impact of Tudor rule in Ireland. It will be a godsend not only for undergraduates and sixth formers, but for their teachers as well.'

A.G.R. Smith, History Today

'In elucidating these complex themes, Ellis's books must be accounted triumphant successes: meticulous narrative and analysis make them models of their kind, and careful provision of lists of officials, maps, glossary and bibliographies ensure the volumes' status as reference works.'

John Guy, Welsh History Review

'a scholarly and deeply-researched account of the way in which a sixteenth-century English province was governed, the nature of colonial life in different areas of this province, and an analysis of Anglo-Irish relations under the Tudor monarchs. . . . In *Tudor Ireland* Dr Ellis has given us two books for the price of one: a fascinating insight into a comparatively unexplored aspect of Irish history is complemented by a valuable addition to the growing body of material now available on the subject of local administration under the Tudors.' *Lydia Skinner*, International Affairs

'well written, closely argued and compellingly readable . . . The problems created by this policy are with us still, and Ellis's book, as well as being a major work in its own right, is a sombre reminder of the relevance of history to contemporary Britain.'

Roger Lockyer, Times Higher Education Supplement

LONGMAN HISTORY OF IRELAND

General Editor: Steven G. Ellis

An analytical account of Ireland from early Christian times to the present, the six volumes of this new series are being written by a team of leading historians in Ireland, Britain and America. The volumes (each substantial enough to make a significant contribution to scholarship without becoming unwieldy for the non-specialist) will tackle a common central agenda, including politics, religion, society, the economy and government. The series will be the obvious starting point for anyone – scholar, student or general reader – wanting an authoritative but accessible introduction to Irish history.

The first volumes to be published in the series are:

EARLY MEDIEVAL IRELAND 400–1200
Dáibhí Ó Cróinín

IRELAND IN THE AGE OF THE TUDORS 1447–1603
ENGLISH EXPANSION AND THE END OF GAELIC RULE
Steven G. Ellis

IRELAND IN THE AGE OF THE TUDORS 1447–1603

ENGLISH EXPANSION AND THE END OF GAELIC RULE

STEVEN G. ELLIS

LONGMAN
London and New York

Addison Wesley Longman Limited,
Edinburgh Gate,
Harlow, Essex CM20 2JE,
United Kingdom
and Associated Companies throughout the world

*Published in the United States of America
by Addison Wesley Longman Inc., New York*

Original version published in 1995 as
Tudor Ireland: Crown, Community and the Conflict of Cultures 1470–1603
© Longman Group Limited 1985

This edition,

Ireland in the Age of the Tudors: English Expansion and the End of Gaelic Rule

First published 1998

© Addison Wesley Longman Limited 1998

ISBN 0 582 01901 X
ISBN 0 582 01902 8

British Library Cataloguing-in-Publication Data

A catalogue record for this book is available from the British Library

Library of Congress Cataloging-in-Publication Data

Ellis, Steven G., 1950–
Ireland in the age of the Tudors, 1447–1603 : English expansion
and the end of Gaelic rule / Steven G. Ellis.
p.   cm. — (Longman history of Ireland)
"Extensively revised and expanded version of a book first
published in 1985 under the title Tudor Ireland"—P. viii.
Includes bibliographical references and index.
ISBN 0–582–01902–8 (csd.). — ISBN 0–582–01901–X (pbk.)
1. Ireland—History—1172–1603.   2. Great Britain—History—
Tudors, 1485–1603.   3. British—Ireland—History—16th century.
I. Ellis, Steven G., 1950– Tudor Ireland.   II. Title.
III. Series. DA935.E58 1998
941.505—dc21   98–23157
                                              CIP

Set by 35 in 10/12pt ITC Garamond Light
Produced by Addison Wesley Longman Singapore (Pte) Ltd.,
Printed in Singapore

CONTENTS

To Emrys Evans

LIST OF MAPS

LIST OF TABLES

LIST OF ABBREVIATIONS

BL   British Library, London.

Carew   *Calendar of the Carew manuscripts preserved in the archiepis-copal library at Lambeth, 1515–74* [etc.] (6 vols, London, 1867–73).

CPR   *Calendar of the patent rolls, 1232–47* [etc.] (London, 1906–).

CSPI   *Calendar of state papers relating to Ireland, 1509–73* [etc.] (24 vols, London, 1860–1912).

Fiants Ire.   'Calendar to fiants of the reign of Henry VIII . . .' [etc.] Reigns Henry VIII to Elizabeth in *Seventh* [to the *Twenty-Second*] *report of the Deputy Keeper of the Public Records in Ireland* (Dublin, 1875–90).

HBC   E.B. Fryde, D.E. Greenway, S. Porter and I. Roy (eds), *Handbook of British Chronology* (3rd edn, London, 1986).

IHS   *Irish Historical Studies*.

LP   *Letters and papers, foreign and domestic, Henry VIII* (21 vols, London, 1862–1932).

NHI   T.W. Moody, F.X. Martin and F.J. Byrne (eds), *A new history of Ireland* (10 vols, Oxford, 1976–).

New DNB The *New Dictionary of National Biography* (Oxford, forthcoming).

PRIA   *Proceedings of the Royal Irish Academy*.

PRO   Public Record Office, London.

Stat. Ire.   *The statutes at large, passed in the parliaments held in Ireland* (20 vols, Dublin, 1786–1801).

StP   *State Papers, Henry VIII* (11 vols, London, 1830–52).

PREFACE

This is an extensively revised and expanded version of a book first published in 1985 under the title *Tudor Ireland: Crown, Community and the Conflict of Cultures, 1470–1603*. *Tudor Ireland* was designed as a general survey for students, and was in fact the first general history of Tudor Ireland to appear since the publication of Richard Bagwell's massive three-volume *Ireland under the Tudors* exactly a century before. Yet it was more than just a student textbook. My purpose was to bridge the traditional divide between medieval and early modern so as to assess how much of the medieval English lordship had survived to serve as a base for the Tudor conquest. In addition, the book's focus on Ireland's changing role within the Tudor state also constituted a significant departure from traditional perspectives on the Tudor contribution to the making of modern Ireland.

Naturally, *Tudor Ireland* was also a response to problems highlighted by ten years of research and teaching on the subject. Yet these general aims also concealed a more fundamental difficulty concerning the writing of *Tudor Ireland*, which was historiographical: how to deal with the competing agendas of two different groups of historians, Irish and Tudor. In helping me to address these problems, however, my teaching commitments in a small history department in the west of Ireland were of considerable assistance: since staff numbers were so small, lecturers were expected to teach a wide range of courses; and beyond my commitment to introductory surveys, I had considerable freedom to offer different kinds of undergraduate courses in English, Irish, or 'four-nations' British history throughout the later medieval and early modern periods. In this context, too, even the ostensibly burdensome condition imposed by the so-called 1929 Act – that courses had to be offered in both English and Gaelic – proved an unexpected advantage, since the need to operate in both languages, with parallel sets of historical terminology, rapidly exposed any woolly thinking in regard to the identification of appropriate themes, terms and concepts.

When I first began work on *Tudor Ireland*, the Tudors were a much livelier field of research than now, with a vigorous debate about Sir Geoffrey Elton's theory of a 'Tudor revolution in government' and an equally important and fruitful controversy concerning the causes of the English Reformation and the advance of protestantism. Moreover, from a Tudor perspective, recent work on relations between the centre and the provinces had raised a series of questions about Ireland as a problem of government within the wider Tudor state. Unfortunately, this work was only beginning to have an impact on our understanding of Tudor Ireland. The conquest of Gaelic Ireland was indeed much the most ambitious undertaking of the Tudor regime, and its execution also offered more general insights into the nature of Tudor rule. Yet in general, Ireland's position in the Tudor state remained unexplored, and Tudor specialists evinced little interest in Irish developments, except at moments of crisis – Lambert Simnel's invasion of England, for instance, or Tyrone's rebellion – when events there had forcibly impressed themselves on the English scene.

By contrast in Ireland, although research and writing on the period remained very uneven, the sixteenth century was beginning to see a revival of interest by Irish historians after 40 years of neglect. Much the most innovative of recent writings had focused on mid-century (1534–76),[1] with some notable skirmishes (chiefly in terms of military history) into the final phase of the Tudor conquest. Yet this left the end of the Gaelic Revival and the first half-century of Tudor rule as a kind of a no man's land between the interests of medievalists and early modernists, with very unfortunate results in terms of wider perspectives. In particular, the conventional division of the Tudor age between a medieval era ending with the collapse of the Kildare ascendancy in 1534 and an early modern period beginning with the inauguration of 'direct rule' had the effect of partitioning the subject between two different historical fields. The Kildare ascendancy was portrayed as the culmination of inherent forces for decline in the medieval lordship while, with hindsight, it had seemed to early modernists that the evident shortcomings of 'aristocratic delegation' prompted Henry VIII in 1534 to impose 'direct rule' and to begin the task of the Tudor conquest. In reality, as closer attention to the evidence suggests, changes in the balance of power between *Gaedhil* (natives) and *Gaill* (settlers) were precisely the reverse of those suggested: early Tudor Ireland witnessed a period of expansion and consolidation of English power and influence, followed by a period of internal weakness and political instability which Gaelic chiefs were quick to exploit.

From a Tudor perspective, a more fundamental difficulty with research and writing which approached sixteenth-century Ireland as part of the making of modern Ireland was its relative neglect of this very Tudor context which made Irish developments most meaningful to contemporaries. For instance, the reasons both for Henry VIII's appointment as governor of Ireland of a leading courtier like the earl of Surrey and, later on, for his recall had far more to do with Tudor court politics and European diplomacy than with developments in Ireland. Moreover, the preoccupation with these 'vertical', Hibernocentric perspectives, to the neglect of other contexts of explanation, led to the development

---

1. I am thinking here in particular of Dr Brendan Bradshaw's two important books focusing on Henry VIII and Ireland (Bradshaw 1974; Bradshaw 1979a) and Professor Nicholas Canny's seminal study of the origins of the Elizabeth conquest (Canny 1976).

of concepts and terminology which were distinctly unhelpful in regard to Ireland's position in the wider Tudor state. Prompted by the wish to study Ireland's medieval settlers as Irishmen in the making, the decision to describe as 'Anglo-Irish separatists' those who saw themselves as 'loyal English lieges' actually amounted to a denial of this Tudor context and of their national identity.

The same can be said about the appropriation of the terms 'nation' and 'national' for the embryonic Irish nation (in the modern sense), at the expense of the two nations of medieval Ireland. Similarly, the coining of the term 'gaelicization', with reference to the phenomenon which contemporary English officials described more generally as 'degeneracy', not only particularized to Ireland what was actually a commonplace of medieval frontier societies but also implied, quite wrongly, that Ireland's settler population (the *Gaill*) were in the process of being accepted as *Gaedhil*. Thus, these various new usages obscured important developments concerning changing Gaelic and English senses of identity and hindered comparisons both with Scottish Gaeldom and also with the political communities of other English provinces, such as the Tudor north or Wales. They meant that Tudor Ireland's frontier character as an outlying province of the Tudor state, and also Gaelic Ireland's position in the wider Gaelic world, were hardly appreciated.

In the circumstances, I felt, when writing *Tudor Ireland*, that the most urgent need was for a survey of Ireland's changing relationship with the wider Tudor state. Indeed, the book amounted to a fairly radical departure from traditional perspectives on Tudor Ireland, both in its identification of new themes and approaches, and even in its restoration of the normal political vocabulary as used by contemporaries and Tudor historians. Substantial portions of it also had to be based on original research. Of course, *Tudor Ireland* had much to say too about the more familiar agenda: ironically, it actually offered a more vigorous critique of Tudor rule from this perspective than conventional accounts in which the power of the Tudor state and conquest and colonization were seen as axiomatic. In the event, *Tudor Ireland* was very well received and immediately established itself as 'the best textbook on its subject'.[2] In terms of Tudor historiography, its wider conclusions about the Tudor state were quickly incorporated into general Tudor surveys. And since then, the appearance of major studies which developed *Tudor Ireland*'s perspectives in respect of different aspects of sixteenth-century Ireland has meant that it is no longer possible for Tudor specialists to write Tudor history as if Ireland were an occasional concern on the margins of the Tudor state.

The importance of *Tudor Ireland* was widely recognized by Irish specialists too: it was even regarded as marking 'a milestone' in the development of the subject. Yet any account of the book's impact on Irish historiography would need to mention the Revisionist Controversy since, in Ireland, the book's departures from the established canon of Irish history inevitably marked it out as a work of 'revisionism'. While *Tudor Ireland* was praised even by its critics for

2. Barnard 1988, p. 486.

its attempt 'to supply a fundamental lack' by providing 'for the first time . . . a conceptual framework for the history of Tudor Ireland', its central thesis that Ireland was transformed 'from a mere borderland region dividing two wider political entities . . . to an integral political entity in its own right' was unacceptable to those Irish historians who 'locate themselves within a nationalist historiographical tradition'.[3]

Revisionism is not of course peculiar to Ireland. Yet as the editors of a recent volume about the subject comment, 'a characteristic of Irish "revisionism"' is that 'the controversy . . . is intensely parochial', and that 'contributions to the debate on both sides have taken place mainly among the Irish themselves', who are 'at one in seeing Irish history as *our* history'.[4] Since the campaign for nationalist orthodoxy was conducted chiefly before invited audiences in summer schools, and the charges were generalized, it was often hard to be sure of the intended target.[5] Nonetheless, *Tudor Ireland* was denounced 'for emptying the evidence of its traumatic content', and for failing to capture the 'catastrophic dimension' of the Irish historical experience.[6] Less surprisingly perhaps, its restoration of Tudor terminological conventions was also disputed.[7] In the circumstances, criticisms of this sort are very understandable: given Ireland's divided present, with two states, each with its separate traditions and popular perceptions of the past, it is scarcely surprising that 'the making of modern Ireland' should also be heavily contested. I would argue, however, that Tudor Ireland is not simply *their* history, and that an English province which was ostensibly run by Englishmen in accordance with English law, political culture and administrative practices has to have a history which is intelligible in an English context. Linguistically too, the same point applies. English was the language of the conqueror, and choice of language carries a penalty: no amount of revising terminology will make the native response to English expansion more intelligible in English than in Gaelic.

The historian who attempts a general survey of Tudor Ireland must necessarily lean heavily on the specialized work of others. The notes and bibliography indicate the extent of my indebtedness to the many scholars whose researches and reflections have deepened our knowledge of the subject; but some more personal obligations require particular acknowledgement here. In preparing the original *Tudor Ireland*, my understanding of political change after 1547 was considerably influenced by the work of Dr Ciarán Brady, who most generously allowed me to consult his outstanding doctoral thesis, since revised and published as *The Chief Governors*. My knowledge of the whole period also benefited greatly from innumerable discussions with Professor

3. Bradshaw 1986, pp. 564–5.
4. Boyce and O'Day 1996, p. 5.
5. I take it, for instance, that *Tudor Ireland* failed to answer the need for the 'kind of history-writing which sustains, energises and bonds a nation', and was accordingly relegated to that category of 'the nationally useless and undermining histories or pseudo-histories of Ireland written by Englishmen': Fennell 1994, p. 187.
6. Bradshaw 1994a, pp. 27–41 (quotation, p. 36); Bradshaw 1994b, pp. 201–3.
7. Bradshaw 1994b, pp. 191–7; Cosgrove 1990–1, pp. 97–111.

Nicholas Canny, while Professor David Quinn kindly allowed me to see his chapters in the *New History of Ireland* vol. 2 in advance of publication. Dr Brendan Bradshaw and Professor A.G.R. Smith very kindly read most of the original book in typescript and made many useful suggestions for improving it, and I am also grateful to Dr Henry Jefferies for reading and commenting on Chapters 8–10 of the new version.

Much more so than monographs, general surveys are synopses of research. They reflect the state of historical knowledge at a particular point in time, and any attempt at a partial revision and updating is a risky undertaking. The appearance since 1985 of an impressive amount of new research, particularly on the later sixteenth century, has inevitably rendered some of *Tudor Ireland*'s more detailed comments less reliable. On the whole, however, I do not think that recent writings on the period – important as they are! – have undermined the book's general arguments or its wider perspectives. Thus the decision of the publishers to commission a six-volume series on Irish history along the lines of *Tudor Ireland* has provided an opportunity both to update the book and also to expand the coverage of certain aspects of Irish history which received rather short shrift in the original book. In particular, I have tried in this new version to offer a fuller account of the late medieval Gaelic world and of the impact of the Tudor conquest on Irish senses of identity. The book's extended chronological coverage, with an additional chapter on the 1447–71 period, reflects my own continuing researches about the end of the Gaelic Revival and the nature of the English recovery. And the decision to split the chapter on religious reform into two chapters focusing on the state of the pre-Reformation church and the progress of the Tudor Reformation was prompted by the need for a fuller discussion of the important work which has recently appeared on religious history. In addition, I have included an extended conclusion with some more general remarks about the Tudor contribution to the making of modern Ireland. Finally, minor changes and revisions have been made in all the other chapters in order to update the book; the book's format, with new subtitles and footnotes, has been recast to make it easier for students to use; and both the Guide to Further Reading and the Bibliography have been entirely rewritten to take account of more recent scholarship.

Steven G. Ellis,
Christmas 1997.

ACKNOWLEDGEMENTS

We are grateful to the editors of *A New History of Ireland* for permission to reproduce tables from *A New History of Ireland*, IX, pp. 478–87 and 601–4 (OUP, 1984).

NOTE ON COINAGE

From 1460, a separate coinage for Ireland circulated there alongside sterling, and I have distinguished between pounds sterling (£) and pounds Irish (IR£): IR£1 was generally worth two-thirds of a pound sterling.

EDITOR'S FOREWORD

In recent years there has been a growing international interest in Irish history. This is reflected in a marked increase in the numbers of scholars and students from outside the island who are engaged in research and study of the subject. *The Longman History of Ireland* is a series of six volumes, written by leading historians of Ireland, which has been devised specifically with this wider audience in mind. Intended primarily for university students of history, it covers Ireland from early Christian times to the present, but it assumes no previous knowledge of Irish history. The aim is to bridge the existing gap between the brief interpretative survey and the weighty collaborative volume which is beyond the pocket of the average student. The series will provide students and teachers alike with a substantial grounding in the subject, an overall interpretation of the period covered, and an assessment of the latest historiographical developments.

There is a further reason for commissioning a new series on Irish history at this time. This relates both to contemporary politics in Ireland and to parallel developments in Irish and British historiography. Inevitably, the growing interest in Irish history reflects in part contemporary concern at the continuing violence in Ireland and the attention which it receives in the news media. The present conflict has a highly developed historical dimension to it which invites the historian's attention, but the writing of history during and about an extended period of civil conflict also presents fundamental difficulties. It is not too much to say that the exceptional circumstances in which the history of Ireland is presently written constitute one of its most salient characteristics and, until very recently, one of the least remarked.

Few countries present the historian with the kind of interpretative challenge offered by Ireland. Its general outlines are of course comparatively familiar – the need to assess the impact of successive waves of colonization; to analyse the endemic unrest, religious strife, and political instability, exemplified in recent times by the partition of the island between rival states; and to evaluate the process of interaction and conflict since the middle ages between two peoples and two cultures, Gaelic and English. In this regard, the principal difficulty lies not so much in recovering and analysing the concerns and values of past societies – though that task presents problems enough! – but in explaining the relationship between the past and competing versions of the present. The polarization of political opinion means that there is at present comparatively little shared historical sense of community between the island's different traditions. These differences have indeed become institutionalized because, like modern states everywhere, the Republic of Ireland and Northern Ireland, through their respective officials and governmental structures, have attempted to invoke history in order to vindicate contemporary aspirations and values and to promote a unifying sense of national identity among their respective peoples. Overall, therefore, the historiographical difficulties attending the writing of Irish history are such as to raise the intrinsic interest of the subject well above the level which might be suggested by Ireland's geographically marginal position on the world stage.

In view of Ireland's contested history, it is surprising that its historiography is not a subject which has attracted much attention among its professional historians – beyond a desire to debunk popular myths. In the last twenty years, however, our understanding of the subject has been advanced considerably by two related developments. The first is the debate among Irish historians about the character of what is called Historical Revisionism. The other concerns the implications for Ireland of the new British history – the attempt to conceive of the development of the United Kingdom in explicitly multi-national terms. In both cases, the result has been to make historians more conscious in their writings of the differing contexts of explanation and also to revise our understanding of the relationship between nation and state in Ireland.

A particular feature of the present series is the attempt to face up more squarely to this historiographical challenge and to make the subject more intelligible to the non-specialist. This does not mean a uniformity of approach. In fact, the authors of individual volumes in the series come from widely differing backgrounds and bring very different sets of assumptions to their work. Each volume, however, pays particular attention, as appropriate, to these historiographical developments. And the series also attempts to ensure that aspects of Ireland's geography, administrative institutions and historical terminology, which might be unfamiliar to outsiders, are properly explained. In addition to the main chapters of narrative and analysis, each volume includes a chronological framework of events, an extensive glossary of technical terms, a number of maps or illustrations, tables of officials and institutions, a critical guide to further reading, an extensive bibliography, and a full index. It is hoped that these aids may also prove useful to those more familiar with the subject.

Steven G. Ellis

FRAMEWORK OF EVENTS

1447 Richard, duke of York, appointed lieutenant (9 Dec).

1448 Richard Nugent, Lord Delvin replaces Richard Talbot, archbishop of Dublin, as deputy-lieutenant.

1449 Succession dispute in east Breffny, following the death of the chief, Owen O'Reilly (17 Mar). Death of Alexander, 3rd lord of the Isles. Richard, duke of York, lands at Howth (6 July). Ulster chiefs submit to York at Drogheda (Aug). Great council at Dublin (17 Oct). Surrender of Rouen, capital of English Normandy (29 Oct).

1450 Parliament at Drogheda passes act of Resumption (24 Apr). Scutage levied for war against Mageoghegan (May). Surrender of Caen, Normandy; and Cade's revolt in England (June–July). Departure of York, leaving Ormond as deputy-lieutenant (late Aug).

1451 Subsidy granted by parliament at Drogheda (26 Mar).

1452 Military progress by Ormond from Co. Limerick through the midlands into Ulster. Captures Owney and Lea castles (spring and summer). Death of 4th earl of Ormond at Ardee (23 Aug); succession of his son, James, 2nd earl of Wiltshire, as earl. Sir Edward FitzEustace appointed deputy-lieutenant.

1453 James, 5th earl of Ormond, appointed lieutenant (12 May), with John Mey, archbishop of Armagh, as his deputy. Battle of Castillon, Gascony, and death of John Talbot, 1st earl of Waterford (17 July). Dispute between Butlers and Geraldines over the Kildare inheritance.

1454 Richard, duke of York, appointed protector of England (27 Mar); confirmed as lieutenant of Ireland (Apr). Thomas Fitzmaurice recognized as 7th earl of Kildare (by July). Death of Edward FitzEustace (25 Oct); Kildare elected justiciar by council.

1455 Earl of Kildare appointed deputy-lieutenant. Battle of St Albans (22 May). Henry O'Neill succeeds his father, Owen, as chief of Tyrone (c. 1 July). Butler raids on Co. Wexford. Parliament at Dublin (17 Oct); address to Henry VI and York.

1457 Richard, duke of York, reappointed lieutenant (6 Mar) for ten years as from 8 Dec.

1

1459   Earl of Kildare defeats and captures O'Connor Faly. Rout of Ludlow (12 Oct); York flees to Ireland, and is attainted by the Coventry parliament (20 Nov). Ormond reappointed lieutenant (4 Dec), and appoints Sir Thomas Bathe and John Bole, archbishop of Armagh, as his deputies.

1460   Parliament at Drogheda (8 Feb, adjourned to Dublin, 23 Feb); confirms York as lieutenant; declaration that Ireland is 'corporate of itself'; acts of Resumption and for separate Irish coinage. Battle of Northampton (10 July). York departs for court (early Sept), leaving Kildare as his deputy. York killed at battle of Wakefield (30 Dec).

1461   Accession of Edward IV (4 Mar). Yorkist victory at Towton (29 Mar); Ormond executed.

1462   George, duke of Clarence, appointed lieutenant (28 Feb), with Roland FitzEustace, promoted Lord Portlester, as his deputy (16 May). Lancastrian risings in the midlands and Meath. Sir John Butler, 'earl of Ormond', captures Waterford for Henry VI. Battle of Pilltown. Treaty of Ardtornish: alliance between Edward IV, John, 4th lord of the Isles, and James, exiled earl of Douglas.

1463   Thomas Fitzgerald succeeds his father, James, as 8th earl of Desmond, and is appointed deputy-lieutenant (1 Apr). Desmond suppresses further Lancastrian risings (summer); Sir John Butler flees to Portugal. Parliament at Wexford (4 Nov), adjourned to Waterford, Naas and Dublin.

1464   Dispute concerning conflicting appointments of Kildare and John Tiptoft, earl of Worcester, as chancellor (Jan). Feud between Desmond and William Sherwood, bishop of Meath, composed at court; Kildare acting deputy (summer). O'Donnell and Burke of Clanrickard visit Dublin.

1466   Desmond captured by O'Connor Faly; rescued by the English of Dublin. O'Brien raids across the Shannon.

1467   Worcester arrives with 700 English archers as deputy-lieutenant (Oct).

1468   Attainder of earls of Desmond and Kildare, and Edward Plunket by parliament at Drogheda (4 Feb); Desmond executed. Widespread Gaelic raids and disturbances among the Englishry. Kildare's attainder reversed.

1469   Renewed fighting among the Yorkists in England.

1470   Clarence dismissed as lieutenant and replaced by Worcester (23 Mar), who is recalled; appoints Sir Edmund Dudley as deputy-lieutenant. Edward IV flees; 'readeption' of Henry VI (3 Oct). Execution of Worcester (18 Oct). Parliament at Dublin (26 Nov), held by Kildare as justiciar of Edward IV. Sir John Butler recognized as earl of Ormond by Henry VI.

1471   Restoration of Edward IV (14 Apr). Earl of Kildare reappointed deputy-lieutenant (Dec).

1474   Brotherhood of Arms of St George founded (18 Mar). Sir Gilbert Debenham appointed chancellor (5 Aug) with retinue of 400 archers.

1475   Bishop Sherwood of Meath appointed deputy-lieutenant (a. 18 Apr). Restoration of 6th earl of Ormond (21 July).

1478　Execution of George, duke of Clarence (18 Feb). Death of 7th earl of Kildare (25 Mar). Altercation between 8th earl of Kildare and Henry, lord Grey concerning the governorship and parliament.

1479　Settlement between Edward IV and earl of Kildare (appointed deputy-lieutenant, *a.* 5 Oct); Ordinances for the Government of Ireland.

1480　Con O'Neill marries Eleanor, sister of earl of Kildare.

1482　Death of Bishop Sherwood of Meath (3 Dec).

1483　Parliament at Limerick (7 Feb). Accession of Edward V (9 Apr). Usurpation of Richard III (25 June).

1484　Mission of Bishop Barrett of Annaghdown from Richard III to Old English lords.

1485　Invasion and accession of Henry VII who defeats Richard III at Bosworth (22 Aug).

1487　Earl of Lincoln with 2,000 mercenaries lands in Ireland (5 May). Lambert Simnel crowned 'King Edward VI' in Christ Church, Dublin (24 May). Edward VI's Yorkist army lands near Furness and is defeated by Henry VII at Stoke (16 June).

1488　Mission of Sir Richard Edgecombe (May–July); pardon of Old English Yorkists (25 May).

1490　Lord Deputy Kildare summoned to court (29 July).

1491　Perkin Warbeck lands at Cork (Nov), posing as Richard IV (Edward IV's son). Sir James Ormond and Thomas Garth appointed with 200 men to govern Cos. Kilkenny and Tipperary (6 Dec).

1492　Earl of Kildare superseded (20 May) by Archbishop FitzSimons of Dublin as deputy-lieutenant and Sir James Ormond as governor. Fighting between Butler and Fitzgerald retainers in Dublin.

1493　Mission of Sir Roger Cotton with 188 archers (Mar). Conditional pardon for treason of earl of Kildare (30 Mar). Parliamentary act of resumption passed in Dublin (28 June). General summons of Old English lords to court (Sept).

1494　Agreement between Henry VII and earl of Kildare (14 May). Pardon of Old English Yorkists (26 Aug). Sir Edward Poynings appointed deputy-lieutenant with army of 653 men; arrives with earl of Kildare and Sir James Ormond (13 Oct). Poynings' parliament meeting at Drogheda passes Poynings' Law (1 Dec) and an act of resumption.

1495　Earl of Kildare arrested in Dublin (27 Feb) and sent to England (5 Mar). Siege of Carlow castle (Mar–July). Reform of Irish finances under William Hattecliffe, appointed undertreasurer (26 Apr). Perkin Warbeck unsuccessfully besieges Waterford (23 July–3 Aug).

1496　Bishop Deane of Bangor succeeds Poynings as justiciar (1 Jan); disbandment of royal army. Sir James Fitzgerald submits (early July). Earl of Kildare marries Elizabeth St John and reappointed deputy-lieutenant (6 Aug).

1497　Sir James Ormond killed by Piers Butler of Polestown (17 July). Perkin Warbeck lands at Cork (26 July); lands in Cornwall with Irish Yorkists (7 Sept).

3

1499 Lord Deputy Kildare captures four castles during campaign in Connaught. Perkin Warbeck executed (23 Nov).
1500 Cork city charter renewed.
1503 Lord Deputy Kildare visits court (May–Aug); his son and heir, Lord Offaly, marries Elizabeth Zouche and returns to Ireland (Aug).
1504 Royal forces defeat Clanrickard and O'Brien in the battle of Knockdoe (19 Aug); Order of the Garter conferred on Lord Deputy Kildare.
1506 Projected Irish expedition by Henry VII with 6,000 men.
1509 Accession of Henry VIII (21 Apr).
1510 Lord Deputy Kildare campaigns in Munster and destroys O'Brien's Bridge.
1513 Death of Lord Deputy Kildare at Athy (3 Sept); succeeded by his son, the 9th earl, appointed deputy (26 Nov).
1515 Lord Deputy Kildare visits court (May–Sept). Death of 7th earl of Ormond (3 Aug); succession disputed between earl's cousin, Sir Piers Butler of Polestown, and his daughters.
1516 Piers Butler recognized in Ireland as 8th earl of Ormond.
1519 Lord Deputy Kildare summoned to court (departs c. Oct).
1520 Thomas Howard, earl of Surrey, arrives as lieutenant (23 May) with 500 men.
1521 Surrey's parliament opens in Dublin (4 June). Surrey visits court for consultations (Dec–Mar 1522).
1522 Earl of Ormond appointed deputy on Surrey's final departure (26 Mar).
1523 Earl of Kildare returns to Ireland (1 Jan). Earl of Desmond's French intrigues ratified in convention with Francis I (20 June).
1524 Visit of royal commissioners to compose differences between Kildare and Ormond (June–Aug). Agreement concerning imposition of coign and livery (July). Earl of Kildare sworn deputy (4 Aug).
1525 MacMurrough Kavanagh surrenders Arklow to earl of Ormond (18 Aug).
1526 Lord Deputy Kildare summoned to court (departs Dec).
1527 Earl of Desmond besieged by Lord James Butler in Dungarvan, escapes to Youghal (4 Dec); bill of attainder prepared against him.
1528 Indenture (18 Feb) between Henry VIII, Piers Butler (8th earl of Ormond) and heirs general of 7th earl of Ormond: Butler created earl of Ossory (23 Feb); Thomas Boleyn, Viscount Rochford, created earl of Ormond. Vice-deputy Delvin captured by O'Connor Faly (12 May). Earl of Ossory appointed deputy (4 Aug). Earl of Desmond requests munitions and defensive alliance with Charles V (11 Nov).
1529 Charles V's chaplain lands in Ireland to negotiate with Desmond (24 Feb). Archbishop Alen of Dublin appointed by Wolsey as vice-legate for Ireland (1 June). 'Secret council' of three officials appointed deputy-lieutenant (4 Aug) to Henry Fitzroy, duke of Richmond and Somerset (appointed titular lieutenant, 22 June). Arrival of royal commissioner, Sir William Skeffington (24 Aug).
1530 Skeffington returns to Ireland as deputy-lieutenant (appointed 22 June) with earl of Kildare.

1531   Submission of O'Donnell to Skeffington at Drogheda (6 May). Skeffington's parliament meets at Dublin (15 Sept).

1532   Earl of Kildare visits court, reappointed deputy-lieutenant (5 July). Marriage of Lord James Butler to Joan, earl of Desmond's daughter. Lord Deputy Kildare wounded by gunshot at siege of Birr castle (*c*. Dec).

1533   Charles V's agent in Ireland to treat with earl of Desmond (June–July). Lord Deputy Kildare summoned to court (*c*. Sept).

1534   Lord Deputy Kildare appoints his son, Thomas, Lord Offaly, as vice-deputy and leaves for court (Feb). Offaly ('Silken Thomas') resigns and repudiates allegiance to Henry VIII (11 June). Kildare arrested and imprisoned in the Tower (29 June). Archbishop Alen killed by Offaly's supporters (28 July). Kildare dies in the Tower (2 Sept). Offaly (10th earl of Kildare) besieges Dublin (Aug–4 Oct). Arrival of Lord Deputy Skeffington (appointed 30 July) with relief army (24 Oct). Parliament at Westminster attaints earl of Kildare and his supporters (*c*. 18 Dec). Truce between Kildare rebels and royal forces (19 Dec–6 Jan 1535). *Ordinances for the Government of Ireland*. Separate debased Irish coinage struck in London.

1535   Siege and capture of Maynooth castle (18–23 Mar). Kildare's envoy in Rome (May) and Spain (June) soliciting aid. Royal commission to suppress nunnery at Graney, Co. Kildare (9 June). Lord Leonard Grey arrives as marshal of the army (28 July). Kildare surrenders (Aug) and is taken to court by Grey. Lord Deputy Skeffington dies (31 Dec).

1536   Grey elected justiciar (1 Jan), appointed deputy-lieutenant (23 Feb). Arrest and removal to England of Kildare's five uncles (Feb). George Browne consecrated archbishop of Dublin at Lambeth (19 Mar). Irish Reformation Parliament meets at Dublin (1st session, 1–31 May); acts attainting Kildare and his supporters, against absentees, and passing English reform legislation. Westminster parliament attaints Kildare's uncles (18 July). Lord Deputy Grey demolishes O'Brien's Bridge (6 Aug).

1537   Kildare and his uncles executed at Tyburn (3 Feb). Visit of four royal commissioners to inquire into state of Ireland (8 Sept–Apr 1538). Last session of Irish Reformation Parliament (13 Oct–20 Dec).

1538   Earl of Ossory restored to earldom of Ormond (22 Feb). Archbishop Browne issues 'Form of the Beads' (*c*. May).

1539   Commission to Lord Chancellor Alen, Archbishop Browne *et al.* to receive surrenders of monasteries (7 Apr). 8th earl of Ormond (and 1st earl of Ossory) dies (26 Aug). Lord Deputy Grey defeats O'Neill and O'Donnell at Bellahoe (Aug).

1540   10th earl of Kildare's fugitive half-brother, Gerald Fitzgerald, escapes to France (Mar). Lord Deputy Grey sails for court (*c*. 1 May). Commission to survey rents and revenues of dissolved religious houses (20 May). Sir Anthony St Leger sworn deputy (*c*. 12 Aug).

1541   Submission of earl of Desmond to St Leger at Cahir (16 Jan). MacGillapatrick created Lord Fitzpatrick of Upper Ossory (11 June) by 'surrender and regrant'. St Leger's Parliament meets at Dublin (13

June–20/23 July); act declaring Henry VIII king of Ireland (18 June). Lord Leonard Grey executed on Tower Hill (28 June). Submission of O'Neill to St Leger at Dundalk (28 Dec).

1542 First Jesuit mission to Ireland (Feb–Mar). O'Neill created earl of Tyrone at Greenwich (1 Oct).

1543 Clanrickard Burke created earl of Clanrickard; O'Brien created earl of Thomond (July). Agreement of O'Neill and O'Donnell before council in Dublin (14 July).

1544 Irish contingent serves in royal army at siege of Boulogne (19 July–14 Sept).

1545 Royal army with Irish contingent defeated by Scots near Jedburgh (27 Feb). Levy of troops under earl of Ormond's command (appointed 5 Sept) for service against Scots.

1546 Lord Justice Brabazon campaigns in Offaly and fortifies Dangan (Fort Governor).

1547 Accession of Edward VI (28 Jan). Arrival with reinforcements of Sir Edward Bellingham as military commander (June).

1548 Order for coining groats in Dublin castle (10 Feb). Bellingham sworn deputy (21 May). Fort Protector established in Leix (May–June). Submission of O'Connor and O'More; sent to England (c. Dec).

1549 Leighlinbridge, Co. Carlow, garrisoned (c. Jan). Order for enforcement of First Book of Common Prayer in Ireland (9 June). Departure of Lord Deputy Bellingham (16 Dec).

1550 French envoys in Ireland conclude treaties with O'Neill, O'Donnell and O'Doherty (Feb). Grant to Humphrey Powell to establish a press in Ireland. Instructions to Lord Deputy St Leger (sworn 10 Sept) for resumption, survey and leasing of Leix-Offaly (July).

1551 Mission of Sir James Croft to survey and fortify Munster ports (Feb–May). Croft sworn deputy (23 May). First Book of Common Prayer printed in Dublin (first book printed in Ireland).

1552 Hugh Goodacre nominated archbishop of Armagh; John Bale nominated bishop of Ossory (Oct). Departure of Lord Deputy Croft (4 Dec).

1553 Death of Edward VI (6 July). Proclamation in Ireland of Lady Jane Grey as queen (27 July). Proclamation in Ireland of Mary I (20 Aug).

1554 Commission to Archbishop Dowdall *et al.* to deprive married clergy (14 Apr). Gerald Fitzgerald created 11th earl of Kildare (13 May).

1555 Hugh Curwin consecrated archbishop of Dublin (Archbishop Browne deprived, 1554) in St Paul's, London (8 Sept).

1556 Sir Henry Sidney appointed undertreasurer (13 Apr). Thomas Radcliffe, Lord Fitzwalter (earl of Sussex from 17 Feb 1557) sworn deputy (26 May).

1557 Sussex's first parliament meets in Dublin (1 June–2 July); acts for settlement of Leix-Offaly, to establish Queen's and King's Counties, and repealing Henrician and Edwardian ecclesiastical reform statutes.

1558 Priory of St John of Jerusalem, Kilmainham, restored (8 Mar; dissolved again 3 June 1559). Expedition by Sussex to western isles of Scotland

(15 Sept–8 Nov). Accession of Elizabeth I (17 Nov). Matthew, Lord Dungannon killed by Shane O'Neill's procurement.

1559 Calvagh O'Donnell captured by Shane O'Neill (14 May). 1st earl of Tyrone dies (*a.* 17 July).

1560 Sussex's second parliament meets in Dublin (11/12 Jan–1 Feb); acts of supremacy and uniformity.

1561 Sussex (appointed lieutenant 6 May 1560) campaigns against O'Neill (June–July); Armagh cathedral garrisoned. Expedition by Sussex to Lough Foyle (Sept).

1562 O'Neill submits to Elizabeth I at Whitehall (6 Jan); returns home (late May). Complaints about Sussex's administration presented to privy council by law students from Ireland (Mar). Brian, Lord Dungannon killed by Turlough Luineach O'Neill (12 Apr). Earls of Ormond and Desmond at court for arbitration (Apr–July). Order for establishment of Court of Castle Chamber (3 July).

1563 Sussex campaigns against Shane O'Neill (Apr). Commission to administer supremacy oath to all ecclesiastics and officials (18 May).

1564 Rising of O'Connors and O'Mores in Leix-Offaly (Feb). Final departure of Lord Lieutenant Sussex (25 May). Order to establish Court of High Commission (6 Oct).

1565 Desmond captured by Ormond at battle of Affane, Co. Waterford (*c.* 8 Feb); both earls summoned to court. O'Neill defeats MacDonalds at Glenshesk, Co. Antrim (2 May); Sorley Boy captured. MacCarthy More created earl of Clancare (24 June). Sir Henry Sidney appointed deputy (13 Oct).

1566 O'Neill requests military assistance from Charles IX of France (25 Apr); negotiates with earl of Argyll and releases Sorley Boy (*c.* June); burns Armagh cathedral (Aug). Col. Edward Randolph's force sails from Bristol for Lough Foyle (6 Sept). Sidney campaigns in Ulster (17 Sept–12 Nov); reaches Derry (12 Oct). Calvagh O'Donnell dies (26 Oct). Randolph killed (Nov).

1567 Sidney arrests Desmond (10 Feb); sent to London (Dec). Garrison at Derry withdraws to Carrickfergus (21 Apr). O'Donnell defeats O'Neill at Farsetmore (8 May). O'Neill killed by MacDonalds (2 June). Bishops' translation of New Testament into Gaelic under way.

1568 James Fitzmaurice, captain of Desmond Fitzgeralds, attacks Lord Lixnaw (1 July). Decree in favour of Sir Peter Carew concerning Idrone barony, Co. Carlow (7 Dec).

1569 Sidney's parliament meets in Dublin (12 Jan–1 Feb); attainder of Shane O'Neill (11 Mar). Earl of Clancare, James Fitzmaurice *et al.* decide to send envoys to Philip II (*c.* Feb). John Hooker licensed to print Irish statutes (20 Mar). Appeal of Irish Catholics presented by Maurice Fitzgibbon (titular bishop of Cashel) to Philip II (*c.* Apr). Sir Edward Fitton appointed president of Connaught (1 June). Fitzmaurice attacks Sir Warham St Leger in Kerrycurrihy (16 June). Sir Edmund Butler attacks Idrone (June). Sidney campaigns in south Leinster and Munster

(July–Sept). Turlough Luineach O'Neill marries Lady Agnes Campbell (*c.* Sept). Humphrey Gilbert appointed colonel of Munster (*c.* Oct). Edmund Campion in Dublin.

1570 Sir Edmund and Piers Butler submit to Lord Deputy Sidney (28 Feb). Earl of Thomond rebels (Feb); proclaimed traitor (June); sails for France; surrenders to Elizabeth (Dec). Sir John Perrot appointed president of Munster (13 Dec).

1571 John Kearney's *Aibidil Gaoidhilge & Caiticiosma* ['Gaelic alphabet and catechism'] published in Dublin: first book in Gaelic printed in Ireland (June). Annaly shired as Co. Longford.

1572 Earl of Clanrickard arrested by Lord President Fitton and sent to Dublin (Mar). Fitton campaigns against Clanrickard's sons (May). Thomas Smith, jun. lands with *c.* 100 colonists at Strangford Lough (31 Aug).

1573 Fitzmaurice submits to Lord President Perrot at Kilmallock (23 Feb). Return of earl of Desmond; rearrested and imprisoned in Dublin (25 Mar). Sorley Boy MacDonald denizized (14 Apr). Departure of Perrot (July). Walter Devereux, earl of Essex, arrives at Carrickfergus to plant Antrim (Aug). Smith killed in the Ards (18 Oct). Desmond escapes from Dublin castle (*c.* 11 Nov).

1574 Desmond submits to Lord Deputy Fitzwilliam (2 Sept). Brian MacPhelim O'Neill of Clandeboye submits, summoned by Essex to Belfast, arrested, executed in Dublin (Nov).

1575 James Fitzmaurice sails for France (Mar). Turlough Luineach submits to Essex (27 June). Rathlin Island massacre (26 July). Sidney reappointed deputy (5 Aug).

1576 Lord Deputy Sidney's progress through Connaught; province shired as Cos. Galway, Mayo, Roscommon, Sligo (Apr). Sir William Drury appointed president of Munster (20 June). Earl of Clanrickard's sons attack Athenry (June). Capt. Nicholas Malby appointed military governor of Connaught (23 July; president, 31 Mar 1579). Clanrickard arrested (Aug). Essex dies in Dublin (22 Sept).

1577 Renewed complaints by Palesmen against cess (11 Jan).

1578 Thomas Stukeley leaves Italy to join James Fitzmaurice (3 Feb); massacre at Mullaghmast, Co. Kildare (Mar); Stukeley arrives Lisbon (*c.* mid Apr), killed at battle of Alcazar in Morocco (4 Aug). Final departure of Lord Deputy Sidney (12 Sept).

1579 Fitzmaurice and Nicholas Sander, papal legate, land near Dingle, Co. Kerry (18 July); fortify Smerwick. Sir Humphrey Gilbert commissioned to attack Fitzmaurice (24 July). Desmond's brothers kill Henry Davells (1 Aug). Fitzmaurice killed in skirmish (18 Aug). O'Reilly's country shired as Co. Cavan (21 Aug). Desmond proclaimed traitor (2 Nov). Ormond campaigns against rebels in Munster (Dec).

1580 Admiral Sir William Winter appointed to cruise off Munster coast (*c.* 17 Mar). Rising of Viscount Baltinglass and Feagh MacHugh O'Byrne in Leinster (July). O'Byrne defeats Lord Grey (deputy elect, appointed

12 Aug) in Glenmalure (25 Aug). Bastiano San Giuseppi's force lands at Smerwick (12–13 Sept). Massacre at Smerwick (10 Nov).

1581   Rising of Kavanaghs, O'Connors and O'Mores (*c.* Mar). Sander dies (*c.* Apr). Baltinglass leaves for Spain (Nov).

1582   Execution for treason of Nicholas Nugent, formerly Chief Justice of Common Pleas (6 Apr).

1583   Desmond killed near Tralee (11 Nov).

1584   Sir John Perrot appointed deputy (7 Jan). Richard Bingham appointed president of Connaught (Mar). Commission to Sir Valentine Browne *et al.* to survey rebels' lands in Munster (19 June). John Norris appointed president of Munster (24 June). Perrot campaigns against Antrim MacDonalds (Aug–Sept).

1585   Perrot's parliament meets in Dublin (26 Apr–25 May); Hugh O'Neill, Lord Dungannon, sits as earl of Tyrone. Commission to Bingham *et al.* for Composition of Connaught (15 July). Scheme for plantation of Munster.

1586   Parliamentary attainder of Desmond and supporters (parliament in session, 26 Apr–14 May). Agreement between Perrot and Sorley Boy MacDonald (18 June); Route divided between Sorley Boy and MacQuillan. Massacre at Ardnaree (22 Sept).

1587   Order to grant Sir Walter Raleigh $3\frac{1}{2}$ seignories in Cos. Cork and Waterford (28 Feb). Patent issued to Dungannon as earl of Tyrone (10 May). Hugh Roe O'Donnell kidnapped at Rathmullen in Tyrconnell (*c.* 22 Sept). Grammar school founded by James Fullerton and James Hamilton in Dublin.

1588   Sir William Fitzwilliam reappointed deputy (17 Feb). About 25 ships of Spanish Armada wrecked off coasts of Ireland (Sept), following their defeat by royal navy off Gravelines (early Aug).

1589   Commission to Lord President Bingham to attack rebels in north Connaught (12 Dec). Progress by Lord Deputy Fitzwilliam to Connaught (23 Dec–14 Jan 1590).

1590   Fitzwilliam orders Bingham to campaign against O'Rourke (14 Mar); O'Rourke flees to Tyrconnell (9 May) and Scotland.

1591   Earl of Tyrone marries Mabel Bagenal, sister of Marshal Henry Bagenal (3 Aug). O'Rourke executed at Tyburn (3 Nov). Hugh Roe O'Donnell escapes from Dublin castle (26 Dec).

1592   Captain Humphrey Willis, sheriff of Fermanagh, expelled from Donegal priory by Hugh Roe O'Donnell (Feb). Charter incorporating Trinity College, Dublin (3 Mar).

1593   Mission of titular archbishop of Tuam from O'Donnell to Philip II (Apr).

1594   Royal force captures Enniskillen (2 Feb); besieged by O'Donnell and Maguire (June); relief force defeated by Maguire on Arny river near Enniskillen (7 Aug).

1595   Tyrone's brother burns Blackwater Fort (16 Feb). Arrival of Sir John Norris as military commander for Ireland (4 May). Enniskillen falls (mid-May). Marshal Bagenal's relief army defeated by confederate army under Tyrone at Clontibret (13 June). Tyrone proclaimed traitor (23 June). Tyrone and O'Donnell offer kingship of Ireland to Archduke Albert, governor of Spanish Netherlands (23 Aug); ask support from Philip II (17 Sept). Death of Turlough Luineach O'Neill (c. 10 Sept).

1596   Tyrone pardoned (12 May). Feagh MacHugh O'Byrne rebels (Sept); killed (8 May 1597). Spanish Armada dispersed by storms (late Oct). Sir Conyers Clifford appointed chief commissioner of Connaught (2 Dec); president (4 Sept 1597).

1597   Two-pronged attack by Lord Deputy Burgh and Clifford on confederate lords (July). Sir Thomas Norris appointed president of Munster (20 Sept). Earl of Ormond appointed military commander (29 Oct).

1598   Marshal Bagenal's relief army for Blackwater Fort defeated by confederate army at the Yellow Ford (14 Aug). James Fitzthomas Fitzgerald established as *súgán* earl of Desmond (10 Oct). Munster plantation overthrown (Oct).

1599   Robert Devereux, earl of Essex, appointed lieutenant (12 Mar); campaigns in Leinster and Munster (9 May–1 July). Phelim MacFeagh O'Byrne routs royal force near Wicklow (29 May). Clifford defeated and killed in Curlew mountains (5 Aug). Parley of Essex and Tyrone, truce agreed (7 Sept). Departure of Essex (24 Sept). Ormond reappointed military commander (24 Sept).

1600   Charles Blount, Lord Mountjoy, appointed deputy (21 Jan). Tyrone campaigns in Munster (Feb–Mar); Maguire killed (1 Mar). Sir George Carew appointed president of Munster (6 Mar). Ormond captured by Owen O'More (10 Apr); released (13 June). Sir Henry Docwra's expeditionary force lands on Lough Foyle (15 May). Mountjoy campaigns against Tyrone (May). Engagement at the Moyry Pass between Mountjoy and Tyrone (25 Sept–2 Oct). James Fitzgerald created 15th earl of Desmond (1 Oct). Neill Garve O'Donnell joins Docwra (3 Oct); captures Lifford (9 Oct).

1601   *Súgán* earl of Desmond captured (29 May). Spanish army under Don Juan del Águila lands at Kinsale (21 Sept). Mountjoy invests Kinsale (26 Oct). O'Donnell eludes Carew in Co. Tipperary (22 Nov). Tyrone joins O'Donnell at Bandonbridge (c. 5 Dec). Mountjoy routs confederate army at Kinsale (24 Dec). O'Donnell sails for Spain (27 Dec).

1602   Águila surrenders to Mountjoy (2 Jan); leaves for Spain (16 Mar). Mountjoy campaigns in Ulster (10 June–c. 15 Sept). Carew captures Dunboy castle (18 June). Rory O'Donnell submits (Dec).

1603   Accession of James I (24 Mar). Tyrone submits to Mountjoy (30 Mar). James I proclaimed king in Dublin (5 Apr).

INTRODUCTION: THE END OF MEDIEVAL IRELAND, AN HISTORIOGRAPHICAL PROBLEM

The attempt to write the history of Ireland in this period is fraught with difficulties. In large measure these stem from the fact that in later medieval and Tudor times the island was divided between separate English and Gaelic worlds. Most of the north and western seaboard had more in common with the Scottish highlands and islands than it had with Dublin and its hinterland, while the lowland parts of Leinster and Munster formed the effective area of English lordship. Politically, a united Ireland was not achieved until 1603, when the whole island came under English rule, and to the present day Ireland has remained culturally divided. The area of Gaelic rule spanned the North Channel: the *Gaedhealtacht*, or Gaeldom, had a common language, law and culture, but was divided into a large number of more or less independent lordships. Elsewhere the sovereignty of the English king was acknowledged, and the English lordship of Ireland formed part of a disparate group of territories comprising the kingdom of England, the principality and marches of Wales, Calais, the Channel Isles, the Isle of Man and, until the mid-fifteenth century, the duchies of Normandy and Gascony. In terms of language, law, customs and governmental institutions, however, the English and Gaelic polities had comparatively little in common.

Like that of most European countries, Irish historiography has inherited from its late nineteenth-century origins as an academic subject a preoccupation with the role of the nation as the decisive force in the making of history.[1] Unfortunately, this traditional focus on 'the growth of the nation' and 'the development of the nation-state' has not been particularly helpful in elucidating developments in Ireland in the period 1447–1603. Late medieval Ireland was a country of two nations – 'Irish' and 'English', or '*Gaedhil*' and '*Gaill*', in its two vernacular languages – and its politics focused on the traditional rivalry between 'native' and 'foreigner'. Yet both nations extended well outside Ireland. The *Gaedhil*, as they described themselves, were a predominantly pastoral, clan-based people inhabiting parts of Ireland and Scotland where, likewise,

1. Kearney 1989, p. 1.

Gaelic land and culture were perceived as being under threat from the *Gaill*, those of the English or Scots language and culture. Regardless of whether they lived in Ireland or Scotland, the *Gaill* described them as 'the Irish', from the primary association of the *Gaedhil* with 'Ireland' (probably Éire-land, from *Éire*, the Gaelic name for Ireland). 'English' also had a broader meaning than it does today: 'the English' were those born in the territories under the allegiance of the crown of England and of English blood and condition.[2] This included the lordship of Ireland and its English-speaking political community, which was of English descent. Thus senses of nationality in late medieval Ireland were predominantly cultural rather than geographical. The Tudor period, however, was to see a marked development of alternative senses of nationality based on the concept of Ireland as the Irish national territory and, at the end of our period and under the impact of the Reformation, even of Catholic nationalism.

Ireland's continuing divisions have meant that its history is to a large extent a contested one of conflict and interaction between two separate civilizations: and because these civilizations both extended outside Ireland, Irish history is also much less self-contained than the history of major European nation-states. The influence of Gaelic Scotland on Ireland was clearly substantial, though little studied. English kings, however, were for long reluctant to become too closely involved, but in the sixteenth century events in Ireland, England and continental Europe gradually pushed them in this direction, and English intervention ultimately determined the fate of medieval Ireland.

In fact, a persistent problem faced by Irish historians is the very basic question of how far, in presentations of Irish history, the history of Ireland can be separated from the history of the Irish. There is no easy answer to this question. In many ways, of course, traditional nationalist historiography offers an appropriate perspective on the patterns of interaction and acculturation between *Gaedhil* and *Gaill* within Ireland and on those long-term developments which were to lead to the emergence of the modern Irish nation and the establishment of an Irish nation-state. Yet for the late middle ages, approaches focusing on the growth of 'Anglo-Irish separatism', 'gaelicization' and the emergence of a common Hiberno-Norman civilization are too narrow, since interaction was rather between separate English and Gaelic worlds extending well beyond Ireland. They also render unintelligible the basic strategy pursued by the English crown and make Tudor policy towards Ireland after 1534 appear far more purposeful than it actually was. Certainly, most English kings entertained vague plans for the future conquest of Gaelic Ireland, but these ambitions have to be seen in the context of the aims, methods, priorities and practicalities of royal government more generally. Change within the lordship was far less important than developments in the wider English state.

In Tudor times, a complicated pattern of development emerged, which witnessed the gradual polarization of a more general rivalry between *Gaedhil* and *Gaill* into separate Irish and Scottish theatres. In Ireland, the circumstances

2. Ellis 1996, p. 4; Hayes-McCoy 1937, pp. 4–5.

of the Tudor conquest brought about a shift in both English and Gaelic senses of identity, so that the Englishness of the earlier English colonists there was increasingly called in question and a wedge was gradually driven between the *Gaedhil* of Ireland and of Scotland. These developments tended towards the restoration of the Ireland-centred rivalry between English and Irish which had characterized the Anglo-Norman period. Yet concurrently, the arrival after 1534 of a second wave of English settlers eventually led to a novel, tripartite pattern of politics between three political groups, the Gaelic Irish, Old English and New English.

In these circumstances, two other perspectives also seem useful in high-lighting Ireland's changing position within the English state. In the Yorkist and early Tudor period, the lordship of Ireland is perhaps best seen as a frontier region, or march – one of a number of 'borderlands', or outlying territories, over which the English monarchy, like other Renaissance states, was trying to centralize its authority. Of course the rule and defence of remote frontier provinces posed special problems for Renaissance monarchy, but arguably 'the Problem of Ireland' was no more intractable than 'the Problem of the North'. The basic error in traditional accounts is the unwarranted assumption that successive kings invariably saw Ireland as a serious problem soluble only by conquering the whole country. In fact, as is suggested below, the Tudors only gradually came to view the problem of Ireland as intractable and requir-ing extraordinary measures. Moreover, this change probably had less to do with Ireland's peculiarities than with developments throughout the English territories. Even a cursory glance at the changing character of the English state goes far towards establishing this point,[3] although as is argued later the Tudors themselves also did much to exacerbate, if not to create, their Irish problem.

In Lancastrian times, the lordship was comparatively well integrated into the English state. Alone of the English territories, it was subject to English common law and so to English legislation. English was the dominant spoken language of the province, the king's subjects there regarded themselves as Englishmen, and the institutions of government there were more closely modelled on those in England than elsewhere. The lordship was of course part of a separate island. It marked England's frontier with the Gaelic world, but as a frontier it was not unique: the kings of France and of Scots were accounted much more formidable adversaries threatening the continental possessions and the north of England respectively. In particular, the English monarchy held the duchies of Gascony and Normandy, laid claim to the crown of France, and had aspira-tions to become a major continental power; but even in the context of Eng-land's emerging position as an insular power, much of English foreign policy was directed to controlling the narrow seas against invasion by maintaining blocks of territory on both sides of the Channel.[4] Control of the major Irish ports and the southern and eastern coastline there was a useful link in this

3. See Ellis 1983b, pp. 201–12; Ellis 1986b, pp. 187–204.
4. Vale 1970, esp. p. 1.

chain of defences, and travel by ship was often easier than by land; but there was less reason strategically or commercially to extend this control to the comparatively remote and barren Gaelic west or north.

Thus, in the wider context, Ireland *c.* 1450 barely surfaced as a problem: its position within the English state was not exceptional; the lordship was less exposed and more recognizably English than most other territories; and the defence of the English interest there was comparatively simple. Within the lordship, it is true, royal control appeared much less secure, but society there was not much more violent nor government much feebler than on the mainland, and arguably the more fundamental difficulties which the Dublin government faced sprang not from Gaelic Ireland but precisely from the fact that English kings did not regard royal government there as seriously threatened and let matters drift accordingly. In a sense they were right: with little exertion or expense, Edward IV and Henry VII stabilized the situation so that after 1496 the lordship was more an asset than a liability.[5]

By Elizabeth's reign, however, the crown's Irish policy was being conducted in a very different context, and changing English perceptions of the problem eventually precipitated a fundamental shift in attitudes towards Ireland. Within Ireland itself, the balance of power was largely unchanged, but the continued survival of an independent Gaelic polity meant that the English districts remained highly militarized by comparison with Tudor England, where strong government had since encouraged the emergence of more settled forms of society. Moreover, the maintenance of English rule in Ireland now required regular financial and military subventions on a scale unknown since 1399.

Within the wider Tudor state, English institutions and culture had since become much more dominant. In part, this was because the crown's continental possessions (hitherto the most obvious exception to the pattern of government in England), whose upkeep had been troublesome and expensive, had since been conquered by France – Normandy and Gascony in 1449–53, Calais in 1558. The loss of Calais finally ended the dreams entertained by kings like Henry VIII of recreating Henry V's continental empire and forced the monarchy to concentrate on the British Isles. Moreover, the most considerable of the remaining dominions, Wales, had effectively been incorporated into England: in 1536 the immunities of the marcher lordships and the official toleration of Welsh law and custom were terminated and English law and administrative structures were extended throughout that country. Concurrently, the feudal franchises of a few favoured prelates in northern England were assimilated into shire ground; and with the advent of generally good relations with the Scottish government after 1560, the difficulties of defending the English monarchy's only other surviving landed frontier in the far north and of taming the wild border clans there were greatly eased. Finally, from the 1530s, the legislation associated with the Reformation had greatly increased the claims

5. Below, Chs 1–3; Richardson & Sayles 1952, p. 162.

of government on the king's subjects throughout the Tudor state, without, in the short term, noticeably strengthening its potential.[6]

Thus by the 1560s the characteristically Tudor pattern of state formation by political centralization, administrative uniformity and cultural imperialism seemed to be making good progress in taming the wild borderers and fostering a more civil society among degenerate English settlers in outlying parts of the Tudor state. These changes had ensured that, over the previous 30 years, the crown's awareness of its Irish problem had greatly intensified, and long-term developments outside Ireland had substantially altered its view of the nature of the problem. Yet in English Ireland levels of public order were now lagging well behind those in England, and structures of government and society were looking increasingly archaic, at a time when the crown was much less tolerant of departures from English norms. In these circumstances, the independent Gaelic chiefs were increasingly identified as the chief obstacle in the path of successive plans to bring order and stability to a backward province, as the Tudor regime gradually came to believe that peace and good government there necessitated a more active intervention in Gaelic Ireland.

English officials had long regarded 'the wild Irish' as an untamed bestial people living in idleness and brutality in their woods and bogs, but hitherto it had been supposed that the extension of English law and government throughout those parts would soon bring the natives, like other primitive peoples such as 'the mere Welsh', to a knowledge of their allegiance and a recognition of the benefits of English civility.[7] Yet, as policy became more interventionist, so Elizabethan officials became increasingly frustrated at the apparent obstinacy of the Gaelic Irish and the continuing failure of successive attempts to extend English rule by reform and persuasion. From the late 1580s, there was a growing disillusion in government circles with traditional Tudor reform strategy and increasing support for the idea that English aims could only be achieved by a massive reassertion of English armed might so as to break Gaelic resistance by military conquest and extensive plantations.[8] Thus, in the wider context of state formation, Elizabeth's reign marks a transitional phase between the classic Tudor pattern of expansion and the emergence in the 1590s of a more aggressive colonialism which was the chief legacy of late Elizabethan Ireland to English colonization in the New World.

The extent to which Gaelic attitudes to the English shifted in this period is much more problematical. Much of the evidence about Gaelic Ireland derives from hostile witnesses – reports of royal ministers and English adventurers. Of the surviving native sources, estimated at only about 100 manuscripts for the entire sixteenth century, many are of little value for an understanding of the workings of Gaelic society.[9] Bardic poetry in particular provides little hard

6. Elton 1982, pp. 31–3, 318–21; Ellis 1995b, pp. 40–63.
7. Ellis 1995a, chs 1–2.
8. Brady 1994a, pp. 291–300.
9. *NHI*, iii, pp. 513–14.

evidence about what chiefs and clansmen actually thought, and attempts to use it to assess the Gaelic reaction to the Elizabethan conquest have proved highly controversial.[10] The annals and the few legal documents are more informative but, even so, it is only in recent years that our knowledge of Gaelic Ireland has begun to extend substantially beyond what was already apparent from English administrative records.[11]

A second main difficulty, however, arises from the predilections of historians of Gaelic Ireland, who have so far shown little interest in comparative studies with Scotland and the clan system, landholding, law and other Gaelic customs there. In many ways a pan-Gaelic perspective is more appropriate to the late medieval period than the separate study of Ireland and Scotland as nations in the making. Just as Irish historians have charted a Gaelic revival in fourteenth-century Ireland, so Scottish historians have noted a parallel Gaelic resurgence in Scotland with the expansion in the power of the Clan Donald lords of the Isles to exercise a supremacy over other western chiefs (and, later, north-east Ulster). This resurgence followed both the collapse of Norse power in the Isles and then of English power in Ulster, so facilitating the restoration of strong ties with Gaelic Ireland. As the Elizabethans quickly discovered, these connections help to explain the resilience of Gaelic Ireland under threat in the sixteenth century, especially the ability of Irish chiefs to recruit Scots mercenary troops, the famous redshanks. Conversely, the revival of strong government in Yorkist and early Tudor England and in Scotland under James IV (1488–1513) put pressure on this Gaelic polity: it led in Ireland to a resurgence of English power during the Kildare ascendancy (1470–1534) and in Scotland to the final forfeiture of the lordship of the Isles in 1493.[12] Nevertheless, as late as 1600, the Gaelic learned classes moved to and fro between Ireland and Scotland. It was perhaps only the increasing pressures exerted by the English and Scottish monarchies, and in particular the emergence of religious differences, that forced the Gaelic peoples to think more consistently in terms of Irish and Scottish politics and so precipitated the gradual emergence of separate Irish and Scots Gaelic identities.[13]

Thus a basic historiographical difficulty concerning Ireland in the period 1447–1603 is one of context and approach. In England and other European nation-states, national history was regularly shaped by internal change, and the interests of the monarchy were more readily identified with those of the nation. Yorkist and Tudor England can be studied in terms of the growth of royal power, the king's relations with the nobles, gentry and towns, and the impact of government on the provinces. Historians sometimes grumble about

10. Bradshaw 1978b, pp. 65–80; Dunne 1980, pp. 7–30; Canny 1982, pp. 91–116. A more recent and comprehensive survey which has evoked an equally critical reaction is O Riordan 1990. For some more sensible comments, see Simms 1987b, pp. 58–75; Leerssen 1994.
11. The most important recent contributions are Simms 1987a and, more controversially, O Riordan 1990.
12. Dickenson 1965, pp. 5, 37–42, 274–98; Smout 1972, pp. 39–40; *NHI*, iii, p. 17; Grant 1988, pp. 118–41.
13. Below, Ch. 2.

Westminster-centred history, and complain that changes in border regions are too frequently ignored except where they relate to 'national' trends, but on the whole the exercise is legitimate. Attempts to write Irish history along similar lines, however, have been criticized more severely: even though in 1500 the English king's authority was more widely recognized than that of any other ruler, the Gaelic chiefs who then controlled about half the island generally denied that he had any right to intervene in their lordships. Moreover, even in the English districts, the capacity and control of the Dublin administration was weaker than royal government in most of England. Thus, in so far as Irish history was not shaped by events outside Ireland, it tended to be the sum of regional histories and their interaction rather than the product of 'national' movements.

In the circumstances, a comprehensive history of Ireland in Yorkist and Tudor times becomes an exceedingly ambitious undertaking (and almost impossible within the compass of this book). What is attempted here is rather to offer a broad canvass on developments concerning Ireland and the Irish. The book focuses especially on English rule, culture and influence in Ireland and on the wider context of Irish identity. Before 1534, Gaelic Ireland is treated mainly as an external problem: a separate description is included of late medieval Gaelic politics and society, and the relationship between English and Gaelic culture is discussed in more detail; but only for the later period, when the Dublin administration was making good its jurisdictional claims there, are the Gaelic areas treated as part of Tudor Ireland. Apart from providing fresh insights into the supposedly familiar story of the Tudor contribution to Irish nationalism, this perspective also permits a fuller consideration of hitherto neglected constitutional themes, such as the impact and revival of crown government or the rule of law. This in turn allows a more comparative approach with regard to those problems of state formation that have recently come to the fore among historians of England or continental Europe.

Thus, the main themes around which the book is organized are, from a Gaelic perspective, the emergence of Ireland as a political entity and of different senses of Irish identity; and from an English perspective, the crown's growing consciousness of its Irish problem, the transformation of that problem from 1534 onwards, the efforts to deal with it, and the success or otherwise that attended these efforts. In this way, it may be possible to make Tudor policy towards Ireland more fully intelligible: that is, to offer an interpretation which does not prejudge the issue of the Elizabethan conquest by suggesting that successive kings had foolishly been trying to govern a totally different form of society as they did England, but which also explains the circumstances that persuaded the later Tudors to abandon the attempt to control the country by traditional methods, and instead to pursue an unconventional strategy of extending royal authority there by force.

CHAPTER 1

THE CROWN'S IRISH PROBLEM IN THE LATER MIDDLE AGES

By 1460 the whole approach of kings of England to the problems of governing Ireland was in urgent need of reconsideration. Since the fourteenth century, English power and influence in Ireland had declined alarmingly, and beginning in the 1420s there had been a disastrous feud among the lordship's leading families. The belated response of Henry VI, the appointment of Richard, duke of York as lieutenant in 1447, in a bid to tackle the lordship's mounting problems, was widely welcomed in Ireland, even though the king's primary purpose was to exclude from influence over the more important French theatre of operations a leading opponent of his policies there. Yet, with the degeneration of English politics into civil war in the 1450s, Richard used the lordship as a base from which to evade arrest and execution as a traitor and to launch an attempt on the throne itself. The duke's career in Ireland illustrated most strikingly the weakness of royal authority there and the dangers that English kings might face if their Irish lordship were finally extinguished.[1]

THE LOSS OF POLITICAL INITIATIVE

Not that this situation was altogether new, for in general English government in Ireland had then been in decline for at least 150 years. At its zenith, c. 1300, the influence of royal government was felt, albeit intermittently in some districts, in about two-thirds of the island, but by 1460 it was confined to much less than half of Ireland. Such statements can, however, be misleading. Under Edward I (1272–1307), the government had exercised some control over many districts which had been only thinly colonized and in which the ruling Gaelic clans had been brought reluctantly to acknowledge the overlordship of a Norman baron: by 1460 English influence was largely reduced to those areas which had earlier witnessed extensive Norman colonization.[2] Moreover, the fourteenth century had witnessed an important change in the lordship's character. Under Edward I the Anglo-Norman colonists had been a dominant

1. See below, Ch. 3.
2. Frame 1981, chs 4–6; Frame 1982, ch. 3; Ellis 1986a, *passim*.

minority exercising an influence in Ireland which was out of all proportion to their numbers: by 1400 this dominance was in many respects a thing of the past. The colonists were fast losing sight of their claim that the lordship of Ireland should extend over the whole island; Gaelic chiefs had recovered many districts conquered in the thirteenth century and were exacting tribute from the king's subjects in others; and the activities of the Dublin administration were increasingly geared to the defence of the principal centre of English influence, the coastline between Bray and Carlingford and its hinterland. In fact the feebleness of royal government under Henry VI (1421–61, 1470–1) meant that the lordship was in some danger of splitting into a series of independent lordships, like Gaelic Ireland, each controlled by a local magnate. Thus although English influence was generally strong throughout much of Leinster and Munster, the particular influence of the Dublin government was intermittent outside 'the four obedient shires', the (medieval) counties of Dublin, Louth, Meath and Kildare, which together were later to comprise the English Pale.[3]

THE NATURE OF THE NORMAN SETTLEMENT

How and why had this situation come about? The answer to this question provides both an insight into the state of Ireland in the later fifteenth century – the king's Irish problem as analysed in the remainder of this chapter – and an indication of why, without any great effort on the king's part, the half-century or so from 1470 should have witnessed a significant revival in the lordship's fortunes. Recent research has made it increasingly clear that the medieval lordship was at no time a peaceful little England across the Irish sea; rather it was a highly regional land in which central government resources had always been fairly limited and its influence correspondingly weak:[4] and since royal government had never been strong, its decline was less precipitous than formerly imagined. In fact the lordship's fragmentation and strong local traditions are largely explained by factors of geography and the piecemeal and partial nature of the Norman invasion and conquest.

The Normans had colonized most heavily the low-lying areas of Munster and Leinster, and these remained the heart of the medieval colony; but the survival of an independent Gaelic civilization in other areas created serious administrative problems. The government responded by encouraging local magnates to recruit and retain troops to defend the marches against Gaelic raids, and at particularly vulnerable points it might organize and pay for a ward itself. In addition, the governor, with the support of the magnates, organized military expeditions to induce Gaelic chiefs to submit and put in pledges to keep the peace. Even in the fourteenth century, however, the government had given priority to Leinster, and in particular to combating raids by the chiefs of

3. Ibid.; Lydon 1972b, *passim.*
4. Esp. Frame 1977, pp. 3–33.

the Leinster mountains. Elsewhere, the various communities under the leader-ship of local lords had primary responsibility for defence, and intervention by the governor was usually confined to moments of crisis.[5]

In part the government was forced to delegate authority and to encourage self-reliance in this way because it lacked the men and money to perform its duties in any other manner: throughout medieval Europe the resources and potential of governments were small and they relied heavily on the unpaid services of wealthy and well-disposed subjects who in return could expect the king's favour in their private interests. What made Ireland different from many regions, however, was the premium placed on armed might for purposes of defence as well as to maintain law and order, although in the marcher areas of northern England, Scotland and Wales conditions were very similar. Thus, because the maintenance of peace and stability was so much more costly and troublesome, the efficiency of government was correspondingly less. Moreover, the private armies of the magnates were frequently used in less acceptable ways – to pursue personal feuds, notably the Geraldine–Butler and Talbot–Ormond feuds of the fifteenth century, to pervert justice or to encroach on the king's rights and interests. In this way the power of the Dublin administration was still further reduced, and Gaelic chiefs could exploit internal dissensions among the colonists.

THE ART OF GOOD GOVERNMENT

Besides the problems arising from inadequate resources, the nature of his adversary confronted the governor with others. Gaelic Ireland was not a cen-tralized monarchy like England, but rather a politically decentralized country in which dozens of independent chiefs pursued their own interests: there was no single individual with whom the governor could negotiate. Instead he had to deal with a score of border chiefs, each of whom was important for the de-fence of a particular march. A good governor set out first to learn the politics of the various border chieftaincies, and much of the art of government consisted in ensuring that chiefs remained at odds with each other and well disposed towards the government, and in correctly predicting trouble and drafting in forces for its containment. Nevertheless, he could not be in two places at once, and an inexperienced governor could do a lot of damage if he mishandled important chiefs like O'Neill, O'Connor or MacMurrough Kavanagh.

Of crucial importance to the government was control of the king's highway down the Barrow valley, the only available overland route connecting 'the four obedient shires' with the other main English districts in the south. This road was swept by Gaelic raids from the midlands and Leinster mountains and by 1400 was almost impassable without an escort. The government had from 1361 relocated the central courts at Carlow, in a bid to provide closer supervision of the area and to facilitate communications, but after reiterated complaints

5. Ibid.; Frame 1975, pp. 748–77.

that the town was unsafe and the king's business impeded, the central administration was moved back to Dublin in 1394. The result was that the lordship became even more fragmented than before, and increasingly communications between Dublin and Waterford or Cork were by sea.[6]

THE LORDSHIP'S POLITICAL DECLINE

Before 1315 the lordship had been a source of profit to the king. But instead of using the money to consolidate his control of border districts and to complete the conquest of Ireland, Edward I had creamed off any surplus revenue to help finance the conquest of Wales (completed in 1282–3) and to support his claim to the overlordship of Scotland. Ireland was for long undergoverned to leave money for these purposes, but the consequent disorders adversely affected the revenues and so further reduced the Dublin government's ability either to assist the king elsewhere or to maintain royal authority in Ireland.[7] Then in 1315 English control over Ireland was jeopardized by the invasion of Edward Bruce, the king of Scots' brother, in an effort to relieve English pressure on Scotland and to destroy the lordship's military and financial value. Although Bruce was eventually killed in 1318 and the Scots expelled, the countryside had been ravaged and English influence gravely weakened. The colony received a further crushing blow from the Black Death which from 1348 affected the lordship's ports, towns and corn-growing areas far more than the largely pastoral districts of the Gaelic west. Mortality probably approached that in the Great Famine of the nineteenth century, and by 1400 successive outbreaks of plague had apparently reduced the population of English Ireland by 50 per cent. Recovery was slow even in the heart of the lordship, and elsewhere English power collapsed as Gaelic chiefs exploited the opportunity and overran border settlements: the balance of power tilted firmly away from the colonists.[8]

England and other parts of Europe were similarly affected by the plague. Recurrent visitations and the trade slump of the period meant that population in England long continued to decline, and the first signs of recovery did not occur until the 1460s.[9] This had important consequences for Ireland: a precondition for Norman expansion there had been the barons' ability to attract tenants from England and Wales to till the lands which they had conquered and organized into manors. These tenants had been attracted by prospects of larger holdings on better terms.[10] But when, during the fourteenth century, population began everywhere to fall, land became more plentiful, rents fell and tenants became scarce. Yet in Ireland the Dublin government was unable to maintain peace or protect the king's subjects in border areas, and this prompted many to abandon their holdings and to seek a better life, either in more settled parts

6. Ibid.; Otway-Ruthven 1980, pp. 160, 287, 327; Empey 1970–1, pp. 174–87.
7. Lydon 1972b, ch. 6.
8. Frame 1981, ch. 6; Otway-Ruthven 1980, pp. 267–70.
9. Hatcher 1977.
10. Bartlett 1993 offers a stimulating reappraisal of this process in its wider European context.

or, because ties between the two countries remained strong, in England itself. Thus began a haemorrhage of English blood out of Ireland which progressively undermined the colony's stability: in 1536 the Irish council reported that

the English blood of the English conquest is in manner worn out of this land.[11]

Without tenants the lords could not defend the land, which was progressively overrun by resurgent Gaelic clans. Rather than suffer this they brought in Gaelic peasants. The native population had in any case been retained on most manors after the conquest, but they had since been at least partially 'anglicized': these population movements, therefore, upset the previous cultural balance between English and Gaelic even in those parts where Anglo-Norman lords managed to hold on to their lands. Irish historians have traditionally but misleadingly described a progressive 'gaelicization' of the lordship, whereby the colonists 'became more Irish than the Irish themselves'. Yet in practice, among the peasantry at least, it was more often a case of the replacement of English by Gaelic. Moreover, the English of Ireland were never accepted as *Gaedhil*, and English officials normally talked about the 'degeneracy' of the English, the loss of their distinguishing characteristics as a people (*'gens'*), and the 'decay' of the body politic.[12] Movements of acculturation were of the essence of medieval frontier societies – in which the English state abounded – but what concerned these officials was the general contrast, in manners and appearance, between the 'civil' inhabitants of lowland England and the 'wild' men of the marches, not the particular differences between different groups of 'savages' in Ireland and Wales.

By 1360 the government was becoming alarmed at the deteriorating situation in Ireland. Of course it failed to appreciate the real nature of the changes taking place – medieval governments had little understanding of social and economic change – but the symptoms of malaise were obvious enough. Where Edward I had drawn over £40,000 from Ireland between 1278 and 1306 (at a time when the internal revenue was usually about £5,000 per annum), after 1315 the revenue barely sufficed to govern and defend the English districts.[13] The king's subjects were leaving Ireland in large numbers, and those who held lands in both countries were neglecting their Irish possessions, which were being overrun by the wild Irish. In other districts the colonists were apparently growing wild and rebellious, adopting Gaelic law and customs and allying with the king's Irish enemies.

THE STATUTES OF KILKENNY

The government attempted to remedy the situation in two main ways. From 1361 it pumped large quantities of men and money into the lordship in a

11. *StP*, ii, 338; Frame 1981, pp. 69–72, 111–13; Lydon 1972b, pp. 201–9.
12. Davies 1994, pp. 1–20; Gillingham 1995, pp. 48–64; McNeill 1931b.
13. Lydon 1972b, pp. 132, 191–2.

heroic but doomed attempt to shore up the tottering structure; and it tried by legislation to arrest the 'degeneracy' of the local Englishry. These two strategies continued to exercise an influence on official thinking well into the Tudor period, and so merit more detailed consideration here. Yet it was social and economic change in the sixteenth century and the pressure of new circumstances, more than the government's persistence with its traditional strategies, that eventually brought about an improvement.

The most celebrated and comprehensive body of legislation was the Statutes of Kilkenny, enacted by the lordship's parliament in 1366. There was little in them that was new, rather they were a codification of laws passed since 1297. The Statutes were essentially defensive in tone: they tried to ensure that the English of Ireland and the lands formerly conquered by them *remained* English, and as far as possible ignored the Gaelic Irish beyond the English districts. In fact, throughout the middle ages, the government's attitude towards the native population was somewhat inconsistent and certainly shortsighted. They were generally treated either as aliens and foreigners or as bondmen and serfs (the distinction is in many ways a fine one), and denied the rights and privileges of the king's subjects. In contrast, in the continental possessions and to an extent in Wales, the indigenous population was more favourably treated and governed by its own law and customs. Sir John Davies, James I's attorney-general, believed that the failure to extend English law to Irishmen was a principal reason why the conquest's completion was so long delayed.[14] In line with their inferior status at English common law, they were officially described as 'the king's Irish enemies' or 'the wild Irish' in contrast to 'the king's English lieges'.

The Statutes forbade any alliance by marriage, fostering children or otherwise between English and Irish, the use of 'march' law (a mixture of English and Gaelic law) or Brehon (Gaelic) law among the English, or the admission of Irishmen to governmental office or to ecclesiastical benefices in the English districts. Englishmen and those loyal Irish living among them were required to speak English and to adopt English names, customs, fashion, manner of riding and dress. The common people in the marches were not to play games called 'hurlings', but were to practise archery, throwing lances and other warlike games. Decisions about war and peace with Gaelic chiefs should rest with the king's council and unauthorized parleys or private battles should cease. Other Statutes dealt with the maintenance of order, the rights of the church, the conduct of officials and their fees and, in general, with the provision of good government. Finally there was legislation to keep down the price of merchandise entering the country, to prevent labourers from leaving the country and to forbid landowners to keep Irish kerne and idlemen except in the marches at their own cost.

The Statutes of Kilkenny mark no real watershed in the lordship's history, but they were remembered by later generations for their comprehensiveness.

14. Davies 1969, pp. 113–21; Otway-Ruthven 1980, pp. 125, 188–90. Cf. Vale 1970, pp. 4–5, 155; Davies 1966, pp. 143–64. Curtis & MacDowell 1968, pp. 52–9 includes the more important Statutes: for commentary, Otway-Ruthven 1980, pp. 290–4; Frame 1981, pp. 132–4.

To modern historians they mark an official recognition of the partial nature of the Norman conquest and what contemporary officials saw as the cause of the colony's troubles. Like the present Republic of Ireland, the lordship claimed a jurisdiction over the whole island which it did not attempt to exercise, according instead a *de facto* recognition to the Irish in their own districts. Thus government reports divided the country into 'the land of peace', the main English districts where 'English civility' was preserved, the marches adjoining the Irishry, and 'the land of war' where the 'wild Irish' lived in savagery and brutality.

ENGLISH SUBVENTIONS

As governments repeatedly discovered, however, it was easy enough to have legislation passed, but quite another thing to see it enforced, particularly when the government was as ineffectual as the Dublin administration. In order to increase that administration's effectiveness, the king began in 1361 to subsidize its operation from his English revenues, and the previous practice of sending over troops to augment the governor's retinue was greatly extended. For example, in 1369–70 William of Windsor as governor had over 600 men in wages and cost the king £12,300 for the year; by 1372 the English exchequer had paid out over £22,000 for Windsor's campaigns.[15] English kings were not prepared for very long to contemplate this level of expenditure on a relatively minor theatre of operations, but it was hoped that by a great effort the king could begin to recover his outlay within two or three years and make Ireland profitable once more. A succession of governors was therefore supported from England, some of whom received considerable sums and brought (by Irish standards) quite large armies. These culminated in the two expeditions to Ireland of Richard II, in 1394–5 and 1399 – the only English king to visit the country between 1210 and 1689. In particular, the 1394 expedition was on a grand scale – the army of around 6,000 men which accompanied the king was comparable with the armies led to France during the Hundred Years War.[16]

The achievements of these expeditions, however, were slight. They were certainly costly, but in fact too little was made available too infrequently to have much effect. The effort was not a concerted one, largely because the king regarded Ireland as unimportant in comparison with the government of England and Wales, the maintenance of his claim to the French crown and the defence of English possessions there. Thus, although Gaelic chiefs periodically found it expedient to submit to a well-equipped governor, when money and men were curtailed the political and military situation quickly deteriorated to its former state.

The effect of these expeditions is illustrated by their impact on royal revenues in Ireland, since the levy of revenue was largely dependent on the government's ability to assert its authority. Between 1315 and 1361 the internal

15. Lydon 1972b, pp. 132, 191–2.
16. Otway-Ruthven 1980, ch. 10.

revenue of the lordship had remained fairly steady at around £2,200 a year – far below the levels of the late thirteenth century – but, apparently in response to stronger government, it rose gradually to an average of £3,600 per annum under William of Windsor (1369–72) before sinking back to barely £2,000 a year during the following twenty years.[17] English subventions had temporarily facilitated revenue collection, but because the effort was not sustained internal revenues fell back to previous levels when the troops went home: seemingly the disturbance caused by the temporary appointment of such an English-born governor almost outweighed the resultant short-term improvements. And when these expeditions failed to achieve the anticipated speedy success, disillusionment quickly set in. This was an experience which was to be repeated many times before the Tudor conquest was finally completed.

In retrospect, however, it would appear that these subventions had the effect of obscuring temporarily the lordship's continuing internal decline. The Dublin government had become increasingly dependent on them to maintain its activities at an artificially high level, and when changed circumstances dictated their curtailment after 1399 there followed an alarming collapse of royal authority. The new Lancastrian dynasty soon found itself short of money and needing to watch the English nobility very carefully to ensure loyalty. While dealing with a series of conspiracies and rebellions at home, the king could spare little time for Ireland, and in fact this neglect continued thereafter for different reasons. From 1415 such revenue as became available was mostly diverted to support the English position in France, where the Hundred Years War had recommenced with a series of sweeping successes for the English. Later, as the war turned against them, the French territories required large sums for defence, and these problems were compounded by follies and feeble government during the personal rule of Henry VI.[18]

THE RULE OF HENRY VI

The later middle ages were very much an age of personal monarchy, in which kings were expected to rule as well as reign. The king aimed to impress both his subjects and foreigners alike by the magnificence and display of his court, which was meant to emphasize his power and God-given authority. He took all important decisions himself and intervened personally to compose the countless disputes and bickering among his wealthier subjects which threatened the peace and stability of his kingdom. It was in fact a major weakness of English rule in Ireland that the king ruled from afar through a viceroy. This meant that government lacked the prestige that a resident court provided, and suffered still further when the king's choice of governor proved unsuitable. Even in England, however, there were certain recognized procedures for government by the king's council during his absence or if he were a minor (as Henry VI

17. Richardson & Sayles 1952, pp. 87–100; Ellis 1982–3, pp. 39–49.
18. Otway-Ruthven 1980, ch. 11; Keen 1973, chs 13–17.

was until 1437), but no provision could be made for what happened after Henry VI came of age. He granted away crown rights and property on an unprecedented scale to his favourites, so that the royal revenues declined alarmingly. He was in many ways easily led, but also unpredictable and liable to intervene inexplicably in minor matters. His choice of ministers was frequently poor and he failed to do justice impartially. Finally, in 1453 and again in 1455 he went insane for a few months, but unfortunately he recovered his sanity on each occasion before the country had had a chance to recover from his government.[19]

The result was that the nobles increasingly took the law into their own hands, built up private armies, and decided disputes on the battlefield; and as the country sank into disorder the prestige and authority of royal government collapsed with it. The fall of the English territories in France was in fact one consequence of this crisis of personal monarchy, but the ignominy of losing so fine a jewel in his crown as France destroyed what remaining credit Henry VI still had. There ensued the so-called Wars of the Roses between York and Lancaster, an intermittent but long-drawn-out civil war which originated in the attempts of a noble faction led by the duke of York to recover influence with the king so as to ensure a fairer distribution of royal patronage, and the efforts of a clique of influential courtiers to prevent it.[20]

Tallies and the growth of coign and livery

The effect of these disorders and lack of direction on royal government in Ireland was equally disastrous. The sharp reductions in English subventions after 1399 had already had serious consequences: the governor was rarely allowed more than 4,000 marks per annum and 300–400 troops, with which he could conduct no more than a holding operation,[21] and the Irish revenues covered only the most basic costs of government. Indeed, between the 1390s and 1420s the ordinary revenue had fallen from an average of £2,000 a year to a little under £1,400 a year, and it continued to decline alarmingly, averaging £1,150 per annum in the 1430s and less than £900 a year down to 1446 (when our sources fail us). By then the administration was collecting little more than was being levied from the far smaller area under English rule in Gascony, it was deeply in debt, ministers remained unpaid for years, and the governor had had to resort to a series of dubious or illegal exactions in order to maintain his retinue.[22]

The king's exchequers at both Westminster and Dublin operated an ingenious system of assignment, designed to prevent large amounts of money being carried about the country and to ensure that revenue was promptly levied. Only sufficient ready cash for emergencies and the king's own needs was

19. Wolffe 1972, pp. 29–48.
20. Goodman 1981.
21. Richardson & Sayles 1952, pp. 152–3, 227–8.
22. Ellis 1986a; Matthew 1984, pp. 97–115; Ellis 1982–3, pp. 39–49. Cf. Vale 1970, pp. 235–7.

customarily kept in the exchequer, and creditors were frequently paid by the issue of tallies cashable by a specified collector of revenue. Provided the government was solvent, the system worked efficiently, but increasingly, under the Lancastrian monarchs, governors of Ireland were paid in tallies which they could not cash because the revenues were overassigned. In turn the unfortunate governors ran up large debts through the practice of purveyance, or 'livery' as it was called in Ireland, by which they requisitioned necessary provisions from the populace. The Irish parliament advised the king in 1474 that a chief cause of the lordship's decline was that those having

> the governance of the same land afore this time for certain years have not paid the commons for their victuals, but shortly departeth out of the land for lack of payment of their wages out of England, for the which [cause] neither they might pay their debts nor continue still for defence of the land, but leave it worse than they find it.

Moreover, an army which the governor could not pay, nor for military reasons disband, was difficult to control and might damage the king's subjects as much as his enemies. The soldiers frequently extorted payment in money or kind from the countryside on which they were quartered, a practice known as 'coign', which was customary in Gaelic Ireland but had repeatedly been forbidden by statute in the lordship.[23]

In these circumstances, the colonists understandably tried to limit royal inter-ference and made a virtue of self-help. Rather than suffer weak government by English-born officials who had little experience of the country nor money and men to back up royal authority, they preferred to govern themselves. In the rule of the provinces, 'self-government at the king's command' was indeed the hallmark of the English tradition.[24] Yet in the government of Ireland there existed considerable potential for friction between king and community in the Dublin administration's anomalous position as both an instrument of provin-cial administration and as a separate central government akin to Westminster. Claims were also made that the king's subjects in Ireland should not be sued by writs out of England, that only those laws enacted by parliament in Ireland should apply there, and that Irish lawsuits should all be determined in the courts there.[25] Had they succeeded, such claims would have established the lordship as a political entity distinct from England but under the same crown, instead of as a lordship or dominion separate from but subordinate to that kingdom, the status it was normally accorded. The nature of Ireland's relation-ship to the crown of England was for long a source of much confusion, but for most of our period such 'separatist' claims were essentially a spasmodic reac-tion to royal misrule rather than a serious political movement based on the first stirrings of nationalist sentiments among the colonists.[26]

23. Otway-Ruthven 1980, p. 351; Richardson & Sayles 1952, pp. 229–33; Bryan 1933, pp. 18–22 (quotation).
24. See now Frame 1992, pp. 1–43 (quotation, p. 5).
25. Lydon 1972b, pp. 262–5; Richardson & Sayles 1952, ch. 16.
26. Lydon 1972a, ch. 5. The most recent contributions on this vexed topic are Cosgrove 1983, pp. 25–41; Ellis 1990–1, pp. 297–9; Lydon 1995, pp. 9–13; Lydon 1994–5, pp. 281–94.

By 1450, the Dublin administration was perforce concentrating almost exclusively on the defence of the English districts nearest to the centre of government, and the 'land of peace' of the fourteenth century had shrunk to 'the four obedient shires' around Dublin. And in default of central government assistance, the outlying communities of English Ireland were organizing themselves for defence into individual, semi-autonomous lordships under the leadership of local magnates.[27] The tendencies towards greater decentralization of power were reinforced by feuds among the magnates. The protracted Talbot–Ormond dispute (1414–47) between Sir John Talbot, created earl of Shrewsbury in 1442, and James Butler, fourth earl of Ormond, was followed by equally disastrous rivalry between the Butlers and the Fitzgerald earls of Desmond and Kildare. These feuds disrupted the peace of the lordship and were ably exploited by the Gaelic border chiefs.[28] One factor in the growth of feuding was that in order to offset the fall in English subventions and the consequent weakness of the Dublin government, the Lancastrian kings recruited their governors from nobles who were Irish-born, or had substantial holdings of Irish land (Talbot and Ormond in particular), and could utilize their own resources in support of government. Noble participation in government made for strong, stable rule, but if it were allowed to degenerate into noble domination, as happened in Lancastrian Ireland, government became an instrument of faction rather than an impartial arbiter, and its estimation was accordingly reduced.

WEAPONS AND WARFARE IN IRELAND

From an Irish perspective, the developments outlined above have usually been seen as part of a grand Gaelic Revival, continuing throughout the middle ages, in which the tide of Norman conquest was first stemmed and then reversed. Certainly this period saw the lordship on the defensive, with a slackening of royal control, territorial expansion by Gaelic clans, and varying degrees of acculturation among the settlers. Yet these changes in fact sprang more from weaknesses in the lordship and from royal neglect and misgovernment rather than from major developments in Gaelic Ireland to meet the challenge posed by the English monarchy. Perhaps the only major exception to this was the introduction in the later thirteenth century of the galloglass, a mailed footsoldier wielding a heavy, long-handled battle axe, which certainly helped to redress the military balance between the two societies. Gaelic chiefs also learned many of the principles of siege warfare, and by 1400 were building their own stone castles. In general, however, it was not so much that Gaelic Ireland revived, but that English Ireland declined, and Gaelic chiefs were thereby able to exploit a situation not of their own making. Otherwise, there would have been much more serious resistance to the Elizabethan conquest.

27. Empey 1970–1, pp. 174–87; Empey & Simms 1975, pp. 161–87.
28. Griffith 1940–1, pp. 376–97; Otway-Ruthven 1980, pp. 385–6, 389; Lydon 1972b, pp. 266–9.

Nevertheless, if there were serious feuds among Old English magnates, among Gaelic chiefs there was almost no political cohesion at all, except when a few chiefs were briefly united by self-interest. Militarily, their weapons were outmoded by European standards. Horsemen rode without stirrups and were therefore unable to couch a lance: instead they carried javelins overarm. The footmen, or kerne, were unarmoured and the bows with which many fought were only about half the length of English longbows and correspondingly less penetrative.[29] Chief Baron Finglas, writing about 1528, dismissed suggestions that Gaelic military techniques or weaponry had improved, remarking that 'in all my days, I never heard that a hundred footmen n[or] horsemen of Irishmen would abide to fight so many Englishmen'.[30] In a pitched battle, the colonists held all the advantages, but the heavily wooded, marshy or mountainous country of the Irishry was much less suitable for English troops. English armies relied chiefly on light cavalry in Ireland and even then could not always follow the small native horses; and the longbow was better suited to open country.

These problems had long been recognized by the government, which regularly employed contingents of Gaelic troops, but many governors got into difficulties beause of their unfamiliarity with the difficult terrain of Gaelic parts. Gaelic chiefs were very adept at exploiting the local terrain: large armies found no one to fight, or faced a series of ambushes, and small armies got beaten. The Dublin government found it hard to penetrate the fastnesses of the clansmen and defeat them militarily, although their frequent but petty raiding seldom seriously challenged English rule and was mostly confined to a campaigning season which lasted from Easter to Michaelmas. In fact most border chieftaincies were poor and weak, and raiding was an important source of income to them: some clans like the O'Tooles probably survived largely by preying on the wealthier colonists.[31]

Thus by the 1450s, English rule in Ireland was in serious difficulties. To the king's officers there, with the collapse of Lancastrian France fresh in their minds, their situation might appear all too similar. York, who had twice served as king's lieutenant in France, wrote in 1450 that failure to pay his salary threatened the lordship's collapse and that rather than preside over this he would return home, 'for it shall never be chronicled nor remain in scripture, by the grace of God, that Ireland was lost by my negligence'.[32] Yet in fact the problems of English rule in the two territories were essentially different. Developments in Ireland had, it is true, led to a grave weakening of royal authority, but there was little likelihood that the Gaelic clans would, as the bards cynically promised, rout the English across the sea. In Normandy, English rule had by the 1440s become largely a military occupation with little local support, and it was defeated by the superior force of a resurgent monarchy whose resources were far greater than those of the English king: English rule in

29. Nicholls 1972, pp. 84–8.
30. Harris 1747, p. 44.
31. Ellis 1986a, pp. 9–10, 49–66; *NHI*, ii; Nicholls 1972, *passim*; Simms 1975–6, pp. 98–108.
32. Otway-Ruthven 1980, p. 382 (quotation).

Ireland, however, was much more than a colonial occupation. It commanded widespread support among a population which was largely anglicized and mainly English by descent.[33] This population might occasionally challenge royal authority and complain about the conduct of government, but it seldom denied the king's right to rule. The key to the king's Irish problem, therefore, was basically the revival of royal authority and the reform of crown government.

33. Ellis 1986a, *passim*; Lydon 1972b, p. 183; Keen 1973, ch. 16.

CHAPTER 2

LAND AND PEOPLE IN TUDOR IRELAND

The social structures of Tudor Ireland were deeply affected by the marcher conditions in which its people lived. Modern historians have tended to stress common features of the Irish economy and society and the similarities that underlay the more apparent ethnic differences. Yet such common features and similarities as emerged during the middle ages were not the characteristics which most impressed contemporaries. In a short excursus on Ireland in his *Anglica Historia*, Polydore Vergil described its inhabitants as of two sorts: 'one is gentle and cultured', living an English manner of life, obedient to the king, and mostly understanding the language (though interestingly he attributed their English-ness simply to frequent contact with England); 'the other type of islander is savage, rude and uncouth', known as '"wild men of the woods"' because of their primitive habits.[1] His remarks summarize what outsiders considered the essential attributes of Ireland's Gaelic and English inhabitants. The English Pale included some of the best land in Ireland, good arable and very similar to parts of lowland England, but quite unlike the stony wastes and bogs of the Gaelic parts. Within the lordship the Normans had replaced Gaelic tribalism with their own brand of feudalism, and the system of landholding there had since developed along English lines. Socially and culturally too, the two peoples exhibited basic differences. Of course the boundaries between Gaelic and English Ireland were now more blurred, and there can have been few parts from which Gaelic influences, or English for that matter, had been totally excluded, but late medieval Irish society cannot be adequately explained merely in terms of an increasing 'gaelicization' of the English districts. In the vast expanse of marchland beyond the more settled parts, society was arguably shaped as much by the existence and proximity of a frontier as by the direct influence of Gaelic Ireland.

THE ENGLISH DISTRICTS

Geography and settlement

The situation and economy of the English districts were determined by a number of factors, of which the geography of the earlier Anglo-Norman settlement

1. Vergil 1950, p. 79.

probably remained the most important. The settlers had of course aimed to acquire profitable land, especially good arable, and intensive occupation had not normally occurred in areas above the 400-foot contour line, or in boggy lowlands. Such districts were also more difficult to control and defend, and as was true of Norman settlement in the Welsh marches, the connection between military and economic considerations which had shaped the original conquest continued to exercise an overriding influence on the lordship's development.[2] In general, settlement in the south and east had been much more intensive than in the north and west, and in those parts where the colonists barely penetrated the power of the magnates amounted to no more than a loose overlordship which was similar in many ways to that later built up by the earls of Kildare. In early Tudor Ireland, the 400-foot contour line still divided the more anglicized districts of Louth, Meath and the Down coastline from the Gaelic areas to the north and west, although in Meath settlement was heavier in the richer, lower-lying land to the east of Trim and Kells. On the southern marches of the Pale, the Wicklow mountains in the east and the bogs of Leix and Offaly in the west continued to determine the pattern of settlement; while in the south the Barrow–Nore–Suir basin, and parts of Cork and Limerick, had been most heavily colonized, with settlement thinning out in the uplands of north Tipperary and south-west Munster.[3]

In these areas good land, comparative peace and peasants of English stock provided the conditions and experience necessary for the introduction of a far more intensive and efficient system of arable farming than continued in Gaelic Ireland: land clearance, relatively high levels of population, and nucleated villages around a church, small castle or other fortified manorial dwelling provided an obvious departure from the scattered population and patterns of land usage elsewhere. In other parts, where the land was poorer and the settlers fewer, continuity with the past was much more apparent. The survival of the manorial system, however, depended on a measure of peace and demographic stability which was increasingly disrupted after 1300 by weak government and adverse economic conditions. Little could be done about plague and famine which by 1450 had greatly reduced the levels of population. The Gaelic chiefs soon picked off isolated settlements, and where lordships were also divided between female heirs or passed to absentees, their raids could set off a chain reaction whereby tenants moved out, individual manors were abandoned, and the defence of whole districts was gradually undermined. Elsewhere, however, a variety of factors – the density of the original settlement, strong lordship, good natural lines of defence, easy communications with England, or substantial assistance from the Dublin administration – combined in differing degrees to ensure the survival, at a reduced level, of the manorial system. By 1500 mixed farming in the traditional English manner was concentrated in the Pale, south Wexford, Kilkenny and Tipperary, with isolated agricultural borough communities in Carlow, Cork, Waterford and Limerick. Here

2. Davies 1978, pp. 302–3.
3. Frame 1981, chs 4, 6; Ellis 1986a, ch. 2; see map, p. 383.

the heavier concentrations of settlers ensured that these territories remained very anglicized, and the continuing absorption into the manorial system of peasants of Gaelic stock also maintained higher levels of population. In other parts the proximity of the Irishry and the shortage of tenants accentuated the swing to pastoralism which was a feature of farming in England too.[4] Thus by the early Tudor period it seemed that the political partition of the island into English and Gaelic was mirrored by a similar landed division between the mixed farming of the more anglicized areas and the marches and Gaelic territories, where pastoralism predominated.

Within the English areas, smallholders were predominantly of English descent. Precise evidence is scarce, but in 1510 29 out of 53 small farmers and cottiers on lands near Geraldstown of a Meath gentleman were English by race, or sufficiently anglicized to adopt the name of a trade or English town as ordered by parliament; as were at least 33 out of 46 tenants of the manor of Danesfort, Co. Kilkenny, in 1443, half of Lord Portlester's tenants and servants near Ballymore Eustace in 1480, and three-quarters of the customary tenants and cottiers on three Dublin manors of the earl of Ormond in the late 1470s. The later fifteenth century perhaps saw a rapid turnover of tenants: on the Kildare manor of Maynooth in 1518, out of 59 cottiers only ten had the same (mostly very common) surnames as tenants there in 1451, and the proportion of tenants with Gaelic surnames rose from 37 to 54 per cent; but in 1540 many of the tenants of 1518 were still there. Where the peasantry was mainly of English descent – in the Pale maghery, south Wexford, and parts of Kilkenny and Tipperary – the countryside remained predominantly English-speaking (despite suggestions to the contrary), as were the towns and cities. By 1550 in most of Kildare and Westmeath, however, Gaelic predominated, which suggests that Kildare expansion had been achieved largely by recruiting Gaelic peasants rather than through any significant increase in the English population. In other English districts, the nobles and gentry could normally speak English, and even Gaelic lords had English-speaking clerks available, though they usually corresponded with the government in an anglicized form of medieval Latin. In Co. Cork in 1535 Lord Barry, a boy of 18 years, could speak 'very good English', as could the young earl of Desmond. Even O'Brien of Thomond found it wise to have written in English a letter of exculpation to Henry VIII for his activities in the recent rebellion, but Gerald Fitzgerald of the Decies could speak 'never a word of English'.[5]

Wealth and landholding in English Ireland

Very little research has yet been done on such basic questions as the distribution of wealth and patterns of landholding among the landed elite, the

---

4. Ellis 1986a, pp. 5–9; Lydon 1972b, chs 5, 7, 9; White 1943, *passim*; PRO, SC 11/934–5, SP 65/3/2. Cf. Bush 1975, ch. 3.
5. *StP*, ii, 281–8 (quotations, pp. 282, 284); Ellis 1986a, pp. 6–7; Empey 1970–1, pp. 184–5; Canny 1975, pp. 2–11; *NHI*, iii, p. 28; Ellis 1995a, pp. 115–16, 130–1.

emergence of a gentry and the concept of a county community. Nonetheless, evidence from the later 1530s concerning the valuations of ecclesiastical bene-fices preserved in the Irish *Valor Ecclesiasticus* points to a marked concentra-tion of wealth in the English Pale, with much lower average values for benefices in the remoter parts of the lordship. In general, marcher conditions encour-aged resident lordship and militated against the more dispersed patterns of landholding common in lowland England. In Co. Kildare *c.* 1500, for instance, there were only around twenty or so substantial gentry families available to serve key offices in local government, such as sheriff or escheator. This was perhaps a small group even by Irish standards: elsewhere the pool of available gentry was probably larger. Meath, a much bigger shire, had in 1511 161 lay and 19 clerical landowners whose landed income was apparently worth the IR£20 a year or more of a 'middling' gentleman.[6]

Estate management too was generally geared more to defence rather than to the maximization of rental income. English tenants, where available, were accustomed to military service, and a loyal and warlike tenantry reduced the need for costly holdings of troops. Yet kerne and galloglass were usually neces-sary to defend exposed marchlands which English tenants found unattractive. And after 1534, with the deployment of a standing garrison by the crown, leading landowners tended to neglect traditional defensive arrangements and to raise rents in line with inflation.

Overall, prevailing conditions meant that the landed incomes of nobles and gentry seemed very low by comparison with landowners in lowland England, but the apparent poverty of the lordship's landed elite frequently disguised relatively large but compact holdings and a numerous tenantry. In this re-gard, the extensive possessions of the ninth earl of Kildare, built up over the previous half-century, were wholly exceptional. Worth *c.* IR£1,585 per annum by 1534, the earl's estates included some land in almost every shire of the medieval lordship, but the bulk of it was concentrated in Kildare (IR£709) and Meath (IR£460), with other clusters of manors in Limerick and Ulster (IR£150). In fact, Earl Gerald's total annual income easily exceeded IR£2,000, making him one of Henry VIII's ten most wealthy subjects: he towered head and shoulders over other magnates in the lordship.

Apart from Kildare, very few of the lordship's leading magnates were worth more than a poor baron in England. Only the two richest ecclesiastical lords, the prior of Kilmainham (worth IR£744 per annum) and the archbishop of Dublin (IR£535), enjoyed what were by English standards respectable landed incomes. The estates of the earldom of Ormond, when regranted to Piers Butler in 1537, were worth only IR£389 a year. When combined with Butler's Polestown estates, they were probably just about adequate to support his dignity; but the landed income of a minor peer like Lord Howth (about IR£100 a year) was less than most English county gentry. Some heads of junior branches of Kildare's extended lineage were also richer than this, including Sir Gerald

6. Trinity College Dublin, MS 594, ff. 25*v*–9*v*; Ellis 1990, pp. 239–65. Cf. Berry 1910, pp. 646–8; Harris 1747, pp. 45–6.

Shanesson, with lands in Carbury barony worth 200 marks (IR), and Thomas FitzMaurice, the earl's cousin, with lands in Kildare and Meath exceeding IR£100 a year. Yet much the wealthiest of these kinsmen was Kildare's half-brother, Sir Thomas Fitzgerald of Leixlip, with extensive possessions worth well over IR£300 in Carlow, Kildare, Louth, Meath and Ulster, as well as Gloucestershire and Warwickshire in England. Sir Thomas was an influential figure in his own right and married the duke of Buckingham's illegitimate daughter.[7] Yet what really mattered in a marcher society was an extensive *manraed* (the men a lord could call on at need for military service) rather than mere rents.

The organization of agriculture

A continuing feature of the late medieval lordship was the extent to which labour services were still required of the manorial tenantry, though they were far less heavy than in Gaelic Ireland or medieval England. At Kells in 1510 fifteen days' work at harvest time was required of some tenants instead of rent, but normally no more than six days a year was demanded. Nevertheless, unlike Gaelic nobles, most English lords had abandoned demesne farming in the fourteenth century, setting their lands to farm, and these services and often some customary renders such as a hen from each tenant at Christmas were received by substantial farmers who took the manor on short lease. A comparatively low money rent was usually the chief burden on the smallholder – commonly between 8*d.* and 16*d.* an acre per annum – and in an age of generally static population levels and a plentiful supply of land after the earlier demographic decline they enjoyed in practice a fair measure of protection from arbitrary eviction and rackrenting, whatever their tenurial rights according to the law. The 1541 commissioners' surveys commonly divided manorial tenants into freeholders and tenants-at-will, though substantial holdings were also entered as let on long leases (usually between 21 and 61 years). In parts of the Pale, Kilkenny, and probably Wexford and Tipperary, the strip holdings of medieval farming communities with scattered plots in common fields survived well into the Tudor period, but as in England, enclosure and the break-up of small customary holdings in favour of larger leasehold farms worked by almost landless labourers was well under way: substantial yeomen farmers were replacing peasant smallholders throughout the English parts of Leinster.[8]

In these areas a normal market economy operated, with trading through the towns in agricultural produce, wool, hides and cloth (both coarse Irish cloth and English cloth imported for finishing). The staple food crop of the Pale was wheat, and barley and rye were also grown, but oats predominated in the rest of the country where barley and rye were rare. In the Pale and the south-east there was much spinning and weaving of both wool and linen. Overall, a considerable export trade was continued in hides, linen and coarse cloths, with

7. Ellis 1995a, ch. 4.
8. Ellis 1986a, p. 7; White 1943, *passim*; PRO, SC 11/934–5, SP 65/3/2 (now printed in Mac Niocaill 1992); Canny 1975, pp. 3–7; Nicholls 1972, p. 116; Otway-Ruthven 1951, pp. 1–11.

butter, tallow, sheepskin and furs also major exports, while staple imports were wine, iron and salt. In years of good harvest corn was exported in quantity, mainly wheat, barley and oats, but cheaper corn, malt, peas and beans were imported, and corn imports of all kinds increased under Elizabeth to feed an enlarged garrison and alleviate shortages caused by war.[9]

As the sixteenth century wore on the Pale landlords took to letting their lands on very short leases and there were complaints that they let holdings decay, expelled the English peasantry, introduced Gaelic tenants, and raised rents and services. Yet the poorer tenantry was predominantly Gaelic, so the acceleration in the dissolution of the medieval farming system, prompted by the Tudor inflation and renewed political instability, may in the lordship have appeared an ethnic phenomenon. There is little evidence, however, that inflation was a significant factor in landlord–tenant relations before 1534: true, the ninth earl of Kildare increased certain rents from their 1518 level about 1530, but then he was known as 'the greatest improver of his lands in this land'.[10] The 1541 commissioners had an interest in seeing that juries found manorial tenants to be tenants-at-will, but other evidence suggests that they were usually copyholders or leaseholders with definite rights and some security of tenure in accordance with customs which varied from manor to manor. Few tenants were still personally unfree, though some serfs remained on church lands in the Pale maghery, and where the manorial system survived social structures were diversified with a peasantry ranging from landless labourers and poor cottiers holding one or two acres to prosperous husbandmen and yeomen able to sue their landlords in the king's courts.[11] In these parts, therefore, society was not unlike parts of lowland England, though it should be remembered that few districts were totally insulated from march warfare. Frequently considerations of lordship and defence were more important than the strict forms of tenure recognized by English law.

TOWNS AND TRADE

A second major difference between the English and Gaelic districts was the comparatively large number of urban settlements in English Ireland. Of course even the English districts were still overwhelmingly rural by continental standards. Yet the lordship included some six or seven towns and cities which English observers accounted important, as well as over 40 significant market towns. Foreign trade was almost entirely in the hands of merchants of these towns. The population of Dublin, the capital, has been plausibly estimated, on the basis of tithe figures, at about 8,000 in 1540, which would make it then about the sixth largest city in the British Isles. Sixty years earlier it may have been *comparatively* more populous: its population was then increasing again

9. Nicholls 1972, pp. 7, 115, 119–20; Nicholls 1982, p. 398; *NHI*, iii, pp. 8, 34, 149.
10. BL, Harleian MS 3756; Hore & Graves 1870, pp. 161–2; *StP*, ii, 300.
11. As note 8.

and in the years 1469 to 1484 admissions to the citizenship (averaging nearly 37 annually) exceeded those to Edinburgh in the 1550s, when Edinburgh was the second or third largest city. Apart from its functions as the administrative capital, Dublin was also an important manufacturing centre and, despite a sand bar, a major port which traded chiefly with Chester, Bristol and later Liverpool, importing mainly luxury items. It was also the focus of a coastal trade which extended northwards to the Bann salmon fishery and south to Wexford and the southern coastal system.[12]

In general, the east coast ports traded mainly with England, exporting little save yarn, fells and tallow. The southern ports had stronger links with the continent and the fishery was the most important economic activity on that coast.[13] Not far behind Dublin in size was Waterford, probably a more flourishing commercial centre with hides and cloth its principal exports. It had a very large hinterland through the confluence of the rivers Barrow, Nore and Suir, and the whole area was, according to Lord Deputy Sidney in 1567, 'full of industry' and the people 'very civil'. New Ross on the Barrow, Kilkenny on the Nore, and Carrick and Clonmel on the Suir – all significant settlements in their own right – were important parts of its interior trade network, while its strongest overseas links were with Bristol. In 1559–60, for example, Bristol imported some 26,556 yards of Irish cloth. New Ross had declined since Edward I's days when it had been the lordship's chief port, but it remained important. Periodically, it disputed (unsuccessfully) Waterford's right to the prisage of wine on the estuaries of the three rivers: until 1536 its lords were the absentee dukes of Norfolk. Kilkenny was the largest inland town in Ireland, thanks partly to Butler efforts in keeping its hinterland relatively peaceful. In 1536 an English commissioner described it as 'well-walled and well replenished of people and wealthy'. The fourteenth century had seen its burgesses roughly halved in number – there were only 118 in 1383–4 – but incomplete entries of admissions to the franchise around 1500 suggest a recent marked recovery. By then Kilkenny proper may have had 3,000 inhabitants, and there was a significant subordinate settlement in Irishtown.[14] The other major settlements, Limerick, Cork, Drogheda and Galway, were all effectively seaports, even though Limerick was 60 miles inland up the Shannon estuary. Both Limerick and Galway traded heavily with the Iberian peninsula and France, but also England, exporting fish, beef and hides (plus corn from Limerick) in exchange for wine. Information about their size is scantier still. Elizabethan Limerick was evidently larger than Cork: the English commissioner described it in 1536 as 'a wondrous proper city . . . and it may be called little London for the situation and the plenty', but an English captain in 1535 was more impressed by Cork. Drogheda had traditionally been a more important port than Dublin: it was overhauled by Dublin

12. Mac Niocaill 1981, pp. 15–19; *NHI*, iii, p. 6; Lynch 1981, pp. 9–14; Longfield 1929, pp. 36–8; Nicholls 1972, p. 119. See now Lennon 1989, ch. 1 on late medieval Dublin.
13. Longfield 1929, pp. 29–40, 200; *NHI*, iii, pp. 6–10.
14. PRO, SP 60/3/120 (*LP*, xi, no. 259); Mac Niocaill 1964a, ii, pp. 335, 456–67, 523–8, 535, 539–88; Mac Niocaill 1981, pp. 8–12; McNeill 1931a, pp. 68–70, 94–142; *NHI*, iii, pp. 8–9; Empey 1970–1, p. 185; Canny 1976, p. 6; Gillespie 1991, p. 6.

in the fifteenth century, but under the early Tudors its trade was only marginally less in volume. By 1611, however, when more precise estimates became available, Dublin's trade outstripped all the other ports, being valued at IR£80,000 a year, as opposed to only IR£20,000 each for Drogheda, Galway and Cork, IR£30,000 for Waterford, and IR£10,000 for Limerick.[15]

Water transport long remained far cheaper than by land, but in Ireland this advantage enjoyed by port towns was accentuated by the relatively disturbed condition of the countryside. For this reason all the major towns and cities and many secondary towns such as Ardee, Navan, Athboy, Mullingar, Trim, Naas, Fethard, Clonmel, Kilmallock (described in 1535 as 'a very poor town') and Athenry were walled; and whereas in England these walls had sometimes been allowed to decay, in Ireland they were maintained stiff and staunch. Wexford, however, was unwalled: it was a secondary settlement, but yet the chief fishing port, with close links with Bristol and a considerable export trade in shipbuilding timber. By 1537 it had recovered sufficiently from the later medieval depression to boast $345\frac{1}{4}$ burgages (against $365\frac{1}{2}$ before 1300) and a population of 500 adult males.[16] With few exceptions, the inland towns were located in the two chief areas of the manorial system – the Pale, and the Ormond region (recently described as 'a second Pale' because of the distinctively English character of its economy and society). This would suggest that the smaller towns at least depended more on the local agricultural economy than on international trade or that with Gaelic Ireland, though small towns like Athboy and Athy were occasionally prosecuted for levying 'through toll' without authority.[17]

ARCHITECTURE AND THE ECONOMIC REVIVAL

The Yorkist and early Tudor period was an age of prosperity by comparison with the fourteenth-century European depression and the locally adverse conditions post-1550, though favourable conditions no doubt benefited the lordship's towns and manorial economy more than the backward Gaelic districts. Apart from the marked growth in trade, illustrated by the rising customs receipts for Dublin and Drogheda, the age also saw an impressive new style of architecture, late Irish Gothic, effectively a subcategory of English Gothic, as the townsmen and nobles invested their new wealth in building projects. For example, in Kilkenny the four gates were rebuilt in 1500, a new tholsel was completed in 1507, a new gate constructed in 1517, and about this time an imposing belfry tower was added to the Black Abbey there, one of the most perfect surviving products of the tower-building period which in Ireland was

15. PRO, SP 60/3/120 (LP, xi, no. 259); StP, ii, 281–6; NHI, iii, pp. 5, 10, 12, 13–14; Gillespie 1991, p. 5; Canny 1976, pp. 2–6; Butlin 1977, pp. 65–6, 70, 72.
16. Butlin 1977, pp. 45–6, 75–6; StP, ii, 284; NHI, iii, pp. 7, 36; PRO, SP 60/4/86 (LP, xii (ii), no. 173); Hore & Graves 1870, p. 59.
17. Empey 1970–1, p. 185 (quotation); Ellis 1986a, p. 128.

largely confined to the period 1400–1600. In Limerick, St Mary's cathedral received more additions during the fifteenth century than any other church in Ireland; and in Galway, St Nicholas's, the second largest parish church in Ireland, was greatly extended in the early Tudor period. The most impressive and elaborate works were sponsored by the older monasteries of the English districts, for example Holy Cross and Kilcooley Abbeys, Co. Tipperary, largely rebuilt c. 1450, but many of the native aristocracy also promoted church building. In the lordship the emphasis was on the improvement of earlier buildings – the addition of belfry towers and cloister arcades – but in sheer bulk of new buildings the foundation of some 40 new friaries, chiefly in the south and west, was a major architectural development. The best documented is the Franciscan friary at Adare, Co. Limerick, built largely at the expense of the seventh earl of Kildare and his wife, but the Franciscan friary at Quin in Clare was sponsored by the local Gaelic chief, MacNamara, and built (exceptionally) within the walls of an old Norman castle. Unlike the earlier urban-based monasteries, these later foundations frequently had Gaelic patrons.

There was also, commencing gradually around 1425, a new spate of castle-building throughout Ireland, notably the towerhouses (also called peles) which were built in great numbers in the more fertile lowland parts of Leinster, Munster, and much of Connaught, as lords and gentry invested in a more secure future in this life too. Towerhouses were largely confined to Ireland, southern Scotland and the English borders where marcher conditions encouraged landowners to maintain fortified dwellings at a time when their counterparts in lowland England were abandoning castles for country houses. Apart from the style of crenellation, Irish towerhouses resembled northern English ones, having the entrance on the ground floor. The great majority were built in the century after 1450, particularly along the coastline south from Carlingford to Galway, presumably against the threat of piracy, with another great sweep running through the Englishry in Cos. Limerick, Tipperary, Kilkenny and Wexford. Within the Pale, however, the majority were situated in the marches, with fewer in the more peaceful maghery where gentry were now building English country houses.[18]

POPULATION TRENDS

The population of late medieval Ireland was comparatively low, perhaps only half a million, though this is mere speculation. From c. 1470 it may have risen slowly with the onset of more settled conditions: certainly the absence for 60 years or so of complaints about emigration from the lordship seems significant. After 1534, however, population levels remained stable or actually fell, against the European trend, with the increasing levels of violence and warfare. Emigration to England resumed. Under Elizabeth, Irish vagrants arrived by the shipload,

18. Leask 1960, *passim*; Leask 1946, chs 9–12; McNeill 1931a, pp. 117, 132, 139; Ellis 1995a, pp. 30–1; Ó Danachair 1979, pp. 158–63; Thompson 1987, esp. p. 23; Ellis 1986a, p. 73; Longfield 1929, p. 25.

presenting a particular problem in the south-west. The 1572 Vagrancy Act ordered that they be punished and sent home. Outbreaks of plague and the 'sweating sickness' also took their toll: in the plague of 1575, for instance, 3,000 people reputedly perished in Dublin alone, around a third of its inhabitants; and the plague of 1602–4 perhaps reduced Ireland's population by 10 per cent. These demographic trends may also explain why, according to the scanty evidence about prices, inflation remained low in late sixteenth-century Ireland, by contrast with England. Yet the overall picture conceals marked regional variations. The English Pale in particular was well populated, and the lordship as a whole, though comprising only a third of the island, probably held over half the total population. The Gaelic districts were very sparsely populated, Antrim and Down in the late sixteenth century particularly so. Some borderlands were almost deserted: during the fifteenth century, districts like Fasagh Bantry and Fasagh Reban had been uninhabited for so long that the original placenames within them were simply forgotten.[19]

CONDITIONS IN GAELIC IRELAND

Overall, English observers found society in the early Tudor lordship still reasonably familiar, if somewhat disordered, but conditions in Gaelic Ireland seemed quite exceptional. Large areas were still covered by scrubby forest, lakes and undrained bog. The population was scanty and shifting, and settlements were scattered and largely impermanent. The economy was predominantly a pastoral one, with great herds of cattle and horses with their herdsmen and escort (known collectively as 'creaghts') wandering over tracts of waste. The creaghts were not everywhere itinerant, but frequent raids and petty warfare placed a premium on mobility, and the indifferent quality of much of the land also encouraged transhumance or 'booleying', the movement of cattle to summer pastures on mountain slopes. It now appears that agriculture was more important in the Gaelic economy than was once thought, but tillage was largely on a shifting or 'long-fallow' basis, and the predominance of small plots cultivated with the spade contrasted with the ploughed open fields or enclosures in areas where heavy Norman settlement had occurred.[20]

Gaelic clans and lordship

Land was owned corporately by agnatic descent groups called clans, all members being descended from a common male ancestor. The clan was a corporate entity with political and legal functions, particularly relating to land, but it also had responsibility for the conduct of its members. Nevertheless, it was not

19. Nicholls 1976, pp. 9–11; *NHI*, ii, pp. 408–11, iii, pp. 4, 34; Gillespie 1991, pp. 9–14; Beier 1985, pp. 10–11, 32–4, 62–5; Canny 1976, p. 3; Ellis 1986a, p. 130; Lennon 1994, p. 8; Lennon 1989, p. 31. For the information about fifteenth-century wastes, I am indebted to a lecture by Mr K.W. Nicholls.
20. Nicholls 1972, pp. 5–7, 114–16; *NHI*, iii, p. 34; Canny 1976, p. 1.

a family in the social sense, and though it might close ranks and collectively seek vengeance against the murderer of one of its members, internal dissension, particularly between cousins, was quite normal. Land was usually held by individual members for a limited term, frequently one year only but sometimes longer, and then redistributed among co-heirs, a practice which militated against intensive exploitation of the land, improvements or substantial buildings: even the nobles lived in cabins made of boughs of trees and covered with turf. Since land was plentiful, however, and peace precarious, there was in any case little incentive to development; but if the co-heirs agreed, a permanent partition of the lands could be made. This practice must frequently have been necessary every two or three generations, and thereafter each co-heir's portion was part-ible among his direct male descendants only. This system of inheritance, found in Wales and Ireland, was referred to by English lawyers as a 'custom in nature of gavelkind' because it seemed to resemble the Kentish custom of gavelkind. Under Gaelic law, however, women were unable to inherit lands. A woman could hold separately from her husband lands purchased during the marriage and on her husband's death redeem any property so bought, but she had no entitlement to her late husband's property, unlike the English custom of dower whereby a woman was entitled to at least a third of her husband's estate. This reflected the low status of women in Gaelic society, and their position was further weakened by the ease with which men could repudiate or divorce their partners: Gaelic law accepted uncanonical 'clandestine' marriages, while concubinage and multiple and trial marriages were also common. With the extension of English power under Elizabeth, however, the refusal of the authorities to tolerate Gaelic custom in this regard allowed aggrieved wives and widows to secure redress, particularly repayment of a dowry, by proceed-ings in chancery. Increasingly, too, dowries were protected by mortgaging land to secure them.[21]

In each lordship election to the chieftaincy lay within the *derbfine* group of the ruling clan, i.e. within descendants, both legitimate and illegitimate, of a common male ancestor in four generations. Theoretically, he who was 'eldest and worthiest' was chosen by the territory's gentry in their assembly, at which both related and unrelated clans of different surname were present. More frequently, a bloody succession struggle decided the issue, a source of serious instability within the lordship and an incentive to outsiders to intervene. In many cases the chief's successor, or tanist, was nominated in his lifetime, but this was no guarantee against strife either.[22]

Lordship in Gaelic Ireland was not a closed and defined territory but a complex of rights, tributes and authority. The chief was entitled to a tribute from each townland in his territory, generally beeves, oats and butter, some-times money or customary labour services of ploughing and reaping. In addi-tion he would levy his travelling expenses on the inhabitants, force them to support his servants and followers, quarter troops on them usually twice a

21. Nicholls 1991, pp. 17–31; Cosgrove 1985b, pp. 25–34; MacCurtain 1985, pp. 51–66.
22. Nicholls 1972, pp. 25–31, 60–4; *NHI*, iii, pp. 34–5; Canny 1976, p. 12.

year, and force them to erect and repair buildings. This system of free services and entertainment was sometimes commuted, frequently adopted by English marchers, and was generally described as 'coign and livery' by English writers. The more powerful provincial chiefs exploited it in the fifteenth and sixteenth centuries to maintain professional armies of kerne and galloglass in preference to traditional hostings of landowning clansmen, thereby eroding their political influence too. 'Coign and livery' constituted one of the principal rights of the chief over his subjects, and if these exactions were not paid he might seize the lands from which they were due as pledge for payment. The chief usually also had some demesne land attached to his office which he cultivated with his own labourers; and he had a right of pre-emption of any goods sold in his lordship which was frequently exercised by granting a particular merchant (a 'grey merchant' in English parlance) the exclusive right of trading within his territory. The burden on the subject varied considerably between lordships, but was usually heavier in Munster border areas, where lordships were generally fragmented and more militarized, than in the Gaelic north and west where lordships were more normally solid blocks of territory. Nevertheless, Gaelic lordship was more a lordship of men than of land, and in the last analysis the extent of a chief's territory was measured by his ability to compel payment of tributes from outlying border clans.[23]

Within each lordship, circumstances such as the burden and indefinite nature of the chief's rights over subjects and the proliferation of his clan stemming from a laxer Celtic tradition concerning marriage prompted the territorial expansion of the ruling clan at the expense of other landowning clans. This ongoing process, found also in modern, primitive clan-based societies, such as in South Africa, led to the gradual displacement of lesser, unrelated landowning clans by the chief's kin and their eventual reduction to the ranks of the landless. The constant transfer of land in this way created a profusion of land titles, especially between the theoretical owners and the actual possessors of the land who might have been intruded by the chief because the owners were unable to satisfy his exactions. It was also customary for the chief to have custody of the lands of an absentee owner, and neighbouring or related clans might occupy for grazing lands lying waste, customs which further complicated the pattern of possession. Theoretically land could only be alienated with the consent of other clansmen, but in practice land was conveyed by means of a pledge or 'mortgage', a device for raising money similar in form and function to the contemporary *prid* or 'Welsh mortgage'. The owners surrendered it in return for a payment in kind or money and might recover it on repayment: in many cases, however, the conditions of redemption were very onerous, and there was no real intention that the pledge would ever be redeemed. Effectively, continuous possession of land over several generations created a (comparatively) secure title.[24]

---

23. Nicholls 1972, pp. 31–40; *NHI*, iii, p. 26; Simms 1987a, pp. 19–20, 59, 93–4.
24. Nicholls 1972, pp. 10–11, 57–60, 65–7; Nicholls 1976, pp. 5–9, 14–17. Cf. Davies 1978, pp. 143–5, 407–12.

Outsiders like the earl of Kildare were thus easily able to penetrate a chieftaincy and establish an overlordship; and in borderlands especially layers of conflicting titles were built up in addition to common law titles. The crown of course recognized only the latter, but when as a result of 'surrender and regrant' in the 1540s it was forced to arbitrate between rival Gaelic titles, it found the task almost impossible. Nevertheless, from a Gaelic perspective, the expansion of Fitzgerald and Butler in the midlands and south Leinster was much the same as that of powerful Gaelic chiefs over their weaker neighbours. The well-known report on the state of Ireland written *c.* 1515 divided the Irishry into over 60 countries ruled by chief captains who each

> maketh war and peace for himself, and holdeth by the sword, and hath imperial jurisdiction within his room, and obeyeth to no other person, English or Irish, except only to such persons as may subdue him by the sword.

To these the report added over 30 'captains of English noble family that followeth the same Irish order'. In practice, however, many of the chiefs listed were acknowledged vassals of others and rarely enjoyed much autonomy, and even the more powerful chiefs were not immune from outside interference. Just as lesser landowning clans were reduced and replaced by the ruling clan, and collateral lines by the chief lineage, so more powerful chieftaincies sought to establish an overlordship over their weaker neighbours and eventually to displace them and acquire their lands. Frequently a series of cattle-raids was executed, until the weaker chief agreed to recognize this overlordship. Thereafter the relationship between overlord and vassal would depend largely on the disparity between their power. Its most important aspect was the overlord's right to quarter troops and followers at will on the vassal, but the overlord might also demand military service, a yearly rent, a proportion of any fines imposed by the chief in his territory, and the nomination of any new chief.[25]

Thus far more transparently than in English society, lordship depended on armed might; and on the pretext of defending his country, the chief gradually extorted land from the subordinate clans in accordance with customs which lent themselves to that purpose. There were, however, certain informal limitations on the chief's power. No doubt the danger that outsiders would exploit internal divisions persuaded some chiefs to moderate their demands, though there is no evidence of this. More tangibly, landowners could at a price buy the protection, or 'slantyaght', of an outside magnate, whereby any injury done to them was treated by their protector as done directly to him, a custom which cut directly across the chief's rights over his subjects. There was, moreover, no shortage of land, but without the stock or dependent labour to exploit it, the land was useless and both of these commodities were in less plentiful supply: 'a chieftain's real wealth lay in the farmers who lived under his protection and the cows they tended'.[26]

25. Nicholls 1972, pp. 21–5; *StP*, ii, 1–31.
26. Simms 1975–6, p. 99 (quotation); Nicholls 1972, pp. 41–3.

Landless and labourers in Gaelic Ireland

Gaelic society was divided fairly sharply between landowners and landless. 'Gavelkind', the lord's exactions, and other economic pressures would gradually force poorer landowners to alienate their lands and become landless labourers: conversely there existed in some parts influential but landless clans who were tenants on demesne lands of powerful lords, and peasants possessing stock might hope to acquire land on pledge from poor landowners and so thrive. Some of the tenantry, moreover, were men of some substance: they negotiated with their landlords on fairly equal terms, and could defend their stock and dependants from raids. The usual form of agricultural tenancy was a form of métayage; and if the tenant provided his own stock and seed, he might retain three-quarters of the crop, giving his lord a quarter. Nevertheless much of the land was cultivated by landowning clans themselves with the help of share-cropping labourers. These 'churls' were effectively tenants-at-will without stock, substance or rights in the land, and entirely dependent on the lord they followed. The great mass of the Gaelic population was of this status, in a particularly weak economic position compared with English peasants. They were not a stable population settled on the land but migrated freely, quite apart from the creaghts: their ties, if any, were to a particular lord, not the land, and usually 'the tenants continue not past three years in one place, but run roving about the country like wild men'.[27] Traditionally they did not bear arms: Sir Henry Sidney remarked that Shane O'Neill was the first Irishman to arm the peasantry of his country, but this was a reaction to mounting disorders in his lordship. Defence was entrusted to landowners who had a general obligation to serve in the 'rising out' or levy of the country, either as horsemen or kerne according to their means, but as English pressure on Gaelic Ireland mounted from the 1540s, the more powerful chiefs particularly in Ulster responded by building up their household troops, hiring redshanks from Scotland (see below, Chapter 10).[28]

The reaction of Gaelic chiefs to less stable conditions and to a growing scarcity of tenants after 1550 seems to have been to redouble efforts to prevent labourers from leaving their lordship, much as the Lancastrian administration had attempted in English Ireland and with equally little success. The prohibition on leaving, coupled with a confusion by contemporary English commentators between the chief's rights over his subjects and a landlord's rights over his tenants, misled modern historians into positing a division in Gaelic society between free and unfree. Despite ambiguities, the evidence militates against the view that there existed an hereditary class of serfs, but it may be that a peasant could contract himself to a landlord in return for land or stock. The landless might therefore be legally free; but in practice they were probably worse off than the remaining villeins on ecclesiastical estates in the Pale. Nevertheless chiefs were, during the sixteenth century, extending to the lands of lesser landowners the labour services, ploughing, weeding and reaping,

27. Nicholls 1976, pp. 9–14 (quotation, p. 11); Nicholls 1972, pp. 68–71, 116.
28. Nicholls 1972, pp. 71, 84–7; Simms 1987a, pp. 126–7.

which their own labourers would normally perform – a strong indication of an acute labour shortage. The evidence, such as it is, all points to a severe under-utilization of the land, a small, highly mobile population, and impermanent settlements.[29]

Gaelic administration

The administration of Gaelic lordships was rudimentary. The chief would appoint a brehon or judge, chiefly to try cases affecting himself or matters of public concern. The brehon's decision was an arbitration to which, theoretic-ally, both parties had given prior consent. If the chief had an interest, he would compel a recalcitrant defendant to accept this, otherwise the plaintiff might take a private distress, i.e. seize the defendant's cattle or goods as a 'pledge for justice' – if he were strong enough. There was no criminal law as such and what English law deemed capital offences were simple torts resolved by payment of compensation much as in primitive Germanic societies. For example, a homicide would result in the murderer's kin paying a fine called an *eric* which varied in accordance with the victim's status like the Anglo-Saxon *wergild*; and the compensation for theft was several times the value of the goods stolen. A proportion of these fines, up to two-thirds for serious injuries, went to the plaintiff's chief and must have formed an important part of his revenues. Accordingly, by the mid-sixteenth century chiefs were imposing man-datary jurisdiction by their own brehons for serious crimes in their territories, and a concept of public justice was emerging. Sometimes, the defendant's kin could not or would not pay the fine, in which case he might be handed over to the injured party, and there are occasional notices of the execution of servants or a cattle-rustler by burning or hanging. The chief would also have a secretary, stewards to levy his rents or tributes, and a marshal to supervise the quartering of his troops on the country; the band of professional household kerne under their captain would collect fines, arrest malefactors and generally execute the chief's orders, and the more powerful chiefs would have con-stables commanding a standing force of mercenary galloglass. Traditionally, the lordship's leading offices had been hereditary, but by the sixteenth century the chief's brehon and marshal were also professionals. Finally the clansmen customarily assembled biennially, at May Day and All Hallows – the terms of the Gaelic year – on a hill to transact any political business requiring their presence, to settle disputes, apportion the chief's levies, or to approve any decrees he made.[30]

The professional learned classes formed a distinctive element in Gaelic society. Their literacy led to a close connection with the clergy, particularly since both groups were often hereditary occupations, and coupled with their mobility throughout the Gaelic world, probably fostered a more cosmopolitan outlook. This mobility was not only prompted by their professions but more

29. Nicholls 1972, pp. 68–71; Nicholls 1976, pp. 13–19. Cf. Hayes-McCoy 1963, pp. 45–61.
30. Nicholls 1972, pp. 40–1, 44–6, 50–7; Simms 1987a, pp. 73–8, 90–5, 143; *NHI*, iii, p. 26.

especially by study: they travelled to attend the schools which many of them kept. Besides the brehons, each chief would also keep poets, historians, musicians and physicians. The head of each profession in the lordship was styled 'ollave', appointed by and serving the chief; the learned men were exempt from military service in the 'rising-out' and were often remunerated in part by lands held free of tribute and exactions. The poets, called 'rhymers' in English ('bards' were inferior poets), were particularly influential as eulogists of the chieftain's activities, inciting him to cattle raids; like an African witchdoctor, they could also compose versified spells (miscalled 'satires') which, it was believed, could injure or kill those 'satirized'. These powers were perhaps pagan in origin and they were regularly invoked along with the church's power of excommunication against violators of treaties: clerks and poets acted as sureties for their performance. The brehons preserved their ancient law texts alongside contemporary Gaelic law as actually practised. These texts were still studied and quarried for legal maxims which could be quoted in pleadings: but behind this 'antiquarian windowdressing', the reality was that late Gaelic law was strongly influenced both by Roman and, as has more recently been demonstrated, by English law. During the period 1350–1500 Gaelic law was evidently transformed, much as Welsh law had been, by the introduction of the pledge as a means of alienating land, the jury, and common law concepts such as *réléas, feofment, aturnae* and *reuersion*. The precise impact of all this is not yet clear, but it seems that common law ideas were adapted to strengthen seigneurial control at the same time as Gaelic law was being modified in accordance with changing structures in Gaelic society. The result was that the amalgam of English and Gaelic customs earlier described as 'march law' had by 1500 gradually ousted pure Gaelic law (and also common law in the lordship's borderlands).[31]

The Gaelic world was intensely local in its politics, but the uniformity of its social and cultural institutions created a substantial racial and cultural unity. And just as the English districts of Ireland were part of a wider English state, so Gaelic Ireland was also part of a wider Gaelic world including the highlands and islands of Scotland. Gaelic identity is discussed more fully below (Chapter 10). This is a highly controversial subject, and the evidence is certainly ambiguous, but perhaps the best estimate is that there were different overlapping senses of identity among the *Gaedhil* in this period – local dynastic, Pan-Irish and Gaelic national. Besides traditional concepts of Ireland, it should be remembered that Gaelic Scotland and Ireland shared a common language with standard literary forms, Irish chiefs had long recruited Scottish mercenaries, and from *c.* 1400 there was substantial 'colonization' by Clan Donald in northeast Ulster.[32] Thus, although the Gaelic annals of Ireland sometimes distinguished between Scottish and Irish Gaels, they also depicted Scottish politics in terms of rivalry between *Gaedhil* and *Gaill*, the Palesmen could be described

31. Nicholls 1972, pp. 44, 79–84; *NHI*, iii, pp. 27–8; Mac Niocaill 1984, pp. 105–17.
32. Freeman 1944, pp. 442, 592–4, 708; Hennessy 1871, ii, pp. 176, 290, 364; *NHI*, iii, pp. 1, 17; Bradshaw 1979, pp. 21–9.

as 'the people of the king of England', and the Elizabethan conquest was seen as a conquest by the *Gaill* of the men of Ireland. Nevertheless in the late sixteenth century, under pressure from Tudor expansion, it was pan-Irish senses of identity that became most prominent.[33]

ANGLO-GAELIC INTERACTION AND ASSIMILATION

Sixteenth-century Ireland, however, was not simply an island divided between two distinct civilizations co-existing in differing degrees of harmony. The villages of Fingal, Co. Dublin, might have little in common with the wandering creaghts of the Gaelic west, but between these English and Gaelic extremes lay an infinite variety of cultural balances which, however, were not only determined by straight interaction. The utter dissimilarity of the two cultures militated sharply against the emergence of any uniform *via media*, a 'Hiberno-Norman civilization', but their co-existence on one small island naturally promoted some degree of interaction and the growth of many features peculiar to society in Ireland. Just as the influx of Gaelic peasantry into the Pale assisted the survival of a Gaelic subculture there, so Gaelic society was influenced by its neighbour to the extent of borrowing English legal concepts, using seals, building castles and training gunners.

In many parts, however, the interaction was more thoroughgoing. Some areas which had been only lightly colonized by the Normans, notably northeast Ulster and north Connaught, were almost totally assimilated into the Gaelic polity. The Dublin administration did not consider them part of the lordship; and the descendants of settlers, where they retained land, generally conformed to Gaelic social patterns. Elsewhere, in parts of Munster or Westmeath, Gaelic influences were so strong that 'gavelkind' had replaced English laws of inheritance, although in most parts of the lordship nobles and gentry clung at least to English land law even where they admitted Gaelic law in personal pleas, used coign and livery, and patronized poets and musicians.[34] The Statutes of Kilcash, local ordinances issued for the Ormond district in 1474, were an amalgam of Gaelic personal law and English land law, and many English magnates also kept brehons. Indeed some practices such as fosterage, patronage of Gaelic learned classes, and the use of the Gaelic tongue were very widespread even in the Pale.[35]

Yet there remain two largely insoluble difficulties about such processes of assimilation: first to determine how far lords and gentry tolerated Gaelic practices simply in order to survive in a frontier situation or to cut a figure in Gaelic society as a means of strengthening colonial dominance, and when this had toppled over into something more thoroughgoing. No doubt most of

33. Hennessy 1871, ii, 136, 324, 460; Freeman 1944, pp. 410, 684 (quotation), 712, 716; below, Ch. 10.
34. Nicholls 1972, pp. 15–19, 37–8, 47–50, 64–5, 81–3, 134–6, 145–51, 177; Canny 1975, pp. 3–9.
35. *NHI*, iii, pp. 8–9; Canny 1976, pp. 10–13, 20, 26–7; Nicholls 1972, pp. 46–50.

the Munster Englishry, Powers of east Waterford, Barrys and Roches in Cork, Fitzmaurices in Kerry and the Desmond Fitzgeralds were frequently found in the latter category under the early Tudors (though some reformed thereafter), whereas Butler and Tobins in Ormond, and Nugents, Plunkets and Eustaces in the Pale marches were more conservative. The second difficulty is that practices analagous to Gaelic ones often develop naturally where power is decentralized and might reflect similar responses to similar problems rather than direct borrowings. For example, the draconian penalties prescribed by the common law were a general weakness of English criminal law, and it did not take Gaelic brehons to advise the earl of Kildare that it might be more sensible to fine a tenant for stealing a sheep or killing a neighbour than to see him hang and his lands go to waste. Lords in England frequently felt the same way, and juries were in any case very reluctant to convict for felonies. Similarly lineages or kinship units like the Gaelic clans developed in other marcher societies besides English Ireland, for instance among English and Scottish border families who accepted joint responsibility for injuries, collectively sought vengeance for wrongdoing, and even developed particular customs of landholding and inheritance. Indeed outside areas of strong manorial control, partible inheritance was quite common among lesser gentry and commoners in England. Royal officials, townsmen, and gentry from the lordship's more settled parts denounced such departures from English norms as 'degenerate' and charged these marchers with 'growing Irish'. In many ways they were right, but the upland and lowland regions of England exhibited differences of social structure which frequently resembled those between the lordship's marches and more settled parts. Ireland was indeed a bye-word for savagery: Archbishop Parker feared in 1560 that, without the speedy appointment of godly bishops, northern England would become 'too much Irish and savage'. It is a mistake to assume that departures from 'English civility' in Ireland were invariably and exclusively the product of Gaelic influences and simplistic to categorize them all as 'gaelicization'.[36]

THE IMPACT OF THE TUDOR CONQUEST

The post-1534 governmental changes further confused an already complicated situation in which each English district had developed its own particular cultural balance. In principle, increased pressures and intervention from Dublin should have reversed the earlier drift to Gaelic customs in favour of a more English way of life, and no doubt this was the general, long-term trend. Ironically, however, the heavier burden of military exactions to feed an enlarged army, and the increasing levels of violence and more destructive forms of warfare which accompanied the Tudor conquest, initially narrowed the differences

---

36. Rae 1966, pp. 5–11; Ellis 1986a, pp. 122–3, 194; Nicholls 1972, pp. 19–20, 35, 46–8, 64, 162–9. Cf. Palliser 1983, pp. 65–6. For an extended discussion of this problem, see now Ellis 1995a, ch. 2 (quotation, p. 68).

between Gaelic and Old English society by undermining the prosperity of the English districts. In the 1530s emigration from the lordship was again a problem. Rising levels of population in England and inflation soon curtailed opportunities there for agricultural labourers, but by 1560 conditions within the Pale had deteriorated so sharply that husbandmen were even migrating into O'Neill's country. Emigration from the Pale was stimulated by heavy exactions as landlords raised rents and shortened leases in response to inflation and quartered troops on tenants in order to maintain private armies for defence, while royal purveyance became an increasing burden as the queen's price, fixed at levels which inflation made increasingly unrealistic, lagged far behind market prices.[37] These changes particularly affected the Pale marches: while Meath remained 'as well inhabited as any shire in England', society in Westmeath and Kildare was transformed partly by the gradual departure of prosperous peasants of English stock and their replacement by beggarly Gaelic tenants who would endure harsher conditions.[38] Increased warfare also encouraged a further decline of tillage at a time when more corn was needed to feed the enlarged army: in years of bad harvest poor tenants 'die[d] in the streets and highways for fault of sustenance'.[39]

Political instability also tended to disrupt such industry as the country possessed, while Elizabeth's government grew increasingly suspicious for political reasons about the continental trade on which the port towns of the south and west depended.[40] Moreover, by the end of the century Irish trade interests were increasingly being subordinated to English interests in accordance with contemporary mercantilist theories. Successive measures were passed to protect weaving and tanning, notably by prohibiting without licence the export of wool and flocks in 1522 and more comprehensively in 1569 by new regulations and the imposition of additional duties on the export of untanned hides, wool, flocks and woollen and linen yarn. In this way the tanning industry was partly revived in the 1570s (only to collapse under the early Stuarts as the oak trees were cut down), but wool and linen yarn were increasingly exported to England for weaving and the native cloth industry declined. For instance, exports of Irish linen yarn, mainly from Ulster, to the increasingly important port of Liverpool rose from 356 packs in 1565–6 to 1,555 packs by 1593–4, while the much less valuable wool exports grew concurrently from 630 stone to 1,506 stone.[41] Overall, however, trade declined steadily from mid-century, disrupted initially by debasement, and the export of primary products became proportionately larger as new exports such as timber replaced declining industries. In most parts the towns decayed, seemingly in accordance with the progress of the Tudor conquest. The decline of the small inland towns of the Pale was initially attributed to the activities of 'grey merchants' who forestalled

---

37. Canny 1976, p. 12; Canny 1975, p. 4 and n. 8.
38. Canny 1975, pp. 8–9 (quotation, p. 9); Canny 1976, pp. 10–12.
39. Canny 1975, p. 7 (quotation); Nicholls 1972, p. 114.
40. Longfield 1929, pp. 27–40.
41. Ibid., pp. 71–93; Gillespie 1991, p. 7; Treadwell 1966, pp. 61, 74; NHI, iii, p. 179.

the market, but by 1567 Lord Deputy Sidney was recommending action by the queen to nurture the important port towns of Connaught and Munster.[42] Economic activity was still further disrupted by measures to crush successive revolts, particularly the Desmond rebellion (1579–83), by which 'a most populous and plentiful country [was] suddenly left void of man or beast', and the Nine Years War (1594–1603).[43] The shipping capacity of the ports declined: whereas local ships had formerly carried much of the overseas trade, by the 1590s foreign vessels predominated in the south and west. Government inquiries revealed that by about 1589 many vessels had been sold to Spain. The chief port towns survived but with reduced populations: Dublin had 6,000 inhabitants c. 1600, Waterford and Cork only c. 2,400, though Galway's population was c. 4,000. Some secondary towns suffered severely: New Ross in 1611 was 'a poor ruined town' and Kinsale 'a poor town ruined by the late rebellion'. These problems were compounded for merchants by two further developments. During 1601–3, in the crisis of Tyrone's rebellion, the government introduced a wretched new silver coinage for Ireland, issuing IR£250,000 in coins only 3 oz. fine (.250), thus supplementing the 'white money' of the mid-Tudor debasement (see below, pp. 145, 269–75) which had continued to circulate in Elizabethan Ireland. Second, the fishery gradually declined c. 1600 as the best shoals deserted the Irish for the Newfoundland banks. As trade was channelled increasingly through England, Dundalk, Carlingford and Carrickfergus prospered and increasing quantities of luxury goods were imported through Dublin, but this was scant compensation for the decline elsewhere.[44]

Thus, far from building on the foundations of the medieval lordship, the efforts of successive governments after mid-century to reform society and increase prosperity had the unintended effect of undermining such influences within the country as had been promoting the ordered commonwealth at which English officials aimed. Though finally conquered, Ireland in 1603 was far less 'civilized' by English standards than it had been in 1534.

42. Longfield 1929, pp. 117–24, 196–212; Canny 1975, p. 7; Canny 1976, pp. 4–5; Treadwell 1966, p. 60.
43. Spenser 1970, p. 104; NHI, iii, pp. 108, 130.
44. Longfield 1929, pp. 39–40, 56 (quotation, p. 39); Dolley 1972, pp. 37–45; Sheehan 1983a, p. 9; NHI, ii, p. 390. For Dublin, see now Lennon 1989, p. 31.

CHAPTER 3

THE CRISIS OF LORDSHIP, 1447–1471

IRISH PEERS AND ENGLISH POLITICS

The appointment in July 1447 of Richard, duke of York, as lieutenant of Ireland marked an important departure in Anglo-Irish relations during Henry VI's disastrous reign. As the king's heir-apparent, York was undoubtedly the 'mighty lord' of English birth for whom the English of Ireland had long petitioned to tackle the lordship's mounting problems. Although his stipend was modest – 4,000 marks for the first year, £2,000 annually thereafter, payable from England – he was appointed for ten years, with full power to appoint to all offices in the Irish administration and to spend the Irish revenues without account. More importantly, given the uncertain prospects for payment by the English exchequer at this time, Richard enjoyed a landed income of £4,000 a year from his extensive possessions in England and Wales; and he was then the crown's only really powerful feudatory in the lordship. As heir to the earldom of Ulster and lordships of Connaught, Trim and Leix, he had title to extensive lands in Ireland, and so had alternative means of building up a powerful retinue and connection there.

Admittedly, his Irish possessions were now worth comparatively little. Most of them, except Trim and south-east Ulster, had long since been overrun by Irish enemies. Yet the Gaelic recovery of lands which had passed into the hands of absentee lords lay at the heart of the lordship's problems, and York's reassertion of his feudal rights there could only strengthen English rule. Moreover, through his long service as the king's lieutenant in France, Richard had vast experience in the rule and defence of frontier societies, and against a much more formidable adversary. Thus, although opinion at court was that York's lieutenancy in France had been terminated and the duke 'exiled from our sovereign lord's presence' for his opposition to Henry's French policy, in the lordship the prospect of his transfer to Ireland was viewed with enthusiasm.[1]

York's appointment seemed to transform the lordship's prospects in another way too, in that he retained the earls of Ormond and Waterford in his service. Until 1444, when Ormond's daughter had married Talbot's son, there had been

1. Johnson 1988, chs 1–3; *NHI*, ii, pp. 557–8; Pugh 1986, pp. 107–41.

a disastrous feud between the other two magnates who were then the most obvious candidates for the lieutenancy of Ireland. John Talbot, created first earl of Shrewsbury in England in 1442 and first earl of Waterford in Ireland in 1446, had been governor of Ireland three times (most recently in 1445–7), while his brother, Richard, archbishop of Dublin, had also frequently served as temporary governor (including in 1444–5 and 1447–8). Talbot, who was also the most successful English commander in France, held the lordship of Wexford in Ireland, while his wife brought him lands in western Meath. His erstwhile opponent, James Butler, fourth earl of Ormond (1411–52), already had an Irish peerage, and held extensive possessions in Tipperary, Kilkenny and Waterford. The Butlers were the most prominent of four families of second rank advanced to an earldom in Ireland between 1316 and 1329, and the only one with extensive estates outside Ireland. Ormond was three times lieutenant of Ireland (most recently in 1442–4), and his son, later the fifth earl (1452–61), was in 1449 to be created earl of Wiltshire in England. Although lesser figures like Archbishop Talbot and Giles Thorndon, the treasurer, attempted for a time to continue the feud, York's appointment seemed to portend strong leadership and renewed cooperation among the English of Ireland, in an age when both qualities had been in noticeably short supply.[2]

Thus, the late 1440s saw the lordship, quite exceptionally, at the centre of national politics, with the heads of the three leading families there both active in Ireland and influential at court. Not for another 200 years was this situation to recur. Yet if the advent of a 'mighty lord' seemed to transform the lordship's prospects, there were also potential difficulties in York's transfer to this neglected outpost of English rule at a time when Henry VI's authority seemed so shaky.

YORK IN IRELAND

Yet York was in no hurry to leave court. It was only in December 1448 that shipping was arrested for his passage to Ireland; and shortly after, a parliament was summoned. Meanwhile, first Archbishop Talbot and then Richard Nugent, baron of Delvin, acted as his deputies. Further delays ensued, so that it was Delvin who presided over the parliament's first session in February.[3] Yet eventually the duke's expedition sailed from Beaumaris in nineteen ships, landing at Howth on 6 July, 'with great glory and pomp' according to Gaelic sources. It is unlikely that he had more than 600 men with him, but these included leading household knights like Sir William Oldhall and Sir Edward Mulso. Oldhall, York's chamberlain, served as his seneschal of Ulster; his brother, Edmund, secured the wealthy bishopric of Meath. Mulso, appointed seneschal of Meath, planned to build a town in Fercullen, in O'Toole's country, called Mulsoescourt.[4]

2. *HBC*, pp. 163, 166, 482, 497; Otway-Ruthven 1980, pp. 348, 375; Griffith 1940–1.
3. Otway-Ruthven 1980, pp. 378–9; Johnson 1988, pp. 70–4.
4. Johnson 1988, pp. 74, 235–6; Berry 1910, pp. 177, 214–23; Otway-Ruthven 1980, pp. 378–9; *HBC*, p. 368; Gorman 1985, pp. 172, 176–7.

Upon arrival, the duke proclaimed a hosting against the Irish of Wicklow. Yet his initial actions were dictated by the military exigencies of the lordship's northern marches, where the English of Louth had become involved in a succession dispute following the death in Cavan on St Patrick's Day of the O'Reilly. The provincial chief, Owen O'Neill, had been consolidating his influence in Ulster and now nominated O'Reilly's son as the new chief, while the English of Louth supported a rival candidate. This prompted a series of raids by O'Neill and his vassal-chiefs on Co. Louth, but the uneasy truce hastily arranged by York's deputy, Delvin, and the earl of Ormond left the duke to mediate between the Ulster chiefs who were nominally his vassals as earl of Ulster and the king's subjects there.[5]

Apprised of the situation there, and conscious of his hereditary claims as palatine lord of the province, York marched north to confront the Ulster chiefs. His approach prompted a mass voluntary submission both of the Gaelic chiefs and of many of the surviving Englishry there to their feudal overlord. By 15 August, Magennis, MacMahon, MacQuillan and both O'Reillys had submitted. Twelve days later, following negotiations between the Ulster chiefs, the archbishop of Armagh, and the earl's seneschal of Ulster, O'Neill's son and successor, Henry, submitted at Drogheda on behalf of the Great O'Neill. In the resultant indenture O'Neill promised to restore all lands, castles, and other rights withheld by the O'Neills from the earldom, the church, and the English of Ulster since the time of the Red Earl (d. 1326), particularly the Fews which adjoined 'English ground' near Dundalk; he promised to render the 'bonnaght of Ulster', the military service traditionally owed by O'Neill to the earl and now quantified as 500 men-at-arms and 500 foot-soldiers; to pay 600 fat cattle for homage and fealty and – in a tacit recognition of O'Neill's claim to be mesne lord between the earl and the other Ulster chiefs – to compel their submission to York. In return, the duke promised to do justice between the O'Neills and the subjects of his earldom in accordance with the laws and customs of his palatinate, and to defend O'Neill against other Irishmen outside his earldom. In effect, the 1449 indenture was the latest in a series of attempts to regularize the relationship between earl and chief by making O'Neill the earl's feudal tenant, holding his lands by military service.[6]

After O'Neill's submission, campaigns in the midlands and Leinster mountains followed, and Gaelic chiefs flocked to submit in the manner of Richard II's visit in 1394–5. O'Byrne of Wicklow undertook that he and his clansmen 'shall wear English array and learn English', and his surrender was followed by that of MacMurrough Kavanagh and other Leinster chiefs. Flushed with this success, the duke wrote triumphantly to the king's council listing 43 leaders, Gaelic and English, who had submitted since his arrival three months before, appending another list of chiefs who had offered a total of 3,620 cattle (1,200 of them from Mageoghegan), and predicting ecstatically that 'with the might of

---

5. Simms 1981, pp. 221–3; Berry 1910, pp. 206–9; Otway-Ruthven 1980, pp. 379–80.
6. Ibid.; Curtis 1931, pp. 87–105; Curtis 1932, pp. 165–8 (which prints extracts from BL, Titus B. XI (I), ff. 38–40); *NHI*, ii, pp. 558–9.

Jesus, ere twelvemonth come to an end, the wildest Irishman in Ireland shall be swore English'.[7]

In fact, York had misinterpreted completely the chiefs' submissions and O'Neill's formal recognition of his historic claims in Ulster. He regarded them as sincere and permanent, constituting a radical reappraisal of traditional views concerning English rule in Ireland. For their part, the chiefs looked to the king's representative for justice between native and settler, and relief from the constant threat of expropriation. O'Neill also hoped to enlist English support for his claims to hegemony throughout Gaelic Ulster, and offered in return protection for the surviving English settlements in east Ulster: thus both sides gained something from the indenture. Yet, no more than any other governor of the period, York never contemplated the long-term investment in time and resources needed to resolve the intractable difficulties souring Anglo-Gaelic relations in Ireland.[8]

THE COLLAPSE OF ENGLISH MORALE

The inevitable sequel to the duke's triumph was a period of growing disillusionment and then withdrawal. In order to consolidate the improved military situation, provision was made at a great council in Dublin in mid-October to curb the abuse of coign, particularly by the marchers of Co. Dublin; for the withdrawal of O'Neill from the Fews; for the safe custody of castles erected by York in the Meath marches; and for the walling of Thomastown, Co. Kilkenny, Fethard, Co. Tipperary, and Newtownards, Co. Down. The newly reconciled earl of Desmond and the earl of Ormond were co-sponsors at the baptism of York's son, George, the future duke of Clarence; and another disruptive influence on the lordship's political community had disappeared with the death in August of Archbishop Talbot. Yet the prevailing optimism quickly evaporated as news arrived of the frightening collapse of the English position in Normandy, where Talbot's brother, Waterford, witnessed the surrender of the capital, Rouen, in October.[9] From Co. Cork, the citizens of Cork, Kinsale and Youghal petitioned the governor and council, claiming that Irish enemies 'now have the whole country under them, but that the Lord Roche, Lord Barry and Lord Courcy do remain': they appealed for a viceregal visit, resident justices and military assistance, warning hysterically, 'if you do not, then we are all cast away, and then farewell Munster for ever!'[10]

Over the winter, as the news from Normandy grew grimmer, York became increasingly concerned at the conduct of 'the Irish enemies, who according to appearances mean to go to war', and the king's failure to pay him his stipulated

---

7. Curtis 1932, pp. 166, 168 (quotations); Johnson 1988, pp. 73–5; Otway-Ruthven 1980, p. 380; *NHI*, ii, pp. 559–60.

8. Simms 1981, pp. 222–4.

9. Berry 1910, pp. 166–77; Otway-Ruthven 1980, pp. 380–1; Johnson 1988, pp. 74–5; Griffiths 1981, pp. 516–18.

10. Gilbert 1865, pp. 356–7 (quotation).

salary which, by May, was 4,700 marks in arrears. Shortage of money severely hampered the duke in dealing with the ensuing Gaelic risings. Knowing that the Irish traditionally began hostilities after Easter, York summoned a parliament which convened in April in an atmosphere of impending crisis. Absentees were fined. Parliament authorized the collection of a scutage in lieu of a subsidy, 'considering the poverty of the common people', and a resumption of royal grants (a radical measure paralleling contemporary opposition demands in the English parliament) to provide money to pay the king's officers. The duke then advanced with the English of Meath against Mageoghegan who, despite his submission the previous autumn, had burned Rathmore and nearby villages with other chiefs and English rebels; but when the chief's son encountered him at Mullingar 'with a great many horsemen well mounted and armed', York could do no better than patch up a peace.[11] In June, as Caen and 3,000 English surrendered in Normandy, York advised his brother-in-law, the earl of Salisbury, that if money were not immediately sent to defend the lordship,

> my power cannot stretch to keep it in the king's obeisance, and very necessity will compel me to come into England to live . . . For I had liever be dead than any inconvenience should fall thereunto by my default . . . [whereby] Ireland was lost by my negligence.[12]

York's departure, however, was finally determined by events in England, where a series of disorders culminated in the Kentish rising led by Jack Cade. Capitalizing on the duke's popularity, Cade claimed to be his cousin, John Mortimer, and York's recall was among the rebels' demands. Perhaps Oldhall and the duke's councillors subsequently established contacts, realizing the possibilities raised by Cade's protest: York later claimed that 'certain persons laboured to indict me of treason', but there is no reliable evidence that he incited Cade's revolt, and his march on London only occurred two months after Cade's death. Meanwhile, in preparation for his return, the duke retained the old earl of Ormond for life, with an annual fee of 100 marks (his son, James, earl of Wiltshire, was already the duke's councillor, but joined the court party soon after); and on 23 August, York appointed Ormond his deputy-lieutenant, with £1,000 for the first year, chiefly from the Irish revenues, plus the profits of his Ulster lordship. Within a week he had landed, unbidden, at Beaumaris and marched on London with a considerable force.[13] Not for another nine years was the duke to return, and then in very different circumstances. His appointment had vividly exposed both the advantages and weaknesses of employing a leading English magnate and politician as governor. It had no long-term impact on the balance of power within Ireland.

11. Berry 1910, pp. 187 (quotation), 259; Otway-Ruthven 1980, pp. 381–2; Johnson 1988, pp. 75–6; *NHI*, ii, p. 560; Griffiths 1981, pp. 387–90, 421–2; Richardson & Sayles 1952, pp. 143–4.
12. Gilbert 1865, p. 362 (quotation); Otway-Ruthven 1980, p. 382; Griffiths 1981, pp. 520–2.
13. Curtis 1932, p. 175 (quotation); Curtis 1932–43, iii, no. 177; Matthew 1984, p. 107; Johnson 1988, pp. 17, 236; Griffiths 1981, pp. 610–19; Otway-Ruthven 1980, p. 383; Gorman 1985, pp. 170–1.

Nevertheless, in the context of the growing factional strife within the English political community, the duke's ability to raise an army in Ireland and his establishment of a considerable following among the English there was to prove important. As the country slid towards civil war, it alerted the opposing parties to Ireland's strategic and military potential, and overall, it certainly brought the lordship closer to the centre of English politics.

THE CRISIS OF LORDSHIP

Despite Archbishop Talbot's notorious gibe eight years before that Ormond was 'aged, unwieldy and unlusty', the experienced deputy-lieutenant worked effectively to rebuild the Dublin administration's shaky finances by extracting more from internal sources. A great council held in November confirmed Ormond's arrangements for payment of ministers' salaries, then much in arrears; and the following March a parliament granted him a subsidy. During spring and summer 1452, he turned to the military situation, embarking on an extended campaign which took him from Limerick into Ulster and belied his advancing years: he recovered Owney castle, Co. Limerick, from O'Mulrian and Lea castle, Co. Kildare, from O'Dempsey; he secured the submissions of O'Farrell, O'Reilly and MacMahon, and then parleyed with O'Neill.[14] His death at Ardee on 23 August, aged about 62, removed the 'best captain of the English nation that was in Ireland and England in those ages'; and the following July the lordship received a further crushing blow in far-away Gascony when his old rival, the earl of Waterford, that 'most famous and renowned English leader . . . one of the most formidable scourges of the French', was slain at Castillon in the final collapse of the English duchy in south-west France. Subsequently, statutes enacting that individual merchants from Gascony, subjects of Henry VI of his crown of France, should be English subjects and pay customs 'as Englishmen born in England and in Ireland' provided a continuing reminder of the tragedy. And the deaths of the two earls were the more keenly felt because neither of their successors ever visited their Irish estates. Thus, around half 'the English ground' was now held by absentee lords, leaving the Englishry destitute of good captains, and precipitating a crisis of lordship.[15]

The nature of this crisis must have been very familiar to the new governor of Ireland, Sir Edward FitzEustace, head of a leading Kildare gentry family who, in default of more substantial candidates, now became York's deputy. Despite the strategic importance of the Barrow valley, Kildare had never been an easy county to keep, vulnerable as it was to raids by the Irish of both the midlands and the Leinster mountains. Yet conditions there had deteriorated alarmingly since the death in 1432 of Gerald Fitzgerald, fifth earl of Kildare, whose daughter and heir-general had married the fourth earl of Ormond.

14. Berry 1910, pp. 250–92; Otway-Ruthven 1980, pp. 372 (quotation), 384–5.
15. Griffiths 1981, pp. 522–33 (quotation, p. 532); Otway-Ruthven 1980, p. 385 (quotation); Ellis 1995a, p. 112; Berry 1910, pp. 386–7 (quotation), 398–401.

Ormond had secured most of the Kildare estates in right of his wife, but the earldom was in abeyance, and without a resident earl to defend it, the land fell sharply in value as the defence of the Kildare–Carlow region gradually collapsed. With the capture of Tullow castle after 1435 and the destruction of Castledermot *c.* 1443, the Gaelic recovery in the Barrow valley swept away outlying English settlements there, leaving the Kavanaghs a clear road into south Kildare. Of Co. Carlow, the inheritance of the dukes of Norfolk, there remained only Carlow castle itself and Baltinglass abbey. To the north-west, O'Dempsey had captured Lea castle, the O'Connors were reconquering the original Fitzgerald patrimony as lords of Offaly, and had recently recovered the manor of Rathangan. They were equally a menace to the Meath community, which bought them off with an annual blackrent of £40, and a coordinated response by the two shires was hampered by the semi-autonomous, partially Gaelic lordship established by the Berminghams of Carbury in north-west Kildare.[16]

Ormond's death signalled the start of a prolonged dispute over possession of the Fitzgerald manors of Maynooth and Rathmore between James Butler, now fifth earl of Ormond, and Thomas Fitzmaurice of the Geraldines, grand-nephew of the last earl of Kildare. And within a few months the situation was exacerbated when the court party ousted York as lieutenant, although his commission still had four years to run, appointing instead Ormond himself, who nominated John Mey, archbishop of Armagh, as his deputy. With little apparent interest or influence in Ireland, Ormond could scarcely control the junior branches of his own family; and repeated complaints to Mey about 'misrule and misgovernance' brought no remedy: 'the true liege people' were afraid to go to the king's court or market towns 'for dread to be slain, take, other spoiled of their goods'.

After the king suffered a mental breakdown in August, however, York's influence began to recover. He still disputed Ormond's appointment, and in January 1454 the community of Kildare appealed to the duke over the heads of Mey and Ormond, telling him that the dispute had

> caused more distruction . . . within short time now late passed . . . than was done by Irish enemies and English rebels of long time before, and is likely to be the final destruction

of Kildare and Meath. Perhaps in response, the question of 'who is and ought to be lieutenant' was raised in the English council. In April York, now lord protector of England during the king's insanity, secured a favourable decision; and when the English parliament met, he also fined peers for absence, in accordance with parliamentary practice in Ireland, to encourage a more representative assembly and endorsement for his policies. FitzEustace resumed office as deputy–lieutenant. An Irish parliament meeting in July began the military reorganization of Kildare by promoting statutes to build castles there,

16. Ellis 1995a, pp. 108–12; Ellis 1986a, pp. 58–60; Richardson & Sayles 1952, pp. 332–65.

for the repair of the key border castles of Tallaght and Ballymore Eustace and, together with the other three 'obedient shires', for taking up labourers to dig trenches and erect fortresses in the marches. By then too, the government had moved to settle the original dispute, recognizing as seventh earl of Kildare Thomas Fitzmaurice, who received a pardon in the parliament. Within four months, he had become governor of Ireland. When FitzEustace died in October, he was elected justiciar, or temporary governor, and then became York's deputy-lieutenant after the duke's appointment was confirmed in December.[17]

Throughout the 1450s, despite sporadic proposals for an expedition to Ireland, the lordship apparently received no military subventions nor, given the state of royal finances, is it likely that successive governors received much financial support. Little could be expected from the governors' private resources either: on his accession, Kildare's ancestral estates were so wasted that their value scarcely exceeded £250 a year, most of which (£133) came from his principal manor of Maynooth located in a more secure district nearer Dublin. Moreover, his appointment as deputy inevitably attracted opposition from the Butlers. Thus the Dublin administration was in an unprecedentedly weak position at this time. Not surprisingly, the great council convened by Kildare in April 1455 and the parliaments in October 1455 and November 1456 were largely concerned with the prevalence of disorders. For instance, a letter to the deputy in October 1455 from the seneschal and sovereign of Wexford complained that the Butlers of Polestown, Dunboyne and Cahir had allied with MacMurrough and burned the county for four days continuously. William Butler of Dunboyne was eventually slain while burning the Englishry with O'Connor, and the others, having once been conditionally pardoned, were still terrorizing Co. Tipperary four years later. Even just outside Dublin city, however, security was so problematic that orders were given for fortifying the bridges of Lucan and Kilmainham and the wall of St Mary's abbey to prevent enemies and rebels from raiding Fingal by night. A parliamentary deputation was also prepared to remind the king and lieutenant 'of the great eminent danger' to the land, which is 'likely to be finally destroyed, unless the most speedy remedy be had out of England for the reformation thereof'.[18]

CIVIL WAR AND YORK'S RETURN

In fact, no effective response was forthcoming. By this time, the crisis in England had finally erupted into open warfare at the battle of St Albans. The evidence concerning developments in Ireland in the later 1450s is very thin. The earl of Kildare continued to serve as York's deputy in Ireland, but the political situation apparently remained largely unchanged until 1459 when a

17. Ellis 1827, ser. 2, I, no. 39 (quotations); Berry 1910, pp. 293, 299; Ellis 1986b, p. 199; Griffiths 1981, pp. 422–3; Wood 1928, pp. 156–7; Otway-Ruthven 1980, pp. 385–6; *NHI*, ii, pp. 562–3.
18. Berry 1910, pp. 300–495, 522–31, 714–19, 734–41 (quotation, pp. 357–9); Ellis 1995a, pp. 110–13; Otway-Ruthven 1980, pp. 385–6.

further crisis in England had major repercussions in Ireland. Initially, the factional struggle focused on attempts to dominate the court and manipulate the king, not to depose him. After the birth of Prince Edward, York was no longer heir-presumptive even though, in 1455–6, Henry's relapse into insanity had prompted the duke's reappointment as protector. His commission as lieutenant of Ireland was also renewed for ten years in March 1457, but by autumn 1458 the court party, now led by Queen Margaret, was in full control: King Henry was no more than a figurehead, and during summer 1459 both sides prepared for war. Queen Margaret enjoyed overwhelming support among the nobles and gentry, but the Yorkists' control of key outposts meant that militarily the two sides were more evenly matched than a roll-call of the English nobility might suggest.

York himself was in a particularly strong position as the lieutenant and leading landowner in Ireland, where he had built up a powerful affinity, including the two resident earls (Desmond and Kildare), and he also held a solid block of marcher lordships in Wales. The two other leading Yorkists, the earls of Warwick (the Kingmaker) and Salisbury, were respectively captain of Calais and warden of the west marches towards Scotland. Even so, when the three lords met at Worcester, they were heavily outnumbered by the royal army, and after retreating to Ludlow, they fled on the eve of battle. York made for Ireland, while the two earls withdrew to Calais, along with the earl of March, York's son and the future Edward IV. They were attainted of treason by the Coventry parliament in October, and so forfeited all their lands and offices. On 4 December the earl of Ormond was reappointed lieutenant, nominating Sir Thomas Bathe and John Bole, archbishop of Armagh, as his deputies, and in January the treasurer of Ireland was ordered to seize all York's lands there.[19]

THE PARLIAMENT OF 1460 AND 'ARISTOCRATIC HOME RULE'

York's response was to convene a parliament at Drogheda in February. Its legislation requires extended consideration here: it constituted nothing less than a radical assault on established constitutional relations between England and Ireland. Chapters four and five of the parliament confirmed York's commission as lieutenant and extended the treason law by enacting that imagining the governor's death or stirring rebellion against him was high treason. The preamble to chapter six asserted the principle that

> the land of Ireland is and at all times has been corporate of itself, by the ancient laws and customs used in the same, freed of the burden of any special law of the realm of England, save only such laws as by the lords spiritual and temporal and the commons of the said land had been in great council or parliament there held, admitted, affirmed and proclaimed, according to sundry ancient statutes thereof made.

19. Gillingham 1981, ch. 7; Pollard 1988, pp. 20–5; *NHI*, ii, p. 564; Berry 1910, pp. 576–637; Gorman 1985, pp. 169–79.

It also noted that 'of ancient custom, privilege and franchise of the said land', Ireland had its own seal, and also its constable and marshal, so that no-one in Ireland should be compelled to answer outside Ireland any appeal of treason or other command 'contrary to the franchises, liberties and ancient customs thereof', except by order under the seal of Ireland, and that appeals of treason should only be determined before the constable and marshal there within Ireland.

Having thus secured his constitutional position, the duke then proceeded to strengthen it militarily and financially by securing further important statutes. The traditional military obligation was extended by requiring landlords to maintain one mounted archer with an English longbow for each £20 of yearly rent. There was also a sweeping act of resumption, justified because, through the king's failure to pay the lieutenant's salary, 'the protection and defence' of Ireland 'depend now solely upon the revenues of the same . . . which revenues are by no means at present of any great yearly value'. The statute also revoked all licences of absence from Ireland, specifying that the revenues of absentees should be applied to its defence.

Finally, chapter eleven enacted that because the lordship was destitute of gold and silver, and to encourage merchants to import bullion, a separate coinage for Ireland should be provided. It should include special pennies called 'Irelands' and halfpennies called 'Patricks', no doubt symbolizing the land of Ireland, plus groats (fourpenny pieces) of the same weight as three pence sterling, and sterling coins tariffed accordingly. Significantly, this coinage was justified on the grounds that

> not only the duchy of Normandy but also the duchy of Guienne [Gascony], when they were under the obedience of the same realm of England were nevertheless separated from the laws and statutes of the same, and had also coins for themselves distinct from the coin of the said realm.[20]

How should this legislation be interpreted? At one level, it is clear, the programme was a device to protect York and his supporters from the political consequences of their defeat by the Lancastrians. Neither his attainder by the English parliament nor any summons under the English seals to answer charges of treason in England would now be valid in Ireland. York was capitalizing on the 'good lordship' he had exercised as lieutenant. Yet, traditionally, 'good lordship' was mutually beneficial; so why should the lordship's political community concur in this risky and revolutionary strategy?

In fact, many did not, as is shown by the acts against Thomas Talbot, prior of Kilmainham (who later submitted to York); Sir Thomas Bathe, Ormond's intended deputy-lieutenant; Chief Baron Cornewalshe; Richard Bermingham, who had allegedly tried to procure an invasion of Ireland; and four others who had similarly brought privy seals into Ireland to procure Irish enemies to make war on York.[21] Nonetheless, the pioneering Irish historian, Edmund Curtis, saw

20. Berry 1910, pp. 638–801 (quotations, pp. 645, 647, 663–5, 719).
21. Berry 1910, pp. 648–61, 740–5, 752–5, 766–7.

the 1460 statute as a declaration of 'legislative independence', the culmination of a movement for 'aristocratic home rule'. Writing around the time of partition and the birth of the modern Irish states, he believed that the fifteenth-century lordship witnessed a struggle for control between an 'Anglo-Irish', 'Home-Rule', or 'Patriot party' led by the fourth earl of Ormond, and a 'Unionist party' led by the first earl of Waterford. 'Finally the Anglo-Irish party was put into the saddle by the action of Richard of York, and not for fifty years did the Unionist party lift up its head again.'[22] Later historians more familiar with English polit-ical culture and administrative traditions were inclined to ignore Curtis's flights of fancy, but since the 1960s historians writing in the nationalist tradition have revived and recast his basic thesis that the 1460 declaration was an expression of 'Anglo-Irish separatism'.[23] —bitchy. bitchy, Steven.

Constitutional relations: lordship, kingdom and crown

Yet how valid historically was this claim that the lordship of Ireland was independent of the realm of England, bound only by legislation in its own parliament? Like the later assertion of the English parliament in 1533 that 'this realm of England is an empire', the claim that the land of Ireland was 'corpor-ate of itself' (a reference to the theory of corporations) was certainly a striking attempt to enunciate a theory of sovereignty in an age before this concept was widely known. The same point was made rather differently in the Irish coinage act by means of a comparison between Ireland, which was 'separate' from but 'under the obedience' of the realm of England, and Normandy and Gascony 'when they were under the obedience of the same realm'. Yet the comparison with Normandy and Gascony was certainly misleading, since these territories had been held by Henry VI as of his crown of France, not of England; and as we have seen, their inhabitants were not English subjects. Undoubtedly too, English constitutional law had previously held that Ireland was a dominion of the English crown, so that English statutes were binding on Ireland without the need for re-enactment. This interpretation was unchallenged in the thirteenth and fourteenth centuries. It was also implicit in the political vocabulary em-ployed to describe the two countries and express their constitutional relation-ship at a later date: Ireland was a mere 'land', or 'lordship', not a 'kingdom' or 'realm' like England; it was a 'member' or 'parcel' of the English crown, part of the one 'body politic'.[24]

During the fifteenth century, however, it became normal practice, when Eng-lish statutes were applied to Ireland, to have them proclaimed by parliament

22. Curtis 1932, p. 164; Curtis 1938, pp. 292, 296, 302–7, 321–5.
23. Cf. Richardson & Sayles 1952, pp. 92–3, 260, 263; Otway-Ruthven 1980, pp. 190, 387 n. 19; Lydon 1972a, pp. 144–5; Lydon 1972b, pp. 263–6; Bradshaw 1979a, p. 29; Cosgrove 1983, pp. 25–41; NHI, ii, pp. 565–6.
24. Ellis 1990–1, pp. 297–300; Berry 1910, pp. 660–7 (quotations, pp. 663, 665); Richardson & Sayles 1952, pp. 92–3; Griffiths 1986, pp. 83–105; Otway-Ruthven 1980, p. 190; NHI, ii, p. 565; and below, p. 93. References in Lydon 1994–5, pp. 289, 291 to 'the land of England' are unsubstantiated by the evidence.

there rather than, as earlier, by the sheriff. No doubt this blurred the distinction between publication and parliamentary consent. A more general source of confusion, however, was the very fact of two separate bureaucracies involved in the government of Ireland: unlike other English provinces, Ireland had its own parliament and a separate central administration based in Dublin, even though Irish affairs regularly came before the king and his ministers at Westminster. Thus, in the circumstances it is not really surprising that even the famous English lawyer, Sir John Fortescue, should give as his opinion that

> the territory of Ireland is separate from the kingdom of England, for if a tenth or a fifteenth be granted here, it shall not bind the people of Ireland, and if a statute be made here, it shall not bind those in Ireland unless they shall approve it in their own parliament, even though the king under his great seal shall send the same statute to Ireland.

Fortescue was alone in this view, but another serjeant argued that Ireland's position was analagous to palatinates like Durham and Chester which were not bound by parliamentary grants of taxation but were nonetheless part of the kingdom.[25]

For political reasons, too, some friction was almost inevitable between Dublin and Westminster: successive governors were naturally anxious to preserve their authority by limiting what were deemed frivolous or vexatious appeals to the king; and the king for his part wished to maintain direct channels of communication with his subjects in Ireland. In 1441, for instance, a great council and then a parliament complained to the king concerning the removal of cases to England by means of writs and privy seals, alleging that this had only been customary upon writs of error or allegations of treason against the king's person. In response, however, the king effectively reserved his prerogative. Yet in 1453, parliament enacted that the matter of any appeal should first be declared before the governor and council and, unless it touched the king's person, sent for determination in the Irish king's bench. Overall, therefore, sufficient confusion undoubtedly existed concerning the validity in Ireland of statutes, seals and appeals from England as to lend colour to the 1460 claim. And despite repeated rulings upholding traditional practice, such doubts continued.[26]

Yet whether such doubts and claims were underpinned by an emerging 'tradition of Anglo-Irish separatism' is quite another matter. Enough has been said already to indicate that, within an English context at least, this terminology raises more difficulties than it solves. 'Separate from the realm of England' the lordship certainly was, but as is abundantly clear from repeated appeals for financial and military assistance from England, the ideology of the lordship's political community was 'loyalist', not 'separatist'. In fact, the conduct of the

25. Cosgrove 1983, pp. 28–31, which includes a good discussion of the implications of this case.
26. Richardson & Sayles 1952, ch. 16; Lydon 1972b, pp. 262–5 (quotation, p. 264); Berry 1910, pp. 295–6; and see below, pp. 79, 116.

English of Ireland suggests that they saw themselves as precisely that – as the English political community resident in Ireland, with their own pronounced sense of regional identity focusing on the lordship and its institutions, which distinguished them from provincial communities elsewhere in the English state – but not as a separate nation. Essentially, their politics revolved around the need to protect their inherited rights and traditions as Englishmen, with all that this entailed. Defence and good government were central to their political aspirations, but so also was the, in part conflicting, tradition of 'self-government at the king's command'. Nevertheless, to judge from the most recent exposition of 'Anglo-Irish separatism', there is now perhaps less disagreement about the *content* of these political ideas than is implied by the continuing debate about the proper terminology to describe them.[27]

IRELAND AND THE WARS OF THE ROSES

Whatever the reasons behind it, however, the decision to back York in the crisis of 1459–61 was to pay dividends in terms of relations between crown and community over the next twenty years. Of course, initially the Yorkist refugees had to be protected from Lancastrian efforts to dislodge them. Ormond's opening attempt to displace York failed when his agent bringing writs for the duke's arrest was himself arrested, convicted of high treason under the new statute, and executed. The Lancastrians then tried unavailingly to incite Gaelic chiefs to rebel and capture leading Yorkists (a blunder exploited by York and Warwick in a propaganda manifesto from Ireland after the chiefs had passed the king's privy seals on to York), before falling back on a prohibition of shipping between England and Ireland to insulate the mainland from a Yorkist invasion. Despite this, however, the earls of Warwick and Salisbury sailed from the other Yorkist bridgehead at Calais in March with a fleet of 26 ships, landing at Waterford with 500 men, in order to plan strategy with York for an invasion. To judge from events, the agreed plan was for a coordinated invasion initiated from Calais, which was much more suitable than Ireland for a strike on the capital, with the aim of securing the throne for York. The invasion succeeded: Warwick defeated the royal army at Northampton on 10 July, capturing the king; so that when the final session of York's parliament opened on 21 July, there was much demand for licences of absence from those wishing to accompany the duke into England.

Leaving Kildare as his deputy, York landed at Chester and marched on London, displaying the royal banner (as the governor of Ireland customarily did, but only in Ireland) and claiming the throne. Eventually, however, an uneasy compromise was confirmed by the English parliament in October whereby Henry would remain king and be succeeded by York in place of

27. Lydon 1994–5, pp. 289–94. For the suggestion that the movement is more aptly termed 'loyalist': Frame 1982, pp. 330–1. Ellis 1995a, pp. 141–5 includes relevant comment for a slightly later period.

Prince Edward.[28] Not surprisingly, however, Queen Margaret refused to accept this disinheritance of her son. Her army surprised the Yorkist lords near Wakefield: York was killed on the field, Salisbury soon after. She then defeated Warwick at St Albans, freeing Henry VI. This left Richard's son, Edward, earl of March, with no alternative but to seize the throne himself. Having secured the Welsh marches against Jaspar Tudor and the earl of Ormond, he entered London, was proclaimed king, raised reinforcements, and departed northwards to encounter the Lancastrians. In the largest battle of the civil war, at Towton on 29 March, the Yorkist victory left Edward IV in control of England.

EDWARD IV, IRELAND AND THE LANCASTRIAN RESPONSE

In large measure, the Yorkist victory in 1460–1 had stemmed from their appreciation and exploitation of the strategic and military value of England's overseas territories. This lesson was not lost on the Lancastrians, and the next three years saw a series of Lancastrian attempts to employ this strategy in reverse. Initially, an opportunity was provided by continued feuding between Neville and Percy in the far north of England, where Carlisle was besieged and Berwick-on-Tweed surrendered in return for Scottish support. The other major campaign of these years, however, was in Ireland, where rivalry between the lordship's leading lineages had likewise become aligned with the dynastic struggle. The Lancastrian earl of Ormond had been attainted and executed after Towton, but in January 1462 his brother and heir, Sir John Butler, styling himself earl of Ormond, attempted to restore the family fortunes by invading the lordship on Henry VI's behalf, so threatening the two Fitzgerald earls. An experienced soldier from the Normandy campaign, Sir John recovered control of the family estates in Kilkenny and Tipperary and captured Waterford city in Henry VI's name. Simultaneously, Lancastrian risings in the midlands, led by the Butlers of Polestown, one of the junior Butler branches, and in Meath by Philip Bermingham, the future chief justice, were staged to coincide with this invasion from England. The acting governor, Kildare, elected by the council on news of York's death, attacked the Meath insurgents and sent the treasurer, Sir Roland FitzEustace, to court to plead for reinforcements. Meanwhile, Thomas Fitzgerald, who had probably just succeeded as seventh earl of Desmond, raised troops against Sir John Butler, who had captured his brother Gerald. In a pitched battle at Pilltown, near Carrick-on-Suir, Desmond defeated the Butlers of Polestown, after which the rising gradually subsided and Sir John Butler departed.[29]

28. Berry 1910, pp. 676–9, 740–5, 792–9; Curtis 1932, pp. 181–3; Griffiths 1981, ch. 25; *NHI*, ii, pp. 567–8.
29. *New DNB, sub* John Butler 6th earl of Ormond; Thomas Fitzgerald, 8th earl of Desmond; *NHI*, ii, p. 599; Gillingham 1981, chs 8–9.

Edward IV (1461–70, 1471–83) was a shrewd, if occasionally impulsive, monarch who worked hard to restore royal finances and authority and to improve the standard of justice. Understandably, he concentrated on doing this nearest the centre of power, in lowland England; and during his first reign, down to 1470, he faced a series of conspiracies culminating in the brief 'readeption' (1470–1) of the feeble Henry VI. He could not therefore spare much time for Ireland, except for moments of crisis when his authority was directly challenged there, but in such circumstances any English king could be expected to react vigorously. Nevertheless, even in the 1460s there were in-dications of a different approach by Edward to his Irish problem. In February 1462 Edward's appointment as nominal lieutenant of his young brother, the duke of Clarence, aged 12, evidently aimed at consolidating the dynasty's close ties with the lordship, since Clarence had been born there; but the decade also saw two important royal interventions aimed at stabilizing English lordship there, firstly by entrusting government to a coalition of local nobles headed by Desmond, and then by appointing a complete outsider as governor. Both experiments had their shortcomings.[30]

The earl of Desmond's deputyship

In the crisis of the Butler rising, however, Edward's initial choice as deputy-lieutenant fell on FitzEustace. He retained him with 300 English archers, grant-ing him Duke Richard's manor of Portlester and other Meath lands as a reward for his previous good service, and raising him to the peerage as baron of Portlester. Thus supported from England, FitzEustace served as deputy for ten months from June. Yet Pilltown was a reminder to Edward of the extent of Desmond power. The sixth earl of Desmond (1421–62) had shown no inclina-tion for affairs of state, despite the crying need for wider noble participation in government. In April 1463, therefore, the king appointed Desmond deputy-lieutenant, despite the risk that the earl was too compromised by close rela-tions with Gaelic chiefs in Munster to command universal support in the lordship. By conferring the governorship on Desmond, traditionally the most isolated of the Irish-based earls, Edward inaugurated an unusual experiment in the crown's efforts to extend the Dublin administration's normal range of operations. Desmond's comparatively meagre landed inheritance around Cos. Kerry, Cork and Limerick offered little help in the primary task of ruling the strategic heartland of English power, around Dublin. Yet this problem was solved by associating with the earl the two previous governors, who both had extensive lands there: Portlester continued as treasurer, while his brother-in-law, Kildare, who was Desmond's kinsman, soon after became chancellor. Edward ordered Desmond to govern with Portlester's advice, having 'a special respect to the observance of our laws and statutes there', and particularly not to impose coign and livery on the king's subjects. In fact, Desmond's deputyship

---

30. Ross 1974; Lander 1980, chs 7–8; *HBC*, pp. 164, 167.

was overshadowed by complaints about his introduction of coign and livery and other exactions into the English Pale.[31]

Desmond immediately faced opposition. A further rising by the commons of Meath formed the prelude to another attempt during the summer by Sir John Butler. Yet after the deputy had spent seventeen days burning the Ormond estates, Sir John fled to Portugal. Charges were also laid before the king of coign and livery imposed on Co. Meath; and in 1464 a feud between Desmond and William Sherwood, the English-born bishop of Meath who spearheaded the Meath gentry's opposition to his rule, led to the killing of nine of Desmond's followers in Fingal. Thus when the governor also ignored Edward's appointment as chancellor of John Tiptoft, earl of Worcester, with Sherwood as his deputy, and appointed Kildare instead, Desmond and Sherwood were summoned to court. Leaving Kildare as acting governor, Desmond departed with a glowing testimonial from parliament, pointedly stressing his good service in upholding law and order and repressing the Lancastrian risings. Yet, thanks largely to his influence in Munster and the Butler eclipse, Desmond also attracted support from some unusual quarters, and his deputyship saw unwontedly vigorous activity by the Dublin administration in outlying English parts. For example, Lord Burke of Clanrickard and O'Donnell both visited Dublin, and the 1463 parliament held sessions at Wexford and Waterford – apparently the first to meet outside the Pale since 1425 – which were comparatively well attended, and paid considerable attention to Munster problems. In autumn 1466 Kildare kept the king's chancery at Cork and Dungarvan instead of Dublin while accompanying Desmond on a progress.[32]

Eventually, Edward confirmed Desmond in office and also rewarded him with an annuity of £100, financed by a life grant of six manors in Co. Meath, so strengthening his hand there. Despite this and a parliamentary act of resumption, however, Desmond remained hard pressed to maintain an adequate retinue without financial support from England; and by mid-1465, when Worcester was appointed to replace him as deputy and then countermanded, Earl Thomas's influence was evidently waning. His continuing difficulties in securing local cooperation were manifested in a considerable disaster which befell the lordship in 1466. While campaigning in Offaly, he was heavily defeated and taken prisoner by O'Connor Faly, although he was later rescued by the English of Dublin. In consequence, O'Connor consolidated his influence in the Meath–Kildare marches, where continuing Gaelic raids called in question Desmond's ability to defend the Pale; and in Munster the O'Briens exploited Desmond's troubles to strengthen their power east of the Shannon. Clearly, Desmond had overreached himself. He was certainly short of money and this probably forced him to quarter his troops on the Pale – hence the complaints about coign and livery. Thus, in spring 1467, Edward decided to replace him, and the earl of

31. *New DNB*, *sub* Portlester, Desmond; Cosgrove 1975, pp. 11–27 (quotation, p. 16); *NHI*, ii, pp. 599–600; Richardson & Sayles 1952, p. 165; Otway-Ruthven 1980, p. 389.
32. *New DNB*, *sub* Desmond; Cosgrove 1975, pp. 11–27; Otway-Ruthven 1980, pp. 390–1; Ellis 1986a, p. 173; *NHI*, ii, pp. 599–600.

Worcester, a prominent Yorkist, arrived in October with the considerable retinue of 700 English archers to restore order.[33]

Desmond's attainder and execution

Despite Worcester's fearsome reputation as 'the butcher', his relations with the Geraldines remained ostensibly civil; and when parliament met before Christmas, he combined with Kildare to found a chantry at Dunshaughlin. Yet when Worcester's parliament reconvened at Drogheda on 4 February 1468, Desmond, Kildare and Edward Plunket of Balrath suddenly found themselves attainted of

> horrible treasons and felonies . . . as well in alliance, fosterage and alterage, with the Irish enemies of the king, as in giving them horses and harness and arms, and supporting them against the king's faithful subjects.[34]

Another, far-fetched, charge against Portlester was that he had treasonably urged Desmond to make himself king of Ireland. Yet, within eight days, Desmond was arrested at the Dominican convent in Drogheda, kept in prison over the weekend 'in daily expectancy of death', and then taken out and beheaded. Plunket was 'flogged through the streets of the town like a villain', but later spared. Kildare was also imprisoned, but escaped during the summer with Portlester's help: the two fled to join Desmond's brother, Gerald Fitzgerald, who burned Meath in revenge, assisted by O'Connor and MacMurrough who were attracted by prospects of plunder.[35]

Apparently Edward had not been consulted beforehand, and we can only speculate at Worcester's reasons for his course of action. Nevertheless, Desmond's execution both shocked and puzzled contemporaries. King Richard III later admitted that he had been 'extortiously slain and murdered by colour of the laws . . . against all manhood, reason and good conscience', and the annals of Ulster related that he was 'killed in treachery by an English earl'. Yet Desmond's imposition of coign and livery was probably the reason: Sir William Darcy later believed, erroneously, that Desmond was the first to impose coign and livery on the Pale, but he may well have extended the practice.[36] At any rate the Meath community bore him a grudge and were perhaps able to manipulate an inexperienced governor.

Worcester, however, soon discovered that royal government in Ireland was as dependent on noble support as in many parts of England: Gaelic Leinster remained disturbed, raids on Louth by O'Reilly and on Tipperary by Gerald

---

33. Cosgrove 1975; *New DNB*, *sub* Desmond, Sherwood; Otway-Ruthven 1980, p. 391; *NHI*, ii, p. 600. Ó Cléirigh 1996 surveys the decline in O'Connor fortunes in the later fifteenth century.

34. Berry & Morrissey 1914, pp. 454–62, 464–6 (quotation, p. 465).

35. Cosgrove 1975 (quotation, p. 23); *New DNB*, *sub* Desmond; Otway-Ruthven 1980, pp. 392–3; *NHI*, ii, p. 600 (quotation, n. 2).

36. MacCarthy 1895, pp. 220–1 (quotation); Gairdner 1861–3, i, pp. 67–70 (quotation); *Carew*, i, no. 2; Cosgrove 1975; *New DNB*, *sub* Desmond.

Fitzgerald followed, and in Lecale the remnant of the Ulster colonists were heavily defeated by O'Neill. The administration seemingly recognized what lay behind the disturbances, and after vainly appealing for English reinforcements it reversed Kildare's attainder on condition that the earl induced the Leinster chiefs to make peace. In Munster, however, the damage was less easily repaired. Edward granted Desmond's son livery of his inheritance even though under age, but Fitzgerald refused to recognize him. A long succession struggle followed which greatly weakened the earl's influence over his tenants and clients: until 1541 successive earls remained estranged from the crown and English influence there was greatly reduced.[37]

IRELAND AND THE 'READEPTION'

By late 1468, growing divisions between leading Yorkists were beginning to destabilize Edward's government. Serious Lancastrian plots were uncovered; there was renewed fighting in 1469–70 between the king and Warwick, now supported by Edward's estranged brother, Clarence; and after Warwick and Clarence had been driven out, a reconciliation in France between Warwick and the exiled Queen Margaret led to another invasion which toppled Edward IV and brought about the brief 'readeption' of Henry VI. As the crisis developed and royal control slackened, so the political situation in the lordship again resembled conditions in 1459–60. The Dublin administration gradually lost the initiative, and attention again shifted to Ireland's military and strategic potential. Money was sent to pay Worcester's retinue in spring 1469, but thereafter his troops remained unpaid; and by March 1470, when he was promoted lieutenant in place of Clarence and concurrently recalled to help Edward against Warwick, Worcester was owed £4,535.

Initially, Worcester left his brother, Sir Edmund Dudley, as deputy-lieutenant, but he too had departed by the time Edward fled to the Netherlands in late September. By 13 October, the Irish council had elected the earl of Kildare as justiciar, and five days later Worcester was executed by the victorious Lancastrians; but Kildare was still holding parliament in Edward's name as late as 26 November. The delicacy of the situation was underlined when Sir John Butler was recognized in England by Henry VI as earl of Ormond and William Butler was arrested in Ireland for calling Portlester a traitor; but on this occasion, Clarence's defection enabled the Lancastrians to exorcise the lordship's growing reputation as a Yorkist bridgehead. By February 1471, the duke had been reappointed lieutenant of Ireland in Henry VI's name, and Kildare was serving as his deputy-lieutenant.[38]

Edward's Irish interventions had been no more successful than his father's lieutenancy, though their fate is instructive. Particularly since the death of

37. Otway-Ruthven 1980, pp. 393–4; *NHI*, ii, p. 601.
38. Pollard 1988, pp. 29–31; Otway-Ruthven 1980, pp. 394–5; *NHI*, ii, p. 601; Ellis 1978a, pp. 23–4; Ellis 1977, pp. 22, 25–7; Ellis 1986a, p. 132.

Talbot and Ormond, political influence in the lordship had increasingly centred on the Pale, and government, to be successful, had had to take account of the Palesmen's interests and sympathies. This region remained particularly conscious of its Englishness, and Desmond's difficulties stemmed in part from his failure fully to respect this consciousness and perhaps also from a comparative neglect of its defence and government. Yet Worcester's deputyship showed how expensive the maintenance of an outsider could be. Political influence in this period was measured in lordship over people as well as land: magnates frequently retained influential gentry and, conversely, the 'good lordship' of influential nobles like Richard of York was eagerly sought, but most landlords could count on the active support of their tenants. Worcester had had no Irish connections and the king had therefore supplied a comparatively large retinue instead. Yet as events in 1468 showed, even 700 men could not keep the peace without the cooperation of the local magnates, and they still cost more than the king was willing to pay on a continuing basis.

A COMMUNITY IN CRISIS

In retrospect, the period 1447–71 marked the nadir of English rule in Ireland. An air of optimism had briefly pervaded the lordship in 1449 during Duke Richard's first visit, and in the 1460s sporadic bouts of activity raised occasional hopes of recovery. Yet in general, the lordship's political community experienced an acute and prolonged crisis of lordship at this time. In many ways, the English of Ireland experienced the same general sense of trauma felt by the English elsewhere at the loss of the French territories, and then at the descent into civil war. But this sense of national disgrace was exacerbated in the lordship by fears arising from the region's endemic insecurity as a frontier zone. Seemingly all was desolation and decay, with loyal English lieges increasingly beset by wild Irish and English rebels. France was gone. Talbot lay dead. The lordship was destitute of good captains. Irish enemies were at the gate. Yet the English were fighting amongst themselves. To harassed exchequer clerks contemplating the king's empty coffers in Dublin castle, or hard-bitten English marchers scanning the Leinster mountains for signs of the next Gaelic raid, the outlook seemed far bleaker than to cultured courtiers safe and secure in the Home Counties.

CHAPTER 4

THE ENGLISH RECOVERY, 1471–1496

THE ENGLISH PALE

Henry VI's 'readeption' soon collapsed, in part because Queen Margaret delayed so long in France. When Edward's small invasion force arrived from Flanders in March, resistance to him was half-hearted, Clarence now declared for his brother, and Warwick and other leading Lancastrians were all killed in the ensuing battles. Upon news of Edward's victory, Kildare had been elected justiciar again, and he became Clarence's deputy-lieutenant after the duke was reappointed lieutenant early in 1472.

The king was initially preoccupied with establishing his position at home. There was no immediate danger from Ireland, but Edward was short of money and would have been mindful of the drawbacks of his experiments in the 1460s with Desmond and Worcester. Not surprisingly, therefore, he aimed to ensure strong but economical government by appointing a Pale noble as governor. So successful did this policy prove that from 1470 until 1534 a Pale landowner was governor for all but nine years.

Initially, Kildare was the obvious choice. Of the three Irish earls, Ormond was still under attainder and Desmond was young and insecure. In the circumstances, to have dismissed Kildare would have been interpreted as a sign of royal distrust and displeasure. Yet circumstances soon altered. After the débâcle of the Readeption, many prominent Lancastrians who had hitherto held out for Henry VI, including Ormond, now made their peace with Edward IV. Thus, in his later years, Edward was very much in control, and by dint of financial reforms he became the first English king since Henry II to die solvent.[1]

The creation of the English Pale

The Dublin administration was in an extremely weak position in 1470–72, principally because Worcester's retinue had been disbanded and Kildare had no money to hire another. Gaelic raids caused widespread disorder in the Pale and beyond: Co. Meath suffered badly, and in Co. Dublin the tenants of Saggart,

---

1. Pollard 1988, pp. 31–3; Gillingham 1981, ch. 12; Lander 1980, p. 101.

a royal manor not 10 miles from the city, concluded a separate truce with O'Toole in default of assistance. The following year the O'Tooles and O'Byrnes burned much of the manor.[2] In the circumstances the administration con centrated, with the king's approval, on building up a defensive system less dependent on English subventions and based on the region later called the English Pale. Some of this work was a resumption of efforts which had been going on piecemeal for most of the century, but there were also some new developments.[3]

By the 1420s, if not before, the administration had tacitly accepted that for military and geographical reasons 'the four shires' should be treated separately from the other English districts, and thereafter their boundaries were increasingly defined. Already by 1428 the region had been vaguely divided into an inner 'land of peace, called "Maghery"' and the marches beyond. The marches lay open to Gaelic raids, but successive parliaments offered subsidies to those who would build towerhouses or small castles commanding the approaches, and ordered the construction of dykes and the fortification of key bridges. They were especially numerous in the Pale marches and were usually single towers about 40 feet high whose role was to give warning of the enemy's approach and later to act as a strongpoint barring his retreat.[4] Similarly, the dykes were not meant to exclude the enemy like a medieval version of Hadrian's Wall, but to prevent him from driving off the cattle which were the principal object of most raids. In this way a chain of defences was built up which insulated the maghery from all but the strongest raids. The term 'Maghery' was simply a transliteration of the Gaelic *machaire*, meaning 'a plain' or 'champaign ground'. Yet significantly, English speakers were now employing this term: quite possibly, they had heard Gaelic marchers refer to what they themselves called 'the English ground' as 'an machaire', and adopted it as a political term.[5]

By 1477 the boundaries of march and maghery had been precisely delineated (see map on p. 383) and were then confirmed by statute. This division within the Pale has not generally been noticed by historians, who have greatly understated its size by equating the maghery with the Pale as a whole and portrayed the area as constantly shrinking down to 1534.[6] In reality the well-known statute of 1488, the Act of Marches and Maghery, which is mistakenly cited as establishing new, shorter boundaries, merely outlined the existing boundaries for the purpose of amending the law concerning coign and livery. Whereas its imposition had formerly been a felony or capital offence, unless by the tenant's free consent, henceforward coign and livery was prohibited

2. Otway-Ruthven 1980, p. 395.
3. For what follows, see Ellis 1986a, ch. 2.
4. Ellis 1995a, pp. 30–2 offers a comparison with the only other English province to see widespread building of towerhouses, the far north of England.
5. Ellis 1986a, p. 52. See also the alternative tautological usage in a tract of Chief Baron Finglas, c. 1528, distinguishing between Englishmen dwelling in the marches and those dwelling 'within *Maghregron*' (i.e. maghery ground), which suggests the term was being employed by monoglot English speakers: Harris 1747, p. 45.
6. Edwards 1973, pp. 89–91.

within the maghery, and in the marches could only be imposed by landlords on their own tenants. Probably the statute reflects stronger government and a growing peace and prosperity in the Pale at this time: coign and livery had earlier spread as a means of maintaining troops to counter raids and disorders.

By the 1520s, so peaceful had the maghery become that there were complaints that its lords were abandoning fortified dwellings for stately houses as in England: they kept 'little ordinary houses, as [if] they were in a land of peace',[7] leaving defence to the marchers. Beyond the marches was the real borderland 'on the frontiers of the march'. By 1495 a second set of defences was being erected in this area: Poynings' parliament required the marchers to build a double rampart and ditch 6 feet high between march and maghery and further ditches 'in the wastes or fasaghe lands' between the marches and the Irishry.[8] There is in fact no reliable evidence to support the widely held view that the English Pale was gradually shrinking under Edward IV and the early Tudors. Rather, the evidence suggests precisely the reverse.

St George, the brotherhood of arms, and English identity

The second aspect of the Pale's new defensive system was the provision of a locally paid and recruited retinue for the governor. All governors were expected to maintain a bodyguard of at least twenty men-at-arms, or their monetary equivalent, out of a salary which was frequently only IR£500 per annum: Lord Deputy Kildare's salary of 1,000 marks (IR) annually (1471–4) payable by the Irish exchequer was little better.[9] By degrees, however, the Palesmen were induced to pay for a larger retinue on the grounds that they benefited from the deputy's habitual residence there. Initially the money was raised by a parliamentary subsidy levied on the Pale. Small numbers of troops were hired for the war season in spring and summer, but late in 1473 Edward responded to an address from the Irish parliament by despatching two royal commissioners, Sir Gilbert Debenham and James Norris, to inspect the lordship's defences. This led in 1474 to the establishment by parliament of the Brotherhood of Arms of St George. The Brotherhood comprised thirteen Pale magnates who would annually elect a captain of a force of 120 archers and 40 horse which was now to be recruited and financed by the extension to Ireland of a new custom called poundage, 12d. in the pound on goods entering or leaving the country.

It has been suggested that the Brotherhood was really a front for a Geraldine standing army, established for Kildare's own interests.[10] This is hardly fair to the earl: he had ultimate responsibility for the lordship's defence and would have been unwise to delegate this responsibility to a rival organization. In fact, the Brotherhood clearly had the king's approval (English kings traditionally maintained that the lordship should contribute more substantially to its

7. *LP*, iv (ii), no. 2405 (quotation).
8. Ellis 1986a, p. 51 (quotation).
9. Ibid., p. 25; for what follows, ibid., ch. 2.
10. Bryan 1933, pp. 14, 24, 51–5.

own defence), not all its members were Geraldines, and its real purpose was manifestly to spread responsibility and secure the active cooperation of the greater landowners.

Parliament also felt the time ripe for a more general royal initiative over Gaelic Ireland and prepared an appropriate address to the king. Until 1494 parliamentary addresses were evidently sent quite frequently. Yet few now survive and that of 1474, seeking approval for the new defensive arrangements and additional royal support, is therefore especially important for its insight into contemporary colonial attitudes. Parliament reminded the king that he was in honour bound to defend his subjects and that England should also contribute because Ireland was 'one of the members of his most noble crown and eldest member thereof'. Since the king's subjects there were 'but petty number in comparison of the great multitude of their Irish enemies, English rebels, and Scots' who were illegally settling in Ulster, he should personally lead an army of 1,000 archers to Ireland or send his lieutenant, Clarence, or some other kinsman. Together with the recent parliamentary grant of pound-age to be employed 'in aiding and sustaining of the said wars and none other-wise', this would suffice until Edward could 'proceed to the whole conquest' of Ireland. The king should also have it proclaimed throughout England that 'all manner persons of Ireland birth', except students at Oxford, Cambridge and London, return to Ireland 'to inhabit such countries as shall [be] con-quered'. Moreover, Ireland, it was thought, had formerly yielded 100,000 marks per annum and would do so again once conquered – an easy task because 'the first conquest thereof was obtained with a full small number of Englishmen' whereas now 'all the cities, castles and walled towns' were 'under the king's obeisance', though interspersed among 'Irish enemies, English rebels and Scots, which been alway divided within themself and not of one power'. The profits from Ireland would then facilitate Edward in 'the subduing of his great enemies of France and Scotland and all their adherent friends'.[11]

The symbolism of the Brotherhood's association with St George was also important, and should be seen in conjunction with that of the separate Irish coinage of 1460 – co-existing regional and national loyalties. All good English-men were in no doubt that God was an Englishman. For how else could Eng-lish success in arms be explained? And in Ireland the cult of St George, patron saint of England, centred on the Guild of St George in St Patrick's cathedral, Dublin. 'St George' was the rallying cry of English armies in Ireland; and by municipal act of 1448 the guild's master and wardens were entitled to one good cow from every prey taken by the city. On St George's Day, when the Brothers assembled to elect a captain from among themselves for the following year, 'St George's Chapel [was] well hanged and apparelled to every purpose with cushions'. The guild also organized the city's annual pageant, witnessed by many pious pilgrims, in which St George rode in procession accompanied by an emperor and empress, king and queen, four horsemen bearing his standard, pole-axe, and the swords of St George and the emperor,

11. Printed, ibid., pp. 18–22.

with a maid leading the dragon. Dublin was 'open' for the pageant, as also for St Patrick's Day and for the city's other main annual pageant, on Corpus Christi Day, when for some obscure reason, St George's dragon got another outing.[12]

From Calais to Ireland: the making of a myth

Finally, the origin and connotations of the very concept of an 'English Pale' demand consideration. The term's application to Ireland, far from representing a forlorn hope by a besieged Englishry in the dark days of Lancastrian lordship, was actually a confident assertion of the region's Englishness by experienced Tudor officials and a recognition of 25 years of English recovery. After the dissolution of Poynings' parliament, the English-born clerk compiling the roll apparently headed the statute for entrenching the four shires: 'ditches to be made about the English Pale', seemingly the first reference to the Pale as a description of the region.[13]

This context also lends support to an earlier suggestion that the Pale in Ireland was inspired by the Pale at Calais[14] – the only territory still held by the English in continental Europe after the loss of Normandy and Gascony, and usually described by the English as 'the territory' or 'dominion' of Calais, while the French called it 'la terre de Calais'. The first recorded reference to the Calais Pale was not until 1494, when Sir Edward Poynings was deputy-lieutenant there.[15] Thus, when Poynings and his troops were redeployed in Ireland later that year, they probably applied the concept to the four shires. Here was another English dominion where prevailing conditions – government, society and geography – apparently resembled lowland England.

In reality, of course, the Pale in Ireland was not a defensive ring of fortifications enclosing a precisely delineated area, like Calais, still less the thin line of modern maps(!), but a typical medieval frontier, a constantly shifting region many miles wide. Yet peculiarly in Ireland, perceptions of an international boundary or borderline were powerfully reinforced by the close coincidence there of geographical, cultural, administrative, political and military boundaries. Nowhere else in the British Isles were the divisions which these different kinds of boundaries reflected clustered quite so thickly together. South of Dublin, for instance, the English lowlands quickly gave place to Gaelic uplands, agriculture to pasture farming; English gentlemen were replaced by Irish clansmen, English-style cloaks by Gaelic mantles; common law gave place to brehon law, country houses to mud huts, and civility to savagery. As Poynings and his staff looked out from this oasis of English civility into darkest Ireland, they may

12. Ellis 1990–1, p. 300; Lydon 1994–5, p. 291.
13. Ellis 1986a, p. 51 (quotation). Dr Elizabeth Matthew has recently shown that the well-known supposed reference in a document of 1446 is actually a Tudor interpolation: Matthew 1994, p. 397. For what follows, see my paper on 'The origins of the English Pale in Ireland' in *IHS* (forthcoming).
14. Lydon 1972a, p. 261.
15. Morgan 1966, p. 7.

well have imagined that the protection of the Pale represented the defence of civilization against the onslaughts of primitive man.

BISHOP SHERWOOD'S DEPUTYSHIP AND THE REFORM OF TAXATION

In 1474, however, when Edward received these proposals for the consolidation and expansion of the lordship, he was preoccupied with negotiations then proceeding with Burgundy and Scotland prior to the invasion of France in 1475. If the conquest of Ireland were so easily accomplished, it could well be postponed until he had nothing better to do. He did, however, retain Debenham and 400 archers paid from England for a year from September, and appointed Debenham chancellor; and in April 1475 a further 100 archers were despatched for the campaigning season. Debenham's appointment apparently led to friction with Kildare, however, and in May 1475 the earl was replaced as deputy by Bishop Sherwood of Meath.[16] His appointment was probably aimed also at assuaging complaints from that quarter, but Sherwood lacked Kildare's Gaelic connections, and the appointment was not altogether successful. It did, however, see the completion of the Pale's new defensive system with the provision of adequate finance for its upkeep.

The troops at the Brotherhood's disposal would normally have cost over IR£1,200 a year, which far exceeded the value of poundage, and the difference was no doubt recouped as before through coign and livery. The king's provision of troops in 1474–5 lessened the need for the Brotherhood, and Sherwood preferred to make his own defence arrangements. In February 1476 poundage was abolished as prejudicial to trade – without the king's knowledge or consent, as Edward later complained – and the Brotherhood disbanded. On the king's instructions both were restored in December 1479, but on this occasion the troops were restricted to the level which could be financed by poundage, and in this form the Brotherhood survived until 1494.[17] In 1476–7, however, Sherwood had had to manage without English subventions, and in order to raise money he initiated a significant reform of taxation in the lordship.[18]

Unlike its English counterpart, which was essentially a tax on personal property, the Irish parliamentary subsidy was primarily a tax on arable land, based on an archaic method of assessment which can be traced back to the *danegeld* levied in Anglo-Saxon England. By the 1470s it was cumbersome and not very remunerative, but the reforms then made enabled it to survive for a century longer. Under Henry VI parliament had customarily granted subsidies, nominally of 700 marks, to help defray the governor's costs in defence; but until 1494 the subsidy was not strictly a royal tax, it was closely linked to

16. Otway-Ruthven 1980, pp. 396–7; Richardson & Sayles 1952, p. 168n.
17. Ellis 1986a, p. 53.
18. Ellis 1986a, pp. 67–70 for the following.

defence and usually granted on condition that the governor eschew coign and livery. In practice a governor was lucky if the actual yield of a subsidy exceeded IR£350. This was because those counties or communities which were absent from particular parliaments very often refused to contribute their quotas to any subsidy agreed there. By 1470, therefore, as the Dublin government gradually relinquished primary responsibility for the defence of outlying shires, the subsidy ceased to be regularly paid outside the Pale, with the exception of small sums from Waterford and Wexford: its yield barely exceeded IR£300 and was entirely inadequate to meet defence costs. From 1477, therefore, successive governors began to demand heavier and more frequent subsidies; the government concentrated on levying subsidies in the Pale, its area of primary responsibility; and the assessment was changed to an open-ended system in which a uniform rate per ploughland of cultivated land replaced the old county quotas. In this way IR£1,357 15s. 4d. was collected from the Pale in 1477 for two subsidies granted in January and October, a total which was probably without precedent in the fifteenth century. This level of taxation soon drew complaints and the governor had to moderate his demands, but the principle of regular and worthwhile subsidies became accepted and was consolidated in the reforms of 1494–5. The governor thus had money to hire troops when, as increasingly happened, none arrived from England.

By early 1477 Lord Deputy Sherwood was having difficulty in keeping order in the lordship, and accompanied by Chief Justice Bermingham, he went to court for consultations, leaving Lord Gormanston as his deputy. The king agreed to provide a force of 200 archers and appointed the new archbishop of Armagh, Edmund Connesburgh, and Alfred Cornburgh, one of the royal squires, as commissioners to investigate and deal with certain strifes and controversies among the magnates in Ireland.[19] What was behind this emerges in the events of 1478. Edward had finally lost patience with his troublesome and unreliable brother, Clarence, who was executed for treason in February. Since Sherwood was technically Clarence's deputy, this annulled his appointment, leaving Ireland without a governor. In such circumstances a custom, known as the Statute of Henry fitz Empress, empowered the king's council there to elect a justiciar, or temporary governor, to act until the king should otherwise provide. On this occasion they elected Kildare which, since Sherwood was undoubtedly the king's nominee, not Clarence's, was effectively a vote of no-confidence in the previous administration. And when Kildare unexpectedly died three weeks later, they elected his son and heir, Gerald, now eighth earl, as justiciar.[20]

RIVALRY BETWEEN GREY AND KILDARE

Edward took the hint and in July 1478 appointed an outsider, Henry, Lord Grey, retainer of his right-hand man Lord Hastings, as deputy-lieutenant to his

19 Otway-Ruthven 1980, p. 397; Quinn 1941a, p. 31; Ellis 1986a, pp. 19, 28, 68.
20. Richardson & Sayles 1952, pp. 168–9, 263–4, 324–31.

infant son, George. Grey's only previous association with Ireland had been in 1473 when Edward had tried to arrest the decline of English influence in east Ulster by giving Grey a 40-year lease of the lands and rights of the earldom of Ulster. The title to this had descended through his father, Richard of York, though the lordship was largely in Gaelic hands. In the 1460s Edward had spent a fair amount of time and money on Ulster, but it was apparent that only a resident lord, lacking since 1333, could contain the ongoing eastward expansion of Clandeboye, a junior O'Neill branch, and settlement by Scottish MacDonalds. Yet Grey knew a bad investment when he saw one and prudently ignored the earldom.[21] He was equally unsuccessful as deputy-lieutenant: he contracted to govern for two years with a retinue of 300 archers in return for a salary of £2,000 in the first year and £1,825 in the second, but left after little more than three months following serious opposition from Kildare.[22]

Earl Gerald was then no more than 22 years old, and while his command of the Fitzgerald connection made him a useful stop-gap governor, the king evidently considered him too inexperienced for a permanent post. Kildare, however, thought otherwise. What followed has been portrayed by historians as a complete capitulation by the king to the might of Kildare,[23] but the outcome was in fact rather more complicated. Edward had apparently been informed of a custom (ignored in 1477) that parliaments should not be convoked nor subsidies granted more frequently than once a year. In order to preserve Grey's options, therefore, the king cancelled Kildare's appointment and ordered him not to hold parliament or impose taxation. Subsequently, Grey's parliament enacted that a justiciar should be elected by a council augmented by the Pale nobility and the mayors of Dublin and Drogheda, and not solely 'by seven persons of the king's council',[24] thus implying that Kildare's election had been invalid. Instructions were ignored, however – their validity was dubious anyway – and a parliament held from May until at least 14 September. Grey had certainly arrived by 15 September, but his commission, apparently, was deemed invalid on a technicality: it was sealed by the king's less formal privy seal and not by the great seal as stipulated in the lieutenant's patent. Lord Chancellor Portlester accordingly refused him access to the Irish great seal which authenticated the governor's commands; the prior of Kilmainham, the outgoing constable of Dublin castle, broke down the bridge, excluding him from the king's palace and the central courts; and when Grey called a parliament some of the sheriffs made no return to his writs of election. Moreover, Kildare had spent much of the subsidy previously granted, and Portlester, as treasurer, had thoughtfully assigned any revenue due at the exchequer. Grey therefore obtained the king's licence to have a new great seal made, and when parliament met he had his own authority confirmed and the acts of Kildare's parliament quashed.

21. Quinn 1935c; *CPR 1467–76*, p. 395.
22. Ellis 1986a, p. 26.
23. Bryan 1933, ch. 3. For what follows, see also Ellis 1986a, pp. 15, 24–6, 36, 69–70, 144, 217; Ellis 1984b, p. 33; Richardson & Sayles 1952, pp. 168–9, 264–6.
24. Richardson & Sayles 1952, p. 168 (quotation).

Edward subsequently overruled the objections concerning Grey's commission but soon realized that, without Kildare's acquiescence, a poorly equipped outsider like Grey stood no chance of exercising effective control. Grey retired to England with Chief Justice Bermingham for consultations, leaving Lord Gormanston, recently created viscount by Edward, as his deputy.

King Edward's settlement

Obviously the situation demanded a new initiative, and in order to obtain a full picture Edward summoned over Kildare and some of his leading associates, the priors of Kilmainham and All Hallows, the archbishop of Dublin, and Alexander Plunket, a future chancellor of Ireland. The review of government which followed was intended to be thorough – after the lieutenant had died in March, Gormanston was reappointed as deputy-lieutenant for four months in May – and afterwards Edward dictated an acceptable compromise between the two factions.

Kildare was appointed deputy-lieutenant, a recognition of his special role as head of the senior Pale family, but Edward guarded against partisan government by appointing the ageing Bishop Sherwood as chancellor and reserving to himself appointments of five of the seven chief officers – the chancellor, treasurer, chief justices of king's bench and common pleas and the chief baron of the exchequer (the others were keeper of the rolls and king's serjeant) – plus, unusually, the master of the mint. Traditionally, the king had empowered his deputy to appoint most of the Irish officers while reserving to himself the top appointments which carried with them a seat on the council: in this way he maintained eyes and ears in the Dublin administration. Under Richard of York, however, the practice of reservations had been allowed to lapse so that the governor had at times almost a free hand. The office of mintmaster was reserved for rather different reasons. Since 1460 mints had operated periodically in the lordship to maintain a supply of coinage: but to prevent their export into the stronger English economy, the Irish coins had a fractionally lower silver content and lighter weight than their English counterparts and normally passed at two-thirds their value. Unfortunately, however, the Dublin government was often unable to exercise adequate control over these English-looking Irish issues, which could be surreptitiously passed in England at par. After various earlier initiatives had failed, Edward eventually appointed an English mintmaster in 1479, ordered that henceforward Irish issues should conform fully to English specifications, and so indirectly prompted a temporary cessation of Irish mint activity.[25]

Thus Edward had begun to reassert royal control over his Irish administration, a policy which was continued piecemeal by the early Tudors. Moreover, with Kildare himself the king drove a hard bargain. Initially, the earl received a kind of probationary contract only until May 1481, but was granted a further four years in August 1480. His salary was a miserly IR£600 a year, payable from

25. Ellis 1978a, pp. 17–36.

the Irish revenues, 'if so be the same revenues will amount thereunto'. He had to maintain a retinue of 120 horsemen from this (though of course the patronage at the governor's disposal would provide him with substantial emoluments), but the king thereby limited his commitment to finding any shortfall on the deputy's salary if the Irish exchequer were unable to pay it in full. In practice £100 a year was sent until 1483, an economy which was in line with arrangements for the wardenships of the marches towards Scotland, where by 1486 the king had also ceased to pay for the upkeep of a private army.[26]

Finally, Edward issued a series of ordinances which were later enrolled in the Irish chancery. The parliament which met in December 1479 gave them statutory authority, in so far as this was constitutionally necessary, but in this period parliament was normally an instrument of royal policy and incapable of sustained opposition. The king confirmed the subsidy granted by Grey's parliament but specifically warned Kildare that

> in no parliament to be holden hereafter there shall no subsidy be asked nor granted in the same upon the commons, nor levied, but one in a year, which shall not exceed the extent of 700 marks as hath been accustomed.

This was a compromise between the governor's needs and what the commons could afford. The governor was limited to a maximum of 700 marks (IR) a year, but this amount was actually realizable, and though in 1485 Kildare received a subsidy of IR£750, no attempt was made to repeat the heavy taxation of 1477. Moreover, to ensure solvency for the future the king resorted to a device which had become very familiar throughout the English territories since 1450, a general act of resumption whereby royal grants made since 1421 were cancelled *en bloc* with provisos made for favoured individuals. Resumptions had in fact been passed by both 1478 parliaments, but the king quashed them as 'more hurting to our subjects there than to us or the weal of the said land profitable'.

He also commanded the repeal of any acts formerly passed in derogation of his royal prerogative, particularly that cancelling poundage and a previous statute (of 1460) restraining the king from summoning people out of Ireland by English writ. Kildare dutifully had parliament reimpose poundage, but the 1460 statute apparently went unrepealed. It is not necessary to believe that in this regard Kildare wilfully disobeyed an inconvenient instruction which struck at a growing separatist movement.[27] The act had been *passed* (the genesis of the principle on which it was based is another matter) to protect Richard of York from the Lancastrians: it had since remained a dead letter.

The remaining instructions provided detailed directions to ministers concerning peace and good government. These tried to ensure that duties were properly performed and that fees and fines were paid at the appropriate rate and properly recorded so that the king's revenues should not suffer. Lord

---

26. Ellis 1986a, pp. 18–19, 25–7, 50; Gilbert 1885, p. 600. Cf. Storey 1957, pp. 593–609.
27. E.g. Lydon 1972a, p. 162; Lydon 1994–5, p. 291.

Treasurer Portlester was ordered to 'remit and forget all malice and evil will' towards Bishop Sherwood and Chief Justice Bermingham, and vice versa, and to abide by the king's arbitration in his disputes with his kinsman, Sir Robert Eustace.[28]

The whole episode serves as a reminder that royal government depended not so much on a developed central bureaucracy as on the king's relations with the nobility and county gentry whose leading role in the preservation of peace and order in the provinces was recognized by their appointment to the unpaid offices of local government. Good relations, built on respect for the monarch, produced effective government: modern notions that the king should have dispensed with aristocratic delegation in favour of more bureaucratic forms of government are misconceived. Edward aimed rather to compose the disputes among the nobles by recognizing their legitimate aspirations, and so to ensure peace, defence and good government for all his subjects. This was all that was expected of medieval monarchy. Kildare in particular seems to have appreciated the nature of the compromise and set out to provide vigorous and impartial government which would justify the king's confidence. In 1483 he even convened parliament at Limerick, which had long been a distant outpost of English rule, an unprecedented step.

KILDARE AND ENGLISH EXPANSION

By the 1480s the chroniclers who had recorded successive depredations on the Pale in the century's middle years had fallen silent, and the reason is not far to seek. Earl Gerald was completing his father's task of consolidating Fitzgerald control of the Kildare marches and initiating its extension into other regions bordering the Pale. This process continued piecemeal down to the 1530s and was part cause and part consequence of an English recovery which originated in the governmental reorganization of the 1470s. Though there were occasionally setbacks, particularly in the years 1491–5 and 1520–8, successive Kildare earls were gradually able to extend the normal range of governmental activity because the administration's base, the Pale, had been secured. This process was first evident in south Leinster, but Kildare domination of Gaelic border clans and expansion in Wicklow, Westmeath and Ulster is best considered in the next chapter in relation to the evidence of the ninth earl's Rental Book, compiled in 1518, even though the seventh and eighth earls were clearly the initiators.

The seventh earl, however, had recovered the border manor of Rathangan, part of the original Fitzgerald patrimony as lords of Offaly, probably in 1459. A substantial towerhouse was also built to cover the ford at Kinnegad, in part by labourers from the barony of Carbury, so that by 1500 the O'Connors had been pushed back westwards and the important ancestral manors and castles of

28. Gilbert 1865, pp. 592–9.

Lea and Moret retaken. Lea castle was rebuilt to serve as the earl's chief military base in the region.[29] By 1519 the earl's justices were even administering English law from Carbury castle. Throughout Kildare, a series of fortifications was erected, particularly at key points in the marches. In Co. Carlow, Leighlin castle was retaken in 1480 and castles were also maintained at Rathvilly and Clonmore. By 1483 the earls had expelled Gaelic clans from many parts of south Kildare and north Carlow, but those with title to land there sometimes made no effort to reoccupy them and they remained waste. Kildare therefore had parliament vest in him all waste lands between Calverstown and Leighlinbridge, unless their owners occupied them within six years. He had also begun by 1485 a substantial castle at Castledermot for 'the true readeption of all the waste lands of the county of Carlow'. And by 1499, so peaceful had the region become that the earl could hold parliament there for the first time in a century.[30]

Historians have tended to discount evidence of Kildare expansion on the grounds that the earls were partially 'gaelicized' and pursuing their own interests and those of 'Ireland' at the expense of the crown.[31] Yet arguments that successive kings were coerced into allowing Kildare a free hand to pursue separatist or 'Home-Rule' policies are false and anachronistic. In late medieval Ireland local loyalties were paramount: there was no real consensus about Ireland as a political entity, and it is unlikely that Kildare saw any clear distinction between his own interests, which he pursued singlemindedly like any other magnate in the English state, and those of the crown and lordship more generally. And since Kildare expansion extended the area in which the king's officers could operate, it tended to strengthen the position of the lordship in the English state. Yet Kildare was continued as deputy because his government proved economical, relatively effective and also safeguarded vital royal interests. If he had failed in this, the king would certainly have been prepared to pay for an alternative.

Thus, cooperation between the crown and the magnates depended on a delicate balance between the crown's rights and interests and magnate aspirations. In this Kildare had a unique role to play because his sphere of influence included the Pale, where the lordship's administrative capital was located, but he was not indispensable. The king needed the cooperation of powerful nobles like Kildare to make royal government work, but equally Kildare's standing among the colonists was greatly enhanced by his appointment as the king's deputy. Normally, therefore, cooperation between king and earl worked to their mutual advantage, but in the decade following Edward IV's death in 1483 this relationship was disrupted by renewed instability in England. Like other magnates, Kildare profited initially from the crown's preoccupations elsewhere, but he eventually overstepped the mark and Henry VII (1485–1509) intervened in force to protect his vital interests.

29. Ellis 1995a, ch. 4 includes a more detailed analysis of Kildare expansion.
30. Ellis 1986a, pp. 58–60 (quotation, p. 59); Richardson & Sayles 1952, pp. 332–65.
31. Bryan 1933, *passim*; Curtis 1938, pp. 331–67.

RICHARD III AND IRELAND

Edward IV died rather unexpectedly on 9 April 1483 and was succeeded by his son Edward V. But on 25 June he was deposed and later executed by his uncle who succeeded him as Richard III. Richard had previously served successfully as the king's lieutenant in the north, and there are signs that, given time, he would have taken a much closer interest in Irish affairs along the lines of his involvement in northern England. For the present, however, his accession did not go unopposed in the south, and he was finally ousted by the last and doubtful heir of the Lancastrians, Henry Tudor, who with French support mounted an invasion through Wales and defeated Richard at Bosworth on 22 August 1485 to become Henry VII.[32]

In July 1483 Richard III confirmed Kildare as deputy-lieutenant, but only for a year because he hoped to intervene in person once he had settled England. He also sent William Lacy, clerk of his council in England, with instructions to negotiate the terms of Kildare's reappointment, to announce that in future the king wished all ministers to hold office during pleasure only, and to order the Irish council to withdraw a recent issue of lightweight and debased English-style coin. In future Irish issues were to be clearly distinguishable from those in England.[33] Kildare, however, was evidently well informed about Richard's difficulties, and as the king's situation deteriorated Kildare exacted substantially better terms than he had got from Edward IV. Bishop Sherwood had died late in 1482 but his replacement as chancellor, Lord Howth, had to secure successive renewals of his commission by Edward V and Richard III before he could be admitted to office. Meanwhile, Kildare as justiciar had appointed his brother, Thomas Fitzgerald, to exercise the office during the vacancy, as he was entitled, but he subsequently refused to admit Howth and claimed to be warranted in so doing by the Statute of Henry fitz Empress. The dispute was referred to the king and council who decided that a justiciar might make an appointment during the king's pleasure only and ordered Kildare to admit Howth, 'assuring you that if ye attempt the contrary . . . we shall provide for such a governance there as shall not presume to derogue, argue or diminish our power royal or prerogative'.[34] Despite this, the king eventually relented: Fitzgerald remained chancellor and in August 1484 Kildare was rewarded by a life grant of the manor of Leixlip, Co. Kildare. The settlement was probably negotiated by the king's councillor, Thomas Barrett, absentee bishop of Annaghdown, who returned in the autumn on a mission to foster loyalty in the lordship and to encourage lords of English descent in Connaught, Munster and east Ulster to use English ways. In particular the king hoped to re-establish good relations with the earl of Desmond: he acknowledged that the earl's father had been judicially murdered, not unlike the king's own brother Clarence in 1478, and sent English clothing and a gold collar if Desmond would promise

32. Lander 1980, pp. 298–330.
33. Gairdner 1861–3, i. pp. 43–6, ii, pp. 286–7.
34. Richardson & Sayles 1952, app. x.

to abandon Gaelic dress. Kildare was ordered to use his influence with O'Neill (who had married his sister) to begin the recovery of the king's inheritance in Ulster and to accept O'Donnell's submission if he could be induced to come in.[35]

HENRY TUDOR'S INVASION AND ACCESSION

By 1485, however, a new danger to Kildare's position had arisen: England stood under threat of invasion by the pretender Henry Tudor. If the invasion succeeded Kildare's commission would lapse with the demise of the crown and his strong Yorkist associations would militate against his reappointment. In June 1485, therefore, he had parliament pass an act which effectively ensured his election as justiciar in such circumstances, although the act contravened previous royal commands and is a revealing insight into Kildare's doubts about the future of Richard's regime. Briefly, the act reaffirmed the Statute of Henry fitz Empress, restricting the franchise for electing a justiciar to the seven principal ministers, chiefly Kildare supporters, and confirmed them in their offices for life. Thus the earl gained a stronger bargaining position from which to negotiate with the new regime.[36]

In a sense events went according to plan, although the mutual mistrust between Kildare and the new king was evident from the start. Two months after Henry VII's accession, Kildare was still holding parliament in Richard's name, and an accompanying anonymous issue of coins from the Dublin mint suggests that Kildare was hesitating about whether to recognize Henry Tudor.[37] His dilemma was by then a familiar one to English nobles, who had shown a growing reluctance to become involved in the dynastic struggle and risk attainder by participating or raising troops from their tenantry. As the king's representative in Ireland, however, Kildare could not stand idly by, and many of his difficulties over the next few years sprang from this and the fact that he was no more adept than most of Europe in predicting Henry Tudor's fate. Initially, however, the earl of Lincoln, Richard's heir and Irish lieutenant, submitted, and this perhaps dictated Kildare's course of action. Lincoln soon changed his mind, but in March 1486 Kildare was appointed deputy to the king's uncle, Jasper, duke of Bedford, and summoned to court. Meanwhile, the king's council was arbitrating between Bristol and Galway in a dispute concerning a Bristol ship seized by Galway merchants the previous December. Yet king and council had more than enough to do in England, and anything other than outright resistance on Kildare's part would no doubt have been tolerated.[38]

35. Ibid.; Gairdner 1861–3, i, pp. 67–78.
36. Richardson & Sayles 1952, app. x.
37. Ibid.; Ellis 1978a, pp. 29–30.
38. Lander 1980, pp. 326–39; Bayne & Dunham 1968, p. 5; Otway-Ruthven 1980, p. 403; Gairdner 1861–3, i, pp. 91–3 (for the date of the letter, Richardson & Sayles 1952, p. 328, n. 19).

The new king had spent most of his life in exile living on his wits. His upbringing inevitably affected his character: he was cautious and calculating, and suspicious of baronial independence, yet his abilities eventually won the fear and respect of subjects and foreigners alike.[39] Kildare asked a high price for his support: he sent a councillor to excuse his absence and present petitions, asking for the deputyship for nine or ten years, an annual salary of IR£1,000, the grant of Leixlip to him and his heirs male, and custody of Wicklow castle with its annual fee of IR£50. Finally, he asked for a safe conduct to court signed by some of the nobles as well as the king. As Henry pointed out in reply, to grant such a safe conduct was inconsistent with the king's honour, but he sent royal letters of protection and urged Kildare to come to court by 1 August, promising to accede to his requests (except for the salary, if IR£1,000 were not available from the Irish revenues). Moreover, notwithstanding the earl's previous activities and associations, he would 'as benignly, tenderly and largely take him into the favour of his grace as ever did King Edward IV'.[40] It does not appear that Kildare went to court, but he sent a statement of the revenue (showing a nominal balance of only IR£185 12s. 8d. available to the deputy) and married his second daughter to Piers Butler of Polestown, cousin and heir male of the earl of Ormond, who as an erstwhile Lancastrian was now back in favour.[41]

LAMBERT SIMNEL, 'EDWARD VI', AND THE BATTLE OF STOKE

Kildare's actions did not go unnoticed by the Yorkists. Edward IV's sister, Duchess Margaret of Burgundy, had a boy trained to impersonate the young earl of Warwick, Edward IV's nephew, then imprisoned in the Tower. The boy, Lambert Simnel, crossed to Ireland early in 1487 where his cause was promoted by Kildare's brother, Thomas Fitzgerald. Henry, whose title to the crown was weak by comparison with Warwick's, had learned of this by 2 February when the English council discussed the plot, and he subsequently had the real earl paraded through London in an effort to dissuade possible sympathizers. Nevertheless, Lincoln fled to Burgundy soon after, where Margaret with assistance from the Emperor Maximilian gathered a force of 2,000 German troops led by Martin Schwarz: accompanied by Lincoln and Lord Lovell, the leader of an unsuccessful rebellion against Henry in March 1486, the force landed at Dublin on 5 May.

Meanwhile Kildare had convened a meeting of the Pale nobility to consider the boy's claims, which were apparently accepted, but until assured of substantial outside assistance (by which time he had little choice in the matter) he avoided openly committing himself. On 24 May, Simnel was solemnly

39. Lander 1980, pp. 280, 320, 323–7, 331.
40. Gairdner 1861–3, i, pp. 91–3.
41. Otway-Ruthven 1980, pp. 165–6, 403.

crowned King Edward VI in Christ Church cathedral, and the courts were kept in Edward's name. Kildare was promoted lieutenant and summoned a parliament which confirmed Edward's title to the crown of England and attainted Thomas and William Butler of treason in adhering to Henry VII. Afterwards, nobles and ministers were very anxious to disclaim any part in the conspiracy, but there does not in fact appear to have been much active opposition to the *coup d'état*. Waterford held out for a time, refusing to contribute troops for a royal expedition into Munster, but messengers sent to remonstrate with Kildare were hanged on Hogges Green on the earl's orders: the city must have capitulated soon after because coins in Edward's name survive from the Waterford mint.

For the invasion of England which followed, Kildare was able to recruit large numbers of Gaelic kerne, reputedly 4,000, but few archers or billmen. Together with Schwarz's German troops and a small contingent of English Yorkists under Lincoln and Lovell, Edward VI set sail on 4 June and landed near Furness in Lancashire on the 11th. After enjoying mixed success in Yorkshire the Yorkist army moved rapidly south, initially surprising the Tudor vanguard under the earl of Oxford at Stoke near Newark. Yet once the main Tudor army arrived, the scales were reversed and the rebels were heavily defeated in a three-hour battle on 16 June. According to an Old English annalist, 'the Irish men did as well as any naked men would do', but without armour they were no match for Henry's forces and their slaughter unnerved the others. Most of the leaders perished with them but Simnel was spared and subsequently given some menial office in the royal household. Kildare held out in Ireland until at least 20 October, but there was no future in a separatist policy – the Irish mints were issuing coins with the arms of England flanked by Geraldine saltires – and he eventually submitted.[42]

THE TUDOR SETTLEMENT OF 1488

Henry was doing what he could at this time to establish Irish links independently of Kildare: the Yorkist earl of Desmond had been murdered in December 1487 and in April 1488 the king allowed his brother and heir to enter his inheritance without payment of the usual feudal dues. He also granted him the constableship of Limerick castle and a commission to arrest and try rebels, appointed Lord Roche as sheriff of Cork, and granted charters of English liberty to two of the more anglophile Gaelic chiefs, Cormac MacCarthy of Muskerry and Florence MacCarthy of Carbery. Moreover, at Henry's instance, Pope Innocent VIII ordered four Irish bishops to collect information about reputedly treasonable activities by the archbishops of Dublin and Armagh and the

---

42. For the Simnel conspiracy and its aftermath, see Bennett 1987. Hayden 1915, pp. 622–38 and (less reliably) Bryan 1933, pp. 99–141 remain useful for events in Ireland. For additional material, Ellis 1978a, pp. 29–30; Ellis 1980a, pp. 103–4. Haigh 1995, ch. 19 gives an account of the Stoke campaign and battle.

bishops of Meath and Kildare, and in August 1487 he issued a bull forbidding, on pain of excommunication, any revolt against Henry and expressly included the inhabitants of Ireland in the order. Eventually, the king issued a general pardon, dated 25 May 1488, to 33 leading lords and ministers in the lordship, and this was brought by Sir Richard Edgecombe with orders to exact bonds and a new oath of allegiance to Henry to prevent a recurrence of plotting.

The battle of Stoke had not ended the Yorkist threat and the revolt had been almost universally supported in the lordship: if Kildare's party had been driven to despair, this might have had serious consequences because Henry could not yet afford an interventionist policy there. There is in fact a significant contrast here between the lenient treatment of Kildare and the decision to rule the northern marches independently of Percy support when the murder of the fourth earl of Northumberland in 1489 presented the king with a similar opportunity to dispense with noble support: it suggests that individual circumstances rather than a settled policy of curbing magnate power dictated the royal response.[43]

Edgecombe landed at Kinsale on 27 June, took the oaths of the townsmen and Lords Barry and Courcy, and sailed round to Dublin via Waterford, arriving on 5 July. Kildare was conveniently absent on a pilgrimage, and when he returned Edgecombe 'made not reverence and courtesy', as was customary to the king's deputy, to show Henry's displeasure. The king expected the leading rebels to enter into bonds by which they should forfeit large sums of money if they again broke their oaths of allegiance – a device much favoured by Henry against noble independence – and the city of Dublin was so bound over in 1,000 marks, but after discussions the nobles flatly refused, telling Edgecombe very significantly that rather than do so 'they would become Irish every [one] of them'.[44] Edgecombe's bargaining position was further weakened by news that Henry's ally, James III of Scotland, was dead, and he eventually decided to deliver the pardons in return for a solemn oath of allegiance and support for Henry. This done, Edgecombe left for home on 30 July.

The settlement was far from satisfactory to Henry, but it was all he could manage. The king's real fears only emerged in the arrangements of 1494–5 when he was in a much stronger position, but plainly the Simnel conspiracy was a startling reminder of the danger of neglecting Ireland. The danger stemmed not simply from Ireland's proximity, but from the fact that the lordship was an English dependency with a ruling elite and political system which were recognizably English: once again the lordship had been used for a descent on the mainland and, despite strong contingents of foreign mercenaries, German and Gaelic, the Yorkist army had found little difficulty in winning local support. Moreover, on this occasion the rebels had legitimized their seizure of power by having a pretender crowned and a parliament called to confirm his claims. Simnel was in fact crowned 'King of England, France and Ireland' instead of the traditional title, 'King of England and France, and lord of

43. Cf. James 1964–5, pp. 80–7.
44. Bryan 1933, p. 130 (quotation).

Ireland',[45] and the incident raised again the whole question of Ireland's constitutional relationship with England.

For the present, Henry attempted by traditional means to foster loyalty in Ireland. In July 1490 he summoned Kildare to court for discussions, but the earl did not reply until June 1491 and then only to excuse his absence on the grounds that he could not be spared: he was needed to compose a dispute between the earl of Desmond and Lord Burke of Clanrickard, so Desmond, Lords Roche and Courcy and Piers Butler affirmed by letter from Limerick, adding that his absence would jeopardize control over lands recently reconquered in east Ulster. Fifteen lords then attending parliament at Dublin also stated that he had recently been ill, from which border chiefs had profited by raiding the Englishry.[46]

PERKIN WARBECK AND THE REORGANIZATION OF 1492

In November 1491, however, there landed at Cork another pretender, Perkin Warbeck, claiming to be Richard, duke of York, Edward IV's second son, who had probably been murdered in the Tower.[47] He was backed by Margaret of Burgundy, Charles VIII of France and James IV of Scotland, and received widespread support in Munster, including from Desmond, while Kildare, even if not openly involved, remained suspiciously inactive. Against Warbeck, however, Henry reacted much more energetically: he immediately despatched Thomas Garth and James Ormond alias Butler, an illegitimate brother of Earl Thomas of Ormond, with 200 men as military governors of Kilkenny and Tipperary which were withdrawn from Kildare's control. In this way he drove a wedge between Desmond and Kildare, and Earl Thomas was also induced to appoint Ormond as his deputy in place of Kildare's ally, Piers Butler. This temporarily thwarted Warbeck, who departed in the spring for the French court, and Henry profited from the respite to dismiss Kildare and his closest supporters. In their places, the archbishop of Dublin, Walter FitzSimons, was appointed deputy in May, Alexander Plunket was made chancellor and in June James Ormond was appointed treasurer instead of Portlester and then joint governor of Ireland with special responsibility for Munster and south Leinster. Henry, however, had tried unsuccessfully to get Earl Thomas himself to serve, and Butler supporters were also appointed to three more key offices. Thus Kildare's influence in government was greatly diminished, and by splitting the governorship, Henry evidently hoped that FitzSimons with his archiepiscopal lands in south Dublin bordering Kildare and Gaelic Wicklow would counter the earl's influence in the Pale, while James Ormond controlled the southern parts.

45 Curtis 1932–43, iii, no. 272.
46. Printed, Bryan 1933, pp. 146–51.
47. The Warbeck conspiracy is the subject of an important study by Arthurson 1994. For Poynings' deputyship see the re-evaluation of Henry VII's Irish policy in Ellis 1981a, pp. 237–54; also *NHI*, ii, ch. 23; Conway 1932.

By mid-1492, therefore, a new administration was in control in Dublin, and Henry VII was apparently aiming at a wider diffusion of power in the lordship, perhaps with the Butlers as the principal governing family as under Henry VI. Kildare was in disgrace and, given his Yorkist background and activities, he was perhaps lucky not to have died a traitor's death. At any rate, as the Tudor regime consolidated its position, Kildare's chances of renewed employment appeared somewhat bleak.

The period after Warbeck's arrival witnessed a gradual increase in royal activity culminating in Sir Edward Poynings' deputyship (October 1494–December 1495), which saw a concerted attempt to strengthen English influence and royal control. Henry's strategy has generally been considered a failure, not least because he found it expedient to reappoint Kildare as governor in 1496 – despite the earl's previous misconduct and his highly controversial activities in the interim. Yet, if the king governed largely without Kildare's support during these years, this was almost the only common strand in his initiatives. It is tempting to assume that Henry VII was following a 'grand design' which aimed at curbing Kildare power – along with the feudal independence of 'overmighty subjects' elsewhere in the Tudor state – and effectively anticipating his son's post-1534 policy of 'direct rule'. The reality, however, was that the first Tudor was no more interested than Henry VIII in acquiring a continuing commitment in Ireland: rather circumstances forced him, most reluctantly, into a more active role (though not a consistent policy), and as soon as the traditional method of government was offered again in a respectable and trusty form he reverted to it.[48]

THE REVIVAL OF THE GERALDINE–BUTLER FEUD

The experiment of dividing the governorship soon proved a failure. After spring 1492 the English retinue was apparently withdrawn, and Kildare influence far outweighed FitzSimons's in the Pale. The king attempted to strengthen Butler influence as a counterweight by granting James Ormond a lavish custody of crown lands and rights in Meath, Kilkenny and Tipperary for two years,[49] but this predictably precipitated another outbreak of the traditional Butler–Fitzgerald feud. Kildare simply withdrew his cooperation, and those Meath gentry who failed to follow his lead received a sharp reminder of the realities of power, finding that 'as soon as the earl abandoned them, they were universally plundered and burned from every quarter by the Irish'.[50] In Dublin city fighting broke out between Fitzgerald and Butler retainers, Ship Street was burned, and the following winter Kildare took Garth prisoner in Offaly and hanged his son. In a letter to Earl Thomas in February 1493 Kildare adopted a pose of injured innocence, disclaiming support for Warbeck; although the king

48. Ellis 1981a, pp. 238, 249–50.
49. *CPR 1485–94*, p. 368.
50. O'Donovan 1851, iv, pp. 1197–9.

had refused to accept this and was imprisoning his messengers. He astutely misrepresented Ormond's efforts to establish his authority in the midlands as Earl Thomas's deputy, asserting that he was inciting trouble there with O'Brien support (his mother was an O'Brien) and planned to usurp the earldom.[51]

Henry responded by dispatching in March 300 troops under Sir Roger Cotton to restore order and issuing a pardon to Kildare on condition (unfulfilled) that he send his son to court within six months. The troops helped to strengthen government control beyond the Pale – the outlying counties were comparatively well represented at a parliament held between June and August, and sheriffs and seneschals from eight of these shires attended at the exchequer as required in 1493–4 – but in Dublin a further outbreak of feuding culminated in a riot in which some of the citizens were killed. This apparently convinced the king that a new strategy was needed, for his principal worry at this time was the threat of invasion by Warbeck from Flanders. With the continuing disorders the Dublin government was in no position to resist this. He therefore determined to arbitrate personally between the warring factions.

Two royal commissioners arrived with reinforcements in early September to survey and stabilize the situation. Viscount Gormanston took over as head of a caretaker administration; and at a council meeting at Trim with Pale lords and gentry, a series of ordinances was passed to promote law and order. Kildare and others gave bonds for their observance (as Henry had unsuccessfully demanded in 1488) in sums ranging from 40 to 1,000 marks (IR). They were also summoned to court: FitzSimons and Ormond apparently sailed for England immediately, and they were followed by Kildare, Gormanston (who left his son as vice-deputy), Garth, Chief Justice Turner, the archbishop of Armagh, the bishop of Kildare, and one or two others.

POYNINGS' EXPEDITION

By May 1494 a satisfactory settlement had apparently been reached. With their quarrels settled, the lords had mostly returned by March, but Kildare remained to help Henry win over Desmond, who had agreed to swear an oath of allegiance and to deliver his son and heir to Kildare as surety (who in turn agreed to send him to Henry if Desmond later defaulted): but before all this could be accomplished Warbeck again threatened invasion and Desmond raised rebellion. The king was back where he had started, having spent nearly £4,000 since 1491, while the Dublin administration remained weak and divided. In these circumstances, Henry reluctantly tried a new tack, the appointment as governor of an English captain, Sir Edward Poynings, with a substantial retinue to hold the country against Warbeck.

This strategy seems to have originated in advice proffered by those summoned to court in winter 1493–4. The colonial community had traditionally argued in favour of greater royal involvement to eliminate the problem of

---

51. Gairdner 1861–3, ii, p. 155.

Gaelic Ireland by conquest, and in August 1494 Henry informed Charles VIII of France that he had decided, on the advice of the magnates there, to pacify Ireland by conquering the wild Irish and extending English order and justice. He advised Dublin that he was sending a 'powerful army for the protection and defence of our land of Ireland and faithful subjects there, to attack and conquer our enemies and rebels and to restore the sovereignty' formerly enjoyed by English kings. Yet Henry had not previously shown much interest in Gaelic Ireland, and his difficulty in 1494 lay rather in the suspect loyalty of his subjects and the feebleness of royal government there. Moreover, the entire English garrison in Ireland in winter 1494–5 amounted to 653 soldiers, plus five or six administrators and lawyers. This perhaps sufficed to hold the English districts against Warbeck but hardly to conquer Gaelic parts as well. In fact conquest and administrative reform, traditionally considered as Henry's aims in 1494–5, were probably no more than a means to an end, increased control at less cost. The colonists had apparently suggested that this end was best accomplished by a general reform policy and (presumably) had argued that a small army with local support would ensure the gradual reduction of Gaelic Ireland at small cost. With a larger area under royal control, the security threat would diminish, and with the administrators overseeing the expansion of English law and order, an increase in royal revenues would follow. Thus (so the argument ran) the conquest would become self-financing and soon achieve a united Ireland under the English crown.

Henry acquiesced in this scheme (despite certain impracticalities which soon appeared) to the extent of issuing grandiose declarations and authorizing expeditions into Gaelic Ireland. The strategy, moreover, encouraged the king's subjects there to unite against his Irish enemies instead of fighting among themselves, but Henry's conduct of policy hardly suggests that he was taken in by colonial propaganda or greatly interested in Gaelic Ireland. The mirage of a self-financing conquest, however, proved a sore temptation to later monarchs, with unfortunate results, though unwittingly the hard-headed Henry VII arguably came nearest to making the strategy work.

In September 1494 the king appointed as lieutenant his 4-year-old son Prince Henry, recently created duke of York, in a bid to discredit Warbeck's pretensions as Richard, duke of York. Sir Edward Poynings, a trusted and able captain who had been serving as deputy-lieutenant of Calais, was now redeployed with his troops as deputy-lieutenant of Ireland, while on the civil side he was well supported by three experienced lawyers as chancellor and chief justices: indeed the chancellor, Henry Deane, bishop elect of Bangor, went on to become archbishop of Canterbury. As treasurer, Henry appointed Sir Hugh Conway – loyal and experienced but also incompetent and effectively replaced in June 1495. Conway's predecessor, Sir James Ormond, was rewarded with a grant of manors in Meath, Kilkenny and Tipperary and appointed constable of Limerick castle to keep an eye on Desmond.

Soon after Poynings' arrival, writs were issued summoning a parliament to meet at Drogheda in December. Meanwhile Poynings surveyed the military situation and negotiated for peace and good relations with Gaelic chiefs. Most of them quickly submitted, giving pledges for their good behaviour, but in November an expedition proved necessary into Ulster, where O'Hanlon and Magennis remained aloof and where O'Donnell was intriguing with James IV of Scotland. Kildare and Ormond accompanied Poynings northwards, and the show of strength together with Kildare's informal approaches to the chiefs achieved the desired result. This minor success, however, was more than offset by a quarrel which arose between Kildare and Poynings in O'Hanlon's country. The deputy learned of Kildare's communications with the chiefs and – understandably considering the earl's previous record – surmised that he was secretly encouraging resistance. He was eventually arrested in February and charged with plotting the deputy's murder, treasonable communications with the king's enemies, and conspiring with the king of Scots and earl of Desmond for an army to overthrow Tudor rule in Ireland. He was shipped to England and attainted of treason by the Irish parliament which added further charges for good measure.[52] This ended any real hopes that the more ambitious military objectives of Poynings' expedition might be realized. If the deputy's army were to be employed in recovering lands in Westmeath or Ulster to which the king had title, he needed Kildare's cooperation and influence to defend the Pale. Without this, Poynings might be hard put just to maintain the status quo.

He was soon put to the test. Within days of Kildare's arrest, his brother Sir James Fitzgerald had seized Carlow castle. The deputy and Ormond besieged the castle throughout the spring and it was eventually retaken in July. By then, however, O'Donnell, O'Neill of Clandeboye and Burke of Clanrickard had identified with Warbeck, and some border chiefs were growing restless – a friar was paid to spy in O'Byrne's country and elsewhere. More seriously, Desmond was rallying support for Warbeck in Munster. After recruiting the coastal towns of Cork and Youghal, Desmond besieged Waterford in late June. The king responded to Poynings' urgent appeals for reinforcements by appointing Sir Roger Cotton to command a relief force of 1,500 men. A month later, 400 troops sailed from Chester but arrived too late to help. On 3 July Warbeck tried unsuccessfully to land at Deal in Kent, and on the 23rd with eleven ships he reinforced Desmond's blockade of Waterford from the sea, and fierce fighting ensued. Poynings hastily summoned the Pale levies to reinforce his army, recruited some Leinster chiefs on his march south, and had by 3 August broken the blockade with his artillery, capturing three of Warbeck's ships. Desmond and Warbeck retreated westwards, and Warbeck then made his way to Scotland via Clanrickard and Tyrconnell. Thus by late August the threat was receding. Poynings continued mopping-up operations throughout the autumn, but was then recalled and sailed for England in late December.

Warbeck had ostensibly attracted widespread support in Ireland, including leading Gaelic chiefs. Yet the motivating factor in Gaelic Ireland was not factions and alignments in English politics but the favourable opportunity these provided to further local dynastic ambitions (discussed in the next chapter). Genuine commitment to Warbeck's cause was probably confined to parts of

---

52. Sayles 1951, pp. 39–47; *NHI*, ii, p. 642; Arthurson 1994, p. 113.

Munster where Richard Hatton, the king's councillor, arrived to negotiate in December. By March, Desmond had agreed to a far from binding pledge for his future good behaviour: he would deliver his son and heir to the city of Cork for a year, and longer if the king granted four petitions which would seriously have circumscribed the royal prerogative. Three days later, in return for the promise of a pardon, he swore an oath of allegiance with detailed clauses about his future conduct, but evaded giving better security. Desmond, Youghal town, and most English magnates in Cos. Cork, Kerry and Waterford, were pardoned in August 1496, but Lord Barry and John Water, mayor of Cork, were specifically excluded: Water was later arrested by Kildare and executed in London with Warbeck in 1499. Cork and Kinsale remained for some time in a kind of legal limbo: Kildare received their oaths in 1498 and Cork finally received a new charter only in 1500.[53] Raids by Fitzgerald on the Pale remained a threat into 1496 and there was the odd incursion by O'Donnell into Co. Louth, but a greatly reduced garrison contained these disturbances increasingly effectively and in early July Fitzgerald eventually submitted. By then the country was comparatively peaceful and Kildare's rehabilitation was almost complete.

THE 1494–5 PARLIAMENT, POYNINGS' LAW, AND ADMINISTRATIVE REFORM

Concurrently with the lordship's pacification and the elimination of support for Warbeck, English officials were conducting an investigation into government there: this resulted in piecemeal administrative reforms and a strengthening of royal control. Much of this programme had been previously agreed in England and, where necessary, bills had been drawn up for approval by parliament. This is quite apparent from the curious and careless wording of its most famous act, chapter 9, subsequently known as Poynings' Law:

> That at the next parliament that there shall be holden by the king's commandment and licence (wherein, amongst other, the king's grace intendeth to have a general resumption of his whole revenues since the last day of the reign of King Edward the Second [i.e. 1327]) no parliament be holden hereafter in the said land but at such season as the king's lieutenant and council there first do certify the king, under the great seal of that land, the causes and considerations and all such acts as them seemeth should pass in the said parliament; and such causes, considerations and acts affirmed by the king and his council to be good and expedient for that land and his licence thereupon (as well in affirmation of the said causes and acts, as to summon the said parliament) under his great seal of England had and obtained, that done, a parliament to be had and holden after the form and effect afore rehearsed; and if any parliament be holden in that land hereafter contrary to the form and provision aforesaid, it be deemed void and of none effect in law.[54]

53. *CPR 1494–1509*, pp. 27, 71, 76, 204–5; Arthurson 1994, pp. 113–15; *NHI*, ii, pp. 642–3; Conway 1932, pp. 49, 94, 221–5; BL, Add. MS 4787, f. 52*v*.
54. See Richardson & Sayles 1952, esp. ch. 17 (quotation, p. 274).

In effect, the act required the king's prior approval before parliament could meet, and that only bills approved by the English council could be considered; but the elaborate procedure employed to translate intention into action was in large measure only worked out in the years following. Quite possibly the act was simply abstracted from instructions given to Poynings when he left for Ireland: 'the next parliament' actually means 'Poynings' parliament', and there is an unnecessary reference to the resumption also passed by parliament. The wording amply illustrates two points about early Tudor parliaments. First, the authorities were as yet comparatively uninterested in precise statutory phraseology (though this was tightened up considerably from 1536): the lifespan of legislation was normally quite short and contemporaries would have been surprised to find Poynings' Law still in force almost three centuries later. Second, though parliaments sometimes refused to grant taxation, particularly if the need appeared insufficiently pressing, very rarely were other government bills rejected (though this also became less uncommon from 1536). Government was not in the modern sense representative and there was no sustained opposition. Parliament's consent was necessary for some purposes, and it frequently offered advice, but the decisions were made by the English and Irish councils. Neither in Ireland nor England was parliament an essential or continuous instrument of government: rather the king employed it to obtain the active cooperation of his chief subjects, and these also found it convenient to pursue private grievances through it. Thus Poynings' Law was not an attempt to muzzle public opinion, but chiefly a reaction to parliament's unauthorized use by recent governors to further private interests; and in particular the Law aimed to prevent Warbeck or any other from emulating Simnel by using parliament to legitimize a *coup d'état*.

Although Poynings' Law was the most notable act of the 1494–5 parliament, a comparatively high proportion of its 48 other acts were of official origin. It was arguably the most important to meet between 1366 and 1536. Some statutes chiefly concerned administration and are discussed in Chapter 7 (including other aspects of Poynings' Law), but other measures, chiefly political in import, require further consideration here. The chief ministers and financial officers were to hold office during pleasure only, and not for life, a change which strengthened royal control over the governor and also conciliar independence of him. Another act repealed the statute of 1460 (see above, pp. 59–62), enjoining obedience to the king's commands regardless of the authenticating seal; and doubts about whether the English parliament could legislate for Ireland were clarified by a statute which, following a decision in the affirmative by the judges in England in 1489, enacted that certain recent English statutes for the common good should now apply (but see also below, p. 225).[55] English legislation against magnate retaining was specially modified for Ireland, where the needs of defence took precedence over efforts to stamp out private warfare and the perversion of justice which retaining seemed to encourage: retaining

---

55. The Legislation of Poynings' parliament is discussed by Chrimes 1972, pp. 264–8. For the interpretation of the act concerning English statutes, see Ellis 1983a, pp. 51–2.

was therefore allowed only in the marches and on condition that lords there certify those in retinue and answer for their conduct (a practice known as 'booking'). Urban autonomy was fostered by prohibiting local lords from retaining citizens and burgesses, and magnate power was further circumscribed by prohibiting the use of handguns and artillery except by licence of the governor.

Some statutes were soon ignored or repealed as impractical. The Statute of Henry fitz Empress was replaced by an act that the treasurer should be governor during a vacancy, but the king was readily persuaded of the need to have a competent captain in charge at such times and the previous custom was statutorily restored in 1499.[56] Another act provided that custody of the chief royal castles at Dublin, Trim, Athlone, Wicklow, Greencastle, Carlingford and Carrickfergus should be restricted to those born in England, which was perhaps practicable only with an English army in the country. Finally, many measures merely re-enacted, with slight modifications, previous statutes for fostering the use of English law, customs and weapons, very often on the pretext that they were being ignored, although surviving court records do not always substantiate this. Chief among these was one confirming the Statutes of Kilkenny (1366), but with the significant exception of clauses proscribing Gaelic speech and requiring the king's subjects to ride in a saddle.

It is impossible to measure accurately the overall impact of Poynings' parliament, but clearly most statutes were far from remaining a dead letter and royal control in the lordship was substantially strengthened. Yet the legislation was not, nor was it intended as, a direct assault on Kildare influence in government. In autumn 1494 when the chief measures were devised there was no intention to redraw the balance of power between king and governor simply so that Kildare or some other unreliable magnate could subsequently be reappointed. As Poynings' commission shows, even he was expected to operate the new procedures: he was licensed to hold only one parliament, to be dissolved by Easter 1495, and he had no specific powers to appoint to offices in Ireland. Neither was the king simply trying to downgrade the governorship: one statute actually strengthened the governor's position as the king's *alter ego* by making it high treason to incite others, especially the Gaelic Irish, to make war on him. Rather the aim was to ensure that such decisions as could and should be made by the king were referred to him, but that the governor also had sufficient power to settle urgent matters on the spot.

As it turned out, Kildare was reappointed in August 1496 on terms which far surpassed those enjoyed by Poynings, but this was neither because the king suddenly admitted defeat, nor because his restoration had been intended all along. It was because the king's main aims had already been achieved, and because Kildare was then the obvious man for the job. To discover how this occurred, we need to turn to the third main strand of Poynings' work, financial reform, and the administration's self-sufficiency, which had always been a major consideration in royal policy.

56. Quinn 1941b, p. 96.

The King's Irish revenues under Poynings

Since 1470 it had become apparent that the days were gone in which English kings were prepared to contemplate regular subventions for Ireland merely to strengthen central authority there. Poynings was adequately provided to resolve the crisis posed by Warbeck, but once this had subsided the continuance of 'direct rule' would depend on finding additional internal sources of revenue sufficient to maintain English administrators and troops. Between August 1494 and Poynings' departure, the king spent £12,000 on Irish affairs, chiefly on the army, because the Irish revenues plus taxation (worth altogether about IR£1,700 a year in the 1480s) did no more than cover normal administrative costs. An annual deficit of around £7,000 was tolerable only in an emergency, and in April 1495 efforts to raise more money in Ireland were intensified. Conway was effectively superseded by the appointment of William Hattecliffe as undertreasurer, and of John Pympe as treasurer-at-war, thus dividing civil and military finance. The groundwork had already been done, however, chiefly in parliament. In return for an undertaking not to impose coign and livery, the Commons granted for five years an annual subsidy on the Pale of two marks (IR) per ploughland, double the previous rate, and on an increased extent of ploughlands: this tax yielded about IR£1,500 a year, surpassing even the level of taxation in 1477.[57] Two acts passed in 1493 and 1494–5 resumed all royal grants of offices, annuities and land since 1422 and 1327 respectively, though with many exceptions for favoured individuals and corporations, and thus saved IR£400 a year. Parliament also granted poundage in perpetuity, and its collection was integrated with the traditional customs duties and the whole system reorganized to deter smuggling. Thus with other incidental windfalls and profits, such as the sale for 140 marks (IR) of three ships captured from Warbeck, Hattecliffe received no less than IR£3,055 15s. 7³/₄d. for the year 1495–6. This was a very creditable performance, but not enough to make ends meet, and in some ways more than could be sustained on a continuing basis: when the subsidy act expired in 1499, the subsidy was modified so that its yield was more than halved. Moreover, the increased level of raids and disorders in the Pale, as Poynings struggled to reassert control, reduced the value of the king's lands and manors, while, financially, reprisals on the Irishry were largely unproductive. But with the lordship's pacification in autumn 1495 substantial economies could be made.

In order to attract skilled administrators and captains for Irish service, Henry had had to offer higher salaries than were normal there, so raising expenses still further, but at the end of December 1495 the army was reduced to 330 English troops and 100 Gaelic kerne, and a further economy was effected by the chancellor acting also as governor after Poynings' departure. The king anticipated that these changes would balance the budget, and they did in fact reduce the deficit to just over IR£1,000 on an annual basis: but Hattecliffe wrote in July that the hiring of additional troops and other unnecessary expenditure after Easter had frustrated this objective. Henry and Hattecliffe were

---

57. Ellis 1986a, pp. 69–70.

undoubtedly right: evidently the new administration was markedly more effi-cient than those installed by Henry VIII in his experiments in 1520 and after 1534, the troops were promptly paid and therefore less mutinous, and the king's involvement in policy was more direct and sustained. Indeed the ad-ministration could have achieved self-sufficiency immediately by reducing the garrison to 270 English archers – adequate for most purposes – but in fact there was no reason why the king should continue to govern in this way. He no longer needed such close control over Irish affairs; it was not normal policy to replace the local nobility with civil servants and a standing army except in an emergency; and to operate such a strategy effectively required stringent supervision (as the later Tudors discovered to their cost).

THE RESTORATION OF THE EARL OF KILDARE

Yet other matters now required Henry's attention, and there was also the ques-tion of what to do with Kildare. Kildare's return would in any case have altered the political complexion of the lordship, necessitating some agreement about his role in government and influence in the Pale. In general, the king was wary in handling the nobles and could be hard, but he was soon convinced that Poynings had, however understandably, misinterpreted Kildare's conduct in Ulster. The earl's lands were not seized after his attainder (despite their value which would have more than covered the deficit in 1496), and as soon as the English parliament met in October 1495, the Irish attainder was reversed. There is in fact little doubt that Henry considered Kildare, properly handled, an important asset, and that commissioning a reliable local noble, adequately supervised, was the normal and most convenient method of government. Thus when it became apparent both that the reduction of Gaelic Ireland was no easy task and that there were no ready pickings available, the king determined on Kildare's reappointment.

To dispel any lingering doubts about the earl's loyalty, Magennis and O'Hanlon were induced to testify in June 1496 concerning Kildare's commun-ications with them in 1494. O'Hanlon swore that Kildare had advised him:

> Do not attempt anything against the deputy that you would not attempt against me myself, for he is a better man than I am, but enter into peace with him and give him your son as surety.[58]

As a signal mark of favour, Henry had three months earlier permitted Kildare to marry his kinswoman, Elizabeth St John (the earl's first wife having recently died). As a dowry, he granted them lands worth 200 marks a year in England and Ireland, plus 600 marks in cash, although he characteristically recouped some of his expenses from the girl's relatives. Kildare settled lands worth 380 marks (IR) in the Pale and Co. Limerick on her as part of the agreement.

58. Printed, Sayles 1951, p. 43.

Nevertheless, the king required a firm guarantee of good behaviour before reappointing the earl as deputy. His son and heir was brought up at court over the next seven years; and on 6 August Kildare swore some detailed articles before the king's council – to defend the land from the king's enemies, rebels and traitors, to arrest any English rebels taking refuge there and send them to England if required, to observe Poynings' Law, to govern impartially and, together with Earl Thomas, Sir James Ormond and Archbishop FitzSimons for their part, to forget old quarrels, particularly that 'betwixt these two noble bloods of the land of Ireland called Butlers and Geraldines'.[59] The terms of his commission as governor, however, were exceptionally generous, reflecting the king's new-found confidence in Kildare. He was appointed for ten years and then during pleasure, he could appoint to all offices save the chancellorship (which was given to FitzSimons), and (in a clause strongly reminiscent of Edward IV's grant to his brother in 1483 of any lands which he could conquer in south-west Scotland) he received a grant of all crown lands which he could recover from the Gaelic Irish.

The long-term consequences of Henry VII's first serious intervention in Ireland were perhaps not so evident as in the north or in south Wales, but the lordship had none the less witnessed a sustained demonstration of royal power. Whatever the precise impact of such a demonstration on the structure of local power might be, the eighth earl certainly took care thereafter that his activities were not seen as those of an 'overmighty subject'.[60]

59. Printed, Conway 1932, p. 226.
60. PRO, C 66/578 m. 12 (*CPR 1494–1509*, p. 62). Cf. Ross 1974, pp. 202–3; James 1964–5, pp. 80–7; Williams 1979, ch. 13.

CHAPTER 5

THE ANATOMY OF IRISH POLITICS:
THE KILDARE ASCENDANCY,
1496–1519

KILDARE AND THE 1496 SETTLEMENT

Kildare landed at Howth on 17 September and took the oath before an afforced council at Drogheda on the 21st. The effect of his reappointment on the border chieftains greatly impressed a courtier, Sir Ralph Verney, who had accompanied the party to Ireland to report on the situation there. Many chiefs sent messengers to Drogheda to sue for peace, and on the 29th at Dundalk some northern chiefs, MacMahon, Magennis, O'Reilly, O'Hanlon and one of the O'Neills surrendered their eldest sons as pledges and swore fealty to Henry VII. Similar guarantees for peace were subsequently given by chiefs from Leinster and the south midlands, MacMurrough, O'More, O'Dempsey, O'Byrne and O'Connor. From further afield O'Donnell, Clandeboye O'Neill, Burke of Clanrickard, the earl of Desmond and others who had been implicated in the Warbeck plot also made overtures. Verney thought that the king

> could have put no man in authority here that in so short space and with so little cost could have set this land in so good order as it is now but this man only.[1]

Yet Verney probably did not fully appreciate the implications of the submissions by border chiefs who were normally under Kildare influence. Gaelic and English concepts of loyalty differed, and the Leinster chiefs in particular probably made no real distinction between submission to Kildare as overlord and to the king in the person of Lord Deputy Kildare. This explains why each new governor had generally to make his own arrangements for peace with border chiefs, and partly also why Kildare could create such trouble if he were dismissed from office. The process might also work the other way of course: in October 1496 Kildare had to mount two raids on MacMurrough and O'Connor before they would submit and surrender Carlow castle with which Poynings had ill-advisedly entrusted them after its capture from Sir James Fitzgerald.

1. Printed, Conway 1932, pp. 232–4. See ibid., pp. 95–8.

98

Nevertheless, in the years following Kildare's restoration Henry reaped the benefit of the settlement so carefully worked out in 1496. The king's vital interests in Ireland were scrupulously protected, Kildare remained cooperative with his old rival Earl Thomas of Ormond, the Pale remained comparatively peaceful and prosperous, and central government control extended more firmly and continuously over a wider area than it had for almost a century. In short, in so far as the problem of governing a distant border province a fortnight's journey away from the centre of power was soluble in this age of personal monarchy, Henry VII had solved his Irish problem. *who is to say how soluble?*

Two difficulties remained to test the strength of the 1496 settlement. Sir James Ormond had undertaken to cooperate with Kildare in the king's service, but the earl's restoration was bound to limit his opportunities for advancement. Presumably Henry and Earl Thomas hoped that he would apply himself to strengthening Butler power in Tipperary against nearby Gaelic chiefs: Sir James was not reappointed to high office, and in Kilkenny Kildare could be expected to favour his son-in-law, Sir Piers Butler of Polestown. Instead of promoting peace and good government as Ormond's deputy, however, Sir James used his powers and influence with O'Brien to interfere with the junior Butler families of Cahir, Dunboyne and Polestown, forcing them to submit to his rule. Early in 1497, acting on complaints by Kildare, Sir Piers and Earl Thomas himself, the king summoned him to court, and after a second unsuccessful summons in May proclamation was made against him. Soon after this he was attacked and killed by Sir Piers, who in a letter of exculpation to Ormond claimed that he had been intriguing with Warbeck and was claiming the earldom for himself. In fact Warbeck reached Cork nine days later, hotly pursued by ships from Waterford, but finding little support he sailed on to Cornwall where he arrived equally inopportunely, just as royal commissioners were settling the county after a major rising. 'Richard IV' was soon defeated and captured, imprisoned in the Tower with the earl of Warwick, and executed in 1499. Kildare informed the king that he and Desmond had taken steps against Warbeck and would have taken him had he stayed longer.[2]

These incidents were not allowed to disturb the settlement, however: cordial letters passed between Ormond and Kildare, horses and hawks were sent to the king, and on one occasion Earl Thomas wrote pointedly to the countess of Kildare, 'praying to God, madam, to send you some good fruit so that my lord and cousin your husband's blood and mine may thereby be increased'.[3] After Sir James's death, Ormond managed his Irish estates through various agents and paid an occasional visit himself, but he remained on good terms with Sir Piers Butler, who had petitioned for the deputyship of his lands in 1497, and eventually reappointed him in 1505. He also granted Butler any lands unlawfully detained from him which Butler could recover, in return for a third of the profits. Kildare also had a particular interest in these arrangements because by the Statute of Absentees passed by the Westminster parliament in

2. Ibid., pp. 111–12, 239–40; Arthurson 1994, chs 13–14; Curtis 1932–43, iv, app. no. 31.
3. Printed, Conway 1932, p. 240.

1380, and periodically renewed by Irish parliaments, the governor was empowered to take two-thirds of the landed profits of absentees from Ireland for costs of defence. In 1504 he had retained Butler and indented with him about these profits should Sir Piers acquire an interest in the lands.[4] In this way Kildare secured Butler cooperation and thereby established an almost unparalleled degree of support for his rule by controlling the most obvious potential focus of opposition.

CENTRAL SUPERVISION AND LOCAL PROSPERITY

The Pale's prosperity at this time can to some extent be gauged by the increased yields of individual items of exchequer revenue. Twelve manors let for annual rents fluctuating between IR£240 and IR£280 between 1484 and 1495 yielded over IR£300 a year by 1501–2, and the value of customs through Dublin port climbed from IR£205 annually in 1494–5 to IR£310 by 1496–7, reflecting greater administrative efficiency and more settled conditions. Beyond the Pale, moreover, the Dublin administration exercised a fair measure of control. Scarce evidence about the precise level of attendance in late medieval parliaments suggests that at the first parliament held in accordance with Poynings' Law, at Dublin in March 1499 and at the recently rebuilt town of Castledermot in August, representation in the commons was 32 out of a possible 46 members, falling to 27 for the second session, while 29 out of 34 lords attended, but only 24 at Castledermot. Eleven dioceses were also represented in the convocation house at Dublin, and eight at Castledermot. The commons were elected, two knights for each shire and two burgesses for each town, in the county or borough courts upon receipt by the sheriff or municipal authorities of a writ of election: thus the continued representation of outlying counties in parliament, even if intermittent, reflects a fairly widespread survival of English local government procedures and structures and continued responsiveness to central control. Moreover, at the exchequer after Easter 1499 the sheriffs and seneschals of almost all the late medieval counties and liberties duly paid their proffers – small, fixed sums of money for exercising their offices before the main process of accounting began.[5] Thus if, c. 1450, there had seemed a danger that English lordship might disintegrate into small, autonomous units, the reorganization under Edward IV and Henry VII had eliminated that danger. Of course the fragmented pattern of English settlement – two largely separate blocks of territory, plus a coastal strip into Ulster and a few isolated enclaves – meant that superficially the lordships controlled by magnates like Kildare and Ormond might resemble the Gaelic lordships elsewhere. The premium on local initiative and self-help in defending the marches ensured that lineage and kindred loyalties remained more powerful than in lowland England (although perhaps no more so than in other areas of consolidated lordship like the

4. Curtis 1932–43, iii, nos. 316, 318–23, iv, app. nos. 31–74.
5. Ellis 1986a, pp. 72–6, 89; Ellis 1991, pp. 297–302.

Scottish borders or Welsh marches), but given effective leadership, the various communities of English Ireland remained capable of pulling together as one lordship.

As the threat to the Pale receded, Kildare spent much of his time in military expeditions far into Gaelic parts and made progresses through outlying shires which in some cases had not been visited by a governor for a generation or longer. In 1498 he visited Cork and also hosted into Ulster where he captured Dungannon castle; in 1499 he took four castles in Connaught including Roscommon; the following year he toured the Ormond districts and issued a series of ordinances for peace and good government there, and also made another expedition into Tyrone. Among the lordship's more remote towns and cities, he also visited Carrickfergus in 1503, Galway and Athenry in 1504, and Limerick in 1510.[6]

O'BRIEN EXPANSION ACROSS THE SHANNON

One measure of the Dublin administration's wider interests at this time was the attempt to contain O'Brien expansion over the Shannon into Limerick and Tipperary. O'Brien had established overlordship there in the 1460s, forcing Co. Limerick to buy off the chief with an annual blackrent of IR£40 which apparently continued to be paid down to 1542. O'Brien's ambitions were further aroused by Sir James Ormond's self-interested efforts to win his support: Kildare, who had property in Co. Limerick, reported in 1498 that the newly elected chief was 'a mortal enemy to all Englishmen and most maliciously disposed of any that ever I heard speak of', and petitioned the king for 300 English archers and 60 gunners 'to be waged at the charge of me and other of my friends' in order to deal with O'Brien raids over the Shannon.[7] The petition was apparently unsuccessful, and the following year the English of Ormond led by Sir Piers were defeated and the sovereign of Kilkenny killed by O'Brien: but in 1504 Kildare did manage to clip the chief's wings at the battle of Knockdoe. By 1506, however, Kildare was again petitioning for assistance against the chief, who had recently constructed O'Brien's Bridge to further his ambitions. Henry observed that 'little advantage or profit hath grown of such armies and captains' as had previously been sent 'for the reduction of' Ireland,[8] but toyed briefly with the idea of leading an expedition in person. Finally, in 1510 Kildare led a large army into Munster, defeated MacCarthy More, and then turned on O'Brien. He broke down O'Brien's Bridge, but the chief inflicted heavy losses on his army in Co. Limerick and retreated across the Shannon; and the earl, having reorganized, then thought better of invading Thomond. Thus, overall, Kildare had little success in curbing O'Brien influence, but it is significant that he should even try.

6. Ellis 1986a, p. 57 and references there cited.
7. Printed Conway 1932, p. 241; Nicholls 1972, p. 157; *NHI*, ii, p. 628; Quinn 1935a, p. 231.
8. Bayne & Dunham 1968, pp. 46–7; *NHI*, ii, pp. 652–4. For the rest of the paragraph, see MacCarthy 1895, iii, pp. 438–9; Bryan 1933, pp. 236–58.

THE PATTERN OF PROVINCIAL POLITICS

Why was Kildare so pre-eminent in Irish politics after his restoration in 1496? The king's confidence and Kildare's unparalleled colonial support counted for much, and from 1488 the deputy could also employ siege artillery to destroy his enemies' castles;[9] but these factors are only part of the answer. The earl's numerous tenantry and landed income (discussed below) and, by contrast, the extreme decentralization and disunity of Gaelic Ireland also allowed him to manipulate and dominate politics there to build up an ascendancy which was far wider than his power base in north Leinster might lead one to expect. It has been suggested that by 1500 politics in Ireland were cutting across the old ethnic divisions, with little regard to the 'national' interests of English kings or Gaelic Ireland, to forge new networks of alliances between native and colonist which furthered merely the dynastic ambitions of the individual participants.[10] There is some truth in this: medieval Ireland had always been a complex of regional balances, but politics were certainly more provincial and dynastic than two centuries earlier. Nevertheless the pattern was more complicated: the overall effect of such political changes as were occurring around 1500 benefited the English interest there, particularly since Kildare generally took care that his campaigning also served the colonists' common interests, even when directed to private ends. *How does he know this?*

Power and lordship in Gaelic Ireland were based on intricate and shifting networks of relationships between the overlord, his kinsmen (who frequently opposed his rule), the vassal-chiefs (*uirritbe*) who presently recognized his overlordship, and their kinsmen and clients. The military and strategic importance to Irish Gaeldom of Clan Donald and Ulster's maritime extension into the western isles is discussed below, in Chapter 10. In the later middle ages power was increasingly decentralized – if the proliferation of lordships is not attributable simply to the increasing weight of evidence. Moreover, the uncertain succession system and continual dissensions within the ruling clans encouraged outside intervention in the internal politics of individual lordships. The most powerful of the Ulster chiefs were the O'Neills of Tyrone, whose rivalry with the O'Donnells of Tyrconnell tended to shape Ulster politics. O'Donnell could usually count on support from at least one dissident O'Neill clan – between 1458 and 1519 this was the Slioght Art, based on Omagh, who were permanently hostile to the ruling clan. Moreover, another sept, Clandeboye O'Neill, had built up an independent lordship east of the Bann largely at the expense of the earldom of Ulster, and usually also allied with O'Donnell. By 1431 the earldom was confined to Carrickfergus and its Pale, the Savages of the Ards and their rivals the Whites of Dufferin,[11] leaving the Pale's northern marches exposed to Gaelic raids. From 1461 English kings were more actively interested in recovering their earldom, although in 1468 the Palesmen had

---

9. Hayes-McCoy 1938–9, pp. 43–65.
10. E.g. Lydon 1972b, pp. 241–2.
11. Nicholls 1972, pp. 130–6 *et passim*.

intimated that the overall military situation was too serious for offensive action of this sort. In the 1470s, however, the two aims were apparently reconciled by a policy of alliance with O'Neill. Besides discouraging further expansion by Clandeboye, this policy facilitated peaceful relations with O'Neill's allies and vassals on the Pale border – Magennis, O'Hanlon, O'Neill of the Fews, and the MacMahons. The alliance was strengthened by the marriage of Kildare's sister to the chief's son, Con, who later succeeded as O'Neill (1483–93). This provided Kildare with considerable leverage in Ulster politics and thereafter his interventions were frequent and effective. For example, Donnell (1498–1509), Art Oge (1513–19) and Con Bacagh (1519–59, the ninth earl's nephew) all relied on Kildare support for their election as O'Neill.[12]

In Connaught, the old ethnic divisions had long broken down, and, though lords of Anglo-Norman descent controlled about half the province, only an isolated area around Galway and Athenry remained significantly anglicized and in regular contact with Dublin. Yet the tendencies towards decentralization were especially pronounced in Connaught, particularly within the old royal house of O'Connor, and since politics there usually also had a north–south axis, they were of comparatively little interest to Dublin. The dominant lordships were those of the rival Burke (de Burgh) families, Burke of Mayo (the Lower MacWilliam) and Burke of Clanrickard (the Upper MacWilliam). By 1500, however, the formerly stronger Mayo Burke was in decline: succession disputes, the replacement of the ruling line of the MacDermots of Moylurg, usually allies, by a line favourable to Clanrickard Burke, and the split with another erstwhile and increasingly powerful ally, O'Donnell, left northern Connaught a prey to outsiders. Under two strong chiefs, Hugh Roe (1461–1505) and Hugh Duff (1505–37), the O'Donnells both held their own against O'Neill and also gradually strengthened their influence in northern Connaught. A key objective of their raids was control of Sligo castle and the imposition of a favourable candidate as the local O'Connor Sligo chief. In turn Clanrickard under two long-lived rulers, Ulick Roe (1429–85) and Ulick Finn (1485–1509) intervened rather unsuccessfully to limit O'Donnell influence. In south Connaught, Clanrickard was frequently in alliance with O'Brien, and also (1492–7) closely associated with Sir James Ormond. His relationship with the Dublin government was anomalous. After 1333 both Burke families had encroached on lands of the earldom of Ulster: their position vis-à-vis the crown's landed claims therefore resembled that of Gaelic nobles. Yet the survival of two royal boroughs, Galway and Athenry, had facilitated the maintenance of an English enclave in Clanrickard; and as sheriff of this small English county of Connaught, the Dublin administration perforce appointed either Clanrickard himself or one of his dependants, the MacHubert Burkes.[13]

The Kildares made occasional expeditions into Connaught after 1496, but apparently more by way of expansion in Westmeath than to maintain royal interests there. In 1499 the eighth earl established his own candidate as O'Connor

12. Ibid., pp. 131–2; Quinn 1935c, *passim*; *NHI*, ii; Simms 1981, pp. 214–36.
13. *NHI*, ii, pp. 625–7; Nicholls 1972, pp. 137–8, 143–50; Ellis 1986a, pp. 199–200.

Roe, and in 1526 the ninth earl intervened in his favour against O'Connor Don. An exception was the Knockdoe campaign. The town of Galway had hitherto been able to maintain its franchises conferred by charter, but in 1504 the Clanrickard Burkes invaded the town. In response Kildare marshalled a large army of Palesmen and Gaelic allies and a rare pitched battle saw Clanrickard and O'Brien defeated at Knockdoe, near Galway, on 19 August. Lord Chancellor FitzSimons was sent to report to the king and Henry rewarded Kildare with election to the Order of the Garter and later with a grant of lands. Apart from its implications for royal policy, the victory was a striking demonstration of Kildare power vis-à-vis other major lords in a remote and unfamiliar part of the island.[14]

Munster politics revolved around the earls of Desmond and Ormond. The province was too distant for Dublin to attempt more than a general supervision of its affairs, but Desmond generally followed the lead of his kinsman, Kildare, and in Ormond English traditions were sufficiently strong to restrict the earls to policies which generally accorded with the local Englishry's interests. The traditional Butler–Fitzgerald rivalry produced sporadic minor clashes, but in general the two earls concentrated on consolidating their power within their own respective spheres of influence. Butler interests were divided between Tipperary, where they dominated the O'Kennedy lordship to the north, and Kilkenny, threatened by O'Carroll and MacGillapatrick to the north and MacMurrough to the east. In general, Butler power expanded under the early Tudors: in particular they recovered important strongholds at Nenagh (by 1505), Tullow (by 1515) and Arklow (in 1525). Desmond however barely held his own against O'Brien expansion into Limerick (despite some support from Kildare) and the activities of the three MacCarthy chiefs to the south-west, MacCarthy More (the latter's traditional enemy), MacCarthy Reagh and MacCarthy of Muskerry, who consistently sought alliance with the crown. And in Waterford the Fitzgeralds of Dromana, descended from a younger son of the sixth earl, gradually established an independent position. Nevertheless, in comparison with Ulster and Connaught, Munster was relatively peaceful and prosperous and its lordships more stable.[15]

Kildare's cross-border ties

In these circumstances, traditional rivalries among the leading Gaelic and gaelicized lords of Ulster and Connaught precluded any general coalition against the Englishry, but in the lordship stronger government and comparative peace and stability left the earls of Kildare well placed to strengthen their control of border areas. With the support of the Palesmen and his traditional clients, vassals and allies in north Leinster, Kildare could bring unprecedented pressure

14. *NHI*, ii, pp. 626, 652–3; Nicholls 1972, ch. 8.
15. *NHI*, ii, pp. 627–32; Nicholls 1972, ch. 9; Ellis 1986a, pp. 60–1.

to bear on the comparatively weak and divided midland chieftaincies. His growing influence in the area is reflected in the section of the Rental Book of 1518 entitled 'The earl of Kildare's duties upon Irishmen'.[16] This lists the annual tributes – frequently a rent of 4*d.* on every cow within the lordship – payable in return for the earl's defending them: many of the tributes were ostensibly agreed with the ninth earl, but in most cases they probably renewed arrangements first made with the seventh and eighth earls. The list – comprising 24 chiefs altogether – includes every significant chief and a host of weaker ones in a wide arc around the Pale, plus a few quite remote chieftaincies – MacDermot and O'Rourke in north-east Connaught, for instance, and O'Dwyre in north Tipperary. In some lordships – those of Maggeoghegan, O'Farrell and O'Reilly – Kildare was buying up lands held in pledge (cf. below, p. 109); and others – MacMahon and O'Farrell – bore his galloglass. These tributes were won and maintained by the continuous campaigning which characterized the Kildare ascendancy and in which the earl impressed the native lords with his military strength; but it should be remembered that fourteenth-century governors had asserted royal authority in similar fashion. The tributes were the reverse of the annual blackrents which some English counties had traditionally paid to neighbouring Gaelic lords for 'defence' (freedom from raids), although, perhaps significantly, evidence survived for the continued payment under the early Tudors of only five of these blackrents.[17]

Of course Kildare's arrangements with border chiefs did not cut out Gaelic raids altogether: in a border situation this was impossible. Many upland clans lived primarily by raiding and robbery on the wealthier lowlanders, like the clans of the Anglo-Scottish marches. Some of the English marchers, the Dillons, Daltons and Delamares of Westmeath and the Harrolds of Wicklow, were hardly more controllable: if the captain of Harrold's country was nominally appointed by the government to defend the marches rather than being elected by his kinsmen, in practice the government had little choice in the matter, and the more settled communities of the Pale maghery frequently found his activities no more acceptable. Yet the contemporary distinction between English and Gaelic marcher lords was evidently still meaningful to Kildare, for in his Rental Dillon, Dalton and Delamare are separately listed in the previous section entitled 'Fees', among those owing the earl an annual fee for his lawful support in their just causes. These two sections of the Rental have created difficulties of interpretation for historians, but 'Duties' were clearly tributes levied for protection on Gaelic chiefs and landowners outside the lordship, while 'Fees' (sometimes reduced if the earl lost the governorship) related to the king's subjects (including English marchers and denizized Irishmen), even though in the marches the distinction was often a fine one. The fees were part of a system of 'bastard feudalism' familiar throughout the Tudor territories, whereby English magnates maintained a following among their tenantry and

16. BL, Harleian MS 3756, at ff. 13–24. A good modern edition is Mac Niocaill 1992.
17. Quinn 1935a, pp. 223, 224, 231.

neighbouring gentry by extending 'good lordship' to tenants, retainers and 'well-willers' in return for service and counsel.[18]

In other circumstances, the exaction of tribute might have presaged re-newed colonization in border areas. As we have seen, this occurred in parts of Kildare and Carlow, and in the Dublin marches the earl recovered Castlekevin and Fassaroe and had built Powerscourt castle by 1500. The north Wexford marches and parts of the Down coast also witnessed some such activity, but these were all areas in which Kildare held or acquired English titles to the land. By 1518 the ninth earl had reorganized the defence and estate management of his principal possessions in the Pale's southern and western marches so that his tenants there were each allocated to one of four castles, Portlester, Rathangan, Kildare and Athy, to which they owed 'suit' for their military and labour ser-vices. Strategically, these arrangements faced west and south-west against a military threat from the Gaelic midlands, reflecting the earl's confidence in his ability to control the Irish of the Leinster mountains. A further interesting fea-ture of these arrangements, perhaps also an innovation by the ninth earl, was the creation of special military holdings in the manors of Rathangan, Kildare and Kilkea for the maintenance of his horsemen: the tenants paid no rent, but were obliged to reside on their holding, not to alienate it, and to be constantly ready for military service. Finally, the relative cohesion of the Kildare lineage was a great help to the earls in the defence of their estates. For instance, many recently reconquered Leinster marchlands were settled on the eighth earl's younger brothers: Oliver received lands in Westmeath and Annaly; Richard had a grant of lands seized from the O'Tooles (notably Powerscourt and Fassaroe), and both Walter and James had lands a little further south in the Dublin–Kildare marches. Similarly, other close relatives had custody of key possessions such as Lea and Morett, the Carlow estates, and the ninth earl's Wexford estates with the captainship of Old Ross.[19] In general, however, the scarcity of English tenants ensured that the earl would continue to exercise a general supremacy over the area, acceptable to both Gaelic and English, rather than build a feudal lordship out of this supremacy, as had developed in Anglo-Norman Ireland. Nevertheless, the unsettled nature of society in these areas, the conflict of cultures, and the insecurity of land titles meant that noble power remained at a premium.

CONCEPTS OF IDENTITY IN IRELAND

Gaedhil and Gaill

The ambiguity of Kildare's position, intelligible in different ways to both English and Gaelic, was the key to his success. It was not that the earl was representative of some emerging Hiberno-Norman civilization with which

18. BL, Harleian MS 3756 (two Gaelic entries were mistakenly duplicated in the Fees section); Morrin 1861, p. 26. Cf. Dunham 1955; James 1978.
19. Ellis 1986a, pp. 59–61; Ellis 1995a, ch. 4.

both cultures could identify,[20] rather he handled Gaelic lords in accordance with their own customs, while retaining his English identity and loyalties. How this could be is strikingly illustrated by the contrast between contemporary accounts of the battle of Knockdoe given by Gaelic annalists and by an ex-chequer clerk, Walter Hussey, in the Old English Book of Howth. Hussey described an English victory over the Irish, achieved by the superior weapons and tactics of the Englishry. The troops supplied by Kildare's Gaelic allies and clients – O'Donnell, O'Neill, Burke of Mayo, O'Connor Faly, O'Reilly, O'Connor Roe, MacDermot, MacMahon, Magennis, O'Hanlon, O'Kelly and O'Farrell – scarcely figure in the account, and the chronicler has no difficulty in classifying Clanrickard as 'Irish'. Kildare places the galloglass in the vanguard, 'for it is less force of their losses than it is of our young men',[21] and is later urged to complete the victory by eliminating the Irish who are with him. In contrast, the Gaelic annalists describe a battle which was chiefly important for the size of the oppos-ing armies and the numbers of natives (*Gaedhil*) and foreigners (*Gaill*) killed.

Among the colonists, their continuing pride in their Englishness included a more developed political dimension which contrasted with Gaelic loyalties. While both English and Gaelic nobles had a highly developed sense of their separate ethnic identities, the ideological mentality of the native lords was, on the evidence of Gaelic annals and poetry, predominantly particularist and dynastic: consciousness of common Gaelic traditions did not precipitate the development of a nationalist movement to rival the ambitions towards colonial domination which remained so clearly a part of English political ideas. None the less, with their historical and political references suitably adapted, Gaelic praise poems were also acceptable to English magnates – the cult of nobility was not peculiar to the Gaelic world. Significantly, however, for an English recipient the poems urged his claims to the deputyship, not to the politically unreal, Gaelic high-kingship of Ireland. This was in effect the traditional Eng-lish conception of nobility as the natural instrument of royal government within the locality, and contrasted with the unlimited claims of rival chiefs in Gaelic Ireland. Nevertheless, the racial animosities which had earlier characterized relations between native and colonist were by 1500 much less pronounced, allowing Kildare to maintain good relations with his Gaelic neighbours and to muster coalitions of *Gaedhil* and *Gaill* against his enemies, as at Knockdoe.[22] To the native lords, the Kildare ascendancy closely resembled those which chiefs like O'Neill and MacMurrough had sometimes built up: had it threatened wholesale expropriation of Gaelic landowners, it might have prompted some collective response based on residual pan-Gaelic loyalties, but Kildare lacked the resources to accomplish what he and other magnates urged on the king. In these circumstances, the earl adapted as best he could to the realities of co-existence and to exploit a system which he could not overthrow.

20. Cf. Edwards 1977, *passim*.
21. *Carew*, vi, 181–4; MacCarthy 1895, iii, p. 469; Freeman 1944, p. 609. Cf. Bradshaw 1979a, p. 64 n. 14.
22. In general, Bradshaw 1979a, ch. 1. For colonial domination (cf. Bradshaw 1979a, p. 27), Ellis 1981a, pp. 242–3; Bryan 1933, pp. 18–22.

To the colonial community, however, Kildare's allegiance and commission as the king's deputy were all-important. Many years ago the claim was advanced that with his prestige and the forces mustered at Knockdoe, Kildare 'could have destroyed England's petty forces in Ireland and made himself a king',[23] and historians have since talked about the Great Earl who was all-but-king of Ireland. If the mistranslation of *Gearóid Mór* (as Kildare is described in Gaelic annals) is a pardonable error not unlike Ethelred the Unready, Kildare's description as all-but-king is quite misleading. The Englishry at large supported the earl because he was the king's representative; and as Desmond discovered in the 1460s, even this might not suffice if he associated too closely with Gaelic chiefs or tried to introduce native customs.[24] Without the king's commission, Kildare could not govern, as was made manifest in the 1534 rebellion. He could certainly stir up trouble by capitalizing on the bastard feudal following which he, like any English magnate, had built up: if the north of England 'knew no prince but a Percy', the Palesmen 'covet[ed] more to see a Geraldine to reign and triumph than to see God come amongst them'.[25] But outright rebellion against established authority was a last desperate gamble, for there was an essential difference between a noble's connection or *manraed* and the support which Kildare needed to govern. Although some members of the ninth earl's household might profess to believe that the eighth earl had built his ascendancy on opposition to the Tudors, magnates like Northumberland and Kildare knew better and actively courted royal support. In 1525, when the ninth earl detected a note of suspicion and displeasure in the king's letter, he replied that he was peculiarly bound to Henry, not only by his allegiance, but by service in his youth, the king's continuing good lordship, and by his first and second wives both kinswomen to Henry.

> And though there were no such cause, yet could I find in my heart to serve your grace before all the princes in the world, as well for the great nobleness, valiant prowess, and equity which I ever noted in your most noble person, as also for the virtuous qualities wherein ye excel all other princes. And besides that I do know right well, if I did the contrary, it should be the destruction of me and my sequel for ever.[26]

Kildare's understanding of the realities of power later proved substantially correct! At bottom, therefore, the extension of Kildare power was a strengthening of the English interest in Ireland.

Kildare's Gaelic identity

Nevertheless, Kildare's acceptance of native customs went deeper than just a thin veneer acquired through occasional contact with Gaelic chiefs. In a marcher

23. Curtis 1923, p. 408.
24. Cosgrove 1975, pp. 11–27; Ellis 1976–7, pp. 260–70.
25. *StP*, iii, 148.
26. *StP*, ii, 125 (quotation), 174–5; James 1966; Weiss 1976, pp. 501–9.

society, a magnate who refused to adapt to his surroundings would soon have lost out; but as the marcher lords of Wales discovered, there were also considerable potential profits in enforcing native law (often in the teeth of native opposition) and restricting English liberties to Englishmen by birth, descent, or denization. Kildare's critics in the Pale later alleged that he had used both Gaelic and English law 'which[ever] he thought most beneficial as the case did require', and the employment of Gaelic judges by lords of the Englishry was clearly very common.[27] Compositions for murder and other capital offences by English law were also frequent, but they can be paralleled in other Tudor borderlands uninfluenced by Gaelic law, and probably reflected primarily the rigidity and unpopularity of crown pleas which was a general feature of the common law. Yet the colonial community was far more conservative in landed litigation and reluctant to jeopardize common law titles to land. Interestingly, there was an active market in titles to quondam properties overrun by Gaelic clans, and significantly the Fitzgeralds, Butlers and no doubt others troubled to acquire these titles for purposes of aggrandizement. Just as the Englishry in Wales were buying up *prid* land, so Kildare and others speculated in Gaelic land which had similarly been pledged for money (cf. above, p. 42). On the Westmeath borders, the earl was buying up disputed marchland in pledge with the Dillons and Daltons, but his sense of constitutional propriety dictated that these transactions should be separated in his Rental from the similar transactions concerning lands in Gaelic territories just a few miles away. One entry vividly expresses the conflict between English tenure and actual possession which eventually brought firm title by native law to 'swordland':

> Kyllynower was in pledge with Gerald fitz Edmund Dillon's sons . . . and beside that the said land was purchased of Maurice Map, rightful heir of the same.[28]

Manifestly, Kildare needed also to be fully conversant with Gaelic law and custom, and this no doubt meant that in minor respects he unconsciously assimilated them. Medieval men expected to be governed by their own law, and in the marches especially the earl's tenants and military retainers included many natives. In his dealings with Gaelic chiefs too, arbitration would necessarily involve recourse to principles of native law. Those who broke Kildare's 'slantyaght' were liable to pay compensation: in two instances recorded in his Rental relating to Maggeoghegan's country, Kildare was awarded damages of 60 and 70 cattle. Politically, there were significant advantages in following the Gaelic custom of fosterage: in 1499 O'Donnell was given Kildare's son, Henry, to foster and duly provided the earl with substantial military support in his expeditions to Clanrickard and Munster in 1504 and 1510. Altogether three of the earl's daughters were married into prominent Gaelic houses and a fourth

27. Hore & Graves 1870, p. 162; Davies 1978, pp. 143–5, 162–3, 182, 407–8; Nicholls 1972, pp. 47–57.
28. BL, Harleian MS 3756, ff. 8–10*v*, 13–24, 42*v*–77 (quotation at f. 51); *NHI*, ii, pp. 632–6; Ellis 1986a, p. 194; Davies 1978, pp. 407–13.

to Burke of Clanrickard. The seventh and ninth earls likewise married their daughters to Gaelic chiefs although, reflecting their enhanced status in early Tudor society, the earls and their heirs now married within English court circles and their younger sons mostly married into the lordship's other leading families.[29]

Through such Gaelic alliances, the earl could expect to win the support of these families in his causes, and these practices introduced a measure of stability into a political system which was notoriously unstable. Since the earl was thus in daily contact with Gaelic nobles, his court inevitably acquired a Gaelic tinge. Like most of the colonial aristocracy (though not apparently the peasantry in more sheltered parts), Kildare spoke and wrote in Gaelic as occasion demanded. His entourage included Gaelic rhymers (poets), a physician, 'rent' receivers, a judge, and captains of his kerne and galloglass.[30] Indeed without such men about him the earl could hardly have cut a figure in Gaelic society, acquired native clients and influenced well-disposed chiefs to visit him in the expectation of entertainment and favour. Kildare's acceptance of Gaelic customs lent credibility to his political ambitions in the Gaelic world, but fundamentally they were geared to the protection of the English interest and identity. His lordship formed a bridge between the English and Gaelic worlds, but this bridge was the means by which the influence of the Dublin administration could be extended over a much wider area than its slender resources would otherwise have permitted.

English identity

Nevertheless, the ease with which English magnates in Ireland could move in Gaelic circles tended to set them apart from their counterparts in England and contributed to the emergence of a separate, but not separatist, provincial identity. With the decline of a cross-channel aristocracy in the fourteenth century, the leadership of the Englishry passed to men whose interests lay primarily with the lordship and who might not agree with decisions reached from the standpoint of the king and nobility in lowland England.[31] Yet between 1470 and 1534 this possibility rarely became a reality because kings of England generally governed the lordship, like other borderlands, through the local community. The earlier clashes with English-born governors who attempted to rule without local consent or adequate resources no longer disturbed Anglo-Irish relations. Indeed the chief colonial grievance at this time was royal neglect. Men like Kildare prided themselves on their status as representatives of the English interest in Ireland and depended on the crown to sustain their position. They looked for greater royal involvement, not less, through a commitment to policies of which they approved. Paradoxically, it was primarily

---

29. BL, Harleian MS 3756, f. 19 *et passim*; Ellis 1995a, pp. 132–7; Bryan 1933, pp. 238, 256–8; Lydon 1972a, pp. 155–6.
30. BL, Harleian MS 3756 *passim*.
31. Frame 1982.

those outside the lordship who saw the English of Ireland as a separate community. Gaelic nobles readily distinguished between the *Gaill* of Ireland, familiar with their customs, and the *Saxain*, who were not. And by 1550 the earlier ethnic sense of Englishness based on language, law and custom was acquiring a more developed geographical dimension from which 'Englishmen born in Ireland' were increasingly excluded. Already under the Lancastrians colonists in England found themselves unintentionally insulted by being labelled 'Irishmen', and occasionally confused with 'wild Irishmen' and other aliens.[32] Yet significant provincial antagonisms were latent in Tudor society, and we should be wary of the idea of a united English nation from which the colonists were now excluded. Under Richard III southerners felt that government was being monopolized by northerners. In 1497 Cornishmen revolted against taxes imposed to defend the north against the Scots, and in 1549 the English Book of Common Prayer provoked rebellion there *inter alia* because many Cornishmen did not understand English. In 1536–7, northern rebels complained about lack of consultation in recent important decisions of government and demanded the holding of a fully representative parliament at York.[33] Similar provincial sentiments in the medieval lordship were thus hardly a major factor in its separate development under the later Tudors. Certainly, we may dismiss suggestions that Henry VII's Irish policy was motivated by fears that his representative there was surreptitiously going native.

PROPOSALS FOR CONQUEST

In 1503 Kildare was summoned to court for extended discussions. He took ship in April, leaving his erstwhile opponent, Lord Chancellor FitzSimons, in charge, and returned in August with his son and heir, Gerald, Lord Offaly, now aged 16, and his newly acquired daughter-in-law, Elizabeth Zouche, Henry's distant relative. The couple received lands in England and Ireland from both king and earl, and soon after Lord Gerald was appointed treasurer of Ireland (the undertreasurer continuing as his deputy) to give him some experience in government. In 1505 the king rewarded Kildare with a grant of Carlingford, Greencastle and Mourne in Co. Down which provided the foundations of a lordship worth over IR£150 annually built up by 1534. And the following year, when his ten-year term as deputy expired, the earl sent important delegations to the king to plead for assistance against O'Brien. In a sense of course this request was an admission of failure, at a time when the renewal of Kildare's commission was under consideration, and suggests a growing conviction by the earl that the reduction of Gaelic Ireland required more active royal support. Henry did indeed decide in principle 'to make a voyage personal in his most noble person for the repress of the wild Irish and redress and sure

32. Ellis 1986b, pp. 187–204; Ellis 1995a, pp. 141–3; Cosgrove 1981a, ch. 5; Canny 1975.
33. Fletcher 1983, *passim*; Pollard 1977, pp. 147–66.

reduction of all the said land',[34] but the council's advice on the logistics of the operation, that he would need a retinue of 6,000 men, plus his household, a large siege train, and back-up for transport, set too high a price and the king changed his mind.

The fate of this proposal may fairly be taken as involving a major royal decision concerning the lordship's future development. We may dismiss suggestions that a royal visit was contemplated because Henry was secretly worried about the great concentration of power in Kildare's hands.[35] The question was rather whether the system of self-sufficient government evolved since 1470 now required replacement by a more interventionist policy. An effective system of defences had been established for the Pale, some key areas beyond had been secured, and the Dublin administration's links with the outlying English districts strengthened (see also below, Ch. 7): yet governmental resources remained small. Kildare could, at some risk and trouble, mount sizeable expeditions far into the Gaelic hinterland, but he could not hope permanently to control these territories, and his piecemeal advances in south-east Ulster and parts of Leinster were unimportant in an all-Ireland context. Yet conquest of Gaelic Ireland would allow the colonial community to maximize their landed profits, dispense with troops for defence, and recover lands in Gaelic occupation to which they had title. Significantly, the proposed royal army of 6,000 men was approximately the size of Richard II's army of conquest in 1394 and precisely the number which the earl of Surrey demanded in 1521 for a rapid conquest. Henry VII's perspective was rather different from the colonists, however: he had already satisfied himself in 1494–5 that 'little advantage or profit' ensued from despatching a force of 650 men to conquer the country.[36] His choice therefore was between continuing the existing economical arrangements or an expensive conquest, and viewed from Westminster the money was better spent elsewhere than in capturing a remote territory inhabited by savages.

Apparently, therefore, Kildare was urged to keep up the good work with the existing resources. Nevertheless, this was easier said than done. Although the king might be satisfied, it is unlikely that the English of Ireland as a whole would rest content with the precarious peace painfully established. In fact, by the ninth earl's day, the political agenda had moved on. Reflecting to a degree contemporary English ideas about the creation of a civil society, complaints against the ninth earl's rule focused on his exploitation of Gaelic practices and his abuse of power rather than, as previously, reflecting a crisis of lordship. Moreover, Kildare's supremacy over the border chiefs was a personal one which would not lightly be accorded to his son, and the good relations built up between the houses of Tudor, Butler and Fitzgerald would certainly come

---

34. Bayne & Dunham 1968, pp. 46–7; Bryan 1933, p. 233; Ellis 1986a, p. 100; Ellis 1980c, p. 518 n. 124; *CPR* 1494–1509, pp. 308, 443; *LP*, i (2nd edn), no. 2055 (95 iii); *Cal. close rolls*, 1500–9, p. 89.
35. Cf. Lydon 1972b, p. 276.
36. Bayne & Dunham 1968, pp. 46–7; Otway-Ruthven 1980, p. 327; above, p. 90.

under strain as leadership passed to men without experience of the lordship's administration in earlier, more troubled times.

THE EIGHTH EARL'S LAST YEARS

Already in the eighth earl's last years there were signs that he was finding it difficult to maintain the position earlier established. In 1508 he was licensed to summon a parliament, the first to meet since 1499, but the four sessions held in 1508–9 resulted only in a renewed ten-year subsidy. Three other bills regulating trade had still not passed when parliament was apparently ended by news of Henry VII's death. Kildare, elected justiciar in June according to custom, informed his successor, Henry VIII, that the state of the country precluded a visit to court. Henry replied with a summons, to which Kildare sent further excuses in June 1510, almost a year later and about the time of his expedition to Munster. In November he was reappointed deputy on almost the same terms as before, while the king remembered his boyhood companion, Lord Gerald, with a grant during pleasure of the royal manor of Ardmullan, Co. Meath. In June 1511 Kildare was again preparing to visit England and again changed his mind, perhaps as a result of a wound he received while campaigning in the midlands.[37]

Over the next two years the Irish council was largely remodelled and certain English-born officials appointed, but these changes were evidently brought about by the deaths of long-serving ministers rather than by any suspicions about Kildare's conduct. Walter FitzSimons died in 1511 and the English-born chief justice, John Topcliffe, in 1513. The king had the Yorkshireman, Bishop William Rokeby of Meath, translated to Dublin and appointed him chancellor in 1512. Two more Englishmen joined Rokeby on the council: Hugh Inge, first of a number of officials who owed their positions to Wolsey's influence, was translated to Meath, and John Rawson became prior of the Knights Hospitallers, Kilmainham.[38] Conditions in Ireland, however, can hardly have been much more disturbed than usual, for in 1511 O'Donnell made a pilgrimage to Rome and was knighted by Henry VIII on his way back, perhaps for his services with Kildare the previous year: it was very exceptional for a Gaelic chief to achieve such control that he could afford long absences from his lordship.

Thus when the eighth earl died, on 3 September 1513, his power and authority were substantially undiminished, as is apparent from the fulsome contemporary tributes to his rule: a Gaelic annalist wrote that 'in power, fame and estimation, he exceeded all the *Gaill*, conquered more territory from the *Gaedhil*, built more castles for the *Gaill*, razed more castles of the *Gaedhil* and kept better justice and law', while Philip Flattisbury, an Old English chronicler, added that as governor for 33 years he had excelled all other governors both in military exploits and by repopulating and re-edifying many towns in divers

37. Quinn 1941b, pp. 104–8; *LP*, i (1st edn), nos. 149, 1313–14; *CSPI*, i, 1; Curtis 1932–43, iv, app. no. 88.
38. *LP*, i (1st edn), nos. 2071–2, 3212, ii, no. 889; Quinn 1960–1, pp. 320–1.

parts of Ireland long devastated, and by constructing castles, bridges and other fortifications particularly on the borders for the weal and defence of the king's English subjects in the future.[39]

HENRY VIII, THE NINTH EARL OF KILDARE, AND IRISH GOVERNMENT

The young ninth earl of Kildare was elected justiciar and two months later appointed deputy by the king on the same terms as his father in 1510. These reserved to the king the chief justiceship of king's bench (in which Topcliffe had been confirmed), and Henry now appointed to the office an able Irish-born lawyer, Patrick Bermingham, who served him well and faithfully for almost twenty years. His nominee as chancellor, Sir William Compton, an absentee courtier, was less distinguished, but Rokeby probably continued as his deputy and regained the office in 1516. Otherwise, the king was content to continue the traditional governmental arrangements.[40]

Accounts of relations between the ninth earl (*Gearóid Óg* in the Gaelic annals) and Henry VIII have been somewhat overinfluenced by attempts to detect in them the origins of the 1534 rebellion. Obviously relations between king and earl were not those of their fathers, and their previous experiences of each other were an important factor in 1534, but it would be unwise to make too much of these supposed long-term causes of revolt.[41] By reason of the growing bulk and variety of the evidence, Henry VIII is a far more vivid character to us than the shadowy late medieval monarchs. He was in general far less suspicious of overmighty subjects than his father, but could be ruthless if his suspicions were aroused. He lacked Henry VII's interest in and application to the details of government and for most of his reign he ruled through a single chief minister, first Thomas Wolsey and then Thomas Cromwell. Neither could rely on the king's invariable acquiescence in their decisions, however. To an extent, Henry could be manipulated, as his courtiers found out; but he was a good judge of character, and on the domestic front at least, a shrewd politician whose judgement in a crisis was better than his ministers'.[42]

The ninth earl has rather unjustly received a generally bad press – for failing to preserve the Kildare ascendancy in changing circumstances over which he often had little control. The eighth earl had been exceptionally fortunate in that Ormond had little interest in government and that Henry VII was a realist prepared to forgive Kildare's earlier disloyalties and to accept the weaknesses and limitations of royal government in Ireland. Henry VIII was more demanding and less appreciative of these difficulties: from 1519 his chief ministers had to reckon on the king's comparatively frequent intervention in Irish affairs,

39. BL, Add. MS 4787, f. 252*v*; MacCarthy 1895, iii, pp. 496–7, 506–7 (my translation); Quinn 1960–1, p. 320.
40. Quinn 1960–1, p. 320; *LP*, i (1st edn), no. 4588; Ellis 1986a, pp. 220–1.
41. Ellis 1976–7, pp. 235–60.
42. Scarisbrick 1968; Elton 1962; Ives 1979.

but his initiatives were rarely sustained and frequently unrealistic. The ninth earl's methods were, predictably, very similar to his father's, and he generally performed well in difficult circumstances: he made mistakes, certainly, but no more than his father, although he was more vindictive and, in the longer term, perhaps his most serious failing was to ignore the vague and intermittent proposals for reform which gradually influenced Henry and his ministers in their conduct of Irish affairs. In this way he gradually began to appear as an obstacle to reform itself.[43]

For six years, however, Kildare ruled the lordship much as his father had. One new element in Anglo-Irish relations was Henry VIII's greater willingness to use Irish offices as a reward for his courtiers. This practice perhaps reflected a heightened perception by the king of the lordship's value, but it hardly helped government there, and some of those who took up residence soon decided that in reality they had been granted a kind of honourable exile. One such was John Kite, appointed archbishop of Armagh in 1514. Kite thought the Pale very fertile and well-stocked with corn and cattle but was appalled by the disorders of the country at large and quickly concluded that the king was as much bound to reform Ireland as to maintain order in England.[44] Indeed the few English-born ministers preferred in early Tudor Ireland may have supported those gentry in the Pale's more sheltered parts and merchants of major towns who argued that Kildare rule was not in the lordship's best interests. These critics acquired two influential spokesmen when the ninth earl dismissed from office and from his baronial council William Darcy, deputy-treasurer (1504–13), and Robert Cowley of Kilkenny. Instead he appointed his father-in-law, Lord Slane, as treasurer; and when, in May 1515, the earl went to court for consultations and with bills for a proposed parliament, his critics got their opportunity.[45]

Complaints against Kildare rule

Viscount Gormanston was elected justiciar in Kildare's absence, and Archbishops Kite and Rokeby, Bishop Inge, Prior Rawson, Sir William Darcy, and possibly Lord Slane were apparently also called over. The earl had to answer questions about his father's estate and his stepmother's claims on it, but Darcy put in articles for a council meeting at Greenwich containing some serious complaints about Kildare rule. He alleged that the deputy was making peace and war without the Irish council's consent, that he had imposed coign and livery, cartage and other unlawful impositions on the king's subjects, that the lords and gentry were becoming Irish, and that within the last 70 or 80 years the earls of Desmond and Ormond had introduced coign and livery and other Gaelic practices in their territories so that the king's laws were not used and his subjects there were as badly off as the wild Irish, while almost the

43. Ellis 1976–7, pp. 235–60; Quinn 1960–1, pp 318–44; Bradshaw 1979a, chs 2–3.
44. *LP*, i (2nd edn), nos. 2907, 2977; Quinn 1960–1; Ellis 1976–7, pp. 246–8.
45. Bradshaw 1979a, ch. 2; Ellis 1981a, pp. 242–3; Ellis 1980–1a, pp. 78–81; Ellis 1986a, pp. 32–3; Frame 1982, pt. i.

entire earldom of Ulster had been reconquered for lack of a resident lord. The impression created was that English rule had a century earlier been fully and most profitably operative in sixteen counties, but that the entire colony had since been swamped by Gaelic practices excepting a small area around Dublin which, with the deputy's help, was now going the same way. Without speedy remedy from the king all would be lost.

In reality the articles were highly misleading and, allowing for the polemical style then usual in such tracts, it does not seem that anything more than a vague feeling that all was not well lay behind them. They were not directed specifically against Kildare – indeed Desmond, with whom Kildare was temporarily and unusually on bad terms, was singled out for criticism. Yet in one sense the articles reflect the dilemma of the colonial community in trying to bring the king to take an interest without being able to say that the real cause of their difficulties (considered in more detail in Ch. 6) was not the malice of the king's enemies nor misgovernment by evil counsellors, but royal neglect.[46]

In any event the king dismissed the complaints, confirmed Kildare as deputy – he was back in office by 20 September – and sent after him, in response to his petitions, a series of royal grants which must have underlined to the Englishry Henry's continuing confidence in the earl. Besides a licence to hold parliament, Kildare received a grant in tail male of Ardmullan manor, of Strangford port, Co. Down, and other rights there and at Ardglass, a licence to found and endow a collegiate church at Maynooth, his principal residence, and charters of incorporation for his boroughs of Kildare and Athy. Rokeby was reappointed chancellor and Kite remained behind, being replaced as archbishop in 1521 by another Englishman, George Cromer.

Parliament met between February and October 1516 and was appropriately receptive to the deputy's legislative proposals. These included an act to confirm Kildare in the lands and liberties enjoyed by the fourth earl (1342–90) and his ancestors. Its purpose was apparently to confirm the liberty of Kildare restored sometime between June 1509 and April 1514. No charter has survived, and the statute's subsequent embezzlement later involved the earl in difficulties, but other evidence suggests that the restored liberty fell short of palatine status, with crown pleas still reserved to the king's justices. In addition the subsidy was renewed for a further ten years, the practice of bringing private suits from Ireland before the council in England was regulated on the grounds that many suits were malicious and designed simply to put defendants to costs, and other acts regulated trade and withdrew previous exemptions from the Statute of Absentees.[47]

46. Quinn 1960–1, pp. 321–2; Ellis 1986a, pp. 22, 32–3; *Carew*, i, no. 2; *LP*, ii, no. 411; *NHI*, ii, pp. 658–60.
47. Quinn 1960–1; *LP*, ii, nos. 996–1001; Quinn 1941b, pp. 108–15; *HBC*, p. 336; Mac Niocaill 1964b, nos. 193–7; Ellis 1986a, pp. 158, 218; Ellis 1981b, pp. 150–61; Ellis 1995a, pp. 110–13. Kildare perhaps had general anxieties about his title because the earldom was in abeyance 1432–53, but the fourth earl was the last to enjoy the palatinate suppressed in 1345. In 1519 Kildare's opponents mutilated the statute roll to spite him.

The Ormond succession dispute

A more worrying development for Kildare was a royal letter of July 1516 ordering Kildare to give his lawful assistance to the seventh earl's daughters, Anne St Leger and Margaret Boleyn, in prosecuting their claim to the Ormond inheritance against the earl's cousin, Sir Piers Butler. The death of Earl Thomas, in August 1515, though not unexpected, was a serious blow. It threatened a re-sumption of disputes and disturbances in the Ormond lordship which had been largely avoided since 1497, and the king's decision to favour the two daughters was even more ominous for Kildare. Margaret's son, Sir Thomas Boleyn, was well connected at court and soon to rise still further as Henry became involved successively with his daughters, Mary and Anne. On the other hand, Sir Piers would expect the good lordship of his brother-in-law (Kildare) in prosecuting his title to the earldom, and the undisputed succession of a resident earl would free Kildare from trouble in supervising Kilkenny and Tipperary: Earl Thomas had required the deputy's assistance on a number of occasions since 1496. If, however, Kildare were to show favour to Sir Piers, there was a fair chance that he would lose the king's.

Besides the political complications, the case posed some difficult legal prob-lems involving, most unusually for this period, a conflict between the custom of Ireland and the law of England. In Edward III's reign, it had been settled that those holding by barony in Ireland were liable to attend parliament there as peers: it followed, if peerages were linked to baronies, that the peerage would pass with the barony, whether or not the heir to the barony was heir to the whole estate. Thus Sir Piers claimed as cousin and heir male on the grounds that the earldom was held in tail male (a popular legal device which altered the normal laws of inheritance to prevent female succession). Ormond, how-ever, also held English lands where he was summoned to parliament as Lord Ormond; and in England the king had sometimes allowed the husband or son of a female heir to inherit a title, a precedent which would favour Boleyn's claims. At any rate, in December 1515 the king granted livery of the Ormond inheritance in England, Wales and Ireland to the two daughters. In Ireland, however, Kildare and the council accepted the claim of Sir Piers and he re-ceived livery of the Irish inheritance in April 1516. Henry then ordered the deputy to have the case heard in council, but if he were obstructed, to com-mand both parties to appear before the English council. The Irish council heard the case in Michaelmas term, respited it pending instructions from the king, and left Sir Piers in possession of most of the Ormond lands in Ireland, while St Leger and Boleyn retained custody of those in England.[48] Here matters rested until about 1526, with Sir Piers being styled earl in royal commissions but the king refusing to recognize him as such. Evidently Sir Piers felt that Kildare had not done enough for his case, however, and sometime before 1520 the two had quarrelled.

48. Ellis 1986a, pp. 157–8.

POINT: actually: Kildare supported the 2 women, hoping to ingratiate himself in court & king supported Piers, who had been sucking up.

Kildare's recall

By 1518 Kildare was again busy replying to complaints about his rule, and in July Henry was dealing personally with correspondence from the earl of Desmond and Cork city. Not that direct communications between the king and the southern towns and lords were all that unusual – in fact disputes about royal charters were *ultra vires* in Dublin – but, exceptionally, Henry VIII was now taking a personal interest in Irish affairs instead of delegating matters to Wolsey. In January 1519 Kildare was summoned to court to discuss these matters, although he was on this occasion commissioned to appoint his own deputy, which suggests that he still retained the king's confidence: it was rumoured that he had come to choose a wife, his first wife having died in 1517.

On his departure in September, he left his uncle, Maurice Fitzgerald, in charge. By then the king had more business to discuss. In another outbreak of the old prisage dispute between Waterford and New Ross the city petitioned the king: Henry ordered Wolsey to hear the case in Star Chamber on the grounds of the city's loyalty during his father's reign and that if the suit were heard in Ireland it would be delayed by the difficulties of journeying to Dublin for fear of the wild Irish. Moreover, it emerged from an investigation into complaints against the deputy's conduct during a progress through the south-east that Kildare had had to intervene to enforce the law in Wexford and to ensure the liberty's defence against Gaelic chiefs to the north. The king had the earl of Shrewsbury (Waterford in Ireland) attend to Wexford's defence, authorizing him to retain 40 armed men to recover parts of his inheritance there. These matters no doubt reminded Henry that his authority in Ireland remained limited, and before Christmas he was debating with his council 'how Ireland may be reduced and restored to good order and obedience'.[49]

The upshot was Kildare's replacement by the earl of Surrey, an able and experienced commander, for a reconnaissance in force. Apparently this followed a dispute between Wolsey and Kildare in council, but whether complaints of misconduct in government provided the real reason for Kildare's dismissal or merely cloaked a clash of personalities is not now ascertainable. At any rate, Kildare was held partly responsible and, instead of being sent back to assist Surrey with his knowledge of the country and experience of politics there, he was detained at court, a mistake which was soon to have serious consequences.

---

49. Quinn 1960–1, pp. 322–30 (quotation, p. 323); *LP*, ii, nos. 3853, 4293, iii, nos. 17, 356, 430; Vergil 1950, p. 265.

CHAPTER 6

NEW PROBLEMS, 1520–1547

SURREY IN IRELAND

The earl of Surrey's lieutenancy (1520–2) originated in one of Henry VIII's spasmodic fits of reforming energy. Besides his candidature at this time for the imperial crown and Wolsey's for the papal tiara the king also exhibited an uncharacteristic interest in the routine of administration; but almost the only tangible result was Surrey's expedition.[1] The expedition is an interesting pointer to Henry VIII's ideas about Ireland on the first occasion when he ventured outside the political assumptions inherited from his father. Some of the questions and problems that arose foreshadowed those he had to consider from 1534 onwards, and in other respects the expedition resembled those of Edward IV's reign, but the overriding impression created is of an expedition mounted without any clear aims or adequate consideration of the consequences. Inadequated planning was a perennial problem of royal government in Ireland throughout the Tudor period.

Surrey reached Ireland on 23 May. His retinue and siege train included three large battery pieces and some 200 yeomen of the guard, part of the king's small bodyguard which was the nearest the Tudors came in England to maintaining a standing army.[2] The earl himself was one of Henry's best generals and could no doubt be spared for service in Ireland only because there was for the present no prospect of military activity on the continent or against Scotland. His orders were, optimistically, to recall outlying lords to their allegiance, to establish peace and levy the king's revenue throughout the island, to reform and anglicize the church, but chiefly 'to inform your highness by which means and ways your grace might reduce this land to obedience and good order'.[3]

It soon emerged, however, that the king was by no means committed to following his advice. At a late stage in the preparations it was decided to confer the more honourable title of king's lieutenant on Surrey, which emphasized

1. Bradshaw 1979a, p. 58.
2. For Surrey's lieutenancy, see in general ibid., ch. 3; Quinn 1960–1, pp. 322–30; *NHI*, ii, pp. 662–8.
3. Ellis 1976–7, p. 239 (quotation).

Henry's high expectations of the expedition but also the difficulties he might face in matching his predecessor's prestige there: Surrey's actual powers were in fact more limited than Kildare had enjoyed. His salary was nominally generous, at £2,000 a year, but this was because, much to his annoyance, he was expected to serve under the old indenture system of military retaining, maintaining a substantial bodyguard at his own expense, besides those troops in the king's pay.[4] He was still haggling with Wolsey about precise numbers of troops after his arrival, but more seriously he soon discovered that the yeomen of the guard were more decorative than effective in Irish warfare. Over half were quickly discharged in favour of light northern and Welsh horse which were more suitable for the difficult terrain of Gaelic Ireland. When the northerners arrived, however, they turned out to be mounted archers, many of them ill-horsed, and not the Northumberland spears whom Surrey had wanted: half of them were soon discharged in favour of locally recruited English and Irish horse. By autumn, therefore, the lieutenant had a more balanced force of around 550 troops in pay, of whom almost half were cavalry.[5]

Surrey spent the summer in attempting to reassert royal authority after the change of governor and in acquainting himself with Irish conditions by three major progresses – northwards against O'Neill, into the midlands against O'More, and to Waterford via Tipperary. Apparently Henry and Wolsey had been lobbied by the colonial community with grandiose proposals similar to those made to Henry VII in 1493–4, though Surrey was evidently unimpressed by them. In 1520, however, Kildare was made a scapegoat for the state of the country, and the king further committed himself by stating publicly that the earl should not for the present return to Ireland. Whatever the merits of the case, the move was unwise because it prompted Kildare to look to protect his standing in the Englishry, and among the Palesmen especially, against an outsider. In turn the Pale aristocracy and Gaelic border chiefs divided between those who sought advancement from the new regime and those who expected Kildare's return. Thus in the hosting against O'More, Surrey received 'the least assistance of the Englishry that ever was seen', only 48 horse and 120 foot, and O'Neill and O'Carroll proved especially troublesome.[6] Yet Surrey received enthusiastic support from some careerist officials, from Sir Piers Butler and his Ormond connection, and from Shrewsbury's seneschal of Wexford. The upshot, however, was that Surrey was kept busy with what in Ireland passed for everyday problems of administration and lacked the necessary power with which to tackle the underlying difficulties of royal government there. Already in July, he was writing to the king that the pacification of Gaelic Ireland would require 'a great puissance of men', money and the political determination by the king to see it through.[7] This report forced Henry and Wolsey to consider more carefully both the aims and the methods of the expedition.

4. Ellis 1986a, pp. 13, 16, 27; PRO, SP 60/3/162 (*LP*, xi, no. 709).
5. *StP*, ii, 31–3, 48, 54–5, 57–8; *LP*, iii, nos. 670, 889.
6. *StP*, ii, 35–6.
7. Ibid., ii, 37.

Surrey had been sent out with sufficient money to cover his wages and those of his troops for only six months, on the understanding that thereafter his administration would be self-sufficient. There were, however, small grounds for optimism on this score. Unlike Poynings, Surrey received very inadequate administrative support from England. Probably at Wolsey's instigation, an executive privy council was established for Ireland which anticipated by fifteen years Thomas Cromwell's initiatives for the creation of an equivalent institution for England. Three of the councillors were to be Englishmen resident in England, and Surrey was not to act without their advice; some of Surrey's retinue received minor administrative posts, but the only Englishman appointed to high office at this time was Sir John Stile, who was no better equipped for the key post of undertreasurer than he had been as Henry's ambassador to Spain.[8] Otherwise, Surrey inherited an administration more schooled in methods of economy and conciliation than in the recovery of the revenue by energetic government. Surrey was unfortunate in that 1520 was a year of plague and dearth, which disrupted billeting arrangements and made it almost impossible for his troops to live on their wages. Rather than increase their pay, the king agreed to the continuance of coign and livery which he had hoped to abolish, but this in turn jeopardized his strategy for increasing the revenue through the calling of parliament.[9]

Parliament and finance

Very little is known about Surrey's parliament apart from the measures proposed and the acts passed. Its meeting was postponed until May 1521 but seven sessions were held before its dissolution in March 1522. The government drafted important money bills to resume the customs and feefarm rents of towns and cities in the south and west (following a proposal made in 1516 but abandoned after opposition) and to establish a royal monopoly on salt imports. But these bills were seemingly rejected, and a proposal to double the parliamentary subsidy in return for the abolition of coign and livery had been abandoned much earlier. In the event, only three relatively innocuous commonwealth measures were enacted.

The fate of the money bills highlighted an important and long-standing difference between king and community. The colonists were ever eager for more vigorous measures by the crown in Ireland, but they felt that the king had a duty to provide for good government and defence throughout his territories, and that the cost of any measures to establish his claims over Gaelic Ireland should be met by all his subjects. Thus, although Henry could count on a measure of financial and military support from the colonists, they saw little logic in the argument (formerly elaborated in the English parliament about Lancastrian France) that the cost of conquering the king's Irish enemies should fall chiefly on his subjects in Ireland.[10] Sir William Darcy, a former undertreasurer,

8. Ibid., ii, 54; Ellis 1986a, pp. 39–42, 220–25; Mattingley 1955, p. 152.

9. PRO, SP 60/1/71 (LP, iii, no. 670 ii).

10. Ibid.; Quinn 1941a, pp. 109–23; StP, ii, 41.

had optimistically informed the king that revenue exceeded ordinary expenditure by 2,000 marks (IR), but Stile complained that there was no evidence that
it had reached even IR£1,600 gross in recent years and that because of war,
plague and dearth it was now worth less than IR£1,400 a year. Stile was himself ignorant of the 'course of the exchequer', and was further hindered because
the few clerks available were so frequently needed for military administration. Matters did improve slightly in 1521–2 and the undertreasurer eventually
accounted for just over IR£3,500 for the two years to Easter 1522, but IR£500
of this was still outstanding in 1538.[11] In these circumstances only some IR£750
per annum was available to meet the wages of Surrey and his retinue. As early
as October 1520 the king had been forced to send over an additional £4,000,[12]
and Henry's hopes of conquest gradually yielded to a preoccupation with
reducing expenses as he realized that the lieutenancy was costing him around
£10,000 a year.

THE ENGLISH CROWN AND THE GAELIC PEOPLE

Moreover, it soon emerged that Surrey and the king disagreed fundamentally
about how Gaelic Ireland was to be reduced. Surrey and many local officials
felt that Gaelic chiefs would be 'brought to no good order, unless it be by
compulsion': Henry replied, in a famous phrase, that it should rather be done
by 'sober ways, politic drifts and amiable persuasions founded in law and
reason'.[13] In the course of this debate, however, the king stumbled upon a
fundamental problem in Anglo-Gaelic relations, namely the question of the
constitutional position of the Gaelic lordships after their incorporation into the
Tudor state. His projected solution, which foreshadowed the 'surrender and
regrant' policy of the 1540s, marked a fundamental departure from traditional
thinking about this question ever since Richard II's visit. The conventional
view among the colonists, uncritically and haphazardly followed by successive
kings, was that the Gaelic people were not the king's natural subjects but a
servile population which had usurped lands rightfully held by Englishmen.
Although in Wales, Edward I had after the conquest found it advisable to recognize certain aspects of Welsh law, he denounced Gaelic law and customs,
which were frequently comparable, as far more 'detestable to God and . . .
contrary to all law'.[14] The Gaelic population was thus denied the rights, liberties and legal protection of Englishmen; their lands and property could be
seized for the crown, and they were legally the *nativi* or villeins of the king or
lord with title by English law to the lands on which they lived. This is broadly
what had happened earlier to the natives in areas settled by the Normans, but
even the most conservative colonists recognized that without some concessions

11. Ellis 1986a, pp. 84–5; *StP*, ii, 77–8, 86–8.
12. *StP*, ii, 54.
13. Ibid., ii, 35, 52.
14. Davies 1966, p. 147.

the reduction of Gaelic Ireland would require a long, bloody and costly campaign. The inducement offered was the denization or enfranchisement of individuals in return for conformity with English ways. Gaelic peasants attracted into the Englishry were normally permitted to purchase their liberty, and occasionally chiefs like O'Neill in 1480 and the two MacCarthys of Muskerry and Carbery in 1488 also received personal grants of English liberty, with the implication that continued conformity might be rewarded by charters to lands occupied by them.[15]

The general proscription of Gaelic law and custom coupled with the piece-meal extension of English liberty to individuals was a useful means of pre-serving the lordship's English identity by regulating contact between native and settler in a two-culture situation, but Henry and Wolsey felt that Gaelic Ireland could be incorporated into the Tudor state more speedily and at less cost if the chiefs could be won over by major political concessions instead of being constrained, as Surrey advocated, by military might. Disregarding the traditional ethnically based classification of his opponents into English rebels and Irish enemies, Henry considered both groups as 'disobeisant subjects' and insisted that Gaelic dissidents were not enemies but rebels.[16] They should be brought round by a mixture of bribery and bullying, and reinforcements would then be sent to crush recalcitrants. Where Surrey urged the colonization of Gaelic Ireland with Englishmen, because both the native population was incorrigible and the country underpopulated if tillage on the English model were to replace Gaelic pastoralism, Henry thought the natives could be drawn to obedience and civility. He expected them to acknowledge his sovereignty, but was prepared to compromise concerning the practical exercise of his judicial lordship. He envisaged a special legal code for the Gaelic and border territ-ories – an amalgam of Gaelic and English customs agreed in consultation with local leaders and possibly inspired by a knowledge of practice in the Welsh and Scottish marches. His compromise concerning land titles, however, failed to address the central problem of the conflict between feudal tenure by Eng-lish law and tribal possession by Gaelic law. Henry was apparently willing to relinquish his title to lands which previous kings had not alienated by feudal grant, but he expected the Gaelic Irish to restore to him any lands which had once been settled and to which the crown had title by escheat or forfeiture, and this begged the question of other English titles to land in Gaelic possession. In Henry's own words:

> Like as we being their sovereign lord and prince, though of our absolute power we be above the laws, yet we will in no wise take anything from them that righteously appertaineth to them, so of good congruence they be bound both by law, fidelity and [al]liegeance to restore unto us our own.[17]

15. Parliament roll, 19 & 20 Edward IV c. 41 (Berry & Morrissey 1939, p. 786); Otway-Ruthven 1980, p. 404.
16. *StP*, ii, 60.
17. Ibid., ii, 53. See Bradshaw 1979a, ch. 3.

By Gaelic law, however, uninterrupted possession of land over a long period conferred ownership, whereas on the king's terms at least a quarter of the island could have reverted to the crown.

Tudor absolutism

In practice, Surrey was never in a sufficiently commanding position seriously to negotiate with Gaelic chiefs; but as political theory, the statement that 'of our absolute power we be above the laws' was an indication that for Ireland too, Henry's personal concept of royal lordship was undergoing change. The effect was to heighten the contrast between royal claims and the realities of Tudor power there. Although crown rights and prerogatives were in theory the same in both countries, the fact that until 1541 the English king was styled lord and not king of Ireland and that Ireland was constitutionally a dependency of England tended to confuse the issue in practical terms. The Yorkist kings and Henry VII had generally been content with the feudal suzerainty which was often the reality of their lordship beyond the Pale: yet even as Henry VIII was groping towards a more absolute expression of his claims upon his subjects throughout the Tudor state, he was discarding the traditional compromise between the theory and practice of English lordship in Ireland, was renewing the claim that this lordship extended throughout the island, and was insisting that the realities of royal power in Ireland should be brought into line with practice in England.

SURREY'S RECALL

All of this, however, was of no practical help to Surrey. By September 1520 the lieutenant had with difficulty restored the administration's usual control in English areas. He soon realized that Kildare influence was behind many of the disorders there, but attempts to obtain proof of this were unavailing. Kildare had been bound in May not to leave the London area, and in July gave fresh bonds to appear before Wolsey on demand. He was apparently imprisoned for a time during Wolsey's examination, but released in November, again suspected of sending messengers to Ireland, and finally cleared in mid-1521, by which time he had rebuilt his credit at court by an astute alliance with the marquis of Dorset whose daughter he was soon to marry.[18] Nevertheless the trouble stirred up by Kildare's supporters merely served to confirm the lieutenant and council in their view that significant progress towards reform would require far more than the peace-keeping force which Surrey disposed. In December 1520 he informed Wolsey that if the king was unwilling to proceed with conquest, he was wasting his time, health, and the king's money in Ireland. Soon after, however, he received news of a projected Scottish invasion under the earl of Argyll to link up with dissident nobles: he sent post-haste for

18. Quinn 1960–1, pp. 329–30.

800 additional troops plus Kildare's return to help stay the growing unrest and resist any invasion.

In fact, by winter 1520–1 the political and diplomatic situation that had landed Surrey in Ireland was rapidly changing. In Europe the peace established by Wolsey in 1518 was collapsing with Charles V and Francis I mobilizing for war and Henry committed to allying against the aggressor, while the background to the threatened Scottish invasion was the expiry of an earlier Anglo-Scottish treaty. Thus, far from contemplating increased involvement in Ireland, Henry was now anxious to cut his losses 'for the advancement of other higher enterprises'.[19] Surrey's inconvenient requests for reinforcements and Kildare's return were turned down, though Surrey later received some munitions and 1,000 marks for emergencies. Sir John Peachey was sent out to explain the king's predicament: Henry's first concern was to make an impact on the continent, on which 'greatly dependeth his honour and estimation' and so England's security, but the king also thought a Scottish invasion of the north more likely and dangerous than one of Ireland. Surrey was assured that he would not be abandoned, but Henry's earlier schemes were quietly dropped and the lieutenant was now ordered to fall back on the defence of the Pale and not to put the king to further charges. Accordingly Surrey patched up truces and treaties with Gaelic chiefs on whatever terms he could get, and after the close of the campaigning season in September the king agreed to his recall.[20]

Though Surrey's expedition was a complete failure – Henry's proposals remained untried and the constitutional status of the Gaelic Irish unaltered – it was an important episode in Tudor policy-making for Ireland which had a significant but adverse impact on the future conduct of government there. In June 1521 Surrey furnished the king with a considered assessment of the difficulties of conquest. The conquest of Wales, he claimed, had taken Edward I in person ten years. Ireland, however, was much larger and separated by sea: piecemeal conquest would require 2,500 men for many years and would probably precipitate a general Gaelic confederacy against the crown; more rapid progress would need an army of 6,000 men fed, financed and equipped from England, castles and towns would have to be built, and English settlers introduced to promote loyalty and civility. Like his predecessors, Henry VIII dismissed the cost of this strategy as far exceeding the prestige and intrinsic value to the crown of conquest. He also informed Surrey that, considering 'the little effect that succeedeth', to maintain an English lieutenant and retinue on such a scale was 'consumption of treasure in vain',[21] a judgement which perhaps reflected more on the circumstances and planning surrounding the experiment than on the possibilities of a more favourable outcome in other circumstances.

Yet while the reduction of Gaelic Ireland sank in the king's mind to the level of a pious aspiration, his conduct of government over the next decade

---

19. Quoted, Ellis 1976–7, p. 329; *StP*, ii, 65–70. See Bradshaw 1979a, ch. 3 for this and what follows.
20. *StP*, ii, 65–72 (quotation, p. 65).
21. Ellis 1976–7, p. 239 (quotation, p. 239); *StP*, ii, 72–5.

would suggest that he also refused to accept the logic of this position. Surrey's expedition had disrupted the political stability previously established, but the king's closer supervision of Irish affairs in the 1520s was directed, not specifically at its restoration, but rather towards ensuring that, without cost to himself, his governor did not altogether lose sight of Henry's ambitions. And since successive governors lacked the time or resources to do more than preserve the status quo, they were placed in an impossible situation. In the longer term, however, the king's suggestions to Surrey resurfaced in the surrender and regrant policy of the 1540s, and the relative merits of rival strategies for a chiefly political or a largely military solution to the Gaelic problem remained at the centre of the debate about Irish policy throughout the Tudor period.

ORMOND'S DEPUTYSHIP

The decision to curtail Surrey's expedition was initially kept secret from the Irish council by the ruse of recalling him temporarily for consultations. His replacement by another Englishman was eventually ruled out on grounds of cost, and the earl of Ormond – to whom the prospect of a favourable settlement of the Ormond succession dispute was briefly held out through a marriage of his son to Anne Boleyn – acted as deputy-lieutenant for two months while Surrey was at court. In March 1522 Surrey returned for a final three weeks to dissolve parliament, disband his retinue, and see Ormond installed with a more powerful commission as the king's deputy. With Kildare in disgrace, Ormond was the only reliable magnate with sufficient standing in the lordship to govern unaided, but the decision to cut off English subventions immediately was certainly ill-advised and drew protests from both deputy and council.[22]

Ormond was soon in difficulties. His estates centring on Kilkenny and Tipperary were of little help in controlling the Pale, which had been greatly weakened by the political changes since 1519, and in Kildare's absence the Geraldines were uncontrollable. Nor was much available from the Irish revenues because the land was 'much waste and the people marvellously poor'. The deputy was soon requesting Kildare's return to control his kinsmen and defend his lands, but this without a settlement between the two earls and concerning the disputed Ormond inheritance merely exchanged one problem for another.[23] Moreover, Desmond, who had kept aloof from Anglo-Irish politics since 1520, exploited the outbreak of hostilities between England and France in 1522 to intrigue with Francis I. On 20 June 1523 he agreed by treaty with the French king to support the claims of the Yorkist pretender, Richard de la Pole, to the English throne.[24] Kildare, having worked his way back into favour with Dorset's help, remained uncooperative and rejected Ormond's

22. Quinn 1960–1, pp. 328–31; *StP*, ii, 88–93.
23. *StP*, ii, 91–3, 95 (quotation); *LP*, iv, no. 81.
24. *NHI*, ii, pp. 672–3.

offer of close cooperation in return for support for the latter's claim to royal recognition.[25] The two earls quarrelled. In October 1523 Henry intervened and Kildare was granted an annuity of IR£100 for defending the Pale, but this settlement soon collapsed when the sheriff of Dublin was murdered by Kildare's brother James while travelling to Kilkenny to spend Christmas with Ormond.[26]

These difficulties coincided with disturbances elsewhere in the Tudor territories against heavy taxation for war against France and Scotland. Wolsey became convinced of the need for firmer control, especially over outlying parts, and this led in 1525 to the restoration of provincial councils in the north under the duke of Richmond and in the Welsh marches with the Princess Mary.[27] In Ireland the initiative was more superficial and even less successful. In a characteristic move by Wolsey, the lordship was visited in summer 1524 by three important commissioners – Dr James Denton and Sir Ralph Egerton, later appointed to the Welsh council, and Sir Anthony Fitzherbert, JKB – with powers to determine all disputes, especially between the two earls, to investigate and reform government in the Pale where Ormond had been unable to control the marcher lords, and to associate Kildare more closely in government. The commissioners seemingly worked thoroughly: 43 marcher lords and Pale gentry were bound over in chancery in sums ranging from IR£40 to IR£200 to uphold the law concerning coign and livery, to appear before the council to answer any charges against them, and to arrest and deliver to Dublin castle any kinsmen and servants so charged; and Kildare and Ormond each gave two bonds in 1,000 marks (IR) before the council to observe the terms of a lengthy composition between them, and to support the king's ministers, uphold the law and not to billet more troops on the country than were necessary for defence.[28]

After the reconciliation of the two earls, Kildare surrendered his brother to the commissioners as an earnest of his intentions, and was then reappointed deputy. The Dublin chronicle reported that

> they kept the council in Christ Church and suddenly the earl of Ossory [= Ormond] was deprived and the earl of Kildare proclaimed and swore deputy. And so O'Neill, being in the council house with them, bare the sword before the deputy till they went to Thomas Court and there dined, and after dinner had a goodly banquet.[29]

James Fitzgerald was led through the streets of London with a noose around his neck but eventually pardoned. Ormond received the lord treasurership, but Kildare soon deprived him of any financial influence by appointing Lord Trimblestone as undertreasurer.[30]

25. StP, ii, 101.
26. Ellis 1976–7, p. 241; Quinn 1960–1, pp. 331–2; Memoranda roll, 15 Henry VIII m. 24 (Public Record Office of Ireland, Ferguson coll., iv, f. 67).
27. Williams 1958, pp. 11–12; Reid 1921, pp. 101–2.
28. StP, ii, 104–18; Ives 1970, pp. 359–62.
29. Trinity College, Dublin, MS 543/2 s.a. 1524; Quinn 1960–1, p. 332.
30. Ellis 1986a, p. 101; Quinn 1960–1, p. 332.

The feud recommenced after a decent interval which the earls used to re-establish their authority in their respective areas of influence, and by April 1525 charges and countercharges were crossing the Irish Sea. The struggle seriously weakened the lordship because Kildare incited his Gaelic clients to raid the estates of Ormond and his supporters and Ormond retaliated likewise. The chiefs needed little encouragement, though Kildare would certainly have given them short shrift earlier.[31]

KILDARE'S RESTORATION

Kildare's reappointment quickly restored order to the Pale, and the earl could resume his interventions in outlying Gaelic lordships: in 1524 he led a hosting against O'Donnell and another into Connaught in 1526, when he also received O'Neill, O'Donnell and other nobles at a council in Dublin.[32] Yet there was a limit to what could be achieved by occasional military forays, and Desmond's conduct placed Kildare in a particularly difficult position. The Yorkist intrigue, a throwback to a previous age, was effectively dead long before de la Pole's death in the French defeat at Pavia in 1525, but by late 1524 Desmond was exploiting Ormond's feud with Kildare to organize a series of raids on Butler territories.[33] The maintenance of what was almost a war on two fronts against the two Fitzgerald earls kept Ormond on the defensive, but he in turn astutely represented to the king that the deputy was in treasonable communication with Desmond. And Kildare's denials seemingly carried less weight because he was unable to apprehend Desmond: he was understandably reluctant to campaign against Desmond to Ormond's benefit, and when he did lead a hosting into Munster, Desmond had ample time in which to disappear.[34] The council could only send the king a draft bill for Desmond's attainder against a projected parliament scheduled to meet before summer 1527, but it gradually became apparent in England that only by getting Ormond and Kildare to work together could Desmond be brought to book, order restored, and the threat of continental intervention ended. By 1528 Ormond's son, Lord James Butler, was in charge of the campaigning, assisted by the sheriff of Cork, Sir John Fitzgerald, and the anglophile MacCarthy chief, Cormac Oge of Muskerry: but Desmond was petitioning Charles V for assistance against Henry and the emperor was sufficiently interested in this possibility of bringing pressure concerning the king's divorce suit from Catherine of Aragon to send his chaplain, Gonzalo Fernandez, to Ireland in February 1529. Four months later, however, the earl died and the desire of his successor for royal recognition temporarily resolved Henry's problem.[35]

31. Ellis 1976–7, p. 241; Quinn 1960–1, p. 333.
32. Ellis 1976–7, p. 249.
33. *NHI*, ii, pp. 672–3; Elton 1969, p. 37.
34. Ellis 1976–7, pp. 241–2 and references there cited.
35. Ibid.; Quinn 1941b, pp. 124–5; *StP*, ii, 147–50; *NHI*, ii, pp. 677–8.

'O'Connor's Wars'

Meanwhile, however, the government had created further trouble by summoning Kildare and Ormond to court and detaining them there. Lord Butler, at court since 1521, returned home to look after the family's interests, and the earl left for London in August 1526. Kildare followed about Christmas, appointing his brother, Sir Thomas Fitzgerald, as vice-deputy, but he was soon superseded, no doubt on the king's orders, by the veteran captain, Lord Delvin. Despite the weakness of his position, Delvin dealt high-handedly with border chiefs, and Kildare's councillors stirred up trouble from O'Neill and O'Connor Faly 'in the hope that he should the rather come home'.[36] In November 1527, facing a second winter without the earls, the council reminded Wolsey of the importance of resident magnates for Tudor rule: through divisions and lack of captains, they warned, the Englishry was never weaker since the conquest, 'for there is none of this land that can or may do for defence of the same so well as [Kildare]'. The two earls, once 'confirmed in amity, should never do our sovereign lord better service . . . than now'. Yet the king did nothing about the earls for over a year, and in February 1528 Lord Chancellor Inge and Chief Justice Bermingham wrote again, lamenting the 'great losses and damages this winter' by Gaelic raids on the Pale, and the disturbances in Tipperary and Kilkenny in Ormond's absence. They begged Wolsey to provide for the lordship, for

the vice-deputy is not of power [i.e. lacks tenants] to defend the Englishry, and yet the poor people is far more charged and oppressed by him than they have been, the earl of Kildare being here. He hath no great lands of his own

and the Irish revenues, since the subsidy had expired in 1526, scarcely sufficed to pay officers' salaries.[37] By this date Henry and Wolsey had imposed a fresh agreement in the Ormond succession dispute, by which Sir Piers Butler relinquished the earldom, but retained two Pale manors and a 30-year lease of most other Ormond lands for a nominal annual rent of £40, and was created instead earl of Ossory. The following year Thomas Boleyn was created earl of Ormond and Wiltshire in England.[38] Ossory could accordingly be sent home in spring 1528 and Wolsey wrote a gentle letter to O'Neill, who replied that Delvin withheld his blackrent and requested Kildare's return.

On departing for court, Kildare had asked his Gaelic allies not to cause trouble until the king's intentions became apparent, and had later sent word to keep the peace until May. In May, O'Connor kidnapped the vice-deputy for stopping his blackrent. The chief was the earl's son-in-law, and 'O'Connor's Wars' (as they were called) were widely thought to have been fomented by Kildare's councillors. In the ensuing crisis, Ossory was too far off, settling his

36. *LP*, iv, no. 3698 (quotation). See Ellis 1976–7, pp. 242–4 for this and what follows.
37. *StP*, ii, 126–8; Ellis 1995a, p. 181.
38. Curtis 1932–43, iv, nos. 115, 136–7, 139–40; *LP*, iv, nos. 2610, 3728, 3950, 3973, 4231; *HBC*, pp. 487, 496.

own lands, to provide any immediate assistance, so because 'the strength, if any be, is by the Geraldines', the council elected Fitzgerald captain and again appealed for aid from England:

> for undoubted, there is no man here now being that can or may defend this land, as well for lack of power as substance.[39]

They requested either Kildare's return or substantial troop reinforcements. Henry, however, refused to be coerced, feeling that Kildare went 'fraudulently about to colour that the king should think that [he] could not be served there, but only by him'.[40] Nor would he foot the bill for an army, and he also vetoed Wolsey's ingenious suggestion that Lord Butler be appointed vice-deputy to Kildare, who should be kept in England, on the grounds that Butler was too young to command the support of the nobles there.[41] A reluctant Ossory was therefore appointed deputy at the king's insistence, though Surrey (since 1524 duke of Norfolk) warned that he would hardly be able to defend his own country, let alone the Pale.

In July, Kildare sent home his daughter Alice with news of Ossory's impending appointment. She rode straight to her husband, O'Connor, who recommenced hostilities; and as captain Fitzgerald failed to organize effective resistance 'by reason of certain intelligence had with O'Connor', as he later admitted, 'contrary to his allegiance'. Gradually, a battle of wills developed between king and earl which resembled Henry's parallel attempt in the west marches towards Scotland to supplant Lord Dacre as warden by the more pliable earl of Cumberland. In both cases, the ruling magnate won out in the ensuing disturbances but later paid a heavy price in the crisis of 1534, following the erosion of trust between king and magnate.

Norfolk's prediction about Ossory's incapacity proved entirely accurate, and by summer 1529 the deputy's inadequacies had again forced Henry to intervene. In a move which resembled Wolsey's initiative for the north in 1525, the king's illegitimate infant son, the duke of Richmond, was appointed lieutenant and a 'secret council' of three ministers – the new chancellor and archbishop of Dublin, John Alen, and Treasurer John Rawson, both Englishmen, and Chief Justice Bermingham – appointed to govern as deputy in his absence. The master of the ordnance, Sir William Skeffington, was sent out to survey the military situation and soon reported that the new administration lacked the money and men to govern effectively. The fall of Wolsey, moreover, removed the architect of this bureaucratic experiment, and in spring 1530 Henry, now advised on Ireland by Norfolk and Wiltshire, appointed Skeffington as deputy with 250 English troops and licensed Kildare's return.[42]

39. *StP*, ii, 129; Ellis 1995a, pp. 182–3.
40. *StP*, ii, 140n.; Ellis 1995a, p. 184.
41. BL, Titus B. XI (II), ff. 349–50 (*LP*, iv, no. 4562); *StP*, ii, 136–40.
42. Ellis 1995a, pp. 182–5 (quotation, p. 183); Quinn 1935b, pp. 175–7; Quinn 1960–1, pp. 336–8; Ellis 1980–1c, pp. 100–3.

SIR WILLIAM SKEFFINGTON'S FIRST DEPUTYSHIP

The circumstances of Skeffington's appointment augured well for stronger government. He had earlier negotiated a settlement between Ossory and the new earl of Desmond, and Ossory had been appointed to supervise government in the Ormond district. Sir Thomas Fitzgerald, summoned to court and then pardoned along with Kildare's daughter and a leading councillor, Meyler Fay of Rathangan, was lavishly rewarded and again entrusted with the Pale's defence.[43] Skeffington's new instructions laid emphasis on the need for good government and strengthening Dublin's control after the vacillations and stop-gap strategies of the last decade. The deputy was to promote good relations between the three Irish earls and secure their cooperation against Gaelic chiefs. His retinue comprised 200 border horsemen from the Carlisle garrison and 50 gunners financed from England, and he also brought two new pieces of heavy siege artillery and other weapons. Nevertheless the aim was primarily to discourage petty raiding, not to stir up trouble by frequent hostings far into the Irishry. Kildare had undertaken to compel the border chiefs to make peace, and the deputy's troops were to be at his disposal for raids whenever Skeffington himself was unavailable. Finally, preparations for calling parliament were ordered, especially for the grant of a subsidy, but since parliament was unlikely to meet until mid-1531 Skeffington was to negotiate (unsuccessfully) for a retroactive extra-parliamentary grant for 1529–30.[44]

For almost a year the arrangement worked well. After being cooped up at court Kildare launched into a furious wave of campaigning, with Desmond and Ossory looking after their own territories and Skeffington active and successful in his own right. The military balance was soon restored. Yet Henry was desperately short of money at this time – Skeffington's salary and retinue was costing him over £3,850 per annum – and with Anglo-Scottish relations deteriorating, both money and men were now needed to defend the northern frontier. In February, with the departure of the northerners, Skeffington's retinue was reduced to a mere 100 horsemen, and the deputy's position was further undermined when one of his chief supporters, Archbishop Alen, was forced to pay a swingeing fine of £1,466 13s. 4d. for offences in exercising Wolsey's legatine authority in Ireland. The king sent over a further £1,550 in May to cover expenses until the anticipated subsidy could be collected, but by July Skeffington and Kildare had fallen out, the Geraldine–Butler feud recommenced and a 'great frey' occurred between the inhabitants of Dublin and English troops.

When parliament met, in September and October 1531, the subsidy bill was thrown out and the government's programme thereby reduced to innocuous commonwealth measures. Skeffington, short of money, adopted the antiquated expedient of levying a scutage; and in the face of a growing reluctance on the part of the Palesmen to attend hostings against the Irishry, an order in council reimposed a graduated scale of fines for absence. Yet Skeffington's deputyship

43. Curtis 1932–43, iv, nos. 149–52; Ellis 1995a, pp. 186–7.
44. *StP*, ii, 147–50; Ellis 1980–1c, pp. 100–3; Ellis 1977, pp. 9–11; Ellis 1995a, pp. 186–8.

became increasingly irrelevant as Kildare mobilized support in the Irish council and from Norfolk and Wiltshire, and Ossory, having secured the deputy's assistance against a common threat, now recognized the danger and set about recovering lost ground at court by developing contacts with the increasingly influential Thomas Cromwell.

During spring 1532 Kildare, Butler, Bermingham and Rawson were summoned to England: Bermingham and Rawson were examined before the council at Greenwich in May concerning the conduct of Skeffington, Kildare and Ossory. They had nothing to say in the deputy's favour, accusing him of serious financial malpractices, partiality, and faking musters. They exonerated Kildare, claiming that he had done good service until recently when provoked by Skeffington's favour for Ossory, and Butler deposed that the deputy was largely responsible for resurrecting the Kildare–Ossory feud. The king concluded that the lordship could be governed more effectively (and £2,000 a year saved) by reappointing Kildare and balancing this by inserting Butler into government as treasurer.[45]

Kildare took up office in August, along with a new chancellor, George Cromer, archbishop of Armagh, in place of the disgraced Archbishop Alen. Attempts by Alen to recover marchlands belonging to his see and increase episcopal revenues had involved litigation against the earl and influential supporters, and he was now troubled by Kildare and the council, to whom the king remitted the matter, for his accounts of £166 13s. 4d. received in 1529–30. Butler was soon edged out of the exchequer by William Bath's appointment as undertreasurer, and Kildare also settled his score with Skeffington 'whereof great mischief came', humiliating him publicly during a muster of his troops before their departure. The 'gunner' was then forced to wait on Kildare until the king's instructions arrived about a sizeable quantity of ordnance and military stores in his custody. Separate inquiries aimed to prove that goods seized for debt had been purloined by Skeffington or his servants, including the Archbishop's namesake, John Alen, formerly clerk of the council. Finally in October, Skeffington entrusted the ordnance to the council and retired to England to add his weight to the campaign begun by the Butlers for Kildare's recall: much of it was later available for use by Kildare's supporters in the rebellion of 1534–5.[46] By late 1532, therefore, the king was back where he had started, with no obvious alternative to a wilful deputy who was growing increasingly suspicious about the king's commitment to peace and good government in Ireland.

THE FAILURE OF HENRY VIII'S POLICY

The chief characteristic of royal policy in the years 1520–32 was its weakness. Henry's reluctance to spend money was a major factor in its failure. Frequent

45. Ellis 1995a, pp. 187–9; Quinn 1960–1, pp. 338–9; Ellis 1976–7, pp. 244–5; Ellis 1977, pp. 9–11, 16; PRO, C. 113/236, box 51, SP 60/1/150 (*LP*, v, no. 1061).
46. Murray 1989, pp. 1–16; Ellis 1995a, pp. 190–1; Ellis 1980c, p. 501 (quotation); Ellis 1986a, pp. 101–2; *LP*, v, nos. 398–9, 657, 779, 838 (10), 1207 (14–17), Add., no. 486.

changes of deputy followed from inadequate royal support and in turn exacerbated administrative difficulties, so that the lordship was worse governed at more cost to the king. Henry's experiments effectively weakened English power in Ireland: the Butlers and others were not strong enough to keep order in the Pale, and the king alienated crown lands in a fruitless attempt to diminish the sources of friction between the earls, so that by 1529 the Irish revenue failed even to pay ministers' fees.

Nevertheless, there are no clear signs that Henry regarded the problems of government there differently from earlier kings or that he was groping towards the post-1534 strategy of paying for an English governor and standing garrison. The contradictions in policy 1522–32 can be explained satisfactorily in terms of Henry's efforts to restore the stability disrupted by Surrey's expedition, Kildare's disgrace and feud with Ossory, and the intrigues of Desmond. Henry had probably developed a surer understanding of Irish problems by the 1530s and royal policy doubtless also weakened Kildare's position, as his determined efforts to regain office suggest, but complaints about Kildare rule alleged his abuse of power, not his ineffectuality as deputy. There is no evidence to support the traditional view that the gradual erosion of Kildare power after 1520 was forcing the king to look to new, more bureaucratic methods of government. Significantly, as late as June 1533 Kildare was granted a subsidy by parliament, at a time when the king had no direct interest in the lordship's finances; yet Surrey had failed to increase taxation and Skeffington had received no grant at all, both at times when Henry was directly concerned and anxious to reduce his financial commitments – an indication of Kildare's continued influence with the colonists. In northern England the Tudors had deliberately weakened the local standing of 'overmighty subjects' by depriving them of offices traditionally theirs, by attracting men into crown service and by developing the king's landed position as a counterweight to the magnates, but in Ireland no systematic effort was made to lift government above the level of competing local interests. Kildare was deprived of office during the years 1520–4 and 1528–32 and detained in England in 1519–23 and 1526–30, but not for this reason and, as became apparent in the 1534 rebellion, without much real impact on his power.

This is significant, for if instead of a periodic summons to the deputy to answer charges of misconduct the king had made a systematic and determined effort to reform government, he should have made progress by careful supervision and for less than his actual outlay during 1520–32. In fact there was little to suggest in 1532–3 that within two years Henry would be embarking on a new policy for Ireland. The Kildare rebellion was not a confused reaction to long-term factors making for change in government and society within the lordship, but the unintended product of a crisis in confidence between king and earl, shaped by the political events of 1533–4 against a background of suspicion and mistrust building up during the 1520s.[47]

47. See Ellis 1976–7, pp. 245–50 for this.

Court faction and the origins of the Kildare rebellion

In 1532 Kildare had mobilized the support of an influential court faction to recover the deputyship, but Henry again made no serious effort to secure his reconciliation with Ossory. Moreover, Norfolk's influence, even on Irish affairs, was declining, and by Christmas the task of supervising the deputy had been delegated to Thomas Cromwell. In view of Cromwell's use of these powers, this change subsequently appeared important, and when rebellion broke out Norfolk attacked him in council for mismanaging Kildare. Cromwell's strategy was opportunist and characterized by attempts to obtain objective reports about Irish affairs, to encourage direct communication with the king instead of through the deputy, and to build up his own patronage network in Ireland. By summer 1533, even Kildare's second wife was petitioning Cromwell to 'labour' the king secretly for the lease of a manor for her son which the earl intended for his heir. Yet much of the mistrust and resentment which these activities aroused in Kildare was no doubt because Secretary Cromwell countenanced the advances of his rivals, Ossory, Skeffington and Archbishop Alen, a fellow retainer in Wolsey's household, whereas Kildare continued to look to Norfolk and Wiltshire for support. As offices fell vacant, Kildare's critics were advanced: John Alen, formerly clerk of the council, was made master of the rolls, and a Butler supporter, Christopher Delahide, became justice of king's bench in a reshuffle following Chief Justice Bermingham's death. The earl could not even be sure of sustaining appointments to lesser offices in his gift. When, however, Chief Justice Dillon died in mid-1533, Kildare appealed to Wiltshire for support, asking him to stay any suit for the office 'unto such time as ye shall be further advertised by the council here', and if Delahide or Chief Baron Finglas petitioned for it he should use all means to prevent it because they were both 'assured unto the earl of Ossory'.[48] Thus although Cromwell was merely pursuing more systematically strategies already outlined by Wolsey and successfully tried elsewhere, their implementation became dependent on the outcome of a faction fight at court: Kildare did not regard him as a neutral figure.

In September, Kildare, Ossory and other officials were summoned to England and the council sent over recommendations for governmental reform and the appointment of an experienced English-born governor. Kildare was already under suspicion and after receiving a reprimand in late August he began transferring ordnance out of Dublin castle into his own strongholds. His response to the summons was to send his wife with excuses alleging that he was prevented from attending by an old gunshot wound received while supporting his son-in-law as O'Carroll, and of which in September 1534 he eventually died; and he continued to delay when Henry rejected these. He also ignored the king's warning, received about November, against removing more armaments from the castle. By then Kildare's dismissal had been agreed, Cromwell had drafted proposals for an extensive reshuffle of ministers, and letters had

48. For this and what follows, ibid., pp. 250–4, 264; Ellis 1995a, pp. 192–7; Ellis 1980c, pp. 500–5; Bradshaw 1977a, pp. 69–79.

gone out to certain Gaelic chiefs soliciting support for a new deputy. A proposal to send out the titular lieutenant, Richmond, was opposed by Norfolk, but the cost of a retinue commensurate with Richmond's status would hardly have commended the idea to Henry, and such was the distaste with which courtiers viewed service in Ireland that Cromwell had to fall back on Skeffington, now over 70 years old, who was 'scantily beloved' at court and quite unacceptable to Kildare.

The arrangements for Skeffington's return, however, depended heavily on the outcome of efforts to secure both Kildare's cooperation and a settlement between Ossory and Kildare. Either Cromwell took Kildare's acquiescence too much for granted, or he underestimated the difficulties confronting an outsider in governing without it, for as late as 25 July 1534 preparations were continuing for Skeffington's despatch with a retinue of only 150 men. Instead of troops to enforce royal authority, he was to go armed with a high-sounding pamphlet, *Ordinances for the government of Ireland*, containing proposals for administrative reform, and a written undertaking by Ossory to support the programme. The significance of the *Ordinances*, however, lay less in their content – a ragbag of instructions of the sort that most incoming deputies received – than in the attempt, through this first use of the press in an Irish context, to secure their wider observance. The will to enforce traditional remedies, not new solutions, was the ingredient hitherto lacking in Henry VIII's Irish policy.

By late 1533 events in Ireland were being overtaken by the political crisis arising from the king's divorce and breach with Rome, and the need to extend ecclesiastical policy to the lordship. The Imperial ambassador, alert for potential supporters of Queen Catherine, had begun to interest himself in Kildare's case, and the earl, now accused of treason, was understandably reluctant to obey the king's summons and risk a third spell in the Tower. He was persuaded, however, by the arrival of a commission empowering him to appoint a deputy to govern in his absence. By deputing in February his heir, Thomas, Lord Offaly, suitably advised, Kildare retained control in his absence. His opponents could only advise the immediate despatch of a successor, and Cromwell minuted accordingly 'a deputy to be sent into Ireland with all speed to set a stay there'. Kildare's infirmities hindered his examination but by May 'manifold enormities' in his conduct had been proved: he was refused licence to depart, but the king, learning that he was 'not like to live long' and no doubt intending to head off trouble from his connection, sent Offaly a summons with instructions for government in his absence. Kildare's response may well have been influenced by the fate of another Norfolk client through Cromwell's manoeuvrings: summoned to court to advise on negotiations for peace with Scotland, Lord Dacre had been arrested without warning and charged with treason for making private treaties with Scots enemies in wartime – precisely the same charge as had been levelled against the earl and his supporters in 1528. Indeed, Kildare's subsequent attainder, reciting that charge, was made retroactive to July 1528.

At one level, the removal of Dacre and Kildare was part of a major reorganization of Tudor provincial government which in the same month saw three new officials appointed to head the government of Ireland, Wales and the far north, followed by other measures to centralize control and reorganize the provincial councils. Yet the two lords were also victims of court faction: in the charged atmosphere of the Reformation crisis, the king became convinced that disaffected nobles were actually plotting against him, and he lashed out against the two magnates he suspected might be his most dangerous opponents. Yet Kildare got a messenger to Offaly advising 'that he should play the best or gentlest part, and . . . not trust to the king's council there' who would send him to England where his life would be in danger, but keep out of the way.[49]

On receiving the king's instructions, Offaly ostensibly complied by summoning a council for 11 June but, guarded by a retinue of horsemen, he used the occasion of his resignation as vice-deputy to denounce the king's policies before the council. There is no real evidence to support the traditional view that the rising followed a conspiracy by Kildare's opponents to goad Offaly into unpremeditated and rash rebellion by circulating a false report of the earl's execution with a similar fate in store for Offaly: this version was coined by the chronicler Stanyhurst in Elizabeth's reign in an attempt to exculpate the family after its restoration. Moreover, Offaly's denunciation and other acts of defiance which followed were probably not intended as outright rebellion but to put further pressure on Henry to confirm Kildare in his traditional office of deputy. Yet they came at a time when Henry was defying both pope and emperor and when Cromwell was steering through parliament a revolutionary strategy to make the king supreme head of a new national church: such 'pressure', therefore, was most unlikely to be construed as anything but open rebellion. Kildare was arrested and sent to the Tower and Offaly, too far committed to draw back, reacted by unleashing a full-scale rising. Archbishop Alen was now a marked man: captured by Offaly after his ship ran aground while leaving for England, he was murdered with his chaplains and servants on 27 July. This, followed by the siege of Dublin castle, marked the effective start of the revolt.

Rebel strategy and the Imperial response

Once the king had decided against compromise, the rebels' chances were greatly diminished. The Pale was too far from the centre of power to present any real threat, even had the king's overthrow been intended, so that their best hope lay in attracting outside support, particularly from dissident nobles on the mainland. Lord Darcy, a chief organizer of the Pilgrimage of Grace in 1536, was implicated, and the rebels evidently felt that they had other supporters and sympathizers in England and Wales. This was no doubt why Offaly claimed to be leading a catholic crusade against heresy, although within the lordship he also tried, somewhat inconsistently, to manipulate local dissatisfaction at royal misgovernment and to whip up regional loyalties and anti-English sentiments.

49. Ellis 1976–7, pp. 255–61 (quotations, pp. 256–7); Ellis 1995a, pp. 185, 194–9, 206, 211; Ellis 1995c, pp. 35–42; Ellis 1980c, p. 505; Ellis 1976, pp. 809–14; Bradshaw 1977a, pp. 69–93.

Following a proclamation that all Englishmen should leave Ireland immediately on pain of death, he 'spareth not to put to death man, woman or child which be born in England'; he denounced the king as a heretic and demanded an oath of allegiance to himself, the pope and the emperor. The crusade won him some support from conservative clerics in Ireland, and also considerable sympathy abroad and from English dissidents.

Outside Ireland it was widely believed that religion was the real cause of the rising: but the agents which Offaly, O'Brien of Thomond and, before his death in December, Desmond despatched to Charles V and Rome, and the three Imperial agents sent by Charles to Ireland, provided little more than prayers, promises and the odd shipload of arms. Nevertheless the king had no means of gauging Charles's intentions in his dealings with the rebels, nor how reliable were the reports from Ireland that an army of 10,000 Spaniards was on its way. He was therefore seriously worried, particularly since the rising took so long to bring under control; but in fact the army which Charles was preparing was for an expedition against the Turks which left for Tunis in May 1535. The emperor viewed the revolt chiefly as a fortuitous development which would ensure that Henry VIII did not combine with Francis I to attack him in the rear. Thus the wider significance of the intrigues with Charles V was that they encouraged the rebels to hold out when a tactical surrender might partly have retrieved their fortunes, and effectively reassured Henry that, despite the divorce, the emperor's aims fell well short of overthrowing the Tudor regime. In this way, as in others, the king was able to profit by his experiences in 1534–5 when dealing with what would otherwise have been the much more serious crisis presented by the northern Pilgrims in 1536.[50]

The siege of Dublin

Nevertheless, even without foreign support, the revolt was serious enough while it lasted. To replace Offaly, the Irish council elected as justiciar the aged Lord Delvin, now over 70, but Offaly brushed aside their feeble attempts to organize resistance: they were soon besieged in Dublin castle while two more rebel armies campaigned in Cos. Louth and Wexford. In early August, a truce with the citizens allowed Offaly to renew the siege from Dublin city. On the king's orders the citizens broke truce in September, and in a final bid to take the city and castle, Offaly besieged Dublin with 15,000 men. Many of the Pale gentry participated unwillingly, shooting headless arrows into the city, but the rebels did considerable damage, breaking into the city before being driven out again.

Until October the action centred on the siege, partly because of the political significance of the lordship's capital but also for control of the military stores there. Despite occasional reverses and periodic resistance from the Butlers, who also faced raids by Desmond, the rebels were gradually able to consolidate

50. Ellis 1976, pp. 812–16, 822–30; Ellis 1976–7, pp. 260, 263–5; Murray 1989, pp. 1–16; Ellis 1996b, p. 128. Ó Siochrú 1996 offers a reappraisal of foreign intrigues in the revolt.

their control over the Pale, Carlow and Wexford. Desmond, supported by O'Brien and the MacCarthies, held the south-west, and other Gaelic chiefs either supported Offaly for their own reasons or were inactive: resistance was largely confined to three urban centres, Dublin, Kilkenny and Waterford. It would probably have collapsed completely if Skeffington's relief army had been much longer delayed. Within the Pale, where very few were not 'personally with Thomas Fitzgerald, or gave him aid of men, money or victuals', rebel control was sufficiently secure as to be institutionalized: acquittances were issued for an aid levied towards the cost of the war, rents were collected, writs of summons required military service, and warrants were issued by Offaly in the style normally reserved for the king or his governor.[51]

The government was slow to appreciate the seriousness of the revolt and completely unprepared for it. It was not until late July that preparations began for a relief army of 1,500 men, and Skeffington, appointed lord deputy for life in a panic reaction, departed for Wales to recruit troops. Meanwhile the king, highly incensed and embarrassed by events, could do no more than parley with the rebels and circularize towns and individuals elsewhere in Ireland urging loyalty. Commissioners reached Offaly in late August and offered a pardon for himself and Kildare in return for his submission. Offaly's counter-proposals have not survived, but they were probably similar to terms negotiated with Dublin city in September: the citizens undertook to obtain Offaly's pardon and the deputyship for life. There is no reason to believe that Henry negotiated any more seriously with Offaly than with the Pilgrims in 1536, but any hopes he might have entertained of driving a wedge between the Palesmen and Kildare's retainers and Gaelic allies were vain because the Palesmen remained unconvinced of the government's determination to suppress the rising.[52]

The character of rebel support

As with most Tudor rebellions, the evidence is too thin to permit a detailed analysis of rebel support. The rising's feudal structure probably explains why only 156 names of those implicated have survived: 107 were Palesmen and their dependants (82 of at least gentry status, including eleven priests, seven knights and Lords Dunsany ad Trimblestone), the rest mainly Gaelic chiefs. Yet clerical participation in the revolt was certainly more extensive than these figures would suggest: at least 61 benefices were vacant after the revolt, mainly in areas where the rebels had strong support. Not all of these vacancies are attributable to government proceedings, but equally members of the secular clergy who were actually executed or deprived for preaching against the king or for other treasonable activities must have constituted a small proportion of the total involved, and there is no statistical evidence at all about the regular clergy's widespread involvement. Other prominent participants, such as

51. Ellis 1976–7, pp. 260–3 (quotation, p. 262); Ellis 1996b, pp. 128–9; Lennon 1989, p. 37; Ellis 1978b, pp. 192–4; Ellis 1980–1c, pp. 100–3.
52. Ellis 1976–7, pp. 264–5, 269–70; Ellis 1981c, p. 515; Ellis 1995a, p. 210.

Sir John Burnell or Sir Christopher Eustace, may also have felt threatened by Archbishop Alen's bid to recover his see's ancient property rights.

More predictably, Kildare's kinsmen and retainers provided substantial support, but an ostensibly more surprising group of supporters was the king's own officials in Ireland. In fact all but the eight most senior offices there were at the deputy's nomination, and Kildare had made recent changes in almost all of the central government posts: small wonder then that, notwithstanding the scanty documentation, a fair sprinkling of clerks and local officials participated. They were joined by a few leading ministers: Richard Delahide, CJCB, a victim of Cromwell's reshuffle, allegedly advised Offaly 'that he shall never come to his purpose except he ruffle the country', but later made his peace. Undertreasurer Bath, however, was tried and executed for having counselled the citizens of Dublin in negotiations for a truce that 'if the Englishmen come, you must do your best to resist them, and let us drink all of one cup'. Lord Chancellor Cromer soon retired to his archiepiscopal duties, advancing clerical supporters of Kildare. Henry replaced him with Trimblestone in August, but Cromer retained the great seal until Skeffington's arrival in October and Trimblestone, having sent troops to Offaly, later had to explain away to the king his attempt to bribe the constable with a safe conduct to surrender Dublin castle. Even Chief Baron Finglas, recently promoted chief justice, doubted the outcome of the siege: he was forced to resign when there came to light a secret composition made with Offaly to convey out himself, his servants and munitions.[53]

The royal army: composition, conduct and equipment

Almost three months after the initial decision to raise it, the arrival in October of a hastily improvised relief army transformed the situation. It eventually comprised around 2,500 men and (following reports that the rebels had captured the king's ordnance in Dublin castle) some powerful artillery (including two demi-cannon), and was probably the largest army sent to Ireland since Richard II's expedition of 1399. Yet it was much less formidable than it seemed: in particular, for a campaign in Ireland with mobility at a premium and few opportunities for a set-piece battle, it was not a balanced force. Difficulties in raising additional troops and in shipping the ordnance had also led to an unfortunate compromise whereby the army sailed in two parts, from Bristol and Chester. The Bristol contingent, comprising 800 footmen plus 100 mounted archers from Wales and the West Country, was intended mainly as a garrison, though it was too large for this. It reached Waterford in early October where it remained until cavalry could be sent down in December to escort it north. The Chester contingent of 1,600 men under the deputy was also predominantly from Wales. It was delayed a further fortnight awaiting shipping and money, then more troops and equipment, and finally the weather.

53. Ellis 1976–7, pp. 257, 268–70 (quotations, p. 266); Murray 1989, p. 15; Ellis 1976, pp. 815–22.

These delays meant a winter campaign, in which footmen could not effect-ively be deployed. Yet following peace with Scotland, half the 900 horse-men were mounted spearmen, veterans from the west marches and much the best troops in the whole army. Their experienced captains included Leonard Musgrave, constable of Penrith (who had previously seen service in Ireland under Surrey and Skeffington but was killed in the abortive landing at Howth Head), and Edward Aglionby (who had also served before under Skeffington), plus Thomas Dacre (newly released from the Tower) and John Musgrave whose transfer to Ireland was probably influenced by their recent rivalry during the Anglo-Scottish war. Yet there were too many mounted archers, including a scratch force from Wales. And long after their arrival, the troops remained poorly equipped and ill-disciplined, especially the Welsh: many longbows proved useless and new supplies were very slow in arriving, there was a great shortage of handguns, many of the horses had died in passage, and the com-panies were soon reduced by sickness and desertion. The troops spent much of the winter uselessly garrisoning the main towns. Skeffington himself lay ill for twelve weeks until March, and only following his partial recovery did the army take the field. Overall, therefore, the revolt was prolonged less by the strength of rebel support than by the failings of the royal army.

The conduct of the campaign

Even so, the despatch of an army showed that, contrary to precedent, the king intended to crush the revolt rather than to negotiate. Rather than risk a pitched battle which might prejudice his chances of outside support, the young earl of Kildare (his father had died on 2 September) withdrew to Maynooth, which had been prepared against a siege, and burned other parts of the Pale 'whereby he thinks to enforce this army to depart'. From then until his surrender in August 1535 Kildare became increasingly dependent on his Gaelic allies, and a rebellion which had effectively started as a demonstration of dissent within a context of overall obedience was transformed into a Gaelic war of independ-ence as chiefs supported Kildare against the threat to their autonomy posed by the royal army. Many Pale gentry had hitherto discerned little difference between this demonstration in favour of the king's usual representative and earlier passive resistance to Ossory as deputy or connivance in O'Connor's kidnapping of Delvin, but they now awoke to find themselves in arms against their anointed prince. Skeffington had Kildare proclaimed a traitor from the High Cross at Drogheda and most of the gentry soon came in, although even after his attainder by the English parliament in December they 'dare[d] not be earnest in resisting of him in doubt that he should have his pardon hereafter as his grandfather, his father and diverse his ancestors have had'.[54]

The one significant military event of the campaign was the ten-day siege of Kildare's principal castle of Maynooth which fell on 23 March. The army

---

54. Ellis 1996b, pp. 122–8; Ellis 1976–7, pp. 257, 268–70 (quotations, pp. 268, 269).

took the basecourt by assault after an artillery bombardment, but the constable was tricked into surrendering the great castle for a bribe, and Skeffington's reputation disappeared with the garrison's summary execution in what was long remembered as 'the pardon of Maynooth'. Thereafter the earl took refuge among the Irishry. His raids on the Pale had little more than nuisance value but were a serious embarrassment to the government because of the wide-spread publicity and sympathy which Kildare's actions had evoked outside Ireland: yet Skeffington's force was ill-suited to the task of hunting down rebels in the independent Gaelic areas.[55] Thus when the earl, despairing of Spanish aid, tried to open negotiations, the council willingly promised him his life.

Kildare surrendered on 24 August and was sent up to London to await his fate. The king, however, found this conditional surrender almost as embarrass-ing as the failure to apprehend him. Norfolk warned against the evil example that would be set if he were pardoned, but also that if he were immediately executed Lord Butler and the marshal of the army, Lord Leonard Grey, who was Kildare's brother-in-law, would lose their credit since they had pledged that he would be spared: relations with the Gaelic chiefs might be so ruptured by this breach of trust that the king would be forced into a general conquest of the country. Norfolk therefore advised a stay of execution, advice which was eventually followed.[56]

The aftermath: executions and reorganization

Nevertheless, there were other factors to be considered besides the king's honour and desire for revenge. Clearly some heads would have to roll, but without Kildare – the one magnate with sufficient resources to govern the lordship unaided – the king might be forced to maintain a regular garrison there for defence or even to conquer the whole country, an even more costly expedient. Henry was probably aware of this difficulty and the advantages of restoring Kildare after a decent interval, but against this the extension to Ireland of the Henrician Reformation and other important legislation would require the consent and cooperation of the lordship's political community at the forthcoming parliament: the council warned that if the Pale gentry were alienated by wholesale executions, the government's legislative programme might be jeopardized. These considerations eventually forced the king to limit executions and attainders to the ringleaders, while other participants were later permitted to purchase their pardons comparatively cheaply. Between January 1535 and May 1536 a handful of rebels were tried and executed, initially small fry *pour encourager les autres*: finally in February 1537, in the aftermath of the Pilgrimage of Grace, Kildare, his five uncles and Sir John Burnell were executed at Tyburn.[57]

55. Ellis 1974, ch. 3.
56. Ellis 1981c, p. 523.
57. Ibid., pp. 517–27 (quotation, p. 527); Ellis 1980c, p. 510.

The sentences meted out to the rebels have attracted the familiar chorus of condemnation from Irish historians, but in fact they were comparatively mild, even by Henry VIII's standards, let alone the bloodbath which followed the German Peasant War of 1525. Whereas 178 executions followed the northern risings of 1536–7, with perhaps three times as many executed following the 1569 revolt, the Kildare rebellion produced only about 75 executions, and 66 people (mostly the same) were attainted by common law or act of parliament. Fines for pardon from perhaps 250 more netted a mere IR£2,377 11s. 5d., and traitors' goods and chattels realized only IR£502 3s. 6d. These sums did not even begin to cover the cost of suppressing the revolt, reputedly £40,000; and in the longer term, although forfeited estates swelled crown revenues by nearly IR£1,250 per annum, the garrison needed for defence after Kildare's demise cost far more. In particular, the value of Kildare's own estates never recovered beyond a derisory IR£895 per annum. Without a resident lord to organize their defence, exposed marchlands were soon overrun; the earl's tributes from border chiefs disappeared; many lands were embezzled because his title deeds could not be found; and even the value of key estates like the manor of Kildare, worth IR£140 a year plus IR£39 allowed for thirteen horsemen for defence before 1534, was reduced to between IR£59 and IR£77 annually through destruction during the rebellion and subsequent Gaelic raids. The result was a renewed crisis of lordship and a 'decay of the borders'.[58]

In the wider context, the proceedings against powerful nobles in the mid-1530s – Kildare, Lord Dacre, the marquis of Exeter and the Percies – appeared to mark a major shift in Tudor policy from the crown's traditional reliance on local magnates in governing outlying regions to more bureaucratic methods. In both Ireland and the north, the king's councils were remodelled after major risings and controlled more firmly from London, while in 1539 a Council in the West was briefly established. All this was part of a broad policy, inspired by Cromwell, which aimed to integrate the borderlands more closely into a unitary realm of England. In Wales, the 1536 act of union abolished the distinction between the Principality and the Marches and extended English law and forms of administration throughout that country; in England, a second act of 1536 effectively assimilated liberties and palatinates into shire ground; and in Ireland, the suppression of the liberty of Kildare in 1534 (an additional source of resentment to the earl because no action was taken against Ossory's liberty of Tipperary), provided the first indication of this general policy. In the English outpost of Calais a series of reforms in civil and military administration followed the visit of commissioners in 1535; and between 1536 and 1543 Calais, Wales and Cheshire were also given representation in the English parliament. The lordship of course had its own parliament, though English legislation could be certified and implemented there (for example two attainders of Irish rebels in 1534 and 1536); but overall the changes suggested and implemented in government and religion in the mid-1530s were so much on a par with what occurred in other borderlands that they have justifiably been treated as part

58. Ellis 1981c, pp. 513, 527–9; Ellis 1995a, pp. 226–7.

of an integrated policy of 'Cromwellian reform', entitled in its Irish context 'unitary sovereignty'.[59]

Yet similar problems breed similar solutions, and we should be wary of the notion that Cromwell's interventions in Ireland represented the step-by-step implementation of a preconceived and comprehensive reform programme. For one thing, Cromwell could never rely on the king's unquestioning support: policy was always subject to the vagaries of faction at court and Henry could also be relied on to baulk at anything that involved increased expenditure. Moreover, there were substantial differences between the methods by which Henry's chief minister hoped to reform government in 1533–4 and what emerged after the government resumed forward planning in 1535. In the event, though Cromwell's plans precipitated fundamental changes in the structure and claims of government in the lordship, the overall effect was to alter the nature of the king's Irish problem and even to exacerbate it rather than to solve it.

With hindsight we can say that the basic change was the replacement of aristocratic delegation as the normal means of government by an English-born deputy with a standing garrison and controlled more firmly from London. The longer this policy of 'direct rule' continued, the more difficult it became to revert to the traditional methods, but as late as 1560 Queen Elizabeth considered reappointing an earl of Kildare as an economy measure. In 1535 the tenth earl's half-brother and next heir had evaded the government's clutches by fleeing to the Irishry: he was eventually restored as eleventh earl in Mary's reign, but in the interim Henry had retained the option of a Fitzgerald deputy by having the younger half-brother raised at court.[60] In theory at least, 'direct rule' facilitated royal control over the deputy, but without the following built up by Kildare a substantially augmented garrison was required for the Pale and, unless the king would bear the additional charge, a corresponding increase in revenue. A partial solution to this problem was conveniently at hand in the projected legislation in parliament. Preparations for a parliament recommenced in June 1535, but with Skeffington's death in December the meeting was postponed, and what is now known as the Irish Reformation Parliament met in May 1536 before Henry's new deputy, Lord Leonard Grey, and was dissolved in December 1537.

THE IRISH REFORMATION PARLIAMENT

Grey's parliament has received considerable attention from historians because of the unique survival of the original statute roll, because of its important ecclesiastical legislation (discussed more fully in Ch. 8), and because of the first appearance there of organized opposition to government policy which became so marked a feature of parliaments in early modern Ireland. The first session in May passed without incident: parliament enacted the chief statutes

59. Cf. Bush 1971, pp. 40–63; Elton 1977, ch. 9; Elton 1982, pp. 32–3; Bradshaw 1979a, ch. 5; Ellis 1986a, pp. 48, 152–4; Ellis 1981b, pp. 150–61.
60. Ellis 1980c, pp. 497–519 *passim*; Bradshaw 1981, pp. 313–15.

of the Henrician Reformation as previously passed in England and attainted Kildare and his accomplices. To facilitate the programme of governmental reform it also agreed to suspend the cumbersome administrative procedures laid down by Poynings' Law. Finally, three financial measures were passed: the parliamentary subsidy was renewed for a further ten years, an act for first fruits required bishops and secular clergy appointed to benefices to pay the first year's income to the crown, and a third act resumed to the crown the landed property of absentee owners – English religious houses, the duke of Norfolk and the earls of Shrewsbury and Wiltshire.

Nevertheless, the untroubled progress of the government's bills seemingly followed an understanding with the council that conformity would be rewarded by a recommendation to the king for a bill to pardon those involved in the rebellion. Henry, however, ignored the recommendation and directed parliament 'to devise how the charges that his grace hath sustained may be partly recompensed'. Three more money bills were introduced in September, to suppress some small and largely derelict monasteries, to resume the customs revenue of outlying port towns, and to establish a 5 per cent land tax. These bills had the effect of uniting different dissidents: the implied threat of more treason trials was ignored, the bills were rejected, and the Commons sent up a deputation to London to explain their position. After a further abortive session (Jan.–Feb. 1537) disrupted by a rumour of a Geraldine restoration, London accepted defeat. The customs bill was dropped, the twentieth land tax was modified to apply only to the clergy and so passed as the equivalent of the English clerical tenth, and the monasteries bill passed after local lawyers and gentry had been reassured that it was not the king's intention to deprive them of lucrative farms and stewardships or to discriminate in favour of the recently arrived English administrators and soldiers.

Thus by modifying his tactics in accordance with the anti-clerical initiatives of the English Reformation Parliament, Henry again made progress. Parliament readily accepted 'commonwealth' legislation for the public good, and an alliance of the crown with secular landed and legal interests overrode clerical opposition to further ecclesiastical measures; but proposals which would have strengthened crown interests at the community's expense were rejected: bills to impose efficiency qualifications on officials, and to bring the Irish currency into line with sterling and so increase the revenue by a third both failed.[61] Thus the Irish Reformation Parliament, like English parliaments of the 1530s, showed both the will and the ability to reject crown measures which it disliked.

CONQUEST OR REFORMATION: FINANCE AND THE POLICY DEBATE

Nevertheless, behind this debate about financing government lay a fundamental disagreement between the king and the Dublin administration about

61. Edwards 1968, pp. 59–84; Bradshaw 1968–9, pp. 285–303; Bradshaw 1979a, pp. 113–14 (quotation, p. 113).

the aims and methods of English rule in Ireland. In the aftermath of the revolt, Henry and Cromwell were bombarded with schemes for consolidating royal control. Irish councillors reported that Gaelic chiefs had been greatly impressed by the might of the king's army so that the time was now more propitious for conquest than in 200 years. A majority of the council favoured complete conquest, to be consolidated thereafter either by extensive colonization or (a cheaper option) by assimilation of the natives. The king, however, was more concerned to learn where the money for all this was coming from and sought an augmentation of the revenues before committing himself to deeper political involvement. In autumn 1535 Cromwell queried 'whether it shall be expedient to begin a conquest or a reformation'. This question went unanswered for over eighteen months as Henry discovered how far the colonial community was prepared to pay for conquest.

Immediately after Kildare's surrender, the army was reduced to 700 men, and soon after debased 'coin of the harp' (nominally fourpences sterling, called groats, minted in London and worth sixpence Irish) were surreptitiously introduced to pay them – the first resort to a policy which was to have disastrous consequences throughout the king's dominions. Perceiving the king's reaction to reverses in parliament, the council concentrated its efforts from summer 1536 on persuading him, as a minimum, to reduce the Gaelic lordships of the Leinster mountains. This would have freed troops defending the Dublin and Wexford marches, facilitated the holding of the Barrow valley, and enhanced the value of crown lands there. In the short term, however, it would also have entailed the maintenance of the existing garrison and new expenditure on castles to dominate the region. Yet for the year to October 1536 £15,000 was eventually provided from England to pay the army, although payment was so long delayed and the troops so mutinous that campaigning over the summer was limited and a hosting into Limerick disrupted. In fact the new revenue sources had little impact on government finances before 1536–7, but by mid-1537 the king had determined that the Dublin administration should restrict its activities to whatever the revenues there would bear.[62]

The King's commissioners, 1537–8

In September 1537 four high-ranking commissioners with powers similar to the Calais commission of 1535 arrived to inquire into and reform abuses in all aspects of government. The period between then and their departure in April 1538 represents the high point of crown involvement in administrative reform there during the reign, and Cromwell's exploitation of the opportunity in terms of patronage and policy-making is underlined by the fact that well over half his extant correspondence for the period consists of letters to the commissioners.

62. Bradshaw 1979a, pp. 106–17 (quotation, p. 107); Ellis 1980c, pp. 507–17; *StP*, ii, 316–17; *NHI*, iii, 408–9. Brady 1994a, ch. 1 includes a reappraisal of the relationship between Cromwell and Grey, arguing that Cromwell's engagement with Ireland was generally spasmodic and reactive, focused on reducing costs and building up a patronage network.

Yet the aims of this initiative were essentially conservative. Against the council's advice, the Dublin administration was to restrict itself to the reformation of the Englishry, to establish a fortified territory on the Calais model: there also the king claimed a much larger territory, the kingdom of France, but only exercised his sovereignty within the Calais Pale. The strategy vis-à-vis the Gaelic lordships would be the maintenance of traditional arrangements: the chiefs would be required to put in pledges to keep the peace, but otherwise there would be no interference. Within the Englishry, however, administrative reform would pave the way for an extension of central control not merely in the Pale but to the rest of English Leinster and Munster where even under strong governors royal government had been comparatively weak.[63]

Almost the first action by the commissioners was to reduce army pay and halve the garrison to 340 men which, it was unrealistically expected, would be adequate for defence and ensure an outright annual surplus of up to 4,000 marks (IR). Two hundred troops would normally accompany the deputy and treasurer, the remainder being posted in border fortresses about the Pale, the Barrow valley and south Wexford. In addition an attempt was made to strengthen the marches by regranting or leasing recently acquired marchlands to English soldiers or local marcher lords. There was no intended discrimination against the colonial community in this policy but, together with the distribution of parcels of confiscated land by way of reward to loyal administrators both English and Irish-born, the effect was to create the nucleus of a distinct New English party which, potentially at least, posed a threat to the Pale politicians by keen competition for the patronage available: hitherto English captains and clerks like Francis Herbert and Thomas Agard had usually departed with the English governor who had brought them. Moreover, parliament was employed to strengthen the colony by re-enacting certain of the Statutes of Kilkenny to recall subjects to their duty: they were to forsake Gaelic customs, lords of marchlands were to reside there, and marriage and fostering with the natives were to be more strictly regulated. In government the commissioners' activities uncovered a whole series of administrative malpractices, a few of which elicited legislation in parliament while others were attended to by less formal means. In this way some financial savings were made and peculation reduced, but in general the investigation did not produce significant reforms.

Continuing financial and military weakness

The revenue administration in particular was subjected to serious criticism by three experienced English officials led by Chief Baron Walsh who visited Ireland as survey commissioners in 1540–1. The king rejected any measures which cost money: proposals sponsored by Cromwell to strengthen government, either by increasing the traditionally low ministerial salaries to attract men of higher calibre or by creating additional posts, remained unimplemented. Thus a central administration which for almost a century had in practice controlled

63. Bradshaw 1979a, pp. 117–21; Brady 1994a, pp. 15–16.

directly only the Pale with a more general oversight elsewhere was suddenly expected to enforce the ecclesiastical changes and govern the entire lordship in accordance with the higher standards now demanded in England but without any worthwhile increase in staffing. Nowhere is the incongruity of this more strikingly illustrated than in the contrast between the new revenue courts established in England to administer the king's new accession of wealth and the position in Ireland where an unreformed exchequer remained the sole debt-collecting agency: yet the moneys which the exchequer was charged with collecting increased fivefold between 1534 and 1542. Cromwell's supervision of the central administration thus produced piecemeal change rather than revolution on the basis of a coherent, planned reform programme.[64]

In terms of local government, the Pale perhaps benefited from having a deputy less directly involved in local politics, so that justice was less frequently manipulated to private ends; but the region certainly suffered from the quartering of the garrison there. The various forms of military exactions known as 'cess' fell increasingly heavily on the Palesmen after 1534 (see Ch. 7), and the irregularly and ill-paid troops also tended to recoup themselves from the inhabitants. English soldiers also proved much less effective outside the open country of the Pale, and cost more than Gaelic troops: the government soon learned the wisdom of maintaining a permanent retinue of Gaelic troops, rather than hiring them for occasional campaigns, and Kildare's kerne and galloglass eventually passed into crown service.

Beyond the Pale the dissolution of the monasteries gave the government a much larger stake in maintaining English law and order, particularly in Cos. Waterford, Wexford, Kilkenny and Tipperary. Partly in consequence, the deputy, councillors and commissioners travelled round the lordship at least once annually from 1535, surveyed the king's new revenues and held sessions. Yet these itinerations, though more intensive, were no novelty and not necessarily very effective in bringing great lords into dependence on the Dublin administration, if only because the latter lacked the resources to replace the magnates as the focus of stability and defence against Gaelic chiefs and other sources of disorder. Ormond (Ossory recovered this title in 1538) actively supported military expeditions into Gaelic Ireland but was unable to prevent all his numerous kinsmen from terrorizing the countryside; the government's attempts to arbitrate between rival claimants to succeed the eleventh earl of Desmond (d. 1534) and so quell disorders had little success; and in east Ulster the lordship built up by the earls of Kildare virtually disappeared. Throughout the English districts large parcels of crown lands, particularly in the marches, were listed in a survey of 1540–1 as destroyed during the rebellion or waste because no-one would live there for fear of the Irish nearby.

Plainly, with the reduced garrison available from 1537, the Dublin administration was unable to defend its landed acquisitions as effectively as their previous owners. Landed revenue climbed spectacularly from IR£400 in 1533–4

---

64. Bradshaw 1979a, pp. 117–33; Ellis 1996b, pp. 132–5; Ellis 1995a, p. 231; Ellis 1980c, pp. 507–17; Bradshaw 1974, pp. 181–3.

to IR£3,100 by 1537, and continuing monastic dissolutions pushed up the nominal valuation of total revenue to IR£4,950 annually in 1537 and no less than IR£7,450 by 1542, but actual receipts fell increasingly short of these valuations: they rose from IR£1,600 to average IR£4,000 a year 1534–7 and IR£4,500 annually 1537–40, but since the ordinary annual charges of government from 1537 were still almost IR£4,400, the administration gradually sank into debt.[65]

LORD LEONARD GREY AND THE GERALDINE LEAGUE

Nemesis, however, was not far away. Grey, a military man like Skeffington and Surrey, was an unfortunate choice to preside over Cromwell's administrative reforms. Directed to keep the peace, reduce the garrison and raise revenues, his best hope of achieving these contradictory objectives was a *rapprochement* with the now leaderless Geraldines. He was gradually drawn into Kildare-like progresses through Gaelic Ireland in a bid to extend royal authority, and ironically his very success with his small retinue led to his downfall. Making skilful use of the royal artillery in difficult terrain, he destroyed O'Connor's new castle at Dangan in Offaly in 1537 and recovered Athlone castle; in 1538 he attacked the MacMahons in Farney, invaded Offaly again and made a longer journey to Galway. In 1539 he journeyed to Armagh and through Munster; and in February 1540 he even reached Dungannon, plundering the heart of O'Neill's lordship. Gaelic chiefs suing to the deputy for peace had to agree to unwontedly severe terms by way of tribute and homage, but Grey's aggressive actions gradually convinced the chiefs, unaccustomed to dealing with a resident English deputy, that the king intended conquest, while councillors complained about useless and expensive journeys. Concurrently Grey's attempt to build up a following for himself by courting the Geraldines alienated the Butlers, who had profited from Kildare's fall, and elicited Lord Butler's famous charge that 'my lord deputy is the earl of Kildare newly born again'.[66]

In reaction, leading Gaelic chiefs banded together to form what is misleadingly called the Geraldine League. Its instigator was Manus O'Donnell, the able young lord of Tyrconnell (1537–55), who married the widowed Eleanor MacCarthy, aunt and guardian of Gerald, the fugitive Fitzgerald heir. O'Donnell thereby acquired some diplomatic leverage against the rival O'Neill chief, Con Bacagh, who had earlier helped to secure his succession. Though Kildare's restoration (and Grey's recall) was the League's nominal aim, unlike in 1534 it was primarily a Gaelic movement with a strong religious dimension (a reaction to the Reformation campaign in the lordship). These developments were potentially very disturbing to the crown. The alignment of O'Neill (Kildare's traditional Ulster ally) and O'Connor Sligo with O'Donnell was a departure from the traditional dynastic mould of Gaelic politics, and with the adherence

---

65. Ellis 1980c, pp. 508–18; Ellis 1995a, pp. 226, 228–9.
66. *StP*, iii, 32; Brady 1994a, pp. 18–21.

of O'Brien of Thomond, O'Connor Faly and many secondary chiefs, the League almost assumed the proportions of a national movement. In August 1539 the Ulster chiefs invaded the Pale, sacking Ardee and Navan and driving off large numbers of cattle. Grey pursued them with half the garrison and Pale levies, surprised them at dawn at Bellahoe, south of Carrickmacross, and routed them.[67]

This ended the immediate threat, but the League did not, as experienced observers expected, then collapse. With Fitzgerald's departure to the continent in summer 1540 and the withdrawal of the Desmond pretender, James Fitz John, and his subsequent recognition by the crown as thirteenth earl (January 1541), the movement became a purely Gaelic phenomenon, but in spring 1540 its leaders proposed to transfer allegiance to the king of Scots. In the event it required a fundamental change of royal policy to disarm the League, a change which followed the arrival of a new deputy, Sir Anthony St Leger, in July 1540. Despite Grey's victory at Bellahoe, the government's strategy was ruined by the events of 1538–9. The king relented and sent over in November 1539 money and reinforcements, and in April 1540 he agreed to increase the wages of troops there. Summoned to court, Grey departed in April to face a long list of treason charges, but the decisive event was the fall of his patron, the king's chief minister, Thomas Cromwell, on 10 June. Grey's arrest followed two days later, leaving the way clear for a new initiative: he pleaded guilty and was executed in June 1541.[68]

ST LEGER'S ADMINISTRATION

St Leger's appointment marked a significant departure from the long line of military governors for Ireland. The head of a prominent Kentish family, the new deputy was essentially an administrator with considerable experience in local government including service as commissioner in Ireland in 1537–8. The basic constraints on the operation of royal government remained the same, even though, unlike many of his successors, St Leger frequently deferred to local politicians for ideas about a long-term solution to the lordship's problems and, at least in terms of stimulating local support for government, was much the most successful English governor of the period. The main features of the new initiative had been suggested in 1537–8, though they accorded broadly with the king's ideas of twenty years earlier; and since, after Cromwell's fall, the Irish administration enjoyed unwonted freedom in determining policy, there followed a speedy and effective response to the crisis of the League.[69]

---

67. Bradshaw 1979a, pp. 174–80; *NHI*, iii, 44–5.
68. Bradshaw 1979a, pp. 179–85; Brady 1994a, pp. 22–5; Ellis 1980c, p. 516.
69. Bradshaw 1973, pp. 264–5 n. 8; Brady 1994a, pp. 25–33. Except where otherwise stated, the rest of this chapter is based on Bradshaw 1979a, pt. iii (modified by Brady 1979, pp. 177–81; Ellis 1980–1a, pp. 78–81). An important critique of Bradshaw's arguments is Brady 1991, and see also Brady 1994a, ch. 1.

Surrender and regrant

The basic aim was to incorporate the Gaelic lordships by consent into a new, fully anglicized kingdom of Ireland comprising the whole island. To this end the Gaelic chiefs had to be induced to hold their lands of the king and the king to forgo many of his ancient but unrealizable feudal claims (a concession which he had refused in 1520) in return for full recognition of his sovereignty. In effect he was to remit what could only be enforced at enormous cost in return for a general acceptance of the status quo and the prospect of stability and a secure patrimony. The initial steps in this programme, to bind individual Gaelic chiefs to cooperate, closely resembled the traditional methods by which governors sought to protect the lordship and which were anyway urgently necessary. Soon after his arrival St Leger mounted a campaign in south Leinster, reducing MacMurrough, O'More and O'Connor to peace. Throughout the next year he reconciled Desmond and Burke of Clanrickard to the crown and brought all the major Gaelic lords to terms, including finally the most important of all, O'Neill, who had rebuffed diplomatic advances in March and May 1541 and only submitted in December after a winter campaign. Each of these chiefs bound himself by indenture to recognize the king as his liege lord, to apply for a crown grant of his lands and a peerage, and meanwhile to attend parliament and resist papal jurisdiction.

This indenture comprised the first stage of what historians have called the policy of surrender and regrant. It was followed by detailed negotiations between government and individual chiefs and the precise terms agreed were then incorporated into another indenture to be signed by the chief before the grant of a charter. By this second indenture the chief agreed to renounce his Gaelic title – the use of the patronymic alone – in return for an English one, to accept, assist and obey the machinery of royal government – courts, writs and laws – throughout his lordship, to do military service and pay rent as specified, to adopt English customs and language, and to encourage tillage, build houses and generally reorganize the socio-economic structure of his territories on more English lines. The charter which he then received granted the lands of his lordship to him to hold of the crown by knight service in perpetuity. Finally, the third phase of the process involved arbitration upon the rights and obligations of the lord vis-à-vis his vassals, kinsmen and other landowners in order to resolve conflicting claims: this was achieved by binding them to him as mesne tenants by a process of subinfeudation. At the same time dynastic alliances under the Gaelic system of clientship were dissolved and disputes between rival chiefs settled.

The implementation of the new programme

Had it been implemented in full, this programme might very well have accomplished a gradual reduction of Gaelic Ireland to English ways at minimal cost. In practice it was suspended in late 1543 when no more than well begun, and in the interim the difficulties of negotiations with individual chiefs and the serious misgivings of Henry VIII himself slowed progress considerably. The initial negotiations were conducted without reference to the king: with St Leger's appointment the Cromwellians on the Irish council lost ground and his right-hand man was Thomas Cusack, a local administrator who was Commons' speaker in the 1541–3 parliament and rose to be lord chancellor in 1550. Bishop Staples of Meath was also influential. While St Leger was campaigning against the Kavanaghs, the king and privy council advised by Norfolk and certain Irish councillors were decreeing exemplary punishment for the Leinster Irishry which contrasted sharply with St Leger's conciliatory handling of chiefs as they submitted.

The reconciliation with Desmond in January 1541, however, required no substantial concessions by the king and could be exploited to influence public opinion. After the recognition of James Fitz John as earl, he signed an indenture similar to that with Ossory in 1534 agreeing to the revival of royal government in his territories and renouncing a liberty which he claimed not to attend parliament. This event was witnessed by the council, four royal commissioners from England, the archbishops of Dublin and Cashel, O'Connor, Clanrickard Burke and some 200 'Irish gentlemen' at Sir Thomas Butler's impressive castle of Cahir. St Leger and Desmond then set out in the snow for Limerick, which received a Desmond earl for the first time in half a century and where negotiations began with Burke and O'Brien of Thomond. Cusack subsequently remarked that 'the winning of the earl of Desmond was the winning of the rest of Munster with small charges'.[70]

The second chief manifestation of the new policy was the parliament which met at Dublin in June 1541 and was continued in eight sessions until November 1543. Preparations for parliament began soon after St Leger's arrival; and on 18 June was enacted a statute to alter the royal style from lord to king of Ireland, so symbolizing the projected revolution in the infrastructure of the medieval lordship. A public holiday and general amnesty for prisoners were proclaimed and the act was promulgated in St Patrick's cathedral, followed by high mass and *Te Deum* attended by 2,000 people, cannonades, bonfires and free wine. The act had originally been proposed by Bishop Staples in 1537 and was justified on two grounds, although until recently historians have seen the act largely as Henry VIII's own initiative in conjunction with religious reform. The preamble justified the act on the grounds that

> lack of naming the king's majesty and his noble progenitors kings of Ireland . . . hath been great occasion that the Irishmen and inhabitants within this realm of Ireland have not been so obedient to the king's highness . . . as they of right and according to their allegiance and bounden duties ought to have been.[71]

In this connection the Irish council pointed out that following a twelfth-century papal grant, sovereign temporal jurisdiction in Ireland was commonly

70. *NHI*, iii, 49 (quotation).
71. *Stat. Ire.*, i, 176; Quinn 1941b, pp. 157–69; Bradshaw 1979a, pp. 233, 264–5; *NHI*, iii, 46–7.

regarded among the Irishry as residing in the papacy: the king's title as mere 'lord of Ireland' seemed to confirm this and encouraged the search by disaffected magnates for an alternative overlord, while the breach with Rome added to doubts. In fact Henry argued that his title to Ireland, as to England, rested on original conquest, and he was very careful – even to the point of ordering a re-enactment of the bill in 1542 with revised wording – to ensure that the act should seem to acknowledge an existing right to sovereign powers long enjoyed rather than appear as a parliamentary grant of new powers. Yet the main reason for the change, which the Irish council failed to spell out, was to affirm the king's new relationship with the Gaelic lords as determined by surrender and regrant.

No sooner had the act passed than Cusack departed for court to explain its full implications, carrying recommendations for legislation and detailed proposals about the initiative already under way. The privy council learned that if the Gaelic population were 'accepted as subjects, where before they were taken as Irish enemies', this would be 'the chiefest mean, by good wisdom, to continue them in peace and obedience'.[72] Instead of the island's effective partition – the political structures, customs and law of the Gaelic parts unrecognized in the lordship and vice versa – there should be a new kingdom of Ireland embracing the whole island and all its inhabitants, governed by English law and institutions, and with the Gaelic population enjoying full constitutional rights under the crown as did the English. Unfortunately, however, wider control required more money from England, at least in the short term.

The negotiations and submissions

Undoubtedly the implications of these proposals were revolutionary, both for royal government in Ireland and for Anglo-Irish constitutional relations. Whether, in practical terms, the actual changes amounted to a 'constitutional revolution', as a leading Irish historian has claimed, shall be considered in the next chapter, and its more general impact on Irish identity is discussed in Chapter 10. Nevertheless, the whole episode is a striking illustration of the extent to which royal control of policy had slackened since Cromwell's fall. A local reform group lobbying for a royal initiative to impose order throughout the island had finally succeeded in committing the crown to just that, despite repeated rebuffs in 1494, 1520 and the mid-1530s.

The king was furious: he roundly rebuked the council for devising 'by an act, to invest in us the name and title of king of Ireland' when the revenues there were not 'sufficient to maintain the state of the same', and he immediately withdrew concessions on surrender and regrant to which he had just agreed.[73] Nevertheless the deed could not be undone, so St Leger's strategy received

72. *StP*, iii, 326.
73. *StP*, iii, 331.

provisional acceptance as the most economical means of incorporating Gaelic Ireland into the Tudor state, and Henry concentrated on driving a harder bargain with Gaelic chiefs to cover costs. The deputy and council were instructed to distinguish in negotiations between border chieftaincies who 'lie so far upon the danger of our power, as you may easily bring them to any reasonable conditions that may be well desired' and more distant lords less easily expelled from their territories who might, if pressed by 'extreme demands, . . . revolt to their former beastliness'.[74] The council replied that albeit in civil countries full constitutional status undoubtedly implied full financial responsibilities by the subject, such a policy would be politically alienating in Ireland. They therefore concentrated on fixing a heavy obligation to military service and a light rent, in accordance with the socio-economic structure of individual lordships: as a concession to Henry token subsidy contributions were demanded (his project of 1520 for a transitional hybrid legal code was also resurrected), but the waiving of customary blackrents was compensated by the grant of royal pensions. After eight months of resistance, the king relented in April 1542, agreed to relinquish on these terms his feudal titles to land in Gaelic occupation, and accepted St Leger's assurances that forbearance now would eventually yield ample financial and political benefits with the gradual emergence of a more stable, ordered and prosperous society.

The actual submissions and issue of charters were carefully staged at court. Desmond preceded the Gaelic lords, visiting court in June to be reconciled with the king: he was well entertained, rewarded handsomely with money and English apparel, and licensed to depart after a week 'for defence of his parts'.[75] O'Neill's arrival in September created an even bigger stir. The king had baulked at creating him earl of Ulster, 'being one of the greatest earldoms of Christendom, and our proper inheritance', but he received the earldom of Tyrone:[76] two Magennises accompanying him were knighted without receiving charters since negotiations with them were uncompleted. The propaganda opportunities of the occasion were also exploited by printing copies of O'Neill's submission, and the French ambassador duly reported home that the greatest lord of the savages who all his life had made war on the English had come to do homage. The next such visit, in June 1543, saw O'Brien and Burke created earls of Thomond and Clanrickard respectively and MacGillapatrick – created baron of Upper Ossory by St Leger in June 1541 before the king had reserved to himself consideration of all applications for tenure – was knighted along with William Wise of Waterford and three secondary Thomond chiefs, MacNamara, O'Grady and O'Shaughnessy. By then, however, Henry was becoming preoccupied with impending war against France and a project to annex Scotland. St Leger dissolved parliament in November, visited court for talks between January and June 1544, and then had to await the conclusion of the wars for further progress.

74. Dunlop 1902, pp. 299, 300 (quotation).
75. *StP*, iii, 389.
76. *StP*, iii, 366.

St Leger's parliament

Nevertheless, while it lasted, the St Leger–Cusack initiative made remarkable progress towards a settlement of the Irish question, particularly in view of the problems faced. Perhaps the clearest indication of this was the proceedings in parliament, although the extent of local support for government was also striking. With the enactment of the bill for the kingly title, the style 'this realm of Ireland' replaced 'this land of Ireland' in legislation and official correspondence, and statutory references to 'the king's Irish enemies' also disappeared. Apart from this act, parliamentary legislation was not especially important, although the tally of 28 statutes enacted despite Poynings' Law suggests a degree of cooperation which was somewhat exceptional and certainly unrepeated in subsequent Tudor parliaments. A further suppression act was passed (see below, p. 213); the parliamentary subsidy was renewed for a further ten years; and Meath, the largest of the medieval counties since the suppression of Duke Richard's liberty of Trim, was divided into the shires of Meath and Westmeath to facilitate administration.[77]

Far more significant, however, was the unprecedented appearance in parliament of Gaelic lords, a striking manifestation of the administration's attempt to create a united kingdom of Ireland.[78] Only Lord Fitzpatrick of Upper Ossory – so created two days before parliament met – sat as of right during the first session, but others attended or sent proctors in response to St Leger's invitation. O'Reilly and, later, O'Connor and Burke of Clanrickard came in person and proctors appeared for MacMurrough, O'More, O'Brien, and disaffected O'Carrolls and O'Neills. The government also rewarded with peerages and monastic lands the service and support of four English gentry families: Thomas Eustace, Viscount Baltinglass, William Bermingham, baron of Carbury, Oliver Plunket, Lord Louth, and Richard, Lord Power of Curraghmore took their seats in the Lords; as did some other peers of ancient stock who had seldom, if ever, attended – Desmond, and Lords Barry, Roche, Fitzmaurice and Bermingham.[79] Thus parliament appeared a far more representative assembly, and an attempt was also made to utilize its administrative and judicial powers to strengthen royal control, to extend participation in government, and to reconcile native and settler. For example, in 1542 short sessions were held at Limerick in February 'to confirm the obedience of the earl of Desmond and many others in those parts' and settle disorders there, and at Trim in June where O'Neill and his vassal-chiefs sought parliamentary arbitration.[80]

Surrender and regrant: the initial Gaelic response

An earlier generation of nationalist historians condemned surrender and regrant as a cynical attempt to sow discord between chiefs and explained its appeal

---

77. Bradshaw 1974, pp. 122–3; Quinn 1941b, pp. 157–69.
78. Bradshaw 1979a, pp. 238–40.
79. Ibid.; Bradshaw 1974, pp. 190, 241; *StP*, iii, 307.
80. *StP*, iii, 311.

to them in terms of bribery: the grant of an English title converted the chief's life interest in his lands into a freehold, while reducing other landowners to tenants-at-will, and the replacement of tanistry by primogeniture deprived his kin of their claims to succession in favour of his common-law heirs. In reality the advantages to the chief were not so clear cut. In a country where power was frequently more important than secure title and certain succession, there were disadvantages in too rigid a succession law, as many Anglo-Norman families had earlier discovered to their cost. St Leger's supporters certainly did not regard primogeniture as a selling point, but they hoped that by the third generation it would be accepted. Meanwhile the tanist was preferred if clearly stronger: thus in Thomond O'Brien's brother, Donough, was created baron of Ibracken with right of succession, and later succeeded the earl without difficulty; but in Tyrone, where O'Neill's eldest but illegitimate son, Matthew, was made baron of Dungannon, his tanist, Shane, later disputed the succession.[81] On the question of tenure, it was never St Leger's intention to weaken the titles of other landowners, even though King Henry once suggested that in return for confirmation of their own titles chiefs should connive at reducing the status of 'meaner gentlemen'.[82] Much later Hugh O'Neill claimed that O'Cahan was his tenant-at-will, but this anomaly resulted from the abandonment of an uncompleted programme. In fact the deputy intended the appointment of commissioners to arbitrate on the division of landholdings and supervise sub-infeudation, as is clear from projected arrangements concerning O'Reilly and O'Toole's countries.

Directly after the king authorized grants of tenure and title, St Leger began negotiations to stabilize internal political relations within individual lordships. For Ulster, arbitration between O'Neills at Trim during a 1542 session of parliament was followed by an agreement in 1543 over the Bann fishery between O'Neill's client, MacQuillan, and O'Donnell's client, O'Cahan, whereby both quitclaimed their rights to the crown in return for pensions; and in July O'Neill and O'Donnell appeared before the council in Dublin and concluded a settlement of their differences, while efforts were also made to resolve a succession dispute in Tyrconnell preparatory to surrender and regrant there. In south Leinster agreement was reached with the Kavanaghs about a settlement of that region, and immediately afterwards the deputy and council departed for Limerick and Galway 'to establish some good orders in those parts whereunto we have been specially required by the earls of Thomond and Clanrickard'.[83] The upshot was an afforced council attended by most of the magnates of Connaught.

Irish troops in Scotland and France

Thus the St Leger–Cusack initiative was making progress, despite the programme's ambitious nature and the enormous problems involved both in

81. Canny 1976, pp. 33–4.
82. Bradshaw 1979a, p. 204 (quotation).
83. *StP*, iii, 486.

retaining royal support for a long-term policy against rival schemes proposed by other factions, whilst at the same time maintaining comparative order throughout the country during the lengthy and difficult process of negotiating with individual lords. Furthermore, the outlook remained encouraging even during the politically more difficult final years of the reign. The English garrison had been reduced to just over 500 men by 1542, but despite strong rumours of foreign invasion or interference no special measures were considered to secure the country during the wars with France and Scotland, and the magnates of outlying parts showed no inclination to resume the foreign intrigues of 1520–40. Indeed, following a suggestion by St Leger, the king decided in March 1544 to raise 1,000 Irish kerne for service in France and Scotland. The Irish council, headed in the deputy's absence by Lord Justice Brabazon, found difficulty in complying speedily with this unusual order, but the earls of Ormond, Desmond and Tyrone, and O'Reilly were persuaded to contribute 500 men, and the rest were raised in smaller numbers from Leinster lords and gentry, Gaelic and English.

The force sailed for England in early May. Six hundred kerne served in France at the siege of Boulogne, prompting French protests that they beheaded prisoners, and 400 were sent north to terrorize the Scots. The French contingent was mostly discharged by October, but in summer 1545 the king decided to recruit a further 2,000 kerne to invade Scotland, and instructed St Leger in September to recruit 'out of the most wild and savage sort of them there, whose absence should rather do good than hurt'.[84] The troops, including 100 of the regular garrison, were scraped together with great difficulty by mid-November – 'for we think, this 200 years, so many men were not embarked and victualled here'[85] – and under the earls of Lennox and Ormond eventually reached Dumbarton. Political developments in Scotland prompted their immediate withdrawal and disbandment, but until 1550 the Edwardian government, short of manpower, also retained Irish contingents in its French and Scottish garrisons.[86]

Thus, by raising troops for service abroad, the Dublin administration cleared the country of disruptive elements, involved the Irish nobility more widely in the business of state, and also supplied the king with tangible proof of the potential value of a reformed Ireland. When St Leger was recalled in spring 1546 he convened an afforced council attended by Desmond, Thomond, Tyrone and the Leinster chiefs to ensure peace in his absence: Cusack could plausibly report that 'those which would not be brought under subjection with 10,000 men, cometh to Dublin with a letter' so that the country 'was never in so good case, nor nothing like, for honest obedience'.[87] Yet, despite Ireland's comparatively peaceful appearance, circumstances again conspired to disrupt a promising initiative and to destabilize politics there at a time when government

---

84. White 1957–8, pp. 213–25 (quotation, p. 223); Ellis 1990–1, p. 306.
85. White 1957–8, p. 223 (quotation).
86. Bush 1975, p. 35.
87. *StP*, iii, 563.

policy was seemingly at last bearing fruit. Irish opposition to St Leger's initiative, disappointment at its relatively slow progress, and financial considerations were all significant forces for change, but the main cause was Henry VIII's death in January 1547. Occurring only seven months after peace with France had permitted a resumption of St Leger's initiative, the king's death also spelled the death of the initiative, for the regency council of his young son had other plans for Ireland.

POLITICAL TENSIONS IN THE DUBLIN ADMINISTRATION

With hindsight, historians have detected a sharp conflict of interest between Old English and New English officials in the Dublin administration after 1534. Both groups stood to gain from conquering Gaelic Ireland, but English-born officials needed to consolidate their influence in Ireland by acquiring land there; and though crown leases of monastic land provided a worthwhile start, the acquisition of Gaelic land seemed in the long term more promising. Thus, the New English had a vested interest in promoting conquest by colonization. The established settlers, however, stood to benefit more by a peaceful reduction of Gaelic Ireland, utilizing their greater familiarity with native customs to consolidate and extend the existing colonial ascendancy with minimal disruption: coercion would require more troops and English officials and so weaken the administration's dependence on local support. Under Elizabeth political opinion did eventually polarize on these lines, with an Old English elite harking back to St Leger's programme and a New English party urging military conquest and colonization. Yet the main aim of the early Tudor period was to commit the crown to conquest; it was far from clear that conquest would tie down vast reserves of English money and manpower (many officials persisted in thinking that the Gaelic lordships would put up little resistance to a serious reform programme); and it would be a travesty to see government officials as motivated solely by 'class' interests.[88]

In fact St Leger was opposed by some Irish-born officials, notably Robert Cowley, master of the rolls, and also had English supporters, including John Goldsmith, clerk of the council, and Thomas Agard, the undertreasurer's chief clerk. What the evidence seems to suggest, as has recently been argued, is that St Leger was attempting to build up a 'King's Party' as a counterweight to traditional factional alignments. In 1546, when St Leger and Ormond were summoned to court to resolve a quarrel which had developed between them, Lord Chancellor Alen laid a series of charges supported by other councillors against the deputy. The St Leger–Ormond differences were resolved, Alen lost the chancellorship, was imprisoned and his charges dismissed, and the deputy returned to Ireland; but within a few months Henry was dead and St Leger was again vulnerable.[89] Moreover, surrender and regrant frequently provoked

88. Brady 1980, p. 27.
89. White 1964–5, pp. 198–200; Brady 1980, pp. 82–3; Brady 1994a, pp. 30–3.

serious disputes because constitutional arrangements did not always reflect the real distribution of power within and between lordships. Particularly in south Leinster the original settlements often broke down and forced St Leger to revise the arrangements.[90] Progress was slower than the deputy had expected, and he attempted to force the pace by recommending the establishment of regional councils for Munster and Connaught and then garrisons for Leix and Offaly, while his private secretary, John Parker, later established a small colony near Carrickfergus. Lord Justice Brabazon's expedition against O'Connor in summer 1546 may have been intended to develop this policy rather than to sabotage the deputy's programme, as has been suggested: despite differences of temperament, Brabazon and St Leger got on reasonably well together and were probably in collusion over financial malpractices. Nevertheless, Brabazon had been more closely identified with Grey's administration and was criticized by St Leger over his handling of O'Connor, so that in effect the expedition amounted to sabotage.[91]

The financial deficit and administrative corruption

As always, the administration's failure to balance the books was a powerful influence on London for change. In 1542 the government of Ireland had cost almost £9,700, but leviable Irish revenues were estimated at only IR£7,450 (£4,967), leaving the king to foot a deficit of almost £4,700. These figures proved fairly typical of St Leger's first deputyship, with expenditure remaining constant, except for 1545 when troops for the Scottish campaign added some £5,000, and Irish revenue declining slightly as arrears increased.[92] Yet at the outset St Leger had had great difficulty in persuading the king to accept even a short-term deficit, and now five years on there was no sign of any improvement in Irish finances. Instead it seemed that Henry's initial fears had been justified: in return for empty promises of fixed rents, crown titles to vast estates, particularly in Ulster and Connaught, had been compromised by St Leger's programme – and in the case of Powerscourt manor, Co. Dublin, lands recovered from the O'Tooles by the earls of Kildare were actually handed back.[93] Fortunately for the deputy, however, the proposals of his rivals held out only vague prospects of long-term gain after heavy initial costs.

Yet it was not only slow progress and the need to conciliate Gaelic opinion that prevented St Leger from making ends meet: part of the reason for his regime's popularity with the local community was its policy over leases of crown land. Brabazon as undertreasurer 1534–51 was at best slack and probably dishonest. He survived one investigation in 1540–1, but then allowed arrears of IR£18,640 to mount up between 1540 and 1547 and leased crown lands at or below the valuations of the 1540–1 survey commissioners. These

90. Brady 1980, pp. 72–9.
91. Ibid., pp. 78–80, 85; Bradshaw 1979a, pp. 243, 258; White 1964–5, pp. 198–9.
92. Carew, i, no. 176; LP, xviii (i), no. 553; BL, Add. MS 4767, f. 71; White 1964–5, p. 208; Bradshaw 1979a, p. 262 n. 13; Brady 1980, p. 88.
93. Bradshaw 1979a, pp. 201–5.

surveys recorded only current values (i.e. nil if waste), not values when leased, and some leases were even made at net values after deductions for monastic pensions had been made, despite the crown's continued payment of pensions.

Those who profited most from this strategy included, predictably, Brabazon himself, St Leger and his brother Robert, Parker, Cusack and Agard, though many others benefited directly or indirectly. In 1554 a commission of inquiry estimated that crown revenues had been depleted by over IR£2,100 per annum by undervalued leases alone. Thus Irish officials, Pale gentry, and those magnates who occupied monastic property but paid little or no rent for it had more than merely an ideological commitment to St Leger's programme. Brabazon died in 1552, a wealthy knight, but charged (with Andrew Wise, his 'Old English' son-in-law, latterly joint undertreasurer) with IR£12,000 owing on his account of 1551; Wise later convinced Mary's government that St Leger really owed most of this, as well as almost IR£5,000 in arrears on his own landed interests on his recall in 1556; and in the conflicts with the government in the 1560s, the most effective spokesmen of the Palesmen were Parker and Agard's son, Francis, who with other 'New English' officials had long since been assimilated into Pale society.[94]

Nevertheless the administration's financial malpractices were not revealed until long after Henry VIII's death. What determined the deputy's recall was the coup by which Edward VI's uncle, Edward Seymour, duke of Somerset, seized power in the regency council in 1547 and St Leger's identification with the rival conservative faction. Thus Irish policy in 1547 was again set to follow a new direction, reacting politically to the failings of surrender and regrant and also promoting a staunchly protestant religious settlement.

TUDOR REFORM: THEORY AND REALITY

Between 1520 and 1547 the nature of Tudor government in Ireland was fundamentally altered and its claims over the inhabitants vastly extended. Following developments in England, successive statements of policy and individual administrative decisions by the king indicated rising royal expectations about the levels of public order and control within the English districts. Henry increasingly demanded that the higher standards now obtaining in England should be extended to the lordship. In practice the increased demands on governors who lacked additional resources indirectly undermined political stability in English Ireland and precipitated rebellion, so forcing the king to increase his commitments there. In political terms the transition from aristocratic delegation to direct rule was successfully effected by Cromwell, but militarily the position remained unstable until Gaelic opposition to an English governor and garrison was exorcized by St Leger, and despite the king's best efforts the lordship's financial self-sufficiency was never restored. In turn, however, the government's

---

94. Brady 1980, pp. 84–96; Brady 1994a, pp. 33–40; White 1964–5, pp. 209–10; Lascelles 1852, i, pt. ii, 42–3; BL, Add. 4767, ff. 75v–78; Bradshaw 1974, pp. 181–3.

response to political instability and rebellion, coupled with developments in England, presented it with new problems. Where Cromwell had envisaged governing outlying English districts like the Pale, St Leger's programme also committed the crown to the reduction and anglicization of the whole island. Again, the extension of the Henrician Reformation to Ireland created problems of enforcement in the lordship in the 1530s and throughout the island thereafter, although as will appear, the conservative reaction in 1540 and St Leger's own conciliatory approach on matters ecclesiastical minimized the government's difficulties in this sphere in Henry VIII's last years.

In sum, the Tudor regime was by 1541 embarked in Ireland on what was administratively a highly ambitious policy, even though governmental resources there were notoriously inadequate and had not been substantially increased after 1534. Indeed, perhaps the main reason why the policy did not immediately break down, but on the contrary began rather well, was the emphasis on economy rather than rapid progress: in particular the king unwittingly assisted in this by vetoing on financial grounds all attempts to force the pace. Nevertheless, when under Edward VI the government attempted to impose a protestant religious settlement while at the same time adopting a more aggressive approach towards Gaelic Ireland, it was quickly confronted with a massive problem of enforcement. Before discussing this, however, a more extended consideration is necessary both of the operation of royal government in Ireland and the nature of the problems which it now faced in enacting and enforcing religious reform.

CHAPTER 7

THE GOVERNMENT OF TUDOR IRELAND

The Tudor period witnessed a profound alteration in the character of royal government in Ireland. In its structure and operation, the Irish administration was in 1500 a small-scale replica of its English counterpart. By 1600, however, its continuing institutional development on English lines disguised some growing contrasts in the essential nature of government. Tudor rule in Ireland developed some of the absolutist characteristics of contemporary continental monarchies, though constitutional changes and administrative reforms also meant that by 1600 the Irish administration was somewhat better adapted to govern the whole island.[1]

THE OFFICE OF GOVERNOR

The Dublin government c. 1500 still claimed jurisdiction throughout Ireland. Indeed royal governors were occasionally able to elicit recognition by Gaelic chiefs of the English king's sovereign rights as lord of Ireland, but in practice the ordinary administrative institutions were geared to govern the main areas of English influence. The aims of government were limited and traditional, ministering justice to the king's subjects, defending his patrimony from external threats, and maintaining such internal order as would inhibit any serious challenge to royal authority. Naturally the lordship's remote geographical position within the Tudor territories and its relative unimportance lowered royal expectations of government there. Even by English standards, resources were decidedly limited and did not even extend to the proper government of the entire lordship. The king was generally satisfied if the administration governed the Pale effectively, discouraged serious Gaelic raids, and exercised a more general oversight of the other English parts: anything more would have required subventions from England.

Unlike the councils recently established to govern the north and Wales, the Dublin government was a complete executive competent to deal in all aspects

1. Except where otherwise stated, this chapter is based on Ellis 1986a.

of the lordship's administration, though subordinate to the Westminster government. The governor, advised by a separate Irish council, was, in the king's absence, both head of the civil administration and military commander of a turbulent border area with a sizeable standing force. The standard Tudor viceregal styles were lieutenant, deputy, and justiciar (popularly 'lord justice'): these had earlier denoted distinct gradations of authority but had since become largely honorific. After, and perhaps because of, York's viceroyalty, the lieutenancy was normally reserved before 1536 for absentee royal princes, and thereafter rarely conferred; most governors were deputies (or deputy-lieutenants), with the justiciarship being a temporary appointment frequently made by the council pending a deputy's appointment. The ambiguity of the Dublin administration's status, as both a subordinate central government and an instrument of provincial government, was reflected in the king's choice of governor. For all but nine years of the period 1470–1534 the effective head of the administration was a Pale magnate. This reflected a deliberate royal decision for economy rather than close control, but it also accorded with the principle of 'self-government at the king's command', which was a hallmark of the English tradition. The king aimed to limit opportunities for misconduct, but this was not always easy without denying his governor essential governmental powers. After 1534 the governor was almost invariably English-born, though the king paid dearly for such additional control as this conferred: like Kildare, long-serving Elizabethan governors pre-empted decisions by manipulating the channels of communication, so precluding the crown from considering what were viewed in Dublin as undesirable options.

The governor's powers were in 1470 little short of those exercised by the king in England, but they were gradually reduced thereafter. Until 1479 the crown had normally limited its commitments in Ireland by farming the lordship to a magnate with local interests: a Talbot, Ormond or Kildare would be retained as governor for a fixed term, serving at his own cost for a fixed salary from England and whatever was available from the Irish revenues. With Edward IV's abandonment of this traditional indenture system, however, deputies were usually appointed during the king's pleasure. Kildare's appointment for ten years (1496) and Skeffington's for life (1534) were unparalleled in Tudor times, although later experiments with programmatic governors (1556–78) almost amounted to a revised indenture system. Before 1534 local magnates had no assistance from England but received the revenues without account; and English governors were supported by English troops and money but had to account for all expenditure.

Edward also took steps to protect the autonomy of the council and chief ministers. Deputies had customarily granted for life important offices carrying a seat on the council, but in 1479 the practice of reserved appointments was revived (see above, p. 78), and Edward also ordered that nothing should be taken as an

act of council, unless the king's lieutenant or his deputy give his assent thereunto by the advice of the more part of the king's council there, 'the more part' being defined as the seven chief ministers (see above, p. 78).[2] In 1478 the nomination of bishops and archbishops was likewise reserved. Edward thereby recovered potential control over the Irish executive, but a determined deputy could still get his way: as late as 1533 the council was allegedly 'partly corrupted with affection towards the earl of Kildare and partly in such dread of him' that they would not oppose his wishes.[3]

The statute of 1494 stipulating that judges and financial officials should hold office during pleasure further strengthened royal control, though the king frequently licensed exceptions. With the increasing practice of appointing ministers by English patent (*ultra vires* in Dublin), this diminished the need for reserved appointments, though all the leading offices were reserved from 1520. In practice the device was of limited value as a check on viceregal activity: Henry VIII vainly used it in attempting to curb the Geraldine–Butler feud in the 1520s, but it did provide the king with additional patronage, and after 1534 there was less need to strengthen a governor's local influence in this way.

From 1494 there were also other restrictions on a governor's powers. He had no power to pardon treasons touching the king's person or counterfeiting the coinage, and increasingly conciliar approval was necessary in pardoning serious offences. He could no longer alienate the crown's landed rights nor grant licences in mortmain. He required licences to hold parliament or introduce bills there. A licence was also required to appoint a deputy if he went to England for talks, but this power almost disappeared after 1534: instead the council elected a justiciar if there was a vacancy, for instance through his death in office or the crown's demise. The precise election procedure varied (see above, pp. 76, 83, 94), but a statute of 1542 forbad the election of a cleric and stipulated an English-born councillor (preferably) or two councillors 'of English blood and surname':[4] given the opportunity, the crown frequently nominated a lord justice after 1534.

With the ousting of local governors in 1534, Irish offices were integrated more closely into the English patronage network, and there occurred a profound change in the status and powers of the governorship. Though the traditional indenture system had long been abandoned and viceregal powers reduced, the essence of the relationship between the king and a magnate like Kildare had remained unchanged: the earl still contracted to govern in return for a share of royal patronage and profits, and successive kings had merely revised terms in their favour. Indeed the system even helped to mitigate the king's absence which in an age of personal monarchy was a major disadvantage of royal government in Ireland. By contrast, later governors were more recognizably salaried officials with far more limited sources of patronage directly at their disposal, although, particularly under programmatic governors like Sussex and Sidney, this transition from provincial viceroy to bureaucratic

---

2. Close roll, 19 Edward IV m. 7d (Gilbert 1865, p. 599; *62nd Report of the Deputy Keeper of the Public Records in Ireland*, p. 569).
3. *StP*, ii, 179.
4. *Stat. Ire.*, i, 207–8. For the later period, see now Crawford 1993, pp. 32–3.

president long remained neither fully appreciated nor, because of the weakness of Irish administrative structures, properly enforced. Nevertheless Lord Deputy Grey was keenly aware of the difference, and in a letter to Henry VIII in 1536 he contrasted his own meagre powers and allowances with those of former governors accountable for the revenue. Previous deputies, he lamented, had appointed farmers of crown lands, customs and other revenues, and used

> to grant liveries of lands, sell custodies of wardships thereof and grant pardons for all manner offences (treason unto your person only excepted), give licences, placards, and all other things that here belong unto your grace's authority . . . The service and obedience of your subjects that should grow unto me

by such powers, he felt, was worth 100 men. Nevertheless, Grey who had 'by your grace's letters patents the same authority that others hath had' had 'no intromeddling accordingly' and so had 'but the name only of your deputy'.[5]

The early Tudor system was cheap and undemanding. The king needed only to ensure that defence was adequate and government not too faction-ridden: but as the experiments under Poynings and Surrey demonstrated, the successful implementation of the post-1534 system depended on the introduction of a much tighter system of control and accounting. Kildare long appeared so indispensable in government because his connection in the Pale enabled him to govern more economically than others. His replacement, even by another local magnate, entailed increased expenditure, a fact which the king found difficult to grasp. In 1522 Lord Deputy Ormond observed that because the revenues were so small, he would have to reward good service with offices, and requested the king not to appoint absentees or alienate further the revenues. In 1534 the deputy designate, Skeffington, complained that warrants drafted for offices reduced his patronage whereby 'I shall neither have profit, strength, love nor thank'.[6] Nevertheless from 1534 governors received a fixed salary, paid through the Dublin exchequer, and the garrison was likewise maintained. Where Lord Grey had indented in 1478 to serve with 300 archers for £2,000 in the first year and £1,825 in the second, in 1540 St Leger received a salary of 1,000 marks with the garrison in wages. Later deputies received more: Croft's salary in 1551 was £1,000, and from 1558 Sussex and then Sidney each received £1,500. Justiciars had traditionally received £500 annually, but the usual salary after 1534 was 100 marks per month.[7]

In practice, however, the resumption of English subventions and the increasing priority accorded from 1534 to military operations in Ireland also raised the standing of the governorship and other posts there: Irish warfare might be small-scale and underfinanced, but by Elizabeth's reign it was almost the only regular theatre of warfare in which nobles and gentry could make their reputations. Unfortunately, however, this development contributed substantially

5. PRO, SP 60/3/168 (*LP*, xi, no. 932).
6. *StP*, ii, 198.
7. Lascelles 1852, i, pt. ii, 1–2; BL, Add. MS 4767, f. 81; *Carew*, i, no. 214; Canny 1976, pp. 45, 52.

to a growing discontinuity of policy. Kildare governed successfully because he was well acquainted with conditions and allowed scope to shape policy in accordance with general royal aims and the limited resources available. Skeffington was twice appointed largely because he was almost the only courtier willing to serve, but by the 1550s the governorship was a coveted office: ambitious novices were being commissioned to implement preconceived programmes, they were controlled far more closely by the privy council, and were increasingly prey to faction both at court and in Ireland.[8]

THE IRISH COUNCIL

The changes in the nature of the governorship in the 1530s also strengthened the council's role in government. There is little evidence about the composition and functions of the council in late medieval Ireland, but until 1494 it was certainly less prominent than its English counterpart. The seven chief ministers, councillors *ex officio*, provided the nucleus of the Tudor council, and this inner circle of lawyers was in Ireland institutionalized by Edward IV's ordinance of 1479 concerning conciliar acts. Particularly under an English governor, however, military captains, the governor's close confidants or royal nominees were admitted even if they held no high office, but since councillors were normally unpaid there was little incentive to attend until the mid-Tudor expansion in the council's role brought increased opportunities of political patronage. By then, however, the earlier undifferentiated council had been succeeded by a distinct privy council and other conciliar courts dealing with particular aspects of the council's work. Medievalists have used the term 'privy council' to denote an inner circle advising the governor on daily administration, but the establishment of a privy council with executive functions only occurred in 1520. Of course, given the circumstances of Irish administration, the council was sometimes hurriedly assembled in Dublin to deal with some emergency while the governor was away campaigning, but from the 1520s the privy council with the chancellor as president regularly transacted business in the deputy's absence, and its growing importance is attested by the experiment in 1529–30 of appointing an executive 'secret council' of three ministers to replace the deputy.

Nevertheless, despite these developments, until 1534 Kildare by his personality was often able to govern as before. It was only with the advent of English governors, coupled with the closer control exercised by Cromwell, that there emerged fully in Ireland the characteristic omnicompetent Tudor privy council, supervising the established courts, receiving and implementing instructions from London, and issuing orders and proclamations in connection with political, military, religious or economic matters. In 1547, the date of the first surviving list of privy councillors, the council's composition resembled the inner circle of 1479, namely, chancellor, archbishop of Dublin, bishop of Meath,

8. Brady 1980, pp. 55–61, 112–14. See now also Brady 1994a, pt. 1.

undertreasurer, both chief justices, chief baron, master of the rolls and a puisne judge, and it evidently remained predominantly ministerial throughout the Tudor period: after 1556 the council doubled in size, partly because of the inclusion of important military men and leading magnates. Down to 1578 the council numbered between 18 and 24.[9]

Its executive functions distinguished the Tudor privy council from both its Yorkist predecessor and its counterparts in other national monarchies of western Europe, and that Irish developments should have anticipated Cromwell's initiative in establishing a privy council in England was understandable given that the king had perforce to delegate most of his executive powers there. Yet, for twenty years at least, two manifestations of the council can be traced at work: for example in 1536 the privy council informed Cromwell that

> except it be for a urgent affair, the whole general council cannot assemble continually together: and over that the matter sometimes may be such as peradventure it is necessary that none shall be privy thereunto but the privy council.[10]

The continuance of a larger governing council alongside the privy council was probably an attempt to associate leading magnates and gentry with government while not restricting the control of king, governor and privy council over policy. As in England the parliamentary peers regarded themselves as the king's natural councillors, and under the later Tudors such sentiments received attenuated expression in the practice of summoning distinct afforced and great councils in connection with the governor's request for purveyance for the garrison and certain other military matters (afforced councils) or to declare a general hosting (great councils).[11]

Clerks and seals

The council was served by a clerk traditionally drawn from chancery but in early Tudor times often the deputy's personal secretary. This presumably created few problems when the council usually attended the deputy, but from 1494 the law courts were normally sedentary at Dublin, making it difficult for the council's lawyers to meet outside Dublin in term time. A second problem arose from the fact that the governor's private seal, kept by his secretary, doubled as a second royal seal: the king's great seal of Ireland, in the chancellor's custody, gradually lost its original force and was increasingly reserved for authenticating the more formal administrative instruments, such as royal grants and commissions. By 1494 a second writing office, separate from chancery, had been created which was now the mainspring of government. In 1479 the king had again unavailingly ordered the chancellor to keep terms in Dublin to seal original writs, but with chancery's development as a court of equity after

9. BL, Add. MS 4801, f. 222*v*; *Carew*, i, nos. 193, 195, 206, 214, 218. Cf. Quinn 1967, p. 97; Crawford 1993, pp. 37–52, app. 4.
10. *StP*, ii, 395.
11. Quinn 1967, pp. 97–102. Crawford 1993, pp. 61–9 has suggested that this distinction between afforced and great councils may be too arbitrary.

1494 its itineration with the governor became increasingly difficult. In England this problem of authenticating orders had been solved by introducing additional royal seals and clerks. The chief secretary kept the signet and resided at court; the keeper of the privy seal attended the council; and the chancellor and great seal were normally at Westminster with the courts. Orders requiring more formal authentication were channelled through the privy seal office and chancery: a signet warrant or conciliar fiat was filed in the privy seal office for each item passing that seal, and chancery both filed privy seal warrants and formally recorded the text of each grant or commission on patent or close rolls. Since they conveyed royal orders, these seals also warranted instructions for Ireland – now the more valuable because the Dublin administration's own records were largely destroyed in 1922. Yet financial considerations prevented the introduction *mutatis mutandis* of this system in Ireland: instead existing institutions were adapted piecemeal.

The governor's orders were written in his name but in the royal style and sealed with the governor's seal – a weakness which was graphically illustrated when Lord Offaly continued to issue such warrants during the 1534 rebellion. Warrants to the chancellor, known as 'fiants', were filed in chancery, but inadequate record-keeping seriously impeded administrative efficiency. As in England, chancery kept patent and close rolls, but grants and commissions were frequently not enrolled to save expensive parchment, and older rolls were cannibalized. Furthermore, no proper records were kept of items passing the governor's seal, and when they departed deputies often took their papers with them, despite suggestions that the clerk of the council should keep them. Thus crown rights were concealed and revenue reduced. Under local governors such disorders and embezzlement was inconvenient, but not much more; magnates like Kildare were more concerned to foster local support than ruthlessly to exploit royal rights. After 1534, however, inadequate records and the continuing shortage of trained clerks seriously hindered efforts to balance the books. Nevertheless, patent and close rolls were better written and other records more systematically preserved. A proper distinction was made between the governor's private secretary and the clerk of the council. Finally in 1560 Elizabeth was persuaded to appoint a secretary of state for Ireland, with custody of a new royal seal, the signet, with which to seal all letters requiring the deputy's warrant. This restored the monarch's explicit authority to such warrants, and the chancellor was forbidden to issue chancery letters without them. In practice, however, the signet was more akin to a conciliar privy seal, and the secretary's role was less important than his English counterpart.[12]

THE JUDICIAL SYSTEM

The common law and the bench

The common law system also saw important developments in Tudor Ireland. In 1470 the lordship's legal system remained much as it had been in 1300: 50

12. Ellis 1978b, pp. 187–94; Crawford 1993, pp. 72–7.

years later its structure had been brought more closely into line with the English system, at a time when the common law overall was beginning a period of fundamental change. These developments created a more flexible system and greatly facilitated the Dublin administration's response to Gaelic law and custom following surrender and regrant. Yet the government's aim was not so much the speedy imposition of impartial justice as to encourage nobles and gentry to resort to law instead of violence and to enforce certain minimum standards which would prevent serious disturbances. In this strategy considerable progress was made before 1534, but under Elizabeth the increasing paralysis of the courts in the face of mounting disorder betrayed a general breakdown of government.

The Irish legal establishment was modest, with around ten established posts for common lawyers, though many others received regular work as justices of feudal franchises, on the regular panel for judicial commissions, or from 1569 on the provincial councils. There were normally two judges on each bench and three exchequer barons, though additional puisne judges were occasionally appointed; and in chancery the master of the rolls was by the 1530s accounted a judge of the four courts. Additionally there were the king's attorney, and a single king's serjeant-at-law and solicitor-general, though from 1537 a separate solicitor-general was appointed.

In general they were poorly paid and depended heavily on fees from litigants: contemporaries both English and Irish thought that Irish-born judges were less learned and more corrupt than Englishmen and there were constant complaints about standards. Lord Chancellor Gerrard asserted in 1577 that 'there were but shadows and shows of justice and judges even at the court at Dublin in term time, much more in sessions abroad'. Barnaby Barnewall (JKB, 1461–92) acquired a reputation for maintenance, wrongful amercement, and procuring vexatious writs and malicious indictments. Nevertheless from 1494 the more specific charges of flagrant corruption declined, following a reorganization of the judiciary. Hitherto the puisne judges had frequently been ill-trained and were rarely promoted chief justice; exchequer barons were regularly recruited from clerks there and were usually skilled more in exchequer methods than the law; and the chancellorship was a political appointment. Thereafter a single career structure was gradually created, although it was not until c. 1534 that common lawyers wrested the top chancery posts from clerics. The mid-Tudor bench enjoyed a fairly high reputation, and increasing numbers of gentlemen's sons attended the Inns of Court in London.[13]

From 1494 the Irish bench included a sprinkling of Englishmen. The chancellor was invariably an Englishman from 1555 – including Elizabeth's exceptional archbishop of Dublin, Adam Loftus, lord keeper for six years altogether during 1573–81, chancellor 1581–1605, and three times justiciar – but despite the ongoing struggle for control of the executive there was until 1603 no settled policy of excluding local lawyers in favour of better-trained outsiders.

13. McNeill 1931b, p. 114 (quotation); Ball 1926, i, pp. 104–53, 231–40; Canny 1975, pp. 13–14.

Nevertheless, complaints about the partiality and ignorance of judges both English and Irish-born increased in the 1560s, although their inactivity was then a more serious problem. Chief Justice Plunket (CJQB, 1559–83) and Chief Justice Dillon (CJCB, 1559–80) were both about 70 when appointed: Lord Deputy Sidney considered them too old in 1567 but yet less inactive than Lord Chancellor Curwin ('speechless and senseless'), the master of the rolls, Henry Draycott ('a very sick and a weak man'), or Chief Baron Bathe ('sick and impotent'), 'so as I am no sooner returned from any journey . . . but that causes of all these courts by swarms fly in unto me'. The notorious trial and execution for treason in 1582 of Nicholas Nugent (CJCB, 1580–1) marked a nadir, and to prevent further feuding among the Palesmen representations recommenced for the appointment of English lawyers; but it was only after 1591 with further Dillon–Nugent feuding that the local ascendancy on the bench was finally broken.[14]

The four courts and litigation

The royal courts in Ireland were generally structured on the English model, but the peculiar conditions of government prompted significant procedural differences. The ancient courts were also hampered by an inadequate mesne process to compel defendants' appearance. In criminal cases indictment before a grand jury led to arrest or outlawry for non-appearance; in civil cases the plaintiff purchased an original writ from chancery giving the desired court cognizance of the case and distresses of defendant's property then secured his appearance; otherwise arrest or outlawry followed. Though formidable in appearance, this process was quite cumbersome in practice, and Elizabethan administrators, aiming for quick results, sometimes overstepped the law. Actions had to be brought in the county in which the cause of action arose, so that arrest was easily evaded by moving to another, even if the sheriff troubled to search properly; and distresses were so trivial (rarely exceeding 2s.) that any freeholder could afford to ignore the first few writs. King's bench had overall charge of criminal cases, including all matters touching life and limb, though powers were regularly delegated by commissions of oyer and terminer and of gaol delivery: in Ireland it tried proportionately more ordinary cases itself and until 1494 still itinerated round the Pale. In the enforcement of royal rights and penal statutes, the exchequer exercised a parallel jurisdiction, proceeding on information or by inquisition: it also appointed special commissioners, but until 1534 exchequer itinerations were not unknown either.

A major weakness of the criminal law system was that many comparatively minor offences carried the death sentence: juries were therefore noticeably reluctant to indict or convict their neighbours. Twenty-five defendants in felony and treason trials in king's bench in 1485–6 were all acquitted, though juries were less lenient with misdemeanours. Nevertheless, even if indictments were malicious, to stand trial was still a hazardous business. The criminal law was

14. Ball 1926, i, pp. 141–2 (quotation); Crawford 1993, p. 104.

far from a dead letter. Before 1534 offenders were punished principally through the purse as governors raised money and curried favour by compounding for pardons. Although felons and traitors were sometimes executed, there were complaints of the evil example whereby 'poor wretches, not having lands ne goods ne friends' had 'the extremities of justice', while the wealthier were pardoned. In dealing with disturbances and rebellion under Elizabeth, how-ever, a determined judge with a jury handpicked by a compliant sheriff could do much to pervert the course of justice: Lord President Perrot of Munster, a military man without legal assistance, commonly despatched 30 felons and traitors at sessions held in 1571–3.[15]

Civil litigation was equally ponderous. The vast majority of cases were merely continued from term to term as the antiquated procedure in mesne process ground its course. In Michaelmas term 1466 the common bench passed judgement in eight cases out of around 165 pending and in only ten cases during four terms, 1479–80, though many cases were no doubt settled out of court.[16] Nevertheless the Irish courts were no more dilatory or ineffective in this than the English. In both regions the ancient courts were losing business to newer tribunals, a trend partly concealed by a general upswing in litigation; though in Ireland the overall pattern was further distorted by the relative weakness of government, which had precipitated an early and more rapid decline of the ancient courts and accentuated the rivalry for a larger share of a declining market. Nevertheless the Pale gentry at least were just as litigious as gentry in England: in the mid-1460s roughly 600 civil actions per term were pending in king's bench, 425 in the exchequer, and 165 in common pleas.

In contrast with the balance at Westminster, king's bench (still peripatetic) was the busiest and had already developed a cheaper form of process analog-ous to the action by bill of Middlesex. The exchequer, still confined to revenue cases in England, also attracted much civil litigation by a similar procedural device based on the writ of *quo minus*. Thus the common bench, specializing in civil suits, found itself almost ousted by courts which had earlier specialized in crown pleas and revenue cases. After the judicial reorganization of 1492–6, however, there followed a significant rise in the business of the ancient courts, with common pleas and the exchequer overhauling the now sedentary king's bench.

Local courts, councils and commissions

Nevertheless cases coming before the central courts were proportionately few. Many local courts – manorial courts, county courts, sheriff's tourns – were still very active with minor litigation in early Tudor times, though much less so even in the Pale under Elizabeth.[17] More importantly, cases which would otherwise have come before the central courts were regularly heard in the

15. *StP*, ii, 192; Canny 1976, pp. 102–3.
16. Ellis 1984b, pp. 21–9.
17. Cf. Canny 1976, p. 18.

localities by itinerant commissioners, so avoiding constant travel to Dublin by jurors and the delays and inconvenience this involved. In Ireland, however, the procedure of *nisi prius*, whereby cases begun at Westminster were dismissed for trial in the locality, was not introduced before 1534. Instead Pale suits generally came before the central courts, and elsewhere annual general commissions were appointed with wide administrative and judicial powers over both civil suits (as commissioners of assize) and criminal cases. In both areas the system was regularly supplemented by special *ad hoc* commissions. The system had its weaknesses, but it was cheap: outlying shires often received no more than a hasty annual visit, and Palesmen were 'much troubled in oft coming to Dublin'. In 1537 Chief Justice Luttrell urged 'all matters except urgent causes to be tried by *nisi prius* except matters within the same shires where the courts do sit', and within a few years justices went on circuit round the Pale as in England.[18] Nevertheless the disturbed conditions deterred many suitors from resorting to distant Dublin, so that private arbitration or awards by Gaelic brehons might be preferable.

Where business warranted it, in Cos. Kilkenny and Waterford in the 1490s, resident commissioners were occasionally appointed, and this device was again tried in Munster in 1551.[19] Nevertheless, the first really substantial attempt to tackle these problems came only, after repeated requests, with the establishment of provincial councils, like those in the north and in the Welsh marches, in Connaught and in Munster in 1569 and 1571. Elizabeth had hitherto baulked at the expense, but the main burden was the additional troops (costing £3,500 annually) provided for the Munster council which significantly altered its character. In Connaught the only extra expenditure was £312 a year for a president, chief and second justices and a clerk of the council who kept the signet. The councils included the bishops and lay magnates of each province, and were empowered to adjudge bills of complaint proffered by subjects residing within their jurisdictions. Additionally they received the normal commissions to try felonies and misdemeanours.[20]

The newer courts

The ancient courts had by 1470 long been reduced almost to a debt-collecting agency, with little business save actions of debt and trespass. Excepting common recoveries, real actions (for title to land) which had formed the staple diet of the common bench around 1300 had almost disappeared. The development of conciliar tribunals offered cheaper, more effective remedies, and initially they were willing to entertain actions over property. By Elizabeth's reign, however, king's bench had recouped itself by extending, by various fictitious devices, the quasi-criminal action of trespass into a general civil jurisdiction. In turn the newer courts – at different times the council, parliament, chancery

18. *StP*, ii, 509.
19. Bradshaw 1976–7a, p. 92.
20. Canny 1976, ch. 5; Irwin 1977, pp. 106–14.

and Castle Chamber – became increasingly specialized and supplemented the traditional system instead of rivalling it.

The king's powers to remedy grievances were not of course exhausted by the establishment of regular common law courts. Subjects deprived of justice could still petition the king for relief. In Ireland, therefore, the governor and council regularly received such petitions; but many preferred to approach the king and council in England directly, and there was constant friction between an Irish council anxious that its authority should not be circumvented and London which feared that damaging information was being suppressed but wished to avoid being inundated by Irish petitions. The conciliar courts thus reflected the council's efforts to deal with such petitions as the practice of litigation expanded; though in Ireland administrative practice was also shaped by the desire that structures should be a faithful representation of those in England even if resources were smaller and the pressures on government different.

The subject, however, saw important procedural differences between the ancient and the newer courts. Instead of obtaining an original writ, the plaintiff exhibited an English bill of complaint to the court (though in Ireland king's bench and common pleas frequently accepted bills) which then issued a writ of *sub poena* for defendant's appearance without specifying cause. This process was cheaper and generally more successful and, instead of trial by jury, the case continued by written pleadings, depositions, sworn examination of witnesses, judgement and decree. Nevertheless the machinery for enforcing decrees was no more effective and the punishments inflicted were largely restricted to imprisonment and fines.

In many ways parliament was the first of these courts, though subsequently more important as a legislature and for its control of taxation. The period 1460–94 witnessed a revival of a quasi-judicial role by the Irish parliament contrasting with the English institution. Parliaments then met annually, with frequently four or five sessions scattered throughout the year, and sessions were often held away from Dublin and Drogheda, the normal Tudor venues, to encourage resort to law. The average parliament passed well over 50 acts but mainly on private petitions, particularly in cases where the ancient courts offered no remedy or were powerless to enforce it; and though most petitions reflected Pale grievances, about 12½ per cent related chiefly to outlying parts, especially Cos. Kilkenny, Limerick, Wexford and Waterford, and Limerick and Waterford cities. No doubt the challenge from Gaelic Ireland contributed to the impotence of the traditional courts, but the same trend appears in England; and as the evidence for landed litigation shows, the main reason was changing patterns of litigation. Between 1470 and 1480, for example, the surviving parliament rolls alone record 36 cases (17 from outside the Pale) in which parliament circumvented common law mesne process by ordering a traditional court to determine title to land. In this way it acted as a clearing house for such disputes and more generally supplied the need for a court with power to override the form of the law in favour of justice.[21]

21. Ellis 1983a, pp. 44–8.

Poynings' Law unintentionally curtailed parliament's judicial work: such activities were not directly precluded, and indeed were deliberately revived in Grey's and St Leger's parliaments, but after 1494 only twelve more parliaments met before 1603, so that parliament was effectively brought to resemble more closely its English counterpart. Instead parliament's judicial and administrative duties largely devolved on the council aided by chancery's development. The court of chancery had traditionally exercised a common law or 'Latin' jurisdiction in cases where subjects sought redress against the crown, but what would in fifteenth-century England have constituted matter for the chancellor's equitable or 'English' jurisdiction was heard by parliament or council. Although there are slight indications before 1494 of chancery's future association with equity, the court's judicial work was then inconsiderable. Its judicial development dated from the appointment in 1494 of Bishop Deane of Bangor as chancellor and of two prominent local clerics as councillors and to the hitherto obscure office of master in chancery. From 1496, moreover, leading clerics were appointed keeper (styled 'master' from 1523) of the rolls, hitherto a promotional post for chancery clerks. Thereafter chancery quickly established itself as a lawcourt – four cases from New Ross, Kilkenny and Co. Meath, 1520–2, yielded IR£55, and in 1533–4 chancery estreats reached 100 marks (IR) a term.

Early chancery cases were frequently matters also determinable by the council – maintenance, embracery and title to land – and if circumstances were at all unusual litigants might be referred to the council. In 1502 Ormond's counsel sued for debt 'in the chancery and court of conscience . . . unto a judgement and, because I might have no judgement' there, before the deputy and council.[22] Nevertheless chancery was increasingly drawn to specialize in supplementing, rather than enforcing, an inflexible common law, particularly by protecting copyhold and enfeoffments to use. By the late 1530s it was already moving towards its major Elizabethan role in reconciling conflicting claims of English and Gaelic law. A Co. Kilkenny jury presentment of 1537 mentioned a *sub poena* served on O'More, who 'not regarding it, took it unreverently and threw it in the mire'.[23] The Elizabethan chancery was very busy with English bills from Gaelic or former border areas seeking the enforcement of Gaelic landed custom or, in more general cases of Anglo-Gaelic legal conflict, other Gaelic claims. In practice, chancery was ready to enforce local custom as a matter of equity, but equally ready to abrogate such customs as it considered inequitable.[24]

Castle Chamber and the differentiation of conciliar business

Although a privy council had been established by 1520, a full differentiation of conciliar business (as between the English privy council and court of Star

22. Curtis 1932–43, iv, app. no. 66.
23. Hore & Graves 1870, p. 104.
24. Nicholls 1970, pp. 105–29.

Chamber) was long delayed. The council dealt with administrative and judicial matters as the need and opportunity arose, and the first surviving council register, for 1556–71, is a miscellaneous record of formal council activities. Scattered early Tudor evidence suggests that the council's judicial business was then primarily in civil suits, especially title to land, but it frequently intervened in disputes which threatened the peace – for example between Ormond and Desmond in 1529–32, between Desmond and a Youghal merchant in 1529, and in a riot between Dublin citizens and men of the archiepiscopal liberty of St Sepulchre in 1525. Yet because of the council's predilections, petitions regularly alleged riot, trespass or forcible entry but turned out to be civil suits not involving a serious threat to order. The extant table of the 1542–56 register adds precision to these suggestions and shows the council most frequently hearing landed disputes of peers (now including Gaelic nobles), plus urban disputes, especially commercial litigation: the age-old prisage dispute between Waterford and New Ross resurfaced in common pleas in 1472, in 1501 in the council, in 1519 in Star Chamber in England, and returned in 1546 to the council. On one occasion the council referred a controversy to Gaelic brehons.[25] Cromwell's 1534 *Ordinances* unavailingly decreed special judicial council sessions modelled on Star Chamber, requiring the chancellor, judges and other councillors to sit twice weekly in the council chamber during term to determine complaints, but in 1537 more formal arrangements were made for the clerk to issue process automatically for the chancellor and council to determine petitions to the deputy.

Nevertheless by 1562 political difficulties and the extension of royal authority were overburdening the council. Lord Lieutenant Sussex therefore requested the establishment of a new court, alleging that 'great numbers of disorders and riots and taking of possession by force be daily committed and left unpunished' because the council was 'occupied with other affairs of greater weight'. Elizabeth consented and a clerk of Castle Chamber was appointed in 1563. The court evidently commenced work but remained subordinated to the council and disappeared entirely after 1566. In 1571, however, it was revived and properly constituted. Its powers and procedure were those of Star Chamber: it sat on Wednesdays and Fridays in term with membership comprising the governor, chancellor, treasurer, chief justices, chief baron and master of the rolls, though other lords, privy councillors or bench justices could be associated as required. A separate entry book was compiled by the clerk (most entries 1573–90 still survive), while the new council register (covering 1571–1619) apparently omitted judicial business. Further differentiation of council records followed in 1581 with a new journal for the privy council's daily business (probably covering 1581–9, of which 1581–6 survives in calendar), while the existing register recorded mainly formal acts, especially agreements of afforced and great councils concerning general hostings and cess. This change perhaps reflected

25. See also Crawford 1980, pp. 29, 46; Gilbert 1897, p. 279; Mac Niocaill 1964a, ii, pp. 335, 456–67, 469, 535, 539–88 *passim*.

the constitutional controversy over cess (see pp. 186–8, 273, 279, 305, 308–9): in consequence entries in the register fell from 40 to 10 pages a year.

Thus from 1571 Castle Chamber was institutionally distinct from the privy council, but with substantially the same membership: the governor's prominence in Castle Chamber was, however, a peculiarity of the Irish court. Attendance averaged five or six, especially the deputy, chancellor and secretary, though the chief justices rarely sat. The court specialized in breaches of public order, especially involving peers, gentlemen and merchants, and cases involving judicial administration – punishing erring jurors and enforcing decrees of other courts – work which was especially important in Elizabethan Ireland because disorders there so frequently verged on rebellion.

The court's preferred punishment was fines (more profitable than imprisonment, but difficult to collect): in 1577 the court imprisoned the foreman of a queen's bench jury for disputing the validity of cess; in 1582 jurors were fined IR£100 each for acquitting Maurice Fitzgerald of high treason in the Baltinglass rebellion against the evidence; and in 1579 Lord Howth was fined IR£1,000 for assault and battery of his wife, child and butler, living with strange women and other 'secret causes . . . not fit to be remembered'. Nevertheless Castle Chamber and the privy council remained more interdependent than their English counterparts: much judicial or quasi-judicial business was still determined in council, and in 1622 James I had to restrain its judicial activity; while basically administrative questions – the cess dispute or questions concerning prise wines and general hostings – came before Castle Chamber. The court was soon bogged down with vexatious suits and delayed by suiters' non-appearance: in 1582 30 or 40 suits were allegedly pending for this reason. Moreover, since it had no separate machinery nor, save its clerk, personnel, its activities effectively constituted a redistribution of the existing conciliar workload rather than a harnessing of new resources to administrative problems. Indeed the majority of cases during 1573–90 involved the well-governed shires of Dublin, Meath and Wexford, though a few suits from outlying or more lawless areas were attracted after 1580.[26]

Finally, the courts in England remained competent to review Irish cases, despite Ireland's erection into a kingdom in 1541. This change certainly implied an alteration in Ireland's constitutional relationship with England, whereby a sovereign kingdom should replace the dependant, medieval lordship; and indeed this vision subsequently inspired separatist sentiments in the Old English community.[27] Yet administrative practice was unchanged: the English king's bench still occasionally reviewed Irish cases, Irish business came before the English privy council and Star Chamber, and orders and patents were still authenticated by the English seals. Moreover, Gaelic clerics and peasants resident in English areas were still prosecuted under Edward VI as Irish enemies, despite the constitutional implications of the 1541 statute, and it was not until

26. Crawford 1980, pp. 34, 38–55 (quotations, pp. 34, 53).
27. Bradshaw 1979a, pt. iii.

Elizabeth's reign that charters of denization ceased to be purchased: such constitutional change as there was came slowly and hardly justifies talk of a 'constitutional revolution'.[28]

LOCAL GOVERNMENT

Central government activity depended heavily for its enforcement not only on local officials or commissioners specially appointed to perform particular duties but also on the cooperation of local nobles and gentry, who in fact predominated in these offices. Outside the Pale where central control was more continuous, early Tudor government aimed to supervise rather than closely control local administration. In these parts defence and good government depended chiefly on the magnates and towns, and their support was assiduously cultivated by appointments to offices and the consolidation of local privileges. Successive royal charters extended the self-government of major towns and cities, so that by 1500 Dublin, Drogheda, Wexford, Waterford, New Ross, Youghal, Cork, Limerick and Galway were largely independent of shire officials. This did not, however, make of them independent city-states.[29] They remained subject to control by Dublin: even in Galway, the most isolated, parliament intervened in law suits there at least five times between 1472 and 1491. Moreover, royal administrative rights were extensively delegated in many other parts of Ireland besides the major population centres, so that altogether about a quarter of the late medieval lordship was withdrawn from Dublin's direct control.

Until the 1530s palatinates were also seen as cheap and effective methods of extending the government's normal reach. Edward IV tried unsuccessfully to continue his father's palatinates of Meath and Ulster after 1461, and he quickly restored as essential to good government those of Kerry, Tipperary and Wexford when they were temporarily in crown hands. Henry VIII permitted the establishment of an effectively new liberty of Kildare (c. 1514–34), and after resuming Wexford liberty in 1536 restored it as a royal liberty in response to local petitions. Furthermore, the Irish palatinates were legally less autonomous than those in England or Wales: four felonies were reserved to the crown, besides proceedings in error, and they were represented and subject to taxation in parliament. In fact liberties long remained popular with litigants because they obviated the need to travel to Dublin and before c. 1550 at least were generally better governed than adjoining royal shires. Despite the hostility of successive governors, their *raison d'être* only disappeared with the establishment of provincial councils, though Tipperary and St Sepulchre survived into the eighteenth century.[30]

28. Ellis 1980–1, pp. 78–81; Morrin 1861, *passim*.
29. Cf. *NHI*, iii, p. 13; Sheehan 1983a, pp. 4–12.
30. Ellis 1981b, pp. 150–61; Canny 1976, pp. 49–50.

The sheriff

For liberties and royal shires alike, the government's chief means of control were the annual general commissions. They were staffed by a mixture of bench justices and local dignitaries, sometimes headed by the governor. They could enter and review the workings of all franchisal jurisdictions. By Elizabeth's reign, however, they were supplemented more regularly by viceregal progresses and special commissioners, sometimes from England. Nevertheless the central government relied especially on the sheriff who, to an extent no longer true in England, remained the principal shire officer. This was largely because in the more disturbed conditions, Irish keepers of the peace, the counterparts of English JPs, had remained chiefly military officials organizing local defence. Peace commissions were usually small and aristocratic and keepers were commonly also commissioners of array: they might inquire of treasons, felonies and trespasses, but outside the towns they were often not empowered to determine them before Edward VI's reign. Pale quarter sessions were begun under Edward VI, but a commission of 1550 for 24 justices to cover all outlying shires can hardly have operated as in England, and under Elizabeth JPs, where appointed, remained comparatively unimportant. For similar reasons the county lieutenancies did not develop in Ireland, although march wardens and county captains or governors were sometimes appointed whose work was evidently similar.[31]

Thus the sheriff remained the normal link between central and local government with important military and judicial besides administrative functions. He led the county *posse*, making 'roads' on the Irish, organizing resistance to their raids; he organized the county levy, computing cartage and military service for general hostings and other 'journeys'.[32] As judge he continued even under Elizabeth to hold his tourn biennially in each county barony (the Irish equivalent of hundreds or wapentakes) to determine lesser crimes, besides presiding over the county court which still heard minor civil pleas. A Kilkenny jury presented in 1537 that there were no quarter sessions in the shire though 'the sheriff sitteth two times a year, but they think it be no session for there be no justices'. And in 1500 an ordinance in the Ormond district required 'that none from henceforth be indicted but in presence of a learned man', to prevent vexatious indictments of 'the poor common people' by sheriff or undersheriff.[33]

Administratively the sheriff was responsible for levying crown revenues, serving writs, and proclaiming statutes, ordinances and proclamations in the county court. Appointments of sheriffs usually reflected local politics because without substantial local influence a sheriff would be unable to organize shire defence let alone execute orders from Dublin. This and the compactness of landholdings in many parts severely limited the government's choice. Pale sheriffs were changed annually, but in the other nine late medieval shires the

31. See also Canny 1976, p. 18.
32. See also Ellis 1977, pp. 5–28.
33. Hore & Graves 1870, p. 126; McNeill 1931a, p. 157.

great landed families dominated the office – Powers in Waterford, Fitzgeralds of Dromana in Cork and Burkes in Connaught. There were, however, no hereditary sheriffs in Ireland, and even before 1534 the government could if necessary find an alternative. Thereafter with the extension of English law and the shiring of Gaelic districts, the sheriff was sometimes a more disruptive influence in local government. The deputy's brother, Robert St Leger, was sheriff of Carlow in 1543–4, in 1545–6 an O'Toole was sheriff of Dublin 'and executed the same right well, according to such knowledge as he had', and a sheriff was also appointed for O'Byrne's country:[34] but similar experiments later were less successful.

After the plantation and shiring in 1557 of Leix and Offaly, military captains were understandably appointed sheriffs, though this hardly increased their acceptability to the dispossessed; but the appointments of Francis Cosby, general of the kerne, as sheriff of Kildare (1560) and of Captain Nicholas Heron as sheriff of Carlow (1559–66) were seen by the local English as an attempt by English adventurers to gain control of local government in obedient shires, as was Richard Grenville's appointment in Cork (1569). As an alternative the sheriffs selected by the president of Connaught for Clare and Galway were an O'Brien and a Burke who were rivals to the earls of Thomond and Clanrickard, a device which helped precipitate rebellion there in the early 1570s.[35] Thus the attempt to find sheriffs who were more controllable and independent of local interests was frequently counterproductive.

THE CIVIL AND MILITARY ESTABLISHMENTS

The friction over shrievalties was part of a wider struggle for office as public opinion in Elizabethan Ireland polarized. The eventual emergence of ideological divisions within government, between a predominantly Old English civil administration and an expanding military administration staffed by English adventurers, detracted seriously from administrative efficiency and undermined efforts to strengthen government. In 1534 the central administration comprised some 34 regular salaried ministers, although (in modern parlance) double-jobbing and freezing vacancies was quite common. In order to consolidate central control and cope with an expected upsurge in business from Gaelic and border districts, a further eight civil posts were created, the most important being the solicitor-general, auditor, surveyor-general and secretary of state. There were of course many unsalaried officers, especially clerks, who depended wholly on fees for services rendered and no doubt increased as Tudor rule expanded, but by comparison with perhaps 450 established posts at Westminster c. 1500 the Dublin administration was exceptionally underdeveloped

---

34. *StP*, iii, 570; Memoranda roll, 35 Henry VIII m. 21 (Public Record Office of Ireland, Ferguson coll., iv, f. 284).
35. Longfield 1960, pp. 20, 52, 57; Canny 1976, pp. 36, 78, 110, 146; Memoranda roll, 13, 14 Elizabeth m. 36 (PROI, Ferguson coll., vi, f. 194).

for the policies pursued after 1534.[36] In marked contrast was the burgeoning military establishment: by 1577 a garrison of 1,600 required two colonels, a general of kerne, marshal, master and clerk of ordnance, clerk of check, nine captains, thirteen petty captains, and nine additional constables of castles, where before 1534 only five constableships had been regular salaried posts.[37]

The effect of these changes was an insidious transformation in the essential character of Tudor rule. The proper planning and execution of so ambitious an undertaking as the Munster plantation (1586–98) would have taxed any sixteenth-century government, but was quite beyond the capacity of the Dublin administration. Private enterprise seemed to offer a cheap solution to the government's difficulties, but even this required supervision: the uncontrolled activities of adventurers in Ulster (1572–3) or acting on grants of concealed lands (1586–98) arguably did more harm than good (below, Chs 11–12). Thus the administration was gradually forced into increasing reliance on coercion to accomplish what could not be done in the normal way: the army and martial law became regular instruments of government.

THE REVENUES

Nevertheless the real measure of the administration's efficiency was, from the king's viewpoint, its revenue-gathering capacity in relation to costs: some remarks on financial administration will set these bureaucratic developments in perspective. The transition in the 1470s from English subsidization of the lordship's defence to the self-sufficiency which characterized early Tudor rule was made possible by a rigorous pruning of expenses and a modest increase in revenue. Crown revenues in early Tudor Ireland were, however, tiny by English standards, nominally c. IR£1,600 in most years, which just covered costs of government. Yet they compared favourably both with the declining revenue of Lancastrian Ireland, when English subsidies averaging c. £2,000 a year failed to reverse the exchequer's mounting indebtedness, and the stagnant revenues and increasingly heavy subsidies after 1547. In many respects the financial recovery after 1470 was based on the same strategies pursued by Edward IV and Henry VII in England, centring on better exploitation of crown lands, customs, prerogative rights and, additionally, a reorganization of parliamentary taxation. After 1534, however, the vast accessions of monastic wealth were not properly exploited and no real effort was made to reform the old exchequer system in line with English developments.

The customs revenue had in the 1280s yielded £1,400 annually, though reduced to c. £100 by 1420. From the 1460s, however, the general upswing in European trade swelled receipts and the administration concentrated on improving collection in the Pale ports while permitting hard-pressed towns elsewhere to appropriate customs revenue for murage and defence costs. Until

36. See also Lascelles 1852, i, pt. ii, pp. 53, 55, 68, 78, 82–3 *et passim*. Cf. Canny 1975, pp. 2–34; Lander 1980, pp. 34–5.
37. McNeill 1931b, pp. 147–55.

1530 the exchequer normally collected customs directly, appointing customers and controllers: thereafter they were farmed at rents which, despite inflation, declined even in nominal value. Poundage was introduced in 1474 (see above, pp. 72–5, 95), and under Poynings the reforms culminated in the enforcement of English customs regulations, and the appointment of a searcher and separate controllers for Dublin and Drogheda: in 1496 the undertreasurer reported the customs 'in much better order than hath been in time past'.[38] Dublin and Drogheda provided most revenue, rising from IR£175 per annum in 1465–6 to c. IR£450 by 1497 before settling back to a farm of IR£285 in the 1530s (see also p. 100); but small sums were also levied at different times from Limerick, Cork, Youghal, Dundalk, Carlingford, Ardglass and Carrickfergus. Altogether the customs yielded an annual average of c. IR£350 1470–1534, but thereafter the government apparently lost interest and by the 1570s they were mostly farmed by officials at rents yielding only IR£320 per annum.[39]

The crown lands 1461–1534 effectively consisted of twenty manors around the Pale, plus certain outlying lands and rights and the feefarm rents of towns and cities. Disregarding dubious claims or lands long in Gaelic occupation, a yield of IR£1,200 was theoretically possible, but as in England crown lands were regarded primarily as a source of patronage. The feefarm rents, worth almost IR£400, were largely remitted for murage and usually yielded c. IR£140 annually, while manors were granted or leased under value to magnates and ministers, though their yields fluctuated anyway due to disturbances. Nevertheless, additional lands were acquired either by reversion (notably the Mortimer inheritance in 1461) or act of resumption (those of 1493 and 1494 netted IR£250 per annum from lands), some farms were increased and waste lands were relet. By 1534 the four Dublin manors of the ancient desmesne yielded IR£125–150 annually, compared with IR£100 in the 1420s; the farms of Mortimer lands in Meath and Ulster increased from c. IR£80 to c. IR£185; and rents of almost IR£60 on lands formerly waste were added (see p. 100). Thus an annual average exceeding IR£500 was available from crown lands.

The reforms of the parliamentary subsidy have largely been considered already (above, pp. 79, 95), but from 1494 with the institution of five- or ten-year levies instead of the customary single grant it became a much more dependable revenue source and 'the substance of the king's revenues, without the which the . . . land may not be defended'. Its total yield (IR£600–630 per annum, 1499–1536) did not of course compare with the English subsidy – though Tudor taxation was light by continental standards – but the Pale was taxed more heavily from 1494 than some of the poorer English shires.[40] In effect these reforms rendered redundant the feudal levy of scutage which had survived in the lordship's more disturbed conditions as an alternative form of taxation. It was levied eight times, 1450–1531, and usually imposed with the consent of parliament or an afforced council in connection with a general

38. Gairdner 1861–3, ii, 69.
39. Treadwell 1976–7, pp. 384–417; Ellis 1980–1b, pp. 271–7.
40. Quinn 1941b, p. 110. See also Quinn 1935a, pp. 219–31.

hosting, though strictly a feudal incident. After 1480 it was confined, like the subsidy, to the Pale, and its yield gradually sank from *c.* IR£300 to *c.* IR£200 per levy.[41]

Royal prerogative rights included fines for homage, livery of lands and reliefs, wardships, escheats and episcopal temporalities – 'casualties', in exchequer terminology, fluctuating considerably in yield. In Ireland the exploitation of these feudal incidents was generally geared to quick profits rather than maximum yield, both because the exchequer could not efficiently administer additional lands in outlying parts and because local governors held office during pleasure. After 1534 English administrators thought that previous administrations had been lax in this matter: wardships were sold for more initially and commissioners sent over in 1537 were instructed to examine feoffments to see that they were not 'fraudulent', designed to evade feudal dues, but since English legislation against enfeoffments to use was not enacted until 1634, little could be done.[42] Nevertheless the profits of temporalities and wardships might be considerable: despite destruction during the rebellion the richest see, Dublin, was still worth IR£350 net per annum when vacant 1534–6; and in two years, 1520–2, four wardships yielded over IR£250, a fifth was sold for IR£200, and eight fines for livery realized IR£175. Over seventeen years, 1558–75, however, annual income from wardships and liveries averaged a mere IR£105.[43]

The only other considerable sources of revenue were the profits of justice, of the mints operating periodically 1460–*c.* 1506, plus two-thirds of the profits of absentees' lands before 1536 (see above, pp. 99–100). Judicial profits generally varied between IR£150 and IR£350 a year, of which the exchequer contributed the bulk in fines on delinquent ministers, and for customs offences, infringements of the king's seigneurial rights, obstructing officials or breaches of penal statutes. Absentees' lands might yield IR£150 in good years and the mint, when operating, was worth IR£90 per annum.

The two major items of expenditure were internal defence costs and ministers' salaries and rewards: before 1534 local governors were expected to maintain a household and defend the lordship out of their salary (effectively the profits of the revenue) and the Dublin administration made no contribution to costs of royal diplomacy or war outside Ireland. By reducing some comparatively large salaries and generally paying officers far less than their English counterparts, the administration kept annual wage costs down to *c.* IR£650. The resumptions of 1493 and 1494 reduced certain annuities from IR£140 to under IR£20 (though IR£50 again by 1534). The balance was available, without account, to the governor as his salary, but governors occasionally needed reminders that other expenses had priority: Kildare agreed in 1524 that the judges should be 'truly and yearly paid their fees and wages' and to spend 40 marks (IR) annually on repairing royal castles and manors.[44] Otherwise,

41. Ellis 1977, pp. 5–28.
42. Kearney 1959, p. 77.
43. McNeill 1931b, pp. 180–1.
44. *StP*, ii, 117.

there was little incentive to keep full records of receipts or even to channel all revenue through the exchequer. Kildare frequently levied certain moneys directly, especially from distant parts where exchequer collection was more difficult, rather than wait for end-of-term assignments on moneys outstanding; and provided the revenue was granted without account, this system worked well and helped mitigate the rigours of exchequer accounting procedures.

In the 1440s, exchequer receipts averaged under £900 a year, excluding taxation, but ministers' salaries alone exceeded this and in 1440–1 an exceptionally high deficit of £1,457 was recorded. Under Edward IV, however, there was a small surplus on ordinary expenditure, so allowing the governor c. IR£900, including taxation, for his salary and defence costs. Surviving accounts and extents are sparse and contain obvious omissions but still list an ordinary revenue of c. IR£1,000 plus over IR£600 in taxation – IR£961 excluding taxation in 1483–4, IR£1,587 inclusive in 1501–2 and c. IR£1,600 in 1533–4. The revenue was thus small but, given the aims and character of government before 1534, adequate for everyday purposes.

The course of the exchequer

Similarly, exchequer accounting procedures were obsolescent, but normally no real disadvantage before 1534. Experiments at direct rule had already demonstrated the limitations of the traditional financial system, and with major governmental changes 1534–41 the need for reform became urgent. Yet the Dublin exchequer retained its accustomed role in Irish finances: indeed its control was extended in 1494–5 to the subsidy and poundage, replacing ad hoc receivers accountable to the governor, and also strengthened over the previously elective sheriffs and escheators. The exchequer was by far the best-staffed and administratively the most important of the central courts, though the constant shortage of trained clerks ensured continued mobility between the courts. Its account procedure was essentially that of the unreformed English exchequer, although speedier and more flexible, and its organization was much less elaborate. Accountants from outside the Pale often accounted infrequently, but generally accounts were rendered and audited promptly within a few months of being closed. They were not allowed to drag on for years as in England.

Traditionally only one memoranda roll was compiled: by 1545 the chief remembrancer was styled king's remembrancer as in England, but the practice of separate King's Remembrancer and Lord Treasurer's Remembrancer rolls was never introduced at all. The only other rolls regularly compiled in the exchequer of audit before 1534 were the pipe rolls, containing all categories of account, though separate subcategories were subsequently introduced. The treasurer's clerk (the equivalent of the English undertreasurer but still firmly under the treasurer's control) headed the receipt where the traditional issue and receipt rolls were still kept, despite their abolition in England. It was the treasurer, for instance, who made assignments, a practice which the Irish exchequer continued on a large scale, despite its abandonment in England for cash balances in the chamber: nevertheless in the period 1470–1534 at least it was well organized, and the earlier problems with bad tallies and mounting exchequer indebtedness did not recur. Yet a development deceptively similar to the English undertreasurer's ousting of his nominal superior saw control of Irish finances also pass to an undertreasurer. Undertreasurer Hattecliffe's appointment to supersede Lord Treasurer Conway in 1495 began the process and by 1534 with Brabazon's appointment as undertreasurer and treasurer-at-war the treasurership had been reduced to an honorary appointment (see also above, pp. 127, 132). From 1534 this combined office controlled finance, recovering some powers which had earlier passed to the governor, and when in 1554 an undertreasurer was recalled to answer charges of corruption, the treasurer had to be ordered to make payments in his absence.

The English administrators who arrived with Skeffington in 1534 were surprised at the laxity of exchequer practices in Dublin. Kildare's undertreasurer, William Bath (1532–4), later executed for treason, had evidently ridden roughshod over formal procedures: Brabazon remarked that on arrival he found 'neither script nor scroll nor no piece of a rental'.[45] Nevertheless instead of introducing modern chamber methods, the administration concentrated on restoring the traditional practices in their entirety, despite their serious weaknesses which Irish conditions only exacerbated. Traditional exchequer process was exceedingly slow, and while debts were eventually driven in, accountants were afforded many opportunities for delay – 'there was never seen so sharp receivers and so slow payers', as one official remarked.[46] The withdrawal of certain revenues from exchequer control had earlier moderated some of the system's worst aspects, but in the late 1530s mounting arrears and the king's refusal to finance the deficit plunged the administration into crisis.[47] Furthermore, the traditional system was ill-adapted to estate management: farming manors at fixed rents was highly inefficient in inflationary times and when potential profits fluctuated so widely. Yet until 1569, when parliament agreed an impost on wines, landed income, including the post-1534 accessions, was much the largest revenue item.

The augmentation of the revenue

By 1542 the annual crown rental stood at an impressive but nominal IR£6,070, rising to IR£8,135 by 1565, though static thereafter until the mid-1580s' forfeitures.[48] Total revenue actually levied fell increasingly short of estimates. It had climbed to IR£4,500 by 1540 and IR£5,395 in 1558–9, but yielded only IR£4,085 in 1561–2 and averaged IR£4,150 annually 1555–70: yet estimates of revenue leviable, 1564–85, constantly predicted a rosy balance of IR£11,000 a

---

45. Quinn 1933, p. 407 (quotation).
46. BL, Cotton MS, Titus B.XI, f. 401 (*LP*, xv, no. 849). I am indebted to Professor W.C. Richardson for this reference.
47. Ellis 1980c, pp. 515–16.
48. *Carew*, i, nos. 176, 250, ii, nos. 34, 597.

year.[49] To improve collection the government appointed a surveyor-general in 1548 to value estates and a clerk of first fruits in 1544 to supervise the new levy on appointees to ecclesiastical benefices (worth *c.* IR£300 a year); and instead of sending over English auditors from the new revenue courts, a resident Irish auditor was appointed in 1547.[50] Nevertheless, the English privy council examining the revenue in 1552 concluded that it was 'rather diminished than increased, which is a marvel, considering the augmentation' forecast from suppressions, conquests and recoveries.[51] The undertreasurer and auditor were dismissed for corruption and an investigation of accounts since 1538 followed, but despite this the decline in revenue continued well into Elizabeth's reign (see also above, pp. 148, 158–9; and Table 3, p. 345 below).[52]

Inquiries and recommendations followed at regular intervals – 1554, 1559, 1565, 1577 – but were altogether without effect on the revenue.[53] The only substantial addition under Elizabeth was the tax on wine imports: this yielded IR£2,470 in 1569–70, even though some ports were without collectors, but by 1575 massive evasion had reduced the yield to IR£835. Overall, total revenue receipts experienced a substantial hiccough, reaching an annual average of IR£6,840, 1569–73, before falling to IR£4,305, 1575–9. The administration therefore farmed the tax for £2,000 sterling per annum 1584–99, reduced to £1,400 in 1600 because of the trade depression.[54] Overall, therefore, the administration became increasingly dependent on English subventions – with important consequences for government.

FINANCE AND THE CHARACTER OF TUDOR RULE

In the event the local community paid a high price for the government's failure to expand the revenue in line with costs: parliamentary control over taxation was gradually undermined and Tudor rule became increasingly arbitrary. After a lean period before 1534, when parliaments rejected many government bills and few others were passed, the parliaments of 1536–7 and 1541–3 had, despite difficulties, been generally successful ones (see above, pp. 143–4, 151–4). Traditionally parliament had been seen as a forum in which the interests of crown and subject could be harmonized; and despite the procedural difficulties imposed by Poynings' Law, Henry VIII made a determined effort to use the Irish parliament as an instrument of policy. The old saying quoted by a member of the 1613–15 parliament – 'Little said soon amended, a subsidy granted the parliament ended' – no doubt reflected the frustrations of Irish

49. Ellis 1980c, pp. 515–17; Longfield 1960, *passim*; Canny 1976, p. 37; *Carew*, i, no. 250, ii, nos. 34, 597.
50. Lascelles 1852, i, pt. ii, pp. 53, 55 *et passim*; Quinn 1941a, pp. 5–6.
51. White 1964–5, p. 208.
52. Lascelles 1852, i, pt. ii, pp. 42–3; Longfield 1960, *passim*; Canny 1976, p. 37.
53. BL, Add. MS 4767, ff. 75–8, 128; McNeill 1931b, pp. 94, 124–5, 180–1; *Carew*, i, nos. 218–20; Canny 1976, p. 43.
54. Longfield 1929, pp. 135–41; Treadwell 1966, pp. 76, 86–7; Canny 1976, p. 155.

MPs 1499–1533, but it also underlined the government's continued reliance on parliament. After 1534, however, the government failed to secure significant increases in taxation, and the widening gap between income and expenditure rendered the parliamentary subsidy increasingly unimportant. In the later 1540s its annual yield rose to c. IR£750, but this was achieved only by agreeing small contributions from outlying counties, not by the tax reforms which were so badly needed: thereafter its decline was even more precipitous than its English counterpart – it yielded barely IR£300 by 1560 – and it was finally abandoned in 1576. By contrast the annual deficit soared from £4,700 in 1542 to £34,700 in 1552: it settled back to average £21,400 a year 1555–65, but rose to £31,800 by the late 1570s, and in these circumstances government policy was increasingly tailored to the interests of the court rather than local interests.[55]

In England the government would have been brought to compromise by its dependence on local support for policy enforcement – in the Taxpayers' Strike of 1525 for instance – but from 1547 the Somerset regime tried a new approach to the Irish problem. Though notably unsuccessful, the strategy incidentally demonstrated the advantages for government of an augmented garrison. In turn this eventually led to a fundamental reappraisal of the nature of the Irish problem and a corresponding alteration in the practice of government. Briefly, the Edwardian government abandoned a basic assumption of early Tudor policy, that the lordship was a borderland posing problems of government essentially similar to those of the north or Wales, and instead embarked on a military solution to the problem. This change was greatly influenced by Protector Somerset's general policy aims which, as Dr Bush argues, broke generally with traditional crown policy by making Scotland the top priority. Relying on his previous military experiences there, Somerset sought to control the country by the more costly strategy of garrisoning lowland Scotland where Henry VIII had relied on periodic punitive raids and invasions to keep the Scots tractable.[56] This policy was also applied in Ireland, where the Gaelic lordships appeared to present a similar problem: the army was greatly reinforced, garrisons were established in key marches, and tentative steps were taken towards the plantation of Leix and Offaly. None of this activity was entirely unprecedented of course, but overall it marked a pronounced shift in policy away from peaceful coexistence or incorporation by consent.

In Scotland the new strategy collapsed with the arrival of a French army, but in Ireland the government soon discovered that a larger army gave it a new freedom of manoeuvre in its dealings both with Gaelic and Old English communities. The restraints on policy imposed by the traditional reliance on local support no longer applied, and in view of the administration's continuing insolvency, this evidently outweighed earlier financial considerations and any additional benefits to be gained through wholehearted Old English co-operation. Thus the question of the crown's relations with the Old English

55. Ellis 1983a, pp. 59–63, on which the rest of this chapter is based; Bagwell 1885–90, i, 379; Canny 1976, p. 155; White 1964–5, p. 208. See also below, Table 3, p. 345.
56. Bush 1975, ch. 2.

gradually became subordinated to the problem of Gaelic Ireland, whereas in England the problem of the north and that of Scotland, though interacting on one another, remained largely separate.

The growth of military government

From 1547, therefore, Tudor policy in Ireland was frequently pursued without reference to Old English wishes and the way was open for military conquest and colonization on a scale which would otherwise have been impossible. The small garrison of 500 men was gradually increased to 2,600 by 1551: despite a brief reduction to 500 men under Mary, the unrest created by government initiatives necessitated its augmentation and under Elizabeth there were rarely less than 1,500 men in pay.

This increase was accompanied by a vast extension in a series of military exactions which both undermined the community's obligation to pay increased parliamentary taxation and lessened the government's dependence on it. Purveyance, or cess as it was known in Ireland, was levied for the provisioning not only of the governor's household but of his retinue too; the duty of ablebodied men aged between 16 and 60 to military service was extended so that the governor by advice of an afforced council could compel service without payment in hostings of 40 days two or three times a year, or exact a fine in lieu; he could likewise require provision of carts to carry provisions, or labourers for defensive building projects; and at need he could quarter troops on the marches for defence. These exactions had originated in the straitened circumstances of the later medieval lordship, and despite provoking occasional disputes, they had generally allowed a more flexible and economical approach to governmental problems which benefited both crown and subject. After 1534, however, the increasing commutation of these services began to challenge the principle of consent to taxation. Holdings of kerne and galloglass on the Pale grew more frequent in the 1540s: in 1546, for example, the Pale contributed over IR£300 to wage 400 galloglass for six weeks. In 1543 the military service of seven counties for a general hosting was commuted for nearly IR£1,000 to allow the government to pay 420 kerne for three months, and the cartage owing from two more counties was commuted for a further IR£500, and in 1554 the entire hosting was commuted to finance an expedition to Limerick.

Purveyance was put on a more regular footing under Lord Deputy Bellingham (1548–9). In 1549, 10,720 pecks of wheat and malt and 2,120 cattle were purveyed for the provisioning of Fort Protector in Leix and fixed prices were agreed. Initially it was the increased incidence of purveyance to feed an enlarged army that caused friction. The Leix garrison was 300 strong but corn and cattle sufficient for 1,000 men for a year were purveyed, though until 1566 the annual levies were rather under 1549 levels. In the 1550s, however, the queen's price for victual lagged behind the market price even in years of reasonable harvest and by 1566, when the levy was substantially increased to feed an enlarged army, the government in effect admitted this by allowing counties to compound for their corn quotas at rates which indicate that it benefited by IR£1,950 per annum from this aspect of purveyance. In an exceptional year, like 1561, the total value of all exactions might even reach IR£20,000.[57]

In these circumstances the government could obtain far more by systematically extending this system of effectively military taxation than was grudgingly granted by parliament, and parliament's role in government declined accordingly. Although a licence to hold parliament was issued in 1548 none met, and relying on the applicability of English legislation to Ireland, the Edwardian government introduced ecclesiastical legislation by proclamation. By the time a parliament next met, in 1557, Mary's government had long since restored catholicism by proclamation. Since Henry VIII had claimed a personal supremacy, there was perhaps more justification for proceeding without reference to parliament in religious matters than in secular, but the contrast with the position in England remains significant. Indeed only four parliaments met in Ireland between 1543 and 1613 and only the 1569–71 parliament passed a reasonable tally of acts. Those of 1557–8 and 1560 were called primarily to settle religion and did little else; deadlock in the 1569–71 parliament was broken only when some opposition leaders switched their opposition to the battlefield, and in 1585–6 the government lost its chief bills. In fact under Elizabeth some of the expedients suggested or employed to secure acceptance of government policies sound distinctly ominous. The commons was packed with non-resident and unrepresentative Englishmen, despite the statutory obligation of residence which in Ireland had been confirmed in 1542, probably to prevent this. For the 1560 parliament the government proposed to create new peers for the duration of parliament or for life and to summon opponents to court. Other measures were enforced without reference to parliament – the establishment of provincial councils in 1569–70, for instance, and the related attempt to suppress the palatinates of Tipperary and Kerry. The government was quick to resort to martial law to quell disorders, and not only in the face of rebellion. In the twenty years following Elizabeth's accession, no less than 259 commissions of martial law were issued; and in the aftermath of the Munster rebellions of 1569–73 and 1579–83 acts of attainder were passed which can only be described as draconian.[58]

The cess controversy

These developments betrayed a breakdown of consensus between crown and community. The Palesmen at least recognized the nature of the change and pleaded for the appointment of a governor who would defer to their interests and reduce the garrison: the cess controversy of the mid-1570s marked something of a *cause célèbre* in this debate. The Palesmen eventually rejected all forms of purveyance as illegal unless granted by parliament or a representative

57. On cess, see now Brady 1985, pp. 11–32; Brady 1994a, ch. 6.
58. Edwards 1997, p. 18.

great council because 'all the laws for purveyors in England were laws in this land' and 'without parliament or grand council there could be no imposition laid upon the subject'.[59] The administration inclined by contrast to regard purveyance as invariably part of the royal prerogative but supported its argument with misleading citations of medieval great council rolls and levies of scutage, plus some more apposite post-1548 precedents. Excluding purveyance for the governor's household, the Palesmen had in fact a strong case, but by then the custom was well established and the issue came to a head in 1577 with the deputy's attempt to enforce, without consent, a partial composition for cess. Local spokesmen were forced into a token submission for denying the prerogative, but a compromise was then agreed whereby an extended great council including Pale lords and gentry approved a temporary annual composition of £2,100 which was subsequently renewed in 1584 and 1586. Despite promises of a parliament to legislate on the issue, none met.[60]

The history of Tudor government in Ireland highlights the importance of particular administrative developments in England in keeping royal government abreast of the new problems posed in the Tudor period. Ireland's remoteness, its relative unimportance and the king's absence meant that informal methods of control, notably court influence, were inevitably less effective; while the formal governmental structures had also been influenced by the pre-1534 system of aristocratic delegation. The machinery of government was thus barely adequate for the tasks expected of it before 1534, but with the failure to initiate major reforms thereafter the system effectively broke down.

From the 1530s the claims of royal government were greatly extended, but the machinery of enforcement remained largely unaltered. Few new posts were created in central government, and the absence of English-style peace commissions and county lieutenancies left the administration dangerously over-dependent on the sheriff in local government. The failure to reform revenue administration or initiate a more efficient system of taxation was crucial: financial self-sufficiency under Lords Deputy Grey and St Leger would effectively have undermined any case for unconventional policies after 1547. Yet such reforms as occurred, particularly the provincial councils, came too late: by 1578 the government had long been employing more coercive methods to extend royal control, methods which had alienated potential Gaelic supporters and aroused deep suspicions in the Old English community. The longer these continued, the harder it became to return to consensus politics, and emerging ideological divisions among landowners undermined still further the effectiveness of ordinary administrative procedures.

Thus the fate of the traditional system of government was in fact largely determined in the period 1547–78, by a combination of royal indifference, local intransigence and the vested interests of key ministers. Under Elizabeth, the option of reforming and rebuilding the existing governmental structures on contemporary English lines in order to extend control was fast dissolving,

59. McNeill 1931b, 132; Quinn 1967, pp. 101–2.
60. Quinn 1967; *Carew*, ii, no. 609.

and the government relied increasingly on new instruments to implement a radical solution: the traditional machinery of government was too weak to make significant progress outside the traditional areas of English influence, but its failure to do so was blamed on Gaelic intransigence and colonial lawlessness. Anglicization was therefore imposed by force. If there was a 'revolution in government' in Tudor Ireland, it occurred under Elizabeth, not under Cromwell.

CHAPTER 8

THE LATE MEDIEVAL CHURCH
AND THE ORIGINS OF TUDOR
REFORM

CONTRASTING HISTORIOGRAPHIES: IRELAND AND
ENGLAND

Reformation historiography is in a state of flux. Traditionally, studies of the Tudor Reformation have been solidly Whig in emphasis, suggesting that protestantism won an easy and early victory in England just as in Ireland it was resolutely resisted from its first imposition.[1] Yet if Irish historians have charted resistance to reform where English historians have concentrated on its early successes, some more recent reappraisals of protestant progress in specific English dioceses (and occasional attempts to apply this approach to Ireland) give grounds for thinking that the early impact of state-sponsored religious reform in the two countries may not have been as dissimilar as formerly suggested.[2]

The prospects in 1534 for the emergence of a protestant Ireland have generally been considered remote. There was no native tradition of heresy, like Lollardy in England, no early toehold established by Lutheranism such as at the universities in England in the 1520s or among English merchants trading with the Netherlands, and no strong tradition of anticlericalism such as provoked the furore following Richard Hunne's murder. Nor did the lordship experience anything similar to the pamphlet war between the ecclesiastical authorities and the early reformers, or the government-inspired propaganda campaign which contributed in England to a public awareness of the issues.[3] The political crisis surrounding the Kildare rebellion inhibited parallel initiatives in Ireland in 1533–4, though the lordship was not altogether isolated from English developments.[4] Moreover, Ireland's politico-cultural divisions accentuated problems of enforcing ecclesiastical legislation: in particular, the

1. Especially Edwards 1935; Dickens 1964.
2. See especially Haigh 1982, pp. 995–1007; Haigh 1993. For Ireland, Jefferies 1997a constitutes a major advance. See also the works of Dr Brendan Bradshaw and Dr James Murray listed below.
3. Watt 1972, p. 216. Cf. Dickens 1964, chs 1–6.
4. See Ellis 1976, pp. 807–13.

190

government could hardly impose its religious reform in Gaelic Ireland without a political conquest; and if Gaelic parts were ignored, the breach in Ireland's religious unity, coupled with new claims on the king's subjects there, would tax still further the administration's limited resources. The prevalence of Gaelic speakers at lower social levels in the lordship also hindered the deployment of two major weapons in the reformers' armoury, the provision of regular sermons by licensed preachers and the promotion of the vernacular in the liturgy. In principle, Gaelic sermons and services could be provided alongside English ones, as happened in Scotland: in practice, bi-lingualism dissipated the reforming impetus and undermined the government's political objective of an English Ireland.

THE PAPACY

At the centre of the pre-Reformation church was the papacy, although its primacy was far more nebulous and its prestige much lower in the aftermath of the Great Schism and the Conciliar Movement than it subsequently became. In Ireland, however, the pope's right to provide to major benefices, overriding the ordinary patrons, remained more important and controversial than in those European states where the emergence of strong monarchies had effectively limited papal patronage. In English Ireland appointments to bishoprics theoretically followed the English compromise between pope and king whereby the king nominated a suitable person for a vacant bishopric and, after papal assent, told the cathedral chapter whom they were to elect. Following papal provision, the bishop then received the temporalities of his see retained by the king during a vacancy. Royal control of temporalities constituted a powerful means of resisting the earlier system of papal provisions, so that pre-Reformation bishops were mostly reliable royal councillors rewarded for loyal service in government. In most of Ireland, however, royal government was too weak to control temporalities and prevent papal provisions. Theoretically the pope might have provided conscientious clerics solicitous for reform, but in practice the system merely encouraged a recrudescence of the worst abuses which the twelfth-century reform movement had aimed to eradicate.[5]

Until very recently, surveys of the pre-Reformation church drew heavily on colourful complaints in the state papers lamenting 'the sorrowful decay in good Christianity' even in a relatively well-ordered diocese like Meath. For instance, the well-known report of 1515 complained that none of the clergy preached the Gospel 'saving the poor friars beggars' and cited a revelation that of all Christian lands Ireland had 'most continual war, root of hate and envy, and of vices contrary to charity', so that Irish souls 'fell down into hell as thick as any hail showers'.[6] Yet *ex parte* statements by self-appointed critics

---

5. Watt 1972, pp. 89–91, 107–8, 135–49, 188–93; Jacob 1961, pp. 264–73.
6. Watt 1972, pp. 181–3; *StP*, ii, 11, 15. For a discussion of the limitations of the state papers as a source for the pre-Reformation church, see now Jefferies 1998a; Jefferies 1997b, p. 123.

are hardly the most reliable form of evidence. Indeed, the application to Irish dioceses of approaches developed by English ecclesiastical historians is now beginning to show that state-paper reports are no more accurate concerning conditions in the parishes than about the reach of royal government. Thus earlier surveys suggesting that the late medieval church was everywhere in serious need of reform have had to be revised in the light of new evidence for revival and renewal in particular areas of church life on the eve of the Reformation. Even so, the basic reasons for the church's overall decline in the later middle ages remain clear: they were largely attributable to the crown's racialist policies, Gaelic custom, a collapse of morale among the religious orders, papal provisions and, above all, the church's poverty.

THE STATUTES OF KILKENNY AND THE IRISH CHURCH

The crown had attempted, by the Statutes of Kilkenny and other legislation, to strengthen English influence in ecclesiastical as well as secular matters. Gaelic clergy were debarred from benefices in English districts without a grant of English law, and in practice this licensing system was operated – effectively in the Pale, less so elsewhere – to exclude them from major benefices while allowing them to serve as curates or in poorer livings which were unattractive to the king's subjects. For instance, of 21 benefices in Co. Louth in the period 1501–31 whose incumbents can be identified, eight were held by Gaelic clerks, thirteen by English; but the eight held by Gaelic clerks were all very poor, worth between IR£1 1s. 1d. and IR£6 6s. 8d. per annum in 1538–44, or about half the average for benefices held by English clerks. Moreover, of 21 un-beneficed priests serving particular parishes as curates or assistant curates in 1518–31, sixteen were Gaelic and only five English.[7] Thus the church remained partially segregated.

Exceptionally in Armagh diocese, separate administrative structures were maintained for the English and Gaelic parts: the primates, who were invariably English, generally lived at Termonfeckin, Co. Louth, and St Peter's parish church, Drogheda, served as a kind of pro-cathedral. They personally ruled Armagh *inter Anglicos* (effectively Co. Louth) aided by an archdeacon and official also drawn from the Englishry. Even though most late medieval primates also visited Armagh regularly (notably Archbishops Mey (1444–56), Bole (1457–71) and Cromer (1521–42)), they had difficulty in controlling the *clerus inter Hibernicos* and were very dependent on O'Neill's support. Thus, in the administration of Armagh *inter Hibernicos*, comprising the Gaelic part, mainly east Tyrone, the dean of Armagh, who was chairman of the cathedral chapter, was a key figure. There was always a Gaelic majority in the chapter, since the four cathedral dignitaries (dean, chancellor, precentor and treasurer) and most of the prebends were in Gaelic hands, as was the priorship of the Culdees whose office, in the 60 years before its suppression, was usually combined with that

7. Calculated from Jefferies 1997a, tables 2, 3 (pp. 33, 40–1). See also Ellis 1986a, pp. 128–31.

of dean. The archbishop's relationship with most of the cathedral chapter was inevitably less intimate than with his archdeacon, who resided near his castle at Termonfeckin. No doubt particular circumstances varied, but similar racial divisions must have complicated the administration of many other Irish dioceses.[8]

Of the other bishops, nine more, mainly in the richer sees of Dublin and Cashel provinces, were English; thirteen sees were invariably held by Gaelic bishops, and the remaining nine had at different times resident English or Gaelic bishops or absentees acting as suffragans in England. One unfortunate consequence of this was a series of conflicting papal provisions to sees in Gaelic or border areas, as candidates represented a see as vacant which was not or were denied peaceful possession by the local lord. Another equally serious result was racial antagonism within the church between English and Gaelic: in 1505 Dean John Alen of St Patrick's, Dublin, made bequests for a poorhouse – not for any poor whatever, but for faithful catholics of good repute, honest life and English nation.[9] By 1500 this antagonism was more muted than two centuries earlier but was still a significant force discernible, for instance, in the Observant movement among the friars, or the failure of reform in the Cistercian order *c.* 1496–8 (see below, pp. 196–8).

At the lordship's height the racial balance between English and Gaelic bishops had never swung beyond 20:14, and thereafter the crown had attempted to retain a disproportionate English influence. The unions sanctioned by the pope of Waterford and Lismore (1363), Cork and Cloyne (1421) and Down and Connor (1453) were one method, also defensible because of the notorious poverty of Irish, especially Gaelic, sees; but more importantly, the crown was from 1492 gradually able to exert a substantial influence over papal provisions even to predominantly Gaelic sees by employing a Cardinal Protector at the Roman Curia to refer and expedite royal nominations to bishoprics including, by virtue of the king's title to Ireland, Irish sees. By 1514 candidates needed royal letters for success, even though Gaelic clerics still frequently sought their own provision. Seemingly tractable prelates might subsequently work against royal interests, royal nominees might not obtain possession of their sees and their nominations frequently reflected a compromise between royal and local interests; yet this system largely eliminated conflicting provisions.[10]

THE CHURCH IN GAELIC IRELAND

Perhaps the most obvious features of the church in Gaelic Ireland were its predominantly rural character and its abject poverty. Reflecting the more dispersed patterns of settlement there, parishes in Gaelic Ireland were generally far larger than in the Englishry. In 1544 in Armagh diocese, for instance, the average size of parishes and chapelries in the two rural deaneries *inter*

---

8. Jefferies 1997a, pp. 83–99; Gwynn 1946, esp. pp. 73–85; Lynch 1982, pp. 7–8.
9. McNeill 1950, pp. 253, 254–5, 258–9; *HBC*, pp. 328–77.
10. Wilkie 1974, pp. 63–80, 161–8; Watt 1972, pp. 108–9, 142, 203.

Hibernicos was well over 10,000 acres, whereas parishes and chapelries *inter Anglicos* averaged less than 2,500 acres. Likewise, the average income of the 22 benefices in Tullyhogue rural deanery, *inter Hibernicos*, was then a mere IR£1 17s. 1d. per annum, and only one rectory there exceeded five marks (IR) a year in value; whereas the average value for benefices *inter Anglicos* as recorded in the Irish *Valor* in the late 1530s was IR£11 18s. 2d. In fact, the incomes for Armagh *inter Hibernicos* are very comparable with the low values recorded for the neighbouring, predominantly Gaelic diocese of Dromore in 1422 (where only one of the 23 parishes had a living worth more than five marks (IR) a year) or for Leighlin diocese as recorded in the *Valor*; and, when inflation is taken into account, they are quite comparable with Gaelic benefices in other parts which were 'taxed' later in the *Valor*.

Thus, by comparison with the richly decorated churches and elaborate ceremonial in the English towns, the prevailing poverty must have imparted a very different character to Gaelic churches and services as well as creating major problems for the clergy in serving large, sprawling parishes. Yet the scanty surviving evidence suggests that they generally managed. The single surviving visitation record from this period, for Armagh *inter Hibernicos* in 1546, reveals that only five of the sixteen churches visited were in satisfactory condition, with three ruinous; but with one possible exception, there were regular celebrations of Mass, Matins and Evensong as required; and apart from celibacy, almost all the clergy were of good conduct. In the circumstances, it is perhaps surprising that conditions were no worse than they were.[11]

Yet in other respects, the Gaelic church lacked many features characteristic of late medieval catholicism elsewhere while exhibiting certain peculiarities and 'abuses' which, at the higher levels, tended to blur distinctions between church and state and also infiltrated outlying English districts. Excepting small parcels of land owned by the clergy, church lands were occupied by various hereditary coarbs and erenaghs who paid fixed dues, furnished refections, helped to maintain churches, and generally constituted the financial linchpin of diocesan administration. Originally the superior of a religious house, a coarb or erenagh was frequently by 1500 a literate layman or in minor orders, and elected by tanistry with episcopal approval from the clan in which the coarbship or erenaghship was vested, although the status, origins and duties of these officers are far more complex than can be explained here.[12]

Within the pre-Reformation clerical profession it became increasingly common for sons of priests and bishops to follow their fathers into the church, despite the earlier work of the twelfth-century reform movement. One example of 'hereditary' clerical families were the Slioght Lachtláin Maguires, descended from an archdeacon of Clogher and Bishop Maguire of Clogher (1433–48), and represented by the prior of Lisgoole (d. 1522) and the vicar of Cleenish (d. 1534). Bishop Turlough O'Brien of Killaloe (1556–69) was the son, by a daughter of

11. Jefferies 1997a, pp. 19–20, 64–5, 70–1, 76–81; Jefferies 1997b, pp. 124–5; Ellis 1990, pp. 248–53; *Valor* 1741.
12. For an adequate summary, see Mooney 1969, pp. 10–15.

an O'Brien chief of Thomond, of Bishop Matthew O'Brien of Kilmacduagh (1503–32), who in turn was the son of Bishop Turlough O'Brien of Killaloe (1483–1526): but this prompts two further observations. Clerical celibacy was widely ignored, despite periodic legislation by provincial synods, and with little sign of any social stigma attaching to concubinage: a clerical compiler of the Annals of Ulster with at least twelve children was lauded by his continuator, in a famous phrase, as 'a gem of purity and a turtle-dove of chastity'. Clergy were also frequently kinsmen and dependents of ruling chiefs. Indeed Bishops O'Farrell of Ardagh (1480–1516) and Barret of Killala (1513–44) were chiefs themselves. Such practices inevitably involved the clergy in dynastic politics: in 1444 Bishop MacCoughlan of Clonmacnois, his son Archdeacon MacCoughlan, two brothers, and the prior of Clontuskert were slain in battle by a rival MacCoughlan faction.[13] Nor was violence excluded from more strictly ecclesiastical matters: Abbot Kavanagh, archdeacon of Leighlin, had his bishop killed on the king's highway in 1525, allegedly so as to obtain his bishopric; but this particularly heinous manifestation of Gaelic bestiality in an English enclave of the diocese provoked an equally savage response from Lord Deputy Kildare. The murderers were flayed alive and then disembowelled in Kildare's presence.[14] In the circumstances it is little wonder that laymen increasingly disregarded the privileges of sanctuary and immunity claimed for church lands and property.[15]

POPULAR RELIGION

Other abuses were perhaps less obviously pernicious than simply superstitious, though these 'superstitions' were chiefly an outgrowth from the low levels of learning in Gaelic society. In 1530 Niall O'Neill was 'most illegally disturbed' by a group of Armagh clerics who fasted and rang bells against him, apparently a not uncommon ecclesiastical sanction;[16] saints' battlers supposedly ensured victory by their presence on the battlefield, but were opposed by rival battlers; doughty warriors and mighty prelates atoned for past sins by burial in friars' habits; water poured into saints' bells cured sick animals; O'Brien of Thomond was killed by the evil eye in 1466; and in 1482 the appearance of a wonder-working holy cross was recorded. But with miracles and signs, prophecies and relics, we reach the commonplaces of Christianity throughout pre-Reformation Europe. Recent work on the western church has emphasized the high level of support for popular religious practices and stressed how closely these accorded with the needs of a non-literate, pre-industrial society.[17] In other words, popular religion was not irrational superstition, as humanists and protestants tended to think. These new insights have certainly helped to

13. Nicholls 1972, pp. 91–101; Mooney 1969, pp. 53–60 (quotation, p. 60).
14. *StP*, ii, 122; Freeman 1944, s.a. 1525; Butler 1849, s.a. 1525.
15. Nicholls 1972, pp. 101–2.
16. Gwynn 1946, p. 203.
17. Good examples are Bossy 1985; and for England, Duffy 1992.

explain the resilience of the pre-Reformation church in the face of concerted attacks by different groups of reformers. Yet they fail to answer their central charge that such practices were contrary to the order of the primitive church, nor do they explain why the Council of Trent likewise prohibited or discouraged them.

Devotional literature provides some insight into contemporary religious preoccupations: prose compositions were usually translations from Latin or, sometimes, English, but much Gaelic poetry was original though criticized none the less by modern historians for its insincerity, spiritual deficiencies, and preoccupation with metrical conventions. One bard translated parts of the Bible into Gaelic, but Christian humanists would probably have found distasteful the emphasis on Mary, the saints, fastings and pilgrimages, not to mention quirks like the description of Christ's crucifixion as the payment of an eric or blood-fine.[18] By contrast, Richard Butler, a colonist who tried his hand at Gaelic poetry, was prepared to sacrifice metre for content: a poem in praise of Christ composed on the day he died included the following verse:

> Whosoever loveth Jesus
> Privily in his heart
> No other love embraceth
> Till the world's end.[19]

The Observant movement

An important exception to the generally depressing state of the Gaelic church was the revival in the mendicant orders. One manifestation of this, the efflorescence of Irish Gothic architecture, has already been discussed (see above, pp. 38–9), though Gaelic buildings were usually less spacious and elaborate than those of English parts. Generally, however, the Gaelic contribution was the more important: beginning in the west and north c. 1400 and spreading rather later into the lordship, a wave of mendicant activity witnessed the foundation of no less than 47 new houses in the period 1400–1508, the majority in the Irishry.

Another manifestation was the reform among the Franciscans, Dominicans and Augustinians (known as the Observant movement because its supporters desired a stricter observance of the Rule prescribed for friars) which also saw many of the lordship's older houses converted to the Observance. Between 1460 and 1536 Observant houses established in the towns alone numbered eleven Franciscan, four Dominican, and four Augustinian.[20] The appeal to the friars of the Gaelic west and north, previously underrepresented in mendicant circles, doubtless arose partly from its remoteness and poverty. Conversely, the movement was, initially at least, a religious manifestation of the increasing

18. Mooney 1969, pp. 32–50; Watt 1972, pp. 211–12.
19. 'Gidhbé gráidhis Ísa/ Na c[h]roidhi go cluthair/ Ní théid [aen] grádh ele ann/ gu dere in domhain': Flower 1947, pp. 134–5 (my translation); Mac Niocaill 1958, pp. 83–8.
20. Watt 1972, pp. 193–9; Gwynn & Hadcock 1970, pp. 220, 240–1, 295.

self-confidence of Gaelic culture: the numerous chiefs who patronized it probably saw the new houses as a spiritual investment – an expiation of sin, a guarantee of continuous prayer for their intentions in life and, afterwards, for the repose of the soul.[21] At a different level, the movement perhaps answered the spiritual needs of the minority who desired more than the basic services and sacraments ministered by ill-educated and poorly paid priests: it attracted support as an isolated light in a naughty world, whereas in English Ireland the spiritual needs of merchants and gentry could find alternative forms of expression (see below, pp. 199–201).

Observantism later took hold in the towns, thus underlining its predominantly spiritual appeal (by the 1530s 56 out of 146 mendicant houses were explicitly Observant),[22] but the original geographical limits of this appeal may well have reflected a politico-cultural bias. Originally the mendicant provinces had been English, their Irish houses predominantly in towns: the vicar provincial was traditionally Old English and subordinate to the English provincial. The later Gaelic foundations finally tipped the balance numerically against the colonists at a time when English lordship was in general decline, and adoption of Observantism freed individual communities from English control. Instead independent Irish Observant congregations were established, reflecting the actual racial balance within each order.[23]

Reflecting their exceptional efforts to maintain the high standards prescribed by their Rules, the Observants and through them friars in general enjoyed a high reputation in pre-Reformation Ireland. In Gaelic parts their clerical privileges continued to be respected, and they were reportedly feared and almost adored even by nobles.[24] Even in the lordship Observant influence was decidedly stronger than in England: an English reformer denounced them in 1538 as 'false and crafty bloodsuckers' whose influence in high places made it 'hard . . . for any poor man to speak against their abusions'.[25] Considering the strenuous resistance to the Henrician Reformation offered by a mere seven Franciscan Observant houses in England, Irish Observantism was probably a significant factor shaping the eventual response to the Tudor Reformation.[26]

The monastic orders

Nevertheless the monastic orders, whose contribution to the vitality of the pre-Reformation church was potentially far weightier, were by then in steep decline. By the Dissolution there were scarcely six communities with six monks or more.[27] Married monks were not uncommon, monks failed to live in the

---

21. Watt 1972, p. 194.
22. Bradshaw 1974, pp. 8–9; Gwynn & Hadcock 1970, pp. 220, 240–1, 286, 295.
23. Bradshaw 1974, pp. 9–10; Watt 1972, pp. 195–8.
24. Bradshaw 1974, pp. 10–14.
25. *StP*, ii, 570.
26. Cf. Knowles 1959, pp. 10–13, 206–11.
27. Bradshaw 1974, pp. 36–7; Watt 1972, p. 188.

monasteries, observe the Rule or wear the habit, abbacies and priorships were sometimes quasi-hereditary, and some of those provided never took orders. For example, the abbey of Lough Key was accidentally burned in 1466 by a canon's wife carrying a lighted candle, and in east Ulster Gelasius Magennis (d. 1527) extended his territorial power by combining the priorships of the Benedictines of Down, the Augustinians of Saul, and the Cistercian abbacy of Newry.[28] In many ways the processes that had earlier provoked the twelfth-century reform movement – the transformation of monastic communities into clans of hereditary coarbs and erenaghs – were seemingly repeating themselves. In marchlands especially, local chiefs were acquiring a controlling interest in what were useful military strongpoints: in the Longford–Westmeath area, for example, O'Farrells held five monasteries by the Dissolution.[29] The Cistercian Order, once in the vanguard of twelfth-century reform, was in a particularly bad way: its General Chapter established a national congregation in 1496 hoping to compensate for its own declining control, and appointed special *reformatores*. Yet racial animosities proved too strong, and the report of Abbot Troy of Mellifont, one of these reformers, was particularly damning. Troy despaired of any remedy for the disorders, stating that only two (English) communities, Dublin and Mellifont, kept the Rule and wore the habit: he complained of ceaseless wars and racial hatred (though at the Dissolution the predominantly English communities of the Pale, Ormond and Wexford usually included Gaelic inmates), lack of adequate leadership, the inordinate influence of lay magnates, and the abandonment of corporate life, the liturgy and hospitality. And he sought dispensation from visiting Gaelic communities because of the risks involved and the violence to which he had been subjected on a previous visitation.[30]

Monasticism was in little better condition in the lordship. The Kildare rebellion precluded visitations like those in England, so the evidence is far scantier; but in autumn 1537 royal commissioners visiting the Ormond district also inquired about monasticism there, no doubt hoping to elicit evidence which would advance the suppression campaign recently begun. They were rewarded by two jury presentments against five houses of serious abuses concerning celibacy and religious observance. At Cistercian Inishlounaght, it was alleged, the liturgy was not celebrated, 'except a few masses by verba', and the abbot and monks each had a concubine and household. Similar complaints were made about Athassel priory and the prior of the Carmelite friars, Clonmel; the priory of Cahir did not celebrate the liturgy; and at St Katherine's, Waterford, the canons had separated and divided their revenues. Nevertheless good reasons have been adduced for not taking these complaints at face value; and even so, the surviving southern jury presentments mention altogether sixteen houses, but only in these five cases were such serious abuses alleged.

---

28. Nicholls 1972, pp. 107–9.
29. Bradshaw 1974, p. 35; Watt 1972, p. 187.
30. Conway 1958, pp. 153–8; Conway 1956, pp. 290–305; Conway 1957, pp. 146–62, 371–84; White 1943, *passim*.

Other evidence occasionally shows the monasteries in a more favourable light. They frequently participated in the late Gothic movement: some sponsored works of great quality in architecture, masonry and monumental sculpture, and the Cistercian abbot of Monasterevin had one of his monks compile at Mellifont an impressive liturgical *manuale* which survives in the Bodleian. Clearly the Ormond monks were not altogether corrupt: one survey of late medieval monasticism in the lordship has convincingly suggested that had the evidence been amenable to analysis like that for England, a similar conclusion – that a basis of truth underlay the smear campaign against the monks, despite exaggerated tales of their corruption – might well have fitted the Irish situation, allowing for differences of culture and religious style.[31]

The fourth reason for religious decline in later medieval Ireland, papal provisions, has already been touched on. Not only did the papacy encourage the resurgence of hereditary clans of Gaelic clerics by devising procedures to circumvent the canon law stipulation that a son should not succeed directly to his father's benefice, it also fostered conflicting provisions by its uncritical examination of self-interested complaints against beneficed clergy. Commonly a petitioner would travel to Rome and denounce an existing incumbent of crimes for which the appropriate canonical penalty was deprivation. The Curia appointed judges-delegate to try the accused, but the petitioner himself often suggested suitable judges: if they found the charges proven, the petitioner would be collated instead.[32] Thus in general, the combination of long-standing abuses in the Gaelic church, its poverty, the region's political instability, and the papacy's lack of interest in the problem precluded any real hope of spontaneous internal reform. Yet ironically, the immediate pre-Reformation period witnessed, through the cardinal protectorships, a quickening of the Anglo-papal cooperation that had been a feature of English rule in Ireland since Pope Adrian's bull *Laudabiliter* granted Henry II its lordship. Thereafter successive kings could generally rely on papal support because the papacy (when it thought about Ireland) regarded this as the best hope for religious reform there: for example in 1487, following the Simnel conspiracy, the papacy commanded ecclesiastics throughout Ireland to give allegiance to Henry VII.[33]

REVIVAL AND RENEWAL IN THE ENGLISHRY

Yet despite overwhelming evidence that the Irish church was in particularly poor shape in the late middle ages, there are also indications that in the century before the Reformation a religious recovery had begun, at least within the lordship's more sheltered parts. Here the state of religion more closely approached accepted European standards, and in the late fifteenth and early sixteenth centuries there was massive lay investment in the parish churches.

31. Bradshaw 1974, p. 27, and pp. 17–27 for this paragraph.
32. Watt 1972, pp. 188–93; Gwynn 1968, pp. 70–4; Nicholls 1972, pp. 103–5.
33. Above, pp. 85–6; Hayden 1915, pp. 632–3. Cf. Watt 1972, pp. 130–49.

In the rural parishes of Co. Louth, for instance, of the remains of 38 pre-Reformation churches so far identified, almost all were constructed in this period, and the others also show contemporary signs of renovation. Significantly, 28 of these churches lay within the maghery, south and east of the Pale ditch. And in addition, the parish churches in the towns of Ardee, Carlingford, Drogheda and Dundalk were evidently all embellished or extended at this time.

The growth in lay spiritual awareness was also reflected in increasing numbers of lay confraternities and Third Order groups in response to the pastoral activities of Observant friars. The foundation of chantries likewise became increasingly common: the most notable example was the Guild of St Anne in St Audoen's parish, Dublin, founded in 1430, which supported six chaplains celebrating masses for deceased benefactors at St Audoen's six side-altars; but St Mary's, Ardee, had five chantries each endowed with revenues of between six and ten marks (IR) a year; there were ten in St Peter's, Drogheda, and five more in St Nicholas's, Dundalk (the last founded c. 1539). Local lords also erected colleges for clergy serving nearby chantries and parish churches, most notably the collegiate chapel at Maynooth, erected by the earl of Kildare in 1518. At St Audoen's, the chaplains lived in a large residence next to the church; and at Ardee the de Verdon family likewise built an impressive college c. 1487 for the chantry priests.

No doubt the growing lay investment in the church also reflected the lordship's increased prosperity and political stability during this period rather than simply an increase in piety. Yet clearly this Irish manifestation of the kind of lay spiritual awareness and promotion of church building which characterized the pre-Reformation church elsewhere in the Tudor state must also have helped to improve the quality of the church's ministry and religious services. Within the English Pale at least, there is no sign of any serious dissatisfaction with the clergy: a recent study of the Co. Louth parish clergy has shown that they were adequately trained, normally resident, and usually conscientious. Even though they did not normally deliver extended sermons, they none the less taught their congregations through homilies: in 1526 Archbishop Cromer directed his clergy to acquire a copy of *Ignorantia sacerdotum*, a manual which was widely used in pre-Reformation England, with a programme for quarterly homilies to instruct the laity concerning the creed, the ten commandments, the seven principal virtues, the seven deadly sins, and the seven sacraments. Similarly, in surviving lay wills from the diocese of Dublin in the late fifteenth century the scale of bequests to the parish clergy and church likewise indicates that they were generally held in high regard. As in England, chantries and guilds marked the feastdays of saints to which they were dedicated by solemn processions and liturgies; and towns and cities like Kilkenny and Dublin celebrated such festivals as Corpus Christi and St George's Day by the enactment of pageants and mystery plays.[34]

34. Jefferies 1997a, ch. 2; Lennon 1991, pp. 10–11; Lennon 1994, pp. 122–4; Berry 1898; *Valor* 1741, pp. 2, 11; Seymour 1929, pp. 118–34; Gwynn 1968, pp. 50–1; Lynch 1982, p. 9.

Although no university was successfully established in medieval Ireland, Oxford and to a lesser degree Cambridge and continental universities remained more accessible to the lordship's beneficed clergy: more of them were gradu ates, though Gaelic parts had their own schools of learning, and it is probably no coincidence that the only extant catalogue of a medieval Irish monastic library comes from a town, Youghal, which held the mother house of the Franciscan Order in Ireland. Dating from 1494, with an addenda of 1523, the list of 130 volumes was long on scholastic theology, preaching literature and scripture, but short on canon law. To judge by its contents, the library, though small, reflected fairly creditably on Franciscan pastoral work. It included con-tributions by local (mainly Old English) friars as well as recent Italian works, though the only contemporary Irish scholar of international repute, Maurice O'Fihilly, archbishop of Tuam (1506–13) and before that professor of theology at Padua, was also the only medieval Gaelic theologian of note.[35]

Prospects for Tudor reform

The evidence for a religious revival in the English Pale and the lordship's towns in the immediate pre-Reformation period also highlights the crucial importance of the leading merchants and gentry of the English community in shaping the local response to Tudor reform. Evidence regarding the distribu-tion of wealth within the pre-Reformation church also points to the same con-clusion. It has long been accepted that the government's ability to enforce its ecclesiastical reforms was to a large extent determined by the value of the benefices and the size of the parishes. Broadly, where livings were sufficiently rich to attract the services of well-qualified or graduate clergy, and where parishes were comparatively small – as in lowland England – more effective instruments of conversion and control could be brought to bear. The evidence already discussed suggests that, even had the necessary degree of political control been established, conditions in Gaelic Ireland were far from conducive to the government's campaign. For English Ireland, the 'taxation' of benefices in the Irish Valor in the late 1530s permits both a more exact assessment of the distribution of ecclesiastical wealth and also a comparison with the English parishes for which the Tudor campaign had originally been designed. Broadly, the English Valor Ecclesiasticus suggests that a benefice worth £13 a year was a comfortable minimum for a rector or vicar with his 'usual' expenses, but that about half the livings in England were worth less than £10 per annum, and in Wales (where conditions approximated more closely to those in much of Ire-land, with larger parishes and poorer livings) the proportion was 70 per cent. By comparison, the Irish Valor suggests that in English Ireland 85 per cent of the livings were worth IR£15 (= £10 sterling) or less. In fact, the average value per benefice was only IR£11 5s. 2½d. a year; and whereas in Wales 23 per cent

35. Bradshaw 1974, pp. 14–16; Gwynn 1968, pp. 36–7, 73–6; Watt 1972, pp. 201–2; Mooney 1969, pp. 21–7, 61; Coleman 1925, pp. 111–20.

Table 1: Annual incomes per benefice in English Ireland[36]

Diocese	Annual income of bishopric	No. benefices listed	Range of income per benefice				Average income per benefice
			over £20	£10–20	£5–10	under £5	
Armagh (*inter Anglicos*)	IR£183 17s. 1½d.	33	1	2	6	24	IR£11 18s. 2d.
Meath	IR£373 12s. 0½d.	106	4	14	29	59	IR£13 9s. 10d.
Dublin	IR£534 15s. 2½d.	70	8	13	20	29	IR£22 8s. 8d.
Kildare	IR£69 11s. 4d.	53	3	3	9	38	IR£8 16s. 2d.
Ossory	IR£66 13s. 4d.	76	2	6	20	48	IR£8 14s. 11d.
Ferns	IR£108 13s. 4d.	81	7	12	17	45	IR£11 3s. 4d.
Leighlin (*inter Anglicos*)	IR£50 0s. 0d.	30	1	0	0	29	IR£4 14s. 1d.
Cashel	IR£66 13s. 4d.	58	1	0	6	51	IR£4 1s. 3d.
Waterford (excl. Lismore)	IR£72 8s. 1d.	34	1	4	7	22	IR£8 4s. 11d.
Total		541	28 (5%)	54 (10%)	114 (21%)	345 (64%)	

36. Calculated from *Valor* 1741; see Ellis 1990, pp. 248–53. Jefferies 1998b also draws attention to the potential role of lay procurators (churchwardens in England) in enforcing reform.

Table 2: Extents of Irish monastic possessions by county

Shire	Gross value	Shire	Gross value
Dublin	IR£1,767 11s. 8¾d.	Meath	IR£1,082 18s. 9d.
Louth	IR£557 15s. 8½d.	Kilkenny	IR£413
Westmeath	IR£282 18s. 9d.	Kildare	IR£238 9s.
Wexford	IR£171 4s. 5d.	Waterford	IR£170 10s. 10d.
Tipperary	IR£117 11s. 10d.	Cork	IR£63 5s. 8½d.
Carlow	IR£41 11s. 4d.	Limerick	IR£24 7s. 3d.
Total	IR£4,929 18s. 10¾d.	*Net* of pensions	IR£4,069 11s. 4¾d.

of the benefices were wretchedly poor, worth £5 or less, in English Ireland no less than 64 per cent were in this category.

This meant that clerical talent was likely to be spread even more thinly in Ireland than in Wales, since the better-qualified clergy would tend to gravitate to the richer livings or leave for greener English pastures. Yet even within the Englishry, marked differences between dioceses occurred in the average wealth of livings, ranging from the modest affluence of Dublin (averaging IR£22 8s. 8d. per benefice) to the abject poverty of Cashel (IR£4 1s. 3d.). Predictably, as Table 1 suggests, clerical wealth was largely concentrated in the Pale maghery, with a smaller concentration around Waterford city, south Wexford and Kilkenny.

Unlike its English counterpart, the Irish *Valor* did not include valuations of religious houses. Yet the 1540–1 survey of dissolved monasteries points to a similar concentration of wealth in the English Pale. As Table 2 shows, by county no less than 58 per cent of the gross value of monastic possessions was concentrated in Dublin and Meath, and of the ten other counties surveyed, only Louth and Kilkenny yielded more than IR£300 a year. By monastery, this inequality was equally marked, with five houses in Cos. Dublin, Louth and Meath in receipt of 55 per cent of the total net income.[37] Thus, the evidence concerning the distribution of ecclesiastical wealth on the eve of the Tudor Reformation suggests that only in the Pale and the towns were conditions comparable with those for which the campaign had originally been designed, so highlighting those richer parts as the decisive theatre in the forthcoming campaign for a reformed church.

Elsewhere, however, the Irish church was manifestly in greater need of reform than other areas where the Reformation succeeded. Indeed, if the fate of state-sponsored reform had depended largely on the condition of the pre-Reformation church, Ireland must surely have appeared a prime target for success. And if the Irish church exhibited little evident anticlericalism or anti-papalism before the 1530s this arose more from secularism, ignorance, and popular indifference to such issues than from any great regard for the senior

---

37. These figures are calculated from White 1943 (esp. p. 376). See Ellis 1990, pp. 248–53.

clergy or the papacy. Indeed the unity of the pre-Reformation church was largely nominal: Fr Mooney concluded that the Gaelic population was 'less sophisticated, more superstitious, more conservative in customs and beliefs', and 'preaching and the liturgy . . . even more neglected than in the Anglo-Irish towns'.[38] Townsmen and Gaelic nobles were no doubt at opposite poles, but if racial strife had by 1500 declined to the extent that religious movements like Observantism could cross ethnic boundaries, there remained real differences in religious life between the lordship's more settled parts and Gaelic Ireland. Thus the chances of united 'national' opposition developing to an alien reform movement seemed remote. There were good reasons for optimism by king and council that Irish opposition to their religious policies would prove less serious and substantial, at least within the lordship, than in other Tudor borderlands.

Although few practical benefits had hitherto accrued from it, the crown's traditional association with religious reform in Ireland perhaps made the Henrician Reformation seem the less innovatory, particularly until it became apparent that English kings were far more interested in quick profits and greater control than in the reforms that were supposed to follow. Indeed the government readily found some support for its policies among those merchants and gentry who had long campaigned for a sustained political initiative to reduce the whole island to civility:[39] since in Ireland the Henrician Reformation coincided with the post-1534 political changes, many settlers saw it, much as was intended, as a welcome (if slightly eccentric) sign that the government was now intent on a thorough reformation of society there. Moreover the loyalist spirit of the colonial community made it particularly receptive to the traditional appeals to loyalty with which the Tudors hoped to secure religious conformity. Thus circumstances there were very favourable to the growth of indigenous support for reform which was so essential an ingredient to protestant progress. Conversely, Gaelic nobles and clerics might be distinctive, conservative, and politically unreliable, but they were also among the most isolated from the intellectual movements of Renaissance Europe, and therefore very vulnerable to a properly coordinated campaign. It would certainly be a mistake to see the eager acceptance by dissident nobles of papal support for successive rebellions in Elizabethan Ireland as a logical outcome of the country's medieval religious divisions: papal links with Gaelic Ireland had hitherto been neither noticeably happy nor strong, so that such a volte-face in policy would necessarily take time to accomplish.

Coupled with the widespread secularism in both English and Gaelic areas, therefore, these considerations suggested that the initial response to the Tudor Reformation would be a largely political one. Contrary to the traditional view, the state of the pre-Reformation church was in general quite susceptible to state-sponsored reform, and at worst ensured that the state authorities would enjoy a substantial respite during which to consolidate their position before

38. Mooney 1969, p. 61.
39. Cf. Bradshaw 1979a, ch. 2.

facing the sort of campaign organized by the Roman church from Elizabeth's last years onwards. Why then did the Church of Ireland fail, even in the Pale and the towns, to hold a majority allegiance of Ireland's inhabitants?

REFORM BY STATUTE: THE IRISH REFORMATION PARLIAMENT

This question is framed advisedly, in view of modern revisionist accounts of the Reformation in Ireland. Against the traditional view that the failure of reform was inevitable,[40] there is now a convincing demonstration that the reformers did in fact make progress under Henry VIII and even under Edward VI, and a further argument that initially at least under Elizabeth this progress was maintained.[41] Though periodization remains unacceptably vague,[42] most historians would now see the years 1580–1600 as decisive.[43] From the outset the government relied heavily in extending its religious policies to Ireland on the royal prerogative and the applicability of English legislation there. In 1534 Lord Deputy Skeffington was simply instructed to resist papal provisions and jurisdiction 'according to the statutes thereupon provided, and the like to be enacted there the next parliament'. The earl of Ossory also undertook to assist in 'reducing the people to Christian manners', but beyond Cromwell's despatch of two chaplains, no special measures were contemplated.[44] This low-key approach almost backfired when the Kildare rebellion suddenly focused international attention on an Irish noble purportedly leading a catholic crusade against English heresy, but in the event the revolt simply served to flush out the very few committed opponents of reform and so smoothed the passage of ecclesiastical legislation in Grey's parliament. The English-born chancellor of St Patrick's cathedral, Dublin, Dr John Travers, who had written in support of the papal primacy, was executed for treason in supporting the rebels[45] and a few more clerics probably suffered similarly; yet despite modern claims of a packed parliament browbeaten by government into passing highly unpopular bills, the opposition was in general remarkably muted by comparison with that in England.

The kernel of the English ecclesiastical legislation was introduced in six bills – many of them identical *mutatis mutandis* with the English measures as eventually enacted – in the first session of parliament. The principle of royal supremacy was laid down in the bill for the supreme head; the succession bill recognized the succession rights of Henry's children by Anne Boleyn and enjoined an oath accepting the validity of the marriage (and, incidentally, the royal supremacy); and the bill for slander made treasonable any opposition to

40. The classic exposition is Edwards 1935.
41. To 1553 see the works of Bradshaw; Canny 1979b, pp. 423–50.
42. Cf. Canny 1979b, p. 450.
43. See now Bottigheimer 1976, pp. 140–49; Bottigheimer 1985, pp. 196–207; Ford 1997.
44. Ellis 1976, pp. 809–11.
45. Edwards 1934, pp. 687–99; Ellis 1976, pp. 812, 815–22.

the marriage or Henry's new titles. More practically, the bill for first fruits replaced papal annates with a revised tax for the new Supreme Head (see above, pp. 143–4); the bill 'in restraint of appeals' substituted chancery for the Roman Curia as the final ecclesiastical court of appeal; and the faculties bill provided for the issue of ecclesiastical dispensations and licences by the crown instead of the pope. All but the last had received the royal assent within a month. Councillors reported parliament's tractability and the king replied with separate letters of thanks to both houses.[46]

The only recorded protest came from the lower clergy who constituted a third house of clerical proctors in the medieval Irish parliament, whereas in England they sat separately in convocation. In subsequent sessions, the Commons rejected a bill to dissolve thirteen monasteries, but their behaviour demonstrated that this opposition was not primarily religious (see above, pp. 143–4): their spokesman, the king's serjeant-at-law, Patrick Barnewall, argued that the royal supremacy conferred a spiritual jurisdiction to reform religious houses but not to interfere with ecclesiastical temporalities by dissolving monasteries. In fact the supremacy had not been intended as a vehicle to suppress monasteries, which were by no means incompatible with the Henrician Reformation; and the wording of the supremacy act meant that Barnewall had a strong case which, following a visit to court in the Commons' deputation, he quietly dropped.

After assurances and concessions by the king the Commons' opposition collapsed, leaving the clergy isolated. The lords spiritual then prevaricated by demanding clarification of the proctors' constitutional position, using their majority to halt business. The proctors' precise status was unclear: the king's lawyers argued that some bills had hitherto passed notwithstanding rejection by the proctors, but as the bishops insisted they may well have had a veto on ecclesiastical matters.[47] The impasse was only broken when royal commissioners arrived with fresh powers and instructions: the commissioners read the king's letters directing the lords and commons to pass such acts as were proposed and to frame themselves to an honest thankful conformity, 'and if anyone will not we shall so look upon him with our princely eye as his ingratitude therein shall be little to his comfort'.[48] Four new bills were then introduced – to extrude the proctors from membership of parliament (a measure which further reduced the Irish institution to conformity with parliament in England), to abrogate papal jurisdiction and impose an oath of Supremacy on

46. Bradshaw 1968–9, pp. 285–303; Bradshaw 1974, pp. 47–65 *et passim*; Edwards 1968, pp. 59–84; Edwards 1935, pp. 5–15.

47. Dr Henry Jefferies (1997a, pp. 137–8) has recently argued that the government's ecclesiastical legislation was blocked in parliament's first session by the proctors' opposition. Yet the council reported specifically that the statutes had passed. He may be right, however, that subsequently doubts about their legality without the proctors' assent delayed their implementation. The succession act in particular could only have passed in the first session since it related to Anne Boloyn: after her execution in mid-May, Cromwell wrote asking that the royal assent be withheld. See also Richardson & Sayles 1952, pp. 183–6.

48. Bradshaw 1974, p. 64 (quotation).

all office-holders in line with a recent English statute, to extend first fruits to superiors of religious houses (since at this stage only a limited dissolution was planned), and to settle the succession on Henry's children by his latest wife, Jane Seymour.

Taxed with ingratitude, the bishops abandoned their subordinates and passed both these bills, the bill dissolving some lesser monasteries, and the amended bill for twentieth parts (see above, Ch. 6). The faculties bill also passed after amendment to allow the alternative issue in Ireland of dispensations where the original bill had specified, like its English counterpart, their issue by the archbishop of Canterbury (in May 1536 the appeals bill had been similarly amended to allow the Irish chancery appellate jurisdiction): apparently these integrationist measures, minor aspects of 'unitary sovereignty', had been resisted by the Irish council.[49] Other English legislation, such as the acts in restraint of annates and for the clergy's submission, were considered unnecessary. In the event, therefore, the lords spiritual showed far less courage in resisting Henry's demands than in England, which was just as well for the king because his influence over the Irish bishops was generally more limited.

THE HENRICIAN REFORMATION

Character and content

Although conservative theologians might fear (justifiably) that the breach with Rome and the royal supremacy presaged the introduction of a continental-style reformation, the state church, while Henry VIII lived, remained far closer doctrinally to Rome than to continental protestants: and to the layman who was more interested in the visible aspects of his religion than in abstruse theological arguments the continuity of the Church of Ireland with its predecessor was even more reassuring. This continuity and the innate loyalty of the colonial community go far towards explaining the jurisdictional success of the Henrician Reformation in Ireland. To spearhead the reform campaign, Henry and Cromwell chose George Browne, the English provincial of the Augustinians, who was appointed to the vacant see of Dublin and reached Ireland in July 1536.[50] Though variously portrayed by historians as an earnest protestant or a vicar of Bray, Browne was like many other secondary figures of the early Reformation period, essentially a civil servant rather than a committed reformer. His approach was authoritarian: his directives closely followed official promulgations in England and he looked to the penal clauses of statutes and the support of the secular arm to secure conformity. By contrast, the other active episcopal supporter of reform, the more conservative Bishop Staples of Meath, advocated progress by consent, explanation and education rather than mere conformity.

49. See also Bradshaw 1979a, pp. 145–6.
50. For the following, Bradshaw 1970, pp. 301–26; and on policy disagreements with Bishop Staples, Bradshaw 1978a, pp. 478–80.

Despite sporadic attempts since 1535 to exercise the royal supremacy,[51] the active phase of reform was eventually inaugurated in September 1537, following the Irish enactment of the ecclesiastical legislation. Browne received a sharp royal reprimand for neither 'giving himself to the instruction of the people in the word of God' nor furthering the king's affairs.[52] In fact he had been unwilling to act before the second succession bill had passed, allowing him to administer the new succession oath, but he soon made amends by inaugurating a campaign of preaching, and by introducing English versions of common prayers. His preaching was in the approved evangelical style, 'moving questions of scripture', in line with the English *Injunctions* which required the clergy to encourage the people to read the Bible, and criticizing current practices concerning the veneration of images, indulgences and auricular confession.[53] Early in 1538 he promoted reform by introducing the 'form of the beads' – revised English bidding prayers which almost amounted to a confession of faith. They were to be read at Sunday Mass before the preface, and affirmed the royal supremacy, the celebrant's personal acceptance of the supremacy, and the abrogation of the bishop of Rome's usurped authority. A section on the vexed question of justification outlined the teaching of the recent English *Bishop's Book* requiring contrition and faith joined with charity (i.e. virtually the catholic position). Auricular confession was not mentioned, but congregations were reminded that remission of sins was through Christ alone and that the pope's 'great thunderclaps of excommunication', his bulls and pardons 'which beforetime, with his juggling, casts of binding and loosing, he sold unto you for your money', were worthless; and they were exhorted to expunge the pope's name from liturgical books and to pray for 'all them that preacheth the word of God purely and sincerely'.[54] Finally in autumn 1538 Cromwell despatched to Ireland a version of the *New Injunctions*, issued in September, which also required incumbents to preach the Gospel quarterly and discouraged superstitious practices such as 'wanderings to pilgrimages, offerings . . . to feigned relics or images', and vain repetition of prayers over beads; but the requirement to provide an English Bible in every parish church was waived in view of the problems of supply and the prevalence of Gaelic in many parts.[55] Browne, however, promulgated the official English translations of the Lord's Prayer, creed, Hail Mary and Ten Commandments, and the clergy were instructed to teach them to their flocks by rote.[56]

The evangelical phase of the Henrician Reformation ended in May 1539 with the English parliament's passing of the Act of Six Articles: this reasserted the state church's essential orthodoxy against Lutheran influences by affirming transubstantiation, communion under one species, private masses, auricular

51. Bradshaw 1974, pp. 42–4, 66–7; Gwynn 1946, p. 211.
52. Bradshaw 1970, p. 312.
53. Bradshaw 1979a, p. 156.
54. *StP*, ii. 564–5.
55. *StP*, iii, 111–12; Bradshaw 1970, pp. 312–13; Bradshaw 1979a, pp. 155–8; Edwards 1935, pp. 22, 49–50, 63–4 (quotations, pp. 22, 49).
56. *StP*, iii, 111–12; Bradshaw 1970, pp. 312–13.

confession, clerical celibacy and the religious vows of chastity, poverty and obedience. In fact the Irish church had not been exposed to committed protestant preachers like Bishops Latimer and Shaxton so no reaction was necessary. Browne, though a Cromwellian, quickly modified his stance and continued to enforce the royal supremacy from his rather less influential position during Henry's last years.[57]

The enforcement of conformity

The enforcement of conformity probably mirrored the government's experience in many parts of England, although the evidence is very sparse except for the activities of Browne and Cromer. Altogether Henry VIII eventually secured some recognition in 24 of the 32 dioceses, either from pre-Reformation bishops who conformed, by successfully nominating bishops himself, or by confirming later papal provisors. Responding to the diplomacy of the Geraldine League, the papacy challenged conforming bishops, and from October 1538 until St Leger's initiative won over Gaelic chiefs (by mid-1542) this policy – a Gaelic harbinger of the developing link between the papacy and religious dissidents in Elizabethan Ireland – had some success. Thereafter, however, St Leger persuaded papal provisors to surrender their bulls for royal patents: where royal nominees were also involved some compromise between the rival candidates was usually agreed, but the few intractable papal bishops lost control of their sees.[58] Some bishops nevertheless managed to remain acceptable to both sides, and even under Elizabeth the last bishop so recognized, Owen O'Hart of Achonry, died only in 1603. Before 1541, however, the full reform campaign was confined to the Pale, Wexford, Ormond and royal towns. Prominent in it were Browne, Staples, and the Irish Augustinian provincial, Richard Nangle, a Gaelic Observant friar whom the king unsuccessfully tried to intrude as bishop of Clonfert; but other bishops were cooperative – Butler of Cashel, Baron of Ossory, Comyn of Waterford, Quin of Limerick, Nugent of Kilmore, and Bodkin of Kilmacduagh whom Henry appointed also to Tuam. Primate Cromer of Armagh (d. 1542) had been implicated in the Kildare rebellion and his archdeacon, Cormac Roth, had participated in the earl's catholic crusade. Subsequently, Cromer's studied inactivity, pleading ill-health while accepting the royal supremacy, did much to insulate this key diocese from aspects of the Henrician campaign. The proctors' opposition in parliament was led by William Hamlin, vicar of St Peter's, Drogheda; and when Roth died c. 1539 Cromer chose as his official principal and commissary another leading conservative, Prior George Dowdall of Ardee, who later succeeded him as primate.[59]

Progress of course was never fast enough for the authorities, and also somewhat hampered by internal dissensions: Browne associated with Grey's rivals

57. Bradshaw 1970, pp. 314–15.
58. Bradshaw 1979a, pp. 246–8; *HBC*, pp. 323–445 *passim*.
59. Edwards 1935, pp. 31, 101–8; Bradshaw 1974, pp. 94–5; Nicholls 1972, p. 103; Jefferies 1997a, pp. 135–48.

on the council and even Staples thought his scriptural disquisitions ill-advised. In Dublin diocese Browne complained, without much exaggeration, that his two cathedral chapters unanimously opposed the changes and that those who formerly 'preache[d] after the old sort and fashion' now kept silence except 'in corners and such company as them liketh'.[60] More serious for the future, however, were the difficulties of attracting committed reformers. An Englishman attracted by Browne's offer of an archdeaconry discovered that it was not worth the promised 100 marks a year and returned.[61] Yet Dublin benefices were the only ones in Ireland generally comparable in value with those in lowland England, which meant that reform in Ireland would be particularly dependent on local efforts.

Overt resistance was another matter: the clergy generally took the supremacy oath and observed a minimal conformity. In one Dublin church, in May 1538, a prebendary of St Patrick's who had refused the supremacy oath now ignored Browne's bidding prayers: he was presented by the parishioners and spent the next fortnight in prison. Bishop Staples' suffragan who publicly prayed for the pope and the king's reconciliation was likewise imprisoned. Despite Browne, however, councillors generally felt that initially leniency would achieve more than severity: the bishop of (?) Annaghdown and a Mullingar friar, arrested for unspecified offences in Meath, were sent up to Dublin castle. Following complaints to the king, they were eventually indicted and arraigned but, to Browne's disgust, only for the lesser offence of *praemunire*, and released after a short imprisonment upon promise of good behaviour.[62] This mild policy made no martyrs, unlike the stir following the execution of leading Geraldines, while forcing opposition underground: an Observant who preached against the changes at Waterford was immediately arrested, 'so as now, what for fear they have to preach their old traditions, and the little or no good will they have to preach the verity, all is put to silence'.[63]

More generally, however, Lord Butler's active support ensured 'good and obedient conformity' in Ormond. Browne could thus move to convert outward conformity into a more positive acceptance of royal supremacy. A highlight of this campaign was the conciliar itineration through the south-east after Christmas 1538, *inter alia* to publish the royal injunctions and advance reform. The archbishop preached at Kilkenny, New Ross, Wexford, Waterford and Clonmel, the councillors remarking the large audiences attracted; and at Clonmel, to which all the Munster bishops were summoned, two archbishops and eight bishops took the oath. The corporations and local bishops at Limerick and Galway had already been sworn six months before and ordered to swear the citizens and diocesan clergy and certify this into chancery; while for Gaelic-speaking parts Nangle of Clonfert preached as Browne's suffragan.[64]

60. *StP*, ii, 539–40, iii, 6–7; Bradshaw 1970, pp. 311, 312.
61. Edwards 1935, pp. 44, 51; Ellis 1976, p. 811.
62. *StP*, iii, 6–9, 102–5; Edwards 1935, pp. 56–8, 62–3; Bradshaw 1974, pp. 94–5.
63. *StP*, ii, 562.
64. *StP*, ii, 561–4, iii, 57–63, 111–18, 123–4 (quotation, p. 112); Edwards 1935, pp. 54–5, 85–8.

Yet in Ireland the friars largely refused to promote reform, and the shortage of suitable preachers severely restricted progress. Some Observants were downright recalcitrant, no doubt encouraged by the visit of the Franciscan Observant General in 1534. In England Browne had countered by integrating them into conventual communities, but in Ireland the Observants predominated and he could only transfer jurisdiction by 'naming them conventuals', an expedient which achieved nothing. He proceeded against some houses in his metropolitan area, swearing them to the supremacy despite lacking the requisite authority, but news of the wholesale dissolution proceeding in England rendered this unnecessary. The Observants themselves were soon demoralized by this news and all but the most dedicated had disbanded.[65]

Another aspect of the reform campaign which might have provoked significant popular reaction was that against images early in 1539. Its nature reflected the *Bishop's Book*, which saw images and relics as useful devotional aids but sought to remedy abuses springing from superstitions and clerical rapacity. It therefore extended only to 'notable images or relics' the subject of superstitious pilgrimages by simple people who were wont 'to lick, kiss or honour [them], contrary to God's honour'. The background, however, was the administration's urgent need to raise money for an army against the Geraldine League. The Irish commission to destroy images, issued in February, was thus occasionally anticipated, as at Limerick; but the Tyrconnell clergy were reportedly elevating the League into a crusade by preaching 'that every man ought, for the salvation of his soul, fight and make war' against the king and loyal subjects. Chancellor Alen feared that colonial resistance might be undermined 'by the enticement and conduct of our friars obstinates [Observants]'. Accordingly the commissioners acted very circumspectly, probably in strict accordance with their commissions, and the operation left no trace of local resentment. The total proceeds from the Pale, the south-east and midlands (excluding Limerick and Waterford cities and Kilkenny town), however, were only IR£346, far less than the proceeds of *one* popular shrine in England; and since the major shrines at Trim (IR£40), Ballyboggan (a mere 26s.) and Christ Church (IR£36) yielded little more than simple parish churches, the commissioners probably confined their activities to local cults.[66]

The dissolution of the monasteries

To a large extent, however, reaction to the Henrician Reformation was shaped by the dissolution of the religious orders, since this doctrinally incidental campaign constituted in practice one of the most visible breaks with tradition. The dissolution is one of the few aspects of the Reformation in Ireland that has been the subject of a detailed, scholarly study.

Ironically, the Pale houses, in which the discrepancy between the Rule and actual practice was less apparent, were the first to attract government

---

65. Bradshaw 1974, pp. 94–7; *StP*, iii, 103; Ellis 1976, pp. 812, 816.
66. Bradshaw 1974, pp. 100–9, 210–11 (quotations, pp. 108, 210–11).

attention. They were in general rich enough to attract a dissolution movement as in England. Even the richest of them, the Knights Hospitallers of Kilmainham, was worth only IR£650 per annum net according to the 1540–1 survey, and only two more houses exceeded the £200 annually thought necessary in England to sustain a viable community of twelve persons;[67] yet a comparatively high proportion of the lordship's landed wealth was invested in defence, and the monasteries' share of the remainder was excessive: the valuation of Cistercian holdings in the Pale, Ormond and Wexford, for example, exceeded that of the Kildare earls. Rumours of dissolution prompted speculation about strengthening marches by reorganizing landholdings there, and once vested interests of local merchants and gentry were assured, the dissolution provoked comparatively little opposition and the monks surrendered quietly enough. The three phases of the process were largely an Irish adaptation of the general English pattern. Excepting isolated individual surrenders, the first stage (which corresponded to the English act dissolving the lesser monasteries (1536)) comprised the seizure of Irish property of English houses and the closure of isolated cells following the 1536 act of resumption, and the suppression (May 1537) of thirteen smaller and mainly decrepit houses in the Pale (9), Wexford (3) and Kilkenny (1).[68]

Long before the king had determined on total suppression, however, parties in Ireland were seeking an extension of suppression to richer houses for financial reasons: Undertreasurer Brabazon hoped to increase crown revenues and Dublin city wished to recoup losses suffered in the Kildare rebellion. Yet the Dublin administration's plans of 1537–8 for a more systematic but still limited campaign to prune out ailing or politically unreliable houses were overtaken by Henry's decision (September 1538) for total closure. The resultant suppression commission for Ireland (issued in April 1539, concurrently with the passage of the greater English monasteries act) had thus long been anticipated: many houses had prepared by making long leases of property at 'give-away' rents to kinsmen and influential supporters, or in return for large cash payments, and had granted annuities to their lay officers. In consequence the value of monastic property to the crown, it was estimated, was reduced by a third.

The crisis of the Geraldine League disrupted the commission's work, but the bulk of the Pale houses surrendered in October–November, and houses in Wexford, Waterford, Kilkenny and Tipperary were hastily dissolved in March 1540. Certain councillors petitioned for the retention of six greater houses as secular colleges, alleging their special social and cultural utility: Christ Church alone was so spared – by the council acting on its own authority and under pressure from the citizens – but the eventual price was the downgrading in 1546 of the secular cathedral, St Patrick's, to a parish church. This phase closed in November 1540 with the surrender of the Knights Hospitallers where the aged but astute grandmaster, Sir John Rawson, an old crown servant, extracted

---

67. White 1943, *passim*; Youings 1971, p. 42.
68. Bradshaw 1974, pp. 32–3, 47–77.

the title Viscount Clontarf, Hospitaller lands there, and a 500 mark (IR) pension. It added some 47 houses to the 16 previously suppressed. Two statutes of St Leger's parliament subsequently confirmed the crown's title to houses which had 'voluntarily surrendered', and permitted ex-religious to earn a living.[69]

The monks usually received an annual pension pending redeployment (if possible) as secular clergy. Its size largely depended on the monastery's revenues, up to IR£50 for superiors of great houses like Mellifont, around IR£6 for lesser superiors, and two or three marks (IR) for ordinary monks: superiors' pensions were evidently ample, and ordinary monks received roughly the same as Dublin monasteries had hitherto paid curates serving parish churches under their care. In practice, the crown's desire to minimize expenditure on pensions tended to preserve continuity of personnel: monks stayed on to serve rural cures as before, served new cures established in previously monastic churches, or received curacies in appropriated parish churches. Even the buildings were frequently left undisturbed: half the churches of monasteries suppressed in the Pale and Ormond in 1539–40 continued to serve as parish churches.[70]

Concurrently with the 1539–40 monastic dissolutions, the mendicant communities were suppressed. Details of this activity have not survived, but altogether 51 houses were closed in the same districts between Carlingford and Dungarvan. Profits to the crown were meagre and the degree of disruption probably greater: because of the friaries' more limited endowment their revenues did not suffice for pensions, and instead legal records noted euphemistically 'the withdrawal of the late prior and convent on their voluntary abandonment of the priory'. In practice, most communities soon dispersed. The majority were situated in urban areas under the more vigilant eye of the authorities and where the buildings were more likely to be demolished or converted to other uses: only four were retained as parish churches, but some were adopted as municipal buildings: Blackfriars, Dublin, became an inn of court; and friaries at Waterford, Mullingar and Naas became a hospital, gaol and shire house respectively. Yet some communities, especially the more remote, entrusted their goods to local wellwishers and withdrew, sometimes temporarily, beyond the government's reach. Probably only eight communities, however, almost all of them Franciscan Observant, survived long enough to re-emerge under Mary. It was only in the changed political circumstances of Elizabeth's reign that friars in Gaelic parts recovered sufficient influence to stiffen papal support.[71]

The final phase (1541–3) was largely a cosmetic exercise by which St Leger aimed to secure political recognition of the crown's ecclesiastical claims by granting the profits to local lords. In so far as the initiative had a religious objective, it ran parallel to the constitutional initiative erecting the lordship into a kingdom. The supremacy act had declared Henry 'the only supreme head

69. Ibid., pp. 78–92, 110–25, 183–5.
70. Ibid., pp. 130–5.
71. Ibid., pp. 137–45, 208–16; Jefferies 1997a, pp. 138–40.

in earth of the whole Church of Ireland', but in the 1530s Irish councillors merely sought nominal submission to the royal supremacy from Gaelic bishops. The full reform campaign was confined to the lordship, and the authorities inclined to treat it ecclesiastically as part of one national church: Browne had congregations pray for the one 'Church of England and Ireland'.[72] From 1540, however, St Leger concentrated doctrinally on the royal supremacy and its juridical acceptance throughout Ireland. He was also more conciliatory, following advice from Bishop Staples who warned that people were saying that 'the supremacy . . . is maintained only by power and not reasoned by learning'.

As an ecclesiastical aspect of surrender and regrant shorn of Lutheran influences, the campaign was generally successful: Gaelic chiefs agreed to resist papal jurisdiction and papal bishops surrendered their bulls; but its religious and financial fruits were tenuous.[73] In Ards and Lecale the religious houses surrendered in 1542–3; Limerick and Cork cities were visited in January and February 1541 and houses in Youghal and Kinsale were merely *surveyed* from Cork; and Cos. Limerick, Cork and Kerry witnessed a cursory visitation, probably in autumn 1542, of a commission headed by Desmond, and four mendicant and four monastic houses out of 50 were nominally suppressed. Two monasteries were leased to English soldiers. Other commissions granted houses to local lords: O'Brien received those in Thomond in exchange for rectories east of the Shannon, and in Connaught and Ulster individual houses were so suppressed. In practice, however, those communities who wished could usually continue either with the connivance of local lords or by securing royal grants transforming them into secular colleges: three colleges were so established in north Ormond, two near Athenry and one in Newry. Such progress as was made, however, represented merely what could be achieved with local consent: when priorities changed during Edward VI's protestant regime, certain houses which had hitherto escaped were also suppressed.[74]

The impact of the dissolution

Altogether the Henrician campaign eventually reached about 55 per cent of Ireland's 140 or so monasteries and 40 per cent of some 200 mendicant communities, but in the Pale, Wexford, Ormond and the south-western seaports it was almost totally effective.[75] There is little sign that the passing of the religious was much regretted, and any feelings of remorse were soon assuaged by the generous grants of church land which landowners, merchants and officials received for their cooperation. In all 44 Palesmen, mainly nobles and gentry but including thirteen merchants, got lands there valued at IR£660 annually, mainly on 21-year leases; and seventeen Englishmen received Pale lands worth IR£794. Other parcels went to three Gaelic lords for town houses, and

72. *StP*, ii, 564–5; *Stat. Ire.*, i, 90; Bradshaw 1979a, pp. 154–63.
73. Bradshaw 1979a, pp. 156, 245; *StP*, iii, 30 (misquoted in Bradshaw 1979a, p. 156).
74. Bradshaw 1974, chs 8–9.
75. Ibid., pp. 206–7.

to Desmond, Ormond, Robert Cowley of Kilkenny and Dublin city.[76] Though leases to Englishmen were generally larger, this reflected not discrimination but the particular preferences of the two groups: the newcomers needed to establish themselves and grabbed whatever they could get, including much marchland; local landowners were more selective, preferring to extend and consolidate existing holdings.

Elsewhere religious property usually went to the local lord or his clientele: conditions in most parts were too disturbed to attract outsiders, and in Ormond the Butlers, having recently gained the earldom from the absentee heirs general, aimed to consolidate their position. In the Leinster marches, however, an interesting initiative aimed to establish order among the Irishry there by using monastic lands for a limited plantation: plantation had been mooted before but St Leger obtained the consent of the Kavanaghs, O'Tooles and O'Byrnes and carefully selected the nine fairly substantial tenants intruded into the Kildare, Carlow and Wexford marches. Perhaps in consequence the tractability of the Kavanaghs was later remarked in contrast with the O'Connors and O'Mores who experienced the first classic colonization scheme involving expropriation and racial segregation.[77] Altogether the net value to the crown of the dissolutions was IR£4,070 per annum according to the 1540–1 survey: property was regularly undervalued and many borderlands remained unlet, but excepting the modest mendicant endowments, licence to purchase (on a 21-year purchase as in England) was in Ireland granted sparingly and only to favoured individuals. In consequence, the redistribution of church land, including leases, tended more to reflect political influence there: few new landowners or younger sons were established.[78]

In terms of community social and pastoral care, the religious were probably missed even less than in England. Polemical assertions that the 'dissolution naturally resulted in the destruction of . . . schools, hospitals, charitable works, and houses for travellers' or 'the retarding of all religious development throughout Ireland, for nearly three centuries'[79] have no foundation in fact. With very few exceptions, the monasteries had long ceased to provide hospitality, and their work in maintaining hospitals and almshouses was passing to others. Secular hospitals and almshouses existed in Dublin, Waterford, Limerick, Galway and Kinsale by 1500, and Dublin, Waterford and Wexford also had leper hospitals. More were founded after the dissolutions; and at the Crutched friars at Newgate, Dublin, where, exceptionally, a hospital of 50 beds was maintained, this was continued. Education presents a similar picture, with well-established grammar schools at Waterford, Kilkenny and Clonmel, and a few surviving monastic schools – at Dublin (Cistercian), Limerick (Franciscan) and the nunnery of Gracedieu – giving place to new schools: a grammar school was endowed from St Patrick's in 1547; the King's Inn, modelled on

76. Calculated from ibid., app. i.
77. Bradshaw 1974, pp. 187–205.
78. Ibid., pp. 187–205; White 1943, p. 376; Brady 1994a, pp. 34–40.
79. Edwards 1935, pp. 72–3.

the London inns of court, from the Dublin Blackfriars; and soon other schools at Galway and Limerick. Pastorally, the government generally ensured uninterrupted service of cures by absorbing formerly monastic parish churches into the ordinary diocesan structure, by endowing new vicarages where necessary, and by intruding monks as stipendiary priests.[80] So ended in the lordship a tradition extending back a thousand years. Not all the monasteries deserved their fate, and a few like St Mary's, Dublin, the lordship's largest community, were of diligent observance.[81]

Thus under Henry VIII the government had made substantial progress. The appearance of religious continuity had been largely maintained, general conformity had been imposed throughout the English districts, and even Gaelic chiefs and bishops had displayed some willingness to conform. St Leger's strategy had dissolved the threatened combination of political and religious malcontents in the Geraldine League and disarmed a vigorous papal riposte to government policy. The papacy's failure was indeed spelled out by the reception accorded the first Jesuit mission to Ireland in 1542: O'Neill and O'Donnell ignored two Jesuits bearing papal letters and they departed after a fruitless four months.[82] The government's general success is strikingly illustrated by the absence in the lordship of any general movement of popular protest akin to the Pilgrimage of Grace.

Even so, the predominantly exploitative character of the crown's campaign must have become increasingly apparent to the local community. Hopes for reform through a vigorous campaign with the establishment of secular colleges, a university, and new schools so as to create a more learned ministry, gradually subsided as all but a fraction of the wealth appropriated from the church was retained by the crown to finance royal government. In particular, the fact that the dissolution stripped of about half their endowments the only two dioceses, Dublin and Meath, in which the clergy enjoyed incomes comparable with those in England represented a crippling blow to prospects for reform. Without adequate stipends, it was far more difficult to attract well-educated and conscientious clergy. In this respect, there was a marked contrast between the king's establishment of six new bishoprics from monastic wealth in response to the problem of overlarge dioceses in England and his failure to address the wretched poverty of numerous small dioceses in Ireland. Indeed, the essential nature of Henry VIII's campaign was again highlighted in 1546 when St Patrick's cathedral was downgraded to a parish church, so netting the crown an additional IR£1,432 2s. $9\frac{1}{2}d.$ a year.[83]

In other respects, too, the prospects for the advance of the Tudor Reformation looked problematic. Although opposition to the changes by both clergy and laity was generally more muted and a good deal less violent than in

---

80. Bradshaw 1974, ch. 12; Hammerstein 1971, pp. 139–41. A recent, more negative assessment of the impact of the dissolution on education is Jefferies 1997a, p. 139.
81. Bradshaw 1974, pp. 136–7.
82. Ibid., pp. 212–14; Bradshaw 1979a, pp. 247–8.
83. Ellis 1990, pp. 252–3.

England, it was no less widespread. Indeed its comparative feebleness perhaps reflected more the slackness with which the settlement was enforced, for royal control there was far less secure than in England. At best there was general acceptance of what parliament had sanctioned, not a growing popular desire for further changes following the infiltration of protestantism, and this left the authorities ill-prepared by comparison with south-east England for the developments that followed.

CHAPTER 9

THE PROGRESS OF THE TUDOR REFORMATION

Despite the break-up of medieval Christendom into rival churches, the polarization of religious opinion, and the outbreak of confessional strife in Europe, Henry VIII had largely succeeded in charting a middle course for the Tudor church between traditional and evangelical versions of Christianity. After his death, however, the Tudor state was ruled in turn by two rancorously partisan regimes which attempted, respectively, to impose an evidently protestant religious settlement under Edward VI, and then to restore an ultra-conservative one under Mary. The consequent erosion of the religious middle ground meant that, by the time of Elizabeth's accession, the crown had little option but to assume the leadership of one of these rival factions; and the circumstances of the queen's birth and upbringing virtually ensured that she would prefer a protestant settlement.

In general, however, the Tudor state conformed to the wider European pattern, encapsulated in the phrase *cuius regio eius religio*, whereby in most parts of Europe the prince eventually managed to impose his own brand of Christianity on his subjects. And Elizabeth's long reign allowed her settlement sufficient time to put down roots, so that after 45 years of protestant services the vast majority of the queen's subjects had grown to accept the Elizabethan church. Ireland and the Netherlands, however, constitute the two most obvious departures from the normal pattern: and arguably in both countries, the religious divisions created by the reformers' comparative failure in Ireland and their overall success in the Low Countries were to bulk large in the events leading to the political partition of the two territories, almost immediately in the case of the Netherlands, much later in Ireland. Nevertheless it would be a mistake to conclude either that the divided state of late medieval Ireland posed insuperable obstacles to reform, or that it necessarily explains why post-Tridentine catholicism came to establish itself most strongly among the Old English merchants and gentry. In fact, as we have seen in the last chapter, the ecclesiastical state of early Tudor Ireland was not uniformly less favourable to reform than England, but contained certain mitigating influences which at least facilitated its initial reception.

THE INTRODUCTION OF THE EDWARDIAN REFORMATION

The introduction of a protestant religious settlement under Edward VI shed a very different light on what had hitherto appeared as the erection of individual provinces of the medieval church into a distinct national church, governed by the territorial ruler as supreme head, but still part of the universal catholic church. Conservative clergy who had accepted the royal supremacy as a means to the religious reform that was so patently necessary now discovered that it might equally be used to promote Zwinglian doctrines; and in Ireland where conservative supporters of the supremacy far outnumbered any protestants, this shift in policy was particularly serious. The administration's difficulties were also compounded by a concurrent change in governmental strategy (see below, Ch. 11) which alienated much local support. Yet the new regime's political priorities and also political unrest in Ireland obliged it to temporize on religion, with the result that change was gradual and its impact in Ireland the less disruptive.[1]

The first major initiative followed an extension of viceregal powers, by which Lord Deputy Bellingham (1548–9) received specific responsibility for the government's religious policy.[2] Accordingly a 'book of reformation' was drawn up by Browne and distributed to his suffragans for enforcement in November 1548: its contents are unknown, but probably provided for the reforms promulgated in England since July 1547 which were certainly all enforced in Dublin by 1550. These aimed to promote religion by proscribing superstitious ceremonies and customs and by introducing the 'Order of the Communion' and its reception in both kinds: all remaining relics and images were swept away, as were pilgrimages, sacramentals such as holy water and bread, palms, ashes and candles, and veneration of saints; and a new vernacular rite for administering communion to the laity was introduced. In Meath Bishop Staples tried to prepare his flock by preaching, but his sermons were denounced as heretical and provoked unrest and he had to write for further instructions.[3] In Armagh the changes presented Archbishop Dowdall with a dilemma similar to that faced by many conservative but conformist bishops in England. George Dowdall had been an influential prior of Ardee, opposed the dissolution, but accepted the supremacy. He visited court with O'Neill in 1542, sued for Armagh to which he was appointed in 1543, and was equally successful there.[4] In 1548, however, Bellingham admonished him for failing 'to set forth the plain, simple and naked truth': he steadfastly refused to implement any of the Edwardian changes, to the government's acute embarrassment, but because of his unwavering loyalty and key role in controlling O'Neill, Bellingham's successor, St Leger (1550–1), and Lord Chancellor Cusack,

---

1. Bush 1975, ch. 5; Bradshaw 1976–7a, pp. 83–99.
2. Bradshaw 1970, pp. 316–19.
3. Bradshaw 1976–7a, pp. 85, 88, 91, 93.
4. Bradshaw 1974, pp. 35, 126–7, 212–13, 220; Jefferies 1997a, pp. 138–9, 148.

Dowdall's cousin, hoped eventually to win him over. They failed, and more vigorous action by Lord Deputy Croft (1551–2) merely precipitated Dowdall's defection and flight.[5]

Besides the growing influence of continental protestantism on the established church after 1547, another new element which probably militated against popular acceptance of reform in Ireland was the exclusive reliance on the royal prerogative for its enforcement. The old king had carefully sought the consent of the local community in parliament, even though broad conformity with English practice was assumed and the implementation of change based on the application of English legislation might sometimes anticipate this consent. Under Edward VI, however, reform measures were imposed exclusively by the prerogative: Bellingham's patent of appointment included powers to convene parliament, but he never exercised them, and Mary, for her own reasons, later followed this precedent in restoring catholicism. Thus the government neglected an important instrument for winning local consent and cooperation. In January 1549 the English parliament passed an act of uniformity requiring the exclusive use from Whit Sunday of the First Book of Common Prayer throughout 'England, Wales, Calais . . . and other the king's dominions': this prayer book was effectively an English translation of the traditional Latin services, simplified and somewhat modified to make them more acceptable to protestants but, as leading conservatives affirmed, still capable of construction in the traditional sense. Accordingly the deputy and council gave directions for abolishing 'idolatry, papistry, the mass sacrament and the like'. The prayer book eventually came into general use in the English districts, but very little evidence has survived about the circumstances of the transition.

St Leger's return saw conciliation and persuasion more in evidence: allegedly he regretted that the government had 'meddled to alter religion' during a minority, but nevertheless worked constructively to ensure local conformity, requiring new appointees to educate the local youth in scripture and true religion. Local men were preferred where available: the aged bishops of Limerick and Waterford were persuaded to resign in favour of more active, local reformers; and even in the midland plantation, where Englishmen were appointed to the sees of Kildare (Thomas Lancaster) and Leighlin (Robert Travers), the existing Gaelic curates were indemnified by grants of denization against the medieval statute excluding them from benefices in the Englishry. Elsewhere, however, Archbishop Butler of Cashel utilized the statute to deprive intractable Gaelic incumbents during a metropolitan visitation late in 1549.[6]

A more fundamental difficulty concerned the availability and intelligibility of the prayer book. Commissioners touring the south and west 'established the king's majesty's orders for religion' generally there in January–February 1551, but the prayer book was confined to English-speaking Galway and Limerick. By establishing the first press in Ireland during 1551, the scarcity of texts was solved, but the use of an English prayer book in Gaelic parts was, by the

5. Bradshaw 1976–7a, pp. 85, 88, 91, 93; Jefferies 1997a, pp. 157–60.
6. Bradshaw 1976–7a, pp. 85–90; Edwards 1935, pp. 122, 131–4.

reformers' lights, 'plainly repugnant to the word of God'. Surprisingly St Leger already had authority to provide a Latin version, and the English council now grudgingly authorized Gaelic services where 'a convenient number' understood no English. Technical difficulties eventually precluded a Gaelic translation, but the Latin version was introduced experimentally in Limerick. The deputy no doubt knew that popular resistance in England to the prayer book had stemmed largely from the dropping of Latin: in Limerick, where some support for reform was apparent, the Latin version was well received; but the old bishop who readily understood the influences behind the studied ambiguities of the revised liturgy strongly opposed it.[7]

The enforcement of reform

Nevertheless, even if the administration was more zealous in promoting reform than was once thought, the results were generally discouraging. Particularly worrying for the government was the attitude of the bishops: many who had accepted the royal supremacy now refused to support the Edwardian reforms, allegedly because they unsettled the people. St Leger's successor, Sir James Croft, was instructed to ensure 'that the bishops and clergy of that realm give good example' in promoting reform, but he faced too many other problems besides religion: his orders were 'so barely looked unto, as the old ceremonies yet remain in many places', and he requested at the least some religious adviser 'the better [to] direct the blind and obstinate bishops'. Dowdall's blank refusal to implement the Edwardian reforms meant that as late as August 1551 the mass and traditional ceremonies continued throughout Armagh diocese. Elsewhere, barely conformist bishops generally refused either to emulate Dowdall's principled stand or to resign in favour of active reformers, and even key sees which did become vacant – Armagh, Cashel and Ossory – remained unfilled 1551–3. In response to Croft's pleas the government sought more urgently for suitable Englishmen to fill Irish sees, but bishoprics there were notoriously poor and the continual rumours emanating of rebellion reflected all too accurately the unrest caused by government political strategies. Nevertheless two reformers accepted the challenge, Hugh Goodacre in Armagh (allegedly poisoned by his own clergy while still in Dublin) and John Bale in Ossory; and Bale's unique account of his Irish experiences gives some indication of what progress was possible in only six months even in unfavourable circumstances.[8]

Bale was a talented protestant scholar and propagandist whose preaching must have considerably disturbed the tranquil airs of Ossory; but his account is apocalyptic, a polemic depicting the forces of Antichrist ranged against him, urging Christians to remain faithful and reminding them that 'continued persecutions and no bodily wealth doth follow the same godly office of bishop'.[9]

7. Bradshaw 1976–7a, pp. 87, 90–1; Edwards 1935, pp. 133–7.
8. Bradshaw 1976–7a, pp. 92–3; Jefferies 1997a, pp. 158–9, 163.
9. For the following, Ellis 1984a.

On Bale's arrival in January 1553, a revised prayer book had been in force for two months in England; but in Waterford he found the 1549 version (still in force in Ireland) so slackly enforced by the bishop, a recent appointee, and city officers that 'the communion . . . was there altogether used like a popish mass'. Since the structures of the two eucharistic liturgies were almost identical, 'counterfeiting the mass' was readily accomplished by mumbling the English text half audibly like the old Latin and restoring the traditional rubrics 'in bowings and beckings, kneelings and knockings'. In the Second Book of Common Prayer, however, the structure had been substantially modified and new rubrics introduced to prevent this: a communion table had replaced the altar and the minister now faced the congregation wearing a surplice instead of the medieval vestments. The 1552 version was thus unambiguously protestant, though too conservative for many continental reformers: conservatives, however, found the old Sarum Use cruelly mangled, while the literary excellence which the two English versions shared went unremarked by anyone at the time. It was not generally used in Ireland, but at Bale's insistence he and Goodacre were consecrated according to the 1552 rite, and many reform-minded Dubliners 'did greatly rejoice of our coming thither'. In Ossory, however, his clergy were reluctant to accept the new version, alleging Browne's continued use of the 1549 version, the want of books, and that the new version had not yet been promulgated in Ireland.

Despite the lack of support from his clergy, however, he evidently built up a considerable following by regular preaching in Kilkenny, especially among the youth; and on his own account open opposition only emerged following news of Edward VI's death. By then the religious polarization of urban politics was evidently threatening the peace: on Queen Mary's proclamation, the young men enacted two of Bale's biblical plays 'to the small contentation of the priests and other papists there'; and after a plot to murder him he was rescued by the sovereign and escorted by psalm-singing youths back to Kilkenny where 'the people in great number stood on both sides . . . shouting praises to God'. In Bale's absence, however, the clergy 'with smilings and laughings most dissolutely . . . brought forth their copes, candlesticks, holy water stock, cross, and censers; [and] mustered forth in general procession . . . with *Sancta Maria, ora pro nobis* and the rest of the Latin litany'; and following a proclamation permitting the celebration of mass alongside the reformed rite, they 'suddenly set up all the altars and images in the cathedral church'. Bale departed for Dublin and exile soon after.

Elsewhere the formal acceptance of the royal supremacy by diocesan clergy had continued apace, especially in outlying areas such as plantation Leighlin and in Limerick and Emly where a rudimentary regional council was operating (see below, p. 270). Indeed, during Croft's administration an unprecedented number acknowledged the royal supremacy in one way or another. Yet acceptance of the supremacy and support for the Edwardian reforms were two different things. An able and enthusiastic preacher like Bale might whip up considerable popular support, but Lord Chancellor Cusack reported that preaching was 'our most lack'. Without preachers the administration was unable to turn minimal conformity into committed support. In this context too, the regime's surprising failure to secure an immediate suppression in Ireland of the chantries and religious guilds, as accomplished by the English act of 1547, was to prove a serious omission: the sale of ecclesiastical property to the laity would have created vested interests in favour of protestantism in much the same way as the sale of monastic lands had underpinned the Henrician Reformation.[10]

THE MARIAN REACTION

Appreciating that protestantism had won only narrow support, the Marian government moved more quickly in Ireland to restore catholicism. Moreover, since the Edwardian reformation had been imposed by the royal prerogative, the same authority could be used to abolish it. In October 1553 St Leger returned as deputy with instructions that religious practice should be that 'of old time used', and Mary as supreme head also filled the sees of Cashel and Ossory (deemed void by Bale's flight) and reinstated Dowdall in Armagh, giving him a life grant of his old priory of Ardee. Dowdall, who was closely linked with Cardinal Pole and the future bishops of Meath and Kildare, Dr William Walsh, Pole's chaplain, and Thomas Leverous, also part of Pole's household in Rome, were the key figures in the Marian reaction.

Immediately after his return, Primate Dowdall held an important provincial synod at St Peter's, Drogheda, which ordered the restoration of traditional rites and practices, the deprivation of married clergy, and the reconciliation of clergy who had used the heretical rites. Besides other decrees of a more traditional character, there were ones ordering the burning of heretical books and, more ominously, the appointment of diocesan and metropolitan inquisitors to compel conformity by seeking out and prosecuting heretics, while a prohibition on fees for administering the sacraments was perhaps a response to protestant propaganda. In April 1554 this initiative was extended throughout Ireland by a royal commission to investigate breaches of canon law. In consequence, Browne, Staples, Lancaster of Kildare and Travers of Leighlin, plus a number of lesser clergy, were deprived for clerical marriage (ironically, considering the prevalence of clerical concubinage) which Edward VI had legalized in 1549. Yet those clergy who did penance and put away their wives were generally allowed to seek other benefices, and Browne ended his days as a prebendary of the diocese he had formerly ruled.[11] The other Henrician bishops and papal provisors who had subsequently conformed all retained their sees; but of the three remaining Edwardian bishops, Casey of Limerick was deprived and his predecessor restored, Burke of Clonfert and Elphin kept Clonfert to which the pope had provided him but his appointment to Elphin in 1552 was ignored, and Walsh of Waterford and Lismore kept his see.[12]

10. Bradshaw 1976–7a, pp. 95–6 (quotation); Lennon 1991; Lennon 1994, pp. 306–7.
11. Jefferies 1997a, ch. 8; Edwards 1935, pp. 52, 160–4; Bradshaw 1970, pp. 322–3; Murray 1929–32, p. 155 (I am grateful to R.J. Hunter for this reference).
12. *HBC*, pp. 378–445.

In general, the Marian reaction in Ireland has been little studied, though not for want of evidence. Recent work by English historians has in many ways undermined the stock charge against Mary – that she merely restored what had been there before, without addressing the problems which had generated the campaign against the church in the first place. In Ireland, however, the growth of heresy presented far less of a problem, but the church's poverty was far more serious: and in the event, although Mary's death likewise cut short some important initiatives, the overall impression is of a more cursory and superficial approach in Ireland to catholic reform.

The crown's relationship with Rome was regularized, so far as Ireland was concerned, in June 1555 when Pope Paul IV erected Ireland into a kingdom, and in July Cardinal Pole was made papal legate for Ireland. In April 1556 the new deputy, Lord Fitzwalter, had orders to prepare for a parliament, to assist the bishops to root out heresy, and to facilitate Cardinal Pole's intended legatine visitation of the Irish church. The visitation never took place, but a parliament eventually met in Dublin in June 1557 to repeal the Henrician Reformation legislation: separate statutes recognized Mary's legitimate birth by repealing the Henrician succession acts in this respect, abolished first fruits and twentieths, restored the papal primacy by repealing all anti-papal statutes passed since 1528, and revived the English anti-heresy laws. No burnings followed, although six English-born councillors and five others received pardons *inter alia* for heresy. In December 1557 commissioners were appointed for every shire to inquire concerning the sale under Edward VI and the present possessors of catholic ornaments and parish church property and lands. Yet the chantries had never been dissolved in Ireland; nor in predominantly Gaelic parts had mass or traditional ceremonies been abolished. Even where they had, if Bishop Bale's experience was typical, the wholesale concealment of altars, images and service books which should have been sold or destroyed would have greatly facilitated the catholic restoration: in England, even comparatively rich parishes could not afford to replace immediately costly items of catholic worship.[13]

Beyond this, however, the regime's achievements look distinctly thin. Little was done to address the growing problem of the church's poverty. Somewhat disturbingly, Dowdall's provincial synod of 1553 had found it necessary to re-enact the laity's long-standing obligation to maintain church naves. His prohibition on fees for sacraments also removed a useful source of income for the parish clergy; and the clergy's increasing difficulty in coping with inflation is suggested by the subsequent re-enactment during the 1554 and 1556 synods of Armagh clergy *inter Anglicos* of traditional decrees concerning payment of procurations and admission to cures by the ordinary. Equally ominous was the re-enactment by these two synods of decrees threatening sequestration of

---

13. Jefferies 1997a, ch. 8; *Fiants Ire., P. & M.*, nos. 172, 176, 181; Morrin 1861, pp. 369–70; Edwards 1935, pp. 165–9; Bagwell 1885–90, I, 394–402; Haigh 1993, chs 12–13; Duffy 1992, ch. 16; Loades 1979, p. 413. Cardinal Pole's register (copy in the Lambeth Library) includes Irish material.

revenues if church chancels were in disrepair: Co. Louth churches had mostly been impropriated to religious houses, so that this duty devolved on their lay successors. By 1566 Lord Deputy Sidney complained that throughout Armagh, Dublin and Meath dioceses, chancels were decayed, 'churches universally in ruin (and some wholly down)'.[14]

A basic difficulty was that the crown could only afford to relinquish a fraction of its church property. Just one of the monasteries was restored, in March 1558, the Knights Hospitallers of Kilmainham, which happened to be in crown hands; though St Patrick's was also re-established as a cathedral. In May 1558, Primate Dowdall's proposal for a university and some free schools was ignored; but when he visited court in August, the queen agreed to fund a new friary for the Carmelite community of Ardee, which had withdrawn into the Irishry in 1540 and returned under Mary, and also to restore Dowdall's old hospital there 'for the better relief of poor and sick people'. Yet with Dowdall's death in London in mid-August, catholic reform was effectively halted.[15]

THE ELIZABETHAN SETTLEMENT

Parliament and legislation

The Elizabethan religious settlement, enacted by the English parliament in 1559, broadly restored the 1552 settlement, but significantly Elizabeth awaited parliamentary assent in Ireland before imposing changes there. Meanwhile Lord Deputy Sussex was instructed that English-born councillors should use the English rites privately. Conscious of the strong opposition encountered in the English parliament, the government prepared the ground carefully, and the queen gave her Irish council further room for manoeuvre by sending over, besides the main supremacy and uniformity bills, an alternative to uniformity in the bill for communion in both kinds and against any villifying the sacrament of Christ's body and blood, modelled on the identically titled English act of 1547. Recommendations in a paper endorsed by Sussex that new peers be created either for parliament's duration or for life and to summon leading catholics to court were apparently ignored, but steps were taken to build 'a strong party' in the Commons where, to judge by a list of returns, the government secured a dependable bloc of twelve New English members, many elected for outlying boroughs or through the good offices of the earls of Ormond, Kildare and Clanrickard, out of a house of 76. The government already had some indication that Marian bishops might prove tractable, although there were no Irish protestant exiles to replace any deprived bishops. Apparently fourteen bishops received summonses, and support by Archbishop Curwin and Bishops O'Fihilly and Walsh of Waterford undermined catholic opposition. Thus, in the event, parliament meeting in January 1560 enacted Elizabeth's English settlement within four weeks. Other bills recognized Elizabeth's

14. Jefferies 1997a, ch. 8 (quotation, pp. 168, 171).
15. Jefferies 1997a, ch. 8 (quotation, p. 170); Bagwell 1885–90, pp. 394–402.

regal title and legitimacy, restored first fruits and twentieths and abolished elections of bishops and archbishops. It was later alleged that the bills had passed on a day when opponents had previously been told that there would be no meeting, but the most recent account of the parliament concludes that there were no irregularities and that opposition was limited. Six days after parliament met, Sussex unexpectedly received an urgent summons to court, and dissolved parliament before departing.[16]

The Irish supremacy act followed the third English one in declaring Elizabeth supreme governor rather than supreme head of the church. It empowered her to visit and correct the church through commissioners, but imposed careful limitations on their powers to adjudge heresy: the Elizabethan supremacy was much more parliamentary and lacked Henry VIII's personal and quasi-papal control. The act also imposed a supremacy oath on all ecclesiastical persons, on temporal officers of state, and on those taking holy orders, university degrees, or minors suing livery of their estates. The uniformity act reimposed the 1552 service book but with minor changes designed to make it more acceptable to conservatives: offensive references to the pope disappeared, the omission of the Knoxian 'Black Rubric' and the combination of the 1549 and 1552 words of administration permitted belief in the real presence, and the new Ornaments Rubric allowed the minister to wear the traditional vestments.

Penalties for refusing the supremacy oath were in Ireland immediate life-long incapacity to hold office, and for not using the prescribed book deprivation of all benefices (for a year at the first offence, permanently thereafter) and imprisonment (for six months, a year, and life, for first, second and third offences respectively): absentees from church forfeited one shilling per Sunday, leviable by the churchwardens for support of the poor; and those openly attacking the Book faced fines of 100 marks (IR), 400 marks (IR), and total forfeiture of goods and life imprisonment for the first, second and third offences respectively. In theory, therefore, the penalties prescribed, with the church's traditional machinery of visitation and presentment, and the newly authorized commissions, constituted an impressive instrument of coercion: in practice the authorities frequently found the machinery too cumbersome for speedy progress even in England.[17]

Change in the parishes: popular perceptions of the settlement

Broadly, the Elizabethan settlement envisaged a church that was doctrinally protestant but liturgically catholic. In Ireland, however, since initially no articles of religion were prescribed, the clergy enjoyed considerable latitude in interpreting the prayer book. Moreover, a special clause for Ireland, perhaps the product of conservative pressure in parliament, permitted ministers ignorant of English to use a Latin version of the prayer book. It is unclear as yet

16. Jefferies 1988–9, pp. 128–41; Edwards 1935, pp. 173–81, 185; Hardiman 1843, app. 2; *Carew*, i, nos. 218–19; Jones 1982, pp. 132–4. Cf. Dickens 1964, pp. 405–15.
17. Jefferies 1988–9, pp. 133, 140; Edwards 1935, pp. 181–5; Dickens 1964, pp. 411–15.

how widely used was this *Liber precum publicarum* (1560), with its more conservative communion rubrics and provisions for the reservation of communion and a requiem eucharist. Yet, had it been widely used to conceal the full extent of the changes, it might perhaps have facilitated the enforcement of the settlement.

Initially too, popular reactions to the Elizabethan settlement were no doubt largely shaped by the common appreciation that this was the fourth attempted settlement of religion in a dozen years, and seemingly with no more prospect of religious stability under Elizabeth than under her brother and sister. In the event, however, the 1560 settlement proved enduring and the problems which had begun to emerge after 1547 soon became far more urgent. Specifically, these concerned the funding of the Elizabethan church and the enforcement of religious uniformity.

By attacking key doctrines like purgatory and transubstantiation, protestant reformers had undermined many of the late medieval church's traditional means of fundraising – through indulgences, votive offerings, trentals and similar pious practices – and so exacerbated long-standing difficulties regarding the church's poverty. At the same time, the bibliocentric thrust of the settlement, with the emphasis on Bibles and sermons, constituted a radical departure from the more visual presentation of late medieval Christianity, with its focus on the miracle of the mass, pilgrimages, pageants and pictures. Under Henry VIII, continuity with the pre-Reformation church had been far more striking and reassuring at parish level than the occasional innovations and piecemeal reforms which the old king had authorized; so the government could expect that traditional habits of obedience and loyalty would gradually work to secure general acceptance of the new order, without the need for more rigorous measures. Under Elizabeth, however, the curate now celebrated the eucharist in English, on a communion table, facing the congregation. A general confession preceded communion, with the laity expected to communicate regularly, in both kinds, instead of the annual confession and communion at Easter. Gone were the old Latin mass and the stone altar where the curate had stood with his back to the people; gone too were the rood screen separating the nave from the chancel, the rood itself, and the statues. And the required appearance instead of the English Bibles and copies of Erasmus's *Paraphrases* with which the authorities hoped to banish these 'monuments of superstition' would have offered small consolation, particularly to illiterate peasants. There was now a royal coat of arms where the 'doom' had been, and scriptural quotations on white walls replaced the other holy pictures. A few popular ceremonies survived, Rogationtide processions and harvest festival for instance, as did the public recitation of the daily offices, but in general traditional ceremonies and saints' days had been greatly pruned.

Thus, in an age when tradition was extolled and innovation distrusted, the ousting of the old Latin mass by the new prayer book services would have appeared far more fundamental and threatening to ordinary people than might appear from the comparatively trivial differences between a modern English mass and an Anglican eucharist. In sum, despite the striking level of continuity with the Marian church in terms of clergy and continued popular attendance at services, the character of the Elizabethan settlement presented the Church of Ireland with an immediate crisis of identity and faced the authorities with a massive problem of enforcement, particularly in the countryside where few people were literate.[18] What was now needed was a full-scale campaign of conversion. Yet for this purpose, the church's administrative machinery had frequently been in poor order even before the 1530s, and had since been further disrupted by successive changes: with clerical morale undermined by reforms which seemed merely to appropriate church property for the crown and lay landowners, and ecclesiastical administration in such rundown condition, the church was in no condition to attempt unaided, in a deteriorating political climate, a major campaign of preaching and evangelization to enforce the changes.

A further difficulty concerned the general background against which the authorities were attempting to impose the new settlement. In part this was, as in England, because the Edwardian changes and the Marian reaction had contributed to a strengthening of ties between the papacy and religious conservatives: experience had taught conservatives that a royal supremacy and national church were no guarantee of religious reform, much less of doctrinal consistency, and the papacy's claims to represent orthodoxy against the infiltration of heresy seemed correspondingly more attractive. In Ireland, however, where secular considerations continued to bulk large in the response of political society to religious reform, the more general shift in government policies from the predominantly conciliatory initiatives of St Leger to the more forceful strategies of his viceregal successors was crucial. Not only did a comparatively weak administration face an even steeper task than in England in trying to impose protestantism on a predominantly conservative population, it was increasingly distracted by political unrest and rebellion. In Gaelic Ireland government ecclesiastical policy was soon identified with military conquest and plantation as part of a general anglicizing policy, and in English Ireland the increasing alienation of the colonial community from the general drift of policy tended to dampen zeal for conformity. As religious opinion polarized in the new age of religious wars, the government had to weigh the additional unrest in an already troubled land which strict enforcement of conformity would initially provoke against less tangible long-term benefits: despite instructions from London and the efforts of zealous individuals, overburdened administrators generally made a virtue of necessity and attended to immediate political problems.

Enforcing the settlement: the potential for reform

Directly after the enactment of the supremacy act commissions issued to administer the oath. Three bishops, Walsh of Meath, Leverous of Kildare (both leading opponents) and Bodkin of Tuam, Kilmacduagh and Annaghdown were immediately tendered it: only Bodkin took it, and the others were deprived.

---

18. Jefferies 1988–9, pp. 133, 140; Haugaard 1968, pp. 112–17. On the character of popular religion in English parishes before the Reformation, see now Duffy 1992.

The evidence is scanty, but the oath was perhaps administered selectively: six bishops certainly accepted the supremacy (Curwin of Dublin, Walsh of Waterford and Lismore, Devereux of Ferns, O'Fihilly of Leighlin, Burke of Clonfert and Elphin, and Bodkin), and probably also Thonery of Ossory and Lacy of Limerick. Armagh was vacant in 1560, Skiddy of Cork and Cloyne had received the temporalities from Mary in 1557 but was not actually consecrated until 1562, while Lacy of Limerick retained his see for political reasons until 1571 when he was replaced by his Edwardian predecessor. Besides the bishops, nine more beneficed clergy had certainly been deprived in English parts by 1562, but an exceptionally large number of appointments were made to other vacant benefices, which may suggest that many incumbents had voluntarily withdrawn.[19] By comparison with the courageous and dignified stand by the Marian bishops in England, a majority of Irish bishops in traditional English areas conformed: even as late as 1560, apparently, the more pragmatic attitudes of the Henrician period still lingered in Ireland, affording the authorities some hope of early success.

There is a serious need for a thorough modern study of the enforcement of the Elizabethan settlement in Ireland. Recent work has uncovered a series of new problems where the received interpretation of unrelenting resistance posed none. If, until 1553, the usual popular response in the Englishry was reluctant conformity, how far into Elizabeth's reign was this practice maintained, and when did recusancy become established? How far did the parochial clergy adhere to the prescribed forms of worship, and how quickly were distinctively catholic customs rooted out? Again, was conservative opposition primarily a survival of pre-Reformation customs, or was it inspired by militant post-Tridentine catholicism? Very recent work is now beginning to address such questions and to advance the debate beyond the exchange and exegesis of contradictory quotations in support of rival hypotheses.[20] Yet in the continued absence of any overall study meeting modern standards, any account of developments can only be conjectural, and notwithstanding its lacing with quotations, the following sketch is largely impressionistic.

Experience in England would suggest that the immediate abandonment of Sunday services at the local parish church in favour of conventicles elsewhere was very much the exception among possible popular responses to the Elizabethan settlement. For one thing, the parish church was the focus of social and political, as well as religious, life in the local community, from which individuals would not lightly dissociate themselves.[21] It also presupposed a clearly perceived distinction between Marian catholicism and Elizabethan anglicanism

---

19. *Fiants Ire., Eliz.*, nos. 199, 226–7, 236, 262 *et passim*; Morrin 1861, pp. 401, 440, 442, 448, 467 *et passim*; Jefferies 1988–9, p. 139; *HBC*, pp. 378–408; Edwards 1935, pp. 187–9, 210–11.
20. In effect, the agenda was set by Bradshaw *v.* Canny: Bradshaw 1978a, pp. 475–502; Canny 1979b, pp. 423–50. Some of the differences apparently are largely terminological. See now Walshe 1988–9, pp. 352–76; Bradshaw 1988, pp. 445–76; Clarke 1989, pp. 105–22; Ellis 1990, pp. 239–65. Murray 1992–3, pp. 345–52 and Ford 1997, pp. 7–20 offer useful historiographical surveys.
21. See especially Haigh 1975, pp. 247–8.

which the illicit continuance of previous practices at parish level or the unauthorized adaptation of the new services would often have obscured: the early Elizabethan Irish church sheltered not only the future Jesuit, Edmund Campion, but also the presbyterian, Thomas Cartright. And it presupposed the speedy establishment of an alternative ecclesiastical structure fostering the regular practice of the traditional faith despite the government's vigilance. Politico-cultural divisions ensured the continuance of Gaelic Ireland's distinctive brand of religion – particularly since the government's post-1547 political initiatives had largely undermined any willingness there to cooperate on ecclesiastical matters – and these areas no doubt constituted a potential springboard from which a catholic counteroffensive might be launched; but any serious campaign would have to overcome the same obstacles as had stymied previous religious movements and which were still a force in Stuart Ireland when urban-based Jesuits were trying to reform the surrounding Gaelic countryside.[22] In borderlands where government control was weak, recusant clergy could no doubt work openly, but these were also the areas in which beneficed clergy could most easily maintain catholic services within the existing parochial structure.

Not even the bishops were above keeping their feet in both camps. Archbishop Bodkin (d. 1572) nominally accepted each successive settlement but could still put on a show in his cathedral for the visiting papal nuncio in 1563 who reported that 'mass is sung and said, and he himself is daily in the choir';[23] Bishop Lacy of Limerick received Lord Deputy Sidney in 1567 with catholic rites; and even Bishop Walsh of Waterford was, according to the papal bishop of Cork, secretly reconciled to Rome: all three received continued recognition in London and Rome.[24] Nevertheless occasional conformity was not an option regularly available to clergy in more anglicized parts where, paradoxically, post-Tridentine catholicism gained its earliest and most secure hold.

Realistically, the authorities might hope in 1560 for no more than a gradual transformation in popular religious practice, beginning in the Pale and royal towns and spreading throughout Ireland with the extension of government control. Any sharp and rigid enforcement of the settlement was beyond the government's resources and perhaps counterproductive anyway: since there was no alternative pool of clergy, not even the proportionately small group of protestant exiles available in England, the government relied on general acquiescence by the existing clergy, most of whom had probably served under three previous settlements. By weeding out the recalcitrant from key positions, introducing instead committed protestants, and weaning conservative clerics away from traditional practices by close supervision and careful instruction, the authorities might hope to establish a basic level of conformity until a graduate protestant clergy could be trained at Oxbridge for the real work of evangelization. Viewed in this light the campaign's initial stages contained both hopeful and disquieting features for the government.

22. See Bossy 1971, pp. 155–69; Collinson 1967, p. 112.
23. Ronan 1930, p. 79 (quotation).
24. Edwards 1935, pp. 210, 220, 241; *HBC*, pp. 400, 407, 437, 444 *passim*.

The initial campaign

Encouragingly, there was no immediate mass exodus of clergy and people from the parishes, despite appalling conditions there. In 1563 English commissioners found 'blind ignorance' but some hope for improvement because 'there appeareth in this people fear to offend'.

> Those we have to do with, we find conformable to laws, and the judges with others of the lawyers ready . . . to execute the laws for religion.

Similarly, Lord Lieutenant Sussex reported in 1562 that

> the people, without discipline, utterly devoid of religion, come to divine service as to a May game. The ministers for disability and greediness be had in contempt, and the wise fear more the impiety of the licentious professors than the superstition of the erroneous papists.[25]

To remedy this situation, the administration requested suitable English ministers to fill Irish bishoprics: in 1560 Archbishop Parker sent a list of names but 'findeth none willing to go', and subsequent efforts were hardly more successful.[26] That the bishops should provide a strong lead was of course essential, but few reliable candidates could be found. To succeed the deprived Marian bishop of Kildare, Elizabeth appointed Alexander Craik, a protégé of Lord Dudley, licensing him to hold the rich deanery of St Patrick's (worth IR£145 per annum) *in commendam* because of the see's poverty (valued at IR£70 c. 1570). By 1561, however, Craik was pleading to be allowed to resign, alleging his ignorance of the language and the lack of preachers, saving his young chaplain, Adam Loftus, recently arrived. Loftus was promoted to the still vacant archbishopric of Armagh in 1562–3 in default of other suitable candidates, and then to Dublin in 1567 when the queen finally acceded to the oft-reiterated request of Archbishop Curwin and translated him to Oxford.[27] To Meath was eventually appointed a local man, Hugh Brady (1563–84), who proved an active and conscientious reformer and an energetic preacher in both English and Gaelic; when death spared Bishop Craik in 1564 another native, Robert Daly (1564–83), also a bilingual preacher, replaced him; and in Armagh Loftus was succeeded by the old Edwardian bishop of Kildare, Thomas Lancaster (1568–84). Only in these sees, however, was adequate leadership provided in Elizabeth's first years, though other suitable natives, Christopher Gaffney (1567–76) and Daniel Kavanagh (1567–87), were soon appointed to Ossory and Leighlin respectively.[28]

To reinforce the bishops' efforts, a series of ecclesiastical commissions was issued between 1561 and 1564 to enforce the settlement in Westmeath,

25. Edwards 1935, p. 234 (quotation); Ronan 1930, pp. 99–100.
26. Edwards 1935, pp. 190, 211–12.
27. Ibid., pp. 207–11; Ronan 1930, pp. 37–9, 54–9, 95–6; *HBC*, pp. 379, 391, 394.
28. Bradshaw 1978a, pp. 484–6; Edwards 1935, pp. 207–8; Ronan 1930, pp. 178–81. On Brady, see now Walshe 1988–9, pp. 352–76.

Armagh province, the shires of south Leinster and Munster, and throughout Connaught and Thomond, and finally in October 1564 a court of high commission was established.[29] Almost nothing is known about the activities of the regional commissions, and little more about the high commission, but in authorizing it Elizabeth informed the administration that the enforcement of conformity should be its first priority. Accordingly the commissioners began by taking presentments from juries empanelled from every parish in the Pale: 'many and great offences' against the settlement were discovered, but not by the most notorious contemners of religion, the nobles and county gentry. Personally examined by the commission, the latter confessed that most of them

> frequented the mass . . . and . . . very few . . . ever received the holy communion or used such kind of public prayer and service as is presently established.[30]

Evidently the Pale aristocracy was mostly evading the settlement by maintaining catholic priests as chaplains: Archbishop Loftus urged the imposition of heavy fines, since they were seducing others by their example. The outcome is unknown, but Lord Deputy Sidney was instructed before his appointment to give precedence to religious reform and replied that it would only be achieved 'by sending learned pastors . . . and giving them competent livings'.[31]

In practice, however, the administration was quite unable to attend to the problem, being distracted throughout Elizabeth's early years by political unrest, particularly Shane O'Neill's activities. The bishops of course were involved in local peacekeeping and justice as peace commissioners, but in Ireland they were further diverted from their principal task by inclusion in commissions for martial law, assizes and regional councils; the bishops of Dublin, Armagh and Meath were also closely involved in affairs of state as councillors, and successive archbishops of Dublin served as lord chancellor long after the practice of appointing ecclesiastics to high temporal office had been abandoned in England.[32] Moreover, lacking close supervision and firm direction, other bishops whose acceptance of the supremacy had represented such a coup for the government, were permitted to do more disservice by remaining than the English Marian bishops had by recusancy.

Clerical poverty and lay control

As ever, the church's poverty was a major obstacle to any kind of reform movement. The overwhelming poverty of the livings, for instance, generally precluded the possibility of attracting well-qualified preaching ministers from England. The Irish *Valor* shows that in those 22 dioceses for which valuations were chiefly made between 1584 and 1630 only nineteen benefices, including

29. Morrin 1861, pp. 446–7, 479, 489–90; *Fiants Ire., Eliz.*, nos. 666–8.
30. Printed, Ronan 1930, pp. 139–40.
31. Ibid., pp. 161–4; Edwards 1935, p. 195.
32. Edwards 1935, pp. 192, 214–15; Gilbert 1897, *passim*.

nine bishoprics, were returned as worth £30 sterling or more per annum. Thus, together with the Henrician returns, these figures suggest that by 1603 the number of Church of Ireland livings capable of attracting resident preachers was little more than 100. And since the number of adequate livings was proportionately small, attempts to advance reform by promoting English outsiders to what was the cream of the Irish ecclesiastical establishment naturally provoked local resentment.

In addition, however, the doctrinal ban on certain traditional sources of clerical income, plus the impact of inflation, also meant that many poorer benefices gradually became inadequate even for less-qualified reading ministers. Inadequate livings were frequently augmented by permitting incumbents to hold additional livings in plurality, but this was a further cause of non-residence: Bishop Craik of Kildare preferred to reside in Dublin where he was dean of St Patrick's, and Elizabeth subsequently appointed a layman as dean to augment his salary as chancellor. In border areas pluralism was often justified simply as a means of excluding papal provisors, but later evidence suggests that one qualified and active, if partially non-resident, minister was often better than two ignoramuses. By 1615, however, the policy of uniting livings to provide the clergy with an adequate income had left the Church of Ireland with only around 800 clergy to serve 2,492 parishes.[33]

In Elizabeth's early years, raids by Shane O'Neill and those subjected to the midlands plantation caused considerable destruction in the Pale, whose 'miserable estate' provoked much official concern. Yet a much more widespread and insidious cause of dilapidation were formerly monastic livings. As has recently been demonstrated, the proportion of impropriate livings in Ireland was far higher than in England – 60 per cent compared with roughly 40 per cent. The potential impact of impropriations is apparent from reports of conditions in the diocese of Meath where, together with Dublin, the only concentrations of rich benefices had been located. Following Meath's union with the neighbouring diocese of Clonmacnois in 1569, Bishop Brady reported in 1576, after personal inquiry throughout his united diocese, that there were 224 parish churches, of which 105 were impropriated to farms held of the crown and served only by curates who lived on the bare altarages. Only eighteen of the curates spoke English, the rest had

> very little Latin, less learning and civility . . . In many places the very walls of the churches [were] down, very few chancels covered, windows and doors ruined and spoiled.

Some 52 churches had endowed vicarages and were in less bad but still poor order, according to Brady, and there were 52 more livings in the gift of others where conditions were barely adequate. This presumably left fifteen parishes of whose state the bishop approved. In response, Lord Deputy Sidney

33. Calculations based on *Valor* 1741; Ford 1997, ch. 4 (see Ellis 1990, pp. 256–7). Ronan 1930, pp. 102, 225–7; Edwards 1935, pp. 219–20; Healy 1908, pp. 213–17.

unsuccessfully urged that where land leases had specified decent spiritual livings and the repair of churches, such clauses should be systematically enforced on the farmers, and in other cases the crown should compensate for their omission.

Brady's successor, Bishop Jones, thought that more than half the churches in his diocese, about 120, had belonged to suppressed abbeys and religious houses: they were mostly farmed to catholic recusants who allowed the curates whom they chose quite inadequate stipends and failed to maintain the chancels. In fact, the royal visitation of 1615 revealed 133 (70.7 per cent) of the rectories impropriate. According to Bishop Jones, there were in 1604 only 31 livings worth £30 sterling or more, and 30 to 40 other vicarages and rectories worth £10 sterling or more. Yet the eastern half of the united see was the richest, most populous and English part of Ireland. Conditions were certainly no better elsewhere, and Bishops Devereux of Ferns (1539–66), Craik of Kildare (1560–4) and Kavanagh of Leighlin (1567–87) were notorious for alienating episcopal lands.[34] In these circumstances, the attitude of the local aristocracy, the lay inheritors of these ex-monastic endowments, was even more crucial than in England to the prospects for a successful Reformation: since the crown and bishops together controlled an even smaller proportion of such wealth as the Irish church enjoyed, the government's campaign was very dependant on a cooperative response by the leading nobles and gentry.

The same point may also be made with regard to church patronage. Even in the richer dioceses of the English Pale, the authorities were frequently unable to control presentations to wealthy livings. In Armagh *inter Anglicos* in 1538–44, for instance, the archbishop's patronage was extremely limited: he could normally present to only two prebends, two rectories and a vicarage; but of these, only the rectory of Clonmore (worth IR£22 13s. 4d.) was financially attractive. In Meath diocese in 1604, the bishop was patron of only four of the richest 33 livings, with the king patron of five and the archbishop of Armagh patron of two more. The patrons of the remaining 22 livings were Old English nobles and gentry, many of whom were catholic recusants. Altogether, these 33 livings supported only eight preaching ministers (one able to preach in Gaelic) and three more described as able to teach (two in Gaelic). By contrast, in Dublin diocese in 1604, where the archbishop was patron of 17 out of the 24 richest livings and the king or the cathedral chapters controlled four more, the position was much more satisfactory: all except one of the incumbents were preachers, with one vacant; and the archbishop had also presented preachers to four lesser prebends of which he was patron. As Sir John Davies complained to Robert Cecil, in many parts the incumbents were poor, unlettered clerks who had, by contract with the patron or ordinary before their institution, alienated the greater part of the profits to laymen or even recusant priests.[35]

34. Meath documents in Healy 1908, pp. 198–9, 213–17. *Valor* 1741, *passim*; Ford 1997, chs 4–5; Canny 1975, pp. 2–12, 35–6; Edwards 1935, p. 218; Ronan 1930, p. 102; Ellis 1990, p. 255. Cf. Bowker 1981, p. 134.
35. Ellis 1990, pp. 255–6; Jefferies 1997a, pp. 33, 42–3.

THE IRISH REFORM DEBATE

Overall, the nature of the Elizabethan settlement presented the Church of Ireland with a series of fundamental but interlocking problems arising from its inheritance of a preponderantly ill-trained, catholic clergy; its seriously deficient, medieval institutional structures; and the pervasiveness of lay control over its property and patronage. These problems were far more fundamental than those encountered by the Church of England, and the ecclesiastical authorities in Ireland were thus faced with a dilemma about how best to proceed to build a reformed national church.[36] In the circumstances, the characteristic Tudor strategy, combining persuasion with coercion to enforce the settlement, soon became disjointed as the authorities cast about for the panacea that the ills of popery, incivility and disorder seemed to require.

The Irish reform debate is poorly documented, but it evidently became increasingly embroiled under Elizabeth in the wider debate about general government policy. Irish-born reformers like Bishop Brady, Lord Chancellor Cusack and Chief Baron Dillon tended to advocate a more persuasive campaign based on preaching, education and the liturgical use of Gaelic to generate popular enthusiasm for reform, though individual English-born councillors like Archbishops Lancaster and Long (1583–9) of Armagh strongly supported them. Brady, Lancaster and Long all promoted projects to endow local schools and campaigned for the establishment of a university (which successive archbishops of Dublin opposed because the endowment of St Patrick's was to be diverted to it). With Lord Chancellor Weston's support, local reformers succeeded in 1570 in securing an act to establish diocesan free schools (its enforcement is another matter), but others to curb non-residence and for repairing parish churches succumbed to opposition by lay impropriators, and the foundation of Trinity College had to wait until 1592.

Towards a Gaelic reformation

The question of Gaelic as a reform medium presumably re-emerged in the 1560 parliament in connection with the act of uniformity: the act apparently ruled out a Gaelic prayer book on grounds of technical difficulties concerning the printing and that few were literate in the language. Antipathy towards a Gaelic liturgy probably reflected Old English prejudices, since reformers generally supported the use of the vernacular and Queen Elizabeth, having authorized the translation of the prayer book and the Bible into Welsh in 1563, then advanced money to the Irish bishops for type and a press for a Gaelic New Testament. When the Welsh prayer book and a New Testament appeared in 1567, and almost simultaneously *Foirrm na n-Urrnuidheadh*, a Gaelic translation of the *Book of Common Order* (1564) by John Carswell, bishop of the Isles, was printed in Edinburgh (see also below, pp. 257–9), the ecclesiastical authorities in Ireland were seriously embarrassed. Politically, the targeting of

36. See esp. Clarke 1989, pp. 105–22.

Carswell's *Foirrm* at Irish as well as Scottish Gaeldom cut across the government's attempts to disrupt Ulster's traditional ties with Gaelic Scotland; its publication also highlighted the government's own inconsistency in demanding the use of the vernacular within the Englishry while retaining Latin for Gaelic parts; and its latent presbyterianism and its origins in John Knox's revision of the 1552 prayer book for use among English protestant exiles in Geneva in effect amounted to a challenge to the regime's own protestant credentials. The queen angrily demanded to know what had happened to the Gaelic New Testament, and threatened the Irish bishops that if it did not presently appear, she should be repaid her money. The type was eventually used in 1571 to print a short Gaelic book compiled by John Kearney, treasurer of St Patrick's, which included translations of the catechism in the Book of Common Prayer, and of Archbishop Parker's twelve articles of religion (1561) and some prayers from Carswell's *Foirrm*.

Although this first Gaelic book printed in Ireland put the authorities 40 years ahead of catholic controversialists, vernacular works were far more central to the reformers' campaign. After long delays, the Gaelic New Testament was reputedly completed in 1587, but not printed until 1603. It was a fine translation but appeared far too late to help the Elizabethan church, while a Gaelic prayer book did not appear until 1608. Nevertheless, by a wholehearted propagation of these policies for reform through education and the use of Gaelic, it was hoped to create an active preaching ministry and a crusading gentry which would then proceed to mop up the surviving pockets of popery in Gaelic parts.[37]

Persuasion or coercion?

Philosophically, the preferences of Old English reformers remained with Erasmian humanism and its English exponent Thomas Starkey, though they soon distanced themselves from the Cromwellian concept of ecclesiastical Ireland as a branch of the English church: against New English assertions that the established church was an English transplant, they favoured a more ancient pedigree which saw the reformed Church of Ireland as a restoration of the independent national church with its more scriptural theology which had flourished between the ages of St Patrick and St Malachy. More practically, protestant Old English who remained influential in government found themselves increasingly isolated from their fellow countrymen as religious attitudes polarized and Old English political influence declined. As local nobles and gentry mostly drifted from occasional conformity into outright recusancy, protestants found it difficult to reconcile their immediate political and religious ambitions: the increase of true religion obviously required the preferment of protestants to the chief offices of state, but this effectively implied the supersession of religiously conservative local politicians by protestant newcomers,

37. Jefferies 1988–9, pp. 133–4; Bradshaw 1978a, pp. 478–502; *NHI*, iii, pp. 511–12, 532–4; Haugaard 1968, p. 126; Mac Craith 1995, pp. 142–8; Jenkins 1995, pp. 118–19; Ronan 1930, pp. 360–1; Treadwell 1966, pp. 74–84.

so undermining the Old English campaign for a resumption by government of St Leger's classic strategy for a political conquest. To preserve their credibility within the local community, therefore, they called for restraint in the enforcement of conformity so as to protect their relatives and friends, actions which attracted the unwarranted charge that they were backward in religion. Even so, officials like Nicholas Walsh who 'answered the expectation of the state' as justice in Munster and speaker of the 1585 parliament frequently lost credibility in Old English circles.[38]

Against the emphasis on persuasion which characterized many Old English reform projects, the New English usually advocated more widespread use of coercion to punish railers against religion and compel others to attend church where they could be converted: yet persuasion and coercion were not conflicting strategies but tensions within the one strategy which conditions in Ireland tended to exacerbate. The chief instrument for the enforcement of the uniformity and supremacy laws was the court of high commission of which Loftus was head. Yet the very sketchy evidence about its operation does not suggest that it was particularly active: it arrested, examined and imprisoned the Marian bishop of Meath in 1565, and Richard Creagh, the papal primate, and David Wolfe, the papal nuncio, in 1567; but Loftus called continually for authority to prosecute offenders more vigorously. Fines imposed by the commission were reportedly never paid, and in 1577 a new commission was issued: for some years thereafter its activities enforced a more general conformity until, in 1591, Elizabeth heard of its action in compelling seven leading Palesmen – notorious recusants all, but not actually caught attending mass – to give bonds in IR£40 each to attend Loftus's scheduled sermon, and ordered more restraint.[39]

Loftus's strategy was strongly supported by his son-in-law, Thomas Jones, promoted bishop of Meath in 1584, and by Sir William Fitzwilliam, lord deputy 1572–5, 1588–94. In 1584–5 Lord Deputy Perrot ordered that prospective JPs take the supremacy oath as required by law, but the administration was unable in consequence to fill peace commissions with Pale gentry. Perrot then haled the recusants before Castle Chamber but earned a royal reprimand for his severity, while Bishop Jones publicly denounced him for not pursuing this assault. In the 1580s three successive governors complained of London's reluctance to allow more coercion in matters ecclesiastical. Compelling leading landowners to take the oath was particularly urged, but by then the widespread and outright recusancy of Pale gentry, the cohesion of colonial society, its alienation from government, and mounting unrest elsewhere were hindering efforts to enforce conformity by the traditional methods of delation, detection and correction, and forcing the administration to advocate more draconian methods.[40]

38. Bradshaw 1978a; Canny 1979b, pp. 423–50 (quotation, p. 430). Cf. Canny 1976–7, pp. 439–63; Canny 1979a, pp. 147–60.
39. Edwards 1935, pp. 198, 228, 230, 247, 273–80; Bradshaw 1978a, pp. 477, 480–1, 485.
40. Edwards 1935, pp. 270–2; Bradshaw 1978a, pp. 481–5; Canny 1979b, pp. 436–7.

Loftus's supporters urged external conformity as the government's primary aim, anticipating that preaching and education would subsequently ensure inward conversion. Nevertheless the paucity of preachers and other instruments of propaganda meant that the popular conception of the reform process was increasingly one of compulsion. By the 1590s Loftus was responding to Lord Burghley's complaints by claiming that preaching was useless unless the people attended church, thus providing the preachers with an audience. Philosophically, these views accorded with the growing emphasis in Elizabethan puritanism on the use of the temporal sword to promote social order and progress among the rude irrational multitude. Perhaps such ideas underpinned Bishop Jones's admission that he preached only quarterly, but more commonly those English ministers who neglected preaching did so for worldly concerns, not because they accepted its ineffectiveness.

A more serious hindrance to reform, however, were those lay officials who argued that reform must await the implantation of civility by military conquest. Edmund Spenser, for example, advocated conquest through war and famine followed by political, social and religious reform, with native ministers to convert by persuasion, instruction and example. Sir William Herbert, a Welsh undertaker, conscientiously strove to implement this strategy during the Munster plantation: he recruited Gaelic-speaking ministers and procured a Gaelic translation of the Prayer Book for the natives, whom he found very tractable. With other earnest English protestants, he condemned planters and soldiers who sought more 'after private gain . . . than the reformation of the country'. Nevertheless advocates of this policy would hope at most merely to contain the religious problem until after military conquest, a strategy which firmly identified religious reform in the popular imagination with racial segregation, expropriation and plantation. It may also explain why some able Elizabethan governors, like Sidney, remained strangely inactive over religious reform, despite repeated instructions and their evident concern for the faith.[41]

THE EMERGENCE OF CATHOLIC RECUSANCY

Nevertheless, though the reform debate (such as it was) and the tensions which it provoked probably prevented the authorities from deploying to best effect the weapons at its disposal, the fact remains that in the crucial period to c. 1590, when a majority of Englishmen became enthusiastic protestants, the resources available to the Dublin administration for a similar task in more trying circumstances were proportionately puny. As Elizabeth's reign progressed, the advocates of coercion apparently became more influential. The reasons for this are unclear, but in part the shift in ecclesiastical policy, evident in the increased activity of the high commission after 1577, probably reflected a more general shift in government policy with the outbreak of the Desmond rebellion

41. Bradshaw 1978a, pp. 480–7; Canny 1979b, pp. 435–6, 447–9 (quotation, p. 449); Edwards 1935, p. 267; Spenser 1970, pp. 91–170; Keaveney & Madden in Herbert 1992.

(1579–83). It also reflected a continuing decline of Old English influence in government, but a third reason was that by the late 1570s outright recusancy was apparently beginning to replace reluctant conformity as the typical response to the Elizabethan settlement. Hitherto conservatives had frequently tried to maintain a foot in both camps by attending public services and secret masses, while even clergy who could not stomach the new rites clung to their livings by hiring curates to conduct services instead. As late as 1574 Nuncio Wolfe regretted that in towns everywhere catholics attended communion and the Lutheran sermons of heretic bishops, despite his grotesque underestimates of those embracing the Lutheran leprosy largely to please Elizabeth.[42] By then, however, reports suggest that private masses were on the increase: in 1580 Lord Justice Pelham (1579–80) reported 'a settled hatred and a general contrariety in religion' among Palesmen, and Barnaby Rich, an adventurer and protestant zealot, wrote that Ireland

> does swarm with Jesuits, seminaries and massing priests, yea, and friars and these do keep such continual and daily buzzing in the poor people's ears that they are not only led from all duty and obedience of their prince, but also drawn from God by superstitious idolatry and so brought headlong by heaps into hell.[43]

Probably the decisive development in the transition from partial conformity to outright recusancy was the novel coincidence of different strands of political and religious opposition, exemplified in the Desmond rebellion, the Baltinglass revolt, and the Nugent conspiracy. Hitherto, local resistance to Tudor centralization and conservative opposition to the Tudor Reformation had been largely distinct. Yet the hysterical overreaction to these revolts of Lord Deputy Grey, convinced of an international catholic conspiracy to overthrow Tudor rule in Ireland, drove separate groups of malcontents to make common cause (see below, pp. 312–18).

At the same time, by 1580 the advent of seminary priests was introducing a new factor into the situation, making general recusancy a more realistic option. To an extent the priests' activities reflect the authorities' failure in a vital aspect of the reform process, that of establishing and maintaining state control of education. For example, one of the most notable Irish grammar schools, that at Kilkenny, was from 1565 run by Peter White, the former dean of Waterford who had refused the supremacy oath; and in 1585 the protestant schoolmaster in Waterford reported that his first 30 pupils had deserted him for the catholic schoolmaster. Traditionally, promising pupils had mostly gone up to Oxford, but in the mid-1570s this practice, hitherto increasing, suddenly declined, while the numbers of Old English merchants' sons attending continental universities greatly increased.[44] The youth which had been attracted by

42. Edwards 1935, pp. 197, 220, 237–8; Bradshaw 1976–7b, pp. 47, 50–2; Canny 1979b, pp. 433–4, 443–4.
43. Hammerstein 1971, pp. 150–1 (quotation); Canny 1979b, pp. 432–3. For the years around 1580 as a watershed, see also Martin 1967, pp. 23–33; Lennon 1975, pp. 101–10.
44. Hammerstein 1971, pp. 137–53; Canny 1975, pp. 26–31; Green 1909, pp. 283–302 (includes a list of Irish students at Oxford); Cregan 1970.

Bale's sermons was now being captured by post-Tridentine catholicism. Thus where the government might have contemplated a ready supply of graduate ministers, it faced instead a stream of returning priests educated in continental seminaries. On Elizabeth's orders an inquiry had begun in 1564 about those organizing the recruitment and training of candidates for the priesthood: it revealed activity centred on Waterford whereby disaffected parish clergy were financing clerical students at Louvain. By 1577 some of these chickens were coming home to roost: the president of Munster described for Secretary Walsingham's benefit how of the 'four principal prelates' of papistry in the Waterford–Clonmel area, three had arrived from Louvain in March 1576, how 'a great number of students of this city' were then maintained there, how 'masses infinite' were held without fear, and how chancing to arrive at five one Sunday morning he saw the inhabitants 'resort out of the [catholic] churches by heaps'.[45] The first Jesuit suffered in Ireland in 1575 and over the next decade at least 49 catholic clergy had been despatched, most of them convicted by martial law or killed out of hand.[46]

These activities were, from the government's viewpoint, the thin end of the wedge. Hitherto catholicism had been practised openly and generally in Gaelic and border areas – in 1574, for example, the government knew of around 60 active abbeys in Connaught[47] – and secretly elsewhere: but such activity was overwhelmingly a continuation of pre-Reformation practice. The existence of independent Gaelic lordships offering a safe haven for catholic priests did of course present a different kind of problem from that faced by Tudor officials in conservative parts of England and Wales. Wales, for instance, produced many seminary priests; but few returned to Wales because, although many Welsh gentry opposed the religious changes, very few had either the resources or the inclination to harbour recusant priests as household chaplains. The continental seminarians returning to Ireland, however, were chiefly merchants' sons from royal towns, few of whom would have been attracted by a life of poverty in remote Gaelic parts. In fact, they took up residence in increasing numbers in Old English areas: the initial advance of Counter-Reformation catholicism re-flected the distribution of Old English catholic nobles, merchants and gentry with the resources to maintain recusant priests. In explaining this development, we may speculate that the two significant differences from the situation in other outlying parts of the Tudor state were, first, the role of the towns and, second, the ability of disaffected landowners and merchants to divert financial resources from the Church of Ireland to the support of an alternative, catholic, ministry.

Towns in Tudor Ireland were generally larger and more numerous than in Wales or the English north; and with their relatively large populations, accumulations of wealth and higher levels of literacy, they exercised a major force in moulding national public opinion. Irish towns, however, were also

45. Ronan 1930, pp. 113–14, 548–9; Hammerstein 1971, pp. 143, 146.
46. Calculated from Edwards 1935, app. i.
47. Ibid., p. 243.

particularly open to outside influences since most were seaports, and many were badly affected by the disruption and insecurity stemming from the Tudor conquest. In Scotland, it is noticeable that the earliest protestant strongholds were the east-coast ports trading with protestant Denmark and north Germany; but in Ireland many of the seaport towns had strong trading links with the catholic parts of continental Europe, as was exemplified by the previously noted activity centred on Waterford.

Second, the conduct of disaffected gentry as impropriators and patrons of church livings has also been noted. Yet the unaccountable failure of the authorities to secure a statute dissolving the chantries allowed recusant merchants and gentry further scope. In terms of revenue, this was probably not a very costly omission. The medieval chantries and guilds were apparently concentrated mainly in the towns; and since, according to the act of uniformity, private masses and conventicles were illegal, in theory the omission simply meant that these endowments should have been diverted to some other charitable purpose. In practice, some at least of them continued to be used for the maintenance of catholic priests and services, most notably the guild of St Anne in St Audoen's parish, Dublin, supporting six chantry priests, which remained quite undetected till 1611.[48]

THE STATE OF RELIGION IN 1603

By 1603 it was clear that the attempt seemingly betrayed by Mary's bishops to 'storm the fort' had failed, so necessitating a siege. Although the government could readily appropriate or dismantle the traditional structures of the old faith in outlying parts, if seminary priests could shepherd conservative merchants and gentry into an underground church in the government's own backyard, the outlook for the Church of Ireland, lacking any substantial measure of indigenous support and opposed by a new militant Counter-Reformation catholicism, would be far bleaker. From the 1590s Rome was actively recovering support in Ireland and the Church of Ireland lost ground as the authorities concentrated on political developments. Thus the 'first', or Tudor, Reformation was undoubtedly a failure.

Yet the outlook was perhaps not quite so bleak as the received interpretation has implied. The completion of the conquest presented the authorities with a new opportunity for a 'second reformation', in which the Church of Ireland might be transformed into a genuinely reformed national church and its structures and finances overhauled. Moreover, though conservative conformists were increasingly opting for recusancy – the Palesmen as early as the mid-1570s, but perhaps not until the 1590s in outlying towns – a significant minority had become enthusiastic protestants. This was especially true in the towns, notably Dublin but still more, and more surprisingly, Galway, which

48. Ellis 1990, pp. 261–3; Williams 1967, pp. 25–7, 55–8; Haigh 1981, pp. 129–47; Bradshaw 1988, pp. 220–52; Lennon 1991.

produced three Elizabethan bishops and seemed to visitors a possible future Geneva; in Munster the principal Barrymore family was included, a junior branch of the O'Briens of Thomond, and some other loyalists during the Desmond rebellion; while in most parts large numbers of native clergy continued to serve the Irish church. In Meath and Clonmacnois in 1604, for example, a third of the top 30 livings were held by Irish-born ministers and proportionately more of the poorer western livings.[49] Men such as these would provide the Church of Ireland with a nucleus of local support in the continuing struggle into the seventeenth century.

In many ways, too, this struggle was still far from reaching its climax: reports on both sides described a battle by a committed minority for the hearts and minds of the uncommitted majority, and we should beware of projecting the seventeenth-century contest back into Elizabeth's reign. Particularly in Gaelic Ireland popular religion still bore little resemblance to the creeds officially propounded by Rome or London. Edmund Tremayne found religion 'totally lacking' in Munster and the people '[n]either papists nor protestants but rather such as have neither fear nor love of God in their hearts'; a Spanish Armada captain described a Donegal girl who rescued him as 'Christian in like manner as Mahomet'; and the first Jesuits active in Ireland wrote significantly of 'this new plantation' of the faith.[50] Finally, in 1603 the Jesuit mission to Ireland had hardly got started,[51] while the government, with the military struggle won, could now turn the full brunt of its resources against this secondary target. Nevertheless the fact remains that in Tudor times the Reformation generally struck only shallow roots in Ireland; and this unenthusiastic local response to the government's ecclesiastical policy seriously exacerbated its political difficulties.

49. Canny 1979b, pp. 429–32, 440–6, 449; Ford 1997, pp. 7–47; Healy 1908, pp. 214–17.
50. Canny 1976, p. 124 (quotation); Bossy 1971, p. 157; Hammerstein 1971, p. 153.
51. Bossy 1971, esp. p. 159.

CHAPTER 10

THE GAELIC RESPONSE TO TUDOR EXPANSION

HISTORIOGRAPHICAL PROBLEMS

The nature of the Gaelic response to the Tudor conquest is presently one of the most emotive issues in Irish history. Until the 1970s, the interpretation of bardic poetry – the most considerable body of contemporary source material available from inside Gaelic society – was generally left to Celtic scholars. Historians concentrated instead on exploiting the much more voluminous but largely hostile Tudor accounts of Gaelic society in the state papers. Since the late 1970s, however, Irish historians have become more interested in the native sources: from being a hopelessly backward, deeply conservative and introverted society incapable of adapting to outside influences, Irish Gaeldom has been historiographically transformed into a dynamic, open society, powerfully influenced by the Renaissance and highly sensitive to the problems of the age.[1] Most recently, the subject has become embroiled in the Revisionism debate: as consensus has collapsed, assessments of the nature and extent of the Gaelic response to the Tudor conquest have exhibited a bewildering variety, ranging from innovative, heroic and successful resistance, to rigid adherence to traditional values and resigned acceptance of a *fait accompli*.[2]

No doubt the debate's character has also been influenced by the intractable nature of the surviving native sources and perhaps also, as is implied, by the technical competence of individual historians.[3] Yet the historiographical

1. The most sweeping presentations of this 1970s revisionism are the studies by Dr Brendan Bradshaw. See esp. Bradshaw 1978b, pp. 65–80; Bradshaw 1979b, pp. 15–36. (Cf. Walsh 1993, pp. 33–50.) More balanced assessments of developments include Nicholls 1972; Simms 1987a; O'Dowd 1986, pp. 120–47.
2. See Bradshaw 1978b, pp. 66–80; Dunne 1980, pp. 7–30; Canny 1982, pp. 91–116; Ó Buachalla 1983, pp. 81–134; Cunningham 1986, pp. 148–70; Simms 1987a; Simms 1987b, pp. 58–75; O Riordan 1990; Ó Buachalla 1992, pp. 149–75; Caball 1993, pp. 87–96; Leerssen 1994; Mac Craith 1995, pp. 139–61; Mac Craith 1996, pp. 50–82. The key contributions in the latest debate are O Riordan 1990; Ó Buachalla 1992; and Caball 1993.
3. We may, however, ignore suggestions (for instance, Whelan 1990, p. 14) that only the more nationally minded historians take account of Gaelic sources and that revisionists disregard them.

problems raised by the debate are actually more fundamental than this: assessments of change over time (continuity or innovation?) and what was realistic in the circumstances are necessarily highly subjective. In addition, the debate's very terms of reference also present a difficulty, since the discussion largely ignores Scottish Gaeldom. In effect, the process of interaction and assimilation between *Gaedhil* and *Gaill* is split into separate Irish and Scottish experiences, but only that part of the process which occurs within 'the national territory' is deemed relevant. Those *Gaedhil* and *Gaill* who were not destined to become Irishmen, because they did not live in Ireland, are excluded from consideration at the outset, with the result that some of the accompanying shifts in Irish senses of identity have perhaps been overlooked.

In the circumstances, rather than offering a detailed commentary on the Revisionist debate, it has seemed preferable in the present chapter to offer a reappraisal of some more fundamental questions concerning the end of Gaelic rule and the nature of Irish identity. Necessarily, the present chapter is unusually speculative. The aim is to set a new agenda; but at the least the restoration of the wider Gaelic context should provide comparisons and contrasts of a peculiarly telling kind. The argument presented below is that the relationship between Irish and Scottish Gaeldom in the late middle ages was in many ways symbiotic. As is well known, 'Irishness' was subtly reconstructed from the later sixteenth century to include the *Gaill* of Ireland, but the fact that the inclusion of Irish 'foreigners' was effected by excluding others traditionally seen as 'Irish' has not generally been noticed. In fact, the key to the fortunes of Irish Gaeldom in our period was the North Channel passage, linking Ulster and the Western Isles. History has not been well served by the historian's practice of dividing up the Gaelic world into modern national units and studying two separate processes of interaction between *Gaedhil* and *Gaill* in Ireland and Scotland, and two composite nations in the making.[4]

THE RISE AND FALL OF CLAN DONALD

In 1493 the MacDonald, John of Islay, fourth and last lord of the Isles, was forfeited and his lands annexed to the Scottish crown. Until his death in 1503 MacDonald remained a pensioner at court, his dependent chiefs received royal charters granting them the lands they held within the lordship, and four new sheriffs were appointed to strengthen royal government in the region.[5] In effect, this strategy anticipated policies later followed by the Tudors in Ireland as a means of integrating Gaeldom into the respective English and Scottish monarchies. Yet the fortunes of the lordship of the Isles were actually much more significant for the wider Gaelic world than its traditional position on the margins of Stewart monarchy might imply. From their power base in the Western

4. My unpublished research on 'The rise and fall of the Gaelic world, 1300–1650' forms the basis of this chapter.
5. Nicholson 1974, pp. 541–8; Munro 1986, pp. lxxi–iii.

Isles, the lords of the Isles had exploited the weakness of Scottish and English kings in this remote maritime region to build up a powerful and aggressive lordship which was far larger and stronger than any of the chieftaincies in Ireland, stretching from the glens of Antrim, along the Scottish west coast from Kintyre to Glenelg, throughout the Hebrides, to the earldom of Ross.

In Antrim, Clan Donald had established a lordship on the ruins of the earldom of Ulster after 1333. This conquest lordship gave them a secure base against the Scottish king and, together with the lordship's authentically Gaelic values, helped to secure Clan Donald a following in Gaelic Ireland. Significantly too, although the title '*dominus Insularum*' or 'lord of the Isles' was adopted in Latin, they retained in their Gaelic style (*Rí Innse Gall*) the traditional title of *Rí* (= 'king') at a time when, by contrast in Ireland, Gaelic chiefs were abandoning it in favour of the title *tighearna* (= 'lord'), which English and Scottish kings found less offensive to their own pretensions.[6]

At the battle of Harlaw in 1411, the lord of the Isles reputedly commanded an army of 10,000 men against a Scottish royal army; and at both Inverlochy in 1431 and Lagebraad in 1480 the lordship's forces routed royal armies. At the same time, however, successive lords intrigued with the English crown – the nominal overlord of their possessions in Antrim – and were claimed by the English as their allies in fifteenth-century Anglo-Scottish truces. Alexander, third lord (1423–49), may also have tried to get the Danish king to reassert Norwegian suzerainty over the Western Isles. In 1462, John, fourth lord (1449–93), concluded a secret tripartite treaty with Edward IV of England and the exiled earl of Douglas, whereby MacDonald and Douglas agreed to become Edward's subjects and to conquer Scotland with English assistance, dividing the region north of the Forth between them and holding it of the English king.[7]

After the 1493 forfeiture, John of Islay was deposed as *Rí Innse Gall*, probably in 1494, and replaced by John Mór of Dunivaig, his *tánaiste*. In turn, Donald Dubh, grandson of the forfeited John, was recognized by the lordship's inhabitants as *Rí Innse Gall*. It was not until 1545, following 50 years of military and political pressure, that the Scottish crown was able to make the 1493 forfeiture effective after Donald Dubh's untimely death at Carrickfergus while treating with Henry VIII against his sovereign.[8]

In his day, John of Islay had contemplated a royal progress to Tara for inauguration as high king of Ireland. Upon his death, this once most powerful of Irish chiefs was eulogized by a bard from Ireland in conventional terms which belied his growing inability to control his own clansmen, reasserting traditional MacDonald claims to sovereignty over the *Gaedhil* of Ireland and Scotland:

6. Munro 1986, p. xx; Bannerman 1977, p. 216; Simms 1987a, ch. 3.
7. Nicholson 1974, pp. 315, 401–2; Bannerman 1977, pp. 216–17. The latest (Scottish nationalist) account of Clan Donald fortunes stresses how much the clan was part of 'the national community', a perspective which is naturally endorsed by the language and terminology of Scottish royal government. Yet the author ignores the Gaelic sources: Grant 1988, pp. 118–41.
8. Bannerman 1977, pp. 213–15.

The sovereignty of the *Gaedhil* to Clann Colla. It is right to proclaim it. They were again in the same battalions, the heroes of *Fodla* [= Ireland]. The sovereignty of Ireland and Scotland of the sunny lands was had by the bloody sharp-bladed tribes, the fighting champions. The sovereignty of the entire tribes was obtained, by John of Islay.[9]

The lords of the Isles and the Gaelic revival

In sum, the growing strength of the lords of the Isles presented an increasingly dangerous challenge to fifteenth-century Scottish kings: it was the most striking manifestation of a wider political and cultural movement, the Gaelic Revival, which from the later thirteenth century had spread throughout late medieval Gaeldom. The changing political and military balance precipitated a remarkable efflorescence of Gaelic culture, attesting to the growing confidence of native society in this period. It was reflected in such areas as architecture, the foundation of friaries, and in the making of the famous great books – compilations like *An Leabhar Breac* (*The Speckled Book*), the Yellow Book of Lecan, and prose compositions such as 'Caithréim Thoirdhealbhaigh' ('The Triumphs of Turlough'). There was also a heightened sense of national consciousness among the *Gaedhil*. And though perhaps getting under way a little later than in Ireland, this renaissance of Gaelic literature, culture and identity was also a feature of Scottish Gaeldom, particularly under the patronage of the lords of the Isles. It was evident in the fifteenth-century building programme at the lordship's priories, notably the recovery and restoration of Iona, in the sculptured stone monuments, and in the compilation of books of history and genealogy, particularly the *Book of the Dean of Lismore*.[10]

Yet despite their aggressive championing of Gaelic values, culture, and even independence against the increasingly lowland values of the Scottish crown, the lords of the Isles were actually quite flexible and eclectic in their pursuit of power. According to circumstances, they could regard themselves as Scots or as enemies to the realm of Scotland. Their greater readiness to adopt feudalized concepts according to circumstances – evident both in surviving charters issued by them and in their acceptance of Scottish royal charters to the earldom of Ross – helped to introduce greater cohesion into the lordship and also to tie it more closely into the Scottish realm. Their maritime traditions also set them apart from the comparatively weak and land-based chieftaincies of Gaelic Ireland, enabling them to deploy both a powerful fleet of galleys and a far larger army than chiefs of Irish lordships, where the lower orders did not bear arms.[11] As late as 1545 the last serious MacDonald pretender, Donald Dubh, brought 4,000 redshanks in 180 galleys with him to Ireland.

9. 'Ceñus Ghaoidheal do chlann cholla, coir a fhógra / síad arís na gcathibh cétna, flatha fodla / ceñus eireñ 7 albuin an fhuiñ ghríanaigh / ata ag an dréim fhuilidh fhaobhraigh cuiridh cliaruidh / Fuair ceñus na haicme uile, Eoin a híle': 'The book of Clanranald', in Cameron 1892–4, pp. 208–10; MacDonald 1911, pp. vi, 6.
10. *NHI*, ii, chs 9, 12; Bannerman 1977, pp. 210–11, 228–30, 233–9; Grant 1984, ch. 8.
11. Munro 1986; Bannerman 1977, pp. 214–15.

Similarly, the earl of Argyll in the mid-sixteenth century could raise an army of 5,000 men.[12]

Redshanks in Ireland

Yet initially, as has been argued, redshanks may have become more readily available to Irish chiefs following the final collapse of the lordship of the Isles after Donald Dubh's rising. The government responded by securing a statute in 1557 to make inter-marriage or hiring of Scots mercenaries a capital offence, but of course this was ignored in Gaelic Ulster. For instance, Shane O'Neill had earlier married one of the MacDonalds of Dunyveg, and was later linked with Catherine MacLean, O'Donnell's wife; while the next O'Neill, Turlough Luineach, married Lady Agnes Campbell, daughter of the fourth earl of Argyll and widow of James MacDonald of Dunyveg, and her daughter by James, Finola, married the next O'Donnell. In each case, the alliances facilitated the recruitment of redshanks, Lady Agnes's dowry being 1,000 Campbells and MacDonalds. Briefly in winter 1569–70, Turlough Luineach reputedly had over 3,000 Scots, between the dowry, his existing Scots mercenaries, and a recently recruited force of MacLeans, plus his traditional Irish kerne and galloglass; but this force overtaxed his resources and he was soon 'eaten out'.[13] Yet, as Anglo-Scottish relations improved and the Scottish government consolidated royal control over its western seaboard, James VI took steps to rein in the islanders, so that the supply of redshanks began to dry up.[14]

The larger numbers of troops available to Scottish Gaeldom suggest that a greater proportion of the population traditionally bore arms than was the case in Ireland, and this presumably reflects a broader basis of support for lordship in Scottish Gaeldom: the right to bear arms conferred a degree of political influence. An account of the election of Donald, second lord, in 1388 suggests a wider degree of consultation than might have been expected of an Irish chieftaincy:

> Raghnald MacEoin . . . summoned the nobles of the Isles and his brethren to the one place, and he gave the rod of lordship to his brother at Cill Donan in Eigg and he was proclaimed MacDonald and Donald of Islay against the view of the men of the Isles.[15]

These remarks about what is, in some ways, a special case help us to understand the potential for change within the Gaelic world in response to outside pressures. The late medieval lordship of the Isles was modernizing

---

12. Munro 1986, p. xli; Hill 1993, p. 30; Mackenzie 1953, p. 98.
13. Hayes-McCoy 1937, pp. 85–109.
14. Ibid., pp. 192–3, 204–5.
15. 'Ragnall mac Eóin . . . do chuir tionol ar úaslibh Iñsibh Gall 7 bhrathribh go haonionadh, 7 tug sé slat an tigernais da bhrathair accill Doñaiñ a neige 7 do goiredh mac Domhnuill de 7 Domhnall ahile anaighuidh baramhla fher Iñsi Gall': Cameron 1892–4, p. 160.

and expanding in broadly the same way as the Stewart monarchy had itself done earlier.

THE MILITARY WEAKNESS OF IRISH GAELDOM

In principle, this course of action was also open to the Irish chieftaincies, and in many ways was later followed by the earl of Tyrone: arguments that Gaelic Ireland was incapable of modernizing or responding to Tudor aggression do not bear serious consideration. Yet the comparison does underline the continued military weakness of Gaelic Ireland at the start of the Tudor conquest. The Gaelic Revival in late medieval Ireland had in fact been erected on extremely flimsy military foundations. Despite the diffusion of armour, siege engines and castle-building skills in Gaelic Ireland, Gaelic kerne, or footsoldiers, were still 'naked men' without armour, and Irish horsemen still rode without stirrups.

Numerically, too, the military capacity of Irish chieftaincies was extremely limited, as is clear from a particularly detailed account of their military potential, entitled 'A description of the power of Irishmen', which dates from around 1490.[16] It lists the military power of 88 Gaelic chieftaincies (besides half a dozen surnames of English descent in Connaught who were 'of no better condition than Irishmen, wearing Irish apparayle') who, collectively, could raise a total of 3,089 horse, 41 battle of galloglass (say, 3,000 men) and 15,744 kerne. The report was evidently intended to emphasize the strength of the Irishry (who 'be for the most part good & hardie men of warre & can live hardly & suffer great miserie') and the weakness of the Englishry, the outlying parts of which were 'so environed wth Irishmen that they cannot answere the kinges deputie, neyther of power to keepe themselves', while even the four shires 'of their owne power be scant hable to susteyne the warres of 3 Irishmen'. What saved the situation, allegedly, was that 'God provides, setting continuall dissension emongst them & mortall warre'. Even so, the power of individual chiefs was quite small: MacMurrough, prince of Leinster, could raise '200 horse well harneysed, a baytayle of galoglas & 300 kerne', O'Brien of Thomond could make '200 h[orse], 2 b[attles of galloglass, and] DC [600] k[erne]', and O'Neill of Tyrone disposed '3 b[attle of galloglass], 200 h[orse, and] 300 k[erne]'. Yet these were the strongest chiefs: a border chief such as O'Toole could make only 24 horse and 80 kerne.

In other words, militarily, the Irish chieftaincies were roughly the equivalent of the English border surnames towards Scotland, with which the Tudor government normally coped quite easily and in much the same way, that is, by booking and taking pledges, and warding peles and castles against them. For instance, when 'booked' in 1528 the surnames numbered 403 clansmen in

16. Price 1932, pp. 202–7 (quotations, pp. 202, 206, 207). I am grateful to Kenneth Nicholls of National University of Ireland, Cork, for help with the dating of this document. My calculations differ slightly from the totals given. The numbers of horsemen available to Leinster chiefs as estimated by the 'description' broadly agree with Chief Baron Finglas's estimate made 40 years later: Harris 1747, p. 44.

Tynedale and 445 in Redesdale.[17] In the absence of muster rolls, the corresponding power of the Englishry cannot be precisely ascertained, but a rough indication is provided by figures for Cumberland (a small, mainly pastoral, border county) which in 1534 had 6,502 able-bodied men of military age, of whom 1,974 were mounted, or Northumberland, an adjacent larger county which in 1538 mustered 2,766 mounted men, excluding Tynedale and Redesdale.[18] Thus bearing in mind that *c.* 1560 Co. Meath was reported to be 'as well inhabited as any shire in England',[19] it is difficult to believe that Gaelic Ireland was capable of mounting any serious military challenge to the English Pale.

Military developments in the sixteenth century

Even so, a professional army of almost 22,000 men, had it ever been assembled, would have been a formidable force: it was around ten times the size of the Tudor bureaucracy and standing forces combined.[20] Yet it was unusual for more than two or three chiefs to combine; and militarily, over 70 per cent of Gaelic troops were unarmoured kerne, whose combat value was decidedly limited. They were good for burning, foraging and taking preys – as English observers noted of their conduct in Henry VIII's armies in France and Scotland in 1544–5[21] – but not for much else. They were also a crippling burden on a Gaelic economy that was less developed and therefore less able to sustain them: no doubt this in turn explains features of Gaelic Ireland which occasioned most comment from foreign travellers – its poverty, lack of towns, and absence of trades.[22]

During the sixteenth century the gradual introduction of gunpowder and firearms began to alter the nature of Irish warfare. By the 1520s, Irish chiefs were beginning to acquire handguns and light field artillery, and Gaelic kerne were gradually converted into 'shot'. Yet Chief Baron Finglas, writing *c.* 1528, thought that 'Irishmen have not such wisdom n[or] policy in war, but Englishmen, when they set themselves thereunto, exceed them far, and touching harness and artillery, exceed them too far'.[23] The changes had little impact on the overall military balance until the 1590s, and even then, the manufacture of heavier siege artillery remained very much under royal control and would have been too expensive for individual chiefs.

Gaelic Ireland was also much less efficient in its use of available manpower: Gaelic peasants did not bear arms until Shane O'Neill began to arm all his subjects in the 1560s, in response to the increasing military pressure from the Tudors.[24] Thus, militarily, Gaelic Ireland remained excessively reliant on Scottish

17. PRO, SP 1/48, ff. 117–340 (*LP*, iv (ii), no. 4336 (21); Ellis 1992a, pp. 253–77.
18. PRO, E 101/549/13; Newton 1974, pp. 8–9, 13. See Ellis 1995a, *passim.*
19. Quoted, Canny 1975, p. 9.
20. Cf. Williams 1979, chs 3–4.
21. See White 1957–8, pp. 213–25; Ellis 1990–1, pp. 289–308.
22. See, for instance, *NHI,* ii, p. 397.
23. Harris 1747, p. 44.
24. Hayes-McCoy 1937, p. ix; Nicholls 1972, p. 71.

Gaeldom, which could provide authentically Gaelic troops and had a long tradition of exporting its surplus manpower to Ireland, from galloglass in the thirteenth century to redshanks in the sixteenth. Indeed, the growing militarization of Irish society during the sixteenth century in response to Tudor expansion only increased this dependency. In 1555, for instance, O'Donnell agreed to maintain 500 of the earl of Argyll's mercenaries in his territory.[25]

There was also a surprising contrast between Scottish Gaeldom's strong maritime tradition and the evident weakness of the Irish chieftaincies in naval power. Prominent on the seal of the lord of the Isles, for instance, was a galley under sail, but the 'description of the power of Irishmen' noted only two chiefs, O'Driscoll and O'Malley, who 'useth long galeys'.[26] Economically, however, the relationship was apparently reversed: the Western Isles were dependent on Irish Gaeldom's larger lordships which had better financial resources and, as we shall see, provided a stronger underpinning for Gaelic culture.

GAELIC SENSES OF IDENTITY AND TERMINOLOGY

This is not really surprising: as the vast bulk of the sources suggest, politics in the Gaelic world remained intensely local, and, in Ireland at least, the *Gaedhil* normally thought primarily in terms of the local dynasty and tribal lordship.[27] In terms of the Gaelic response to Tudor expansion, however, it is the more muted evidence concerning wider 'national' senses of identity among the *Gaedhil* that is perhaps more significant.

In the first place, there was a sense of national identity which identified the *Gaedhil* with the land of Ireland (apostrophized as *Inis Fáil, Banbha* or *Fódla*). This Gaelic sense of Irishness was underpinned by an ancient literature and a long-established tradition focusing on a high kingship and a 'national' history about the occupation and defence of Ireland against the foreigner, or *Gaill*. Racial and cultural unity was also fostered by the uniformity of Gaelic Ireland's social, legal and cultural institutions. These traditional concepts of Irishness were most evident in the poetry of the period in which, for instance, the bards extolled the claims of individual chiefs to the high kingship of Ireland. Bardic poetry can be read as both local and national: local because, politically, it was clan-specific, aimed at extolling the prowess of the particular lord, the poet's patron; national because it was a reflex of Gaelic national culture. Yet, although this Irish sense of identity sharpened in the face of the Tudor conquest, the last attempt to revive the high kingship of Ireland had been in 1315 – for Edward Bruce. The identity of the would-be king is significant: Gaelic Scotland and Ireland shared a common language with standard literary forms, Irish

25. Mackenzie 1953, p. 98.
26. Price 1932, pp. 203, 204; Munro 1986, pp. lxxi, 318–20.
27. A recent, sensitive discussion of many of the problems raised by this evidence is Leerssen 1994, esp. pp. 5–16.

chiefs had long recruited Scottish mercenaries, and by 1400 there was substantial 'colonization' by the MacDonalds in north-east Ulster.

These reflections in turn prompt the question as to whether senses of Irishness focused primarily on Ireland and its peoples or on an Irish nation. The fact that the Gaelic annals persisted in dividing the island's inhabitants into *Gaedhil* ('Irish' or 'Gaels') and *Gaill* ('foreigners', of English or Scots speech and culture), even though the geographical term *Éireannaigh* ('Irishmen') was available to describe the *Gaedhil* and the *Gaill* collectively, indicates that we are not talking about Irishness in the modern sense. The *Gaedhil*, as they described themselves, inhabited Ireland and Scotland where, likewise, Gaelic land and culture were threatened by *Gaill*. And regardless of whether they lived in Scotland or Ireland, the *Gaill* described the *Gaedhil*, their culture and language as 'Irish' (or 'Erse', a variant), from the primary association of the *Gaedhil* with 'Ireland'. For instance, in the Scottish army at the battle of Solway Moss in 1542, most of the estimated 12,000 'Irishmen' contemptuously described by English spies as 'very slaves and no men of good order' had probably never set foot in Ireland.[28] And both traditional and modern usages can be seen in such phrases as the description in 1545 of Donald Dubh as king of 'the Scottish Irish'. 'Ireland' too was sometimes extended to include the highlands and islands of Scotland (*Scotia*, the land of the *Scoti*, or 'Irish').[29]

Of course, Gaelic sources could distinguish between *Gaedhil na hÉireann* ('the Irish of Ireland') and *Gaedhil na hAlban* ('the Irish of Scotland'), or between *Gaill* and *Sasanaigh* ('Englishmen'), even though the English were usually described as *Gaill*. Yet these distinctions, though no doubt significant, were in fact rarely made. Politics in both countries normally revolved around 'the war of the *Gaedhil* against the *Gaill*', so that late medieval Gaeldom apparently thought more in terms of a Gaelic world (*Gaedhealtacht*) surrounded by *Gaill* than of an Irish polity threatened by Englishmen. An entry in the annals of Connaught neatly illustrates these overlapping senses of identity: 'the king of Scotland summoned the nobles of the Scottish race, and they came to the harbour and boarded the king's ship and the king took them prisoner, both *Gaill* and *Gaedhil*, and released the *Gaill* after a while'.[30] It was only from *c.* 1560 when Gaelic Ireland first came under serious political pressure from England that conditions developed which were more conducive to the emergence of a distinctive Gaelic Irish identity, separate from Scots Gaelic, in opposition to the English state.

---

28. Ellis 1995a, pp. 60–1.
29. *LP. Hen. VIII*, xix (ii) no. 795. For another instance, see below, p. 278. For other references to 'Irish' as applied to the *Gaedhil* in Scotland and to 'Ireland' as applied to the Scottish highlands, see Hayes-McCoy 1937, pp. 4–5.
30. 'Ri Alpan do chor gharma ar maithib an chinidh Alpanaigh et a techt chuigi aran cuan a roibhe se, et dul annsa loing a roibhe an Ri doibh et an Ri da ngabail itir Gall 7 Ghaoídel, 7 na Goill do lecin amac a cinn tamaill 'na diaigh sin': Freeman 1944, p. 716 (my translation). Ellis 1994, pp. 169–70. As late as the eighteenth century, Gaelic-speaking highlanders still referred to Scottish lowlanders as *Sasanaigh*; Colley 1992, pp. 14–15.

Gaelic national identity

Thus, alongside traditional expressions of national sentiment focusing on the land of Ireland, the *Gaedhealtacht* witnessed, during the period of the Gaelic Revival, a different kind of ethnic, cultural nationalism, fostered by the restoration of Gaelic Ulster's traditional ties with the Western Isles after the collapse of the earldom of Ulster in the fourteenth century. It was this that provided the real dynamic within the Gaelic world. In this connection, it is hardly coincidence that from the later fifteenth century there are once again obits of leading Gaelic *literati* in the Irish annals, implying that they operated in a pan-Gaelic context – 'the head of the schools of Ireland and Scotland', 'the teacher of Ireland and Scotland in poetry', 'the professor of music for Ireland and Scotland' – a practice which had ceased with the Anglo-Norman conquest of east Ulster in the late twelfth century.[31] And significantly, none of the great Gaelic books and collections of poetry that were so prominent a feature of the Gaelic Revival in Ireland survive from a Scottish source before *The Book of the Dean of Lismore*, a collection of poems by poets based in Ireland and Scotland, which dates from the early sixteenth century.[32]

The ambiguity between these different senses of national identity in the late medieval *Gaedhealtacht*, which is probably quite deliberate, is epitomized by Clan Donald pretensions. John of Islay's claim to be high king of Ireland reflected the traditional pinnacle of poetic ambition, even though the pretensions of Gaelic chiefs in Scotland did not normally extend to Ireland; but his styling in a prose account as 'áird rígh . . . Gaoidheal' (high king of the *Gaedhil*) is evidence of even wider ambitions. In the poetry composed by his hereditary MacMhuirich bard, Scottish and Irish themes are interwoven to stress the lord's overarching position throughout the *Gaedhealtacht*:

> Pride of the *Gaedhil* / the champion of Ulster / . . . The sun of the *Gaedhil*, / the countenance of O'Colla, / by the banks of the Bann, / quick are his ships / an angry hound that checks plunders, / a modest heart, / the tree of *Banbha*. / The land with fire-brands is red after him, / his prime purpose is to come to Tara [where, traditionally, high kings of Ireland were inaugurated] / putting Meath in commotion, / the leopard of Islay.[33]

Of course poets based in Ireland were also conscious of this pan-Gaelic dimension, although they might choose to describe it rather differently. Teague Dall O'Higgin (1550–91) reminded Sorley MacDonald, head of the Antrim MacDonalds, of the oppressions which *Banbha* now suffered and her ancient claim on Scotland. In an age in which concepts of Ireland as the national

31. Hennessy 1871, i, pp. 162, 168, ii, pp. 176, 290, 364 ('cend scoile Erenn ocus Alban'; 'oide fer nErenn ocus nAlban re dán'; 'ollam Erenn ocus Alban re sinm').
32. For example, Watson 1937, pp. 6–12; Quiggin 1937.
33. 'Guaire Gaoidheal, aoinfher uladh . . . / Grian na nGaoidheal . gnúis í cholla / fa bhruach baña . luath a longa / cuilen confuigh . choisger foghla / croidhe cuñla bile banbha / tir na teñal deirg na dheghaidh / a bhert bunaidh techt go temhair / measgadh midhe onchu íle': Cameron 1892–4, pp. 260, 264.

territory were rather different, the poet wondered whether she would claim 'the islands to the east between *Fódla* and Scotland' and all of Islay or Kintyre. He recalled the departure of the three Collas to Scotland, the return of two, but the continued absence of the choicest, 'the king whom *Banbha* is expecting', whose strange allegiance to a foreign land deprived her of a spouse:

> The best-loved of Conn's dwelling
> Sorley, son of MacDonald,
> the expected spouse from *Monadh*'s plain,
> he for whom Ireland is waiting.

Sorley's return, he prophesied, would discharge Scotland's debt to Ireland and provide her with a husband.[34] Over a century earlier, much the same themes and sentiments had been developed – rather more diplomatically – by Teague Oge O'Higgin in a poem addressed to Alexander MacDonald, lord of the Isles (*c.* 1423–49):

> The path of the three who came from the east
> to conquer *Fódla* from Scotland;
> the stars of the race of Conn will come
> in the same way to us.[35]

Thus, in the late middle ages, the Irishry of western Scotland may be seen as an extension of the Irishry of Ireland, rather like the relationship between the English districts of Ireland and the English mainland. This, however, was a source of strength to the *Gaedhil*, not of weakness – even though the suggestion that the concept of 'Ireland' as the national territory of the *Gaedhil* was, from a modern perspective, less geographically specific might imply the opposite.

During the sixteenth century, however, those economic and political trends that had favoured late medieval Gaeldom vis-à-vis the *Galltacht*, the regions of English culture, now became increasingly unfavourable to Gaelic Ireland. The economic upswing of the late fifteenth century fostered trade and the prosperity of the lordship's towns, while demographic growth throughout the Tudor state led to rising food prices, land hunger and reduced labour costs, so tilting the economics of farming back towards agriculture and prompting a renewed interest in colonization schemes for Ireland. Politically too, the English revival in Ireland and the parallel suppression of the lordship of the Isles in Scotland were underpinned by a gradual Anglo-Scottish *rapprochement*: exemplified by the short-lived treaty of 1502, the first formal peace between the two nations since 1333, and the more durable treaty of Edinburgh in 1560, this *rapprochement* was of fundamental importance to the *Gaedhealtacht* because it prompted a new cooperation within the *Galltacht* against a common adversary. The

34. 'Rogha leannáin Leasa Cuinn / Somhairle mhac Meic Domhnuill / brath céile do Mhoigh Mhonaidh / 's re bhfoil Éire ag anamhain': Knott 1922–6, i, pp. 173–9, ii, pp. 115–19.
35. 'Slighe an trír tháinig a-noir / go ghabháil Fhódla a hAlbain / tiocfa réalda cinidh Chuinn sa slighidh gcéadna chuguinn': McKenna 1939–40, i, pp. 114–18, ii, pp. 69–71.

Stewart monarchy was consolidating its control over the kingdom's western periphery at the same time as similar pressures were being exerted on Gaelic society in Ireland.

SURRENDER AND REGRANT: CREATING AN IRISH IDENTITY

Even though they were to bring about its division into separate Irish and Scottish entities, however, these long-term shifts in the balance of power can only have been dimly discerned within late medieval Gaeldom, if at all. From a Gaelic perspective, the 'surrender and regrant' initiative was perhaps the most salient development in the gradual expansion of the Tudor state. This offered confirmation to the landowning elites of their existing titles to land in return for their acceptance of Tudor sovereignty and the new English kingdom of Ireland: instead of being aliens in their own land, they were to become full subjects of Henry VIII, entitled to his protection and access to the king's courts.

Yet the initiative also had much wider implications, both concerning concepts of nationality and in regard to political and social structures. No doubt more by accident than design, the Tudor creation of a new dependent kingdom which was co-extensive with the island of Ireland proved to be a particularly seductive piece of statecraft. It promoted the concept of a unitary kingdom of Ireland, embracing both *Gaedhil* and *Gaill* there as common Irish subjects of the crown, with Ireland as the national territory of this new composite nation.[36] Hitherto, 'Irish enemies' had been consistently denied the rights of freeborn Englishmen because, English lawyers argued, nationality was conferred by 'blood' (parentage) and allegiance: Englishness was a legal status enjoyed by those (including the English of Ireland) of free birth, born within the territories under the allegiance of the king of England, and of English blood and condition. Yet the legislation associated with Henry VIII's establishment of a kingdom of Ireland in 1541 and the parallel 1536 statute for Wales, the so-called Welsh Act of Union, now created a situation in which large numbers of non-English, namely the 'mere Irish' and the 'mere Welsh', enjoyed with Englishmen the same free status as the king's subjects.

In the longer term, the effect of the statutes was to foster more geographical senses of nationality in both England and Ireland, based on the *patria* or native land, at the expense of traditional ethnic concepts of identity. And this process later accelerated under the impact of the Reformation. After the 1530s, Englishness came to be more narrowly focused on England itself, and it later acquired a pronounced religious character, the product of protestant perceptions of England as God's elect nation.[37] In Ireland, the concept of an English-speaking Irishman was born, and Irishness was increasingly identified with

c f. p3210.

36. On these developments, see Bradshaw 1979a, part III, which construes the evidence rather differently.
37. Ellis 1986b, pp. 187–204; Ellis 1995a, ch. 4.

catholicism. Propagandists for the new order could invoke earlier Gaelic traditions centring on the older and narrower, but politically more innocuous, Hibernocentric senses of Irish identity: these ideas were combined with traditional English structures of government to create a new kingdom and nation comprised of the island's English and Gaelic inhabitants. Yet equally novel was the increasing exclusion of Scottish Gaeldom from this new nationalism: the Irish of Scotland, who saw themselves as Irish as well as Scottish, and their traditional ties with Ireland were simply ignored.

Nevertheless, it still took a considerable amount of state pressure exerted by the English and Scottish governments throughout the early modern period to partition the *Gaedhil* and the *Gaedhealtacht* between separate 'national' units – that is, to convince those *Gaedhil* living in Scotland that they were purely Scottish and not Irish, and to persuade those *Gaedhil* and *Gaill* living in Ireland that they were really all *Éireannaigh* (Irishmen).

Gaelic society and surrender and regrant

Even more problematic for the Gaelic elite was the likely impact of this anglicizing process on politics, government and society in the locality. Undoubtedly, Tudor perceptions of 'civil society', lordship and 'good governance' were far removed from Gaelic ones, but how visible were these differences in Gaelic Ireland?

The model of English provincial society most familiar to Gaelic chiefs was of course English Ireland, in much of which the existing patterns of compact landholding, extended lineages and marcher lordship (sometimes bolstered by palatine jurisdictions) seemed to promise substantial continuity with traditional Gaelic power structures. Indeed, it is significant that surrender and regrant was more successful in those lordships, such as Thomond, where the government attempted to work within existing power structures rather than against them; and later on, Hugh O'Neill's price for an English Ulster was apparently a presidency or palatine jurisdiction for himself.[38] Yet even in Ireland, the destruction of the Kildares would have alerted the Gaelic chiefs to the government's preference for an alternative manifestation of English society that was much less congenial to the Gaelic elite. As the power of great magnates like Kildare was eroded, so English provincial society was increasingly dominated by coalitions of lesser landowners, especially the county gentry, such as had long ruled individual Irish shires like Co. Louth. And within this model of 'civil' society, even quite humble freeholders had access to the king's courts and also some input into the political process, either through their election to minor office as constable or churchwarden, or through service on grand or petty juries. Thus to the political elite of a society which remained extremely hierarchical, tribal and autocratic, the implications of this anglicizing process must have been extremely unwelcome.

38. See below, pp. 334–7.

The Gaelic response

To judge from some of the poetry, the Gaelic *literati* were acutely sensitive to the implications of surrender and regrant. As early as 1542, an anonymous poet condemned those chiefs now collaborating with the English:

> Shame on you, men of the *Gaedhil*,
> none of you is alive;
> the *Gaill* are dividing up your land;
> you are like a crowd of fairies . . .

> *Banbha*'s O'Brien lineage under Murrough [the chief]
> is covenanted to the king of England,
> they have turned their backs on their ancestral inheritance
> – and the surrender is pitiful . . .

> O'Neill of Oileach and Eamhain [Macha],
> the king of Tara and Tailte,
> in foolish submission has exchanged his kingship
> for the earldom of Ulster . . .

> Shame on the grey foreign gun,
> shame on the golden chain,
> shame on the court without English speech,
> shame for the denial of Mary's son.

> O nobles of the island of old Art,
> unworthy is your altered rank,
> you weak misguided crowd,
> henceforth say nothing but 'shame'.[39]

Apparently dated by the reference to O'Neill as earl of Ulster, this remarkably perceptive satire alluded succinctly to all the major implications of the Tudor initiative – the chiefs' abandonment of their inheritance, royal lineage, land, culture and religion, in return for English earldoms. No wonder that Tudor officials regarded Irish 'rhymers' as dangerous subversives.[40] This, contemporary Gaelic annals, and a number of other, slightly later poems show that the Gaelic learned classes were well aware of the major changes concerning language, religion, and ethnicity occurring in sixteenth-century Gaelic society.

---

39. 'Fúbún fúibh, a shluagh Gaoidheal, / ní mhaireann aoinneach agaibh; / Goill ag comhroinn bhur gcríche; / re sluagh síthe bhur samhail . . . Síol mBriain Bhanbha fá Mhurchadh / I gcunnradh do rígh Shacsan, / tugsad – 's is truagh an toirbheart – / druim re hoighreacht a n-athar . . . Ó Néill Oiligh is Eamhna, / rí Teamhrach agus Tailtean, / tugsad ar iarlacht Uladh / ríoghacht go humhal aimhghlic . . . Fúbún fán ngunna ngallghlas, / fúbún fán slabhra mbuidhe, / fúbún fán gcúirt gan Bhéarla, / fúbún séana Mheic Mhuire. A uaisle Inse sean Airt, / neamhmaith bhur gcéim ar gclaochlúdh, / a shluagh míthreórach meat, / ná habraidh feasta acht "faobún"': Ó Cuív 1974, pp. 272–3 (my translation).
40. *NHI*, iii, pp. 520–1.

Given that the work of individual poets was usually tailored to the views of their patrons, however, the poetry generally exhibited a wide variety of responses, ranging from the vigorous denunciation outlined above to the cynical recapitulation of traditional bardic themes when local circumstances apparently dictated discreet silence in respect of Tudor reform. For instance, a remarkable poem in honour of Connor O'Brien, the protestant third earl of Thomond (1553–81), is quite unlike a traditional bardic inaugural ode. Instead of exhorting him to great deeds like banishing his foes from Ireland, it is indiscriminately admiring of *Gaedhil* and *Gaill* alike, pointedly describes him as earl of Thomond rather than O'Brien, and commemorates his accession to the earldom along with other earls, Ormond, Desmond and Clanrickard, and Lord Deputy Sussex. Although Thomond patronized the poets, his rule was marked by contradictions between English law and Gaelic custom, and in response to his hanging of three poets in 1572, Ulster poets composed satires against him.

Even so, as the Tudor conquest progressed and Anglo-Gaelic relations plummeted, the tone of the poetry became more urgently anti-English. For instance, a Franciscan poet, Owen O'Duffy (*d.* 1590), portrayed the Church of Ireland clergy as English blow-ins, employing English terms to ridicule them: 'Those clergymen who come here now / a blind clergy shrouded in fog / respect Mary less than a *dog* / but *by God*, they shall not get away with it.' By the 1590s, there are occasional indications of a new nationalist ideology articulated in the poetry.[41]

THE BEGINNINGS OF THE GAELIC REFORMATION

In other respects, however, the initial Gaelic response to religious change was surprisingly muted, given its central role in the creation of more modern 'faith and fatherland' expressions of Irish nationalism. In part, this may be because, initially, efforts to transform the medieval church in Ireland into the national Church of Ireland had not proceeded very far at parish level. By the 1560s, however, religious change was impinging on Irish Gaeldom not simply in the form of the Tudor Reformation but also from a quite unexpected quarter.

In 1567 the publication in Edinburgh of Bishop John Carswell's Gaelic translation of John Knox's *Book of Common Order* marked the advance of the Reformation in sections of Scottish Gaeldom, notably Clan Campbell. *Foirm na n-Urrnuidheadh* was the first printed book in Gaelic. It was clearly intended for use throughout the *Gaedhealtacht*, even though dedicated to the earl of Argyll. For this reason, the translation was rendered into classical common Gaelic, the standard literary language, and not the Scottish or Irish dialects that

---

41. 'An cliar-sa anois tig anall / cliar dhall ar a ndeachaigh ceo / ní mó leo Muire ná *dog* / dar *by God*, ní rachaidh leo': Caball 1993, p. 92 (my translation); Leerssen 1994, pp. 10–11, 28, 37–8; Ó Buachalla 1992, pp. 160–1; Bradshaw 1978b, pp. 66, 78; Mac Craith 1996, pp. 76–8; O'Dowd 1986, p. 137.

later predominated. It also preserved Gaelic orthography, but its abandonment of traditional Gaelic script in favour of Roman type set a standard for Gaelic writings in Scotland.

For Ireland, Elizabeth's approval of Gaelic type for the press on which Kearney's Gaelic Catechism was presently printed also set a standard, and this had the effect of introducing a further difference between Irish and Scottish practices. The *Foirm*'s intended audience was also emphasized by the translator's introduction, in which Carswell observed that the translation was made 'especially for the men of Scotland and Ireland' and related at length the disadvantages 'to us, the *Gaedhil* of Scotland and Ireland . . . that our Gaelic language has never been put into print'. In particular, 'we suffer a greater want than any other, that we have not the Holy Bible printed in Gaelic, as it has been printed in Latin & English . . . and likewise that the history of our ancestors has never been printed, although a certain amount of the history of the *Gaedhil* of Scotland and Ireland has been written in manuscripts'. In consequence, instead of preserving the word of God and the truth, Gaelic writers were preoccupied with lying worldly tales composed about Tuatha Dé Danann, the sons of Milesius, and Finn McCool and his Fianna.[42] Yet differences between Irish and Scottish Gaeldom were reflected in Carswell's intrusion of a prayer for the blessing of a ship and, more significantly, in the poem he composed for his *Foirm* which, already in 1567, recognized the rooted opposition to the Reformation of the friars in Ireland. After travelling throughout Scotland, he urged the book westward:

> After that, travel over each wave
> to the land of Ireland, of the liberal bounds;
> although the friars hate you,
> move westward within their sight.[43]

In other ways too, Carswell's *Foirm* reflected the comparative openness of Gaelic culture in Scotland to outside influences. This was apparent also in the very odd-looking orthography of *The Book of the Dean of Lismore* – in the

---

42. 'atá uireasbhuidh is mó iná gach uireasbhuidh oraind gan an Bíobla naomhtha do bheith a gcló Gaoidheilge againd, mar tá sé a gcló Laidne agas Bhérla . . . agas fós gan seanchus ar sean nó ar sindsear do bheith mar an gcédna a gcló againd riamh, acht gé tá cuid éigin do tseanchus Ghaoidheal Alban agas Eireand sgríobhtha a leabhruibh lámh': Thomson 1970, pp. 10–11. In a novel reappraisal of Ireland's religious milieu from a social and cultural perspective, Professor Meigs has now offered a strikingly different interpretation of the Gaelic response to reform. The marked resilience of Irish catholicism in the face of state-sponsored reform, she argues, stemmed from the peculiar role of the Gaelic learned classes in transmitting religious beliefs and practices, thus imbuing Irish Christianity with a distinctively Gaelic, bardic tradition: Meigs 1997. One apparent difficulty with this thesis, however – highlighted by the author's worrying failure to address the evidence outlined here – is that in Scotland the same bardic tradition was successfully harnessed to the cause of reform: see, for instance, Dawson 1994.

43. Thomson 1970, pp. 13, 110–17. 'Dá éis sin taisdil gach tond / go crích Eireand na bfond bfial; / gé beag ar na bráithribh thú / gluais ar amharc a súl siar.': ibid., p. 13.

ordinary Scots hand and spelling of the period, and not unlike Manx Gaelic –
which was clearly an attempt to make the Gaelic language more readable and
intelligible to English speakers.[44]

The impact of confessional divisions

The advance of the Reformation too began to erode traditional ties between
Ulster and western Scotland. In principle, as both Elizabeth and James recognized, Calvinism's potential for subversion (notably the doctrines of the Cov-
enant, a parity of ministers, and independent kirk sessions) furnished Irish
Gaeldom with a perfect ideological justification for opposition to Tudor expansion. Yet as we have seen, Gaelic lordship and society in Ireland were
markedly more autocratic and hierarchical than their Scottish counterparts, and
the democratic potential of Scottish Calvinism would also have eroded chiefly
power. Perhaps this is one reason why the Irish chiefs increasingly looked to
Rome and the absolutist monarchies of catholic Europe with their far greater
resources.

By and large, Scotland accepted the Reformation, Ireland resisted, with the
result that Scottish and Irish Gaeldom were increasingly divided by religion.
The strong political support for the Gaelic Reformation provided by the most
powerful lord within Scottish Gaeldom, the earl of Argyll, meant that by 1600
Gaelic Scotland was increasingly Calvinist.[45] And the importance of religious
divisions within the *Gaedhealtacht* as a solvent of pan-Gaelic identity was recognized by the bards themselves. Arriving in Scotland on a professional visit,
Fergal Oge MacAward soon came to regret his journey when he found that
Mass was not available:

> Alas, Scotland does not believe, as she ought,
> that the blood of the High King
> enters into the host,
> but I cling to the law He made.

Better to beg from door to door at home, he concluded, than to live like a king
in an heretical land.[46]

THE ORIGINS OF 'FAITH AND FATHERLAND'

Paradoxically, the impact of the Reformation meant that by 1600, in both
Scotland and Ireland religion was coming to be seen as a force for unity

---

44. See Quiggin 1937. For a seventeenth-century example of Gaelic writing in Scots orthography, see Cameron 1892–4, ii, pp. 1–137; Ross 1939, p. xv.
45. See esp. Dawson 1994, pp. 231–53; Kirk 1989, ch. 12.
46. 'Ní chreideann Alba fa-ríor' go dtig tonn d'fhuil [an] Airdríogh / san abhluinn mar as
dleacht dí / adhruim don reacht do-rinne': McKenna 1939–40, i, pp. 204–7, ii, pp. 120–2. See
also Mac Craith 1995, p. 158.

between *Gaedhil* and *Gaill* – it was just that the religion in each case was different. Within Ireland, the survival of catholicism and then its gradual trans-formation under the impact of the Counter-Reformation encouraged the Gaelic chiefs to look to their co-religionists for support, both within Ireland where the Old English were increasingly disaffected, and also abroad, from the contin-ental catholic powers, notably Spain. To qualify for such assistance, however, the defence of the traditional Gaelic order, local chiefs, and the privileges of the Gaelic learned classes had to be transformed into a more broadly based movement.

Much the most important and successful attempt to modernize Irish Gaeldom was the Ulster confederacy led by Hugh O'Neill, earl of Tyrone.[47] The military aspects of this response are discussed in Chapter 12. Yet Tyrone was not a traditional Gaelic chief: he had been fostered by the Hovenden family in the English Pale, and subsequently he advanced his career by studious loyalty in government service. In this capacity, and while attending the parliaments con-vened by Sidney and Perrot, O'Neill would have been exposed to the patriotic ideas of the commonwealth reformers focusing on Ireland as their native country (see below, pp. 282–4).

This movement to create a unitary Irish kingdom was undermined by the activities of New English adventurers. Yet in the 1570s, the small militant band of Old English exiles plotting on the continent against Tudor centralization took up the patriotic ideal and combined it with the religious ideals of the Counter-Reformation to create a new faith-and-fatherland ideology, which was then repatriated to Ireland by James Fitzmaurice. For instance, Fitzmaurice's requests for mercenary aid emphasized in three Gaelic letters, *sinne ag cosnamh ár gcreidimh 7 ár ndúthaighe* – 'we are defending our faith and our territory'.[48]

As an island, 'Ireland was the perfect invention for the renaissance concept of the *patria*' – unlike the disparate Netherland provinces with which contem-porary Dutch patriots had to wrestle. Yet the very idea of a 'fatherland' cut directly across the bardic tradition's portrayal of Ireland as a woman and its focus on the politics of ethnicity. Indeed, there is no evidence that O'Neill ever patronized the poets, whose praise of traditional Gaelic lordship was of little value to an earl who only became chief in 1595. Instead, in letters and pro-clamations, Tyrone appealed to the Old English, during the offensive phase of the Nine Years War from 1596 onwards, in their own commonwealth rhetoric, stressing Ireland and the Irish, a common fatherland and a common faith, and ignoring traditional differences of race and culture. For instance, a letter to James FitzPiers, sheriff of Kildare, asserted that 'we Irishmen are exiled and made bond slaves and servitors to a strange and foreign prince': accordingly, he intended 'to reform all things to the will of God and goodness of the com-monwealth', reminding FitzPiers that provision was made 'in hell for all sinners and offenders against God's commandments and the commonwealth'. And when Pope Clement VIII refused to excommunicate catholics who supported Queen

47. On the following, see Morgan 1993a, pp. 21–37.
48. Mac Craith 1995, pp. 144–5. For the meaning of *dúthaig*, see also below, p. 261.

Elizabeth, Tyrone commissioned the Old English academic, Peter Lombard, professor of theology at Louvain, to argue his case.

The resultant book, *De regno Hiberniae, sanctorum insula, commentarius* ('A memoir about the kingdom of Ireland, the isle of saints'), written in Rome in 1600 but only published in 1632, offered a detailed exposition of the Irish nationalist position. Ireland and its inhabitants, once referred to as *Scotia* and *Scoti* (though the terms now applied to Scotland) and also called 'the island of saints' because its monasteries were centres of learning for the conversion of British and continental pagans, had been subjected by the English pope, Adrian IV, to England on condition that the English king would reform the Irish church. Yet English rule, he asserted, had reduced Ireland to a state of barbarism, and then Henry VIII had attempted to seduce the Irish from their faith. Under James Fitzmaurice, the Irish had begun a military and spiritual campaign to free their country; but this liberation struggle in Munster had been crushed by terrible massacres and colonization, so that now only Ulster was free of English control. Originally, O'Neill had taken up arms to protect his inheritance, he admitted, but he was a good catholic and an able captain, so that now his private interests and the church's were irrevocably linked.

In reward, Lombard was appointed papal archbishop of Armagh, and O'Neill was recognized as 'captain-general of the Catholic army in Ireland', but this response was inadequate to win over Old English catholics who viewed Tyrone as a traitor and his crusade as rebellion.[49]

Gaelic terminology and the new nationalism

In practice, faith and fatherland had a minimal impact on the Old English in the Nine Years War; but in the aftermath of Kinsale the new nationalist ideology was rapidly absorbed by the Gaelic learned classes, and history was rewritten. The poets quietly decided that the *Gaill* were not really foreigners after all, but Irish catholics like the *Gaedhil*, to whom the common denomination *Éireannaigh* now applied. The real foreigners, for whom the term *Gaill* was now reserved, were the New English; and the traditional prophesies of the banishment from Ireland of the foreigners were redeployed against the *Sasanaigh*, the followers of Luther and Calvin, and other heretics. Within 30 years too, a Gaelic biography of Red Hugh O'Donnell described the Ulster chiefs as fighting to defend their faith and fatherland (*ag cosnamh a nirsi 7 a nathardha*) against enemies bent on conquest and perverting them from the Roman Catholic faith (*creidemh catholocda Romhanda*).[50] The new political vocabulary was created by recycling traditional terms like *dúthaigh* and *athartha*, which had meant 'territory' and 'patrimony', to denote 'native land' and 'fatherland', as has been suggested.[51]

49. Quotations, Morgan 1993a, pp. 24, 27, 32.
50. Ó Buachalla 1992, pp. 160–1; Mac Craith 1995, pp. 146–8.
51. Mac Craith 1995, pp. 139–61.

No doubt the currency in Ireland of these Gaelic equivalents for patriotic concepts reflected the spread of the new nationalism after Fitzmaurice's campaign. Yet by 1513 the terms themselves were already current in Scottish Gaeldom in their more modern sense. For instance, a *brosnachadh catha* (incitement to battle) on the eve of Flodden urged that even the Leinster *Gaedhil* should be summoned to strengthen Gaelic resistance to the English and defend Scotland:

> Against *Gaill*, I tell you,
> Before they have conquered our native land [*ar ndúthaigh*].
> Let us not yield up our native land.
> Let us make terrible war
> After the manner of the *Gaedhil* of *Banbha*.
> Let us watch over our fatherland [*ar n-athartha*] . . .
> Drive the *Gaill* westward over the high sea
> So that Scotland may suffer no division.[52]

Given the greater cohesion of the Scottish kingdom, it is hardly surprising to find a more developed, political sense of national identity and the national territory among Scottish Gaeldom. Yet by the time of the War of the Three Kingdoms (1638–51), the new nationalism was steadily eroding Ireland's traditional ethnic and factional divisions, even though in Ireland it was applied in a narrower, more exclusive sense.

The decline of Gaelic national identity

After 1603, the bards continued to compose their traditional praise poems for as long as anyone could be found to buy them. Yet King James's *coróin na dtrí ríoghachta* (crown of the three kingdoms) exerted novel pressures on the *Gaedhealtacht*. The collapse of the Gaelic chieftaincies undermined the traditional role of the bard and his poetry which was increasingly out of tune with the new political realities. In his account of Gaelic resistance to the Scottish Covenanters in the War of the Three Kingdoms (1638–51), even Niall MacMhuirich, hereditary bard to the Clanranald branch of the MacDonalds, was driven to use prose and the new terminology to describe the political alignments that had destroyed the *Gaedhealtacht*:

> The Scots [*Albanaigh*] were the soonest to begin this war of the three kingdoms, and not the English [*Sasanaigh*] or Irish [*Éireannaigh*]. For, after the making of the Covenant or league against the king and the English in order to remove the bishops and replace them with presbyteries, they sent for all the Scottish officers in the other kingdoms overseas & they made commander in chief Alexander Leslie, an old soldier who had long experience of war abroad'.[53]

52. 'Ré Gallaibh adeirim ribh / sul ghabhadar ar ndúthaigh; / ná léigmid ar ndúthaigh dhínn / déinmid ardchogadh ainmhín / ar aithris Gaoidheal mBanbha / caithris ar ar n-athartha . . . / cuir siar thar ardmhuir na Goill / nach biadh ar Albain athroinn': Watson 1937, pp. 158–64.
53. 'gur ab íad na halbanuidh is taosga do thionsgain cogadh sa na tri Rioghachtuibh 7 nar bhíad sagsanuigh no eireañaigh; oir tair eis coibhinent no comhchengal do ghenamh anaghaidh an ríogh 7 Shagsanach um na heasbaguidh do chur ar cúl 7 Presbetri do chur na

Yet briefly, when pressure and cooperation between Dublin and Edinburgh were relaxed, Irish *Gaedhil* once again served with *Gaedhil* from Scotland under the marquis of Montrose, and MacMhuirich could recount Gaelic successes in the traditional way: 'The victories of those two battles [at Perth and Aberdeen] raised the courage and spirit of the *Gaedhil* thereafter.'[54] In Scotland, where Gaelic was likewise condemned as a chief cause 'of the continuance of barbarity and incivility amongst the inhabitants of the Isles and Highlands', the cultural leadership of the professional bards was soon challenged by the emergence of a brand of vernacular poetry with a strong political content which broke with bardic conventions. Irish vernacular poetry followed.[55] Consciousness of a common Gaeldom spanning the North Channel gradually faded away, to be replaced by new senses of Irish and Scottish nationality.

Significantly, traditional ties survived longest – at least until 1660, if not 1691 – where religious divisions were less apparent. In the 1620s and 1630s, Irish Franciscan missionaries were accorded a sympathetic reception in the southern Hebrides where Scottish clans, such as the MacNeills and the MacDonalds of Clanranald, remained catholic.[56] Similarly, catholic poets from Scotland still sometimes visited Ireland in the 1640s.[57] And within the Reformed tradition too, the translation from the Isles of successive bishops of Raphoe at this time also underscores the importance of these emerging ideological divisions.[58]

CONCLUSION

In retrospect, we can see that although the traditional Gaelic world responded vigorously to the growing threat from the Tudor state, the nature of this reaction was simply inadequate to halt the tide of Tudor expansion. There were several reasons for this.

First, despite appearances, the military successes of the Gaelic revival rested on comparatively narrow economic foundations. Once the Tudor regime began to take more seriously the defence of its northern and western frontiers, Irish Gaeldom's traditional but growing reliance on Scots mercenaries and seapower proved very inadequate. There is some evidence too that chiefs felt constrained in their response by the desire to preserve the traditional privileges of the political elite: the average Irishman had comparatively little stake in Gaelic society, being entirely excluded from the political process, with no rights in the land nor effective access to the law.[59] Yet it was not simply that

---

nionad gur chuiredar fios ar an rabh doifigechuibh albanach sna ríoghachtuibh oile taobh thall dairge 7 go ndenadar ard chommandair dalasduir Leislí .i. sensoigdeir do bhí fada accogadh ar choigcrich': Cameron 1892–4, p. 176.

54. 'do mhétuidh búaidh an da chatha sin misnech 7 menmna Ghaóidheal o sin amach': Cameron 1892–4, p. 178. See Stevenson 1980, *passim.*

55. Macinnes 1988, pp. 59–94 (quotation, p. 62); Leerssen 1994, p. 64.

56. Dawson 1994, pp. 248–9; Giblin 1964, *passim.*

57. *NHI*, iii, p. 541; O'Rahilly 1942, pp. 113–18.

58. *HBC*, pp. 315, 405.

59. See, in general, Nicholls 1972, *passim.*

Gaelic Ireland had too many lordships, with political influence restricted to the landowning elite: in terms of military technology and tactics too, attempts to modernize proved too little too late. Whether, even in 1500, the military situation was recoverable is debatable. Yet the experience of Scottish Gaeldom, which in key respects was manifestly more open to outside influences, shows what might have been attempted. It is possible to envisage, for instance, that in other circumstances the lordship of the Isles might have been transformed, not unlike the Stewart monarchy itself, into a centralized maritime kingdom in the north-west, which could have checked Tudor and Stewart expansion.

Indeed, such success as Irish Gaeldom enjoyed against the Tudors owed much to its symbiotic relationship with Scottish Gaeldom. These traditional ties rested on more open, ethnic and cultural senses of identity, of a historic Gaelic nation focused on but not confined to Ireland – concepts which were essentially inimical to more modern ideas of faith and fatherland. In this regard, the increasing identification of Irish Gaeldom with Counter-Reformation catholicism, far from facilitating resistance to Tudor rule, simply helped to isolate the Ulster chiefs from their traditional military bases in Scotland, without securing for them any significant support from religious dissidents in the *Galltacht*.[60] In consequence, after 1603 the same Stewart regime could impose on Irish Gaeldom a much more radical settlement than in Scotland – in terms of law and administration, landholding, language and culture.

In other respects, however, the response of Irish Gaeldom to Tudor expansion was quite impressive. When it eventually came, the Gaelic military response as exemplified in the Nine Years War was a quite extraordinary achievement (discussed below, pp. 334–51). In sum, Tyrone created a modern army which came close to defeating the English, nearly bankrupted Elizabeth, and forced Mountjoy to concede comparatively generous terms of surrender. Equally striking was the ideological response, the moulding of a new sense of Irish identity in opposition to the Tudor conquest.

At one level of course, Irish identity in the modern sense was very evidently the creation of the Tudor state, being an outgrowth of the politico-cultural assimilation of those *Gaedhil* and *Gaill* living in Ireland that was prescribed by the statute of 1541. Whereas in 1450 the 'Irish' were the *Gaedhil*, a people distinguishable by language, law and culture living in Ireland and Scotland, by 1650 the 'Irish' were the catholic peoples of Ireland, whether of English or Gaelic speech or culture, the descendants of the medieval *Gaedhil* and *Gaill*. The Irish of Scotland were no longer Irish because they were neither catholics, nor lived in Ireland. Yet remarkably, in opposition to English attempts to transform Ireland into a *Saxa nua* (a new England),[61] the Gaelic learned classes were able to construct a new sense of Irishness based on faith and fatherland and to create a new political vocabulary which dressed up revolution as a restoration of ancient, pre-Norman traditions.

60. Morgan 1993a, pp. 1–17.
61. Ó Buachalla 1992, p. 155 (quotation).

CHAPTER 11

THE BREAKDOWN OF CONSENSUS POLITICS, 1547–1579

Notwithstanding the important policy developments of Henry VIII's reign, the old king had ensured broad continuity simply by imposing practical, especially financial, limitations on the operation of new policies. In the decade following, however, successive regimes proved less able to resist the demands of influential politicians with Irish interests, and Irish patronage became established as a significant prize in court politics. Increased expenditure on Ireland allowed English newcomers to consolidate their influence, but at the expense of local politicians who grew alienated from an executive heavily dependent financially on London and increasingly unresponsive to local needs. By Elizabeth's reign, the government was embarked on a highly ambitious and demanding stategy which was quite unjustifiable by the normal lights of Tudor policy. The government's central purpose remained the reduction of Ireland to English rule by reform and the gradual extension of the common law and English administrative structures, not by military conquest; but the increased resort to coercion to accelerate the pace of change gradually undermined local confidence in the government's good intentions. And as political opinion in Ireland polarized and confidence declined, the queen found it politically difficult to scale down operations so as to recover local confidence and financially impossible to maintain the establishment demanded by successive governors to speed change.

The result was pronounced discontinuity of policy, encouraging the growth of an articulate opposition movement which cut across traditional factional politics, undermined respect for the viceroyalty, and threatened to unite Gaelic and Old English opinion against Tudor rule. By 1579 traditional consensus politics were near collapse and a political climate was emerging which was conducive to the spread of novel ideological forms of opposition.

THE LEIX–OFFALY PLANTATION

St Leger was initially confirmed as deputy in 1547, but his days were numbered. Protector Somerset's preoccupation with the Scottish war (1542–50) caused him to temporize on other problems, but events in Ireland appeared to present another opportunity to try his favoured garrison strategy (see above, p. 185). In turn this prompted a shift in policy aims within the Dublin administration from gradual but general progress in assimilating Gaelic Ireland to concentration on reducing the border chieftaincies in order to insulate the Pale from Gaelic raids. This initiative arose from disturbances in the midlands in 1546–7 which rapidly escalated into a war against O'Connor and O'More. Lord Justice Brabazon captured and garrisoned Dangan in Offaly and Ballyadams in Leix in summer 1546 (see above, pp. 158, 185), a traditional temporary expedient in such circumstances, but the revolt's continuance excited Somerset's interest. In March 1547 the privy council gave orders to establish English garrisons 'in most meet places of service without the English pale' so as to screen it from a principal source of disorder, and in June it sent out Sir Edward Bellingham, a soldier-administrator and privy councillor, with troops, money and supplies as captain-general in Ireland.[1] In November an auditor was appointed to inquire into Irish finances and when, with Bellingham's connivance, Brabazon mounted another attack about December on St Leger's conduct of policy, the privy council agreed to St Leger's recall.

Bellingham returned as deputy in May and until his departure in December 1549, soon after Somerset's fall, he was allowed considerable latitude and ample supplies of money and men to impose a soldier's solution in the midlands. By autumn 1548 elaborate fortifications, houses and breweries had been built at Dangan and Ballyadams (renamed Forts Governor and Protector respectively) to house garrisons costing a princely IR£8,300 a year; and smaller garrisons were established at Nenagh and Athlone in 1547–8. After fighting throughout the midlands in summer and autumn 1548, O'Connor submitted and O'More soon after. They were shipped to England and given pensions, though O'Connor's brother, Cahir, was executed for instigating another revolt. Bellingham then placed another garrison at Leighlin Bridge to control the Kavanaghs. Thus by spring 1549 military control of the whole midlands area was established and the administration could turn to questions of settlement.

Initially the surveyor-general, Walter Cowley, proposed minor settlements around the forts but envisaged regranting most of the area to the native proprietors on terms, and in June the privy council sanctioned grants to conformable Gaelic lords. Nevertheless Bellingham gave leases to a handful of Englishmen, made provision for settlers in Shillelagh barony in Kavanagh's country, and planted Nicholas Bagenal in Newry and Andrew Brereton in Lecale. This was enough to provoke Gaelic fears of a general plantation, and the stop-gap administration (December 1549–September 1550), headed successively by Marshal Francis Bryan and Brabazon, faced a combination of chiefs intriguing for French and Scottish aid: the English ambassador in Paris reported their agent as saying that 'they looked for none other but to be driven out of their

---

1. Bush 1975, pp. 133–4. See also White 1964–5, pp. 198–205; Quinn 1946–7, pp. 307–10; Ellis 1983a, pp. 59–60; Dunlop 1891, pp. 61–5; Bagwell 1885–90, i, pp. 326–7, and for the following.

ancient possessions . . . as had lately been served to O'More and O'Connor'.[2] St Leger's return temporarily calmed most chieftains, but it reflected no real change in policy, simply a divided privy council playing for time. Indeed he was instructed to consider Leix–Offaly confiscated, to have a survey drawn up, and to make 21-year leases to suitable tenants of English stock.

By 1551 the privy council was growing alarmed (needlessly, as it transpired) about rumours of a French invasion with Scottish aid in Ulster, and in February it despatched a military expedition under Sir James Croft, a supporter of Somerset's successor, Warwick, with orders to fortify the Munster and then Ulster ports. Meanwhile, following a complaint by Tyrone against Brereton's conduct, St Leger secured his removal and return to England, remarking to Secretary Cecil that 'such handling of wild men hath done much harm in Ireland'. Cowley completed a rough survey, and the deputy, having had his own proposals about Leix–Offaly rejected, then made token leases of substantial estates to army captains and Palesmen. By April, however, Brereton had through Sir William Herbert talked the privy council into reinstating him and recalling St Leger. Croft was appointed deputy instead and, with military reinforcements, continued where Bellingham had left off: to withstand invasion he had no less than 2,134 English troops and 484 Irish in pay.[3]

Renewed instability in Ulster

The rapid build-up of troops since 1547 allowed the administration to dominate the country 'betwixt the Shannon and St George's Channel'. The Irishry was overawed, and in May 1552 Lord Chancellor Cusack could make a circuit of Ireland including Tyrone and Tyrconnell. He recommended just dealings to make Gaelic lords obedient subjects and the extension of shire ground throughout Ireland, especially to Leix–Offaly, to promote civility. The privy council, however, had no intention of reverting to St Leger-style 'truth and gentleness', and received news of Gaelic submissions by remarking that 'we win them not by their wills but by our power . . . then shall they obey because they cannot choose'.

In fact Croft could do little about the continued infiltration of west Highland MacDonalds into Antrim which facilitated the recruitment by Irish chiefs of Scottish mercenaries known as 'redshanks'. Redshanks, distinguishable from resident galloglass families, had been recruited by successive O'Donnell chiefs in the fifteenth century, but the vast expansion in their recruitment which worried successive governors from the 1550s probably reflected renewed instability in Irish politics and the final collapse of the lordship of the Isles.[4]

2. White 1964–5, p. 204 (quotation); Quinn 1946–7, p. 308; Bagwell 1885–90, i, pp. 337, 345–7; Potter 1983, pp. 161–7.
3. White 1964–5, pp. 204–6 (quotation, p. 205); Quinn 1946–7, p. 309; Potter 1983, pp. 168–76; Dunlop 1891, pp. 64–5; Bradshaw 1979a, p. 260; Ellis 1983a, p. 60.
4. White 1964–5, pp. 206–7 (quotation); Simms 1987a, pp. 126–7; Hayes–McCoy 1937; Cosgrove 1981a, pp. 83–4; Nicholls 1972, pp. 88, 134–6; PRO, SP 60/2/143 (*LP*, x, no. 1143(3)); Brady 1996a, p. 27.

These developments were initially seen in England as part of a projected Franco-Scottish invasion since, to English officials, Gaelic clans from the Western Isles were not simply *Gaedhil* but subjects of the Scottish crown. Croft proclaimed a hosting against the 'Scots' from Carrickfergus in summer 1551 but they melted away and his attempt to seize Rathlin, the island stronghold of James MacDonald of Dunyveg, failed for lack of shipping.

He was equally unsuccessful in attempts to pacify Tyrone, where Earl Con was fast losing his grip and the lordship was wasted by a succession dispute between his youngest son, Shane, now emerging as the tanist, and Matthew, the eldest but probably illegitimate son by the wife of a Dundalk blacksmith, who had been created baron of Dungannon with right of succession to the earldom: this threatened a direct conflict between English and Gaelic succession laws. Most Ulster chiefs repaired to Croft at Carrickfergus for arbitration: he left a garrison there, another in Armagh under Marshal Bagenal who was commissioned with Lord Dungannon to restore order in Tyrone, and enticed Tyrone to Dublin where he was detained for over a year.[5] Yet in general Croft was unable to exert sufficient continuous pressure in Ulster to make much impact in this remote area of operations.

The colonization debate

In Leix–Offaly Croft was instructed to report on progress and the best way of planting the area. Earlier a syndicate of 23 officials, English soldiers and local gentlemen had petitioned for a freehold grant of Leix in return for clearing Gaelic proprietors from the greater part, maintaining Fort Protector and its garrison, and paying an annual rent of IR£600. Considering the subsequent cost to the crown, the government might have been well advised to accept this first project for a corporate private plantation in Ireland; but Croft criticized haphazard lettings on short leases and recommended substantial freeholds to provide the necessary incentive to develop the land. It emerged in a protracted debate that the government feared lest large freeholds create undesirable vested interests among settlers: it therefore compromised by stipulating small estates with copyhold tenure for not more than three lives, saving remote parts where copyhold in tail male might be allowed. The shiring of Leix–Offaly was also authorized.

A notable contribution to this debate was made by Edward Walshe, a Waterford gentleman, whose 'conjectures' are the earliest known attempt in Ireland either to generalize from an experiment to solve particular problems in Leix–Offaly to a policy for colonization elsewhere or to invoke classical precedent for colonial settlement. Instead of large estates on short leases, he urged 'great numbers' of smallholders with secure tenancies at low rent 'planted thick together' as the only economical and effective means of extending English influence by plantation, but plantation had to be accompanied by the introduction of English law. These views perhaps marked a slight advance on traditional proposals for the planting of Englishmen in small fortified settlements, but they fell far short of the ambitious schemes from the 1580s onwards for

5. Bagwell 1885–90, i, pp. 360–4; *NHI*, iii, pp. 71–3; Brady 1996a, pp. 22–4.

wholesale confiscation and plantation. Within a few years, however, support had collapsed in Old English circles for proposals for accelerating the pace of Tudor reform by plantation. Old English spokesmen increasingly urged a reversion to St Leger's original reform strategy, arguing that the extension of an effective system of law enforcement throughout Ireland needed no military conquest – a view already articulated in an anonymous treatise of 1554–5 and, with a different emphasis, in the slightly later tracts by Roland White.

In practice the authorities long viewed the Leix–Offaly plantation merely as a particular solution to a particular problem: little progress was made before Croft was recalled for consultations in December 1552. Even so, garrisoning was firmly established as a means of extending government control, when in Scotland Somerset's strategy had been abandoned: its costliness eventually curtailed its use in Ireland too, but the idea of controlling the country by settlement was to play an increasing role in the shaping of future policy.[6]

Financial retrenchment and the aristocratic reaction

By 1552, however, the privy council was becoming aware of the appalling cost of its military strategy in Ireland. In part its policies were financed by debasing the coinage: between 1548 and 1552 a mint operated in Dublin and struck English-style coins with Henry VIII's portrait in silver only 4 oz (.333) and later 3 oz (.250) fine. Profits amounted to c. IR£50,000 in five years but at a cost of galloping inflation and a dramatic slump in trade which was exacerbated when the government offloaded a consignment of debased York pennies after the partial revaluation in England. The administration also hoped to make a profit from mining silver at Clonmines, Co. Wexford, but lost almost IR£6,000 in two years. Forts Governor and Protector alone, despite a paper rental exceeding £1,000 sterling, were still costing 7,000 marks (IR) annually in 1552, though the areas they protected were small; and from September 1550 to March 1552 Brabazon paid out IR£43,000 in military expenses alone. The deputy feared that but for the army's unprecedented size, the country was 'never liker to have turned to a revolt by mean of the money and decay of the cities and towns'; yet when the annual deficit reached IR£52,000 in 1552 the government was forced to reconsider its policies. Lords Justices Cusack and Aylmer presided over a caretaker administration as the privy council debated how both to cut costs and pacify Gaelic chiefs. They decided on St Leger's reappointment, although Mary had succeeded Edward before he eventually returned.[7]

In England the mid-Tudor period witnessed something of an aristocratic reaction, especially in the north where Percy and Dacre were rehabilitated and regained the wardenships and Neville became lieutenant-general. The government apparently decided that in Ireland too the absence or inactivity of

6. Quinn 1946–7, pp. 309–22; Dunlop 1891, pp. 65–6; Bush 1975, p. 134. Cf. Bradshaw 1981a, pp. 299–315; Canny 1976–7, pp. 439–63; Canny 1979a, pp. 147–60; Brady 1994a, pp. 248–50.

7. White 1964–5, pp. 207–11 (quotation, p. 207); NHI, iii, p. 411; Bagwell 1885–90, i, pp. 370–2, 379; Quinn 1946–7, p. 310; CSPI, i, 130.

great magnates was a major cause of disorder. Accordingly, there returned in 1554 the young earl of Ormond, still under age, and Lord Fitzpatrick of Upper Ossory – raised at court with Edward VI – and Gerald, eleventh earl of Kildare. Kildare's return from exile had been sanctioned by Protector Somerset, following the traditional practice of restoring fallen noble families after a decent interval, but also after rumours that foreign powers sought to use him to raise rebellion in Ireland: he received a pardon for treason and an annuity of £300, was restored in blood in 1552, and to his title and most of his estates in 1554. He remained a major figure in the defence of the Pale until his death in 1585, but he lacked the connection and landed base of his father and grandfather. In addition, where Croft had established small wards in Kavanagh's country, the chief, Cahir MacArt, was soothed with a life peerage as baron of Ballyan, and the government even released old Brian O'Connor, imprisoned in the Tower since 1548. O'Connor, however, was quickly rearrested on a charge of fomenting disturbances in Offaly and incarcerated in Dublin castle.

St Leger's third deputyship (November 1553–April 1556) has been little studied, but Mary's instructions suggest that he was allowed to follow the more conciliatory policies of the 1540s, if only to save money. The army was to be reduced to 500 men, extraordinary garrisons discharged altogether and coign and livery eradicated. In Leix–Offaly, the government was now prepared to allow freeholds to attract tenants: St Leger was to grant lands 'piecemeal' but to bind tenants to introduce tillage and build houses for husbandmen. In Munster three captains and 250 men supported by the earl of Desmond had been established as an embryonic regional council in 1551: the deputy was to weigh the advantages of developing this initiative, particularly since the murder in April 1553 of the tractable second earl of Thomond by his brother Donald, who sought royal confirmation of his election as O'Brien against Thomond's son and heir. This development split the clan, involved the Butlers in support of the young third earl, grandson of Piers, eighth earl of Ormond, and threatened a repetition of the disorders in Tyrone.[8]

Nor were Kildare and Ormond's return altogether helpful to St Leger: Kildare lost no time in reasserting the traditional Kildare dominance in the midlands, where disturbances ensued, and also showed signs of reviving the O'Neill alliance by supporting Shane O'Neill against a dissident junior O'Neill clan. Periodic trouble between Ormond and Desmond was pacified by Ormond's mother whose third husband was Desmond, but Ormond and St Leger were soon on bad terms. Moreover in Ulster the situation deteriorated as disorders in Tyrone spread to Tyrconnell where O'Donnell was ousted by his son Calvagh, supported by the MacDonalds.[9]

St Leger's return preceded the establishment in August 1554 of a privy council committee to reduce expenditure and reform government in Ireland,

8. Bagwell 1885–90, i, pp. 379, 385–6, 393; Dunlop 1891, p. 66; Bradshaw 1976–7a, p. 92.
9. Bagwell 1885–90, i, pp. 346, 375, 385, 392–3, 395–6, 406; Bush 1975, pp. 129, 131, 142; Dunlop 1891, pp. 63, 66–7; Brady 1980, p. 78; *Carew*, i, nos. 196, 200, 225; Loades 1979, pp. 97, 107; *CSPI*, i, 132; Morrin 1861, p. 342; Potter 1983, pp. 162, 174.

where an investigation of Undertreasurer Wise's accounts followed his dismissal for corruption. Continuing disorder prevented St Leger from reducing the army below 1,060 men initially, but overall military expenditure was drastically curtailed, from IR£36,000 in 1554–5 to IR£16,000 in 1555–6. Administrative reforms also helped, so that the English subvention of £12,000 in 1556–7 was about a third that in 1553–4; but actual receipts in Ireland showed little improvement and the deficit was in fact artificially depressed by occasional land sales and, more especially, by further debasement despite the English revaluation: in March 1555 *c.* £6,700 in base English money was recoined into double its nominal value in Irish money 3 oz (.250) fine. Nevertheless these economies took time to bite and were not readily attributable to St Leger's efforts. The deputy was also implicated in Wise's misdeeds following renewed charges of financial corruption – he owed the crown almost IR£5,000 on his Irish landed interests. His recall, however, was finally determined by the ambition of the young Sir Thomas Radcliffe, Lord Fitzwalter, who saw Ireland's problems as a golden opportunity for glory and gain.[10]

SUSSEX'S VICEROYALTY

Fitzwalter (earl of Sussex from 1557) was much the most important courtier to hold Irish office since the earl of Surrey, and was accompanied by another newcomer, Sir Henry Sidney, as undertreasurer. These two, together with the recently arrived and equally youthful Sir William Fitzwilliam, were to dominate the Irish viceroyalty for the next 22 years. Their appointments reflected the opportunities created by the crown's new-found willingness to spend money there, but since Sussex was a complete novice as governor his appointment was also something of a gamble.[11] His instructions reflected alleged failings in St Leger's administration, requiring him to make justice more widely available, to pursue the queen's profit, and to prepare for a parliament.

Beyond administrative reform, the expulsion of the 'Scots' from Ulster, and the midland plantation, the aims and novelty of Sussex's policies are difficult to assess because of the relative dearth of evidence about his predecessors' activities since 1547 and because of his tendency to appropriate ideas and publicize his own achievements.[12] Nevertheless he intended to hasten change, a strategy found counterproductive by St Leger, and his advent presaged a wave of military activity, in preparation for which the army was doubled. He lost no time in proclaiming a hosting into Antrim against James MacDonald, who promptly withdrew into Scotland but returned to attack Sussex's rearguard on its withdrawal: to Sussex's military mind these Scottish cousins of local chiefs

10. Loades 1979, pp. 184, 304, 305, 310–11; Brady 1980, pp. 95–6, 105–7, 131; Gilbert 1897, p. 281; *CSPI*, i, 132–3. Brady 1994a, ch. 3 offers a detailed and persuasive reassessment of the importance of Sussex's viceroyalty. For a more favourable view of Sussex, see Crawford 1993.
11. Canny 1976, p. 45; Brady 1980, p. 112; Crawford 1993, pp. 45–52.
12. *Carew*, i, no. 206; *CSPI*, i, 133–4; Canny 1976, p. 35; Brady 1980, pp. 110, 117–18.

– not even nominally the queen's subjects – should be excluded by a chain of forts from Dundalk to Lough Foyle, an impossibly expensive operation. Thereafter he turned to Leix–Offaly where he hoped to turn the garrisons into self-sufficient colonies. His instructions were that, provided the local clansmen proved tractable, they should be allotted the western third of their territories along the Shannon, individual clansmen to receive in common socage smallish estates not exceeding two ploughlands (or 240 medieval acres) at 2*d.* an acre annually: on pain of forfeiture they were to use English law and customs, build houses in stone or timber, avoid the woods, and not to retain idlemen. Outside these Gaelic reservations, six ploughlands were to be assigned to Forts Governor and Protector, and the rest distributed among 'Englishmen born in England or Ireland' in estates not exceeding three ploughlands held on similar terms but retaining for each ploughland one native English archer 'and not above one of the Irish blood and birth'. Any lands recovered elsewhere from 'rebels, traitors, and enemies' would be distributed in similar proportions.[13]

Opposition to Sussex

Initially chieftains and clansmen seemed to accept this drastically altered form of surrender and regrant, but by Christmas general revolt had ensued. Sussex hunted the rebels down, captured O'More and hanged him, with a dissident Kavanagh leader, in chains at Leighlin. He then invaded Offaly. The 1557 parliament passed acts permitting the deputy to make leases in Leix–Offaly, shiring the two lordships as Queen's and King's Counties respectively, renaming Forts Governor and Protector Philipstown and Maryborough, and authorizing the issue of commissions to shire other territories. Yet by then the O'Mores and the O'Connors, entrenched in their woods and bogs, made enforcement almost impossible. In July 1557 Sussex made a spoiling raid into Offaly, and in October he twice burned Armagh in search of Shane O'Neill who reappeared near Dundalk within a week and retreated to his woods when pursued. Three more expeditions to ravage the midlands followed, where O'Carroll and O'Molloy had joined the rebels, after which Sussex went to court for consultations, leaving Archbishop Curwin and Sidney as lords justices.[14]

By then Sussex's conduct was encountering strong but uncoordinated Old English opposition. Desmond, Archbishop Dowdall, Kildare, and St Leger in England argued that his military exploits were counterproductive, needlessly arousing general fear and suspicion among Gaelic chiefs, and urged a return to St Leger's gradualist approach and the delegation of authority to local lords whom they respected: Dowdall eventually complained that since 1539–40 Ireland was 'never in my remembrance in worse case', Ulster 'as far out of frame as ever it was' and Leix–Offaly 'destroyed and burned'. Yet opposition in the Irish council had merely infuriated Sussex and encouraged his inclination to

13. Dunlop 1891, pp. 67–70 (quotations, p. 68); Bagwell 1885–90, i, pp. 397–405; *CSPI*, i, pp. 134–5.
14. Ibid.

purge the administration of St Leger's supporters and rely excessively on relatives and supporters brought over and gradually inserted into important, mainly military posts: these included his brother, Henry, commander of the Leix–Offaly forts; his brothers-in-law, Sidney and Sir William Fitzwilliam; Marshal George Stanley; and Captains Wingfield and Heron, who were soon entrusted with Gaelic Leinster. All were made councillors. The council's size was thereby increased, although without affecting the existing balance between local and outside interests. To combat disorders, the army was increased to 1,500 in mid-1557 and to 2,500 in May 1558; and debasement was stepped up to pay the troops. Between March 1556 and April 1558 IR£85,000 in coinage 3 oz fine (.250) was shipped to Ireland, but Lord Justice Sidney still appealed for more, 'though it be as base as counters'.[15]

By 1557 increased purveyance and other military exactions for an enlarged army were provoking fierce local resentment, particularly among the Palesmen who had already suffered disproportionately from Sussex's purge and who contributed the bulk of the cesses and lost out as inflation fuelled by debasement eroded the real value of the queen's price. Parliament offered some hope of redress: yet considering the deputy's usual attitude to publicity, a suspicious absence of evidence cloaks its proceedings (partially repeated in Sussex's 1560 parliament), though hints of opposition survive. Parliament met at Dublin on 1 June, with a second session in July; it was prorogued to Limerick for 10 November but then prorogued the same day to Drogheda for 1 March and dissolved automatically by Sussex's prior departure from Ireland. The sixteen acts mainly concerned the ecclesiastical settlement and plantation (see above, pp. 224, 272), but other significant acts were a ten-year subsidy act, a statute clarifying the interpretation of Poynings' Law and formally authorizing procedures already in use *de facto*, and an act to prohibit marriage and fosterage with the Gaelic Irish. The latter, which was certainly against the spirit of legislation in St Leger's parliament, was mysteriously extracted from the statute roll and could not be enforced, while the transmiss of the bill entitling the crown to Leix–Offaly twice disappeared on reaching Dublin and was only presented to parliament after transmission a third time. Otherwise nothing is known about parliament's proceedings.[16]

Nevertheless Sussex had somehow secured the enactment of the government's programme, and after his temporary recall the opposition switched to court. Despite the local community's justifiable grievances against an inexperienced deputy whose costly policies had caused much trouble and achieved virtually nothing, his conduct was vindicated. A less influential governor would probably have succumbed, but Mary could hardly afford the disgrace of a leading English earl over actions in a minor theatre of operations, and anyway circumstances were in 1557–8 particularly unfavourable to the opposition.

15. *CSPI*, i, pp. 136–42 (quotations, pp. 140, 142); *Carew*, ii, no. 61; Bradshaw 1979a, pp. 268–75; Canny 1976, pp. 35–6; Canny 1975, pp. 15, 21; Brady 1980, pp. 127–9, 131, 134–7; Ellis 1983a, pp. 60–2; Gilbert 1897, pp. 1–74 *passim*.
16. *Stat. Ire.*, i, pp. 239–74; Bradshaw 1979a, pp. 274–5; Bradshaw 1973, pp. 79–80; Edwards & Moody 1940–1, pp. 419–20.

Besides the opposition's manifestly self-interested complaints, and St Leger's efforts to exculpate himself, war had broken out with France and Scotland and Calais was lost in January 1558. Lord Justice Sidney feared an invasion, reported that James MacDonald was expected in Ulster with French and Scottish allies, and insinuated that the Palesmen's disaffection was through sympathy with dissident Gaelic chiefs who had an agent, George Paris, in France soliciting aid: earlier Sussex had misconstrued Dowdall's conciliatory contacts with northern chiefs through his Gaelic dean and his troops had ransacked Armagh cathedral in search of incriminating evidence. In these circumstances the government was disinclined to listen to suggestions that the army be reduced and rebels appeased. St Leger's criticisms were rejected with the help of Sussex's backers on the privy council, Desmond's proposal for an impartial commission of inquiry was ignored, and Dowdall, summoned to court in April to explain his complaints, was drawn into discussions about founding schools and a university and later mollified with orders concerning a hospital at Ardee and a college at Termonfeckin; but these lapsed with his death in August.[17]

On his return Sussex was instructed to keep on the move so as to promote peace and justice. Army pay was increased and viceregal residences were authorized for Roscommon, Athlone, Monasterevan, Maryborough, Philipstown, Ferns, Enniscorthy and Carlow, all places which before 1534 had been distinctly marginal or comfortably within the Irishry, but indicating also that regular government activity had not yet expanded far beyond its traditional limits. Sussex returned to find his brother besieged in Maryborough, though the garrison beat off the O'Mores and O'Connors after a stiff fight. In June and July he visited Limerick and Galway on an expedition into Thomond to place the young earl in possession of the earldom disputed by his uncle; and a far more adventurous but less effectual autumn expedition took him into the Scottish isles against the MacDonalds. For this purpose the queen provided shipping and he sailed from Dublin with 1,100 men on 14 September for Islay: wind and weather frustrated this object, but he burned unopposed much of Kintyre, Arran, Bute and the Cumbrays and then set back into Antrim hoping to chase the Scots out of the Route. The fleet returned the worse for wear after a rough passage, a transport foundered, 700 soldiers were ill after drinking foul water, and Sussex hoped for better luck in a second attempt. Mary then licensed him to visit England, but Desmond's death necessitated a progress to Waterford in late November to receive the homage of young Earl Gerald. Soon after, news arrived of Mary's death, and Sussex hastened to court to safeguard his position, leaving Sidney as justiciar.[18]

Ireland on Elizabeth's accession

On Elizabeth's accession England was in a sorry state, almost bankrupt following earlier financial mismanagement under Edward; at war with France and

17. *CSPI*, i, pp. 140–8; Bradshaw 1979a, pp. 269–75 (which revises Quinn 1958, p. 26); Bagwell 1885–90, i, pp. 405–8; Jefferies 1997a, pp. 169–70.
18. *CSPI*, i, pp. 145–51; *Carew*, i, nos. 214–15; Bagwell 1885–90, i, pp. 408–12.

Scotland and with French troops in Scotland; and with the new regime's stability very much in doubt. In consequence, no major change was contemplated for Ireland, save to economize so far as was consistent with security. Sussex relieved Sidney in May, returning with detailed instructions. Elizabeth's parsimony was amply displayed in lengthy orders about ways and means of increasing the revenue and reducing costs. She even delivered Sussex a book describing the course of the English exchequer and each officer's duties, and ordered the assimilation of Irish exchequer procedures. Considering the government's parlous financial condition and Sussex's manifest failure hitherto to reform administrative malpractices detected under St Leger, this emphasis was necessary, but subsequently Elizabeth's parsimony involved the administration in needless difficulties. The army was reduced to 1,500 men, paid initially by further issues of 'white money', and Sussex was ordered to keep expenditure below IR£1,500 per month and nearer IR£1,000 if possible. Perhaps suspecting that her deputy had hitherto acted less than evenhandedly, Elizabeth also appointed an exceptionally large council to advise him, replied favourably to petitions from temporal peers, bishops and towns, and authorized Sussex to offer earldoms to Shane O'Neill and MacCarthy More. In lesser matters Sussex was given considerable latitude: he should proceed with the midland plantation, but further plantation, especially in Ulster which Elizabeth admitted was necessary to restrain the Scots, was postponed on financial grounds.[19]

Besides the ecclesiastical settlement, the government's main problem was Shane O'Neill. Parliament, which might have debated problems and priorities, met only briefly (12 Jan.–1 Feb. 1560) to settle religion, during which Sussex was suddenly recalled for consultations (see above, pp. 225–6). The O'Neill problem arose from Dungannon's murder in 1558 and Tyrone's death early in 1559, by which time the lordship had long been effectively controlled by Shane O'Neill. Shane's ambition was the traditional one of establishing O'Neill supremacy throughout Ulster: with careful handling, he might well have accepted, like his father, the changes implied by the grant of an earldom. When Sidney visited him, Shane petitioned for recognition as earl, alleging that Matthew was no O'Neill but a blacksmith's son and learnedly remarking that creation patents of peers normally specified succession to the grantee's heirs male, not illegitimate offspring; but he agreed to abide by the queen's decision. Elizabeth inclined to reject the claim of Dungannon's son, Brian, and to recognize the common-law heir who was also Con's successor by Gaelic law, but she was dissuaded by Sussex who had apparently conceived a deep personal dislike of Shane and whose destruction, he believed, would be an example to others.

Shane was thus driven to intrigue, through the earl of Argyll, with Mary queen of Scots, French pretender to the English crown and Elizabeth's next heir: and the government, despite overtures from Sorley Boy, James's brother, to hold the MacDonald lordship in Antrim as Elizabeth's subject, feared an

19. *Carew*, i, nos. 218–20; *NHI*, iii, pp. 412–13; Crawford 1993, p. 40. Cf. MacCaffrey 1969, ch. 1.

extension to Ulster of the threat of French encirclement. These fears were fuelled in spring 1560 by rumours of French aid for Donald O'Brien and other dissidents returning from France, by the truculent attitude of the Fitzgerald earls, by contacts between all three and O'Neill who was Kildare's cousin, and by O'Connor's escape from Dublin castle; all of which could conceivably suggest (as older historians accepted) a general conspiracy against the government. Elizabeth's position improved considerably, however, following the peace of Câteau Cambrésis with France (March 1559) and an English invasion of Scotland and the departure of French troops after the treaty of Edinburgh (July 1560). Even so she was being manoeuvred towards an interventionist policy in an inaccessible part of Ireland where English influence had always been particularly weak.[20]

Despite renewed Old English objections, Sussex was promoted lieutenant of Ireland and returned in June 1560 to relieve Lord Justice Fitzwilliam, Sidney's successor as undertreasurer in 1559. There was some hope in the Pale that Kildare would be appointed governor, or at least allowed greater influence in government. The augmented army and the midlands plantation caused friction between Sussex and Kildare because they restricted Kildare's traditional role in defence through a hegemony over the border chiefs: his supporters boasted

> that 'tis the earl and not the English power that preserveth the [Pale] from burnings and other mischiefs, affirming that the subjects shall never live quietly till the earl have the governance of the realm.

Even those outside the Kildare connection felt that Sussex's defence arrangements were inadequate and excessively onerous. By 1560, however, Sussex had evolved a strategy which he expected would solve the principal problems in governing Ireland; and believing that opposition would soon fade with evidence of rapid progress, he persuaded Elizabeth to ignore it. His new instructions descended to still greater detail about reducing governmental costs, and Elizabeth then despatched Gilbert Gerrard, attorney-general in England, to investigate the revenues. Leix–Offaly, still without tenants, was to be planted, Shane O'Neill reduced by diplomacy or force, the earl of Thomond supported, and some of the 300 additional troops provided were to guard Limerick, Waterford and Cork. Sussex was also authorized to negotiate a further bout of surrender and regrant, and secretly instructed to induce Kildare to repair to court. In fact suspicions about Kildare's loyalty soon evaporated: he did not depart until April 1561, but before this Sussex and the council used him in negotiations with O'Neill.[21]

20. *Carew*, i, nos. 223–8; *CSPI*, i, pp. 156–60; Canny 1976, pp. 37–9; Bagwell 1885–90, ii, pp. 2–12; *NHI*, iii, pp. 80–1; Hogan 1947, pp. 156–7; Silke 1966, pp. 5–6; Brady 1996a, pp. 36–7.
21. *CSPI*, i, pp. 157–61; Hore & Graves 1870, p. 175 (quotation); *Carew*, i, nos. 223–5; Bagwell 1885–90, ii, pp. 7–12.

Confrontation in Ulster: Shane O'Neill

Elizabeth's belated consent to military operations against O'Neill arrived too late in the season, though diplomatic efforts were made by Secretary Cecil working with the earl of Argyll to isolate O'Neill from Gaelic supporters in Ulster and Scotland. To gain time O'Neill was granted a safe-conduct to visit court: he pointedly contrasted Tyrone's peaceful state with the Pale. Sussex felt obliged to defend himself against charges of bad faith, but after a spring vacation he returned in June with 600 more soldiers. By then Shane had gained further room for manoeuvre by capturing O'Donnell in a skirmish, and when the lieutenant's long-awaited hosting set out for Armagh in July he simply withdrew with his cattle to the borders of Tyrconnell. Shortage of victuals eventually forced Sussex to retire, and the garrison left in Armagh merely presented him with the problem of how to keep it supplied.

Upon learning of this failure, Elizabeth supplied 200 more troops from Berwick for a second expedition but also entrusted revived negotiations to Kildare with whom Sussex was ordered to cooperate, forgetting private malice. The second expedition in September was hardly more successful: after an unsuccessful attempt to have O'Neill assassinated, Sussex set out with an exceptionally large force accompanied by Ormond, Desmond, Thomond and Clanrickard. O'Neill promptly disappeared, but Tyrone was burned and Sussex penetrated to Lough Foyle, where a victualling fleet missed an appointed rendezvous: according to Sussex, Shane had lost 5,000 cattle, but immediately after the expedition's dispersal he raided Co. Meath.[22]

Kildare shortly returned with a plenary commission to negotiate for O'Neill's visit to court and quickly concluded terms which were deeply humiliating to Sussex, who remonstrated that 'if Shane be overthrown, all is settled; if Shane settle, all is overthrown'. Yet together with Elizabeth's evident annoyance and her small thanks for his service, this seemed to augur disgrace and Sussex quickly obtained licence to follow O'Neill to court, leaving Fitzwilliam as justiciar again (January–July 1562). Fortunately for Sussex, the agreed terms, though Kildare presented them as a diplomatic triumph for Elizabeth, so reflected on her honour as to make it extremely difficult for her to conclude a lasting agreement with Shane without appearing to lose face. He was, for example, to receive a loan of £2,000, a pardon, and a safe-conduct signed by the five Irish earls: he left Dublin for court in December. The wild appearance of his galloglass, and O'Neill's howling confession of rebellion made after prostrating himself before Elizabeth created general astonishment at court, but his speech in Gaelic, when eventually translated, proved acceptable: it included thanks for his pardon, promise of good conduct, a petition for favour, and he also did homage to Elizabeth.

A lengthy examination by Secretary Cecil followed, with Sussex responding to O'Neill's replies, and an even longer investigation of crown rights in Ulster and Shane's claims by Gaelic custom, before Elizabeth decided that she could

---

22. Bagwell 1885–90, ii, pp. 14–30; *NHI*, iii, pp. 80–1; *CSPI*, i, pp. 161–81; Dawson 1987, pp. 113–38; Dawson 1989, pp. 196–216.

not fairly adjudicate concerning Tyrone in young Dungannon's absence. By then O'Neill was clamouring for licence to depart, rightly fearing procrastination by the government and that his continued absence would weaken his control of Tyrone where his tanist, Turlough Luineach, was strengthening his position. When news arrived of Dungannon's murder by Turlough Luineach, an indenture was drawn up and O'Neill returned to Ireland in May: O'Neill was recognized as captain of Tyrone, with a reservation regarding the rights of Hugh, Dungannon's younger brother and future second earl (1585–1614), but his authority was only generally defined. His claims to overlordship throughout Ulster except Tyrconnell – of which, most exceptionally, Gaelic documentation has survived in the tract known as *Ceart Uí Néill* – were tacitly rejected, and his disputes with O'Donnell and O'Reilly remitted to arbitrators. In fact Sussex's return in July virtually ensured that the agreement would not last.[23]

Sussex and O'Neill soon disagreed about the indenture's terms, the English garrison at Armagh and Shane's claims over other chiefs being particular sources of friction. The lieutenant reported that tractable border chiefs who had resisted O'Neill's pretensions and hung on the queen's promises felt betrayed: the loyal MacDonald chief in Down, Alaster MacRandal Boy – 'a Scot who is as wise and subtle an Irishman as any' according to Sussex – also complained but was murdered soon after by Brereton in Lecale. O'Neill quickly recommenced raids on neighbouring chiefs, and the government's earlier diplomatic efforts collapsed as they submitted or, like the MacDonalds, negotiated agreements with him. By late 1562 it was becoming very evident that Sussex's strategy was bankrupt: parleys with O'Neill had no effect – Shane entirely distrusted him, and sought other mediators with Elizabeth – and he lacked the resources for an effective campaign, while the colonial community, even Ormond who had hitherto been very cooperative, increasingly distanced itself from the lieutenant. Sussex organized a further hosting against O'Neill in April 1563 and another in June, but all without significant effect. Elizabeth then listened to Sir Thomas Cusack who visited court to advocate conciliation and sent him back with extensive powers to negotiate. Cusack and Kildare accordingly met Shane and patched up a treaty in September by which the crown effectively capitulated, acknowledging him as O'Neill with all the powers ever exercised under that name.[24]

Sussex's departure and the Leix–Offaly settlement

O'Neill, however, was not the only Irish problem under consideration at court in spring 1562. A second source of unrest was renewed rivalry between Ormond and Desmond which earned them both a summons to court, where Desmond

---

23. Hogan 1947, pp. 154–70; Canny 1976, p. 40 (quotation); Bagwell 1885–90, ii, pp. 30–41; *NHI*, iii, pp. 81–3. *Ceart Uí Néill* is printed in Ó Donnchadha 1931; English translations and commentary in Dillion 1966, pp. 1–18; Ó Doibhlin 1970, pp. 324–58. Brady 1996a, pp. 36–47 now offers a plausible interpretation of the manoeuvrings surrounding Shane O'Neill's visit to court.

24. Bagwell 1885–90, ii, pp. 51–64; Brady 1996a, pp. 51–2.

was detained for contumacy before the council. He was eventually released in December 1563, upon promise of good behaviour, because his absence rather fuelled than quelled disorders in Munster.

More worrying, however, was the Pale's miserable condition because of increased cess contributions as the government sought to curtail military expenditure. The Palesmen, anticipating a change of policy, pointedly argued that government should be entrusted to 'such as need no aid nor impositions of the country' and the queen 'disburdened of her superfluous garrisons'. A renewed, more organized campaign had begun for Sussex's dismissal, with the English-born master of the rolls, John Parker, prominent: 27 law students in London complained to the council about his conduct and sought a full inquiry. Two months later 27 Pale gentlemen reiterated the demand, and Elizabeth eventually appointed Sir Nicholas Arnold to investigate complaints about the army.

Irish problems at this time were complicated by Lord Robert Dudley's selfish support of Sussex's critics in Ireland, both newcomers and Old English: factional alignments both at court and in the Irish council thus ensured that Old English grievances received a ready hearing, but also hindered their resolution since the queen's decision in a minor theatre appeared to reflect on her courtiers. In this case the inquiry dragged on for almost a year and implicated Sussex in financial malpractices. In October 1563, therefore, Elizabeth appointed Arnold and other administrators to inquire into all aspects of government. When the commission eventually arrived in February Sussex soon read this and other signs and conveniently went on sick leave in May never to return.[25]

The other major event of 1563 was the final plantation of Leix–Offaly, further delayed since 1561 by the discovery that the original survey was so defective as to be useless. By then hardly any of the original 21-year lessees were left. The new conditions of tenure – in tail male by knight service with a rent rising to $3d.$ per acre after seven years – differed little from those projected in 1556, but were slightly more onerous. Altogether 88 individuals got estates, but the distribution was a further source of discontent to the Palesmen who had expected that Kildare would direct the project: in fact Sussex placed his brother in charge and 44 soldiers received estates compared with 29 Gaelic grantees and only 15 Palesmen. These grants formed the basis of a struggling English colony which initially provoked some favourable comment about the increase in tillage and good order, but overall was an expensive failure. Vast sums had been spent on constructing forts and, as Lord Deputy Sidney commented in 1576, maintenance costs far exceeded rents 'so that the purchase of that plot is and hath been very dear'. More generally, the expropriation of leading midland clansmen poisoned the government's relations with Gaelic Ireland and, while the plantation attracted periodic Gaelic raids when the authorities relaxed their vigilance, it proved largely unsuccessful in screening the Pale. The general conclusion was that garrisoning was prohibitively expensive, and that its transformation into a state-sponsored quasi-military colony by redistributing

25. Canny 1976, pp. 36–41 (quotations, p. 39); Canny 1975, p. 15; Bagwell 1885–90, ii, pp. 46–51, 57–8, 65–74.

the land to turn soldiers into self-sufficient settlers who would also dominate the Gaelic reservations simply did not work. Later Elizabethan colonizing initiatives tried to exploit the potential of private enterprise.[26]

Sussex's programmes for reform

In September 1560 Sussex had sent over by Gerrard his programme for reforming Ireland and reducing Elizabeth's charges there. It comprised an ignorant and superficial three-year plan to eliminate the major problems, after which the country could be readily reduced to civility: but because it was based on a series of false premises it was highly unlikely to achieve results.

Sussex believed that Ireland was divided between rival Butler and Geraldine factions, except the earls of Clanrickard and Thomond whose recent peerages had attracted them into the royal service: granting earldoms to other magnates, especially O'Donnell and MacCarthy More, would weaken the two factions and bring others to look directly to the crown. Yet the Geraldines were allegedly of unconquered Irish blood, their faction included all the troublemakers and conspirators against English power, and they maintained Shane O'Neill and Donald O'Brien against the rightful earls: conversely, the more loyal and conformable people who detested foreign intrigues were linked to the Butlers, who were mostly English or conforming Irish and supported the feudal heirs to Tyrone and Thomond. Therefore the queen should displace Geraldines and advance reliable men to prevent conspiracies, removing O'Neill especially so as to weaken the Geraldines. Kildare, who sought to overthrow all English government, to discredit Sussex, and to secure the governorship himself, was most dangerous and should be removed from Irish politics by exchanging his estates for lands in England: otherwise the French would eventually exploit internal disaffection to seize Ireland, 'which I have often wished to be sunk in the sea', both as an entry into Scotland and to strangle English trade by blockade. Certain English lords and gentlemen should be planted in other key places, besides the midlands, the army reduced to 600 men, and coign and livery abolished. After the wild Irish had been conquered, a special code of English and Gaelic law (above, pp. 123, 153) could be introduced by consent for their government: this recommendation reversed the strategy advocated by St Leger and most Old English spokesmen who hoped to wean chiefs away from their traditional practices by making English justice more widely available. The revenues could be raised from IR£8,000 to IR£12,500 annually by commuting for IR£4,000 certain galloglass-billeting rights ('bonaughts') on border chieftaincies, and leasing Leix–Offaly (IR£500): this would reduce to £1,050 the annual deficit on maintaining a lieutenant and 600 men. Otherwise, Sussex believed that Kildare's appointment as governor was the only way to reduce costs, but at the price of sacrificing royal control.[27]

---

26. Dunlop 1891, pp. 71–96; Canny 1976, pp. 36–41; Begwell 1885–90, ii, p. 311 (quotation).
27. *Carew*, i, no. 227.

In part Sussex's antipathy to Kildare stemmed from the fact that local English politics still reflected, albeit sometimes eccentrically, faction at court, where a group headed by the duke of Norfolk and including Sussex and Ormond competed for patronage with that led by Lord Dudley (created earl of Leicester, 1564) to which Kildare and Desmond attached themselves.[28] Yet even in Ireland factionalism was seldom so rabid in a governor and seemingly reflected a transient phase: Sussex's recommendations of 1562 ignored this theme. Nevertheless the lieutenant was evidently still relatively unfamiliar with Irish politics after four years. The alacrity with which he employed force to extend royal authority soured relations with Gaelic chiefs, though even he eventually realized that more diplomacy and less coercion achieved better results.

His eighteen-month plan of 1562 was more moderate, detailed and precise: while still urging O'Neill's expulsion, he now advocated, alongside his earlier proposals, the establishment of three regional councils as the chief instrument of reformation. That for Ulster at Armagh should have a martial Englishman as president, with 800 men available, but those for Connaught and Munster should comprise the leading lords and bishops of each province under an English president, a retinue of 40 horsemen, and should execute martial law only in an emergency and against those without property. In Leinster an English captain had recently been appointed to govern Kavanagh's country and the Kavanaghs resorted to the Dublin courts and served on inquests and juries; likewise the O'Byrnes and O'Tooles. Captains should be continued there and in the midlands to encourage resort to law. Nevertheless all this would require an army of 2,000 men, and would cost IR£22,500 a year: his proposals for levying this money were decidedly optimistic, his expectation that all Ireland would become obedient within eighteen months even more so, but he had at last a coherent and viable strategy to bring the country under English rule.[29]

TENSIONS IN GOVERNMENT: LONDON AND DUBLIN

Before his recall, therefore, Sussex had managed to adapt for more general use ideas and experience about garrisoning and plantation gained chiefly under Edwardian governors. He had combined them with instruments for assimilating Gaelic lordships devised under St Leger, and so framed a strategy which employed effectively the additional resources and influence that he had earlier disposed. He could thus contemplate a somewhat speedier conquest of the country than had St Leger.

Sussex's device, subsequently adopted by Sidney, of detailing ways, means and deadlines in a comprehensive programme for conquest has prompted one modern historian to label Sussex, very aptly, the first of the 'programmatic governors', by contrast with St Leger's empirical, gradualist approach.[30] Yet by

28. Canny 1976, pp. 42–4; Canny 1975, p. 16; Brady 1980–1, pp. 298–303.
29. *Carew*, i, no. 236.
30. Brady 1980, esp. ch. 4.

1562 the various circumstances which since 1547 had brought Ireland more into prominence in English political circles were changing, and expenditure was again being curtailed. Sidney and Fitzwilliam, who headed successive administrations in 1566–78, could to some extent learn from Sussex's mistakes: yet the circumstances of Elizabeth's accession – with a leading courtier entrenched in Dublin castle, amply supplied with English money and men, and advocating more coercive methods to accelerate the expansion of English rule – preconditioned the new regime to adapt existing policies rather than revert to the more economical Henrician initiatives. Seventeen years during which the dominant outlook in governing circles had been to pay for quick results created powerful vested interests in favour of a rapid reformation – among the burgeoning Irish military establishment, among English adventurers hoping to get rich quick on Irish land, and among courtiers who had discovered a lucrative new area of patronage. Deficit financing with a vengeance transformed the Irish service from an area of honourable exile for middling or mediocre talents into a likely place for ambitious English aristocrats: by 1560, therefore, Ireland was established as a significant prize in court faction-fighting, where under Henry VIII its politics and problems had received only reluctant consideration.

In these circumstances Elizabeth found it hard to follow the counsels of local politicians and their English allies against her courtiers: St Leger's 'truth and gentleness' had obvious financial attractions to her, but its advocates were apparently no less self-seeking and generally less influential at court. Her reaction was to endorse in principle Sussex's methods, but to seek to implement some variation of his programme more cheaply: understandably, however, Elizabethan governors tended to plan in accordance with the resources that he had commanded rather than those formerly available. The result was sharp discontinuity of policy and, as is clear in retrospect, a *pis aller* which attracted all the opposition of Sussex's lieutenancy and none of the local support cultivated by St Leger, while leaving the administration insufficiently equipped to achieve its aims. For the plain truth of the matter was that the conquest of Ireland was not a sufficiently consistent priority of government to warrant the long-term military commitments necessary to implement Sussex's strategy. In order to secure temporarily the requisite resources, he and later Sidney misled the queen by submitting absurdly optimistic assessments of costs and deadlines. In practice, therefore, not only had the crown remarkably little to show for the vast sums squandered on Ireland since 1547, but its aims continued to outstrip available resources, and its methods also exacted a heavy price in terms of royal relations with the Old English and Gaelic communities.

THE ORIGINS OF OLD ENGLISH IDENTITY

By 1564 the trend of government policy since 1547 had largely confirmed Gaelic chieftains in their view that St Leger's initiatives were a flash in the pan and that, whatever her ministers said or did, Elizabeth's aim was the traditional English one of military conquest and expropriation of Gaelic land. And as opinion in governing circles increasingly polarized between conciliatory and coercive strategies of conquest, excluding the option of peaceful co-existence in separate English and Gaelic polities, the deteriorating political climate gradually destroyed hopes of progress by conciliation: after Sussex's lieutenancy its advocates never commanded sufficient influence in government to restore Anglo-Gaelic relations, and Elizabeth's periodic doubts about the cost and effectiveness of coercion were soon dispelled when Gaelic chiefs mistook for weakness her dallying with conciliation. Moreover, under Sussex and Sidney the Old English community was becoming dangerously alienated by the government's increasing reliance on unorthodox methods – the frequent imposition of heavy military cesses, its gradual exclusion from any real political influence, and attempts to muzzle complaints by impugning Old English loyalty. One result of this was the increasing influence in politics of new forms of regionalist sentiments as the local community lobbied against its comparative exclusion by newcomers from political power.

In large measure the politics which precipitated the gradual emergence under Elizabeth of a self-consciously separate Old English community with a distinctive ideology can be explained, as Professor Canny has shown, without recourse to concepts of nationalism. Modern discussions of a separate colonial identity and consciousness in the later medieval lordship expose no significant differences between colonial attitudes and regionalist sentiments elsewhere in the English state: the fundamental problem was that an augmented military establishment, necessary to reduce Gaelic Ireland, seemed to threaten the dominance of local nobles in the Englishry, and so to transgress an unwritten law of English government, that the rule of the counties lay in the hands of their native elites.[31] Yet a good case has none the less been made for the increasing influence of an embryonic concept of nationalism on Old English political ideas under Elizabeth. In the present survey, the practice has been to distinguish, where necessary, between those of English stock born, raised and resident in Ireland, and Englishmen born, by describing the former as Old English, even though they described themselves as English without qualification: by the middle of Elizabeth's reign, however, the gradual polarization of local reform politics between Old English advocates of conciliation and newcomers supporting tougher measures was prompting the search for new labels to denote the differing approach of each group. There had in England long been a tendency to describe 'Englishmen born in Ireland' geographically rather than ethnically as Irish, and the post-1534 newcomers called the older colonists English-Irish; but after some hesitation, the latter eventually began to describe themselves generally in the 1590s as 'the Old English' or, even as early as 1568, 'old ancient faithful English subjects'.[32]

These changes reflected an increasing Old English awareness of their separate interests, and as successive governors seemed to abandon the reform programme agreed with St Leger, the Old English invoked its constitutional

31. Pollard 1977, pp. 147–66. Cf. Frame 1982.
32. Canny 1975, p. 31 (quotation); Cosgrove 1981a, ch. 5; Brady 1985, p. 30 (quotation).

implications to defend their privileged position in government. Concurrently the concept of the *patria*, the native country, which was ousting older ethnic forms of community consciousness in early Tudor England, was adapted for the same purpose. Thus by the 1550s Old English spokesmen frequently prefaced remarks on political reform by some expression of their 'natural affection' for their 'native country', 'poor Ireland',[33] though they baulked at suggestions that their Irish birth detracted from their Englishness: some would be called 'Ireland men', though 'in no wise Irishmen', but the description of their Englishness as 'Old' was intended to impugn undesirable novelties in England. Linguistic borrowings, for example, were transforming mainland English into a language that was 'not at all English', where the Old English vernacular preserved 'the dregs of the old ancient Chaucer English'.[34]

More important, the erection of Ireland into a kingdom had fostered Old English notions of Ireland as a commonwealth separate from England but with the same monarch as 'the head of our common weal': the two countries were apparently regarded as a dual monarchy, even though in practice constitutional arrangements spelled out very clearly Ireland's continuing subordination to England. Thus Sussex's efforts to pack the administration with his own supporters drew complaints from the Palesmen 'that their kingdom was kept from them by force and by such as be strangers in blood to them', arguments which recalled reaction in Marian England to Philip II's Spanish courtiers. And against continued encroachments on their position the Old English styled themselves 'commonwealth-men' to denote their defence of the traditional order and government against innovation during clashes with later governors over cess.[35]

Eventually in the seventeenth century, the erosion of Old English political influence, their increasing estrangement from government, a devotion to Ireland shared with the Gaelic community, and the breakdown of religious division with the gradual spread of post-Tridentine catholicism helped to dissolve remaining Gaelic–Old English antagonisms and promote a shared Irish sense of identity and patriotism. Already by the 1580s Richard Stanyhurst's writings betray clear signs of a shift in this direction; but Stanyhurst, a member of a long-established Dublin patrician family, who forsook political advancement for religious exile in Antwerp, was a highly untypical figure, and in general such ideas made little headway in Tudor times.[36]

MID-TUDOR PERCEPTIONS OF THE IRISH PROBLEM

Although short-term factors such as political ambition and the vagaries of court faction adequately explain the government's dalliance with Sussex's plans,

33. Bradshaw 1979a, ch. 9 (quotations, pp. 276, 277).
34. Lennon 1978–9, pp. 121–43 (quotations, pp. 127, 131).
35. Canny 1975 (quotation, p. 24); Canny 1976, pp. 38–9 (quotation, p. 38); Bradshaw 1977b, pp. 43–9 (which revises Canny). Cf. Loades 1979, James 1973, pp. 61–8.
36. Bradshaw 1979a, ch. 9; Lennon 1981, pt. ii.

more deep-seated influences were beginning to alter its whole perception of the problem at this time and to predispose it towards 'solutions' generally advocated by English adventurers. In principle, there was no reason why Old English and Gaelic society should not have been gradually and peacefully assimilated as were Wales and the north, with Irish magnates retaining considerable political influence by adopting the social and cultural values of lowland England. Indeed the view of Ireland as an unruly feudal fief received some further confirmation following the successful assimilation of Wales from the 1530s, when English forms of administration were imposed throughout Wales accompanied by more vigorous action by the provincial council there to curtail lawlessness.

Yet there were important differences between Welsh gentry and Gaelic nobles. Although Wales remained culturally Celtic, politically it had largely been integrated into the English system; whereas Gaelic Ireland remained independent, and the nobles' armed bands were necessary for defence even if, as in Wales, they also fomented disorders. In consequence, efforts to apply a 'Welsh solution' met with more strenuous resistance in Ireland.[37] Under Elizabeth, however, the impact of the New World discoveries and renewed European colonization began to reawaken latent colonialist attitudes in England: it was remembered that Ireland had once before been the subject of English colonization. Thus, as the other English borderlands were gradually assimilated by traditional Tudor methods when Ireland remained seemingly unresponsive to Tudor reform, so the predominant early Tudor perception of the country as a borderland gradually lost ground to ideas of Ireland as an old colony gone wrong. Very gradually, plantation projects began to exercise a wider influence in official circles, despite the unfortunate experiences in Leix–Offaly. And as the different strategies of Sussex's successors all failed to recover the momentum of St Leger's initiative, so Ireland came to be seen as a region ripe for plantation in accordance with contemporary colonial theory.

In this context there existed another obvious contemporary analogy for the Tudor conquest of Ireland, demonstrably influential in shaping government policy, but also perhaps even more misleading than the borderland analogy. Certain features of Gaelic society – in particular its highly individual religious practices, transhumance (which was mistaken for nomadism), and the insubstantial dwellings even of chiefs – had long suggested to English officials that Ireland's indigenous peoples were not a civilized society but primitive savages. Accordingly, the New World discoveries and the methods of Spanish *conquistadores* in subduing the Amerindians seemed to indicate an alternative blueprint for the reform of Ireland which was much more congenial to English adventurers. Yet if Gaelic civilization appeared very backward, it was much better equipped for resistance than were the Indians, as would-be colonists quickly discovered.[38]

---

37. Quinn 1958, pp. 5–6. The continuing influence of the 'Welsh policy' on Elizabethan Ireland has recently been explored in Brady 1995, pp. 64–86.
38. Ibid., pp. 3–15; Canny 1976, pp. 93–8, 117–36; Ellis 1995a, ch. 2.

SIR NICHOLAS ARNOLD AND THE REACTION TO SUSSEX

Upon Sussex's departure, Elizabeth appointed Commissioner Arnold as justiciar. Arnold was a Dudley protégé, but comparatively unimportant at court and hamstrung by a much reduced military establishment. He virtually ignored Gaelic Ireland and courted popularity and local support by encouraging the inevitable reaction which swept Sussex's supporters out of office. The Palesmen were gratified by Kildare's appointment to supervise their defence; William Bermingham was allowed to direct the commission's inquiry into the conduct of government; and Sir Thomas Cusack and John Parker were influential in the administration's dealings with the magnates. The commission uncovered serious and long-standing irregularities concerning the army: large numbers of Irishmen had been recruited; companies were well below strength; the aged, the blind, the dead, even Archbishop Loftus, were in pay; and accounting was quite inadequate. Some captains were imprisoned, including Sussex's brother, though the privy council thought this high-handed and Leicester and Cecil urged moderation.[39]

While the army was being thus purged, however, Lord Justice Arnold was rapidly losing control elsewhere. In Ulster, where the government failed to honour all the terms agreed in September 1563, Shane O'Neill consolidated his position on the pretext of doing service. He besieged and captured Lifford, ransomed O'Donnell who went to court to seek Elizabeth's support, and plundered Carlingford. But then, to the government's satisfaction, he attacked the 'Scots' and eventually in May 1565 decisively defeated them at Glenshesk in north Antrim: James and Sorley Boy MacDonald were captured and two MacLeod chiefs killed. In Leix–Offaly a new rising threatened, but the clansmen were dispersed by a hosting. And in Munster there was renewed trouble between the earls. Desmond maintained the O'Brien tanist against the weak and incompetent earl of Thomond who was supported by Clanrickard; but following Lady Desmond's death the Ormond–Desmond feud erupted into open war over Desmond's claims in the Decies. The two earls mustered their retinues and met in battle at Affane in spring 1565 where Desmond was wounded and captured. Elizabeth was furious at this outburst of noble violence – the last private battle, as it happened, between Tudor nobles – and angrily summoned both earls to court. Affane apparently discredited Arnold, and after this brief experiment with peaceful co-existence Elizabeth was again ready for new initiatives.[40]

SIR HENRY SIDNEY'S PROGRAMME FOR GOVERNMENT

Arnold's failure encouraged Sussex to hope for reappointment, but Leicester thwarted this by supporting the candidature of his sister's husband, Sir Henry

39. Brady 1980, pp. 158–70; Canny 1976, p. 41; Bagwell 1885–90, ii, ch. 22.
40. Bagwell 1885–90, ii, pp. 74–91.

Sidney, whose previous experience equipped him well for the post. After service under Sussex, his other brother-in-law, Sidney had in 1560 been appointed president of the council in the Welsh marches and so escaped some of the odium that befell Sussex's followers.[41] Nevertheless, hoping to avoid difficulties experienced by previous governors, Sidney required a larger army, regular subventions, and unqualified privy council support before agreeing to serve. Professor Canny has argued that Sidney's deputyship marked a 'new departure' in Tudor policy involving 'a programme for the conquest of Ireland' which, while disappointing government expectations, none the less saw 'a pattern established, 1565–76' for the eventual reduction of Ireland. The argument is ingenious, but more recent research has established that the 'new departure' had been anticipated by Sussex and was less novel or systematically pursued than had been thought. In fact Sidney appropriated Sussex's 1562 programme, proposing to develop existing policies and initiatives in predictable ways, although he hoped initially at least to retain the local support built up by Arnold. Like Sussex he advocated controlling Ulster by expelling Gaelic Scots and overthrowing Shane O'Neill, followed by limited strategic colonization, particularly in east Ulster. In Leix–Offaly he thought that the plantation should be continued and transformed into a model community which would draw Gaelic parts to civility by example. Thus the argument that Sidney's deputyship marked a shift from traditional reform government to conquest and colonization is perhaps overstated: but as recent work has revealed, the government's excessive reliance on martial law in this period and Sidney's acquiescence in the increasingly vicious campaign against the O'Mores hardly accord with traditional Tudor methods either. Local perceptions of Tudor reform may have differed sharply from original intentions.[42]

By 1565 the various attempts to control Gaelic Leinster and the midlands by establishing captainries and wards had developed into a system of seneschalcies, with five English captains appointed seneschals over separate districts, each with a fort and garrison financed, as far as possible, from exactions formerly collected by the chiefs. The seneschals had power of martial law and followed the English practice of 'booking' whereby the gentry were required to lodge lists of dependents for whose conduct they accepted responsibility: masterless men were then executed or expelled. Sidney continued this system but, having secured a measure of external control over border chiefs to secure the Pale from attack, he envisaged gradually introducing common law processes plus a further bout of surrender and regrant following the submissions of various Leinster chiefs in spring 1566. He also modified surrender and regrant to try to make crown tenants of all the major Gaelic landowners, not just leading chiefs, so that claims to overlordship would be eroded and the gentry induced to look to the government for protection: St Leger's practice of creating mesne tenures

---

41. Williams 1958, pp. 251–2; Canny 1976, pp. 46–7; Brady 1980, pp. 169–70, 173.
42. Canny 1976; Brady 1980. Brady 1994a, ch. 4 restates the case for continuity and the primacy of reform government under Sidney; Canny 1987a, ch. 4; Canny 1988a; Canny 1996–7 argue for a shift to conquest and colonization. And see now Edwards 1997; Carey forthcoming.

by subinfeudation had of course confirmed the chiefs' influence under the Gaelic system, but by attacking the existing social hierarchy so as to speed change Sidney risked alienating the very chiefs on whose support the initial acceptance of anglicization depended. Surrender and regrant so modified was to operate also in border areas of Munster and south Connaught where English local government would be promoted by introducing provincial councils.[43]

Overall, therefore, Elizabeth had seemingly committed herself, by appointing Sidney, to a programme for extending English rule throughout Ireland, whereas Sussex (and Arnold) had been preoccupied with the Pale's defence. Yet the contrast is more apparent than real because Sussex had effectively been denied the resources to implement his policies, and Sidney soon discovered that he had been fobbed off with half-promises. His formal powers as deputy were almost identical to Sussex's, and his instructions (incorporating many of his own recommendations) were not inconsistent with his overall programme, but it soon became apparent that he was being judged on short-term performance, particularly regarding Shane O'Neill and the Ormond–Desmond feud, rather than progress towards long-term goals. The military establishment remained at 882 soldiers plus 300 kerne – 'beggar-like and insolent' as Sidney complained – but from these and the civil administration great things were expected. He was to establish religion, purge the bench of partial judges, reform the finances and ease the subject but without further charge to the queen. The courts' jurisdiction should be extended into the midland Irishry by joining lordships administratively to existing shires and replacing Gaelic customs, landholding and exactions with English manners, tenures and fixed payments. Sidney was to temporize with O'Neill and the Scots, but to support O'Donnell and consolidate royal influence in east Ulster. Elizabeth also approved a provincial council for Munster, and perhaps Connaught.[44]

Like Sussex, Sidney immediately began to establish a dependable clique in the Irish executive: yet circumstances allowed its accomplishment with less friction, and the changes fell well short of packing the administration with inexperienced English adventurers. Arnold had already dismissed many Sussex appointees from senior army posts, and few of Sussex's captains wished to stay. Sir Nicholas Bagenal returned as marshal and a councillor following Stanley's dismissal, but exceptionally Undertreasurer Fitzwilliam survived – he was Sidney's brother-in-law. Kildare retained the military responsibilities given him under Arnold; Cusack and Francis Agard remained influential; and Archbishop Loftus, Bishop Brady and Desmond were added to the council.[45]

Desmond–Ormond rivalry and the Munster council

Following a long examination, the earls of Desmond and Ormond had been released and bound over in IR£20,000 each to keep the peace and abide the

43. Canny 1976, pp. 34–5, 47–57; Brady 1980, pp. 174–8.
44. Bagwell 1885–90, ii, pp. 94–8; Canny 1976, ch. 3; Falls 1950, p. 94 (quotation).
45. Canny 1976, pp. 52–4; Brady 1980, pp. 174–5. Crawford 1993, pp. 45–52 stresses the extraordinary continuity and accumulated experience among Irish councillors, 1556–78.

queen's award in their controversies. In June 1565 MacCarthy More had been created earl of Clancare following his surrender and regrant, a move which limited Desmond overlordship there. Moreover, Elizabeth privately instructed Sidney to favour Ormond – Black Tom, her kinsman, whom she always liked.

Desmond was in fact in a difficult position. Arrears on monastic leases inherited from his father burdened his lordship with a debt to the crown of almost IR£2,400 by 1565, and by his previous misconduct he was held to have forfeited an earlier recognizance of IR£12,000. Yet in 1568 commissioners valued his properties at less than IR£1,000 per annum. Hitherto he had maintained his estate by ruthlessly exploiting Gaelic exactions and feudal services customarily paid by neighbouring Old English and Gaelic landlords, but with the revival of crown government in Munster these revenues were increasingly withheld and Desmond's overlordship questioned. His obvious response, a major demonstration of his power, drew Elizabeth's displeasure at efforts to settle disputes by violence; but if he obeyed the law his debts mounted and his vassals mistook his behaviour for weakness. Thus Desmond's chronic rebelliousness culminating in outright insurrection in 1579 is explained, not as the actions of the archetypal overmighty subject resisting Tudor centralization, but by his attempts to resolve this dilemma. Much more than in Ormond, Desmond's power depended on overlordship over a predominantly Gaelic population; and the earl, dim-witted, barely literate, more a captain than a courtier, was no match for Ormond who winked at discreet Butler support for his opponents. Nevertheless Desmond was not unwilling to become a landlord instead of a warlord, provided his political influence was safeguarded; and he proved responsive to approaches from the Dudley faction by Arnold, Sidney and Cusack.[46]

The argument that the Munster council aimed chiefly to undermine established magnate power has recently been attacked for confusing intention with effect. Sidney's choice as president, Sir Warham St Leger, the former governor's son, actually discharged the office throughout 1566 before being countermanded, and Desmond, already on friendly terms with St Leger, cooperated fully: indeed without local support it is difficult to see how the council could have functioned. Although the president had power of martial law (unlike his English counterparts), his instructions severely circumscribed its use, and his small retinue of 50 troops hardly allowed him much freedom of action. In reality the Munster council was conceived *mutatis mutandis* on the English model: St Leger would preside over a council comprising three Munster bishops, the earls, and two salaried lawyers to supply the necessary legal expertise. The council's jurisdiction extended over Thomond and Cos. Cork, Kerry, Limerick, Tipperary and Waterford, where regular sessions would be conducted; and in upholding English law and local government the president was expected to cultivate local support and draw nobles to the crown.

Nevertheless Ormond soon detected an unfavourable wind, particularly when his brothers were arrested for imposing coign and livery, although the Fitzgeralds

46. Brady 1980–1, pp. 289–303 (which revises MacCurtain 1975, pp. 28–44; McGurk 1979, pp. 578–85, 670–5); Bagwell 1885–90, ii, pp. 92–8; Canny 1976, ch. 3.

were equally guilty. He counterattacked shrewdly by objecting to Sidney's choice of president, alleging the old St Leger claim of 1515 to the Ormond inheritance (see above, p. 117). Yet his real fear, apparently, was for his palatinate of Tipperary whose operation would certainly be more closely supervised by the council and whose suppression as an anachronism (with the Desmond palatinate of Kerry) Sidney had earlier recommended. Furthermore, Ormond's complaints coincided with a reverse for Leicester at court, which Norfolk and Sussex exploited by attempting to discredit Sidney and break his grip on the important Irish patronage.[47]

Ormond's complaints immediately aroused Elizabeth's suspicions, and in May 1566 she ordered all disputes between Ormond and Desmond referred to London: she later rebuked Sidney for not investigating complaints against Desmond and finally had St Leger withdrawn altogether, so saving the council's costs. At court a series of bitter personal attacks on Sidney followed and he eventually challenged Sussex to a duel, but to save his administration he quietly abandoned Desmond. At assizes held at Waterford in spring 1567 the earl was adjudged guilty of misconduct during 1566 whereby his bond of IR£20,000 was forfeit, and when Desmond dissented Sidney arrested him on a charge of plotting treason, so anticipating a warrant from the queen. Desmond was sent up to London and incarcerated in the Tower, but Sidney knighted his able brother, Sir John Fitzgerald, and appointed him special commissioner of the peace in the lordship with lesser Munster lords, pending a new president.[48]

THE CAMPAIGN AGAINST SHANE O'NEILL

With his programme for Munster effectively countermanded, Sidney had no option but to concentrate on Ulster where O'Neill's activities could hardly be ignored. Shane was posing as defender of the faith against English heresy, had offered the crown of Ireland to Charles IX in return for French troops, and was also intriguing at the Scots court where Mary encouraged him as a useful diversion for Elizabeth. Most exceptionally, he also began training and arming the Tyrone peasantry, 'the first that ever did so of an Irishman'. Sidney began negotiations, chiefly for Elizabeth's benefit, but made little or no progress, and his reports of O'Neill's overweening pride and ambition soon galvanized the privy council into supporting military measures. Elizabeth thereupon dispatched her vice-chamberlain, Sir Francis Knollys, as special commissioner to discover if war was really necessary and to investigate Sidney's requests for more money, regular army pay, and a competent chancellor to replace Archbishop Curwin. Knollys reported favourably about the deputy's activities and endorsed his plan for a winter campaign – a permanent settlement by Lough Foyle to alleviate supply difficulties and break O'Neill domination of Tyrconnell, and a naval blockade to prevent Scottish redshanks from reinforcing O'Neill.

47. Brady 1980, pp. 295–6, 301; Canny 1976, pp. 49–57, 95–100.
48. Brady 1980–1, pp. 290, 293, 301–2, 308; Canny 1976, p. 56.

With O'Neill ravaging the Pale and even laying siege to Drogheda, the plan was approved and Elizabeth grudgingly granted £6,000 for the war. Reinforcements were despatched, and an expeditionary force of 700 men under Edward Randolph sailed direct to Lough Foyle to establish a garrison. Upon news of its arrival, the deputy with Kildare, O'Donnell and the army advanced to burn Tyrone, and reinforce and supply Randolph for the winter, leaving Desmond and St Leger to defend the Pale. Marching unopposed via Armagh, Benburb (Shane's chief residence), Omagh and Lifford, the deputy left Randolph at Derry with six weeks' provisions, restored O'Donnell, and reached Dublin again in mid-November by Donegal, Sligo (where O'Connor Sligo surrendered the castle and was promised a royal charter as independent lord of his country), Boyle and Athlone.[49]

This first large-scale amphibious operation of the reign was a great success: the demonstration of revived royal power and O'Neill's failure to make a stand encouraged many of his vassal-chiefs to desert him. The chief desperately attempted to recover his position by attacking Randolph's garrison, hoping then to exploit O'Donnell's recent death and reassert overlordship over Tyrconnell. The assault merely highlighted the traditional Gaelic weakness against defended earthworks, but Randolph was unluckily killed in the ensuing slaughter and thereafter sickness and shortages of supplies and equipment gradually undermined morale. The following April an accidental explosion destroyed the fort and the survivors withdrew to Carrickfergus. O'Neill quickly gathered an army and advanced into Tyrconnell, but after crossing the river Swilly at Farsetmore near Letterkenny his army was surprised and routed (8 May) by the O'Donnells. Shane himself escaped but was driven to negotiate with MacDonald for reinforcements, offering Sorley Boy's release in return for 1,000 galloglass. Apparently unofficial English offers of recognition for the 'Scots' colony weighed more with the chief than Shane's promises. O'Neill was cut down in a parley (2 June) and Glenshesk thereby avenged. Subsequently his body was exhumed and his head sent 'pickled in a pipkin' to embellish Dublin castle. Sir James Ware later calculated that overall the queen spent IR£147,000 against O'Neill and lost 3,500 soldiers.[50] Shane was very able, but fortunately for Elizabeth his ambitions were also very traditional, in contrast with Tyrone 30 years later: yet his career amply illustrated the dangers of an over-rigid insistence on anglicization and English succession laws in a remote area. Shane's tanist, Turlough Luineach, succeeded him and along with other Ulster chiefs submitted and offered to compound for his pardon.

The Ulster settlement and the advance of colonization

Ten years' campaigning in Ulster had done little to advance royal influence there, but Shane's fortuitous assassination removed a serious international

49. Bagwell 1885–90, ii, pp. 102–11; Canny 1976, pp. 58–9; *NHI*, iii, pp. 84–6 (quotation, p. 84); Brady 1982–3, pp. 116–23; Brady 1996a, pp. 59–61.
50. Bagwell 1885–90, ii, pp. 115–19; *NHI*, iii, p. 86; Canny 1976, p. 59; Brady 1982–3; Brady 1996a, pp. 64–5.

embarrassment to the government and left Elizabeth well placed to exploit the ensuing alterations in the balance of power. While the privy council debated how best to exploit the opportunity, however, the chance was missed. Understandably, Sidney required a firm commitment of support for a modified programme before continuing as deputy, and departed for court in October, leaving as lords justices Fitzwilliam and the recently appointed chancellor, the aged Dr Robert Weston. Sir Humphrey Gilbert, one of many West Countrymen promoting colonizing projects in Elizabethan Ireland, was appointed governor of Ulster pending its settlement.

Among those Englishmen who saw Ireland as a New World ripe for colonization on the Spanish model, Sidney was accounted an influential ally, having spent three years as Mary's emissary in Spain. The deputy valued the additional support, but carefully avoided complete identification with one policy: it was Secretary Cecil who urged the moderate extension in the role of colonization that characterized Sidney's deputyship. The experiment was earmarked for Ulster whose geography, natural and political, Cecil had carefully studied. Cecil proposed Tyrone's division between O'Neill's vassal-chiefs and junior O'Neill lineages, all to become crown tenants by surrender and regrant; the MacDonalds should be expelled from Antrim in favour of English colonies; and fourteen garrisons established in strategically situated forts to protect both colonists and Gaelic tenants. Elsewhere the projected regional councils by which Sidney set great store were to earn their keep by inquiring into 'concealed land' – monastic or escheated property wrongfully detained from the crown – on which English colonies might be introduced.

Characteristically, Elizabeth instructed Sidney to implement a cheaper version of the scheme, with fortifications only at Carrickfergus, Armagh and Olderfleet. He should summon a parliament to confirm the crown's title to Ulster, increase the revenue and promote civility by legislation for building churches, schools and a university; and he was to reduce military expenditure and exploit crown lands more effectively.[51]

The deputy sailed direct to Carrickfergus and during September and October 1568 was preoccupied with Ulster affairs, especially negotiations with Turlough Luineach. He quickly decided, however, that three forts were insufficient to control the province and proposed instead eight forts garrisoned by 2,000 colonists supplied by English nobles and gentry at their own expense. Initially this suggestion was 'better liked than thought likely', and disorders elsewhere which the justices had been unable to control soon drew him south; but the idea of establishing self-sufficient colonies to hold strategically important areas against outside intervention was applicable elsewhere, especially in Munster. There the threat of a Spanish landing to exploit local discontent exercised the government increasingly in the 1570s as Anglo-Spanish relations deteriorated. In fact small private colonies, though potentially disruptive, stood a better chance in the half-anglicized south than in turbulent Ulster, and Munster witnessed the earliest attempts to introduce oases of English civility

51. Canny 1976, pp. 60–7, 72; Brady 1980, pp. 191–8, 201–2.

to supplement the major instruments of royal control. St Leger's interest in Munster had not ended with his dismissal as president, for Desmond leased the manor of Kerrycurrihy near Cork to him in settlement of a debt. On this and adjoining churchlands which he claimed, he established a small English settlement which was soon reinforced by Sir Richard Grenville's arrival with 106 followers. With other adventurers such as Gilbert and Sir Peter Carew, they then proposed a much more ambitious corporate settlement further west near Baltimore, approved in principle by the privy council in April 1569. The idea was to confiscate Gaelic land (following legal proceedings to expose defective titles), expel 'the wild and rebel enemy', and introduce English colonists. Meanwhile Desmond's brother had also been arrested: thus Desmond power devolved entirely on the earl's captain-general, his landless cousin James Fitzmaurice Fitzgerald, the previous tenant of Kerrycurrihy, whose activities Grenville, now appointed sheriff, attempted to restrain.

Of more general concern in Old English circles, however, were Carew's other activities. With Sidney's encouragement, Carew had come to Ireland in 1568 and laid claim to lands once held by Anglo-Norman Carews in the Pale, Carlow and Munster. He began proceedings before the deputy and council against an influential Pale gentleman, Sir Christopher Cheevers, for the manor of Maston, Co. Meath, arguing that he could obtain no fair trial at common law. Realizing Sidney's hostility, Cheevers soon capitulated and compounded with Carew for Maston, but these proceedings effectively prejudged the larger issue of Carew's claim to Idrone barony, Co. Carlow, occupied mostly by the Kavanaghs but in part by their overlord, Sir Edmund Butler, the earl of Ormond's brother and heir. Notwithstanding previous agreements and the peerage granted to an earlier chief, prescription and Gaelic title were ignored in favour of a dubious common-law claim. Supported by the seneschal of Kavanagh's country, Thomas Stukeley, whom he succeeded, Carew then took up residence in Idrone and began proceedings against Butler for an adjoining tract of land.[52]

SIDNEY'S PARLIAMENT: THE EARLY SESSIONS

Thus by late 1568 the government was perceived to be bent on small-scale but widespread plantation, overturning the rights of existing proprietors, Old English as well as Gaelic. The projected regional councils, moreover, were seemingly directed to the same end, although a Munster president might well have restrained Fitzmaurice if Elizabeth had not delayed the appointment on financial grounds. Concurrently, preparations were proceeding for a parliament in January 1569 in which Sidney had licence to introduce certain contentious bills which promised an extension of divisive central interference in southern shires. Already before parliament met, therefore, relations between the executive and the local English were seriously strained. Fitzmaurice and Butler were on

52. Canny 1976, pp. 64–9, 77–8; Quinn 1945, pp. 543–5; Brady 1980–1, pp. 304–5; Bagwell 1885–90, ii, pp. 139–45, 156–8; Piveronus 1979, pp. 15–36 (quotation, p. 21).

the verge of rebellion: both defied the government by raising troops and reimposing coign and livery.[53]

In fact Sidney had high hopes of substantial socio-political reform in parliament, despite Elizabeth's insistence on economy, but when parliament assembled the government immediately faced an organized coalition of landowners in the Commons led by Butler and the Palesman, Sir Christopher Barnewall, which unsuccessfully challenged the official nominee as Speaker and then attacked the credentials of government supporters. Subsequent events in parliament confirmed mounting suspicions that Sidney, like Sussex, was intent on overriding local opposition and so strengthened rebel support in the ensuing revolts. Apparently Sidney had developed Sussex's electoral strategy for the previous parliament and the Commons included a substantial block of New English members, notably Carew's solicitor, John Hooker, member for Athenry, while in the Lords the replacement of catholic by protestant bishops had since created an adequate government majority for most purposes. The Commons opposition, however, forced Sidney to exclude self-returned mayors and sheriffs and representatives of unincorporated boroughs, but he rejected the demand that non-resident Englishmen be excluded. The ruling accorded with English practice but ignored the recent confirmation by the Irish parliament of the statutory obligation of residence (see above, p. 187); furthermore, circumstances were clearly different. Even so, the changes were enough to frustrate the government's intentions: when a vote was taken on the crucial bill to suspend Poynings' Law, it was defeated by four votes (44–48).[54]

Following Elizabeth's instructions, Sidney had planned a short, six-week parliament in which the government's programme would be expedited as in 1536, by the procedural device of suspending Poynings' Law for public bills. Against this, the English council had reduced to 20 the 46 bills originally certified in spring 1568. The plan was to pass the suspension bill and then the other transmitted bills which, if amended, would be recertified to England for the royal assent. Thus the suspension bill's rejection jeopardized the whole programme. Hooker, whose speech eulogizing Elizabeth's power and wisdom was larded with slighting references to the natives of Ireland, reported that 'every bill furthered by the English gentlemen was stopped and hindered' by the Old English. In fact the programme included significant socio-economic measures to revitalize the towns and eradicate Gaelic practices, notably a wines' impost and the suppression of coign and livery, but after a month parliament was bogged down in procedural disputes about the ousting of local custom by English parliamentary usages. It had passed only minor measures against retaining Scots, fosterage, and 'grey merchants' (see above, p. 42) plus a modest subsidy bill.

To maintain the major bills, and perhaps also his own credit at court if parliament were dissolved in these circumstances, Sidney exploited some slack drafting to engineer an unauthorized extension in parliament's intended

53. Treadwell 1966, pp. 67–8; Canny 1976, pp. 99–101, 143–4.
54. Treadwell 1966, pp. 66–9; Brady 1980, pp. 200, 204.

powers under the suspension bill and thereby encourage its passage. The effect was to allow parliament to pass public bills *before*, as well as after, certification from England, and so initiate new bills. In consequence a session in February–March saw seven new bills passed – notably one to prohibit the future introduction of suspension bills except by formal resolutions in both houses – to all of which Elizabeth eventually assented. The government also dropped a mysterious but very controversial bill to confirm certain English statutes – possibly concerning the problems of Uses which had reduced crown profits from wardships and other feudal incidents. Yet Sidney's embarrassment and the concessions extracted did little to restore local confidence in the administration's good intentions, and only six more transmitted bills were passed, after amendments. These comprised the attainders of Shane O'Neill and Thomas Fitzgerald, Knight of Glin, bills for shiring Gaelic lordships and to suppress 'captainries' of countries (except patentee appointments) and their exactions within shire ground, a bill to allow the deputy to appoint to ecclesiastical dignities in Connaught and Munster for ten years, and a useful mercantilist measure to promote industry and lower food prices by forbidding the export of certain provisions and raw materials (see also above, p. 49). In addition, one vital measure was unresolved, a bill to establish a differential duty on wines imported in aliens' and subjects' ships, which would augment the revenue, encourage loyal mercantile interests, and discourage strategically dangerous trade by Spanish ships.

Parliament was eventually prolonged over eight sessions and two years, but long before then the political climate had been transformed by a series of rebellions in the south and west.[55]

REVOLT IN THE SOUTH

Sidney's high-handed proceedings had provoked concerted opposition by different Old English interests, but not all were prepared to hazard a protest in arms, despite the ineffectiveness of conventional, constitutional opposition. Fitzmaurice had concerted action with Butler and announced that 'the Butlers are become friends to the Geraldines', but in order to win essential support from the earl of Clancare and lesser chiefs he was driven to behave like a Gaelic lord. Landless and with little to lose, he maintained such uncompromising opposition to the crown that he soon forfeited any hope of general Old English support.

In June 1569, the day after Grenville sailed for England, Fitzmaurice and Clancare – who now assumed his old title, MacCarthy More – plus two lesser Fitzgerald heads, the White Knight and the Seneschal of Imokilly, descended on Kerrycurrihy with 2,000 men. They overthrew the garrison and colony and chased the survivors into Cork, which stood siege rather than surrender them. A pious catholic, Fitzmaurice charged in a proclamation to the citizens that the

---

55. Treadwell 1966, pp. 55–75 (quotation, p. 68).

queen intended to impose 'another newly invented kind of religion', and urged them to expel 'all therein that be Huguenots' and restore the old faith. In fact the towns remained loyal, clinging to the prospect of relief from feudal disorders which Sidney's programme offered, though Kilmallock was burned. Major landowners who had profited from Desmond's decline – Viscounts Barry and Decies, and Lord Roche – also stood aloof; others 'remained, or they seemed, sound, yet their young and loose people went to [Fitzmaurice]'; and after Sidney's arrival most landowners came in. Fitzmaurice sent Maurice Fitzgibbon, papal archbishop of Cashel, to Philip II and declared that Spanish aid was coming: his religious appeals aimed to exploit an emerging popular reaction to anglicizing and centralizing influences. Yet the archbishop's memorial, asking Philip to nominate a new king of Ireland for papal confirmation, and listing every leading lord as supposedly supporting the request, was no more representative than a similar appeal in 1559, and Philip ignored it.

The revolts in the south-west have not yet attracted a detailed study, but notwithstanding his religious appeals Fitzmaurice's main support was apparently neo-feudal. Butler's remark – that he would not meddle in matters of religion – seems more typical, and his less radical conduct won him wider support. Despite the papal bull of 1570 excommunicating Elizabeth, another decade was to elapse before Irish dissidents would generally identify political and religious grievances and actively support the developing Counter-Reformation movement.[56]

Concurrently, Sir Edmund unleashed the Butler connection on English colonists and loyalist merchants around Ormond. The Carew settlement in Idrone suffered a similar fate to Kerrycurrihy, while Edmund's younger brothers overawed the south-east. Parts of Cos. Carlow, Dublin and Kildare were destroyed, but the Leix–Offaly plantation became a special target: settlers were led about in halters or killed and 'their hose and doublets, being stuffed and trussed, he would set up as marks for his kernes to throw their darts at'. In July Butler joined Fitzmaurice and Clancare in an unsuccessful siege of Kilkenny, but overall his revolt assumed more the character of a vendetta against Carew and a local loyalist, Sir Barnaby Fitzpatrick, and he soon attempted to draw back. Ormond, then at court, was seriously embarrassed but claimed that Sidney and Carew deliberately fomented the revolt to gain more land for plantation, and that his brother had despaired of justice at the deputy's hands. Four hundred troops were hastily despatched from England, and in August, when the earl arrived home to restore order, his brothers came in to him. In the event, Ormond managed to limit the damage to his reputation and family. On his orders, 165 rebels were killed outright or executed after surrender, and coign and livery was later abolished within his lordship. Yet his brothers, though eventually pardoned, were attainted by parliament; and thereafter Ormond's career as a courtier was hampered by his need to supervise their conduct and the rule of his lordship.

56. Canny 1976, pp. 142–50 (quotations, pp. 145, 147); Silke 1966, pp. 5–6, 10–11; Bagwell 1885–90, ii, ch. 26; Brady 1980–1, pp. 305–6; Piveronus 1979, pp. 28–31.

Very probably, the revolts of 1569–70 were an Irish manifestation of the court intrigues that culminated in the Northern Rising of 1569–70: Sir Edmund claimed that he was defending the queen from her enemies, and Sidney reported that he feared that Leicester would marry Elizabeth and make Sidney king of Ireland. Two Northern Rebels later joined Fitzmaurice. In the circumstances the stock justification of Tudor rebels – that they were merely protesting against the unauthorized activities of evil and corrupt officials – was not perhaps altogether unrealistic: but with Norfolk's fall and the Northern Rising, Sidney's position was secure and Ormond concentrated on saving his brothers.[57]

Sidney's tardy appearance in Munster with 600 men soon broke rebel control of the countryside. He took and garrisoned some Fitzgerald castles, relieved Cork and pushed on to Limerick where major figures of the Munster Englishry submitted – notably Desmond's half-brother, Thomas, Burke of Clanwilliam, and Lord Lixnaw – as did Desmond's galloglass captain. Unexpectedly, Turlough Luineach in Ulster merely continued to consolidate his power there. He married MacDonald's widow who brought a dowry of 1,200 redshanks, and warily hired other mercenaries against English intervention; but Sidney had neither opportunity nor money for the interventionist policies of Shane's day, and once the traditional nature of O'Neill's ambitions became apparent, he withdrew Gilbert and in September appointed him colonel to pacify Munster. Gilbert's chief success was to break an attempted siege of Kilmallock, after which Fitzmaurice's support fell away, but his ruthless campaigning – apparently with an eye to more forfeited land for plantation – was more appropriate to Gaelic Ulster than the punishment of unruly subjects unaccustomed to sustained central supervision. Until February 1571 the entire province remained exclusively under martial law, an unprecedented departure from established practices of English government.

Gilbert was certainly effective: within six weeks he had captured 23 castles without artillery, slaughtering the occupants, man, woman, and child, of any that resisted. By December 1569 Clancare and most Geraldines had submitted, and Fitzmaurice – 'a silly wood-kerne' – was sheltering in the glen of Aherlow in Tipperary. Sidney reported that 'the iron is now hot, apt to receive what print shall be stricken', but the campaigning had been expensive, and Elizabeth was in no hurry to despatch the new president, Sir John Perrot. Perrot only assumed office in February 1571, and with Fitzmaurice still at large he remained primarily a soldier, fruitlessly chasing Fitzmaurice around Munster. In desperation he called for Sir John Fitzgerald's return and even challenged Fitzmaurice to a quasi-tourney. Even when he held assizes, 30 executions regularly followed, and by April 1573 he had despatched an estimated 800 traitors by common or martial law, besides those killed in battle. Thus Perrot's 'rule of law' – he lacked even a trained lawyer initially – hardly differed

---

57. Canny 1976, pp. 142–52 (quotation, pp. 145–6); Begwell 1885–90, ii, ch. 26; Falls 1950, pp. 123–4, 138–41. Edwards 1992–3, pp. 228–55 adds considerably to our understanding of the Butler rising.

from Gilbert's administration and did little to endear Munstermen to the presidency.[58]

REVOLT IN THE WEST

In Connaught the council's intended base, Athlone, already disposed a garrison which could double as the president's retinue. Thus Sir Edward Fitton's installation in December 1569 with Justices Ralph Rokeby, from the council in the north, and Robert Dillon, a Gaelic-speaking Palesman, cost relatively little (see above, p. 171). However, Fitton, Burghley's client, proved tactless and inflexible; and perhaps only the anomalous position of the western earls – requiring government support for their English titles against local opposition – prevented an immediate conflagration. Fitton began by erecting the more anglicized south into Cos. Clare, Galway and Roscommon, held sessions, and took pledges and bonds worth IR£9,000 from the major landowners for the conduct of their dependents, who were booked. Less acceptable was his zeal in purging Connaught of popery before he had the means to promote true religion: monuments of superstition were consigned to the flames and friars expelled. Civility was imposed by proscribing coign and livery, Gaelic law and custom, and requiring all who submitted to cut their hair as a 'first token of obedience'.

Surprisingly, the earl of Clanrickard remained cooperative, willing 'to leave all unreasonable exactions and lewd Irish customs' (though his Gaelic sobriquet, Richard Sassenach, speaks for itself), and Galway was almost civility itself; but even Clanrickard grew restive when Fitton appointed his rival, John Burke, sheriff of Galway, with power of martial law, and exempted Burke's lands from his control. When Fitton likewise appointed Teig O'Brien, another would-be tanist, sheriff of Clare to counterbalance the earl of Thomond's authority, Thomond was less patient. He tolerated Fitton's assizes held at Ennis, but refused to appear or negotiate, and starved him into withdrawing. Then, wearing the proscribed Gaelic habit, he arrested the sheriff and provost-marshal, declaring 'that he would do nothing with the lord deputy nor lord president but as the duke of Norfolk would say'.[59]

Thomond's resistance signalled the start of general opposition to Fitton's presidency, and after O'Rourke and some of the Burkes had come out, he began to lose control. In response to Fitton's appeals, Sidney sent reinforcements and entrusted Thomond's subjection to the earl's cousin, Ormond, newly reconciled to Sidney. Thomond readily submitted on Ormond's appearance (April 1570), understanding that Ormond should have custody of his country. He departed for court to beg his pardon, fled to France, changed his mind,

58. Bagwell 1885–90, ii, pp. 163–9, 179–89, 207–10; Falls 1950, pp. 106–10; Canny 1976, pp. 101–3 (quotation, p. 101); Quinn 1940, i, introduction.
59. Canny 1976, pp. 108–11, 143, 146, 150 (quotations, pp. 109, 150); Brady 1980, pp. 209–11.

submitted and was pardoned and bound over in IR£10,000 for his future good behaviour. Ormond pardoned most of the clansmen and vassals, garrisoned the castles, and wrote pointedly to Sidney: 'The queen hath many good subjects here, if they were but cherished and not overpressed.'

Elsewhere in Connaught, Fitton found he could win battles, notably against Burke of Mayo, but not restore order. Rokeby recommended that only 'fire and sword', not the rule of law, was appropriate in such conditions. The garrison was gradually increased, martial law extended, and Connaught soon came almost to resemble Munster under Gilbert.[60]

SIDNEY'S PARLIAMENT: THE LATER SESSIONS

With leading opponents abandoning it for the battlefield, however, parliament's later sessions were comparatively tranquil. Continued constitutional opposition risked identification with Fitzmaurice, but equally the government found it harder to resist the demands of loyal magnates and towns: a precarious consensus was re-established. A three-week session in October 1569 saw the formal reversal of the Kildare attainder of 1536 – a reward for the eleventh earl's service and support – and the enactment and immediate enforcement of the unpopular but lucrative wines impost. Yet the government had to agree to substantial reductions in the duties payable, duty-free allowances for nobles, and its amendment to a ten-year, not perpetual, levy (see also above, p. 184).

The next major session, in May–June 1570, was a disappointment for the government. Its chief success was an act establishing diocesan free schools, but only after the deputy had surrendered to bishops of Pale dioceses the nomination of schoolmasters there, while other aspects of a worthwhile programme to revitalize the Irish church (see above, Ch. 9) were frustrated by vested interests. An act authorizing the deputy to execute the surrender and regrant of Gaelic estates probably aimed to scotch rumours about wholesale expropriations of Gaelic landowners, but it also augmented crown landed profits. The third major measure was a ferocious coercion bill, an ultimatum to rebels who had not yet submitted, which, even as amended by the Lords, provided that all who failed to appear before the deputy to answer treason charges within 40 days of proclamation should stand attainted without trial.

Rejected bills included Sidney's long-delayed project to abolish all forms of coign and livery, with which was associated a privately sponsored bill concerning tenure, the price of Ormond's consent to abolition: not that Old English landowners wished to preserve Gaelic exactions, but in many parts the lord's right to coign was a major item in leases and compensation might threaten land titles. Moreover, the hated government cesses, which the Palesmen thought illegal, would be replaced by regular taxation to maintain a standing army: the overall effect might therefore be simply to disband the retinues of loyal

---

60. Bagwell 1885–90, ii, pp. 170–3 (quotation, p. 173); Falls 1950, pp. 106–8; Canny 1976, pp. 110–11 (quotation, p. 110).

subjects and leave them defenceless against both rebels and the indisciplined and oversized army of an authoritarian administration. Another bill to create a staple monopoly of cloth and leather exports to compensate merchants of the five staple towns for the 1569 act restricting exports failed when the government added a clause imposing new customs duties on these exports.

In November–December Sidney attempted a last rescue bid, holding further sessions, but the outcome was hardly more satisfactory. Two of the five acts passed were attainders endorsing God's judgement on the White Knight and Thomas Comerford respectively who had inconveniently evaded parliament's previous judgement by dying, while two more reflected a bargain between the government and corporate towns. The government, worried about smuggling, was allowed to tighten the export act, supplementing the prohibitive duties on exporting raw materials by making smuggling a felony and introducing coastal cockets to regulate the coastal trade in such commodities: in return corporate towns were aided by widening the proposed restriction on exporting manufactures to include merchants resident there, while deleting the new customs duties.[61]

PACIFICATION AND SIDNEY'S RECALL

By 1571 Ireland was sufficiently quiet to permit Sidney's recall, decided the previous summer. The deputy installed Perrot in Munster, concluded a treaty with Turlough Luineach, and departed in April leaving Fitzwilliam as justiciar. In fact Sidney was disillusioned by the councils' failure as an effective instrument of socio-political reform and by parliament's intractability; and particularly after the outbreak of rebellion, his administration was much less economical than Elizabeth had intended. The garrison now numbered 2,031 men, costing IR£32,500 per annum, and since Sidney's return in 1568 Elizabeth had spent no less than IR£148,000, with debts of IR£73,000 still outstanding. The attempt to govern Connaught and Munster through regional councils, though realistic, failed because their belated introduction coincided with a deteriorating political climate with which neither president had the experience nor ability to cope: to win support in England Sidney had sanctioned supposedly complementary but peripheral colonization projects, but these poisoned relations with local leaders by seeming to threaten common-law land titles. As had happened so often since 1547, the government was attempting too much with too little too quickly.

Elizabeth soon realized her mistake: Sidney was sharply reprimanded for meddling in common-law matters, and Carew discreetly disappeared. 'Rash dealings in matters of land' by adventurers were subsequently restricted to 'mere Irish' areas like Ulster and more adequately supervised. This in turn restored the traditional pattern of politics – momentarily disrupted by a threatened combination of rebellious Old English and Gaelic lords – as the government

61. Treadwell 1966.

reverted to its usual strategy of involving the more loyal and tractable elements in an administration strengthened by English clerks and captains: but the damage to crown–community relations of seeming to treat loyal subjects as Irish enemies was less easily repaired.[62]

Nevertheless leading officials were baffled by Sidney's apparent failure, and another Arnold-style experiment followed with government almost decentralized into autonomous provinces. There was no rush to succeed Sidney, and eventually in December 1571 Fitzwilliam had to be promoted lord deputy: excepting Sidney's second deputyship (1575–8), the governorship was to remain with secondary figures until 1599. Fitzwilliam, a dependant of Sussex, was expected to economize, but was immediately hamstrung by the summons of his chief supporter, Ormond, to court, followed by the army's reduction to 1,300 men. He could therefore do little to help Fitton or Perrot, nor to maintain peace in Ulster where earlier plantation schemes now reached fruition in the Ards project. In Connaught revolt now centred on Clanrickard's two sons John and Ulick, whom the old earl could not control. Fitton merely compounded his difficulties by arresting Clanrickard for complicity and quarrelling with Fitzwilliam. The president was shut up in Galway, but when the Mayo Burkes joined the revolt he retired first to Athlone and then, following Fitzmaurice's intervention, to Dublin and England. Elizabeth reprimanded him for Clanrickard's arrest, and after six months' detention in Dublin the earl was sent home with a commission to grant pardons at discretion. Yet with Connaught at their command, Clanrickard's sons voluntarily submitted to Fitzwilliam in November, and the earl wrote to ask for another president.

In Munster, where English traditions were much stronger, Perrot received ready support against Fitzmaurice: he lacked the manpower to flush Fitzmaurice out of his fastnesses, but the province grew more peaceful despite his authoritarian rule. By late 1572, however, Elizabeth had decided on the earl of Desmond's restoration, much to the annoyance of Fitzwilliam and Perrot. Desmond and his brother were released after five years' detention – in the Tower and, latterly, Sir Warham St Leger's house – and reached Dublin the following March, the earl having agreed to support the religious settlement, to crush Fitzmaurice, and to levy his dues only by legal process without molesting neighbouring lords. In fact Fitzmaurice and Imokilly had submitted on news of Desmond's release, but with Munster finally under control, Perrot and Fitzwilliam now imposed additional conditions on Desmond which would have left him militarily and legally powerless there. When the earl demurred, he was reinterned, but fearing treachery he escaped from Dublin in November to rally Desmond to his defence. Ironically Perrot departed the same day, having resigned office, and within weeks all traces of his work had disappeared. Fitton had returned to Ireland with Desmond, but primarily as undertreasurer: following their reconciliation, Clanrickard, Thomond and Fitton received a

---

62. Bagwell 1885–90, ii, pp. 181–2; Treadwell 1966, pp. 80, 85–6 (quotations, p. 86); Brady 1980, pp. 200–9; Falls 1950, p. 110. Recent work by Crawford 1993, pp. 124–9 throws further light on the political manoeuvrings surrounding this episode.

commission of oyer and terminer for Connaught, but the council ceased. Thus attempts to speed change by regional councils proved costly and counterproductive: pressure of circumstances produced a complete transformation in their essential nature, and Elizabeth discontinued them as an expensive luxury.[63]

THE ULSTER PROJECTS

In Ulster, Sir Thomas Smith's attempt to plant the easily defended Ards peninsula was approved as a pilot scheme for private colonization and commenced in late summer 1572. It reflected an increasing pessimism in court circles about the possibility of assimilating Gaelic Ireland by persuasion and education. Moreover, of the fashionable get-rich-quick schemes for surplus capital, like alchemy and piracy, colonization alone could provide land and also appeared a pious work and a remedy for the overpopulation then worrying thinking Englishmen. Classicist, civil lawyer and secretary of state, Smith was influenced both by Caesar and Cicero and by recent plantation experience, and envisaged his incompetent son, Thomas, leading out a colony to Ulster like a Roman general extending the empire.

Following privy council approval and a grant of the Ards, the Smiths assembled some 750 adventurers at Liverpool by May 1572 through an intensive and novel campaign of propaganda pamphlets. The idea was to raise money by subscription on the recently developed joint-stock principle, to cover transportation, victualling and fortification until the colony should be self-sufficient, hopefully within two years. Individual horsemen and footmen would contribute £20 and £10 each respectively, and non-participating investors 25 marks: in return they would each receive estates of two, one, and one ploughland respectively, holding of Smith as tenant-in-chief. These adventurers would form an aristocratic elite, retaining servile Gaelic tenants to work the soil, though English husbandmen were not excluded. They would first expel the 'wicked, barbarous and uncivil people, some Scottish and some wild Irish' and establish a kind of *encomienda* system like Spanish America in which the 'Irish churl', 'a very simple and toilsome man', would be 'gently entertained' and 'well rewarded' for ploughing and labour, but not enfranchised, allowed English dress, nor to bear arms or office, nor purchase land.

By March 1572, however, the local chief, Sir Brian O'Neill of Clandeboye ('a true subject') had obtained a copy of Smith's pamphlet and vigorously protested his loyalty and service against Shane and Turlough Luineach O'Neill, while other chiefs made mutual pacts and braced themselves for resistance. Following Fitzwilliam's warning that rebellion would follow, Elizabeth belatedly countermanded the expedition, and before Secretary Smith could get this decision reversed, most adventurers had gone home or joined Sir Humphrey Gilbert's volunteers for the Netherlands. Only 100 men landed in Co. Down

63. Bagwell 1885–90, ii, chs 29–30; Brady 1980, p. 219; Brady 1980–1; Canny 1976, pp. 103–4; Cunningham 1979, p. 23. See now also Morgan 1985, pp. 261–78 concerning Smith's project.

on 30 August and Sir Brian soon drove them into Carrickfergus whence Smith appealed unavailingly for Fitzwilliam's assistance. The settlers eventually regrouped south of Newtownards, but in autumn 1573 Smith was suddenly attacked and killed by his household 'churls' who boiled up his body and fed it to their dogs. Despite two attempts by his father in 1573 and 1574 to reinforce the colony, it fizzled out.[64]

By then, however, Walter Devereux, earl of Essex, had landed in August 1573 as leader of a much more grandiose scheme. Essex financed his venture by mortgaging his estates to Elizabeth for £10,000 and engaged to conquer and colonize all Antrim save Carrickfergus with 1,200 troops, financed jointly by himself and the queen: in return he received an extensive grant of rights and privileges there with five areas reserved to Elizabeth and some others to the adventurers. These included *conquistadores* like Carew and St Leger, plus such courtiers as Lord Rich, Lord Hunsdon's two sons and Knollys's son.

A storm dispersed Essex's fleet, but eventually about 1,100 men, including labourers, and kerne supplied by Lord Dungannon, assembled at Carrickfergus. A chivalrous but unthinking knight, Essex promised not to 'imbrue his hands with more blood than the necessity of the cause requireth', and expected to achieve his objective principally by expelling Gaelic Scots rather than by expropriating the Clandeboye O'Neills. Initially Sir Brian remained tractable, considering Essex's proposal for a crusade against Clan Donald while he weighed the earl's real strength. Yet, finding that Antrim was no garden of Eden, many of the 400 adventurers went home. Essex's troops included many ill-armed recruits, and he soon faced a combination of Turlough Luineach, Sir Brian and MacDonald, who asserted that they were 'no rebels' and the war not the queen's. Accordingly, early in 1574 Elizabeth appointed Essex governor of Ulster with quasi-presidential authority and sent reinforcements, but the earl then found no-one to fight. Sir Brian again submitted and Dungannon proved serviceable, but Essex's colonists were marooned in Carrickfergus; supplies grew scarce; and Elizabeth, realizing that the project's successful conclusion would be prohibitively expensive, sought how to extricate herself honourably without ruining Essex or his reputation. Fitzwilliam could offer little assistance, nor wished to, while Elizabeth ignored suggestions that the earl be appointed deputy instead.

In desperation, Essex treacherously slaughtered Sir Brian's company at a feast in November and sent the chief to a traitor's death in Dublin. In July 1575 he despatched an expedition against the Rathlin Scots commanded by Captain Francis Drake with troops under Captain John Norris: they massacred the island's entire population of 600. This, however, was the last act in the tragedy. By 1575 Essex was spending more time in the Pale, making sporadic raids against Turlough Luineach. In May Elizabeth countermanded his project, and a reasonable peace was patched up with Turlough Luineach which interpreted narrowly the chief's claims to overlordship.

64. Quinn 1945, pp. 543–60 (quotations, pp. 548, 551, 553); Quinn 1958, p. 10; Canny 1976, pp. 66–92, 139; Bagwell 1885–90, ii, pp. 211–16, 231–3, 247.

The Ulster projects proved an expensive failure: the queen spent over IR£130,000 in Ireland over two and a half years to September 1575, besides internal revenues and unpaid debts. Ill-conceived and incompetently executed, the projects marked the abandonment of the private-enterprise colony in Ireland. Overall, their significance was chiefly to point the way to the Hakluyts, Gilbert, Grenville and Raleigh in colonizing America: in Ireland, however, the harsher attitude to and treatment of the Gaelic population by English adventurers, and Essex's atrocities, precipitated a further deterioration in Anglo-Gaelic relations. Gaelic troops replied in kind: according to Essex, they mutilated dead soldiers, 'cut off their privy parts, set up their heads and put them in their mouths'. The rules of Irish warfare had traditionally differed from continental conventions, but by treating the natives as savages and persistently infringing all military conventions Elizabethan armies precipitated the savagery that characterized the conquest's eventual completion.[65]

SIDNEY'S RETURN: COMPOSITION

1575 also witnessed a new programmatic initiative which aimed to turn the unfortunate experiences with regional councils to good account through schemes for composition. Fitzwilliam had recognized that intrusive presidents who attempted to undermine the influence of great magnates would necessarily provoke disorders: lacking the resources to quell rebellion, he had temporized by allowing the institutions to lapse. Within the Pale too, Fitzwilliam backed away from confrontation in the cess controversy: rather than attempting to exploit rights of purveyance more effectively to reduce costs he courted local support. A promising initiative by which Kildare was commissioned to defend the Pale ended needlessly in the earl's arrest: he fell under suspicion in 1574 concerning communications with Gaelic chiefs, was arrested by Essex, and sent to London. Nevertheless, Fitzwilliam's administration was judged on expense and effectiveness, and therefore fell an unsurprising victim to a further campaign by the Leicester faction to recover control of Irish patronage by Sidney's reappointment.

Sidney had been impressed by the views of his former secretary, Edmund Tremayne, clerk of the privy council, who argued that the extension of crown government was inimical to the interests of feudal magnates, but that if coign and livery were abolished, they would be powerless to oppose it. Supposedly, this explained the failure of regional councils. In Connaught, however, Fitton had briefly tried to raise money for an increased retinue by surveying Thomond and Clanrickard, dividing them into ploughlands, and demanding an annual tax of one mark (IR) per ploughland. Tremayne proposed a general campaign to abolish coign and livery and make the garrison self-supporting by a series of

65. Bagwell 1885–90, ii, pp. 239–47, 257–61, 269–76, 284–96, 300, 324–7 (quotations, pp. 243, 259); Canny 1976, pp. 88–90, 137–9, 160–1 (quotation, p. 139); Quinn 1945, p. 560.

agreements known as 'compositions': in effect the presidents would act as superior warlords, emulating the magnates with their private armies, but offering to commute, for a fixed annual rent, the rights of billeting, purveyance and military service which they would exact. In turn, Tremayne expected, the magnates would be induced to seek corresponding commutations from their dependants, leading to a universal composition and the rapid emergence of more civil forms of society under royal control.[66]

Composition was destined to form a major plank in Elizabeth's Irish policy over the next twenty years, but in order to try out these theories Sidney had to outbid his rivals to secure his own reappointment. Rashly, he offered to make Ireland self-supporting within three years for IR£60,000 and 1,100 troops, and returned in September. Financial exigencies, therefore, and the desire for early success to impress Elizabeth forced him to exceed discretion in pressing composition. The scheme was initially tried in the Pale, following earlier suggestions for a commutation of cess: Sidney offered to abolish all exactions there – household and general cesses, hosting money, cartage, and cesses of labourers – in return for a composition rent of IR£5 per ploughland, which compared very favourably with their estimated real cost to the country of IR£8. Unfortunately for Sidney, he arrived after two successive bad harvests followed by plague. Moreover, his offer in effect belied the administration's traditional defence of cess as an assorted collection of unfortunate though temporary impositions, confirming the Palesmen's oft-repeated fears that cess was an alternative extra-parliamentary form of taxation (see above, pp. 186–8). The Palesmen rejected both Sidney's offer and his exorbitant cess demands, designed in reality to force a composition. The respective arguments about cess were soon reformulated in the most uncompromising terms: Sidney stated baldly that all aspects of cess depended solely on the royal prerogative, while the Palesmen asserted that all such exactions were illegal unless agreed by parliament.[67]

Fitzwilliam had been blamed for inactivity, and Sidney, like a new broom, soon departed to view east Ulster, which he reported much wasted and depopulated by the recent warfare. Generally he recommended recognition of the existing chiefs, including Sorley Boy MacDonald in the Glens of Antrim, with peerages for Turlough Luineach and Magennis, and other chiefs holding directly of the queen by surrender and regrant. He also withdrew the garrison from Rathlin and recommended revocation of land grants in Co. Down to English adventurers, saving Marshal Nicholas Bagenal at the strategically important outpost of Newry where a well-built town had grown up.[68]

In late autumn Sidney departed on another progress through the south and west which was intended to facilitate the reintroduction of the provincial councils he continually requested. In Munster he held court for six weeks at Cork, whither repaired almost all the magnates, Gaelic and English, lesser chiefs, and

---

66. Brady 1980–1, pp. 296, 306–7; Brady 1980, pp. 210–18; Canny 1976, pp. 78, 112; Bagwell 1885–90, ii, pp. 297–8.
67. Brady 1985; Brady 1980, pp. 221–8; Quinn 1967, pp. 101–2.
68. Bagwell 1885–90, ii, pp. 300–6.

'many of the ruined relics of the ancient English inhabitants of this province'. Elizabeth, having decided on Desmond's rehabilitation, had disapproved of his handling by Perrot and accepted his submission in September 1574 negotiated through Kildare and his brother, and Essex; and shortly before Sidney's return two commissioners settled outstanding disputes, upholding Desmond's rights on certain important issues, notably the palatinate of Kerry. Thus the deputy found Desmond tractable: he was already disbanding his armed retainers maintained by coign and livery as previously required, and was willing to undertake a commutation of his customary exactions as overlord. Thus abandoned, the earl's leading retainers, Fitzmaurice, Imokilly and the White Knight's son, fled to France in March 1575 to intrigue for foreign intervention, while erstwhile swordsmen were forced into grudging conformity. At Cork Sidney secured a general undertaking by landowners to disband private armies and eschew coign and livery, he booked dependants and promised a president to maintain order. The landowners also agreed to a composition rent to maintain 150 English troops instead of military service, although Desmond was tactfully excluded. Thus when Sir William Drury arrived as president in July 1576 his task appeared relatively straightforward – to consolidate previous progress by bridling retainers and facilitating the magnates' transition from warlords to landlords.

Against Tremayne's advice, however, composition negotiations in Munster were delegated to the president, thus reinforcing the institution's exploitative image. Thomond, where Sidney appointed the earl's brother, Sir Donald O'Brien, as sheriff and induced the landowners to bear the charge of a provost marshal to prosecute idle men, was transferred to Drury's jurisdiction: but Ormond was now exempted, and Sidney's pleas for the suppression of palatinates were prudently ignored. Drury combined long military service with previous experience of a provincial council in England. His imposition of cess antagonized the province, his formal composition was refused and, following booking, executions of masterless men continued at an exceptional rate – 400 in twenty months by martial and common law, Drury boasted – but the president was less tactless than Perrot and further rebellion was – just – avoided.

The crisis came in 1577 when Sir John Fitzgerald, disillusioned and ill-rewarded for his services, was arrested for complicity with revolt in Connaught: Desmond retired into Kerry, raised troops, refused taxes, and disobeyed summonses, but on Sidney's advice Drury held back and a reconciliation was effected. By March 1578, Drury had reached individual settlements with all the Munster lords outside Tipperary, and had secured an annual rent of IR£1,170 towards the council's costs of IR£3,815, with a further IR£1,120 expected in rents from monastic lands. Desmond became not merely compliant but actively cooperative: he kept the government informed about rumours of foreign intervention, referred to Dublin cases exempted from his palatine jurisdiction, and completed a commutation of his customary exactions through which he could expect an unwontedly large annual revenue of IR£2,000. Elizabeth wrote personally to praise his conduct and promise further favour for continued service. Overall, the Munster council was seemingly accepted and effective, and the nobles, no longer threatened by English adventurers, were apparently conformable; but appearances were deceptive.[69]

From Cork Sidney travelled via Thomond to Galway where he received the principal Connaught landowners, including many from north Connaught – hitherto relatively free from government interference. Burke of Mayo, O'Malley and others submitted, surrendered their lands, and agreed to hold them of the queen following an inquisition to determine the freehold rights of lesser lords. In April 1576 Sidney erected the shires of Mayo and Sligo, appointing an English sheriff of Mayo at Burke's request, and sanctioned the demarcation of the four Connaught counties. These arrangements were intended to facilitate the extension of conciliar activity throughout Connaught, but Clanrickard whom Sidney adjudged overmighty was harshly treated. His two sons were taken prisoners to Dublin, his two strongest castles garrisoned, his vassal, O'Shaughnessy, promised an independent grant of his lordship, cess imposed on the earl's immune demesne lands, and IR£10,000 arrears of monastic rents demanded, plus a fine of IR£6,000 for rebuilding Athenry, destroyed in the last rebellion.

The deputy returned via Roscommon and Athlone, where O'Connor Don, O'Connor Roe, and MacDermot attended him, while O'Connor Sligo and O'Rourke submitted at Dublin and offered rent for security of tenure. Yet the delay in appointing a president proved a false economy: in June Clanrickard's sons escaped, attempted to raise the province, and burned Athenry again, while the earl weakly remonstrated about Sidney's exhorbitant financial demands. The deputy reacted sharply: he hurried west, taking hostages from other landowners to contain the revolt. The Burkes were soon dependent on Scottish mercenaries for support, and the experienced Captain Nicholas Malby, appointed colonel with 300 troops by Sidney and hastily promoted president in July, had little difficulty in breaking the revolt. Clanrickard submitted immediately and was imprisoned for failure to arrest his sons, who retreated to their fastnesses. Malby methodically burned both districts, slaughtering all the inhabitants, after which peace prevailed and Clanrickard's sons remained inactive. Despite the uncertainty about the earl's fate, Sidney was then able to impose a composition. In 1577 the Connaught landowners reluctantly agreed to pay annual rent and provisions to support the president and to maintain specified numbers of troops, arrangements which yielded IR£1,140 a year: further revenue was expected from 'concealed' lands.[70] Thus, despite the operation's indifferent management, the regional councils had been re-established, without repetition of the major revolts of 1569–72, but they were not yet self-sufficient, nor were local suspicions allayed concerning their exploitative nature.

69. Brady 1980–1, pp. 295–7, 306–9; Brady 1980, pp. 228–31, 234–5; Canny 1976, pp. 104–8; Bagwell 1885–90, ii, pp. 307–17, 322–4, 336–8, 345 (quotation, p. 314).
70. Canny 1976, pp. 112–14, 147; Brady 1980, pp. 229–30; Cunningham 1979, pp. 25, 64–70; Bagwell 1885–90, ii, pp. 316–23, 338–40.

Confrontation in the English Pale

While Connaught and Munster landowners were being thus pressed into composition agreements, Sidney's similar demands in the Pale were meeting intransigent opposition. Under pressure, the deputy had made concessions over the levels of cess, but many landowners simply refused to pay, regardless of what had been agreed in great council. Leading lords like Baltinglass, Delvin and Howth actively organized resistance in their own shires, and a small group of lawyers prepared a legal defence of their actions, while in London courtiers like Kildare and Ormond lent discreet support. Thus 'the country cause', as the Palesmen labelled their movement, spread rapidly, and increasingly cut across traditional factional divisions within the Old English community to create a combination recalling the opposition to Sussex and similar to that faced by Sidney in the last parliament. Not that revolt in the Pale seemed likely, although the continental intrigues of Fitzmaurice, Fitzgibbon and the renegade Thomas Stukeley posed a distinct threat in the half-pacified south-west, but the deputy could afford no compromise because his programme depended on composition. Opposition in council to cess merely underlined the local community's declining influence in the Dublin administration: Old English councillors like Nicholas White and Nicholas Nugent who supported the country's cause lost the deputy's confidence, while Luke Dillon who retained it did so only by ignoring cess complaints. Once again, therefore, the Old English community was driven to subvert the governor's programme and circumvent his authority. Early in 1577 three lawyers, Barnaby Scurlock, Richard Netterville and Henry Burnell, were chosen to petition the privy council, while others attempted to indict the executive of levying illegal exactions. Elizabeth, however, was already defaulting on payments and complaining about the costs of Sidney's government, increased by revolt in Connaught and shortfalls on cess. Accordingly the lawyers were treated mildly, and the deputy had to mount a strong campaign at court to discredit them, whereupon they were consigned to the Tower. In the Pale four lords and some leading gentry were likewise committed to the Castle for challenging the prerogative; but once they and the lawyers had submitted, Elizabeth proved sympathetic to complaints about the *abuse* of cess and the burden that it constituted in time of scarcity. The Palesmen counterattacked by agreeing to a year's composition and proposing an alternative scheme to supplement the pay of 1,000 soldiers by 1*d.* sterling per day. They also renewed an offer made during Fitzwilliam's deputyship to undertake a victualling contract themselves.

These offers made room for compromise, for which the queen was anxious – she had already reprimanded Sidney for bringing the controversy to a head and so publicizing undeniable grievances. More seriously for Sidney, however, she now doubted whether the difficulties of governing Ireland were wholly inherent in the situation, suspecting rather his abrasive style of government. These doubts were reinforced by the views of William Gerrard, appointed chancellor in 1576 after long service as Sidney's vice-president of the Welsh council. Sent to court in July 1577 to promote the deputy's programme, Gerrard was by then more critical of it, condemning its extravagance, its failure to reform the central courts, and its over-reliance on coercion and martial law: he urged instead a more limited, economical and decentralized approach to government.

In fact by Michaelmas 1577 Sidney had exceeded his estimates by IR£14,000 and was almost IR£9,000 in debt, and even in defending the Pale his administration had not been notably successful. The O'More pretender to Leix, Rory Oge, who led an outlaw band supported at times by his brother-in-law, the dissident O'Byrne chief, Feagh MacHugh, and the O'Connor pretender, Connor MacCormac, had long eluded Fitzwilliam, but in 1577 he broke loose to burn Naas, Leighlinbridge and, in 1578, Carlow, before Lord Fitzpatrick cornered him. His reputation as the Robin Hood of Ireland hardly flattered Sidney, nor did the massacre of over 40 O'Mores summoned to Mullaghmast in March 1578 for military service and slaughtered by Captain Francis Cosby and the O'Dempseys by virtue of a commission of martial law. Thus by March 1578 Sidney's recall was determined and he finally departed under official disapproval in September, leaving Drury as justiciar.[71]

THE REACTION TO PROGRAMMATIC GOVERNMENT

Sidney's recall marked a clear reaction to the programmatic methods of government over the previous twenty years. Gerrard advocated instead concentration on the Pale and those areas most amenable to government, reliance on judicial circuits to extend the common law's operation ('by little and little to stretch the Pale further'), restricting a reduced garrison to peacekeeping and protection, and relying instead on local support, cultivated by persuasion and good example, to contain obstreperous chiefs. Accordingly Drury, Gerrard, and other chief ministers were given wide discretionary powers to govern by the traditional Tudor methods which programmatic governors had abandoned, priority being restored to administrative reforms that cut costs and exploited efficiently existing sources of revenue. The Palesmen's alternative scheme for composition and their victualling proposal were accepted and efforts made to restore relations with the local community.

Yet the belated abandonment of ambitious programmes which outstripped available resources was singularly ill-timed and executed. Fitzmaurice's long-threatened invasion was at last materializing with papal support, but with Drury's promotion his expected landfall was left unguarded at the critical moment and anyway the governor had only 600 troops immediately available. Given the innate loyalty of the Old English community and the traditionally localized nature of Gaelic politics, a major political crisis might still have been avoided, but that previous programmatic initiatives had antagonized all shades of political opinion in Ireland, thereby providing a focus for new forms of

71. Brady 1985, pp. 11–32; Brady 1980, pp. 230–39; Bagwell 1885–90, ii, pp. 327–52; Carey forthcoming.

nationalist resistance. Moreover abrupt changes of policy had created profound uncertainty, seriously undermining confidence in the viceroyalty and even calling in question Elizabeth's good intentions. When Fitzmaurice landed at Smerwick in July 1579, Drury's administration soon broke down: the resultant crisis saw the collapse of traditional consensus politics within the Englishry and the emergence of novel forms of opposition.[72] In the political atmosphere of Elizabeth's later years, with the regime struggling for survival against the Enterprise of England and other catholic intrigues, counsels of moderation and compromise in Ireland fell increasingly on deaf ears.

72. Brady 1985, pp. 11–32; Brady 1980, pp. 240–51; Bagwell 1885–90, iii, pp. 333, 346–8 (quotation, p. 335), ii, chs 36–7.

CHAPTER 12

PACATA HIBERNIA, 1579–1603

THE PROSPECTS FOR FOREIGN INTERVENTION

By 1579, with leading magnates antagonized or totally alienated and traditional supporters exasperated and bewildered by the recent conduct of government, the Dublin administration was sitting on a powder keg. Yet, as recent campaigning had again confirmed, Gaelic levies were no match for English armies, and there was therefore small prospect of successful rebellion without foreign support. Substantial foreign assistance for Irish dissidents effectively depended on the attitude of the major continental powers, France and Spain. Intrigues by Mary Queen of Scots with Shane O'Neill were certainly worrying to the government, but Scotland alone lacked the resources to mount a serious challenge. Moreover, although successive governors found Ulster the least anglicized and accessible province, it was also a comparatively remote landfall for continental powers. Anyway, European politics during the 1560s were generally discouraging to Irish dissidents. Ireland was always a peripheral concern to European princes, and the potential benefits of intriguing there had to be weighed against the possibility of English reprisals elsewhere. During the period of intermittent Anglo-French hostilities, 1549–59, French intervention in Ireland had seemed a distinct possibility, but thereafter peace and the onset of the French Wars of Religion had eliminated the threat from that quarter. O'Neill, Fitzgibbon and Fitzmaurice all in turn requested French assistance, but the French were no longer in a position to provide it.

Ostensibly more hopeful for rebels was the attitude of England's erstwhile ally, Spain, under Philip II. Spanish influence in Europe had strengthened with France's eclipse and Philip saw himself as defender of catholic Europe against the twin threats from Islam and Protestantism. Thus, it was chiefly on religious grounds that Irish dissidents appealed to Philip in 1559 and 1569 to nominate a new king of Ireland to replace the heretic Elizabeth, even though political unrest was far more serious in early Elizabethan Ireland. Yet Philip had serious preoccupations elsewhere, notably in the Mediterranean, where he was attempting to break Turkish naval power, and in the Netherlands, where his inept handling of local nobles and towns had created a situation not unlike that in English Ireland. Despite his detestation of heresy, therefore, he was

311

anxious for good relations with England and managed, until 1570, to dissuade successive popes from excommunicating Elizabeth.

Even after Anglo-Spanish relations deteriorated following English attacks on Spanish shipping and Alba's arrival with an army to crush the Dutch revolt, Philip feared that vigorous reprisals would simply promote Anglo-French friendship and greater support for Dutch rebels. Yet, despairing of Spanish assistance, a more militant pope, Gregory XIII (1572–85), was by 1577 prepared to use his own limited resources to back an expedition to Ireland by the most experienced (though least reliable) of Ireland's would-be liberators, Thomas Stukeley. Stukeley recruited 1,000 Italian swordsmen, but after reaching Lisbon he was persuaded by King Sebastian of Portugal to support an expedition to Morocco where he fell in battle. Fitzmaurice secured the remnants of his force and, with Philip's connivance, set sail from Spain with some 60 Italian and Spanish troops plus Dr Nicholas Sander, the eminent English clerical exile.[1]

THE ORIGINS OF THE DESMOND REBELLION

Fitzmaurice's band landed at Smerwick (17 July 1579) where they constructed a fort, while Sander composed letters and proclamations calling on the princes and people of Ireland to rally to the papal banner against Elizabeth, 'a she-tyrant who has deservedly lost her royal power by refusing to listen to Christ in the person of his vicar'. The initial response was discouraging: in particular, Desmond immediately summoned his kinsmen and informed Lord Justice Drury of his intention to crush the invaders. Drury's response was as vigorous as circumstances permitted: he commissioned Sir Humphrey Gilbert to attack Fitzmaurice, despatched Sir Henry Davells to advise Desmond, and mustered the Palesmen so as to release garrison troops for a field army. Malby with the Connaught garrison awaited Drury's arrival at Limerick; but while attempting to pass into Connaught, Fitzmaurice was killed in a skirmish with the Burkes of Castleconnell.

Nevertheless, the delay in fielding an army against Fitzmaurice, coupled with the fragility of royal control in Munster, eventually drove Desmond into revolt. Unassisted, the earl dared not trust his retainers against Fitzmaurice, while former friends deserted him and rivals secretly encouraged the rebels. In August Desmond's problems were greatly increased when Sir John Fitzgerald assassinated Davells and assumed leadership of the revolt, probably hoping thereby to commit the earl. By late September, Desmond's able brother had 2,000 choice troops under him, and the ailing Drury, with only 500 men and Kildare, prudently halted at Cork and patrolled east Munster. He encouraged Desmond to crush the revolt in his own way, while awaiting reinforcements from England – initially 2,500 men, plus five frigates to cruise off Munster – which were twice ordered, countermanded, and reordered, as reports arrived of Fitzmaurice's progress. Yet as reinforcements dribbled in, Drury was carried away to die at Waterford.

1. Silke 1966, pp. 3–14; Falls 1950, pp. 123–6; Bagwell 1885–90, iii, pp. 1–13.

Malby, appointed temporary governor of Munster, began a vigorous Perrot-style campaign: with 1,000 men he defeated the main rebel army, which uncharacteristically offered battle, at Monasternenagh (3 October), but his campaigning also made it impossible for Desmond to restrain his tenants. The irresolute earl's behaviour became increasingly erratic. Eventually, on Malby's advice he was proclaimed a traitor (2 November) by Sir William Pelham, a recently arrived expert in fortifications who was hastily elected justiciar in the emergency. By sacking Youghal in mid-November, Desmond seemingly burned his boats.[2]

Recalling earlier occasions when abrasive conduct by unsympathetic officials had driven magnates to revolt, Elizabeth was sceptical of tendentious indictments drawn up to convince her that Desmond had never reconciled himself to ecclesiastical or political reform and had conspired with Fitzmaurice from the first. Shrewdly but tardily, she appointed Ormond general of Munster. Yet Ormand was too late to prevent Desmond's proclamation, for which Malby was disgraced and Pelham reprimanded. He was forced to take the field in December without the troops necessary to back his diplomacy by force. Nominally he disposed 950 men ('sickly, unapparelled, and almost utterly unvictualled'), but lacking ordnance and supplies he could do little. Meanwhile, in letters to France and Spain Sander preached a crusade and extolled rebel successes, spreading rumours in Ireland of a great fleet coming from Spain and Italy; but news of these 'false libels' did at least help to convince Elizabeth of the need for adequate supplies and reinforcements. By February the garrison numbered 2,800: Lord Justice Pelham brought up more troops to Limerick and, operating independently of Ormond, systematically burned Desmond's estates there, butchered the inhabitants ('blind and feeble men, women, boys, and girls, sick persons, idiots, and old people', as a Gaelic annalist observed), took and garrisoned the earl's castles on the Shannon with naval support, and gradually forced Desmond back into Kerry. By summer the revolt seemed almost over: amid Desmond's overtures for peace and in a starving countryside, rebel support ebbed away, as chiefs and lords came in upon offer of a pardon. Only Geraldines and Barries held out, blockaded by a fleet under Admiral Sir William Winter.[3]

THE BALTINGLASS REVOLT AND THE MASSACRE AT SMERWICK

Then, quite unexpectedly, a new rebellion broke out in Leinster. James Eustace, third Viscount Baltinglass, had earlier contacted the rebels, and in late July joined the disaffected O'Byrne chief, Feagh MacHugh, to attack the oppressive

2. Bagwell 1885–90, iii, pp. 13–35 (quotation, p. 16); Brady 1980–1, pp. 309–12; Silke 1966, pp. 13–14; Falls 1950, pp. 126–32.
3. Bagwell 1885–90, iii, pp. 32–58 (quotations, pp. 32, 36); Brady 1980–1, pp. 311–12; Falls 1950, pp. 130–5; MacCurtain 1975, pp. 38–9.

New English seneschal of Wicklow. An enthusiastic young catholic, recently returned from Rome, Baltinglass displayed the papal banner, invited Kildare's support, and bluntly informed Ormond that 'a woman uncapax of all holy orders' could not be supreme governor of the church and that Ireland under Elizabeth had witnessed 'more oppressing of poor subjects under pretence of justice' than ever before.

The administration had been expecting trouble in Ulster, where disorders increased and Turlough Luineach hired Gaelic reinforcements from Scotland, or in Connaught, where Malby easily crushed an attempted rising. Baltinglass, however, was an important Tudor noble, his family traditional enemies of the O'Byrnes: his grandfather had received extensive grants of monastic land, a barony and a viscountcy for loyalty and service under Henry VIII.[4] He was soon joined by Sander and Fitzgerald, who evaded the government's net and reached Wicklow with O'More help. O'Neill, O'Donnell, O'Rourke and O'Connor Sligo were reportedly also sworn to Baltinglass, but provided no direct assistance.

In fact the revolt was a fiasco, almost confined to Gaelic clansmen, with the Pale unsympathetic. It quickly collapsed, and its only notable event was MacHugh's defeat of Arthur, Baron Grey de Wilton, in rocky, thickly wooded Glenmalure (25 August). Against Grey's appointment as deputy in July, 2,100 reinforcements had been prepared – the largest levy for Ireland since 1534 – but on arrival Grey could not take office until Lord Justice Pelham in Munster surrendered the sword of state. Nevertheless, distrusting Kildare who was defending the Pale's southern marches but whose best captain had deserted to the rebels, Grey decided to attack them immediately. Against expert advice, he entered Glenmalure where his raw recruits, readily distinguishable in red and blue coats, were soon picked off. The losses were not heavy, but the defeat encouraged renewed trouble in Ulster, where Turlough Luineach reasserted O'Neill claims to overlordship and attacked loyalist chiefs; O'Rourke rose, as did Clanrickard's sons in Connaught; while in Leinster Fitzgerald, the O'Mores and O'Connors besieged Maryborough. Munster alone remained subdued, but then Winter's fleet departed to refit, notwithstanding an expected invasion: a week later (10 September) one of Stukeley's captains, Bastiano di San Giuseppi, arrived with 600 Italian and Spanish troops raised on his own initiative and reoccupied Fitzmaurice's fort at Smerwick. With further reinforcements, Grey had 6,437 men by mid-October, and he easily contained the invaders in the Dingle peninsula, awaiting Winter's return with artillery to assault the fort. Following this, Smerwick surrendered in the expectation of mercy (10 November), but Grey, a stern Puritan, massacred the entire garrison.[5]

Militarily, Grey's administration – properly supplied for once – had little difficulty in controlling the situation, and rebellion wilted with news of

4. Bradshaw 1974, pp. 76, 111, 190, 193, 203.
5. Bagwell 1885–90, iii, pp. 51–79 (quotations, pp. 51–2); Walshe 1990, pp. 26–52; Lennon 1994, pp. 202–5; Brady 1985, pp. 26–8; Falls 1950, pp. 61–2, 135–8, 142–5; Silke 1966, p. 14; Bradshaw 1978b, pp. 65–80; Bradshaw 1978a, p. 484. The latest study of the Baltinglass revolt is O'Connor 1989.

Smerwick. Politically, however, the consequences for crown–community relations were disastrous. To the vast majority of the Palesmen rebellion was anathema, and throughout the Englishry Fitzmaurice's views had won little support. Yet the Pale composition scheme had serious implications for individual marcher captains: even ministers admitted that 'cess and the oppression of the soldier' were the 'chief original' of unrest in the Pale during 1580–1. Equally, a holy war was attractive for different reasons to a tiny group of young scholars influenced by the Counter-Reformation (see above, pp. 238–42). When, exceptionally, the two influences combined, the result was explosive. Thus Baltinglass drew support from a motley group including marcher gentry, fervently catholic Pale lawyers involved in the earlier cess controversy, and the expropriated Gaelic O'Connor and O'More clans, while two leading Dublin merchants, William FitzSimon and Alderman Walter Sedgrave, supplied the viscount with weapons and powder. Their response prefigured the emergence of a militant nationalist tradition and betrayed a growing impatience within the Englishry at the conduct of Tudor government. Ironically, however, the administration's overreaction to the hazy plotting of hot-headed idealists triggered the very reaction that Elizabeth's mediation had aimed to avoid.[6]

THE NUGENT CONSPIRACY

Both Delvin and Kildare had been deeply implicated in Baltinglass's original plans, though reluctant to engage in outright rebellion. Delvin's brother, William Nugent, was less clearly implicated, but also suspected by the government. Thus when, in December, Delvin and Kildare were arrested in council, Nugent, forewarned, eluded the sheriff's posse and gathered a company, hoping to secure his brother's release. Ex-courtier and Oxford graduate, who composed English sonnets and Gaelic poems in the then novel exile genre, Nugent was apparently less aggrieved about religious change than about the growing New English hold on administrative offices in Dublin, to which younger sons of Pale landowners had traditionally aspired. Yet other young gentlemen participated in the ensuing conspiracy for 'the cause of religion', notably its key figure, John Cusack of Ellistonrede. The eventual plan was for a combined revolt spearheaded by minor Pale gentry and a Gaelic inroad by Turlough Luineach, O'Rourke and O'Reilly in late summer to release Delvin and Kildare.

By contrast with Grey's conduct in Munster, the administration's initial response to these disturbances about the Pale was surprisingly moderate. Nine gentlemen suffered eventually for their part in the Baltinglass revolt, plus others of 'mean calling' 'executed by martial law'. By November a further 25 gentlemen had been arrested, as the government gradually unravelled the threads of the Nugent conspiracy; and the seven executed mostly died unrepentantly, asserting that they were catholic martyrs. In January 1582, however,

6. O'Connor 1989; Lennon 1994, pp. 202–5; Lennon 1989, pp. 118–19; Mathew 1933, ch. 10; Murphy 1948–52, pp. 8–15; Brady 1985, pp. 26–8; Bradshaw 1979a, pp. 285–8.

John Cusack's arrest and decision to turn queen's evidence in return for a pardon apparently disclosed over twenty more conspirators, including important men like Chief Justice Nicholas Nugent and Lord Dunsany.

These purported revelations convinced Grey, quite wrongly, of a widespread catholic conspiracy in the Pale. A fresh wave of arrests and trials followed against the sons of leading gentry and lawyers, while lesser men were summarily executed. Concurrently, old scores were settled: leading commonwealth men, including Scurlock and Netterville, lost relatives, and the trial and execution of Chief Justice Nugent was an utter travesty of justice. Yet Grey's practice of redistributing the confiscated goods and even lands of Nugents, Cusacks and Eustaces among his officers disappointed the hopes of established officials like Wallop who complained to London; and in April the privy council halted the executions and, alongside a reduction in the army, ordered a general pardon. Altogether, seventeen gentry had been executed; others, notably William Nugent, among the sixteen excluded from the pardon, escaped; and at least 45 gentlemen paid fines for their pardons. Yet Grey remained convinced that severity alone would achieve results in Ireland. Moreover, following the Palesmen's cess agitation, this discovery of a seemingly general catholic conspiracy in which Gaelic and Old English lords had united provided New English officials with an excellent opportunity to discredit the entire Old English political community. They urged the abandonment of the privileged treatment hitherto granted the Old English: the queen should 'use a sharp and a severe course without respect of any man's greatness', reproving the 'arrogant zeal to popish government' of local politicians, relying solely on English officers and soldiers, and not 'leave the Irish to tumble to their own sensual government'.[7]

In particular Ormond's conduct as general of Munster was bitterly attacked: allegedly he was too closely connected with other local magnates, was reluctant to prosecute the rebels, and hindered Grey's grants of traitors' lands to deserving servitors like Captain Walter Raleigh, the executioner at Smerwick. Eventually Elizabeth revoked Ormond's commission (May 1581), though chiefly to save money: she appointed no English president and tempered Ormond's dismissal with a proclamation offering a general pardon. Thus the previous *pis aller* was substantially preserved: Grey largely thwarted the intended amnesty by excepting several other individuals from its terms besides the three (Desmond, Fitzgerald, and Baltinglass) named by Elizabeth. In consequence it had little effect beyond the Pale where many gentry sued pardons as insurance against Grey's continuing witch-hunt.

Following Ormond's dismissal and with Grey's encouragement the army was given its head, and in five counties whatever had hitherto escaped the ruthless exaction of cess, the soldiers' extortions and the rebels' raids was systematically destroyed in a bid to starve the rebels into submission. The policy was less effective than Grey had anticipated, partly because Elizabeth reduced the

7. Walshe 1990, pp. 26–52; Bagwell 1885–90, iii, pp. 82, 88, 89 (quotations); Brady 1985, pp. 26–8; Canny 1983, pp. 11–14; Mathew 1933, ch. 10.

army prematurely: between summer 1581 and spring 1582 4,600 troops were discharged. Rather, the Munster peasantry was decimated in the ensuing famine and even hard-headed officials were moved to pity. Sir Warham St Leger, lately returned, reported that in Cork between 20 and 70 died daily of starvation and that Munster was ruined almost beyond recovery. Grey's secretary, the poet Edmund Spenser, wrote that from

> woods and glens [the people] came creeping forth upon their hands, for their legs could not bear them. They looked anatomies of death, they spake like ghosts crying out of their graves, they did eat of the dead carrions . . . yea and one another soon after in so much as the very carcasses they spared not to scrape out of their graves . . . In short space there were none almost left and a most populous and plentiful country suddenly left void of man or beast.[8]

Far more died of famine than by the sword, but without the manpower to hunt down the ringleaders, the army's conduct simply drove previously loyal landowners into rebellion to replace those caught. Nevertheless by 1582 revolt was again confined to Munster. In April 1581 Dr Sander had died of dysentery, Baltinglass fled to the continent in November and eventually reached Spain while Nugent, after two years in France and Rome, returned and was eventually pardoned. In Connaught Malby contained the two rebellions there, drove Scottish mercenaries back into Ulster, and arbitrated between rival claimants for the Mayo Burke chieftaincy; and in Ulster Grey patched up peace with Turlough Luineach. In January 1582 the government had a further success when Fitzgerald was accidentally encountered and killed: his head was made a new-year gift for Grey. Yet rebellion dragged on and Elizabeth, increasingly impatient at the apparently fruitless expense, recalled Grey: Archbishop Loftus, recently appointed chancellor on Gerard's death, and Sir Henry Wallop, the new undertreasurer, succeeded him as lords justices in August.

Grey's recall was unlamented: his unsparing repression disturbed even New English officials, who found him inefficient, while the local community regarded him as 'a bloody man [who] regarded not the life of [the queen's] subjects, no more than dogs'. On Grey's own admission, he executed almost 1,500 'chief men and gentlemen' by martial law during his two years as governor 'not accounting . . . killing of churls, which were innumerable'. To the dismay of New English officials, however, Elizabeth appointed Ormond as governor of Munster in December with 1,000 troops and power to pardon all rebels save Desmond himself. Adopting his usual tactics, Ormond soon weakened rebel support. Desmond had recently disposed over 2,000 men, but night raids quickly broke up rebel bands: Ormond cleared them out of Tipperary and Waterford, and in February Desmond fell back into Kerry. By late May 206 gentry had been killed, but 921 had submitted and been pardoned, including Lord Lixnaw and Desmond's countess; and when the earl's last prominent adherent, Imokilly, submitted in June, Desmond was reduced to a small

8. Bagwell 1885–90, iii, pp. 81–99, 104–5; Spenser 1970, p. 104 (quotation); MacCurtain 1975, pp. 41–2.

fugitive band, penned into west Cork and Kerry. The final act in the tragedy took place amid renewed intrigues by St Leger, Wallop and Secretary Fenton to have Ormond recalled on financial grounds; but Burghley dissuaded Elizabeth from this and Desmond, who refused unconditional surrender, was eventually hunted down and killed near Tralee (11 November 1583). His head was sent to Elizabeth and placed on London Bridge.[9]

The intrigues against Ormond reflected the almost complete polarization of loyalist political opinion in Ireland since 1579: New English officials feared that the earl would be appointed deputy and would seek to discredit them. The Pale composition had collapsed with Fitzmaurice's return, billeting was reintroduced and cess revived, and the Pale community remained sullenly hostile under Grey's unprecedentedly oppressive administration. Yet the experience fundamentally altered Old English attitudes to crown government and, ironically, this in the longer term strengthened New English influence. Hitherto the Old English leadership had rested with men who remembered the more optimistic political climate of St Leger's days. Yet recent events had seemingly justified the assertions of younger men that English government was necessarily hostile to the local community. Moreover, the commonwealth leadership included a disproportionate number of lawyers who were committed catholics, like Scurlock, Netterville and Burnell, and their victimization during the repression enhanced their status. The catalyst that precipitated the final fusion of separate political and religious protests was Perrot's parliament.

THE DEPUTYSHIP OF SIR JOHN PERROT

Sir John Perrot's appointment as deputy in January 1584 had long seemed likely. Reputed by stature and temperament the illegitimate son of Henry VIII, his previous experience as provincial president equipped him well for the administration's most pressing task, the settlement of Munster; and his long acquaintance and, for the present, friendly relations with Ormond might also prove useful in promoting better Old English–New English relations. Against this, however, stood his ambition, his notorious temper, and his abrasive conduct. Accompanying Perrot were the famous Norris brothers, John and Thomas, appointed president and vice-president of Munster respectively; while Malby, having 'placed all Connaught under bondage', died in March 1584 and was succeeded by Sir Richard Bingham, an experienced military and naval captain.

Perrot's return marked the initiation of another bout of programmatic government, for which he had long been campaigning. His programme included the familiar detailed estimate of costs, favourable prediction of increased revenues, and optimistic timetable for the resolution of key problems, in this case the settlement of Ulster. The general thrust of these plans included a renewed campaign of surrender and regrant, and also a revival of Sidney's composition

9. Bagwell 1885–90, iii, pp. 91–115; Falls 1950, pp. 146–52; Sheehan 1983b, pp. 106–10; Edwards 1997, p. 20 (quotation); Spenser 1970, p. 106 (quotation).

scheme, for which he hoped to equalize the burden of composition by establishing a uniform unit of assessment throughout Ireland. The threat of catholic conspiracy would also be curbed by a general campaign for religious conformity. His initial priorities, however, were the settlement of Munster and the holding of parliament, by which he hoped also to cultivate local support and endorsement of his programme.

In the event, Perrot's plans were crippled almost from the outset by the looming confrontation with Spain. By late 1584, the government was increasingly preoccupied with the Dutch crisis and the growing likelihood of an English expedition to the Netherlands, which materialized in 1585. And for the rest of her reign, Elizabeth was at war with Europe's most powerful, and militantly catholic, monarchy. The cost and conduct of the war gradually threw the government into crisis: English money and men were increasingly committed in the Netherlands, and then also in France, until by the mid-1590s, when the outbreak of the Nine Years War in Ireland coincided with four years of dearth and famine at home, the very survival of the regime was at stake. Moreover, whereas in her first two decades Elizabeth's personality – her innate conservatism and indecisiveness, combined with a fierce determination to hold the strings of policy – had frequently worked in her favour; during the war years, when commanders needed to make spot decisions, Elizabeth's conduct of Irish affairs was much less fortunate. In any event, the queen and council now had little time for enterprises in Ireland, and the instructions to Perrot and his successors were above all to economize and keep Ireland quiet.[10]

The deputy's installation speech, in which he stated that Elizabeth regarded equally her subjects of Ireland and of England, was conciliatory, and among Gaelic chiefs and the commonalty Perrot soon acquired a reputation for fair dealing. His overbearing and occasionally violent conduct in council, however, alienated key New English officials, notably Undertreasurer Wallop, Secretary Fenton, and Chancellor Loftus who resolutely opposed his plans to dissolve St Patrick's to endow a university. He thus became increasingly reliant on locally born officials, while support in the privy council for his programme also gradually dissolved.

Initially, Perrot had intended 'for a time to look through my fingers at Ulster', until Munster and Connaught had been settled. Yet almost immediately the arrival of large numbers of redshanks in Lough Foyle attracted his attention and he was gradually drawn into a campaign to expel the 'Scots' and settle Ulster. Failing to catch the redshanks, he launched an unprovoked attack on Sorley Boy MacDonald, and then imposed a 'composition' on the Ulster chiefs whereby they would supply victuals worth £13,000 to maintain 1,100 English soldiers there and so keep out the 'Scots'. Underpinning this device, Perrot had intended constructing seven forts and towns, with a garrison of 2,400; but

---

10. There are important reappraisals of aspects of Perrot's viceroyalty in Morgan 1993b, ch. 3; Brady 1994a, pp. 291–300; Treadwell 1985, pp. 259–308. See also Brady 1985, pp. 28–30; Bagwell 1885–90, iii, pp. 105–6, 116, 122–3, 128–9, 136–7, 146; *NHI*, iii, p. 112. On the wider Tudor context of the war years, see now MacCaffrey 1992.

Elizabeth vetoed this. Accordingly, the soldiers were left under the command of the local chiefs and expected to collect their own allowances. Concurrently, most of Ulster was divided up into three lieutenancies – Antrim and Down under Sir Nicholas Bagenal; the future Tyrone, Fermanagh and Coleraine under Turlough Luineach; and what became Armagh and Monaghan under the baron of Dungannon. These lieutenancies, however, co-existed uneasily with traditional Gaelic claims to overlordship; and the following year the five territories, plus Donegal, were named shires. Finally, Perrot promoted surrender and regrant on a general basis, gradually negotiating settlements with all the major lords of Ulster, the north midlands, and Connaught who had remained unaffected by the policy, excepting O'Donnell, O'Cahan and O'Rourke.

In practice, however, most of the new arrangements proved insubstantial. Within a year, harvest failure had caused the number of composition troops to be halved; individual lords then began to eject their companies; and finally the companies were transferred to the Netherlands in return for annual rents promised by the chiefs. These rents remained unpaid, however, as also did most of the £3,000 rental negotiated through surrender and regrant arrangements. And the new shires lacked sheriffs or any other instruments of English common law. By summer 1585, moreover, Elizabeth had agreed the so-called treaty of Berwick and an English pension for James VI, and Perrot was instructed to reach 'some reasonable composition with Angus MacDonald, Sorley and the rest of the principal persons of that province': in 1586 Angus and Sorley were finally denizened and granted parts of the Route and the Glens of Antrim respectively.

Equally humiliating for Perrot was the creation of Dungannon as earl of Tyrone with the same rights as his grandfather. Dungannon had been styled earl in 1585, but both Perrot and Bagenal, for different reasons, had hoped to divide up Tyrone. In the event, given Dungannon's clear title by English law, and the risk of antagonizing him when fear of a Spanish invasion was increasing, the privy council agreed to his demands, leaving Turlough Luineach with the captaincy of Tyrone for life.[11]

Ironically, however, it was Old English opposition in parliament that finally destroyed the deputy's programme. Perrot's parliament ran a similar course to Sidney's, but the deadlock was even more complete. Reflecting the continued expansion of English influence, the extension of the parliamentary franchise provided an obvious opportunity to strengthen government support. Compared with 1560, 36 boroughs and cities were represented instead of 29, and 27 counties instead of 20: in particular Connaught now comprised four counties, and the O'Reilly, O'Farrell and O'Byrne lordships were shired as Cavan, Longford and Wicklow. Yet in 1585 the polarization of political opinion precluded the return of New English officials for borough seats, so confining New English influence practically to some seventeen knights returned mainly for shires where adventurers had secured land. Eight Gaelic knights and six burgesses were also returned, but the Old English majority in the Commons

11. Morgan 1993b, ch. 3; Treadwell 1985, pp. 268–9, 291.

was still overwhelming. In the Lords, sixteen bishops attended and 23 peers participated, if only by proxy. They were predominantly Old English; but besides the five Gaelic peers, Perrot summoned the other substantial chiefs to attend as observers – dressed in English clothes, 'which they embraced like fetters'.[12]

Parliament opened on 26 April 1585 amid wild rumours about extortionate rates of composition and following rigorous action by Perrot against Pale recusants. Despite opposition, the government's nominee, Nicholas Walsh, chief justice of Munster, was elected speaker; but the conventional Poynings' Law suspension bill fell victim to a well-prepared campaign led by the 'countrymen', Netterville and Burnell, who argued that Perrot wished to suppress both their ancient constitutional liberties and freedom of conscience. After much manipulation, the bill passed the Lords by one vote, but failed by 35 votes in the Commons. Disgusted, Perrot then prorogued parliament briefly to allow the bill's reintroduction, but neither intimidation, arrest nor compromise had much effect, and the session ended on 25 May. Only two bills had passed, notably the Baltinglass attainder, but the composition bill failed, as did another extending to Ireland the English parliament's harsher anti-catholic legislation. The deputy urged firmness to break the opposition, but Elizabeth had no wish for renewed trouble in Ireland at this juncture, and representations from the Pale procured a directive to abandon the composition and anti-catholic bills and not to press the supremacy oath.

When parliament eventually reconvened for three weeks in April–May 1586, the outcome was very similar. Of sixteen bills transmitted, five were defeated, two substantially amended and one withdrawn: the remainder were innocuous commonwealth measures. In 1585, substantial amendments to the Desmond attainder had prompted its withdrawal, but as passed in 1586 the attainder certainly exceeded earlier attainders in ferocity, though, oddly, it now comprised separate acts. The first attainted the earl and 37 gentry supporters in the five south-western counties, many without trial by common or martial law: the second, against a further 102 gentlemen of the same shires, was similarly framed but also included all their unidentified associates.[13] Otherwise, the renewal of Sidney's wines impost constituted Perrot's only success.

Not surprisingly, after this fiasco no parliament was held in Ireland for 27 years. The decisive defeat of an ambitious and autocratic governor restored the Palesmen's confidence in conservative constitutional opposition vis-à-vis Baltinglass's desperate methods: but, ironically, Perrot's twin attack on recusancy and constitutional liberty also helped to identify catholicism as an important item in the country cause. As Archbishop Loftus later observed: despite an earlier

12. There is now a detailed modern account of Perrot's parliament: Treadwell 1985, pp. 259–308. See also Moody 1939–40, pp. 44–5; Hardiman 1843, app. ii–iii; Bagwell 1885–90, iii, pp. 123–7, 131–5, 140–2, 157–61; NHI, iii, p. 112 (quotation); Mathew 1933, ch. 11.
13. Treadwell 1985, pp. 259–308; Moody 1939–40, pp. 47–8; Brady 1985, pp. 27–30; Stat. Ire, i, pp. 391–430; Bagwell 1885–90, iii, pp. 142–5 (quotation, p. 143), 149–50; Ellis 1983a, pp. 56–7.

general disposition to popery ... this general recusancy ... began in the second year of Sir John Perrot's government in the beginning of the parliament holden by him, before which time ... there were not in the Pale the number of twelve recusants, gentlemen of account.[14]

Thus the crisis of 1579–86 saw the final emergence of a distinct Old English community centring on the Pale, overwhelmingly and tenaciously catholic, but loyal, eschewing dealings with Gaelic rebels, and asserting its primacy in defending English civility in Ireland and its unique ability to secure a peaceful reformation of the Irishry. Notwithstanding his religious conformity, Speaker Walsh's closing speech in parliament neatly epitomized this Old English outlook. The machinery of government, he argued, rested on constitutional principles which, if respected, provided against despotism. Constitutional government should seek, chiefly, not to destroy its enemies but to preserve the subject: and since the basis of privilege was the subject's constitutional status, this precluded discrimination between subject and subject. Moreover, Ireland was politically autonomous, Her Majesty 'head of this body politic and in that respect allied to all': her governor, therefore, should 'accept in the same sort of us, without any differences or distinctions of persons'. The speech was both a reproach to Perrot's methods and a refutation of the constitutional theories of New English lawyers like John Hooker who saw Ireland as a dependency and sought to undermine Old English influence by appealing to the royal prerogative.[15]

The Composition of Connaught

Meanwhile, the failure of the composition bill had left Perrot with pressing financial commitments. His demands for cess, however, provoked widespread resistance in the Pale and he was forced to compound for a mere IR£1,500 in lieu of all cesses there, a particular composition which was renewed for two years without prejudice after parliament's dissolution. Concurrently, Perrot pressed ahead with composition in Connaught; where his arrangements built on more substantial foundations than was the case in Ulster. The Composition of Connaught, an improved version of the 1577 composition which had collapsed on Malby's death, constituted the major success of Perrot's viceroyalty. Sidney's more limited composition had ignored the earl of Clanrickard, imprisoned 1576–82, compounding instead with lesser landowners. By transferring the military obligations of lordship from earl to president, however, it had attempted to undermine the earl's traditional authority over lesser lords, a characteristic of Sidney's policies. The political circumstances in which the 1585 commission for composition issued were, however, very different. Disliking Bingham personally, and having quarrelled with Loftus and Wallop, Perrot was unusually dependent on local councillors. Reversing his stance of the 1570s, he sided for once against the New English officials on the reform

14. PRO, SP 63/94/37. I am grateful to Dr Ciarán Brady for this quotation. See now Brady 1985, p. 11.
15. Bradshaw 1973, pp. 85–6 (quotations, p. 85); Brady 1985; Canny 1979b, pp. 429–31.

question. Moreover, the western earldoms were in different hands: the court-educated, protestant, fourth earl of Thomond had succeeded his father in 1581. Clanrickard died shortly after his release in 1582, and in a settlement between his sons, the eastern barony of Leitrim was granted to the younger absolutely, while the elder became third earl. Accordingly the Old English reformers, Nicholas White and Thomas Dillon, chief justice of Connaught, overruled Bingham's objections to negotiate a moderate agreement for anglicization which safeguarded the earls' traditional influence.[16]

The 1585 composition comprised a series of individual indentures, usually divided into five sections, between the deputy and the landowners in the various Connaught lordships – Clanrickard, Thomond, Hymany (O'Kelly), and so on. In the Thomond indenture, for instance, the first section surveyed the lordship, barony by barony, measuring the land in 'quarters' of *c.* 120 acres besides bog and woodland. The second agreed an annual rent of 10*s.* (IR) per quarter of inhabited land payable to the president instead of all arbitrary exactions and customary garrison charges. The third abolished all Gaelic captainries, jurisdictions, elections and customary divisions of land, and instead compensated the magnates with 'freedoms' for certain of their lands from composition rent and by imposing an additional annual rent on the lands of freeholders, payable to the chief lord in lieu of chiefry rights: in Thomond this rent was a uniform 5*s.* (IR) per quarter, in Clanrickard it ranged from 3*s.* to 13*s.* 4*d.* a quarter, reflecting no doubt the relative strength of the earl's authority in different baronies. In politically fragmented Mayo, the picture was still more complicated. Additionally, important vassal-chiefs – in Thomond, the two MacNamaras and MacMahons, and O'Loughlin – received their own 'freedoms'. Some also received the additional rents: in Thomond, Lord Inchiquin and Sir Turlough O'Brien of Corcomroe, collaterals, had secured these rents within their own baronies, following earlier grants of independent lordship, the price of their acceptance of primogeniture in surrender and regrant. In Clanrickard, Leitrim barony, following the 1582 settlement, and two more areas were similarly autonomous. The remaining sections were apparently later additions of further autonomies and 'freedoms', such as those for the Thomond bishops of Killaloe and Kilfenora, or of special provisions for favoured individuals.[17]

The annual composition rent alone was calculated at IR£3,645 in 1586, and since this was applied directly to cover the council's administrative costs of IR£3,167, Bingham enjoyed a large measure of financial autonomy. Connaught actually paid for itself for most of Bingham's presidency (1584–96) until north Connaught became involved in Tyrone's rebellion in 1593. From the earls' viewpoint, too, the 1585 composition consolidated their local influence, since their own rents (a novelty in 1585) apparently reflected fairly the extent of their real power under the Gaelic system, and their 'freedoms' were, as Bingham complained, distinctly generous: small wonder that the earls soon supported composition enthusiastically. Moreover, in a severely underpopulated region,

16. Cunningham 1979, pp. 64–107, 132–5; Brady 1985.
17. Cunningham 1979, pp. 64–106, 110–12.

the typically mobile Gaelic peasantry 'doth choose rather to dwell upon the great freedom': the 'freedoms' therefore assured the lords an adequate supply of tenants and so benefited them at the crown's expense, because uninhabited lands did not bear rent. Indeed, with the farming of the crown's rent, always difficult to collect, in the 1590s, responsibility for the Composition devolved increasingly on the earls, who were now assured of maintaining their local influence in an English Ireland. The crown rent totalled far more than under Sidney's composition, but this caused little friction because it was achieved by extending its incidence, chiefly in north Connaught, not by increasing the rent per quarter. In north Connaught, however, the anglicizing aspect of composition was less effective: crown rent was paid, but chiefly as a guarantee against cess, and disputes over the MacWilliamship and other Gaelic titles continued.

Contrary to the conventional interpretation, however, it has recently been shown that the Composition did not settle Connaught land titles. Of course the problem of Gaelic landholding, addressed by surrender and regrant, was closely intertwined with that of Gaelic lordship, which composition addressed; but since no plantation threatened, Connaught landowners were generally unconcerned about common-law tenures. Defective land titles, which Lord Deputy Wentworth exploited in his abortive plantation of the 1630, was not an issue in late Elizabethan Connaught. Nevertheless, the Composition by no means excluded outsiders, and already by 1585 at least 24 New English or Palesmen had purchased land in Connaught. This process, whereby substantial outsiders, especially officials, speculated privately, was encouraged chiefly by the English administrative presence, although the council's increased stability following Composition accelerated the process. Private colonization caused little local resentment in an underpopulated and undeveloped region, though it was more prevalent in areas of weak lordship like east Galway, Roscommon and, later, Mayo. On the other hand the activities of mean men, 'hungry fellows' bent on making their fortune by swindling local lords through grants of concealments (see below, p. 333), provoked fierce resentment.[18]

Notwithstanding the Composition, President Bingham ruled Connaught with an iron rod. His attempts to establish his authority throughout north Connaught cut across a complicated succession dispute over the now proscribed MacWilliamship and were resisted. Yet even in Galway 70 were executed at the sessions, and when the Mayo Burkes refused to attend, Bingham proceeded against them by martial law. Perrot peremptorily ordered conciliation, but rebellion flared and Bingham again took the field. He had all but crushed the revolt when 2,000 redshanks intervened: with 600 men, including 300 reinforcements from Munster, Bingham cornered and massacred the Scots at Ardnaree (22 September 1586), 'the only piece of service, next to Smerwick, that hath been done in this land in many years'.

Perrot objected to Bingham's proceedings, and against the council's advice arrived to conduct a fruitless inquiry in Galway. A protracted dispute followed, temporarily eased in 1587 when Bingham was encouraged to serve in Holland

18. Ibid., pp. 30–4, 83 (quotation), 88–105, 169–209.

and an Old English official deputized. Throughout, however, Bingham's presidency was characterized by general disregard for constitutional forms and ruthless severity – too harsh even for some New English officials – but a secure base in south Connaught, following the earls' support for Composition, enabled Bingham to crush later revolts in Mayo in 1588–9 and in Leitrim in 1589–90 and so dominate the whole province until 1593. Clanrickard and Thomond remained loyal during Tyrone's rebellion and, paradoxically, ensured that seventeenth-century Connaught became a bastion of Old English influence, while Munster, hitherto the more anglicized province, was partly recolonized following revolts in 1579–83 and 1598–1602.[19]

The Munster plantation: theory and planning

The impending Munster settlement was a central issue in the continuing New English–Old English rivalry that dominated Perrot's deputyship. With the polarization of loyalist political opinion, New English influence was dangerously dependent on its court connections and the vagaries of faction there; but an extensive Munster plantation would secure them a strong landed base to challenge Old English power. Not surprisingly, therefore, attempts to discredit Old English politicians as disloyal papists and plotters drew a vigorous counterattack. The thrust of this was that no catholic conspiracy had existed, but that well-disposed local lords were being goaded into rebellion by harsh, ill-advised and frequently illegal actions of self-seeking English servitors. Investigations also produced some evidence to substantiate this case. Lord Grey was of course an obvious target, but Old English politicians also pressed for an official inquiry into Bingham's conduct. Quite apart from the excesses of particular adventurers, the argument was particularly well directed because of Elizabeth's innate conservatism. Already in 1581 Sir Nicholas White was reminding Burghley that 'innovations hath been in all ages accounted dangerous, and the busiest men that way be not the profitablest ministers': he urged the merits of 'temperate and peaceable government' against 'the rooting out of ancient nobility' by 'violent and warlike government'.

Undeniably, the reduction of Old English lords and gentry by military conquest and colonization ran clean contrary to accepted ideas of Tudor government: in court circles reform meant conservative measures aimed at preserving the exiting order of society, not social revolution by a disreputable band of rash, needy soldiers. Thrown back on to the defensive, New English spokesmen like William Herbert and Edmund Spenser argued that the moral imperatives of the particular situation necessitated innovation (see also above, pp. 184–9, and below, pp. 330–3). Contemptuous dismissal of Gaelic people as 'heathen or rather savage and brute beasts' was a commonplace in official circles but, in order to justify the extension of conquest and colonization to the Englishry, New English officials now attempted to detract from their Englishness.

19. Bagwell 1885–90, iii, pp. 151–9, 166–7, 175–95, 203–16; Cunningham 1979, pp. 31–5, 189; Bradshaw 1978a, pp. 483–4; *NHI* iii, p. 112 (quotation); Falls 1950, pp. 158–60.

Allegedly, the Old English, who had once occupied mid-point on the social scale from savagery to civility, had so degenerated by contact, marriage and fosterage with Gaelic society that Ireland's 'chiefest abuses' 'are grown from the English, and the English that were are now much more lawless and licentious than the very wild Irish'. Despite their civil appearance, there was never 'Irishman in authority which upon trial had proved a true subject', but only papists or time-servers, given to 'any kind of treason or mischief' and nourishing a 'burning hatred and malice against all the English nation'. In part, the contrast between Spenser's pessimistic outlook on Ireland's inhabitants and the more optimistic assumptions of Old English thinkers may reflect, as Brendan Bradshaw has argued, the Puritan mentality of the new colonizers. Yet Spenser's *View of the present state of Ireland* (1596) was above all a persuasive rationalization of the particular circumstances in which the New English now found themselves, hence its continuing popularity in planter circles.[20]

While the controversy continued, preparations proceeded for a Munster settlement. Perrot had begun by issuing a general pardon, and following Ormond's advice his instructions envisaged redistributing forfeited estates to reward loyalty and service by local landowners besides English servitors. New English officials, however, pressed for a more extensive plantation of exclusively English-born colonists under their own supervision.

In the event, the privy council assumed direct control, as with earlier Ulster ventures, and compromised by relying chiefly on English-based landowners. About a third of the eventual undertakers had previous experience of Munster, but Ormond, who had some claim to the Desmond inheritance as heir-general to Earl James, received only 3,000 acres in Tipperary and some poor land in Kerry, while other Munster lords got nothing. Elizabeth commissioned Sir Valentine Browne and other officials to prepare a rough survey of forfeited lands, but bad weather, local hostility, and interminable difficulties over title and fraudulent conveyances delayed the commissioners: assuming that widespread concealment had and would occur, they included almost everything in sight and reported in October 1585 that 574,645 acres of land, worth precisely IR£9,887 11s. 11½d., were available for settlement, scattered chiefly throughout Cos. Limerick, Kerry and Cork.

Concurrently, Burghley tried to interest substantial men in acting as chief undertakers for individual western counties from Hampshire to Chester: each would persuade county JPs to recruit sufficient volunteers from the local tenantry to plant seignories of 12,000 profitable English acres each under the county's chief undertaker. Despite the survey, the number of seignories originally envisaged varied from 43 to 62, each held in common socage at a small annual rent, but some were later split into smaller seignories of 4,000 acres or more, with allowances for mountain, bogland and other wastes. Concurrently, Burghley's inquiries had identified 86 gentlemen applicants for seignories, covering over 0.75 million acres of land. The aim was to plant each full seignory with 90 tenants and their families, plus the undertaker – six freeholders with

20. Canny 1983 (quotations, pp. 2, 8, 9, 13, 14); Bradshaw 1978a; Bradshaw 1981b, pp. 240–3.

300 acres each, six farmers (400 acres), 42 copyholders (100 acres) and 36 cottagers (10, 25 or 50 acres).

Thus the government aimed initially to introduce c. 8,400 settlers into Munster, a formidable undertaking by comparison with the 108 persons landed in 1585 on Roanoke Island, the first English settlement in North America. The allotment of particular estates to chief and lesser undertakers was based on the Browne survey, and in December 1585 the conditions of settlement were substantially determined. Yet the detailed measuring and division of estates did not begin until September 1586 and only c. 63,000 acres had been properly plotted when the undertakers, impatient at the delays, secured Elizabeth's approval of a more expeditious plan whereby each would itemize the lands he claimed, agree them with neighbouring undertakers, and secure a royal grant on this basis.

On paper, therefore, the plantation appeared well organized, with a total initial investment of c. £60,000, almost every contingency provided for, the numbers and categories of tenants specified and even the undertaker's exact costs itemized. When the undertakers attempted to translate intention into effect, however, they ran into serious difficulties. Obtaining the necessary permits to export household goods, building materials, livestock, grain, money and people caused many delays, particularly with the Spanish Armada threatening, but those planters who reached Munster then had great difficulty even in locating and establishing title to their estates. The underlying problem was the Browne survey which included as forfeit not only freehold lands, but also lands unlawfully detained or 'chargeable lands' on which Desmond claimed Gaelic exactions, while the valuations consisted principally of customary dues, services and exactions rather than rent charges. The commissioners had bought time by promising a further hearing later and full allowance of good titles; but when in 1586 new inquisitions had to be taken, Old English juries proved much less cooperative in finding for the crown once it became apparent that the land was destined for New English outsiders. Moreover, the general pardon, with numerous verbal promises of restitution by Perrot, further complicated matters. And in 1583 rebel estates had frequently been depopulated, whereas not all tenants has starved: some estates remained waste for five years before their costly reclamation by undertakers, but elsewhere the tenantry subsequently drifted back.

Thus, despite Munster's partly English appearance, the newcomers faced a hostile population, with no-one quite certain which titles were valid and who were squatters, particularly in districts where Gaelic landholding had survived. Attempts by settlers to establish themselves in 1586 all failed, but a few succeeded in 1587, more in 1588, and by 1589 the plantation was a going concern. Eventually, there were 35 successful undertakers who received a total of 298,653 acres. They included seventeen with previous service in the Irish administration, but only thirteen English county gentlemen.[21]

---

21. The authoritative account of the Munster plantation is now MacCarthy-Morrogh 1986. Chs 1-4 cover the Tudor plantation; see also Dunlop 1888, pp. 250-69; Quinn 1966b, pp. 19-40; Sheehan 1982-3a, pp. 297-318; MacCurtain 1975, p. 43.

FITZWILLIAM'S SECOND TERM AS DEPUTY

By 1589 certain other difficulties had been resolved. Perrot had been hamstrung by local distrust of his policies, and failure in parliament frustrated hopes of any constructive alternative to plantation. Yet he found opportunity enough for delay, and many local officials proved downright obstructive. His disputes with other councillors also threatened to bring government into disrepute, particularly when he had Secretary Fenton arrested for debt and came to blows in council with old Marshal Bagenal: his health was poor, his temper worse, and Elizabeth eventually decided that his replacement by Sir William Fitzwilliam might reunite the council and speed plantation while still keeping the country quiet.

Despite Fitzwilliam's reputation for corruption, the appointment for a second term as deputy of this lacklustre, but most experienced Irish official seemed a shrewd move at this juncture, since his pragmatic, minimalist style of government promised to reduce both costs and friction with petulant provincial officials like Bingham. Yet Fitzwilliam still owed £1,778 from his previous spell as undertreasurer, following the discovery of a serious shortfall on his account in 1571; and mindful of the way in which Sidney had undermined his previous deputyship and secured a second term, he deeply resented the renewed interventions in Irish affairs by Perrot after his appointment to the privy council. Thus the two were soon at loggerheads, and Fitzwilliam's early years saw a continuation of factional strife in the Irish council. Perrot's influence only collapsed in mid-1590 after the deputy had procured a renegade priest, Sir Denis O'Roughan, to allege treasonable correspondence between Perrot and Philip II. Perrot was eventually tried and convicted of treason in 1592, but died in the Tower.

From 1590, therefore, Fitzwilliam had a much freer hand in Ireland which he used to mend his fortunes by a range of corrupt practices. Yet immediately after Fitzwilliam's arrival in June 1588 had come the Armada crisis. Even after the threat of a landing in England receded, the government feared that the fleet might regroup off Scotland and invade Ireland, where the garrison numbered only 1,761. Accordingly, most of the half-starved wretches who struggled ashore from some 25 shipwrecks around Irish coasts were simply slaughtered by the troops or executed by martial law; others were stripped by the natives; but in parts of Ulster and north Connaught they were harboured. In mid-September, Secretary Fenton reported 6,194 Spaniards 'drowned, killed or taken', certainly an underestimate: well over 6,000 may have drowned from the twelve ships that foundered off Connaught, while over 700 were executed there by George Bingham, the vice-president. Yet *c.* 3,000 were later sheltered in Ulster, of whom perhaps 500 escaped to Scotland – 'miserable, ragged creatures, utterly spoiled by the Irishry'. With the Armada defeated, however, attention returned to Munster.[22]

22. Bagwell 1885–90, iii, pp. 157–61, 166–8, 172–95; Morgan 1993b, pt. 1; Morgan 1995, pp. 109–25; Flanagan 1988, pp. 16–24; Falls 1950, pp. 162–7; Mathew 1933, ch. 11.

The Munster plantation: practice and performance

By 1588, the clamour for a full inquiry concerning land titles there was so great that Elizabeth sent over Chief Justice Anderson to head an important special commission for determining controversies. Previous commissioners sitting in 1587 had been surprised by the many suits, 'fair and very lawlike', for traversing the queen's title on the grounds that the rebels had wrongfully detained estates from their rightful owners. To preserve title, they simply refused to hear witnesses and put undertakers in possession, hoping that upon arrival the undertakers might expose perjury or fraud. In 1588, however, Anderson was instructed to admit only official court records as evidence in such cases: by this means and by the peremptory dismissal of suits based on Gaelic custom or those improperly drawn or presented, the commission managed to reject 80 of the 81 claims heard. Yet by attempting to uphold the Browne survey instead of remedying its deficiencies, the commissioners simply brought the law into disrepute. Litigation was driven elsewhere, chiefly to the privy council as director of the plantation. The result was a series of well-meaning but contradictory interventions, aimed at rectifying the more blatant injustices: lacking proper information about Irish land titles, however, the council usually relied for information on the suitors then before it, and so kept reversing its own decisions. Overall, many decisions restored native claimants: but where undertakers' titles were confirmed, squatters frequently refused to leave, could not be ejected, and were eventually accepted as tenants, so defeating the aim of the plantation.

Nevertheless privy council decisions only affected a small minority of claimants, and in 1592 another commission comprising experienced Irish officials investigated all aspects of the plantation, including land titles. Altogether it heard 115, mostly new, suits, mainly against undertakers, restoring native claimants in 28 cases. Thus almost all undertakers lost land at some stage, either by legal process or through squatting; and, exceptionally, St Leger's seignory was halved, and Hugh Cuffe's reduced to a mere 1,953 acres. As D.B. Quinn remarked, 'the Munster plantation is an excellent example of the ideas of a sixteenth-century government outrunning its capacity for performance', a frequent occurrence in Tudor Ireland.[23]

The extent of the settler population is hard to determine, but three incomplete sets of returns give some indication and suggest that it never approached the projected levels. The 1589 returns show that on eighteen out of the 31 seignories c. 515 'Englishmen' then resided, although swamped even here by native tenants; those of 1590 list 662 'people' on twelve seignories (the same seignories in nine cases); those of 1592 listed 245 'tenants' on twelve seignories (three were different seignories again). The terms 'Englishmen', 'people' and 'tenants' relating to settlers are unclear, but one might conjecture, by correlating the lists, a total planter population of c. 2,000 people by 1590 and that by 1592 the 31 undertakers had still only c. 775 English tenants instead of the

---

23. Sheehan 1982–3a; Quinn 1966b (quotation, p. 24).

1,720 (86 × 20) originally envisaged. One undated report mentions a 'certificate' (of ?1594) that the plantation then comprised '5,000 able Englishmen, besides women and children': but this hardly seems more than an optimistic guess, and the author added ominously that 'at the first there was more resort thither than hath been now of late', blaming undertakers for preferring Irish to English tenants.

The plantation conditions had stipulated tenants of English birth and no alienation of land to the Gaelic Irish, but the difficulties over native claims frustrated this objective. In fact, after the expense and delay hitherto experienced, the undertakers recouped themselves as best they could, neglecting conditions of tenure, extorting the local population, and generally breaking the law. The administration lacked the resources for proper supervision, but from 1594 crown rents yielded c. £1,900 annually. As with later plantation projects, the government found it easier to find new landowners than to recruit new tenants. Men like Lord Chancellor Hatton were anyway in no position to give their seignories adequate attention; but even conscientious undertakers found thriving farmers quite reluctant to sell up and risk all on a dubious Irish venture, while the poorer sort were, as William Herbert lamented, ill-equipped to purvey 'piety, justice, inhabitation and civility with comfort and good example'.

Dispersed among a warlike and hostile population, the settlers were unable to defend themselves when, in 1598, rebellion returned to Munster. Nevertheless, if the plantation fell far short of government expectations, it was certainly comparable with the more successful of contemporary European colonization ventures, notably to the New World, and had a considerable impact on the Munster economy. The settlers imported both ploughs for tillage and also sheep in considerable quantities, besides other English livestock. On some estates rents increased fivefold in ten years, the new town of Tallow held 120 able Englishmen, and a new export trade in prepared planking sprang up with sawmills and wharves established to exploit the woods.[24]

Sir William Herbert's Croftus

A unique insight into the plans and prejudices of the plantation's leading undertakers in its early years is provided by a long Latin tract, *Croftus sive de Hibernia Liber*, composed by Sir William Herbert in 1591. From a Welsh county gentry family, Herbert had been sheriff, JP, and twice member of parliament before receiving a seignory of 113,276 acres at Castleisland, Co. Kerry, where he likewise served as sheriff, JP, and on the Munster council. Essentially, *Croftus* urged the need for more colonization in order to plant 'English civility' throughout the south-western corner of Ireland: its achievement was to weave together into an effective piece of propaganda three distinct and, in part,

24. Dunlop 1888, pp. 250–69 (quotations, pp. 262, 266); Quinn 1966b, pp. 19–40 (quotations, pp. 24, 30); Sheehan 1982–3a; Sheehan 1982, pp. 102–17 (on which my calculations of population and tenants are based); Sheehan 1982–3b, p. 17.

discordant strands of thought, of which two were commonplace among Elizabethan officials, the third much less so. His starting point is the classic Tudor strategy of state formation: that outlying territories can best be assimilated by imposing on them standard English administrative structures and common law, building towns and promoting tillage, all of which would somehow automatically promote 'English civility', turning the wild Irish into loyal English subjects. This strategy, allegedly, was clearly justified because it had brought England to the height of perfection and happiness, whereas the Irish were wicked and barbarous – like all primitive peoples unacquainted with a cultured way of life.

Unfortunately, it was not just the Irish who remained unconvinced about the efficacy of these conventional Tudor methods of state formation. If coercion was necessary to bring savages to appreciate the benefits of English civility, more problematic was the fact that princes elsewhere also seemed to believe that the laws and administrative structures of a particular region generally reflected the topography, settlement patterns and social structures of that region, and that therefore the laws and customs of a conquered territory should first be confirmed and then gradually remodelled, not proscribed and eradicated. Besides, if English government was so patently superior, why did it need supporting – uniquely in Ireland – by a standing army and draconian measures for wholesale colonization and expropriation of the natives, all of which was foreign to the Tudor tradition?

To this question, the obstinacy of the wild Irish offered only a partial answer, particularly since the Munster plantation was chiefly directed against the Old English. Herbert's extensive citation of classical authors was designed to deal with such inconvenient questions. Recognizing the high esteem in which the philosophies of the ancients were held throughout Renaissance Europe, he rummaged around for classical texts in support of his preconceptions, harnessing the classical tradition of colonization in support of English plantation in Ireland. To this end, Machiavelli's *Prince* also underwent a substantial rehabilitation.

Yet Roman colonization schemes to civilize primitive peoples around the Mediterranean appeared to Herbert to offer only general support for his projects. Hence, the third strand in his thought, 'the Welsh model', which was more original (at least in the detailed way Herbert exploited it) but required careful handling if it was to prove what Herbert wanted it to prove. In a general way, of course, Tudor officials had long accepted that the process by which Wales had been reformed and civilized offered a blueprint for Ireland. Yet Herbert was much more familiar with the planting of Englishries and conquest towns in medieval Wales. He thought that, as in Wales, native law, habits and customs should be rooted out and replaced by English. His attitude to the Gaelic language, however, was more sympathetic, no doubt because of his familiarity with the recent Reformation literature in Welsh, notably the Bible and the Prayer Book: he wanted the Bible and common prayers read to the Irish in their own language, with singing of Gaelic hymns and psalms accompanied by the harp.

Yet overall, given the comparative success of Tudor reform in Wales, Herbert's difficulty is to explain why this same strategy proved far less effective in Ireland. The reality of course was that Tudor Ireland was not Wales, despite some cultural parallels: it was far more like the far north of England where, likewise, a long military frontier fostered the very kind of marcher lordship and lineage society that Herbert denigrated as 'degenerate' among the Old English of Ireland. Unfortunately, the far north could hardly serve as a model for Ireland, since Tudor rule had equally failed there to foster the kind of 'civil society' that Herbert desired.

He states the problem fairly enough, noting that Henry VIII 'held the same opinion' about Ireland and Wales,

> deciding to proceed by one and the same road in the reform of each country, so that under one king, one law, one fair, wise and moderate administration but different sceptres they would become citizens of one happy and flourishing state.

Yet he then offers a highly selective history of medieval Ireland, asserting that English law and government had been less widely planted in Ireland, that the natives there had been controlled more by castles and garrison troops than by plantations of English settlers, and that English government had been too feeble. Allegedly, such colonies as had been planted had not been adequately planned and protected, so they had gone native. Thus the remedy for Ireland's miserable estate was more colonization, properly established and supported, for which purpose the lands of such traitors as Desmond, Baltinglass and O'Rourke, plus the Essex inheritance in Ulster, were now all available. What was in fact a monumental failure of Tudor policy was presented as a golden opportunity.

Finally, Herbert offers detailed proposals for a 'hearts and minds' policy with, as its centrepiece, the founding of two universities, with three colleges each, at Dublin and Limerick to foster 'virtue, learning and civilization'. Even so, the impact of all this would have been negated by his other main recommendation: that 'the poor and the people as a whole' should not be called to parliament, hold office, bear arms or act in defence of the state. Thus, having manipulated the evidence to establish why the land should become English, he then proposes to transform Ireland into a classic colony by reducing the natives to the status of Gaelic Man-Fridays![25]

Herbert's *Croftus* was, in point of composition, the first of three tracts written about Ireland in the 1590s by New English officials with personal experience of the Munster plantation. Many of the same themes and preoccupations are found in the treatises of two other undertakers, Richard Beacon, who published *Solon his follie, a political discourse* (Oxford, 1594), and Edmund Spenser, whose *View of the present state of Ireland* was composed in 1596.

25. Keaveney & Madden in Herbert 1992 (quotations, pp. 39, 101, 111). For the conventional Tudor strategy of state formation, see Ellis 1995b, pp. 40–63.

Instead of relying on administrative and legal reforms to effect a peaceful 'reformation' of Ireland, all three favoured military conquest and were enthusiastic proponents of widespread colonization. Although Beacon and Herbert were much more moderate in their views than Edmund Spenser's notorious tract, which coldly advocated a policy of general starvation, wholesale expropriation and ruthless transplantation of the natives, perhaps the essential point is that all three writers were deeply distrustful of local magnates and envisaged a sharply diminished role for them in the emerging new Ireland.[26]

Yet plantation, and the government's frequently arbitrary decisions in this regard, were not the only source of social unrest in late Elizabethan Munster. With the failure of programmatic government, the privy council re-examined resumption as a possible means of extending crown lands in regions already subjugated. In England, the resumption campaign by which Edward IV and Henry VII had restored crown solvency had been directed by numerous well-paid receivers, surveyors and auditors. Yet in Ireland, despite the manifest weakness of many land titles, there existed one poorly paid escheator-general and his deputy. Burghley therefore attempted to harness private greed for public gain by exploiting grants of concealments to transform hitherto sporadic escheats activity into a major campaign (1586–96). These grants in effect commissioned private individuals to search out and establish the queen's title to concealed lands at their own expense: in return, the grantee would normally receive a 21-year lease of these lands at a low rent. Thus at no cost the queen would immediately profit from an increased rental and, when the lease expired, from the lands' full market value.

In the aftermath of a major rebellion, however, this campaign was most ill-advised, because the chances of alienating potential supporters by misdirected activity far outweighed the likely profits. The search for concealments soon provoked serious protests even from New English officials, soldiers and settlers, as the campaign uncovered numerous examples of petty official corruption. Yet the campaign's financial rewards were largely diverted to enrich a small clique, the seventeenth-century adventurer class. The procedures used by an ambitious but penniless rogue like Richard Boyle to swindle the crown, the church and local landowners out of substantial sums and extensive properties are extremely technical, involving *inter alia* extensive bribery, collusion of minor officials, gross undervaluation of estates, securing false verdicts from corrupt juries, withholding certificates of concealment and antedating returns. They provoked fierce local resentment in Connaught and Munster, on which activity was concentrated, and were a contributory cause of the rebellions there in 1595–6 and 1598 respectively.[27]

26. There are now good modern editions of the Beacon and Herbert tracts. See Beacon 1996; Herbert 1992; Spenser 1970. For an illuminating debate concerning Spenser's writings and the different opinions of Beacon and Herbert, see Brady 1986, pp. 17–49; Canny 1988b, pp. 201–9; Brady 1988, pp. 210–15.
27. Ranger 1956–7, pp. 257–97. For the complicity of Burghley and Fitzwilliam in this, see Morgan 1995, pp. 124–5.

THE NINE YEARS WAR

Ulster before the Nine Years War

With the Munster plantation and the consolidation of presidential control in north Connaught, it seemed that Tudor rule might shortly be extended throughout Ireland without further serious trouble. By 1590 English local administration operated everywhere outside Ulster and a system of garrisons and devolved government had been created to contain and localize disturbances. Although there was little confidence in the government's good intentions, so that Tudor rule seemed little more than a military occupation, English armies had apparently adjusted to the difficult terrain of Gaelic Ireland. Thus barring a Spanish invasion and the loss of military supremacy, it might seem that the rapid reduction of Gaelic Ulster must surely follow.

Indeed, the government was already embarked on extending its bridgehead in this least accessible province, offering composition and surrender and regrant as inducements. Sheriffs had long operated in Down and part of Antrim and, more recently, in Cavan; and nominally, the remaining lordships were shired in 1585. Carrickfergus and Newry were useful northern bases, Blackwater Fort a recent addition, and in 1588, following the death of its chief, Sir Donald O'Connor Sligo, a royal grantee, the administration seized Sligo castle commanding the passage from Ulster into Connaught. Within Ulster, moreover, an agreement of 1585 had effectively divided the strongest lordship there between the Pale-educated earl of Tyrone and Turlough Luineach, with the earl appointed tanist.

In 1589 O'Rourke's rebellion and the death of MacMahon provided fresh opportunities for encroachment. Sir Ross MacMahon, the old chief, had accepted surrender and regrant, but his brother and heir, Hugh Roe, was opposed by a tanist, and Fitzwilliam canvassed a partition between subordinate MacMahon heads. The MacMahons rejected this, whereupon Fitzwilliam recognized Hugh Roe and sent troops to support him. When, however, Hugh Roe resisted the recently introduced sheriff and began border raids ('distraining for his right according to custom', as Tyrone observed), the deputy again upheld the law, having him arrested, tried and hanged at Monaghan sessions. Subsequently, it was alleged that Fitzwilliam had accepted Hugh Roe's bribe of 800 cattle to prefer him to the tanist as chief, but that he had failed to deliver. In any event, the episode showed the Ulster chiefs that failure to adhere to surrender and regrant agreements by upholding Gaelic custom could now be construed as treason.

In 1591 the lordship was divided between eight chief lords, each having large demesnes, with 280 clansmen planted as freeholders, owing rents of $1\frac{1}{2}d.$ and $2\frac{1}{2}d.$ per acre to the queen and lords respectively. Significantly, in the longer term, this 'native plantation' proved far less vexatious than other Tudor plantations, but the land settlement also constituted a devastating attack on the social structure of Gaelic lordship, on Tyrone's landed interests there, and on his rights as overlord. O'Rourke, on the northern confines of Bingham's jurisdiction, had long been disaffected, withholding Composition rent, exclud-ing a sheriff, and maintaining redshanks and Spaniards. Perrot had restrained Bingham, but in March 1590 Fitzwilliam authorized a campaign: O'Rourke fled to Tyrconnell and then Scotland, where James VI surrendered him, and he suffered a traitor's death at Tyburn in November 1591. In this instance, the lordship's division was restricted to the chief lords, but the request for appoint-ment as O'Rourke by the chief's son was ignored, so that Gaelic lordship was again the loser.[28]

While the government's grip on Ulster was tightening, it was becoming clear that the general response there to anglicization would depend on the ambitious and very talented earl of Tyrone. Quite exceptionally among Gaelic chiefs, Tyrone was well connected both at court and in Dublin: he had been fostered by an English settler family, the Hovendens, in Queen's County, and had since built up credit with New English officials like Sir Henry Harrington and Warham St Leger, while visits to court in 1567–8, 1587 and 1590 had forged connections with the earls of Leicester and Essex, Sir Christopher Hatton, and Sir Francis Walsingham. The queen too had been impressed by the earl during his visit to court to negotiate a final settlement of his inheritance in 1587. This settlement apparently secured his position in Tyrone.

Earl Hugh had previously depended heavily on government backing, but officials in Dublin who had supported him as a useful counterpoise to Turlough Luineach now began to work against him. In 1590 the earl moved to neutralize an obvious rival interest by asking to marry Mabel Bagenal, sister of Sir Henry who had just been appointed to the council and to his father's office of marshal; but despite Sir Henry's refusal, she became his third wife anyway. Within Ulster, the other leading chief, Hugh Roe O'Donnell, and an important vassal-chief, Hugh Maguire, were Tyrone's sons-in-law. Both were young and disaffected: O'Donnell had been kidnapped and imprisoned (1587–91) as a hostage for his father's conduct, while Maguire was antagonized by Fitzwilliam's imposition of an obstreperous English captain as sheriff of Fermanagh. In December 1591, however, Hugh Roe escaped from Dublin castle, drove Captain Willis, who had since occupied Donegal priory, from Ulster, and was inaugurated O'Donnell in May on his father's resignation. In Tyrone, however, a threatened succession dispute with Shane O'Neill's sons and Turlough Luineach's sons was avoided in May 1593 when Turlough resigned in Tyrone's favour, although he was not formally elected O'Neill until Turlough's death in September 1595.

Thus Tyrone's new dual position as apparent leader of a Gaelic confederacy and an English earl gave him an unwonted freedom of manoeuvre. Without Tyrone's support, O'Donnell and Maguire had little chance of successful re-bellion, despite their enthusiasm for the conspiracy now being hatched by the papal archbishop of Tuam to secure military assistance from Philip II.

28. Bagwell 1885–90, iii, pp. 146, 170–1, 201–3 (quotation, p. 202), 208–9, 212–17; Morgan 1993b, pp. 61–73, 92–3; Morgan 1987, pp. 285–301; Falls 1950, pp. 168–9, 171; *NHI*, iii, pp. 112, 116, 119, 166.

Although Tyrone was aware of the plot, to the experienced earl a catholic confederacy to establish an independent Ireland under Spanish suzerainty must have seemed an enormous gamble, particularly if by negotiation he might maintain his ascendancy in an English Ulster. Yet the prospects for this were less than encouraging. Tyrone was far better able than other Gaelic lords to detect the subtle shifts in factional alignments at court and in Dublin and to understand the conflicting pressures that lay behind Elizabeth's Irish policy. Particularly in Ireland, however, recent trends had been unfavourable. The dawn of an English Ulster was raising hopes among New English officials that the break-up of traditional Gaelic overlordships like Tyrone's would again release extensive lands for plantation.

Recent developments also underlined just how little sympathy there was in Dublin for the problems of Gaelic lords in adapting to English rule and English-style politics and how potent a weapon the common law could be in the hands of New English officials. The unwavering loyalty of the English-educated and protestant earl of Thomond constantly surprised English officials, but was not rewarded by high office, while Desmond had failed to adapt from warlord to landlord. Ormond had long been the only Irish earl with any real influence in government, but his strong claims to be deputy had been consistently overlooked, even though he was Elizabeth's cousin. In Tudor England successful nobles were exchanging their regional autonomy for influence at court, but Elizabethan Ireland was increasingly dominated by minor English officials on the make – not an attractive prospect to Tyrone who wrote of the Monaghan plantation that 'every peddling merchant and other men of no account' had a share of the land.

In these circumstances, the earl was understandably reluctant to commit himself in the struggle now beginning. His best hope was perhaps to allow events in Ulster to highlight his importance by allowing O'Donnell, Maguire and other O'Neill clans to create disturbances which he could then settle. Once his key role in a potential settlement was apparent, he could then exploit his court connections to appeal over the heads of unsympathetic officials in Dublin and reach an understanding that would safeguard his ascendancy in the new English Ulster.[29]

The first phase of the war

The first round in the struggle began in May 1593 when Maguire mounted a pre-emptive strike against encroaching officials, raiding Sligo and Roscommon. Fitzwilliam commissioned Tyrone to bring him in, but Maguire attacked the Monaghan garrison instead, whereupon Marshal Bagenal and Tyrone defeated

---

29. Our understanding of the outbreak of the Nine Years War has been substantially advanced by Morgan 1993b. See esp. chs 4–8 (quotation, p. 70) for these two paragraphs; also Bagwell 1885–90, iii, pp. 197, 218–28, 233, 237; Falls 1950, pp. 172–5, 190; *NHI*, iii, pp. 117–18; Cunningham 1979, pp. 39–40, 47–51, 128–33. A useful short discussion of Ormond's career is Brady 1989, pp. 49–60.

him near Belleek (10 October) and invested Enniskillen castle which eventually surrendered in February. The earl was wounded near Belleek and retired to Dungannon, complaining that his services were ill-regarded. In part this followed Bagenal's refusal to acknowledge his assistance: Tyrone subsequently claimed that Fitzwilliam and Bagenal were conspiring against him, while his friends on the privy council, Leicester, Hatton and Walsingham, were all dead. An English captain on close terms with the earl sent Elizabeth a report which quite possibly reflected Tyrone's own views in 1593–4: allegedly an Ulster war would prove costly and troublesome, but only Tyrone, O'Hanlon and Magennis were well affected. Indeed, Ulster could only be governed with Tyrone's support and he should therefore have overall charge, after which he would readily accept a sheriff and regular assizes at Dungannon.

Elizabeth was by now very concerned about the earl's conduct, and Burghley wrote to Ormond to use his influence with Tyrone to head off trouble. Concurrently Fitzwilliam was superseded (May 1594): his health had broken down and in March he had had to appoint commissioners to negotiate with Tyrone at Dundalk. His successor, Sir William Russell, the earl of Bedford's fourth son, was a capable soldier but without Irish experience, and clearly not intended to work miracles with the 1,100 troops available outside Connaught and Munster. Elizabeth instructed him to inform Tyrone that, of his foes, Fitzwilliam had been withdrawn and Bagenal forbidden to act against him. Yet the earl received no positive recognition or support, and before Russell's installation in August events in Ulster were pressing him towards rebellion.[30]

By May 1593, O'Donnell and the papal archbishop of Armagh had organized another appeal for Spanish military assistance by a confederacy which included Maguire, the last O'Rourke's son, Brian Oge, a Mayo Burke chief and six more papal bishops. The archbishop supposed that Philip II would send an army if the chiefs rebelled, although he was in fact preoccupied in the Netherlands and Brittany. In June 1594, therefore, O'Donnell joined Maguire in besieging Enniskillen, and two months later Maguire, assisted by Tyrone's brother, ambushed an English relief force at a ford south of Enniskillen, killing 56 soldiers. Although the castle was shortly relieved by Russell with 1,200 men, this success certainly heartened the confederates. Eight days later, however, Tyrone appeared unexpectedly in Dublin and submitted to Russell. He promised to restore peace in Ulster, to expel Gaelic Scots – 3,000 of whom had recently arrived to support O'Donnell – to pay composition rent, to send his eldest son for education at Oxford or Cambridge, and to receive a sheriff provided his lordship was not split into separate shires of Armagh and Tyrone.

Elizabeth afterwards reprimanded Russell for not detaining the earl who subsequently ignored his promises. Tyrone apparently aimed at an exclusive commission to govern Ulster, but when this was withheld his ambivalent stance gradually became untenable and by May 1595 he was in open rebellion. Nevertheless, his caution had at least won time: exploiting a previous concession which allowed him to maintain a peace-keeping force, he began militarizing

30. Bagwell 1885–90, iii, pp. 233–42; Falls 1950, pp. 175–84.

his lordship, buying arms, ammunition and equipment in lowland Scotland, and later in English and Irish towns, and hiring redshanks. By 1595 he was reputedly maintaining 1,000 pikemen, 4,000 musketeers and 1,000 cavalry, and had re-established control over the traditional O'Neill vassal-chiefs: Elizabeth, however, only began to reinforce the garrison in March, and for long maintained Tyrone's pretence of negotiations, hoping to save money and outmanoeuvre him. Thus the earl was effectively allowed to fight on his own terms.[31]

Tyrone made good use of the opportunity. In February 1595 another of his brothers captured Blackwater Fort, Enniskillen was retaken in May, and soon after Tyrone himself invested Monaghan. To relieve it, Bagenal set out from Dundalk via Newry with 1,750 men, reached Monaghan with some difficulty, but was almost overwhelmed at Clontibret on the return journey. Tyrone astonished his opponents by fielding a force of musketeers clad 'in red coats like English soldiers' and by his skilful deployment of cavalry and 'shot'. Bagenal's force was severely mauled and only reached Newry, apparently, because the earl's troops ran out of powder: from there it was extricated by sea.

The government now discovered that Tyrone had secretly transformed his levies into a disciplined army. Instead of relying on outsiders for galloglass and Gaelic Scots to supplement the traditional O'Neill 'rising out', the earl had built up a professional standing army, a volunteer force raised by proclamation and formed in companies on the English model. Instead of fighting 'with stones, casting spears and galloglass axes', these troops had modern matchlock calivers, muskets and pikes like Elizabeth's army, in which the traditional bills and bows had largely disappeared in the 1560s, although traditional Gaelic levies with bows and javelins lingered on. For training he had had the services of six English captains to drill his erstwhile peace-keeping force, plus some Spanish officers and Irishmen formerly in Spanish service: these were later supplemented by deserters from Elizabeth's army, particularly Irishmen recruited into the more experienced companies. His cavalry, again starting from an English-trained nucleus, was considered better-horsed and more numerous than the queen's, and if powder and firearms were occasionally hard to obtain, the major limiting factor was the north's ability to feed the confederate forces. Government officials frequently predicted that he would soon be 'eaten out', but while his defences remained intact sound commissariat arrangements allowed him to support far more troops than was anticipated. Thus the military balance in Ireland had been transformed. Tyrone was now capable of confronting an English army in the field, although his preferred strategy was to avoid unnecessary risks, and the Ulster terrain gave him a distinct advantage. The confederate troops whom formerly the English 'were wont by great odds to beat' were now 'most ready, well disciplined, and as good marksmen as France, Flanders or Spain can show'.[32]

---

31. Silke 1959, pp. 279–90, 362–71; Falls 1950, pp. 184–5; Bagwell 1885–90, iii, pp. 242–4.
32. Hayes-McCoy 1949–53, pp. 105–17 (quotations, pp. 105, 113); Hayes-McCoy 1969, pp. 87–105; Falls 1950, pp. 187–8.

In June, Armagh was fortified, Blackwater Fort regarrisoned, and Tyrone proclaimed a traitor; but Sligo was lost and Bingham's control over north Connaught reduced to a few castles with O'Donnell dominating the countryside. The government had already sent 1,600 veterans from Brittany and responded to Russell's requests for a senior commander by returning Lord President Norris, although with an independent commission for Ulster which annoyed the deputy. Yet the reinforcements sent following Clontibret were raw conscripts ('poor old ploughmen and rogues'). Thus although the administration had 657 horse and 4,040 foot available in October, the companies had been strengthened with twenty Irishmen apiece and many had small combat value. The MacMahons recovered Monaghan in December, but in fact small isolated garrisons were now a liability, since another Clontibret was risked each time they required resupplying.

In these circumstances, the government gratefully responded to Tyrone's overtures for a pardon: despite recent offers by Tyrone and O'Donnell of the kingdom of Ireland in return for a Spanish force of 2,000 to 3,000 with money and arms, a truce was agreed until the new year, later extended until May. While Elizabeth saved money, however, the truce effectively played into the chiefs' hands. From a confederate perspective, the first phase of the war from 1593 to 1596 was essentially defensive, designed to keep the English crown out of Ulster while conserving their strength and awaiting a diplomatic climate more favourable to their appeals for Spanish aid.[33]

Spanish intervention and the war's middle phase

During winter 1595-6, however, the two sides edged closer to a settlement which promised to protect the confederates' position and Tyrone's ascendancy while establishing Tudor sovereignty throughout Ireland. Increasingly aware of the potential costs of crushing the confederacy and the threat of Spanish intervention, particularly after the government obtained hard evidence of the confederate approach to Spain in September 1595, Elizabeth instructed Lord Deputy Russell to negotiate and gradually moderated her terms, blaming Fitzwilliam's corrupt dealings for the crisis in Ulster. In March, she commissioned Norris and Fenton to agree a settlement with Tyrone, even though Russell thought he was dissembling. Gradually, a potential settlement emerged whereby the confederates would all submit, acknowledge their offences, make reparations and pay rents, dropping their recent and highly embarrassing demand for liberty of conscience and accepting Tudor sovereignty. In return, the garrisons would be withdrawn, including eventually from Armagh provided there was peace there and the archbishop's lands were restored. The Gaelic lordships would be shired, although Armagh and Tyrone would not be divided and a countryman would be sheriff, but Tyrone would retain substantial local control, including over those vassal-chiefs previously under Turlough Luineach, while agreeing to arrest and surrender any rebels entering his territories. There

33. Morgan 1993b, ch. 8; Falls 1950, pp. 188-94 (quotation, p. 189); *NHI*, iii, p. 121.

was also a promise to investigate O'Donnell's claims to rents out of Sligo, and the political division of Monaghan would be revised in favour of the MacMahon pretender.

As the settlement was being finalized in May 1596, however, the negotiations collapsed when Philip II – his interest aroused by Elizabeth's failure to crush Tyrone – sent three separate missions to the confederates, to encourage them to continue resistance, to assess their military strength, and to survey the coasts and harbours for a possible Spanish invasion. Exceeding his brief, the Spanish envoy also informed them that Philip had already raised soldiers and prepared a fleet to assist them. As a result, Tyrone and O'Donnell decided to abandon their agreement with Elizabeth and commit the confederacy to an alliance with Spain. They informed Philip they would renew the war. They asked for immediate assistance, with a Spanish army to follow when ready, and offered the crown of Ireland to Cardinal Archduke Albert, Philip's nephew and governor of the Netherlands.[34]

Accordingly, the confederates embarked on a more offensive strategy in the second phase of the war. It was already apparent that Tyrone's claim to be acting as the queen's lieutenant could no longer be maintained in the face of the government's proclamation of the earl as a traitor. Moreover, while his inauguration in September 1595 as the O'Neill at Tullaghoge allowed him to claim Gaelic rights of overlordship which were independent of the crown, these were traditionally confined to Ulster. Tyrone therefore moved to internationalize the confederate campaign, attempting to rally all the Gaelic lords throughout Ireland and to extend its appeal to the Old English towns. This involved stressing the religious dimension of the struggle, as a war to defend catholicism. The main thrust of his propaganda was his ingenious attempt to adapt Old English commonwealth ideas to develop a new faith-and-fatherland nationalist ideology which was discussed in a previous chapter (Ch. 9). Yet alongside this, Tyrone also attempted to extend his rights of overlordship, particularly after the struggle extended to Leinster and Munster in 1598. His most notable creation was James FitzThomas as earl of Desmond; but he also nominated Florence MacCarthy as the MacCarthy More and deposed the government's O'Carroll in favour of his own candidate. Ironically, government officials made the same mistake as Tyrone, fearing that the earl's campaign would precipitate a widespread revolt among the Old English who were seen as Irish rather than English. In the event the vast majority of the Old English held aloof, viewing the earl's campaign as a revolutionary threat to the social order.[35]

During the summer Philip sent further military missions to secure information for a projected invasion. They conferred with Tyrone, O'Donnell, Maguire and O'Rourke and, convinced that the rebellion was truly a religious war, cutting across traditional dynastic politics and commanding widespread support, they recommended Spanish aid. After considering the possible northern ports

34. Morgan 1993b, ch. 9.
35. Morgan 1993a, pp. 21–37.

of embarkation – the harbours' suitability, defences if any, ease of transport inland – Limerick was mutually agreed as most suitable, since it could berth a large armada, while O'Donnell's nominee as MacWilliam (Theobald Burke of Mayo, established in 1595) could provide close support. The confederate leaders claimed to have 6,000 foot and 1,200 cavalry available, against 6,000–7,000 *English* troops (in fact, because of sickness and desertion, the *total* government muster in December 1596 was still only 5,732 foot and 617 horse, despite substantial reinforcements), but they argued that loyalist catholics would desert once the armada arrived. Ironically, Elizabeth's perseverance in 1596 with negotiations stemmed partly from the great expenses incurred in organizing an expedition to Cadiz, but the expedition's successful conclusion in July virtually ensured Philip's support for an armada to Ireland in revenge. A total of 100 ships duly departed in late October (along with an armada for England), but a protestant wind dispersed the fleet, overwhelmed 32 ships, and blew the rest back into Spanish ports.[36]

Meanwhile counsels were divided in the Dublin administration as Tyrone sought to extend his support outside Ulster. The command structure, with Norris in charge of suppressing revolt in Ulster but under Russell in Munster, caused friction and undermined cooperation much as had Essex's independent Ulster command in the 1570s. The spread of rebellion into Connaught, moreover, precipitated another, this time successful, attack on Bingham's conduct as president. Bingham believed that revolt there reflected O'Donnell influence following Sligo's loss, plus Russell's failure to supply sufficient troops to defend the province. His enemies led by Fenton argued, however, that fear of Bingham had driven the Connaught rebels into O'Donnell's arms. Bingham's 'fire and sword' reputation finally got the better of him and he was suspended in May 1596 and imprisoned in September following his unauthorized departure from Ireland. His successor, Sir Conyers Clifford, had long experience in Connaught and, lacking the resources to attack O'Donnell, attempted by diplomacy to win over his clients in north Connaught – Burke of Mayo, O'Rourke, MacDermot and O'Connor Don – while conciliating Clanrickard and Thomond.

In July 1596 the confederate leaders had issued a circular urging others, especially the 'gentlemen of Munster', to join them in defending 'Christ's Catholic religion', and they also petitioned the pope to grant them the patronage of Irish benefices. The circular apparently encouraged further disturbances in the south, where attacks began on Munster settlers; and in Wicklow Feagh MacHugh O'Byrne broke out again in September but was eventually cornered and killed in May 1597. Old English catholics overwhelmingly opposed the confederacy, arguing that Tyrone was no crusader but bent on establishing his own supremacy. Exploiting a changing political climate in Rome, they successfully lobbied against the confederates' petition and also later requests designed to force them to support Tyrone. Nevertheless, with an enlarged, ill-disciplined

---

36. Silke 1966, pp. 19–23; Silke 1970, pp. 28–31; Falls 1950, pp. 193–7; Bagwell 1885–90, iii, pp. 260–8, 273.

garrison oppressing the Englishry, Burghley could foresee previous patterns of revolt recurring and 'the queen's loyal subjects in the English Pale tempted to rebel'.[37]

Thus by 1597 the situation in Ireland was critical, and the privy council attempted to meet the emergency in two ways. The commissions of both Russell and Norris in Ulster were revoked and a unified command re-established with the arrival in May as deputy of Thomas, Lord Burgh, an energetic soldier-administrator. Second, efforts were made to improve supplies, army discipline and musters to keep companies at proper strength. Burgh concentrated on the northern problem, where 'deluding parleys' had virtually replaced military activity since 1595. Very ambitiously, however, he planned to repeat Sidney's two-pronged assault on O'Neill in 1566 by marching from Newry through Dungannon to link up near Lifford with Clifford who would meanwhile have crossed the Erne at Ballyshannon. Burgh proclaimed a general hosting and departed in July with 3,500 men, leaving the now obsolescent Pale levies to defend the marches. His progress apparently surprised Tyrone: regarrisoning Armagh within a day, he reached the Blackwater by night march, assaulted the ford and then took a defended earthwork before daylight; but after skirmishing with Tyrone's main force which now blocked the way, Burgh finally realized that he faced an army far superior to his own half-trained force and wisely abandoned his plans. Meanwhile Clifford had delayed to await reinforcements and supplies. He had previously strengthened his position in north Connaught, recovering Sligo in March; but O'Donnell now held the Erne fords against him, he failed to take Ballyshannon, lost Lord Inchiquin, an important loyalist, and only some skilful manoeuvres enabled his 1,200 men to escape envelopment by confederate forces and retreat ignominiously into Connaught.

Burgh spent the following months building and provisioning a new Blackwater Fort, part of a chain of garrisons.[38] In October, however, his unexpected death from typhus seriously exacerbated the administration's difficulties: despite his industry, his new-found reliance on garrisons to reduce Tyrone repeated Protector Somerset's mistake in Scotland, while the obvious alternative commander, Norris, had also recently died. The council initially elected as justiciar Norris's brother, Sir Thomas, newly promoted president of Munster, with Ormond, now aged 66, as lieutenant-general. Elizabeth, however, ordered Norris back to Munster, then threatened by another Spanish armada which was again dispersed by storm in late October: instead Loftus and Chief Justice Gardiner were appointed justices.

The administration's major problem was now Blackwater Fort, which Tyrone had blockaded: its ill-equipped garrison of 150 men was barely adequate to defend the bare earthwork, let alone for aggressive action, while any relief army would be costly – 'raiding journeys' in Ulster had already cost Elizabeth

37. Bagwell 1885–90, iii, pp. 242–79 (quotation, p. 274); Falls 1950, pp. 185–6, 191–201; Cunningham 1979, pp. 34–8.
38. Falls 1950, pp. 201–7; Hayes-McCoy 1969, pp. 112–15; *NHI*, iii, pp. 123–4 (quotation, p. 123).

£300,000 – and risked battle on the difficult terrain of Tyrone's choosing. The council was for abandoning Burgh's 'scurvy fort', despite the inevitable loss of face, but the decision was postponed when Elizabeth authorized renewed negotiations which resulted in Tyrone's submission to Ormond in December. The truce was progressively extended, but when it expired in June 1598 Tyrone immediately besieged Cavan, sending a force to blockade Blackwater Fort and another, quickly defeated by Ormond, to fan rebellion among the O'Mores, Kavanaghs and O'Byrnes. Now that all Tyrone's forces were assembled, the war reputedly cost him £500 a day, but with the Ulster economy reorganized he could raise £80,000 a year there. Ormond had meanwhile reorganized the queen's army, disbanding companies to restore the remainder to strength, but it was reportedly three-quarters Irish following Burgh's heavy local recruitment, and Ormond had received only 600 English reinforcements, veterans from Picardy.[39]

The cost of the war likewise represented an enormous burden to the Tudor state, particularly from 1596 onwards when warfare in Ireland was the largest single expense in the wider military struggle against Spain. In the period 1594–1602, there were sixteen separate infantry levies of between 1,000 and 6,350 troops each for Ireland, amounting to 30,592 soldiers from 36 English counties and 6,611 soldiers from thirteen counties in Wales. In addition, nearly 3,000 troops were redeployed from the Low Countries, and 1,880 horse bands were levied, making a grand total of 42,558 troops shipped from English ports, mainly Chester (47%) and Bristol (26%), to Ireland. If the total number of able-bodied men eligible for military service was then around 225,000 in England and Wales, these levies involved 19 per cent of the available manpower.

The privy council took some pains to see that the burden of the levies was evenly distributed, but it was obviously more convenient to levy troops for Ireland from the western maritime counties, and shires elsewhere made larger contributions to other theatres of war. Thus 25 per cent of the English infantry levies came from six western counties, while the Welsh levies were proportionately even larger, representing 2.9 per cent of the *total* population of Wales (*c.* 225,000), as opposed to only 0.76 per cent of the English population. For the most part, the soldiers were raw conscripts, apart from some veterans from Brittany and the Low Countries; but as the crisis continued, the government even resorted to raiding the trained bands which were the nearest Tudor equivalent to a professional soldiery and had hitherto been exempt from service abroad. The recruitment and transport of such large levies also demanded a degree of uniform and centralized control. The privy council's advice was for choice of sons of yeomen, husbandmen, and farmers at the musters, seasoned ideally with some volunteers; but in practice there was such reluctance to serve in Ireland, and so much corruption and evasion, that the actual drafts were tantamount to a policy of social cleansing. Thus a report concerning one levy mustered prior to embarkation at Bristol remarked that

39. Falls 1950, pp. 206–11; Hayes-McCoy 1969, pp. 114–16 (quotation, p. 114); *NHI*, iii, pp. 124–5. Cf. Bush 1975, pp. 32–9.

There was never beheld such strange creatures brought to any muster . . . they are most of them either lame, diseased, boys, or common rogues. Few of them have any clothes; small weak starved bodies taken up in fairs, markets and highways to supply the places of better men kept at home.[40]

The habitual practice of ridding the provinces of idlers, miscreants and the sickly also helps to explain the unsatisfactory conduct of these levies in Ireland, and the high wastage rates in sickness and desertion. Yet able or not, the levies all had to be equipped and transported, and most of the initial charges fell on the soldiers' home county in what amounted to a system of local taxation akin to that practised in Ireland. For instance, in Kent the cost of raising, equipping and sending 56 horse and 600 foot to Ireland 1595–1602 amounted to £3,324, or about one-third of its total expenses for the wider war effort. A poor but large county like Lancashire spent over £5,500 for Irish levies of 20 horse and 1,403 foot, but its contribution to other theatres was only 300 foot.

Faced with repeated demands for men, money and arms for Ireland, together with numerous other assessments for poor relief, purveyance, ship-money tax, gunpowder tax, privy-seal loans, and the heavy burden of national taxation in these years, there were growing complaints by the local gentry charged with organizing all this, a general feeling of war-weariness and, frequently, direct refusals to pay the assessments. The cost of the Irish levies alone (at £3 10s. per footman, and £30 per horse) amounted to almost £152,000 in local taxation. On top of this, the government's own expenditure in Ireland also soared during the war years. As Table 3 shows, Irish military expenditure under Elizabeth generally hovered at between IR£35,000 and IR£52,000, apart from the period of the Desmond war and its aftermath. Most of this cost was borne by the English exchequer, although the proportion raised from local sources gradually increased from less than 10 per cent to almost 35 per cent by the mid-1590s. Thereafter, however, sterling payments from England *averaged* almost £104,000 a year, with peaks of £196,000 in 1598–9 and £188,000 in 1599–1600. Only with the massive debasement in the last years of the war did they begin to fall.

In sum, the traditional machinery of Tudor government was operating at the very limit of its capacity in these years. Indeed, by 1600 the war could only be sustained by overriding local privileges and exemptions so as to develop a system of military taxation. Concurrently, a system of compulsory relief for disabled soldiers was created (by statutes of 1593, 1597 and 1601), while in many areas provost marshals had to be appointed to control able-bodied ex-soldiers. Of course much of this machinery gradually lapsed after 1603, to be revived in mid-century, but as in other parts of Europe, the demands of the war furthered, at least in minor ways, the development of a more centralized and powerful state.[41]

---

40. McGurk 1997, esp. pp. 32–5 (quotation, p. 33), 55–65, 96–7, 138–40, 262–4.
41. McGurk 1997, esp. pp. 99–102, 119, 262–4; Sheehan 1990, p. 47.

Table 3: Irish military expenditure, 1559–1603:[1] *average per annum in four-year periods*

Period	Irish revenues 'clear remain'	Payments from England	
		Irish pounds	Pounds sterling
1559–63	IR£3,964	IR£40,897[2]	£23,230
1563–67	IR£4,625	IR£35,468	£26,597
1567–71	IR£5,700	IR£29,758	£22,319
1571–75	IR£4,856	IR£45,497	£34,123
1575–79	IR£9,419	IR£40,073	£30,024
1579–83	IR£10,510	IR£65,129	£48,847
1583–87	IR£8,026	IR£57,029	£42,772
1587–91	IR£11,963	IR£39,602	£29,701
1591–95	IR£13,295	IR£38,649	£28,987
1595–99	IR£9,315	IR£138,368	£103,776
1599–1603	n/a	IR£160,922[3]	£83,334

[1] Calculated from Sheehan 1990, Tables 1 and 2. The 'clear remain' was the balance on the net Irish revenues after payment of the civil establishment (i.e. fees, pensions, annuities, and expenses of officers of the courts). Payments from England came mainly from the exchequer, with small amounts from other sources, mainly from Wards and Liveries.

[2] Includes IR£60,000 in debased coins (worth £15,000 sterling, or IR£20,000 normal fineness), issued in summer 1559.

[3] Includes IR£307,000 in debased coins (worth £80,519 sterling, or IR£94,026 normal fineness), issued in 1601–3.

Crisis: the battle of the Yellow Ford and its aftermath

In spring 1598, the crisis of the war was fast approaching: when, at length, 1,850 recruits arrived from England, the council decided to relieve and rein-force Blackwater Fort. Ormond unwisely endorsed acceptance of Marshal Bagenal's offer to command the relief army of 4,200 men, although Bagenal was 'better experienced in the knowledge of that country than in the command of an army' which, though well-equipped, included the 1,850 recruits, untrained and unruly.

Bagenal reached Armagh without incident, but halfway to the Blackwater he was attacked by Tyrone, O'Donnell and Maguire with *c.* 5,000 men. Allow-ing his regiments to sprawl back excessively, he lost control, was beaten to a standstill, and the vanguard routed (14 August). About 830 men were killed, including Bagenal, 400 wounded, and 300 Irish deserted to Tyrone: *c.* 2,000 struggled back to Armagh, having lost most of their equipment and supplies. The consequences were disastrous. The council feared a descent on Dublin, almost defenceless with Ormond away campaigning in Leinster. In fact Tyrone, worried about a projected landing on Lough Foyle, missed his opportunity: but while O'Donnell secured almost complete control of Connaught and the

O'Mores attacked the Leix–Offaly settlement, he responded to requests from dissident Munster men by sending Owen MacRory O'More with a flying column of *c.* 700 men from Queen's Co. to Limerick to overturn the plantation and establish a Desmond pretender, James Fitzthomas, nephew of the last earl. Preoccupied with Ulster, the council had long ignored the president's appeals for money and men to control a deteriorating situation, but the military collapse in October was frighteningly swift. The settlers, numbering *c.* 3,000, were suddenly attacked by confederates, their own Irish tenants, and forces hastily assembled by the *súgán* ('straw rope') earl. Most simply abandoned everything, fleeing to Cork, Youghal, Waterford and England, or were killed or mutilated en route. Although small companies rallied to hold isolated castles, fourteen years' work disappeared in a few days.[42]

Bagenal's defeat at the Yellow Ford confronted Elizabeth with the unpalatable fact, increasingly apparent to shrewd observers since Clontibret, that her Irish problem had largely transformed itself into a straight military contest against a disciplined and resourceful adversary. In this war, the geography of the confederacy's Ulster base helped to minimize the effect of vastly superior English resources. Moreover, a Spanish landing could easily have tipped the balance. In the longer term English seapower was a crucial factor, but given the prevailing winds, it was far from certain that a Spanish army operating in Ireland could not be supplied. Following news of the Yellow Ford disaster, Elizabeth diverted to Dublin 1,900 men intended for Lough Foyle, and further reinforcements followed, of reasonable quality and well equipped – 1,300 in October, 2,000 in December and 3,000 in January including 1,500 Netherlands veterans. With these, Ormond prevented the Munster rebellion from spreading throughout Leinster and even recovered the initiative in Munster during December. The queen, however, long hesitated about Burgh's replacement. Bingham, an ailing man of 70, returned to replace Bagenal and died soon after, but finally in March she appointed as lieutenant Robert Devereux, second earl of Essex, a royal favourite and popular hero of the Cadiz expedition, with the largest army to leave England during the reign, 17,300 men.

Elizabeth's response: Essex and Mountjoy

Nevertheless, Essex was an indifferent soldier surrounded by indifferent advisers, a novice in Irish warfare, without any clear strategy for winning the war. 'By God, I will beat Tyrone in the field' was his boast, but on arrival in April he distributed over half his army in garrisons and turned south. His eight-week progress through Munster and south Leinster simply wore out his troops without improving on Ormond's success with far smaller forces. During the summer, moreover, the queen's forces suffered some embarrassing setbacks in Essex's absence: near Wicklow Phelim MacFeagh O'Byrne repeated his father's success of 1580; and in Roscommon Clifford, ordered to relieve Sir Donough

---

42. Falls 1950, pp. 215–24; Hayes-McCoy 1969, pp. 116–28 (quotation, pp. 116–17); Sheehan 1982–3b, pp. 11–22; Quinn 1966b, pp. 33–4.

O'Connor Sligo who was besieged by O'Donnell in Collooney, was killed in an engagement in the Curlew mountains and lost nearly a third of his 1,700 men. In August Essex held a council of war which decided that because of sickness and increasing desertion, there was little hope of putting a force into Lough Foyle or successfully confronting Tyrone on the Blackwater that year. Astonished, Elizabeth peremptorily ordered Essex north, but when in early September the earl marched north with 4,000 men, he encountered Tyrone with a much larger force near Louth, was surprised into a parley, and conversed privately with Tyrone for 30 minutes. The result was a shameful truce permitting the confederates to hold all they possessed. Following this, however, Essex apparently reconsidered the implications of Elizabeth's annoyance at his previous inaction, his manifest failure and ostensibly suspicious conduct in talking privately with Tyrone, and then the arrival of a royal letter forbidding him to leave his post without licence. He concluded that rivals were exploiting his absence from court to plot against him, deserted his post, and hurried to London to defend himself against Elizabeth's fury.[43]

Essex was among the more spectacular examples of English commanders whose reputations were ruined in Ireland. He left, under Ormond's command, a demoralized army, much reduced by desertion, with Loftus and Sir George Carey, the new treasurer, elected justices. Ormond was so little impressed by the administration's military preparedness that he negotiated extensions of the truce until January 1600 while warning Elizabeth against hopes of a negotiated settlement. Moreover, when the truce expired, Tyrone marched south unopposed with 2,000 men, burned the lands of loyalists in Westmeath, north Tipperary and Cork, and camped near Kinsale to receive the submissions and hostages of local landowners – a feat that would have been quite unthinkable three years before.

In February, Charles Blount, Lord Mountjoy, arrived as deputy, Elizabeth's last and, as it proved, most successful governor. Yet, with royal authority hardly extending beyond the major towns, Mountjoy's prospects seemed unattractive. Passed over in Essex's favour in 1599, Mountjoy had, despite considerable military service, little experience of high command; and if his 13,200 troops included fewer raw recruits, that was because the nucleus of his smaller army was the demoralized force bequeathed by Essex. Indeed by 1600 the problems of English rule in Ireland looked suspiciously like those of Spanish rule in the Netherlands. Tyrone had recently managed to inspire a remarkable degree of unity and support for an independent catholic Ireland and, despite his failure to win over the catholic but traditionally loyal Old English, the confederacy had effectively become a nationalist uprising against a foreign and protestant power. The confederates fought 'for the maintenance of their tanist law and old Irish customs' and that 'this island Ireland shall be at our direction and counsel as Irishmen'.

Thus a stalemate seemed likely: perhaps the most likely outcome was that Mountjoy would succeed in consolidating royal control over the more

43. Falls 1950, pp. 225–47 (quotation, p. 228); *NHI*, iii, pp. 127–9.

anglicized east and south, while elsewhere the confederacy would hold out with Spanish aid – the arms and ammunition that continued to reach Tyrone, and perhaps eventually an armada – to establish a Gaelic free state.[44] However, Mountjoy was far more purposeful than Essex and better served by subordinates. Exploiting his advantages in resources while avoiding risks, the deputy maintained pressure on Tyrone through winter campaigns, he systematically wasted Tyrone's lordship, utilized seapower and planted garrisons effectively to break up confederate strongholds. Accompanying Mountjoy was a new president of Munster, Sir George Carew, cousin of the adventurer and an able soldier and politician. Before Carew's installation in April, however, Tyrone's son-in-law, Maguire, had been killed in a chance encounter and Tyrone departed precipitately to avoid envelopment by loyalist armies under Ormond and Mountjoy. With 3,000 reinforcements, easy communications, and the backing of major towns and local loyalists, Carew had a relatively easy task against the *súgán* earl and his supporters, particularly since he could temporize initially with the other major figure, Florence MacCarthy, successor of the earl of Clancare (*d.* 1596), who tried to play with both sides. There was little enthusiasm in Munster for another Desmond rebellion, and the *súgán* earl's main supporters were 800 mercenaries left by Tyrone and 1,000 Connaught mercenaries who departed in August. Carew's diplomacy and, in October, the restoration, as fifteenth earl, of Desmond's son, James, as a counterpoise, steadily undermined Fitzthomas's support. Earl James, a colourless individual whose protestantism alienated potential adherents, returned to England in March 1601, his fugitive rival was captured in May, and the young earl then solved the government's problem over the future Munster settlement by conveniently dying.[45]

Nevertheless, Munster, where Carew could in the main repeat the successes of earlier presidents against scratch forces fighting in the traditional Gaelic manner, was a much easier proposition than Ulster, where Mountjoy had to buy his experience. Mountjoy's first move, in May, was a feint towards the Blackwater to distract Tyrone while Sir Henry Docwra effected the long-threatened landing of 4,000 men in Lough Foyle. Mountjoy's outward march was unmolested, and Docwra's landing entirely successful, but in the Moyry pass north of Dundalk Tyrone attacked a following convoy of supplies for Newry and only withdrew on Mountjoy's timely appearance. Docwra fortified himself in Derry, prudently remaining on the defensive during the summer while winning over dissident confederates – Sir Arthur O'Neill, Turlough Luineach's son, and Neill Garve O'Donnell, Hugh Roe's cousin. Docwra's force was soon depleted by sickness and desertion, however, and O'Donnell felt confident enough to raid the territories of Thomond and Clanrickard in June–July, although in October Docwra sent Neill Garve to take Lifford. During summer Mountjoy campaigned in Leinster where O'More had recently kidnapped Ormond during a parley but

---

44. Falls 1950, pp. 247–54; *NHI*, iii, p. 129; Hayes-McCoy 1969, pp. 144–6 (quotations, p. 146).
45. Falls 1950, pp. 253–8, 282–9; *NHI*, iii, pp. 129–30.

then released him: the O'Mores dispersed with their chief mortally wounded. By September Mountjoy was ready for a trial of strength with Tyrone and departed north with 3,300 men to re-establish an Armagh garrison. Though hard pressed, Tyrone was strong enough to oppose him at the Moyry pass, which was heavily fortified, and resisted *inter alia* two major assaults before Mountjoy retired to Dundalk, ordered up reinforcements and sent a regiment into Newry by Carlingford Lough. Thereupon Tyrone retired north towards Armagh; Mountjoy dismantled the Moyry fortifications, marched into Newry, and then contented himself with building a new fort at Mountnorris, eight miles beyond Newry.

The battle of Kinsale

During the campaign Mountjoy had lost some 75 killed and 300 wounded without attaining his objective, but in the months following Tyrone was closely surrounded and his lordship continually pillaged: a new Blackwater Fort was established, with other forts to the south, while Sir Arthur Chichester in Carrickfergus raided across Lough Neagh. The confederacy's fate now depended on Spain where Philip III considered whether, instead of simply encouraging Tyrone in order to distract Elizabeth, the landing of a Spanish army might force the recall of English troops from the Netherlands while establishing a Spanish base for an assault on England itself. In January 1601 the necessary troops became available, and Philip finally agreed to send an army of 6,000 to Ireland: during the following months Mountjoy and Tyrone prepared themselves for the expected invasion. Tyrone and O'Donnell had earlier advised that an army of 6,000 should land in Munster, but if only 4,000 it should land on the Shannon, while 2,000 men could be reinforced more speedily if landed in Donegal Bay. By May 1601, however, the confederacy was almost dead in Munster and when the armada at last sailed from Lisbon on 3 September, the 6,000 – already considered too few for both a field army and garrison – had shrunk to 4,432. Moreover, some ships became separated in a storm, including those carrying most of the munitions, so that the Spanish army under Don Juan del Águila, who landed unopposed at Kinsale on 21 September, eventually numbered only some 3,400, albeit experienced, troops. Disappointed to learn that Fitzthomas and MacCarthy had since been captured, Águila felt too weak to take the field and fortified himself in Kinsale to await reinforcements from Ulster or Spain.[46]

Nevertheless, Mountjoy's position soon became critical. Fearing that anything other than resolute action would precipitate general insurrection, the deputy departed immediately for Cork with a small force, leaving the army to follow. An adequate field army could only be scraped together by the dangerous expedient of stripping the garrisons, including 1,400 men from south Tyrone; but since he could not expect immediate reinforcement, Mountjoy's best hope

46. Falls 1950, pp. 262–95; Silke 1970, pp. 90–110; Hayes-McCoy 1969, pp. 132–43.

was to defeat Águila before Tyrone joined him, regardless of the consequences elsewhere. By late October he was besieging Kinsale with 7,000 men. Águila's army was weaker than Tyrone had hoped, but nevertheless transformed the military situation: instead of conserving his strength and hoping that Elizabeth would, in despair, offer favourable terms, or die and be replaced by a more accommodating successor, Tyrone now had a fighting chance of beating Mountjoy in the open field. And if Kinsale was a long march away, the earl had long known that Elizabeth could not be defeated simply by defensive victories in Ulster.

Accordingly, after making such defensive arrangements for Ulster as they might, Tyrone and O'Donnell took the considerable risk of marching south in mid-winter, leaving behind them loyalist pretenders and the recently reinforced garrisons at Carrickfergus and Derry. O'Donnell departed on 2 November, marched south via Roscommon, Galway and Tipperary, eluded Carew and 2,500 men whom Mountjoy detached to oppose him, and reached Bandon-bridge with 2,200 men. Tyrone left a week later, and after vainly attempting to distract Mountjoy by raiding the Pale, joined O'Donnell in early December. Reinforced by 500 Munstermen and 200 out of 600 Spanish reinforcements who had just landed at Castlehaven, the confederate army numbered perhaps 6,500 as it approached Kinsale on the 21st.

Although since strengthened from England, Elizabeth's army in two camps commanded by Mountjoy and the earl of Thomond was now virtually cut off between the Spaniards and the confederates. Águila was short of supplies but resisted stoutly, while the loyalists were exposed and exhausted, reduced by cold, sickness and desertion to 6,600 effectives, and their horses near starvation. Yet Tyrone abandoned his usual caution and agreed to a coordinated operation to relieve Águila by attacking the two camps while the Spaniards sallied out. To do this he had to risk a formal battle, but he hoped for wholesale desertions of Irishmen to the confederates. Mountjoy could detach no more than 2,000 men to oppose him, but it did give his heavier cavalry, under Marshal Wingfield and the earl of Clanrickard, an opportunity to fight on favourable ground.

Moving out quickly to parry Tyrone's 'surprise' dawn attack on the 24th, Mountjoy caught the confederate army as it was deploying, clumsily, in three divisions organized like Spanish *tercios*. Clearly Tyrone's men had some training for the pitched battles of formal warfare, but the *tercio* formation was particularly complicated and his three 'battles' too widely separated. When the loyalist cavalry charged, the confederate horse turned tail and fell in on their own mainward, disordering it. The mainward was then attacked from the rear and broke, whereupon the vanguard and rearward retired and scattered with heavy loss. It was all over very quickly. Águila made no move because the confederates never approached the appointed rendezvous: instead he negotiated favourable terms with Mountjoy and surrendered on 2 January.[47]

47. Hayes-McCoy 1969, pp. 144–73; Falls 1950, pp. 295–318; Silke 1970, pp. 111–75; McGurk 1997, pp. 246–7.

From Kinsale to Mellifont: the end of the war

Kinsale effectively broke the rebellion. O'Donnell left for Spain to seek further aid from Philip III, and died soon after, but Philip lost interest after news of Águila's surrender and his return in March. Remnants of the confederate army struggled home and Tyrone soon tried to negotiate a pardon. The pacification of Munster, entrusted to Lord President Carew, received priority for fear of another Spanish landing, but with the capture of Dunboy castle in June resistance there was almost ended. Meanwhile Mountjoy prepared to harry Ulster, and crossed the Blackwater in June with 3,000 men. Tyrone offered no resistance but took to the woods while Mountjoy's men again wasted the country, finding 'everywhere men dead of famine'. His chief adherents gradually submitted, notably O'Donnell's brother and successor, Rory, in December.

Elizabeth intended to continue the war against Tyrone, but authorized Mountjoy to pardon other rebels at his discretion. Yet Tyrone's continued resistance forestalled plans for settling Ulster, and in February she relented and authorized him to offer Tyrone life, liberty and pardon on terms. In fact negotiations had been continuing unofficially, and in March, Tyrone agreed generally to the terms previously outlined. Mountjoy sent him a safe-conduct and he submitted at Mellifont on the 30th. By then Elizabeth had been dead six days, as Mountjoy had learned unofficially but Tyrone had not. Tyrone renounced the title of O'Neill, authority over his vassal-chiefs and dependence on the Spanish king, and he agreed to support the queen's sheriffs and garrisons: in return Mountjoy promised the queen's pardon to him and his followers and restoration to his earldom. Six days later formal notification arrived of Elizabeth's death.

Nevertheless, Mountjoy, rendered pliable by reports that Elizabeth was dying and rumours of Spanish reinforcements, had made two vital concessions: acceptance of Tyrone as full owner of his lordship, and of the lordship of O'Cahan, his principal vassal-chief, as part of Tyrone. The terms, couched in deliberately vague phraseology, could hardly have been more generous: the earl was denied the palatine jurisdiction he had earlier sought, but he preserved his lordship against Mountjoy's intention to divide it among junior O'Neills and so reward native loyalists. Moreover, Dublin's plans for an Ulster council were quietly dropped when it appeared that King James might appoint Tyrone himself president. Thus, paradoxically, the settlement increased rather than diminished the earl's local authority, granting him more than Gaelic law had allowed, at the expense of O'Cahan, Sir Arthur O'Neill and others. On Mountjoy's recommendation, this settlement was repeated in Tyrconnell, where Rory O'Donnell was created earl of Tyrconnell in September and Neill Garve abandoned to the tender mercies of his cousin. The war had cost Elizabeth c. £2 million, by far the heaviest expense of her last years, but the eventual peace terms, uncritically accepted by James, hardly differed from what Tyrone had sought in 1594 – recognition of his paramount position in an English Ulster.[48]

48. Canny 1969–70, pp. 249–62; Falls 1950, pp. 307–34; *NHI*, iii, pp. 135–6 (quotation, p. 135); Smith 1984, p. 248.

CONCLUSION: THE TUDOR
FAILURE

Militarily, Tyrone's submission at Mellifont signalled the completion of the Tudor conquest, but politically it marked, not the solution of the crown's Irish problem, but simply the start of a new phase of anglicization. To establish political stability in the aftermath of military conquest, the Dublin administration faced a very difficult task: it commanded wholehearted support in Ireland only among the numerically small New English group and a small minority of older settlers, while many natives were totally alienated from government and provided a receptive audience for further conspiracies. In these circumstances James I might most easily have won support by timely political concessions to Gaelic and Old English lords, coupled with a firm enforcement of anglicizing policies in religion and government. Yet this would have involved close supervision and, initially at least, a substantial army to prevent disorders and enforce conformity, neither of which James was willing to provide. To save money, the army was quickly reduced to 1,100 men, and this imposed severe restraints on policy options. Instead, the government generally favoured the New English interest, allowing officials and adventurers ample scope to exploit the weakness of native land titles and so to strengthen their position politically and numerically by expropriation and plantation. The Old English community was excluded by religion from office and influence, but in practice the generous measure of religious toleration accorded it forestalled serious unrest. In general, this uneasy but economical compromise between interest and expediency promoted the gradual anglicization of Gaelic Ireland, but it did little to inspire local confidence in royal justice or to conciliate Gaelic and Old English lords. Thus, by 1641, when the political crisis in England gave Irish dissidents another opportunity, the basis of local support painfully built up by the Dublin administration was still too narrow to withstand major rebellion.[1]

Nevertheless, the completion of the conquest, despite Spanish intervention at Kinsale, was a major achievement of the Tudor regime, and one which is undiminished by the subsequent failure to establish a stable political settlement in Ireland. As Penry Williams has argued, Mountjoy's defeat of Tyrone's rebellion enabled Elizabeth 'to hand to her successor a kingdom effectively

---

1. *NHI*, iii, pp. 142–288; Beckett 1966, chs 2–3.

united and secure – for the time being – from internal threats'.[2] Undoubtedly, the planning, preparation and execution of Mountjoy's campaign was an extraordinary feat of government. Yet it placed an enormous strain on the English economy and on the crown's limited financial resources.[3] Moreover, if, as shall be argued, a more conventional approach to government in Ireland could well have obviated the need for military conquest, it follows that the cost of victory was unacceptably high. Large parts of Ireland had been devastated, crops burned, cattle slaughtered, buildings razed: Ulster was almost a wilderness, Munster west of Cork almost uninhabited, trade disrupted, the coinage debased, towns ruined or declining, and the population decimated by famine. The contrast with England could hardly have been starker.

Even if we leave aside Elizabeth's last years as untypical, the Tudor achievement in Ireland remains distinctly unimpressive. The concerns of sixteenth-century governments were very limited, particularly in Ireland where the border's proximity imposed additional constraints on inadequate resources. Yet kings were traditionally expected to do justice, maintain order, and defend their subjects from invasion and insurrection: and an additional Tudor preoccupation was the maintenance of religious uniformity. Tudor government clearly made little progress in these tasks, even within the traditional English regions, and still less in Gaelic and border lands. Elizabeth's Irish bench had a poor reputation for impartial justice, the council was distracted by more urgent problems, and the frequent resort to martial law brought the whole system into disrepute. The government did perhaps succeed in curbing aristocratic feuds after 1565, but this was hardly because disputes were now pursued in the lawcourts: rather the polarization of political opinion under Elizabeth prompted Old English magnates to close ranks and redirect their energies against the newcomers or to engage in outright rebellion. Indeed Irish politics were punctuated by revolt throughout the Tudor period, and perhaps the main reason why Elizabethan governors (aided by wind and weather) were not more troubled by foreign invasion was that continental powers regarded the strategic possibilities of Irish unrest as strictly limited. The failure of the established church to strike firm roots in local society also contributed its share of unrest and disorder. Thus between the various revolts, petty raiding, and the disorders of the garrisons, Elizabethan Ireland enjoyed remarkably few sustained periods of peace and stability.

The sharp contrast between the Tudor regime's comparative success in England and its dismal record in Ireland must surely cast doubt on its general policies there. The consensus of historical opinion has been that geographical, cultural and social differences within the island and between Ireland and England created conditions that were so extraordinary by English standards as to constitute an intractable problem of government: Tudor government failed in Ireland because it failed to appreciate the need for extraordinary remedies for exceptional problems. Of course there is some truth in this argument, but also

2. Williams 1979, p. 462.
3. Smith 1984, pp. 233–8.

much Whiggery. Undoubtedly, the particular combination of exceptions to English norms *was* peculiar to Ireland: but individually marcher conditions and differences of law and language had all been encountered elsewhere, and Irish problems were not so different from those successfully resolved in other Tudor borderlands. Moreover, in the early Tudor lordship the traditional techniques of English government *had* brought about a gradual improvement in conditions, discernible in the areas of justice, order and defence. Why then did Tudor policies subsequently break down?

Clearly there is no short answer to this question, but arguably the general thrust of later Tudor policy for Ireland was fundamentally misplaced. From being a distinctly peripheral consideration under Edward IV and Henry VII, Irish affairs became increasingly more important thereafter, and the Tudors spent increasingly large amounts on government there. Yet almost invariably after 1534 the demands made of successive governors grossly outstripped the resources available to them to perform their duties, and this led to the erratic operation of government and frequent reversals of policy. To evaluate the relative merits of the various strategies attempted by the Tudors is a highly subjective exercise, but it should be said that most of them were inherently workable: usually Tudor policies failed in Ireland because they were not given the chance to succeed. Yet the policies of successive governors did become increasingly ambitious (even taking into account that Tudor government everywhere became gradually more intensive), while Tudor monarchs remained reluctant to contemplate Irish government as a *long-term* drain on their resources. It is perhaps in this context that the various policy options may best be evaluated.

The Kildare ascendancy proved that the late medieval lordship could be administered out of its own resources, even if the resultant standard of government was comparatively low. To make any real progress in reducing Gaelic Ireland, however, required English subventions. The options were wide, but financial considerations still determined what was practicable. Theoretically the king could, as Surrey advocated in 1520, despatch an army of 6,000 men and keep it there until Gaelic Ireland had been conquered and remodelled to his liking. This would certainly have been more effective and less expensive than the gradual build-up to the Elizabethan conquest, which gave Gaelic chiefs ample opportunity to prepare resistance: but no monarch could have accepted such substantial and ongoing commitments in Ireland. Unfortunately, however, Elizabeth did allow herself to be persuaded that Gaelic Ireland could be conquered within three years by a smaller army! In practical terms, the cheapest option was probably something akin to St Leger's surrender and regrant scheme, because this strategy attempted (with some success) to win the support of Gaelic chiefs for anglicization by helping them also to consolidate their local power base: concurrently, the support of the Englishry was assured, despite the expense and inconvenience of an enlarged garrison, because the scheme promised increased stability and security, and an enhanced political standing for the local leadership within an extended Tudor state.

It also had two major disadvantages, however. First, by supporting the chiefs against their local rivals, it threatened to create overmighty subjects; although in borderlands English kings had traditionally viewed strong government by potentially overmighty subjects as preferable to disorder or the expense of intervention. Sidney's modification of the approach eliminated this threat by aiming to create directly a 'civil' gentry-dominated society, but its initial impact on Gaelic society was consequently more disruptive and its implementation therefore more costly. Second, progress was unspectacular, but this was chiefly because Henry VIII denied St Leger's administration the means to move more quickly.

The major political mistakes were made during the mid-Tudor period of weak government (1547–60), when influential outsiders attempted by new methods to accelerate the change already taking place. A poor and remote borderland was always likely to appear backward and unruly to cultured courtiers; but by dissociating local lords and gentry from their environment, English administrators could persuade themselves that corruption and disloyalty among local politicians, rather than inadequate resources, were chiefly responsible for the slow progress. Allegedly, if the campaign were directed by trusted and impartial outsiders, Gaelic Ireland would be quickly and efficiently civilized. In terms of overall policy these considerations were marginal: but much more serious was the precipitate manner in which the newcomers were packed into key positions. This development antagonized the local community and initiated a ruinous power struggle within the Dublin administration between New and Old English politicians. Thus the additional money and men provided after 1547 were largely squandered in internal feuding. Disgruntled local lords withheld their cooperation, while the vast majority of the newcomers were seemingly men of modest means more intent on making their fortunes than civilizing the natives. Unfortunately for these adventurers, Gaelic Ireland was too poor to offer significant pickings in booty and ransoms, but it did offer ample opportunity for land-grabbing. Moreover, the grossly undermanned Dublin administration was quite unable to curtail disruptive private ventures by its own officials, while the queen and privy council often lacked the information to intervene effectively. The result was that the later Tudors were gradually manoeuvred by their chief ministers in Ireland into pursuing a strategy for conquest which, although inherently sound, far outstripped the resources available. Henry VIII had sanctioned a gradualist strategy to assimilate Gaelic Ireland culturally and politically into the Tudor state: his daughter was eventually committed to an exceedingly ambitious strategy which entailed breaking Old English political influence in order to establish a new political elite preparatory to a costly military conquest of the country. Unfortunately, however, the region in which the Tudors attempted their most ambitious policies was that in which royal government was weakest.

Considering the overall failure of Tudor policy in Ireland, it is hardly surprising that few rulers or ministers emerge with much credit from their interventions there. Most notably, Elizabeth's rule by faction, parsimony, and irresolute conduct of government proved particularly disastrous in Ireland and certainly strengthens the revisionist interpretation beginning to emerge of a queen who made serious mistakes as well as enjoying spectacular successes. Of her councillors, Lord Burghley was particularly well-informed and influential in policy-making for Ireland, but his advocacy of some ill-considered plantation schemes involved Elizabeth in much fruitless expense. Ironically, the ruler who was most successful in Ireland was probably the man who attempted least there: Henry VII required merely that his vital interests be protected and the traditional authority of English kings there preserved, and after 1495 he achieved his ambitions. Henry VIII was, from 1519, more demanding of his governors and less realistic in his policies; but by keeping a tight rein on English subventions for the lordship, he effectively forestalled some of the sillier, programmatic initiatives sponsored by Sussex and Sidney. Of his chief advisers, Norfolk (albeit after service there) had the best grasp of Irish political realities, but his advice was too often ignored. Cromwell was also interested and informed, although his sponsorship of 'direct rule' (1534–40) was comparatively less successful than the similar experiment by Henry VII (1494–6). Protector Somerset's garrison strategy for Gaelic Ireland – an adaptation of his Scottish policy to what superficially appeared a similar problem – was an expensive mistake; and neither Northumberland nor Mary, apparently, were able for long to resist similar demands for ambitious but ill-conceived experiments. Of the various Tudor governors, most performed competently in a difficult office which afforded innumerable avenues to financial ruin, military defeat or political disgrace but offered small opportunity for glory and gain. Yet in their different ways, the eighth earl of Kildare, St Leger and Mountjoy proved outstanding governors, while the conduct of Sussex, Grey de Wilton and Essex ought perhaps to warrant their consignment to a viceregal rogues' gallery.

Overall, the Tudor conquest of Ireland had a substantial impact, both on the making of modern Ireland and also on the development of the contemporary English state. Most obviously, in Ireland itself the manner of its execution and the subsequent settlement under James I caused great bitterness and long-term alienation from royal government of the Gaelic and Old English communities. Within the Englishry, particularist sentiments sharpened into a distinct Old English identity. Concurrently, the different pressures exerted on the traditional Gaelic world by centralizing monarchy in England and Scotland assisted its break-up and the incorporation of the *Gaedhil* of Ireland and Scotland into different political units. In effect, the *Gaedhealtacht* was partitioned and the Gaelic people were marginalized in separate composite kingdoms of *Gaedhil* and *Gaill*. Yet, while London and Edinburgh in this way defused the most dangerous threat to their power and pretensions in the region, these developments also promoted conditions conducive to the gradual emergence, mainly after 1603, of a new Irish nation with a nationalist ideology based on faith and fatherland.

In other ways too, the Tudor conquest continued to set the political agenda. In its aftermath, English law and administrative structures were quickly extended to the former Gaelic lordships. Compared with the ruthless, autocratic rule of the old Gaelic chiefs, the application of the English model of local government ('self-government at the king's command') implied a considerable defusion of power: the leading Gaelic clansmen would be transformed into an English county gentry, representing the new shires in parliament and ruling them as sheriffs and justices of the peace as part of a county community. Likewise, the model envisaged the growth of a politically aware 'middling sort' elected to minor office, as constables or churchwardens for instance, and serving on grand and petty juries.[4] Initially, hopes of just such a transformation may have been raised among previously disenfranchised sections of Gaelic society.[5] Yet in practice, this development was stymied by the very instrument intended to advance it, plantation. On the pretext of 'civilizing the natives', small cliques of English and Scottish colonists attempted to manipulate local government so as to avoid sharing power with rival elites whose interests were diametrically opposed, in terms of politics, culture and religion. The resultant struggle for power eventually precipitated the 1641 rising – significantly, the first popular insurrection in Gaelic history. Yet ironically, this struggle revolved around the administrative structures of this new English kingdom: by 1641, political discourse was conducted entirely within this framework, with no support for the restoration of traditional Gaelic lordship. Thus, in this respect too, the shape of the Tudor conquest set a pattern for Irish politics which, in Northern Ireland at least, has persisted down to the present.

Within a wider context too, the conquest had a major impact both on Tudor England and also, in the context of the 1603 Union of the Crowns, on English patterns of state formation. The conquest was influential in shaping the characteristics of English nationality as it developed in Tudor times. Before the Reformation, the Tudor territories were united principally by a common allegiance to the English crown and by a dominant culture and system of government that were recognizably English. Despite conflict between geographical and cultural criteria of nationality, a generally wide sense of 'Englishness' prevailed which included the Englishry of Ireland. After the breach with Rome, however, and the growing consciousness of differentiation from continental Europe that accompanied the Elizabethan idea of an 'elect nation', a narrower definition of 'Englishness' evolved, from which the catholic Old English were clearly excluded. Yet this new English 'nation-state' might have developed very differently if, as seemed very predictable c. 1534, the Reformation had succeeded in Ireland and the lordship, together with its local elite, had been peacefully absorbed, like Wales and the north, into a unitary realm of England. As it was, Ireland developed differently, with the unfortunate results that are painfully apparent today. To the Tudor specialist, however, the fate of Irish variations on familiar constitutional themes, illustrated by the cess controversy, the decline of parliament, the growth of a standing army, and the abuse of martial law, do at least underline the very delicate nature of the balance between

---

4. Ellis 1992b, pp. 141–3, reviewing a recent case-study of the transformation from Gaelic lordship to English shire which, unfortunately, simply ignores this perspective.
5. See, for instance, the remarks in *NHI*, iii, pp. 535–7, 555–6; Dunne 1980, pp. 24–5.

crown and community, on which political change in Tudor England was founded. Similarly the Tudor failure in Ireland shows how barely adequate were the English government's resources to tackle the serious problems that it faced elsewhere.

Finally, the Tudor conquest also reinforced an emerging English pattern of state formation (evident also in the treatment of Wales and the English north) by centralization, administrative uniformity, and cultural imperialism. In Ireland, this took the form of the imposition of the highly centralized structures of English government on remote and 'uncivilized' Gaelic lordships and their integration, together with the English lordship there, into a dependant kingdom. The new kingdom of Ireland, controlled from London but without a substantial input into the political process there, proved a serious and continuing source of instability in the developing British state. The device of a dependent kingdom set an unfortunate precedent, offering a misleading model much favoured by English politicians, for the incorporation of Scotland into a wider English state following the Union of the Crowns in 1603. Thus, in many ways, the eventual shape of the Tudor conquest left as its legacy a series of unresolved tensions between King James's three kingdoms which later came back to haunt the Stewart monarchy, precipitating its collapse and the creation of a republic (1638–51).[6]

6. Ellis 1995b, pp. 61–3.

GLOSSARY OF TERMS

assignment exchequer device for anticipating revenue by issuing a tally (q.v.) in advance of payment by an accountant.

attainder formal declaration, without trial and especially by parliament, that a man is a traitor.

bill (see also **writs**) formal petition, usually in English, used to initiate legal proceedings, especially in prerogative court.

Bill of Middlesex legal device used to give king's bench cognizance of a case normally determined elsewhere.

blackrent rent illegally extorted, commonly by Gaelic chiefs on English marchers in return for 'protection'.

booking administrative device whereby lords and gentry were required to indicate those dependants for whose conduct they would answer.

brehonlaw name given to the legal system used in Gaelic parts (*breitheamh(ain)* = judge(s)).

bull solemn papal document.

cess (= assess) general term used in Ireland to refer to a range of government impositions, notably purveyance (q.v.), **cartage** (the levy of carts for transport) and **cesses of labourers** (the organization of labour services for building works).

chantry endowment of a priest to say mass for the soul of the founder.

clan the basic Gaelic corporate family group of unilineal descent, with political and legal functions.

coarb literally, the successor (*comharba*) of the patron saint, an office of high spiritual prestige.

coign (and livery) general term for the various Gaelic exactions arising from the free quartering of the chief's dependants on the country (*coin-mheadh* = billeting; livery = purveyance, q.v.).

(common) socage (see also **knight-service**) form of landholding whereby the tenant's chief obligation was to pay rent, and in which the incidents of tenure were less onerous, excluding wardship (q.v.; see also **feudal incidents**).

359

concealments land that was rightfully forfeited or escheated by common law but secretly detained.

copyholder tenant who held land on terms set out in a copy of the manorial court roll.

cottiers category of poor tenant holding a small parcel of land with a cottage on a short lease.

creaghts (caoruigheachta) herds of cattle with their keepers.

demesne lands and rights retained for direct exploitation by the lord.

deposition sworn statement given in evidence.

distress confiscation of movables by court order.

embracery corruption of juries.

erenagh hereditary tenant of church lands.

escheat return of a tenant's lands to his lord in default of an heir or if convicted of felony (q.v.).

felony criminal offence carrying the death penalty.

feudal incidents dues owed by tenants for their lands, notably relief, escheat and wardship (q.v.).

first fruits the first year's revenue of all ecclesiastical benefices paid as royal taxation; this replaced similar payments called **annates** to the papacy for certain greater benefices at the Reformation.

fosterage Gaelic custom whereby nobles committed the upbringing of their children to others with the aim of developing a political connection.

franchises and liberties areas where subjects exercised quasi-independent administrative and judicial authority.

Gaedhil and **Gaill** Gaelic names for the peoples, native and settler respectively, of Ireland and Scotland.

galloglass Gaelic professional foot-soldiers, of Scottish descent, who fought with a distinctive axe.

gavelkind system of partible inheritance prevailing in Kent but extended in English usage to denote the system of joint and equal inheritance among males found in Ireland and Wales.

hosting military expedition, especially by royal army which included contingents of militia; also the obligation to unpaid military service by able-bodied men to defend Tudor Ireland. The equivalent obligation in Gaelic lordships was called the **rising-out**.

husbandman category of fairly prosperous peasant who commonly held 20–30 acres of land on long lease or copyhold (q.v.).

idlemen term used by English officials of professional soldiers who apparently contravened the statutes against poverty and vagrancy.

impropriate annexation of ecclesiastical property into lay hands.

indenture document used to record a contract or lease between two parties.

indictment formal accusation which began criminal proceedings.

inquisition formal inquiry by sworn evidence before a jury.

kerne unarmoured Gaelic footmen, equipped with sword, bow or javelin.

knight-service originally unpaid military service owed in return for tenure of land; in Tudor times it denoted the form of tenure itself, which was now distinguished by heavier feudal dues on the tenant, notably wardship and (in Ireland until 1531) scutage (q.v.). See also **feudal incidents**.

livery 1. surrender to heir of lands in knight-service; also payment exacted for this. 2. purveyance (q.v.).

maintenance use of influence or threats in support of a lawsuit with the aim of perverting justice.

maghery (*machaire* = champaigne ground) the innermost region of the Pale, insulated from Gaelic raids by fortifications, dykes and ditches.

march frontier or border region.

march law an amalgam of brehon and common (English) law.

mark money of account, worth 13s. 4d. or two-thirds of a pound.

mesne process (*mesne* = intermediate) the legal procedure by which a court aimed to secure defendant's appearance.

misdemeanour criminal offence which was less serious than a felony and carried a lesser penalty.

***nisi prius* procedure** practice whereby juries were summoned to Dublin or Westminster unless the matter had previously been settled at the local assizes, as it usually was.

Observant mendicant house which adhered strictly to the Rule of the founder (v. **conventual**, which did not).

oyer and terminer literally, to hear and determine; a commission to try and judge criminal cases. Assize judges commonly acted also as commissioners of **gaol delivery** (to try prisoners held in gaol) and of **assize** (to try civil suits).

palatinate category of liberty (q.v.) in which almost all royal rights were delegated to the subject.

Pale English Pale in Ireland comprising the four medieval counties of Dublin, Kildare, Louth and Meath and divided into march (q.v.) and maghery (q.v.; *machaire* = plain).

pledge person, goods or land retained as surety for performance of agreement by the donor; also mortgage of land in Gaelic Ireland.

ploughland (also **carucate, quarter**) measure of land, commonly 120 medieval acres.

poundage custom of 12d. per pound value levied on imports and exports.

praemunire strictly, a writ designed to prevent invasions of royal jurisdictional rights; more generally, offences by clergy against the king's authority.

presentment formal finding or statement by grand jury in reply to charge.

primogeniture system of inheritance by which the eldest son succeeds to all his father's landed property.

provisor person appointed ('provided') by the pope to an ecclesiastical benefice, especially without royal permission.

purveyance king's right to pre-empt food and procure transportation for his household below market price; extended in Ireland to provision the governor's retinue.

quo minus (writ of) legal device used to give the exchequer cognizance of an action for debt normally determined elsewhere.

redshanks Scots Highland mercenary foot-soldiers serving with Irish.

sanctuary right of criminals to shelter in a church or other area from which royal officials were excluded; also applied to the place of refuge.

scutage commutation of knight-service (q.v.) owed; also called **royal service** in Ireland.

slantyaght protection extended by a magnate to a lesser man.

Statute of Henry FitzEmpress custom whereby the Irish council elected a justiciar or temporary governor to serve during the king's pleasure if the land was left without a governor.

subinfeudation process whereby the king and great lords distributed lands to their followers, and these in turn to their own men, to hold by knight-service.

sub poena writ ordering defendant's appearance before prerogative court without stating cause.

surrender and regrant modern name for the process whereby Henry VIII and his successors regularized titles by Gaelic law to land.

tail male form of dividing estates whereby they are reserved to the direct male descendants of the original grantee.

tally small wooden stick issued by the exchequer as a receipt for money paid in.

tanist literally, second (*tánaiste*), but usually denoted the successor-designate of a Gaelic chief. Tudor writers used **tanistry** generally to refer to the system of succession by seniority.

temporalities resources of a church, especially a greater benefice, held in return for secular services such as feudal dues.

twentieths one-twentieth of the annual value of Irish benefices paid yearly as royal taxation after the Reformation. In England a **tenth** was payable.

use legal device designed to keep land out of wardship by granting it to trustees for the use of the effective owner.

villein (also **native, betagh**) serf or unfree peasant bound to lord or estate.

wardship lord's right to guardianship of those tenants by knight-service who succeeded to their lands as minors, involving the administration of the lands and the right to arrange their marriages.

writs standardized legal letters, usually in Latin, conveying formal royal orders. **Original writs**, sealed in chancery, were used to give particular court cognizance of a case; **judicial writs**, sealed in court, executed its orders.

yeoman prosperous peasant who held land in freehold.

TABLES

KEY TO TABLES

a.	ante, before
c.	circa, around
C	afforced council
cons.	consecrated
cr.	created
D.	deputy
D.L.	deputy-lieutenant
depr.	deprived
d.s.p. leg.	died without legitimate posterity
d.s.p.m.	died without masculine posterity
d.s.p.s.	died without surviving posterity
forf.	forfeited
G.C.	great council
J.	justiciar/justice
L.	lieutenant
nom.	nominated
p.	post, after
P	parliament
prov.	provided
recog.	recognized
res.	resigned
rest.	restored
s. & h.	son and heir
st.	styled
temp.	temporalities restored
trs.	translated
( )	date in brackets denotes officer acting by that date

CHIEF GOVERNORS

monarch	governor	date of appointment	period of office
Hen. VI	John, e. of Shrewsbury, L.	21 May 1445	a. 18 Nov. 1446 – p. 20 Oct. 1447
	Richard Talbot, abp of Dublin, D.L.		c. Nov. 1447–1448
	Richard, d. of York, L.	9 Dec. 1447	c. 9 July 1449 – c. 8 Sept. 1450
	Richard Nugent, Ld Delvin, D.L.		a. 23 Dec. 1448 – ? 6 July 1449
	James, 4th e. of Ormond, D.L.	23 Aug. 1450	c. 8 Sept. 1450 – 23 Aug. 1452
	Edward FitzEustace, D.L.		p. 23 Aug. 1452 – p. 25 May 1453
	James, 5th e. of Ormond, L.	12 May 1453	a. 14 Sept. 1453 – p. 8 Mar. 1454
	John Mey, abp of Armagh, D.L.		
	Richard, d. of York, L.	1 Dec. 1454	c. Dec. 1459 – early Sept. 1460
	Edward FitzEustace, D.L.	23 Apr. 1454	22 May 1454 – 25 Oct. 1454
	Thomas, 7th e. of Kildare, J.		a. 6 Nov. 1454 – p. 13 Feb. 1455
	Thomas, 7th e. of Kildare, D.L.		a. 18 Apr. 1455 – autumn 1459
	(James, 5th e. of Ormond, L.)		
	(Thomas Bathe and John Bole, abp of Armagh, D.L.)		
	Thomas, 7th e. of Kildare, D.L.	4 Dec. 1459	Sept. – Dec. 1460
	Thomas, 7th e. of Kildare, J.		Jan. – ?Mar. 1461
	Thomas, 7th e. of Kildare, J.		?Mar. 1461 – 12 June 1462
Edw. IV	George, d. of Clarence, L.	28 Feb. 1462	12 June 1462 – Apr. 1463
	Roland FitzEustace, Ld Portlester, D.L.	16 May 1462	
	Thomas, e. of Desmond, D.L.	1 Apr. 1463	? Apr. 1463 – p. 13 Oct. 1467
	Thomas, e. of Kildare, D. to Desmond		p. 24 June 1464 – late summer 1464
	(John, e. of Worcester, D.L.)		
	John, e. of Worcester, D.L.	? May 1465	
	John, e. of Worcester, L.	spring 1467	a. 31 Oct. 1467 – p. 9 Jan. 1470
	Edmund Dudley, D.L.		spring – summer 1470
	Thomas, e. of Kildare, J.	? 23 May 1470	a. 13 Oct. 1470 – p. 3 Dec. 1470

monarch	governor	date of appointment	period of office
Hen. VI	George, d. of Clarence, L.	18 Feb. 1471	a. 7 Feb. 1471 – ? Apr. 1471
Edw. IV	Thomas, e. of Kildare, D.L.		a. 12 May 1471 – 22–28 Dec. 1471
	Thomas, e. of Kildare, J.	16 Mar. 1472	22 x 28 Dec. 1471 – ? May 1475
	George, d. of Clarence, L.		? May 1475 – Feb. 1478
	Thomas, e. of Kildare, D.L.	a. 18 Apr. 1475	1477
	William Sherwood, bp of Meath, D.L.		? Feb. 1478 – 25 Mar. 1478
	Robert Preston, Ld Gormanston, D. to Sherwood		
	Thomas, e. of Kildare, J.	10 Mar. 1478	c. 25 Mar. 1478 – a. 15 Sept. 1478
	(John, d. of Suffolk, L.)		
	Gerald, e. of Kildare, J.		
	George, son of Edward IV, L.	6 July 1478	a. 15 Sept. 1478 – p. 15 Dec. 1478
	Henry, Ld Grey of Ruthin, D.L.		a. 14 Jan. 1479 – p. Mar. 1479
	Robert Preston, Visct Gormanston, D. to Grey	5 May 1479 – p. Mar. 1479	
	Richard, d. of York, L.	7 May 1479	? 1 June 1479 – p. 18 Oct. 1479
	Robert Preston, Visct Gormanston, D.L.	a. 5 Oct. 1479	p. 18 Oct. 1479 – p. 9 Apr. 1483
	Gerald, e. of Kildare, D.L.		p. 9 Apr. 1483 – 31 Aug. 1483
Ric. III	Gerald, e. of Kildare, J.	19 July 1483	
	Edward, son of Richard III, L.	31 Aug. 1483	31 Aug. 1483 – Mar. 1484
	Gerald, e. of Kildare, D.L.		? Mar. 1484 – p. 15 Oct. 1484
	Gerald, e. of Kildare, J.	21 Aug. 1484	
	John, e. of Lincoln, L.	c. 22 Sept. 1484	p. 22 Oct. 1484 – ? 24 Oct. 1485
Hen. VII	Gerald, e. of Kildare, D.L.		a. 18 Dec. 1485 – ? Mar. 1486
	Gerald, e. of Kildare, J.	11 Mar. 1486	? Mar. 1486 – 20 May 1492
	Jasper, d. of Bedford, L.		a. 24 May 1487 – p. 13 Aug. 1487
	Gerald, e. of Kildare, D.L.		
[Edw. VI]	(Gerald, e. of Kildare, L.)	20 May 1492	20 May 1492 – p. 3 Sept. 1493
	Walter FitzSimons, abp of Dublin, D.L.		a. 6 July 1492 – p 3 Sept. 1493
	James Ormond, governor		

	Name	Appointment	Term
	Robert Preston, Visct Gormanston, D.L.	a. 12 Sept. 1493	a. 12 Sept. 1493 – a. 12 Oct. 1494
	William Preston, D. to Gormanston		c. Nov. 1493 – a. 20 Feb. 1494
	Henry, d. of York, L.	12 Sept. 1494	a. 12 Oct. 1494 – p. 20 Dec. 1495
	Edward Poynings, D.	13 Sept. 1494	1 Jan. 1496 – p. 4 July 1496
	Henry Deane, bp of Bangor, J.	1 Jan. 1496	6 July 1496 – 21 Sept. 1496
	Gilbert Nugent, Ld Delvin, commr		21 Sept. 1496 – p. 21 Apr. 1509
	Gerald, e. of Kildare, D.	6 Aug. 1496	? Apr. 1503 – Aug. 1503
	Walter FitzSimons, abp of Dublin, D. to Kildare		a. 1 June 1509 – Nov. 1510
Hen VIII	Gerald, e. of Kildare, J.	8 Nov. 1510	? Nov. 1510 – 3 Sept. 1513
	Gerald, e. of Kildare, D.	4 Sept. 1513	4 Sept. 1513 – p. 26 Nov. 1513
	Gerald, e. of Kildare, J.	26 Nov. 1513	a. 13 Jan. 1514 – p. 5 May 1515
	Gerald, e. of Kildare, D.	13 Apr. 1515	a. 14 May 1515 – a. 20 Sept. 1515
	William Preston, Visct Gormanston, J.		a. 20 Sept. 1515 – p. 10 Sept. 1519
	Gerald, e. of Kildare, D.		a. 20 Dec. 1519 – 23 May 1520
	Maurice FitzGerald, D. to Kildare	10 Mar. 1520	24 May 1520 – p. 21 Mar. 1522
	Thomas, e. of Surrey, L.		p. 21 Dec. 1521 – a. 9 Mar. 1522
	Piers, e. of Ormond, D.L.	6 Mar. 1522	6 Mar. 1522 – 4 Aug. 1524
	Piers, e. of Ormond, D.	13 May 1524	4 Aug. 1524 – p. 20 Dec. 1526
	Gerald, e. of Kildare, D.		p. 20 Dec. 1526 – ? a. 14 Sept. 1527
	Thomas FitzGerald, D. to Kildare	?	p. 14 Sept. 1527 – ? p. 10 June 1528
	Richard Nugent, Ld Delvin, D. to Kildare	15 May 1528	15 May 1528 – a. 14 Oct. 1528
	Thomas FitzGerald, captain	4 Aug. 1528	a. 14 Oct. 1528 – a. 4 Sept. 1529
	Piers, e. of Ossory, D.	22 June 1529	
	Henry, d. of Richmond, L.	secret council as D.	a. 4 Sept. 1529 – 24 Aug. 1530
	John Alen, abp of Dublin		
	Patrick Bermingham		
	John Rawson		
	William Skeffington, D.	22 June 1530	24 Aug. 1530 – 18 Aug. 1532
	Gerald, e. of Kildare, D.	5 July 1532	18 Aug. 1532 – 11 June 1534
	Thomas FitzGerald, Ld Offaly, D. to Kildare		mid-Feb. 1532 – 11 June 1534

monarch	governor	date of appointment	period of office
	Richard Nugent, Ld Delvin, governor		?11 June 1534 – ? early Aug. 1534
	John Barnewall, Ld Trimblestone, ?governor		? early Aug. 1534 – 24 Oct. 1534
	William Skeffington, D.	23 July 1534	24 Oct. 1534 – 31 Dec. 1535
	Leonard, Ld Grey, J.	1 Jan. 1536	1 Jan. 1536 – c. Mar. 1536
	Leonard, Ld Grey, D.	23 Feb. 1536	c. Mar. 1536 – Apr. 1540
	William Brereton, J.	1 Apr. 1540	2 May 1540 – c. 12 Aug. 1540
	Anthony St Leger, D.	7 July 1540	c. 12 Aug. 1540 – 10 Feb. 1544
	William Brabazon, J.	12 Oct. 1543	10 Feb. 1544 – 11 Aug. 1544
	Anthony St Leger, D.	3 July 1544	11 Aug. 1544 – 1 Apr. 1546
	William Brabazon, J.	16 Feb. 1546	1 Apr. 1546 – 16 Dec. 1546
	Anthony St Leger, D.	7 Nov. 1546	16 Dec. 1546 – Mar. 1547
Edw. VI	Anthony St Leger, J.		Mar. 1547 – Apr. 1547
	Anthony St Leger, D.	7 Apr. 1547	Apr. 1547 – 21 May 1548
	Edward Bellingham, D.	22 Apr. 1548	21 May 1548 – 29 Dec. 1549
	Francis Bryan, J.	27 Dec. 1549	29 Dec. 1549 – 2 Feb. 1550
	William Brabazon, J.	2 Feb. 1550	2 Feb. 1550 – 10 Sept. 1550
	Anthony St Leger, D.	4 Aug. 1550	10 Sept. 1550 – 23 May 1551
	James Croft, D.	29 Apr. 1551	23 May 1551 – 9 Dec. 1552
	Thomas Cusack and Gerald Aylmer, J.	6 Dec. 1552	9 Dec. 1552 – c. 25 July 1553
[Jane]	Thomas Cusack and Gerald Aylmer, J.		c. 25 July 1553 – c. ? 18 Aug. 1553
Mary	Thomas Cusack and Gerald Aylmer, J.		c. 18 Aug. 1553 – 19 Nov. 1553
	Anthony St Leger, D.	1 Sept. 1553	19 Nov. 1553 – 26 May 1556
	Thomas Radcliffe, Ld Fitzwalter (e. of Sussex, 1557)	21 Apr. 1556	26 May 1556 – 5 Dec. 1557
	Hugh Curwin, abp of Dublin, and Henry Sidney, J.	12 Nov. 1557	5 Dec. 1557 – 6 Feb. 1558
	Henry Sidney, J.	18 Jan. 1558	6 Feb. 1558 – 26 May 1558
	Thomas, e. of Sussex, D.	9 Mar. 1558	26 May 1558 – 18 Sept. 1558
	Henry Sidney, J.	4 Aug. 1558	18 Sept. 1558 – 10 Nov. 1558
	Thomas, e. of Sussex, D.	17 Aug. 1558	10 Nov. 1558 – 12 Dec. 1558

Eliz. I			
Henry Sidney, J.	12 Dec. 1558	13 Dec. 1558 – 30 Aug. 1559
Thomas, e. of Sussex, D.	3 July 1559	30 Aug. 1559 – 15 Feb. 1560
William Fitzwilliam, J.	18 Jan. 1560	15 Feb. 1560 – 25 June 1560
Thomas, e. of Sussex, L.	6 May 1560	25 June 1560 – 2 Feb. 1561
William Fitzwilliam, J.	10 Jan. 1561	2 Feb. 1561 – 5 June 1561
Thomas, e. of Sussex, L.	24 May 1561	5 June 1561 – 22 Jan. 1562
William Fitzwilliam, J.	20 Dec. 1561	22 Jan. 1562 – 29 July 1562
Thomas, e. of Sussex, L.	4 July 1562	29 July 1562 – 25 May 1564
Nicholas Arnold, J.	2 May 1564	25 May 1564 – 20 Jan. 1566
Henry Sidney, D.	13 Oct. 1565	20 Jan. 1566 – 14 Oct. 1567
Robert Weston and William Fitzwilliam, J.	9 Oct. 1567	14 Oct. 1567 – 28 Oct. 1568
Henry Sidney, D.	17 Apr. 1568	28 Oct. 1568 – 1 Apr. 1571
William Fitzwilliam, J.	1 Apr. 1571	1 Apr. 1571 – 13 Jan. 1572
William Fitzwilliam, D.	11 Dec. 1571	13 Jan. 1572 – 18 Sept. 1575
Henry Sidney, D.	5 Aug. 1575	18 Sept. 1575 – 14 Sept. 1578
William Drury, J.	27 Apr. 1578	14 Sept. 1578 – 3 Oct. 1579
William Pelham, J.	11 Oct. 1579	11 Oct. 1579 – 7 Sept. 1580
Arthur, Ld Grey de Wilton, D.	15 July 1580	7 Sept. 1580 – 31 Aug. 1582
Adam Loftus, abp of Dublin, and Henry Wallop, J.	25 Aug. 1582	31 Aug. 1582 – 21 June 1584
John Perrot, D.	7 Jan. 1584	21 June 1584 – 30 June 1588
William Fitzwilliam, D.	17 Feb. 1588	30 June 1588 – 11 Aug. 1594
William Russell, D.	16 May 1594	11 Aug. 1594 – 22 May 1597
Thomas, Ld Burgh, D.	5 Mar. 1597	22 May 1597 – 13 Oct. 1597
Thomas Norris, J.	29 Oct. 1597	30 Oct. 1597 – 27 Nov. 1597
Adam Loftus, abp of Dublin, and Robert Gardiner, J.	26 Nov. 1597	27 Nov. 1597 – 15 Apr. 1599
Robert, e. of Essex, L.	12 Mar. 1599	15 Apr. 1599 – 25 Sept. 1599
Adam Loftus, abp of Dublin, and George Carey, J.	24 Sept. 1599	25 Sept. 1599 – 27 Feb. 1600
Charles Blount, Ld Mountjoy, D.	21 Jan. 1600	28 Feb. 1600 – 5 Apr. 1603

(*Source:* Ellis 1986a app. i; *HBC*, pp. 163–7; *NHI*, ix, pp. 479–87)

LORD CHANCELLORS AND KEEPERS OF
THE GREAT SEAL

2 Sept. 1446	John Talbot (e. of Shrewsbury from July 1453)
a. 13 Jan. 1447	Robert Dyke (deputy)
6 Nov. 1451	Thomas Talbot, prior of Kilmainham (deputy)
7 Aug. 1454	William Welles (deputy)
5 Apr. 1458	Michael Tregury, abp of Dublin (deputy)
5 Apr. 1448	Thomas Fitzgerald, prior of Kilmainham (office granted in reversion)
24 Feb. 1460	Edmund, e. of Rutland
5 Nov. 1460	John Dinham
2 May 1461	John Dinham
2 May 1461	Robert Preston, Ld Gormanston (deputy)
18 July 1461	William Welles
?	Walter Devereux
25 Jan. 1464	Thomas, 7th e. of Kildare
31 Jan. 1464	(John, e. of Worcester)
26 Jan. 1464	(William Sherwood, bp of Meath)
?	Edmund Dudley
16 Apr. 1472	Roland FitzEustace, Ld Portlester, & John Tapton
5 Aug. 1474	Gilbert Debenham
15 Feb. 1478	Richard Martyn
5 Oct. 1479	William Sherwood, bp of Meath
1482	Walter Champfleur, abb. of St Mary's, Dublin (keeper)
25 Aug. 1482	William Sherwood, bp of Meath
11 Jan. 1483	Robert St Lawrence, Ld Howth
1482/3	Thomas Fitzgerald
1486/7	Rowland FitzEustace, Ld Portlester
11 June 1492	Alexander Plunket
13 Sept. 1494	Henry Deane, bp of Bangor
6 Aug. 1496	Walter FitzSimons, abp of Dublin
(16 Apr. 1505)	John Payne, bp of Meath (keeper)
21 May 1512	William Rokeby, abp of Dublin
6 Nov. 1513	William Compton
8 Feb. 1522	Hugh Inge, bp of Meath
19 Sept. 1528	John Alen, abp of Dublin
5 July 1532	George Cromer, abp of Armagh
16 Aug. 1534	John Barnewall, Ld Trimblestone
31 Aug. 1538	John Alen (keeper)
18 Oct. 1538	John Alen
1 May 1546	Thomas Cusack (keeper)
6 Nov. 1546	Richard Rede
22 Apr. 1548	John Alen
4 Aug. 1550	Thomas Cusack
7 Aug. 1555	William Fitzwilliams (keeper)
13 Sept. 1555	Hugh Curwin, abp of Dublin
10 June 1567	Robert Weston
25 May 1573	Adam Loftus, abp of Dublin (keeper)
23 Apr. 1576	William Gerrard

15 Sept. 1577	Adam Loftus, abp of Dublin (keeper)
?	William Gerrard
10 Oct. 1579	Adam Loftus, abp of Dublin (keeper)
?	William Gerrard
6 Mar. 1581	Adam Loftus, abp of Dublin (keeper)
1581	Adam Loftus, abp of Dublin

(*Source:* Ellis 1986a, app. i; *NHI*, ix, pp. 505–6)

LORD TREASURERS

1444	Giles Thorndon
1452	Roland FitzEustace
1 May 1461	Roland FitzEustace
21 Dec. 1461	Idem et John, Ld Wenlock
(Dec. 1479)	Roland FitzEustace
(14 Jan. 1484)	Robert Dovedall (deputy)
11 June 1492	Thomas, e. of Ormond
15 June 1492	James Ormond
(10 Mar. 1494)	William Preston (deputy)
13 Sept. 1494	Hugh Conway
28 Feb. 1504	Gerald Fitzgerald
(25 Nov. 1505)	William Darcy (deputy)
13 Jan. 1514	Christopher Fleming, Ld Slane
(11 Feb. 1516)	Bartholomew Dillon (deputy)
8 Feb. 1522	John Rawson
13 May 1524	Piers, e. of Ormond
19 Sept. 1528	John Rawson
5 July 1532	James, Ld Butler (e. of Ormond, 1539–46)
29 Mar. 1547	James, e. of Desmond
26 Aug. 1559	Thomas, e. of Ormond

(*Source:* Ellis 1986a, app. i; Lascelles 1852, i, pt. ii. p. 41, *IHS*, ii, p. 377)

UNDERTREASURERS

26 Apr. 1495	William Hattecliffe
2 July 1516	Bartholomew Dillon
11 Mar. 1520	John Stile
(13 Oct. 1523)	William Darcy
3 Sept. 1524	John Barnewall, Ld Trimblestone
(East. 1529)	Bartholomew Dillon
11 Sept. 1532	William Bath
26 Aug. 1534	William Brabazon
20 Jan. 1551	*Idem et* Andrew Wise
12 Dec. 1553	Edmund Rouse
13 Apr. 1556	Henry Sidney

24 July 1559	William Fitzwilliam
5 Aug. 1575	Edward Fitton
10 Aug. 1579	Henry Wallop
1 Mar. 1598	George Carey

(*Source:* Ellis 1986a, app. i; Lascelles 1852, i. pt. ii, pp. 42–3)

PARLIAMENTS AND GREAT COUNCILS, 1447–1603

year	regnal year	date of opening	place	
1447	25 Hen. VI	13 Jan.	Trim	P
1447	26 Hen. VI	20 Oct.	Naas	G.C.
1449	27 Hen. VI	28 Feb.	Dublin	P
1449	28 Hen. VI	17 Oct.	Dublin	G.C.
1450	28 Hen. VI	24 Apr.	Drogheda	P
1450	29 Hen. VI	27 Nov.	Drogheda	G.C.
		adjourned to 14 Dec.	Dublin	P
1451	29 Hen. VI	26 Mar.	Drogheda	P
1451/2	30 Hen. VI	?	Dublin	P
1453	31 Hen. VI	25 May	Dublin	G.C.
1454	32 Hen. VI	5 July	Dublin	P
1455	33 Hen. VI	14 Feb.	Dublin	P
1455	34 Hen. VI	18 Apr.	Dublin	G.C.
1456	35 Hen. VI	5 Nov.	Naas	P
1457	35 Hen. VI	28 Jan.	Dublin	P
1458	36 Hen. VI	3 Feb.	Dublin	P
1459	37 Hen. VI	9 Feb.	Dublin	P

year	regnal year	dates of session	place	
1460	38 Hen. VI	8 Feb. – [ ]	Drogheda	P
		23 Feb. – [ ]	Dublin	
		3 Mar. – 7 Mar.		
		28 Apr. – 28 Apr.		
		9 June – 11 June		
		21 July – [ ]		
1461	1 Edw. IV	12 June – [ ]	Naas	P
1462	1–2 Edw. IV	8 Jan. – [ ]	Dublin	G.C.
		8 Mar. – [ ]		
		3 May – [ ]		
1462	2 Edw. IV	15 Oct. – [ ]	Dublin	P
1463	3 Edw. IV	4 Nov. – 10 Nov.	Wexford	P
		14 Nov. – 19 Nov.	Waterford	
1464		20 Feb. – 24 Feb.	Naas	
		27 Feb. – 3 Mar.	Dublin	
1465	5 Edw. IV	12 Aug. – 17 Aug.	Trim	P
		14 Oct. – 22 Oct.	Dublin	
		18 Nov. – [ ]	Drogheda	

year	regnal year	dates of session	place	
1467	7–8 Edward IV	11 Dec. – 23 Dec.	Dublin	P
1468		4 Feb. – 22 or 23 Feb.	Drogheda	
		2 May – 3 May		
		30 May – 31 May		
		20 June – 28 June		
		11 July – 13 July		
		26 or 27 July – 29 or 30 July		
		1 Sept. – 3 Sept.		
		3 Oct. – 5 Oct.		
		3 or 7 Nov. – 15 Nov.		
1469	8 Edw. IV	27 Jan. – [ ]	Drogheda	P
		adjourned to	Dublin	
		unspecified dates	Bray	
		diss. *a.* 10 Jan. 1470	Dublin	
1470	10 Edw. IV	26 Nov. – [ ]	Dublin	P
1471	11–12 Edw. IV	29 Nov. – 10 Dec.	Dublin	P
1472		2 Mar. – 6 Mar.		
		25 May – 29 May		
		13 July – 17 July		
		12 Oct. – 22 Oct.		
1472	12–13 Edw. IV	4 Dec. – [ ]	Naas	P
1473		11 Mar. – 16 Mar.	Dublin	
		12 July – [ ]		
		25 Oct. – 29 Oct.		
1474	14 Edw. IV	18 Mar. – [ ]	Dublin	P
		[ ] – [ ]	Kilmainham	
1475	15–16 Edw. IV	21 July – [ ]	Dublin	P
		23 Oct. – [ ]	Drogheda	
1476		5 Feb. – [ ]	Dublin	
		6 May – [ ]		
		17 June – [ ]		
1476	16–17 Edw. IV	6 Dec. – [ ]	Drogheda	P
1477		14 Jan. – [ ]	Dublin	
		13 Oct. – [ ]		
1478	18 Edw. IV	29 May – [ ]	Naas	P
		6 July – [ ]	Dublin	
		14 Sept. – [ ]	Connell	
1478	18–19 Edw. IV	6 Nov. – [ ]	Trim	P
		19 Nov. – [ ]	Drogheda	
1479		31 May – [ ]	Dublin	
1479	19–20 Edw. IV	10 Dec. – [ ]	Dublin	P
1480		7 Feb. – [ ]	Dublin	
		8 May – 8 May	Naas	
		15 May – [ ]		
		10 July – [ ]	Dublin	
1481		15 Jan. – [ ]		
1481	21–22 Edw. IV	19 Oct. – [ ]	Dublin	P

year	regnal year	dates of session	place	
1482		4 Feb. – [ ]		
		3 June – [ ]		
1483	22–23 Edw. IV	7 Feb. – [ ]	Limerick	P
1483	1 Rich. III	[c. Aug.]	?	G.C.
1484	1–2 Rich. III	19 Mar. – [ ]	Dublin	P
		30 Aug. – [ ]	Naas	
1484	2 Rich. III	15 Oct. – [ ]	Naas	G.C.
1485	2–3 Rich. III	18 Mar. – [ ]	Dublin	P
		6 June – [ ]	Trim	
		8 Aug. – 8 Aug.	Trim	
		24 Oct. – [ ]	Dublin	
1486	1–2 Hen. VII	14 July – [ ]	Dublin	P
		24 Nov. – [ ]		
[1487	1 Edw. VI	[May or June]	[Dublin]	P]
[1487	1 Edw. VI	[June – Oct.]	[? Dublin]	G.C.]
1488	3 Hen. VII	11 Jan. – [ ]	Drogheda	P
1488	3 Hen. VII	17 July – 30 July	Dublin	C or G.C.
1489	4 Hen. VII	[?16] Jan. – [ ]	Drogheda	P
1490	5 Hen. VII	8 Jan. – [ ]	Trim	P
		2 Mar. – [ ]	Dublin	
1491	6–7 Hen. VII	14 Jan. – [ ]	Dublin	P
		4 June – [ ]	Dublin	
		[ ] – 8 Nov.	[? Dublin]	
1492	7 Hen. VII	13 Jan. – [ ]	Trim	P
1493	8 Hen. VII	28 June – [ ]	Dublin	P
		5 Aug. – [ ]		
1493	9 Hen. VII	12 Sept. – [ ]	Trim	C
1494	10 Hen. VII	[c. Sept.]	Drogheda	P
1494	10 Hen. VII	1 Dec. – [ ]	Drogheda	P
1495		[ ] – late Mar. or early Apr.		
1499	14–15 Hen. VII	1 Mar. – [ ]	Dublin	P
		26 Aug. – [ ]	Castledermot	
1508	24 Hen. VII	6 Oct. – [ ]	Dublin	P
		23 Oct. – [ ]		
1509		26 Feb. – [ ]		
		26 July – [ ]	Castledermot	
1516	7–8 Hen. VIII	25 Feb. – 7 Mar.	Dublin	P
		1 July – 1 July		
		25 Sept. – 2 Oct.		
1521	13 Hen. VIII	4 June – 14 June	Dublin	P
		5 Aug. – 5 Aug.		
		17 Oct. – [ ]		
1522		25 Jan. – 29 Jan.		
		13 Feb. – 13 Feb.		
		17 Feb. – 17 Feb.		
		21 Mar. – 21 Mar.		

year	regnal year	dates of session	place	
1531	23 Hen. VIII	15 Sept. – 13 Oct.	Dublin	P
		27 Oct. – 31 Oct.	Drogheda	
1533	25 Hen. VIII	19 May – [ ]	Dublin	P
		5 June – [ ]		
		2 Oct. – [ ]		
1536	28–9 Hen. VIII	1 May – 31 May	Dublin	P
		25 July – 26 July	Kilkenny	
		28 July – 28 July	Cashel	
		2 Aug. – 19 Aug.	Limerick	
		15 Sept. – 28 Sept.	Dublin	
1537		20 Jan. – 5 or 6 Feb.		
		1 May – 8 May		
		20 July – 21 July		
		13 Oct. – 20 Dec.		
1541	33–5 Hen. VIII	13 June – 20 or 23 July	Dublin	P
		7 Nov. – 7 Nov.		
		22 Dec. – 22 Dec.		
1542		15 Feb. – 7/10 Mar.	Limerick	
		12 June – 21 June	Trim	
		6 Nov. – 18 Nov.	Dublin	
1543		17 Apr. – 2 May		
		6 Nov. – 19 Nov.		
1557	3&4–4&5	1 June – 2 July	Dublin	P
	Philip &	10 Nov. – 10 Nov.	Limerick	
1558	Mary	1 Mar. – 1 Mar.	Drogheda	
1560	2 Eliz. I	11/12 Jan. – 1 Feb.	Dublin	P
1569	11–13 Eliz. I	17 Jan. – 17 Jan.	Dublin	P
		20 Jan. – 17 Feb.		
		21 Feb. – 21 Feb.		
		23 Feb. – 11 Mar.		
		10 Oct. – 31 Oct.		
1570		13 Feb. – 15 Feb.	Drogheda	
		26 May – 26 June	Dublin	
		6 Nov. – 2 Dec.		
		5 Dec. – 12 Dec.		
1571		25 Apr. – 25 Apr.		
1585	27–8 Eliz. I	26 Apr. – 25 May	Dublin	P
		27 May – 27 May		
		29 May – 29 May		
		3 Nov. – 3 Nov.	Drogheda	
1586		17 Feb. – 17 Feb.		
		21 Mar. – 21 Mar.	Dublin	
		26 Apr. – 14 May		

(*Source: NHI*, ix, pp. 600–4)

THE CHURCH

Archbishops of Armagh

	accession	date of death
John Mey	prov. 26 Aug. 1443; cons. 20 June 1444	1456
John Bole (Bull)	prov. 2 May 1457; cons. *a.* 13 June 1457	18 Feb. 1471
John Foxhalls (Foxholes)	prov. 16 Dec. 1471; cons. *p.* Dec. 1471	*a.* 23 Nov. 1474
Edmund Connesburgh	prov. 5 June 1475; cons. *c.* 1475; (did not get possession); (suffr. Norwich; Ely 1477)	res. Nov. 1477
Octavian de Palatio	prov. 3 July 1478; cons. *a.* Jan. 1480	June 1513
John Kite	prov. 24 Oct. 1513; cons. *p.* Oct. 1513	trs. to Carlisle 12 July 1521
George Cromer	prov. 2 Oct. 1521; cons. *c.* Dec. 1521	16 Mar. 1542
George Dowdall	nom. 19 Apr. 1542; cons. Dec. 1542	deemed to have deserted see *a.* 28 July 1551
Hugh Goodacre	nom. 28 Oct. 1552	1 May 1553
George Dowdall (reinstated)	rest. 23 Oct. 1553	15 Aug. 1558
Adam Loftus	nom. 30 Oct. 1562; cons. 2 Mar. 1563	trs. to Dublin 9 Aug. 1567
Thomas Lancaster	nom. 12 Mar. 1568; cons. 13 June 1568	1584
John Long	nom. 7 July 1584; cons. 13 July 1584	*a.* 16 Jan. 1589
John Garvey	trs. from Kilmore; nom. 24 Mar. 1589; l.p. 10 May 1589	2 Mar. 1595
Henry Ussher	nom. 24 May 1595; cons. Aug. 1595	2 Apr. 1613

(*Source: HBC*, pp. 335–6, 379–80)

Archbishops of Dublin

Richard Talbot	prov. 20 Dec. 1417; cons. *a.* Aug. 1413	15 Aug. 1449
Michael Tregury	prov. *a.* 24 Oct. 1449; temp. 10 Feb. 1450	21 Dec. 1471
John Walton	prov. 4 May 1472; cons. *a.* 27 Aug. 1472; temp. 15 Aug. 1474; temp. (again) 20 May 1477	res. 14 June 1484
Walter FitzSimons	prov. 14 June 1484; cons. 26 Sept. 1484	14 May 1511
William Rokeby	trs. from Meath 28 Jan. 1512; temp. 22 June 1512	29 Nov. 1521
Hugh Inge	trs. from Meath 27 Feb. 1523	3 Aug. 1528
John Alen	prov. 3 Sept. 1529; cons. 13 Mar. 1530	28 July 1534

George Browne	nom. 11 Jan. 1536; cons. 19 Mar. 1536	depr. 10 May × 10 July 1554; d. *a.* 1558
Hugh Curwin	prov. 21 June 1555; cons. 8 Sept. 1555	trs. to Oxford 1 Sept. 1567
Adam Loftus	trs. from Armagh; nom. 5 June 1567; l.p. 9 Aug. 1567	5 Apr. 1605

(*Source: HBC*, pp. 351, 391)

Bishops of Meath

William Silk	prov. 22 Sept. 1433; cons. *p.* 14 Oct. 1434	9 May 1450
Edmund Oldhall	prov. 7 Aug. 1450	9 Aug. 1459
William Sherwood	prov. 26 Mar. 1460	3 Dec. 1482
John Payne	prov. 17 Mar. 1483; temp. 16 July 1483; cons. *a.* 4 Aug. 1483	6 May 1507
William Rokeby	prov. 28 May 1507	trs. to Dublin 28 Jan. 1512
Hugh Inge	prov. 28 Jan. 1512	trs. to Dublin 27 Feb. 1523
Richard Wilson	prov. 27 Feb. 1523	res. *a.* Sept. 1529
Edward Staples	prov. 3 Sept. 1529	depr. 29 June 1554; d. *c.* 1560
William Walsh	l.p. 22 Nov. 1554	depr. 1560; d. 4 Jan. 1577
Hugh Brady	nom. 21 Oct. 1563; cons. 19 Dec. 1563	14 Feb. 1584
Thomas Jones	nom. 18 Apr. 1584; cons. 12 May 1584	trs. to Dublin 8 Nov. 1605

(*Source: HBC*, pp. 368–9, 402)

EARLDOMS OF IRELAND

Clancare

1. **Donald MacCarthy More**; cr. 24 June 1565; res. 1597; d.s.p.m. bef. 12 Feb. 1597

Clanrickard

1. **Ulick Burke** or de Burgh; cr. 1 July 1543; d. 19 Oct. 1544
2. **Richard Burke** or de Burgh, s. & h.; b. aft. 16 Sept. 1527; d. 24 July 1582
3. **Ulick Burke** or de Burgh, s. & h.; st. 1585; d. 20 May 1601
4. **Richard Burke** or de Burgh, 1st surv. s. & h.; b. 1572; d. 12 Nov. 1635

Desmond

6. **James Fitzgerald**, uncle & h.; b. bef. Dec. 1388; st. 1 Apr. 1421; d. 1463
7. **Thomas FitzJames Fitzgerald**, s. & h.; st. 2 Aug. 1462; exec. 15 Feb. 1468
8. **James FitzThomas Fitzgerald**, s. & h.; b. *c.* 1459; d.s.p.m. 7 Dec. 1487

9. **Maurice FitzThomas Fitzgerald**, br. & h. male; lic. of entry 7 Apr. 1488; d. 1520
10. **James FitzMaurice Fitzgerald**, only surv. s. & h.; d.s.p.m. 18 June 1529
11. **Thomas FitzThomas Fitzgerald**, uncle & h. male; d. 1534
12. **James FitzMaurice Fitzgerald**, gds. & h.; d.s.p.m. 19 Mar. 1540
13. **James FitzJohn Fitzgerald**, cons. & h. male, d. 14 Oct. 1558
14. **Gerald FitzJames Fitzgerald**, son by 2nd wife; b. *c.* 1533; recog. 12 Jan. 1560; forf. 15 Nov. 1582; d. 11 Nov. 1583
15. **James Fitzgerald**, s. & h.; b. 1570–1; cr. 1 Oct. 1600; d. unm. *c.* Nov. 1601
Súgán earl James FitzThomas Fitzgerald, gds. of 13 by 1st wife; att. 10 Mar. 1601; d.s.p. leg. Apr. 1607

Kildare

7. **Thomas FitzMaurice Fitzgerald**, recog. ?spring 1454; forf. Feb. 1468, rest. shortly aft. Feb. 1468; d. 25 Mar. 1478
8. **Gerald FitzMaurice Fitzgerald**, s. & h.; b. prob. aft. Jan. 1456; forf. *c.* Feb. 1495; rest. Oct. 1495; d. 3 Sept. 1513
9. **Gerald Fitzgerald**, s. & h.; b. 1487; d. 2 Sept. 1534
10. **Thomas Fitzgerald**, s. & h.; b. 1513; forf. 1 May 1536; d. 3 Feb. 1537
11. **Gerald Fitzgerald**, half-br. & h.; b. 28 Feb. 1525; cr. 13 May 1554; d. 16 Nov. 1585
12. **Henry Fitzgerald**, 1st surv. s. & h. male; b. 1562; d.s.p.m. 1 Aug. 1597
13. **William Fitzgerald**, br. & h. male; d. unm. early in Apr. 1599
14. **Gerald Fitzgerald**, cous. & h. male; d. 11 Feb. 1612

Ormond

4. **James Butler**, s. & h.; b. prob. 1390; liv. 8 Aug. 1411; d. 23 Aug. 1452
5. **James Butler**, s. & h.; b. 24 Nov. 1420; liv. 3 May 1452; exec. *c.* 1 May 1461 and forf.
6. **John Butler**, br. & h.; recog. during the Lancastrian restoration Oct. 1470–May 1471; pardoned by Edw. IV bef. 23 Nov. 1474; formally rest. 21 July 1475; d. bef. 15 June 1477 (poss. 14 Oct. 1476)
7. **Thomas Butler**, br. & h.; b. *c.* 1424; lic. entry 15 June 1477; d.s.p.m. 3 Aug. 1515
8. **Piers Butler** (see Ossory), cous. & h. male of 7; b. *c.* 1467; res. 18 Feb. 1528; st. 23 Oct. 1537; rest. 22 Feb. 1538; d. 26 Aug. 1539
9. **Thomas Boleyn**, Viscount Rochford, gds. of 7; b. 1477; cr. 8 Dec. 1529; d.s.p.m. 12 Mar. 1539
10. **James Butler**, s. & h. of 8; b. bef. 20 July 1504; d. 28 Oct. 1546
11. **Thomas Butler**, s. & h.; b. 1531; d.s.p.m. leg. s. 22 Nov. 1614

Ossory [see Ormond]

1. **Piers Butler**, b. *c.* 1467; cr. 23 Feb. 1528; d. 26 Aug. 1539 [The earldom of Ossory descended with that of Ormond]

Thomond

1. **Murrough O'Brien**; cr. 1 July 1543; d. 26 June × 28 Oct. 1551
2. **Donough O'Brien**, neph. & h. to earldom; res. bef. or on 7 Jan. 1552 and cr. again 7 Jan. 1552; d. 1 Apr. 1553
3. **Connor O'Brien**, s. & h.; b. *c.* 1535; d. Jan. 1581
4. **Donough O'Brien**, s. & h.; b. aft. 1560; d. 5 Sept. 1624

Tyrone

1. **Con Bacagh O'Neill**; b. *c.* 1484; cr. 1 Oct. 1542; d. bef. 16 July 1559
2. **Hugh O'Neill**, gds.; b. *c.* 1550; st. 1585; forf. 28 Oct. 1614; d. 20 July 1616

Waterford

1. **John Talbot**; b. 1390; cr. 17 July 1446; d. 17 July 1453.

(The earldom of Waterford descended with that of Shrewsbury, but later earls were absentees.)

GAELIC CHIEFTAINCIES

O'Brien of Thomond

Turlough Bog	1444–1459
Teague	1459–1466, s. of T.B.
Connor More	1466–1496, br. of T.
Turlough Oge	1496–1498, br. of C.M.
Turlough Don	1498–1528, neph. of T.O.
Connor	1528–1539, s. of T.D.
Murrough	1539–1551, br. of C.

(see earls of Thomond thereafter)

O'Donnell of Tyrconnell

Naughton	1439–1452
Rory	1452–1454, br. of N.
Donnell	1454–1456, cous. of R.
Turlough	1456–1461, s. of N.
Hugh Roe	1461–1497, 1497–1505
Con	1497 s. of H.R.
Hugh Duff	1505–1537, s. of H.R.
Manus	1537–1555, s. of H.D.
Calvagh	1555–1566, s. of M.
Hugh	1566–1592, half-br. of C.
Hugh Roe	1592–1601, s. of H.
Rory	1601–1603, br. of H.R.

O'Neill of Tyrone

Owen	1432–1455
Henry	1455–1483, s. of O.
Con	1483–1493, s. of H.
Henry Oge	1493–1498, half-br. of C.
Donnell	1498–1509, br. of H.O.
Art	1509–1513, cous. of D.
Art Oge	1513–1519, s. of Con
Con Bacagh	1519–1559, half-br. of A.O.
Shane	1559–1567, s. of C.B.
Turlough Luineach	1567–1595
Hugh	1595–1603

(see also earls of Tyrone)

Burke of Clanrickard — Ellis said @ beginning that Burke was an English lord.

Ulick Roe	1429–1485
Ulick Finn	1485–1509, s. of U.R.
Richard Oge	1509–1519, br. of U.F.
Ulick Oge	1519–1520, s. of U.F.
Richard More	1520–1530, br. of R.O.
John	1530–1536
Richard Bacagh	1536–1538
Ulick MacWilliam	1538–1544

(see earls of Clanrickard thereafter)

MAPS

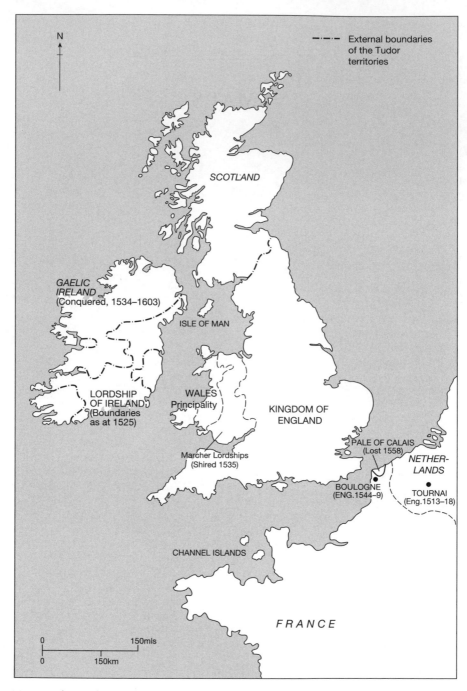

Map 1 The Tudor territories

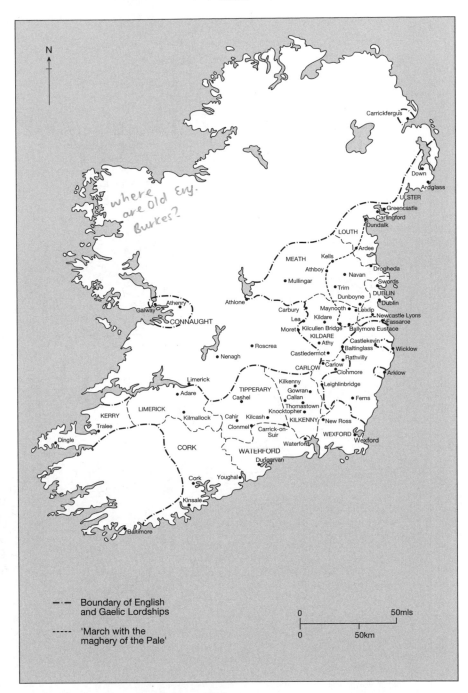

Map 2 The Lordship of Ireland, *c.* 1525

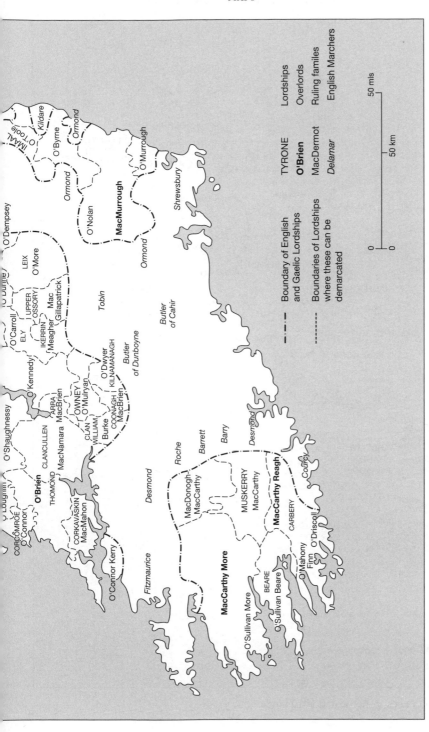

Map 3 Gaelic lordships, c. 1534, with prominent English Marchers

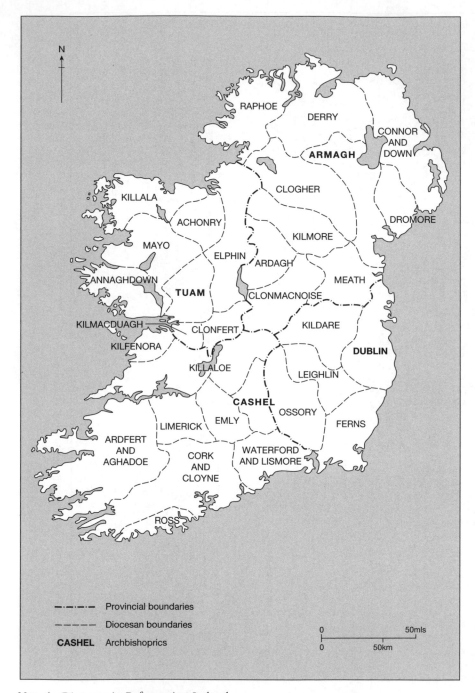

N

RAPHOE

DERRY

CONNOR
AND
DOWN

ARMAGH

CLOGHER

DROMORE

KILLALA

ACHONRY

KILMORE

MAYO

ELPHIN

ARDAGH

MEATH

ANNAGHDOWN

TUAM

CLONMACNOISE

KILMACDUAGH

CLONFERT

KILDARE

KILFENORA

DUBLIN

KILLALOE

LEIGHLIN

CASHEL

OSSORY

LIMERICK

EMLY

FERNS

ARDFERT
AND
AGHADOE

CORK
AND
CLOYNE

WATERFORD
AND LISMORE

ROSS

–·–·–·–   Provincial boundaries

– – – – –   Diocesan boundaries

CASHEL   Archbishoprics

0   50mls

0   50km

Map 4   Dioceses in Reformation Ireland

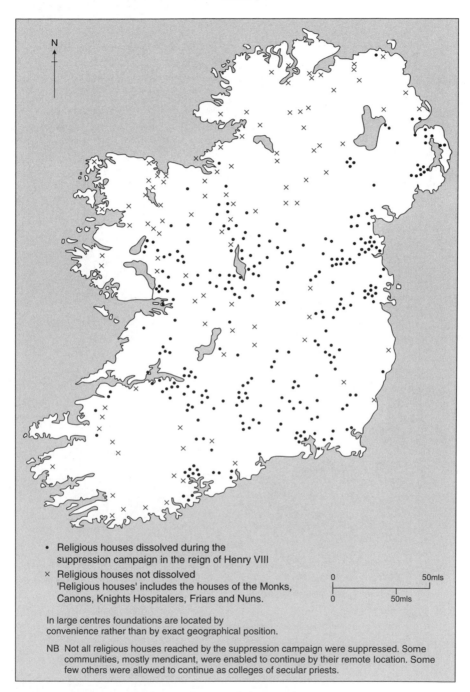

* Religious houses dissolved during the
  suppression campaign in the reign of Henry VIII
× Religious houses not dissolved
  'Religious houses' includes the houses of the Monks,
  Canons, Knights Hospitalers, Friars and Nuns.

In large centres foundations are located by
convenience rather than by exact geographical position.

NB Not all religious houses reached by the suppression campaign were suppressed. Some
   communities, mostly mendicant, were enabled to continue by their remote location. Some
   few others were allowed to continue as colleges of secular priests.

Map 5 Irish religious houses on the eve of the Dissolution

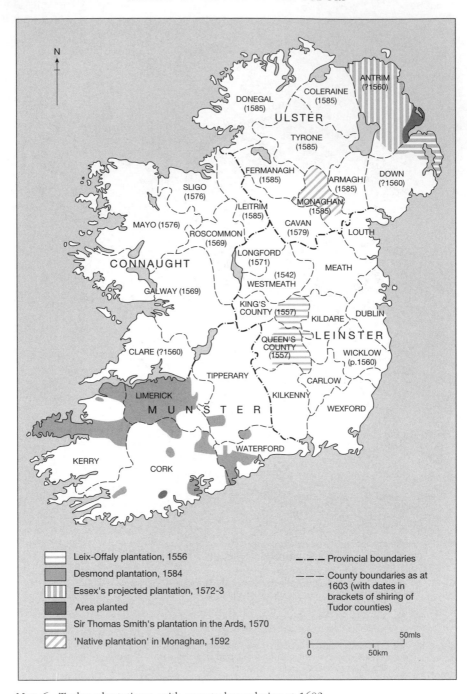

N

ANTRIM
(?1560)

COLERAINE
(1585)

DONEGAL
(1585)

ULSTER

TYRONE
(1585)

DOWN
(?1560)

FERMANAGH
(1585)

ARMAGH
(1585)

SLIGO
(1576)

LEITRIM
(1585)

MONAGHAN
(1585)

MAYO (1576)

ROSCOMMON
(1569)

CAVAN
(1579)

LOUTH

CONNAUGHT

LONGFORD
(1571)

MEATH

(1542)
WESTMEATH

GALWAY (1569)

KING'S
COUNTY (1557)

KILDARE

DUBLIN

LEINSTER

QUEEN'S
COUNTY
(1557)

WICKLOW
(p.1560)

CLARE (?1560)

TIPPERARY

CARLOW

LIMERICK

KILKENNY

M U N S T E R

WEXFORD

WATERFORD

KERRY

CORK

Leix-Offaly plantation, 1556

Desmond plantation, 1584

Essex's projected plantation, 1572-3

Area planted

Sir Thomas Smith's plantation in the Ards, 1570

'Native plantation' in Monaghan, 1592

—·—·— Provincial boundaries

——— County boundaries as at
1603 (with dates in
brackets of shiring of
Tudor counties)

0   50mls

0   50km

Map 6   Tudor plantations, with county boundaries at 1603

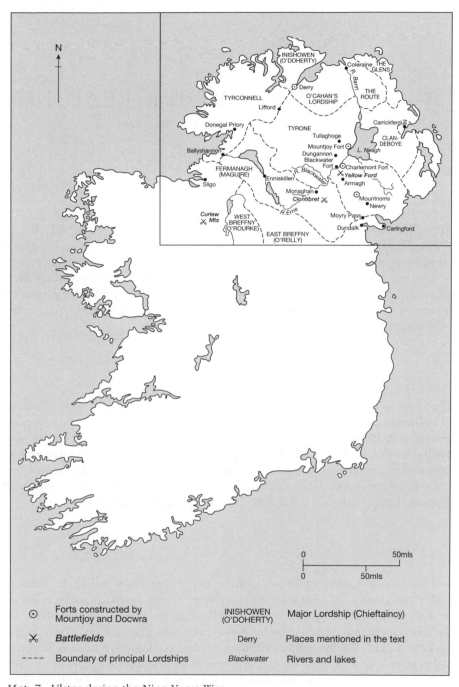

Map 7 Ulster during the Nine Years War

A GUIDE TO FURTHER READING

Although the weight of writing on Tudor Ireland cannot compare with that on Tudor England, the Irish literature is at present not only much more lively and controversial but also raises a series of basic questions relating to the practice of history. The following Guide is merely a selection from a secondary literature that has expanded greatly over the past 25 years, with the emphasis on recent work. Full bibliographic details for each title listed will be found in the Bibliography (pp. 397–416).

1. GUIDES

The *New history of Ireland*, volumes II (1169–1534; Oxford 1987) and III (1534–1691; Oxford 1976) include very full bibliographies. The latest impressions (1993, 1991) include an updated 'Bibliographical supplement' to 1990 and 1989 respectively. Asplin, *Medieval Ireland, c. 1170–1495*, a critical bibliography of secondary works, also remains useful; and for the later period Edwards and O'Dowd, *Sources for early modern Irish history* is an important survey of printed sources, with chapters on archival collections and historiography.

2. SURVEYS

Not surprisingly, modern surveys of the period generally reflect, in their insights and depth, the character and quality of recent research and writing on individual topics. Whereas the late middle ages have seen comparatively little serious research, later Tudor Ireland is presently an extremely cluttered and contested field. The nearest modern equivalent to Bagwell's mammoth three-volume *Ireland under the Tudors* of 1885–90 are the relevant parts of the *New history of Ireland*, which unfortunately divides at 1534. Volume II has been well characterized as 'a gigantic lucky-dip', but among its prizes are the four narrative chapters covering 1460–1534 by David B. Quinn, the finest Irish historian of his generation. Volume III is more dated, and longer and stronger on the seventeenth century, but the Tudor section remains useful. The approaches of other, more manageable surveys which include part of the Tudor age in their timespan likewise reflect the period's partition between decline in the medieval lordship and the origins of the modern Irish problem. Of the two relevant volumes in the Helicon History, Cosgrove, *Late medieval Ireland*, chs 4–7 still offers a good brief introduction, while Canny, *From Reformation to Restoration*, chs 1–5 is stimulating and provocative. In the New Gill History of Ireland, one thin and woefully inadequate medieval volume has succeeded the three sparkling volumes of the original series, but New Gill's second volume, Lennon, *Sixteenth-century Ireland* offers a comprehensive survey which is particularly strong on urban history religious change and the local impact of later Tudor reform policies. Finally, two recent English surveys, Guy, *Tudor England* and Williams, *The later Tudors*, both make some attempt to go beyond English nationalist history and to integrate Irish developments into the wider Tudor picture.

3. POLITICS

Recent work has tended to highlight the differences between politics in English and Gaelic Ireland in the period before the Tudor conquest. The subject has been transformed in the past 25 years by the publication of some half-dozen substantial monographs written from different perspectives and offering apparently conflicting reappraisals of particular topics. For the earlier period, the almost simultaneous publication of Simms, *From kings to warlords* on Gaelic developments and Ellis, *Reform and revival* on the English lordship (both heavy going!) provoked one medievalist to ask pertinently 'if the two authors were writing about the same country' (Cosgrove 1990–1, p. 101). Just so! The English dimension of the Kildare ascendancy is further explored in Ellis, *Tudor frontiers and noble power*, a pioneering comparative study of the English Pale and the far north of England as frontier societies. Bradshaw, *Irish constitutional revolution* is a bold analysis of the relationship between constitutional change and ideology centring on the period 1520–47. Some of its conclusions have since been undermined by Brady's challenging book, *The chief governors*, the most important recent contribution to our understanding of mid-Tudor politics. Brady also includes a penetrating critique of the colonial thesis expounded in Canny, *Elizabethan conquest of Ireland*. Canny's arguments have since been reformulated in his *Kingdom and colony*, and 'Identity formation in Ireland'. The final phase of the Tudor conquest is best approached through Morgan, *Tyrone's rebellion*, which unfortunately ends at 1596, but see also MacCaffrey (below). Morgan, 'Hugh O'Neill and the Nine Years War' offers a brilliant comparison with the Dutch revolt.

These works can be supplemented on particular episodes by Johnson, *Duke Richard of York*; Bennett, *Lambert Simnel and the battle of Stoke*; Arthurson, *The Perkin Warbeck conspiracy* (all of which focus on the wider picture); and Brady, *Shane O'Neill*. There are also some useful collections of essays which add breadth and depth to the topic: most notably, Brady and Gillespie (ed.), *Natives and newcomers*; MacCurtain and O'Dowd (ed.), *Women in early modern Ireland*; and from a New British perspective, Ellis and Barber (ed.), *Conquest and union*; and Bradshaw and Morrill (ed.), *The British problem*.

4. THE GAELIC WORLD

The starting point remains Nicholls, *Gaelic and gaelicised Ireland*, a brilliant sketch of Gaelic society, supplemented on the late medieval background by Simms (above). O'Riordan's important but controversial *Gaelic mind and the collapse of the Gaelic world* also assesses the Gaelic response to conquest: for a 'blood and guts' review, see Ó Buachalla 1992. Other conflicting interpretations of the evidence are Bradshaw, 'Native reaction to the Westward Enterprise', Dunne, 'The Gaelic response to conquest and colonisation', and Canny, 'The formation of the Irish mind'. Leerssen, *Mere Irish and Fíor-Ghael* is a major work on identity. None of these address Scottish Gaeldom, nor surprisingly does Hill, *Fire and sword: Sorley Boy MacDonnell*. In default, Bannerman, 'Lordship of the Isles' and Munro (ed.), *Acts of the lords of the Isles* provide comparative material. Leerssen, *Contention of the bards* and Simms, 'Bardic poetry as a historical source' offer sensible advice about a notoriously difficult source. On Gaelic law and custom, see also Nicholls, *Land, law and society* and Mac Niocaill, 'Land transfer in sixteenth-century Thomond'.

5. MILITARY HISTORY AND FOREIGN AFFAIRS

Reflecting its escalating importance as a war zone, Tudor Ireland's military history has been well studied, thanks largely to the labours of G. A. Hayes-McCoy. His account of six battles from Knockdoe to Kinsale in *Irish battles* effectively surveys the main technological developments, while his *Scots mercenary forces in Ireland* discusses one of the reasons for the remarkable resilience of the antiquated Gaelic military organization. The chapters in Bartlett and Jeffery (ed.), *Military history of Ireland* add depth, and include a study of the 1534–5 campaign, but early Tudor expeditions to Ireland have generally attracted little attention. McGurk, *Elizabethan conquest of Ireland* has transformed our understanding of the recruitment and supply of Elizabeth's Irish army. The general character and context of the Elizabethan response is well captured in MacCaffrey, *Elizabeth I: war and politics*, although Falls, *Elizabeth's Irish wars* remains useful. On foreign affairs, the latest work, Palmer, *Problem of Ireland in Tudor foreign policy* emphasizes Ireland's growing importance in this context, but Wernham, *Before the Armada* remains useful. Dawson, 'Two kingdoms or three?' discusses Ireland's role at a turning point in Anglo-Scottish relations, while Silke, *Kinsale* investigates a turning point in Irish history from Spanish sources.

6. CONSTITUTIONAL AND INSTITUTIONAL HISTORY

Bradshaw, *Irish constitutional revolution* opens up the topic of constitutional change but is not altogether reliable. See Brady, 'Decline of the Irish kingdom'. On the late medieval background, Bradshaw can be supplemented by Richardson and Sayles, *Irish parliament in the middle ages*, which is more wide-ranging than the title suggests and also sparked a debate about Anglo-Irish constitutional relations and the 1460 parliament: see Lydon, '"Ireland corporate of itself": the parliament of 1460'; Cosgrove, 'Parliament and the Anglo-Irish community'; Lydon, 'Ireland and the English crown'. Tudor parliamentary developments are outlined by Bradshaw, 'Beginnings of modern Ireland', and parliament's institutional importance and later decline are emphasized in Ellis, 'Parliament and community'. There are excellent accounts of Sidney's parliament and Perrot's parliament by Treadwell ((1966) and (1985)). Edwards discusses 'The Irish Reformation parliament'. Poynings' Law has been discussed by Quinn, 'Early interpretation of Poynings' law', and Edwards and Moody, 'History of Poynings' law'. Ellis, *Reform and revival* is a detailed study of the lordship's institutional history, though in this field too, many of David Quinn's pioneering studies remain useful, especially his 'Irish parliamentary subsidy' and 'Government printing and the publication of the Irish statutes'. On finance, see also Matthew, 'The financing of the lordship of Ireland under Henry V and Henry VI', Sheehan, 'Irish revenues and English subventions', and Ellis, 'Taxation and defence in late medieval Ireland'. On the later period, the starting point is now Crawford, *Anglicizing the government of Ireland*, but Kenny, *King's Inns* is useful on the law. Morgan, 'Extradition and treason-trial of a Gaelic lord' adds a new dimension.

7. RELIGION

The literature on this topic has improved considerably in recent years, but who will write a survey to replace Edwards, *Church and state in Tudor Ireland?* On the pre-Reformation church, Watt, *The church in medieval Ireland*; Gwynn, *Anglo-Irish church life*; and Mooney, *The church in Gaelic Ireland*, provide introductions; while particular aspects are treated in Gwynn, *Medieval province of Armagh* (a comparatively well-documented province); [Conway], *Story of Mellifont* (about Cistercian decline); Empey, 'The sacred and the secular: the Augustinian priory of Kells in Ossory'; and Wilkie, *The Cardinal Protectors of England.*

On the early Reformation, Bradshaw, *Dissolution of the religious orders* includes some more general remarks, besides being a model study of that particular episode. Jefferies, *Priest and prelates of Armagh* extends to Ireland the diocesan approach of English historians and constitutes an important reassessment both of the state of the pre-Reformation church and the initial impact of Tudor reform: Bradshaw has also written a number of individual studies: in particular, 'George Browne, first Reformation archbishop of Dublin' appraises a leading English-born reformer; 'The Edwardian Reformation' outlines a serious attempt to promote protestant reform'; and 'Sword, word and strategy' explores tensions within reform circles. Important case-studies on the origins and enforcement of reform are Murray, 'Ecclesiastical justice and the enforcement of the reformation' and 'Archbishop Alen, Tudor reform and the Kildare rebellion'; Walsh, 'Enforcing the Elizabethan settlement'. A stimulating debate on protestant progress under Elizabeth was begun by Canny, 'Why the Reformation failed in Ireland'; see also Bottigheimer, 'The failure of the Reformation in Ireland'; Bradshaw, 'Reformation in the cities'. The basic internal inadequacies of the Church of Ireland are outlined in Clarke, 'Varieties of uniformity'; and its weak economic base in Ellis, 'Economic problems of the church', on which see also Murray, 'Sources of clerical income in the Tudor diocese of Dublin'. Jefferies, 'The Irish parliament of 1560: the Anglican reforms authorised' and Lennon, 'Chantries in the Irish Reformation' discuss other aspects of the problem. In their different ways, Ford, *The Protestant Reformation in Ireland* and Lennon, *Lords of Dublin in the age of the Reformation* are major studies of the impact of religious divisions in the later period.

8. POLITICAL IDEAS, PATRIOTISM AND ENGLISH EXPANSION

These themes also lack a satisfactory survey, but Canny, *Kingdom and colony*, chs 1–3, reformulating Bottigheimer's perceptive 'Kingdom and colony . . . 1536–1660', opens up particular areas of the subject. See also Quinn, 'Ireland and sixteenth-century European expansion'; and Ellis, 'Crown, community and government in the English territories' on the English background. The stimulating debate on the implications of persuasion *v.* coercion is best approached through Bradshaw, *Irish constitutional revolution* and Canny, *Elizabethan conquest.* Two fine new editions of important New English tracts have advanced our understanding of their views on Tudor reform: Carroll and Carey (ed.), *Richard Beacon Solon his follie*; Keaveney and Madden, *Sir William Herbert Croftus sive de Hibernia liber.* On Edmund Spenser, a stimulating debate between Brady ('Spenser's Irish crisis'; 'Reply to Nicholas Canny') and Canny ('Spenser's Irish crisis') appeared in *Past & Present*, and there is also a useful collection of essays: Coughlan (ed.), *Spenser and Ireland.* Old English views have likewise been elucidated chiefly by editions of contemporary reform proposals: Canny, 'Rowland White's "Discors touching Ireland"' and 'Rowland White's "The dysorders of the Irisshery"' (White was an Old English protestant); Bradshaw, '"A treatise for the reformation of Ireland"'.

On the emergence of a separate Old English identity, the Bradshaw–Canny debate is best approached through Canny, *Formation of the Old English elite* and Bradshaw, *Irish constitutional revolution*, but Lennon, 'Richard Stanyhurst . . . and Old English identity' expounds the views of its most prolific but untypical writer and also provides a biography and translation of a major work by him, *Richard Stanyhurst, the Dubliner.* An interesting sidelight is Quinn, 'Edward Walshe's *The office and duety in fightyng for our countrey*'.

9. PLANTATION

The best introduction to this topic is Loeber, *The geography and practice of English colonisation*. There is also a model study of the most important Tudor colonization project: MacCarthy-Morrogh, *The Munster plantation*. On other projects see Morgan, 'The colonial venture of Sir Thomas Smith', Duffy, 'Territorial organisation of Gaelic landownership and its transformation in County Monaghan', and the work of the great Manchester historian, Robert Dunlop: 'Plantation of Leix and Offaly', 'Sixteenth-century schemes for the plantation of Ulster' and 'Plantation of Munster'. The work of another pioneer, David Quinn, remains important on the evolution of plantation policy: 'Edward Walshe's "Conjectures"'; and 'Sir Thomas Smith . . . and the beginnings of English colonial theory'; also Canny, 'The ideology of English colonization'. Quinn, 'Renaissance influences in English colonization' and Canny, 'The permissive frontier' and 'Dominant minorities: English settlers in Ireland and Virginia' add important comparative dimensions.

10. SOCIETY AND THE ECONOMY

This remains a poorly researched field, although there are a number of useful sketches. Perhaps the best is now Lennon, *Sixteenth-century Ireland*. Gaelic society is well treated in Nicholls, *Gaelic and gaelicised Ireland*, and his pamphlet, *Land, law and society* includes some important insights confusingly presented. Quinn, *Elizabethans and the Irish* is an important study of Elizabethan views of Gaelic Ireland. The surveys of colonial society in the later middle ages, 1534 and 1558 respectively included in Lydon, *Lordship of Ireland*, by Quinn and Nicholls in *New history of Ireland*, iii, and Canny, *Elizabethan conquest* exhibit sharp differences of emphasis even allowing for ongoing historical development. On economic history, Gillespie, *Transformation of the Irish economy* is no more than a start. On the towns, there are short surveys in Butlin, *Development of the Irish town* and Sheehan, 'Irish towns in a period of change'. Lennon, *Lords of Dublin* is a major study on the capital. For later medieval trade, see now O'Neill's lively *Merchants and mariners in medieval Ireland*. Longfield's pioneering *Anglo-Irish trade in the sixteenth century* has not been followed up, but Woodward, *Trade of Elizabethan Chester* includes much Irish material. Mac Niocaill, 'Socio-economic problems of the late medieval Irish town' offers preliminary remarks on a range of new questions by applying new evidential techniques.

11. HISTORIOGRAPHY

The starting point here is Bradshaw's brilliant reply, 'Nationalism and historical scholarship in modern Ireland' to my 'Nationalist historiography', which highlights the fundamental differences among professional historians of the character and purpose of history. These and other contributions to the debate are reprinted with an important introduction in Brady (ed.), *Interpreting Irish history: the debate on historical revisionism*. Ellis, 'Representations of the past in Ireland: whose past and whose present?' is a rejoinder to Bradshaw, while Cosgrove, 'Writing of Irish medieval history' looks at the medieval implications. Irish revisionism's protean character is inadvertently illustrated by Canny, 'Revising the revisionist'. Other significant contributions are Bradshaw, 'Revising Irish history', Ellis, 'Writing Irish history', and the 'Introduction' to Boyce and O'Day (ed.), *The making of modern Irish history.*

BIBLIOGRAPHY

Andrews, K.R., Canny, N.P. and Hair, P.E.H. (eds) (1978), *The Westward Enterprise: English activities in Ireland, the Atlantic and America, 1480–1650* (Liverpool).

Appleby, J.C. and O'Dowd, M. (1984–5), 'The Irish admiralty: its organisation and development, *c.* 1570–1640' in *IHS*, xxiv.

Arthurson, I. (1994), *The Perkin Warbeck conspiracy, 1491–1499* (Stroud).

Asplin, P.W. (1971), *Medieval Ireland, c. 1170–1495* (Dublin).

Bagwell, R. (1885–90), *Ireland under the Tudors* (3 vols) (London).

Ball, F.E. (1926), *The judges in Ireland, 1221–1921* (2 vols) (London).

Bannerman, J.M.W. (1977), 'The lordship of the Isles' in J.M. Brown (ed.), *Scottish society in the fifteenth century* (London), pp. 209–40.

Barnard, T.C. (1988), review of S.G. Ellis, *Tudor Ireland* (1985) in *English Historical Review*, ciii, pp. 486–8.

Bartlett, R. (1993), *The making of Europe: conquest, colonization and cultural change, 950–1350* (London).

Bartlett, T. and Jeffery, K. (eds) (1996), *A military history of Ireland* (Cambridge).

Bayne, C.G. and Dunham, W.H., Jr (ed.) (1968), *Select cases in the council of Henry VII* (Selden Soc., 75) (London).

Beacon, R. (1996), *Solon his follie, or, A politique discourse touching the Reformation of common-weales conquered, declined or corrupted*, ed. C. Carroll and V. Carey (Binghamton, NY).

Beckett, J.C. (1966), *The making of modern Ireland, 1603–1923* (London).

Beier, A.L. (1985), *Masterless men: the vagrancy problem in England, 1560–1640* (London).

Bennett, M. (1987), *Lambert Simnel and the battle of Stoke* (Gloucester).

Berry, H.F. (1898), *Register of wills and inventories of the diocese of Dublin in the time of Archbishops Tregury and Walton, 1457–1483* (Dublin).

Berry, H.F. (ed.) (1910), *Statute rolls of the parliament of Ireland, reign of King Henry VI* (Dublin).

Berry, H.F. and Morrissey, J.F. (eds) (1914, 1939), *Statute rolls of the parliament of Ireland . . . reign of King Edward IV* (2 vols) (Dublin).

Bindoff, S.T., Hurstfield, J. and Williams, C.H. (eds) (1961), *Elizabethan government and society* (London).

Bossy, J. (1971), 'The Counter-Reformation and the people of Catholic Ireland, 1596–1641' in *Historical Studies*, viii.

Bossy, J. (1985), *Christianity in the West, 1400–1700* (Oxford).

Bottigheimer, K.S. (1976), 'The Reformation in Ireland revisited' in *Journal of British Studies*, xv.

Bottigheimer, K.S. (1978), 'Kingdom and colony: Ireland in the Westward Enterprise, 1536–1660' in Andrews, Canny & Hair.

Bottigheimer, K.S. (1985) 'The failure of the Reformation in Ireland: *une question bien posée*' in *Journal of Ecclesiastical History*, xxxvi.

Bowker, M. (1981), *The Henrician Reformation: the diocese of Lincoln under John Longland, 1521–1547* (Cambridge).

Boyce, D.G. and O'Day, A. (1996), 'Introduction: "Revisionism" and the "revisionist" controversy' in D.G. Boyce and A. O'Day (eds), *The making of modern Irish history: Revisionism and the revisionist controversy* (London), pp. 1–14.

Bradshaw, B. (1968–9), 'The opposition to the ecclesiastical legislation in the Irish Reformation Parliament' in *IHS*, xvi.

Bradshaw, B. (1970), 'George Browne, first Reformation archbishop of Dublin, 1536–1554' in *Journal of Ecclesiastical History*, xxi.

Bradshaw, B. (1973), 'The beginnings of modern Ireland' in Farrell.

Bradshaw, B. (1974), *The dissolution of the religious orders in Ireland under Henry VIII* (Cambridge).

Bradshaw, B. (1976–7a), 'The Edwardian Reformation in Ireland' in *Archivium Hibernicum*, xxxiv.

Bradshaw, B. (1976–7b), 'Fr. Wolfe's description of Limerick, 1574' in *North Munster Antiquarian Journal*, xvii.

Bradshaw, B. (1977a), 'Cromwellian reform and the origins of the Kildare rebellion, 1533–4' in *Transactions of the Royal Historical Society*, 5th ser., xxvii.

Bradshaw, B. (1977b), 'The Elizabethans and the Irish' in *Studies*, lxv.

Bradshaw, B. (1978a), 'Sword, word and strategy in the Reformation in Ireland' in *Historical Journal*, xxi.

Bradshaw, B. (1978b), 'Native reaction to the Westward Enterprise: a case-study in Gaelic ideology' in Andrews, Canny & Hair.

Bradshaw, B. (1979a), *The Irish constitutional revolution of the sixteenth century* (Cambridge).

Bradshaw, B. (1979b), 'Manus "the magnificent": O'Donnell as Renaissance Prince' in Art Cosgrove and Donal McCartney (eds), *Studies in Irish history presented to R. Dudley Edwards* (Dublin), pp. 15–36.

Bradshaw, B. (1981a), ' "A treatise for the Reformation of Ireland, 1554–5" ' in *Irish Jurist*, n.s., xvi.

Bradshaw, B. (1981b), 'The Elizabethans and the Irish: a muddled model' in *Studies*, xx.

Bradshaw, B. (1986), review of Ellis, *Tudor Ireland* in *Studies*, pp. 564–5.

Bradshaw, B. (1988), 'The reformation in the cities: Cork, Limerick and Galway, 1534–1603' in J. Bradley (ed.), *Settlement and society in medieval*

Ireland: studies presented to Francis Xavier Martin, O.S.A. (Kilkenny), pp. 445–76.

Bradshaw, B. (1994a), 'Revising Irish history' in D. Ó Ceallaigh (ed.), *Reconsiderations of Irish history and culture* (Dublin), pp. 27–41.

Bradshaw, B. (1994b), 'Nationalism and historical scholarship in modern Ireland' in Brady (1994b), pp. 191–216.

Bradshaw, B. and Morrill, J. (eds) (1996), *The British problem c. 1534–1707: state formation in the Atlantic archipelago* (Basingstoke).

Brady, C. (1979), review of Bradshaw 1979, in *Studia Hibernica*, xix.

Brady, C. (1980), 'The government of Ireland, c. 1540–1583', unpublished PhD thesis, University of Dublin.

Brady, C. (1980–1), 'Faction and the origins of the Desmond rebellion of 1579' in *IHS*.

Brady, C. (1982), 'The government of Ireland, c. 1540–83' in *Irish History Thesis Abstracts*, iii.

Brady, C. (1982–3), 'The killing of Shane O'Neill: some new evidence' in *Irish Sword*, xv.

Brady, C. (1985), 'Conservative subversives: the community of the Pale and the Dublin administration, 1556–86' in P.J. Corish (ed.), *Radicals, rebels and establishments: Historical Studies XV* (Belfast), pp. 11–32.

Brady, C. (1986), 'Spenser's Irish crisis: humanism and experience in the 1590s' in *Past & Present*, no. 111, pp. 16–49.

Brady, C. (1988), 'Reply to Nicholas Canny' in *Past & Present*, no. 120, pp. 210–15.

Brady, C. (1989), 'Thomas Butler, tenth earl of Ormond (1531–1614) and reform in Tudor Ireland' in C. Brady (ed.), *Worsted in the game: losers in Irish history* (Dublin, 1989), pp. 49–60.

Brady, C. (1991), 'The decline of the Irish kingdom' in M. Greengrass (ed.), *Conquest and coalescence: the shaping of the state in early modern Europe* (London).

Brady, C. (1994a), *The chief governors: the rise and fall of reform government in Tudor Ireland, 1536–1588* (Cambridge).

Brady, C. (ed.) (1994b), *Interpreting Irish history: the debate on historical revisionism, 1938–1994* (Blackrock).

Brady, C. (1995), 'Comparable histories?: Tudor reform in Wales and Ireland' in Ellis and Barber (1995), pp. 64–86.

Brady, C. (1996a), *Shane O'Neill* (Dundalk).

Brady, C. (1996b), 'The captains' games: army and society in Elizabethan Ireland' in Bartlett and Jeffery (1996), pp. 136–59.

Brady, C. and Gillespie, R. (eds) (1986), *Natives and newcomers: essays on the making of Irish colonial society, 1534–1641* (Dublin).

Bryan, D. (1933), *Gerald FitzGerald, the Great Earl of Kildare, 1456–1513* (Dublin).

Bush, M.L. (1971), 'The problem of the Far North: a study of the crisis of 1537 and its consequences' in *Northern History*, vi.

Bush, M.L. (1975), *The government policy of Protector Somerset* (London).

Butler, R. (ed.) (1849), *Thady Dowling, Annals of Ireland* (Dublin).

Butlin, R.A. (ed.) (1977), *The development of the Irish town* (London).

Caball, M. (1993), 'The Gaelic mind and the collapse of the Gaelic world: an appraisal' in *Cambridge Medieval Celtic Studies*, xxv (Summer 1993), pp. 87–96.

Calendar of state papers relating to Ireland, 1509–73 [etc.] (=*CSPI*) (1860–1912) (24 vols) (London).

Calendar of the Carew manuscripts preserved in the archiepiscopal library at Lambeth, 1515–74 [etc.] (=*Carew*) (1867–73) (6 vols) (London).

Calendar of the close rolls, 1500–09 (1963) (London).

Calendar of the patent rolls, 1232–47 [etc.] (=*CPR*) (1906–) (London).

Cameron, A. (1892–4), *Reliquiae Celticae: texts, papers, and studies in Gaelic literature and philosophy*, ed. Alexander MacBain and John Kennedy (2 vols) (Inverness).

Canny, N.P. (1969–70), 'The treaty of Mellifont and the reorganisation of Ulster, 1603' in *Irish Sword*, ix.

Canny, N.P. (1973), 'The ideology of English colonization; from Ireland to America' in *William and Mary Quarterly*, 3rd ser., xxx.

Canny, N.P. (1975), *The formation of the Old English elite in Ireland* (Dublin).

Canny, N.P. (1976), *The Elizabethan conquest of Ireland: a pattern established, 1565–76* (Hassocks).

Canny, N.P. (1976–7), 'Rowland White's "Discors touching Ireland" c. 1569' in *IHS*, xx.

Canny, N.P. (1978a), 'Dominant minorities: English settlers in Ireland and Virginia, 1550–1650' in Hepburn.

Canny, N.P. (1978b), 'The permissive frontier: social control in English settlements in Ireland and Virginia, 1550–1650' in Andrews, Canny & Hair.

Canny, N.P. (1979a), 'Rowland White's "The dysorders of the Irisshery" 1571' in *Studia Hibernica*, xix.

Canny, N.P. (1979b), 'Why the Reformation failed in Ireland: une question mal posée' in *Journal of Ecclesiastical History*, xxx.

Canny, N.P. (1982), 'The formation of the Irish mind: religion, politics and Gaelic Irish literature, 1580–1750' in *Past & Present, no.* 95.

Canny, N.P. (1983), 'Edmund Spenser and the development of an Anglo-Irish identity' in *The Yearbook of English Studies*, xiii.

Canny, N.P. (1985), 'Migration and opportunity: Britain, Ireland and the New World' in *Irish Economic and Social History*, xii.

Canny, N.P. (1987a), *From Reformation to Restoration: Ireland, 1534–1660* (Dublin).

Canny, N.P. (1987b), 'Identity formation in Ireland: the emergence of the Anglo-Irish' in Canny and A. Pagden (eds), *Colonial identity in the Atlantic world, 1500–1800* (Princeton).

Canny, N.P. (1988a), *Kingdom and colony: Ireland in the Atlantic world, 1560–1800* (Baltimore).

Canny, N.P. (1988b), 'Debate: Spenser's Irish crisis: humanism and experience in the 1590s' in *Past & Present*, no. 120, pp. 201–9.

Canny, N.P. (1996–7), 'Revising the revisionist' in *IHS*, xxx, pp. 242–54.

Carey, V. (1991), 'Local elites and central authority: Gerald XI earl of Kildare and Tudor rule in Ireland, 1547–1586' (PhD thesis, State University of New York at Stony Brook).

Carey, V. (forthcoming), 'The road to Mullaghmast: Sir Henry Sidney, John Derricke's *Image of Irelande* and the resort to massacre in the Elizabethan conquest of Ireland' in *IHS*.

Chrimes, S.B. (1972), *Henry VII* (London).

Chrimes, S.B., Ross, C.D. and Griffiths, R.A. (eds) (1972), *Fifteenth-century England, 1399–1509* (Manchester).

Clarke, A. (1981), 'Ireland, 1534–1660' in Lee.

Clarke, A. (1989), 'Varieties of uniformity: the first century of the Church of Ireland' in W.J. Sheils and D. Wood (eds), *The churches, Ireland and the Irish: studies in church history*, vol. xxv (Oxford), pp. 105–22.

Clarke, A., Gillespie, R. and McGuire, J. (1991), *A new history of Ireland: bibliographical supplement, 1534–1691* (Oxford).

Coleman, J. (1925), 'A medieval Irish library catalogue' in *Bibliographical Society of Ireland*, ii.

Colley, L. (1992), *Britons: forging the nation, 1707–1837* (New Haven, Conn.).

Collinson, P. (1967), *The Elizabethan Puritan movement* (London).

Comerford, R.V., Cullen, M., Hill, J.R. and Lennon, C. (eds) (1990), *Religion, conflict and coexistence: essays presented to Monsignor Patrick J. Corish* (Dublin).

Conway, A. (1932), *Henry VII's relations with Scotland and Ireland, 1485–1498* (Cambridge).

Conway, C. [Colmcille] (1956, 1957), 'Decline and attempted reform of the Irish Cistercians, 1445–1531' in *Collectanea Ordinis Cisterciensium Reformatorum*, xviii (1956), xix (1957).

Conway, C. [Colmcille] (1958), *The story of Mellifont* (Dublin).

Cosgrove, A. (1975), 'The execution of the earl of Desmond, 1468' in *Journal of the Kerry Archaeological and Historical Society*, viii.

Cosgrove, A. (1981a), *Late medieval Ireland, 1370–1541* (Dublin).

Cosgrove, A. (1981b), 'Medieval Ireland, 1169–1534' in Lee.

Cosgrove, A. (1983), 'Parliament and the Anglo-Irish community: the declaration of 1460' in Cosgrove and McGuire (1983), pp. 25–41.

Cosgrove, A. (ed.) (1985a), *Marriage in Ireland* (Dublin).

Cosgrove, A. (1985b), 'Marriage in medieval Ireland' in Cosgrove (ed.) (1985a), pp. 25–34.

Cosgrove, A. (ed.) (1987), *A new history of Ireland, II. Medieval Ireland, 1169–1534* (Oxford).

Cosgrove, A. (1990–1), 'The writing of Irish medieval history' in *IHS*, xxvii, pp. 97–111.

Cosgrove, A. and McGuire, J.I. (eds) (1983), *Parliament and community: Historical Studies XIV* (Belfast).

Coughlan, P. (ed.) (1989), *Spenser and Ireland: an interdisciplinary perspective* (Cork).

Cowan, I.B. (1978), *Regional aspects of the Scottish Reformation* (London).

Crawford, J.G. (1980), 'The origins of the court of Castle Chamber: a Star Chamber jurisdiction in Ireland' in *American Journal of Legal History*, xxiv.

Crawford, J.G. (1993), *Anglicizing the government of Ireland: the Irish privy council and the expansion of Tudor rule, 1556–1578* (Blackrock).

Cregan, D.F. (1970), 'Irish Catholic admissions to the English Inns of Court, 1558–1625' in *Irish Jurist*, v.

Cruickshank, C.G. (1966), *Elizabeth's army* (2nd edn) (Oxford).

Cunningham, B. (1979), 'Political and social change in the lordships of Clanricard and Thomond, 1569–1641', unpublished MA thesis, National University of Ireland.

Cunningham, B. (1984–5), 'The Composition of Connacht in the lordships of Clanricard and Thomond, 1577–1641' in *IHS*, xxiv.

Cunningham, B. (1986), 'Native culture and political change in Ireland, 1580–1640' in Brady & Gillespie (1986), pp. 148–70.

Curtis, E. (1923), *A history of medieval Ireland* (1st edn) (London).

Curtis, E. (1931), 'The "Bonnaght" of Ulster' in *Hermathena*, xxi, pp. 87–105.

Curtis, E. (1932), 'Richard duke of York as viceroy of Ireland, 1447–60' in *Journal of the Royal Society of Antiquaries of Ireland*, lxii, pp. 158–86.

Curtis, E. (ed.) (1932–43), *Calendar of Ormond deeds, 1172–1350* [etc.] (6 vols) (Dublin).

Curtis, E. (1938), *A history of medieval Ireland from 1086 to 1513* (2nd edn) (London).

Curtis, E. and MacDowell, R.B. (1968), *Irish historical documents, 1172–1922* (2nd edn) (London).

Davies, J. (1969), *A discovery of the true causes why Ireland was not entirely subdued* (London, 1612; facsimile reprint, Shannon, 1969).

Davies, R.R. (1966), 'The twilight of Welsh law, 1284–1536' in *History*, li.

Davies, R.R. (1978), *Lordship and society in the March of Wales, 1282–1400* (Oxford).

Davies, R.R. (ed.) (1988), *The British Isles, 1100–1500: comparisons, contrasts and connections* (Edinburgh).

Davies, R.R. (1994), 'The peoples of Britain and Ireland, 1100–1400. 1. Identities' in *Transactions of the Royal Historical Society*, 6th ser., iv, pp. 1–20.

Dawson, J.E.A. (1987), 'Two kingdoms or three? Ireland in Anglo-Scottish relations in the middle of the sixteenth century' in R.A. Mason (ed.), *Scotland and England, 1286–1815* (Edinburgh).

Dawson, J.E.A. (1989), 'William Cecil and the British dimension of early Elizabethan foreign policy' in *History*, lxxiv, pp. 196–216.

Dawson, J.E.A. (1994), 'Calvinism and the Gaidhealtachd in Scotland' in A. Pettegree, A. Duke and G. Lewis (eds), *Calvinism in Europe, 1540–1620* (Cambridge), pp. 231–53.

Dickens, A.G. (1964), *The English Reformation* (London).

Dickenson, W.C. (1965), *Scotland from the earliest times to 1603* (2nd edn) (London).

Dillon, M. (1966), 'Ceart Uí Néill' in *Studia Celtica*, i.

Dolley, M. (1972), *Medieval Anglo-Irish coins* (London).

Duffy, E. (1992), *The stripping of the altars: traditional religion in England, 1400–1580* (New Haven, Conn.).

Duffy, P.J. (1981), 'The territorial organisation of Gaelic landownership and its transformation in County Monaghan, 1591–1640' in *Irish Geography*, xiv.

Dunham, W.H. (1955), *Lord Hastings' indentured retainers, 1461–1483* (New Haven, Conn.).

Dunlop, R. (1888), 'The plantation of Munster, 1584–1589' in *English Historical Review*, iii.

Dunlop, R. (1891), 'The plantation of Leix and Offaly' in *English Historical Review*, vi.

Dunlop, R. (1902), 'Some aspects of Henry VIII's Irish policy' in Tout & Tait.

Dunlop, R. (1924), 'Sixteenth-century schemes for the plantation of Ulster' in *Scottish Historical Review*, xxi.

Dunne, T.J. (1980), 'The Gaelic response to conquest and colonisation: the evidence of the poetry' in *Studia Hibernica*, xx.

Dunne, T. (ed.) (1987), *The writer as witness: literature as historical evidence* (Cork).

Edwards, D. (1992–3), 'The Butler revolt of 1569' in *IHS*, xxviii.

Edwards, D. (1997), 'Beyond reform: martial law and the Tudor reconquest of Ireland' in *History Ireland*, v(2), pp. 16–21.

Edwards, R.D. (1934), 'Venerable John Travers and the rebellion of Silken Thomas' in *Studies*, xxiii.

Edwards, R.D. (1935), *Church and state in Tudor Ireland* (Dublin).

Edwards, R.D. (1961), 'Ireland, Elizabeth I and the Counter-Reformation' in Bindoff, Hurstfield & Williams.

Edwards, R.D. (1968), 'The Irish Reformation Parliament of Henry VIII, 1536–7' in *Historical Studies*, vi.

Edwards, R.D. (1977), *Ireland in the age of the Tudors: the destruction of Hiberno-Norman civilization* (London).

Edwards, R.D. and Moody, T.W. (1940–1), 'The history of Poynings' law: part I, 1494–1615' in *IHS*, ii.

Edwards, R.D. and Quinn, D.B. (1971), 'Sixteenth-century Ireland, 1485–1603' in Moody.

Edwards, R.W.D. and O'Dowd, M. (1985), *Sources for early modern Irish history, 1534–1641* (Cambridge).

Edwards, Ruth D. (1973), *An atlas of Irish history* (London).

Ellis, H. (1827), *Original letters illustrative of English history* (2nd ser., London).

Ellis, S.G. (1974), 'The Kildare rebellion, 1534', unpublished MA thesis, University of Manchester.

Ellis, S.G. (1976), 'The Kildare rebellion and the early Henrician Reformation' in *Historical Journal*, xix.

Ellis, S.G. (1976–7), 'Tudor policy and the Kildare ascendancy in the lordship of Ireland, 1496–1534' in *IHS*, xx.

Ellis, S.G. (1977), 'Taxation and defence in late medieval Ireland: the survival of scutage' in *Journal of the Royal Society of Antiquaries of Ireland*, cvii.

Ellis, S.G. (1978a), 'The struggle for control of the Irish mint, 1460–*c*. 1506' in *PRIA*, lxxviii C.

Ellis, S.G. (1978b), 'Privy seals of chief governors in Ireland, 1392–1560' in *Bulletin of the Institute of Historical Research*, li.

Ellis, S.G. (1980a), 'Parliaments and great councils, 1483–99: addenda et corrigenda' in *Analecta Hibernica*, xxix.

Ellis, S.G. (1980b), review of Williams 1979, in *Studia Hibernica*, xx.

Ellis, S.G. (1980c), 'Thomas Cromwell and Ireland, 1532–40' in *Historical Journal*, xxiii.

Ellis, S.G. (1980–1a), review of Bradshaw 1979, in *IHS*, xxii.

Ellis, S.G. (1980–1b), 'The Irish customs administration under the early Tudors' in *IHS*, xxii.

Ellis, S.G. (1980–1c), 'An indenture concerning the king's munitions in Ireland, 1532' in *Irish Sword*, xiv.

Ellis, S.G. (1981a), 'Henry VII and Ireland, 1491–1496' in Lydon (ed.) (1981).

Ellis, S.G. (1981b), 'The destruction of the liberties: some further evidence' in *Bulletin of the Institute of Historical Research*, lvi.

Ellis, S.G. (1981c), 'Henry VIII, rebellion and the rule of law' in *Historical Journal*, xxiv.

Ellis, S.G. (1982–3), 'Ioncam na hÉireann, 1384–1534' [The Irish revenue, 1384–1534] in *Studia Hibernica*, xxii/iii, pp. 39–49.

Ellis, S.G. (1983a), 'Parliament and community in Yorkist and Tudor Ireland' in Cosgrove & McGuire.

Ellis, S.G. (1983b), 'England in the Tudor state' in *Historical Journal*, xxvi.

Ellis, S.G. (1984a), 'John Bale, bishop of Ossory, 1552–3' in *Journal of the Butler Society*, ii (3).

Ellis, S.G. (1984b), 'The common bench plea roll of 19 Edward IV (1479–80)' in *Analecta Hibernica*, xxxiii.

Ellis, S.G. (1986a), *Reform and revival: English government in Ireland, 1470–1534* (London).

Ellis, S.G. (1986b), 'Crown, community and government in the English territories, 1450–1575' in *History*, lxxi, pp. 187–204.

Ellis, S.G. (1990), 'Economic problems of the church: why the Reformation failed in Ireland' in *Journal of Ecclesiastical History*, xli, pp. 239–65.

Ellis, S.G. (1990–1), 'Historiographical debate: representations of the past in Ireland: whose past and whose present?' in *IHS*, xxvii, pp. 289–308.

Ellis, S.G. (1991), 'Ionadaíocht i bparlaimint na hÉireann ag deireadh na meán-aoise' in *PRIA*, xci C.

Ellis, S.G. (1992a), 'A border baron and the Tudor state: the rise and fall of Lord Dacre of the North' in *Historical Journal*, xxxv, pp. 253–77.

Ellis, S.G. (1992b), 'The shock of the new' in *The Irish Review*, no. 12 (spring/summer 1992), pp. 141–3.

Ellis, S.G. (1994) 'Nationalist historiography and the English and Gaelic worlds in the late middle ages' in Brady 1994b, pp. 161–80.

Ellis, S.G. (1995a), *Tudor frontiers and noble power: the making of the British state* (Oxford).

Ellis, S.G. (1995b), 'Tudor state formation and the shaping of the British Isles' in Ellis & Barber (1995), pp. 40–63.

Ellis, S.G. (1995c), 'Frontiers and power in the early Tudor state' in *History Today*, xlv (4), pp. 35–42.

Ellis, S.G. (1996a), 'Writing Irish history: revisionism, colonialism, and the British Isles' in *The Irish Review*, xix, pp. 1–21.

Ellis, S.G. (1996b), 'The Tudors and the origins of the modern Irish states' in Bartlett & Jeffery (1996), pp. 116–35.

Ellis, S.G. and Barber, S. (eds) (1995), *Conquest and union: fashioning a British state, 1485–1725* (London).

Elton, G.R. (1962), *Henry VIII* (Historical Association Pamphlet, London).

Elton, G.R. (1969), *England under the Tudors* (2nd edn) (London).

Elton, G.R. (1977), *Reform and Reformation: England 1509–58* (London).

Elton, G.R. (1982), *The Tudor constitution: documents and commentary* (2nd edn) (Cambridge).

Empey, C.A. (1970–1), 'The Butler lordship' in *Journal of the Butler Society*, i.

Empey, C.A. (1984), 'From rags to riches: Piers Butler, earl of Ormond, 1515–39' in *Journal of the Butler Society*, ii (3).

Empey, C. A. (1984–5), 'The sacred and the secular: the Augustinian priory of Kells in Ossory, 1193–1541' in *IHS*, xxiv.

Empey, C.A. and Simms, K. (1975), 'The ordinances of the White Earl and the problem of coign in the later middle ages' in *PRIA*, lxxv C.

Falls, C. (1950), *Elizabeth's Irish wars* (London).

Farrell, B. (ed.) (1973), *The Irish parliamentary tradition* (Dublin).

Fennell, D. (1994), 'Against revisionism' in Brady (1994b), pp. 181–90.

Flanagan, L. (1988), *Ireland's Armada legacy* (Dublin).

Fletcher, A. (1983), *Tudor rebellions* (3rd edn) (London).

Flower, Robin (1947), *The Irish tradition* (Oxford).

Ford, A. (1985), *The Protestant Reformation in Ireland, 1590–1641* (Frankfurt).

Ford, A. (1997), *The Protestant Reformation in Ireland, 1590–1641* (2nd edn), (Dublin).

Frame, R.F. (1975), 'English officials and Irish chiefs in the fourteenth century' in *English Historical Review*, xc.

Frame, R.F. (1977), 'Power and society in the lordship of Ireland, 1272–1377' in *Past & Present*, no. 76.

Frame, R.F. (1981), *Colonial Ireland, 1169–1369* (Dublin).

Frame, R.F. (1982), *English lordship in Ireland, 1318–1361* (Oxford).

Frame, R. (1992), 'Commissions of the peace in Ireland, 1302–1461' in *Analecta Hibernica*, xxxv (1992), pp. 1–43.

Freeman, A.M. (ed.) (1944), *Annála Connacht: the annals of Connacht, 1224–1544* (Dublin).

Fryde, E.B., Greenway, D.E., Porter, S. and Roy, I. (1986), *Handbook of British chronology* (3rd edn) (London).

Gairdner, J. (ed.) (1861–3), *Letters and papers illustrative of the reigns of Richard III and Henry VII* (2 vols) (London).

Giblin, C. (ed.) (1964), *Irish Franciscan mission to Scotland, 1619–1646: documents from the Roman Archives* (Dublin).

Gilbert, J.T. (1865), *History of the viceroys of Ireland* (Dublin).

Gilbert, J.T. (ed.) (1897), 'Acts of the privy council in Ireland, 1556–71' in *Historical Manuscripts Commission, 15th report*, app. iii (London).

Gillespie, R. (1991), *The transformation of the Irish economy, 1550–1700* (Dundalk).

Gillingham, J. (1981), *The Wars of the Roses: peace and conflict in fifteenth-century England* (London).

Gillingham, J. (1995), 'Foundations of a disunited kingdom' in A. Grant and K. Stringer (eds), *Uniting the kingdom? The making of British history* (London), pp. 48–64.

Goodman, A. (1981), *The Wars of the Roses: military activity and English society, 1452–97* (London).

Gorman, V. (1985), 'Richard, duke of York, and the development of an Irish faction' in *PRIA*, lxxxv C, pp. 169–79.

Grant, A. (1984), *Independence and nationhood: Scotland, 1306–1469* (London).

Grant, A. (1988), 'Scotland's "Celtic fringe" in the late middle ages: the Macdonald lords of the Isles and the kingdom of Scotland' in Davies (ed.) (1988), pp. 118–41.

Green, A.S. (1909), *The making of Ireland and its undoing, 1200–1600* (London).

Griffith, M.C. (1940–1), 'The Talbot–Ormond struggle for control of the Anglo-Irish government, 1414–47' in *IHS*, ii.

Griffiths, R.A. (1981), *The reign of King Henry VI* (London).

Griffiths, R.A. (1986), 'The English realm and dominions and the king's subjects in the later middle ages' in John Rowe (ed.) Aspects of government and society in later medieval England: essays in honour of J.R. Lander (Toronto, 1986), pp. 83–105.

Guy, J. (1988), *Tudor England* (Oxford).

Gwynn, A. (1946), *The medieval province of Armagh, 1470–1545* (Dundalk).

Gwynn, A. (1968), *Anglo-Irish church life 14th and 15th centuries* (A History of Irish Catholicism, ii, pt. 4) (Dublin).

Gwynn, A. and Hadcock, R.N. (1970), *Medieval religious houses: Ireland* (London).

Haigh, C. (1975), *Reformation and resistance in Tudor Lancashire* (Cambridge).

Haigh, C. (1981), 'From monopoly to minority: catholicism in early modern England' in *Transactions of the Royal Historical Society*, 5th ser., xxxi, pp. 129–47.

Haigh, C. (1982), 'The recent historiography of the English Reformation' in *Historical Journal*, xxv.

Haigh, C. (1993), *English Reformations: religion, politics and society under the Tudors* (Oxford).

Haigh, P.A. (1995), *The military campaigns of the Wars of the Roses* (Stroud).

Hammerstein, H. (1971), 'Aspects of the continental education of Irish students in the reign of Queen Elizabeth I' in *Historical Studies*, viii.

Hardiman, J. (ed.) (1843), 'Statutes of Kilkenny' in *Tracts relating to Ireland* ii (Dublin).

Harkness, D.W. and O'Dowd, M. (eds) (1981), *The town in Ireland: Historical Studies XIII* (Belfast).

Harris, W. (ed.) (1747), *Hibernica: or some ancient pieces relating to Ireland* (1st edn) (Dublin).

Hatcher, J. (1977), *Plague, population and the English economy, 1348–1530* (London).

Haugaard, W.P. (1968), *Elizabeth and the English Reformation* (Cambridge).

Hayden, M.T. (1915), 'Lambert Simnel in Ireland' in *Studies*, iv.

Hayes-McCoy, G.A. (1937), *Scots mercenary forces in Ireland, 1565–1603* (Dublin).

Hayes-McCoy, G.A. (1938–9), 'The early history of guns in Ireland' in *Galway Archaeological Society Journal*, xviii.

Hayes-McCoy, G.A. (1949–53), 'The army of Ulster, 1593–1601' in *Irish Sword*, i.

Hayes-McCoy, G.A. (1963), 'Gaelic society in Ireland in the late sixteenth century' in *Historical Studies*, iv.

Hayes-McCoy, G.A. (1969), *Irish battles* (London).

Healy, J. (1908), *History of the diocese of Meath*, i.

Hennessy, W.M. (ed.) (1871), *The annals of Loch Cé* (2 vols) (London).

Hepburn, A.C. (ed.) (1978), *Minorities in history: Historical Studies XII* (London).

Herbert, W. (1992), *Croftus sive de Hibernia liber*, ed. A. Keaveney and J.A. Madden (Dublin).

Hill, J.M. (1993), *Fire and sword: Sorley Boy MacDonnell and the rise of Clan Ian More, 1538–1590* (London).

Hogan, J. (1947), 'Shane O'Neill comes to the court of Elizabeth' in Pender.

Hore, H.F. and Graves, J. (eds) (1870), *The social state of the southern and eastern counties of Ireland in the sixteenth century* (Dublin).

Irwin, L. (1977), 'The Irish presidency courts, 1569–1672' in *Irish Jurist*, n.s., xii.

Ives, E.W. (1970), 'Patronage at the court of Henry VIII: the case of Sir Ralph Egerton of Ridley' in *Bulletin of the John Rylands Library*, lii.

Ives, E.W. (1979), *Faction in Tudor England* (Historical Association Pamphlet) (London).

Jacob, E.F. (1961), *The fifteenth century, 1399–1485* (Oxford).

James, M.E. (1964–5), 'The murder at Cocklodge, 28th April 1489' in *Durham University Journal*, lvii.

James, M.E. (1966), *A Tudor magnate and the Tudor state, Henry Percy fifth earl of Northumberland* (Borthwick Paper) (York).

James, M.E. (1973), 'The concept of order and the Northern Rising' in *Past & Present*, no. 60.

James, M.E. (1978), *English politics and the concept of honour, 1485–1642* (*Past & Present* supplement 3) (Oxford).

Jefferies, H. (1988–9), 'The Irish parliament of 1560: the Anglican reforms authorised' in *IHS*, xxvi.

Jefferies, H. (1997a), *Priests and prelates of Armagh in the age of Reformations, 1518–1558* (Dublin).

Jefferies, H. (1997b), 'The diocese of Dromore on the eve of the Tudor Reformation' in L. Proudfoot (ed.), *Down history and society: interdisciplinary essays on the history of an Irish county* (Dublin), pp. 123–40.

Jefferies, H. (1998a), 'The Armagh registers and the re-writing of Irish church history on the eve of the Tudor Reformations' in *Seanchas Ard Mhacha*, xvii.

Jefferies, H. (1998b), 'The laity in the parishes of Armagh *inter Anglicos* on the eve of the Tudor Reformations' in *Archivium Hibernicum*, lii.

Jenkins, P. (1995), 'The anglican church and the unity of Britain: the Welsh experience, 1560–1714' in Ellis & Barber (1995), pp. 115–38.

Johnson, P.A. (1988), *Duke Richard of York, 1411–1460* (Oxford).

Jones, N.L. (1982), *Faith by statute: parliament and the settlement of religion, 1559* (London).

Kearney, H. (1989), *The British Isles: a history of four nations* (Cambridge).

Kearney, H.F. (1959), *Strafford in Ireland, 1633–41: a study in absolutism* (Manchester).

Keen, M.H. (1973), *England in the later middle ages* (London).

Kenny, C. (1992), *King's Inns and the kingdom of Ireland: the Irish 'Inn of court', 1541–1800* (Blackrock).

Kirk, J. (1989), *Patterns of reform: continuity and change in the Reformation kirk* (Edinburgh).

Knott, E. (ed.) (1922–6), *The bardic poems of Tadhg Dall Ó Huiginn (1550–91)* (2 vols) (London).

Knowles, D. (1959), *The religious orders in England*, iii.

Lander, J.R. (1980), *Government and community: England, 1450–1509* (London).

Lascelles, R. (ed.) (1852), *Liber munerum publicorum Hiberniae* (2 vols) (London).

Leask, H.G. (1946), *Irish castles* (Dundalk).

Leask, H.G. (1960), *Irish churches and monastic buildings. III Medieval Gothic, the last phases* (Dundalk).

Lee, J. (ed.) (1981), *Irish historiography, 1970–79* (Cork).

Leerssen, J. (1994), *The Contention of the Bards (Iomarbhágh na bhFileadh) and its place in Irish political and literary history* (London).

Leerssen, J. (1996), *Mere Irish and Fíor-Ghael: studies in the idea of Irish nationality* (Cork).

Lennon, C. (1975), 'Recusancy and the Dublin Stanihursts' in *Archivium Hibernicum*, xxxiii.

Lennon, C. (1978–9), 'Richard Stanihurst (1547–1618) and Old English identity' in *IHS*, xxi.

Lennon, C. (1981), *Richard Stanihurst, the Dubliner, 1547–1618* (Dublin).

Lennon, C. (1989), *The lords of Dublin in the age of the Reformation* (Blackrock).

Lennon, C. (1991), 'The chantries in the Irish Reformation: the case of St. Anne's Guild, Dublin, 1550–1630' in Comerford *et al.* (eds) (1990), pp. 6–25.

Lennon, C. (1994), *Sixteenth-century Ireland: the incomplete conquest* (Dublin).

Letters and papers, foreign and domestic, Henry VIII (=LP) (21 vols) (London, 1862–1932).

Loades, D.M. (1979), *The reign of Mary Tudor: politics, government, and religion in England, 1553–1558* (London).

Loeber, R. (1991), *The geography and practice of English colonisation in Ireland from 1534 to 1609* (Athlone).

Longfield, A.K. (1929), *Anglo-Irish trade in the sixteenth century* (London).

Longfield, A.K. (ed.) (1960), *Fitzwilliam accounts, 1560–65* (Dublin).

Lydon, J.F. (1972a), *Ireland in the later middle ages* (Dublin).

Lydon, J.F. (1972b), *The lordship of Ireland in the middle ages* (Dublin).

Lydon, J.F. (ed.) (1981), *England and Ireland in the later middle ages* (Dublin).

Lydon, J.F. (ed.) (1984), *The English in medieval Ireland* (Dublin).

Lydon, J.F. (1994–5), 'Ireland and the English crown, 1191–1541' in *IHS*, xxix, pp. 281–94.

Lydon, J.F. (1995), '"Ireland corporate of itself": the parliament of 1460' in *History Ireland*, iii (2), pp. 9–12.

Lynch, A. (1982), 'The province and diocese of Armagh, 1417–71' in *Irish History Thesis Abstracts*, iii.

Lynch, M. (1981), *Edinburgh and the Reformation* (Edinburgh).

MacCaffrey, W. (1969), *The shaping of the Elizabethan regime* (London).

MacCaffrey, W. (1992), *Elizabeth I, war and politics, 1588–1603* (Princeton).

MacCarthy, B. (ed.) (1895), *Annála Uladh; Annals of Ulster*, iii (Dublin).

MacCarthy-Morrogh, M. (1986), *The Munster plantation: English migration to southern Ireland, 1583–1641* (Oxford).

Mac Craith, M. (1995), 'The Gaelic reaction to the Reformation' in Ellis & Barber (1995), pp. 139–61.

Mac Craith, M. (1996), 'Litríocht an 17ú hAois: Tonnbhriseadh an tSeangh-náthaimh nó Tonnchruthú an Nuaghnáthaimh' in R. Ó hUiginn (ed.), *Léann na Gaeilge: súil siar, súil chun cinn* (Maynooth, 1996), pp. 50–82.

MacCurtain, M. (1958), 'Dhá dhán le Risteard Buitléar' in *Éigse*, ix.

MacCurtain, M. (1972), *Tudor and Stuart Ireland* (Dublin).

MacCurtain, M. (1975), 'The fall of the house of Desmond' in *Kerry Archaeological Society Journal*, viii.

MacCurtain, M. (1985), 'Marriage in Tudor Ireland' in Cosgrove (ed.) (1985a), pp. 51–66.

MacCurtain, M. and O'Dowd, M. (eds) (1991), *Women in early modern Ireland* (Edinburgh).

MacDonald, A.M. (ed.) (1911), *The MacDonald collection of Gaelic poetry* (Inverness).

Macinnes, A. (1988), 'Scottish Gaeldom, 1638–1651: the vernacular response to the Covenanting dynamic' in J. Dwyer, R.A. Mason and A. Murdoch (eds), *New perspectives on the politics and culture of early modern Scotland* (Edinburgh), pp. 59–94.

Mackenzie, J. (1953), 'Treaty between Argyll and O'Donnell' in *Scottish Gaelic Studies*, vii.

Mac Niocaill, G. (ed.) (1992), *Crown surveys of lands, 1540–41 with the Kildare Rental begun in 1518* (Dublin).

Mac Niocaill, G. (1964a), *Na Buirgéisí* (2 vols) (Dublin).

Mac Niocaill, G. (ed.) (1964b), *The Red Book of the earls of Kildare* (Dublin).

Mac Niocaill, G. (1975), 'Land transfer in sixteenth-century Thomond: the case of Domhnall Óg Ó Cearnaigh' in *North Munster Antiquarian Journal*, xvii.

Mac Niocaill, G. (1981), 'Socio-economic problems of the late medieval Irish town' in Harkness & O'Dowd.

Mac Niocaill, G. (1984), 'The interaction of laws' in Lydon.

McGurk, J.J.N. (1979), 'The fall of the noble house of Desmond, 1579–83' in *History Today*, xxix.

McGurk, J. (1997), *The Elizabethan conquest of Ireland: the 1590s crisis* (Manchester).

McKenna, L. (ed.) (1939–40), *Aithdioghluim Dána* (2 vols) (Dublin).

McNeill, C. (ed.) (1931a), *Kilkenny city records; Liber primus Kilkenniensis* (Dublin).

McNeill, C. (ed.) (1931b), 'Lord Chancellor Gerrard's notes of his report on Ireland' in *Analecta Hibernica*, ii.

McNeill, C. (ed.) (1950), *Calendar of Archbishop Alen's register, c. 1172–1534* (Dublin).

Martin, F.X. (1967), 'Ireland, the Renaissance and the Counter-Reformation' in *Topic 13: studies in Irish history* (Washington).

Mathew, D. (1933), *The Celtic peoples and Renaissance Europe* (London).

Matthew, E. (1984), 'The financing of the lordship of Ireland under Henry V and Henry VI' in A.J. Pollard (ed.), *Property and politics: essays in later medieval English history* (Gloucester), pp. 97–115.

Matthew, E. (1994), 'The governing of the Lancastrian lordship of Ireland in the time of James Butler, fourth earl of Ormond c. 1420–1452 (unpublished PhD thesis, Durham University).

Mattingley, G. (1955), *Renaissance diplomacy* (London).

Meigs, S.A. (1997), *The Reformations in Ireland: tradition and confessionalism, 1400–1690* (London).

Moody, T.W. (1939–40), 'The Irish parliament under Elizabeth and James I: a general survey' in *PRIA*, xlv C.

Moody, T.W. (ed.) (1971), *Irish historiography, 1936–70* (Dublin).

Moody, T.W., Martin, F.X. and Byrne, F.J. (eds) (1976), *A new history of Ireland, III. Early modern Ireland, 1534–1691* (Oxford) (= *NHI*).

Moody, T.W., Martin, F.X. and Byrne, F.J. (eds) (1984), *A new history of Ireland, IX. Maps, Genealogies, Lists* (Oxford) (= *NHI*).

Mooney, C. (1969), *The church in Gaelic Ireland 13th to 15th centuries* (A History of Irish Catholicism, ii. pt. 5) (Dublin).

Morgan, H. (1985), 'The colonial venture of Sir Thomas Smith, 1571–1575' in *Historical Journal*, xxviii.

Morgan, H. (1987), 'Extradition and treason-trial of a Gaelic lord: the case of Brian O'Rourke' in *The Irish Jurist*, xxii (new ser.), pp. 285–301.

Morgan, H. (1993a), 'Hugh O'Neill and the Nine Years War in Tudor Ireland' in *Historical Journal*, xxxvi, pp. 1–17.

Morgan, H. (1993b), *Tyrone's rebellion: the outbreak of the Nine Years War in Tudor Ireland* (London).

Morgan, H. (1995), 'The fall of Sir John Perrot' in J. Guy (ed.), *The reign of Elizabeth I: court and culture in the last decade* (Cambridge), pp. 109–25.

Morgan, P.T.J. (1966), 'The government of Calais, 1485–1558' (unpublished DPhil thesis, Oxford University).

Morrin, J. (ed.) (1861), *Calendar of patent and close rolls of chancery in Ireland, Henry VIII to 18th Elizabeth* (Dublin).

Munro, J. and R.W. (eds) (1986), *Acts of the Lords of the Isles, 1336–1493* (Edinburgh).

Murphy, G. (ed.) (1948–52), 'Poems of exile by Uilliam Nuinseann Mac Barúin Dealbhna' in *Éigse*, vi.

Murray, J. (1989), 'Archbishop Alen, Tudor reform and the Kildare rebellion' in *PRIA*, lxxxix, sect. pp. 1–16.

Murray, J. (1991–2), 'The sources of clerical income in the Tudor diocese of Dublin, c. 1530–1600' in *Archivium Hibernicum*, xli, pp. 139–60.

Murray, J. (1992–3), 'The Church of Ireland: a critical bibliography . . . I, 1536–1603' in *IHS*, xxviii, pp. 345–52.

Murray, J. (1995), 'Ecclesiastical justice and the enforcement of the reformation: the case of Archbishop Browne and the clergy of Dublin' in A. Ford, J. McGuire and K. Milne (eds), *As by law established: the Church of Ireland since the reformation* (Dublin).

Murray, J. (1996), 'Historical revisit: R. Dudley Edwards, *Church and state in Tudor Ireland*' in *IHS*, xxx (1996–7), pp. 233–41.

Murray, L.P. (ed.) (1929–32), 'Calendar of the register of Primate Dowdall' in *Journal of the County Louth Archaeological Society*, xii.

Newton, Robert (1974), 'The decay of the borders: Tudor Northumberland in transition' in C.W. Chalklin and M.A. Havinden (eds), *Rural change and urban growth, 1500–1800* (London).

Nicholls, K.W. (1970), 'Some documents on Irish law and custom in the sixteenth century' in *Analecta Hibernica*, xxvi.

Nicholls, K.W. (1972), *Gaelic and gaelicised Ireland in the middle ages* (Dublin).

Nicholls, K.W. (1976), *Land law and society in sixteenth-century Ireland* (Dublin).

Nicholls, K.W. (1982), 'Anglo-French Ireland and after' in *Peritia*, i.

Nicholls, K.W. (1991), 'Irishwomen and property in the sixteenth century' in MacCurtain and O'Dowd (eds) (1991), pp. 17–31.

Nicholson, R. (1974), *Scotland: the later middle ages* (Edinburgh).

Ó Buachalla, B. (1983), 'Na Stíobhartaigh agus an tAos Léinn: Cing Séamas' in *PRIA*, lxxxiii C, pp. 81–134.

Ó Buachalla, B. (1992), 'Poetry and politics in early modern Ireland' in *Eighteenth-century Ireland: Iris an dá chultúr*, vii, pp. 149–75.

Ó Cléirigh, C. (1996), 'The O'Connor Faly lordship of Offaly, 1395–1513' in *PRIA*, xcvi C, pp. 87–102.

O'Connor, E. (1989), 'The rebellion of James Eustace, Viscount Baltinglass, 1580–81' (MA thesis, St Patrick's College, Maynooth).

Ó Cuív, B. (1974), 'A sixteenth-century political poem' in *Éigse*, xv, pp. 261–76.

Ó Danachair, C. (1979), 'Irish tower houses and their regional distribution' in *Béalóideas*, xlv–vii, pp. 158–63.

Ó Doibhlin, E.(1970), 'Ceart Uí Néill' in *Seanchas Ard Mhacha*, v.

Ó Donnchadha, T. (ed.) (1931), *Leabhar Cloinne Aodha Buidhe* (Dublin).

O'Donovan, J. (ed.) (1851), *Annála ríoghachta Éireann: annals of the kingdom of Ireland by the Four Masters from the earliest period to the year 1616* (7 vols) (Dublin).

O'Dowd, M. (1986), 'Gaelic economy and society' in Brady & Gillespie (eds) (1986), pp. 120–47.

O'Neill, T. (1987), *Merchants and mariners in medieval Ireland* (Dublin).

O'Rahilly, T.F. (1942), 'A poem by Piaras Feiritéar' in *Ériu*, xiii, pp. 113–18.

O Riordan, M. (1990), *The Gaelic mind and the collapse of the Gaelic world* (Cork).

Ó Siochrú, M. (1996), 'Foreign involvement in the revolt of Silken Thomas, 1534–5' in *PRIA*, xcvi C, pp. 49–62.

Otway-Ruthven, A.J. (1951), 'The organization of Anglo-Irish agriculture in the middle ages' in *Journal of the Royal Society of Antiquaries of Ireland*, lxxxi.

Otway-Ruthven, A.J. (1980), *A history of medieval Ireland* (2nd edn) (London).

Palliser, D.M. (1983), *The age of Elizabeth: England under the later Tudors, 1547–1603* (London).

Palmer, W. (1994), *The problem of Ireland in Tudor foreign policy, 1485–1603* (Woodbridge).

Pender, S. (ed.) (1947), *Essays and studies presented to Professor Tadhg Ua Donnchadha (Torna)* (Cork).

Piveronus, P.J. (1979), 'Sir Warham St. Leger and the first Munster plantation, 1568–69' in *Éire-Ireland*, xiv.

Pollard, A.J. (1977), 'The tyranny of Richard III' in *Journal of Medieval History*, iii.

Pollard, A.J. (1988), *The Wars of the Roses* (Basingstoke).

Potter, D. (1983), 'French intrigue in Ireland during the reign of Henri II, 1547–1559' in *The International History Review*, v.

Price, L. (1932), 'Armed forces of Irish chiefs in the early sixteenth century' in *Journal of the Royal Society of Antiquaries of Ireland*, lxii, pp. 202–7.

Pugh, T.B. (1986), 'Richard Plantagenet (1411–60), duke of York, as king's lieutenant in France and Ireland' in J.G. Rowe (ed.), *Aspects of late medieval government and society* (Toronto), pp. 107–41.

Quiggin, E.C. (1937), *Poems from the Book of the Dean of Lismore*, ed. J. Fraser (Cambridge).

Quinn, D.B. (1933), 'Tudor rule in Ireland, 1485–1547', unpublished PhD thesis, University of London.

Quinn, D.B. (1935a), 'The Irish parliamentary subsidy in the fifteenth and sixteenth centuries' in *PRIA*, xlii C.

Quinn, D.B. (1935b), 'Henry Fitzroy, duke of Richmond, and his connexion with Ireland, 1529–30' in *Bulletin of the Institute of Historical Research*, xii.

Quinn, D.B. (1935c), *Ulster, 1460–1550* (Belfast).

Quinn, D.B. (1940), *The voyages and colonizing enterprise of Sir Humphrey Gilbert* (London).

Quinn, D.B. (1940–1), 'The early interpretation of Poynings' law, 1494–1534' in *IHS*, ii.

Quinn, D.B. (ed.) (1941a), 'Guide to English financial records for Irish history, 1461–1558 with illustrative extracts, 1461–1509' in *Analecta Hibernica*, x.

Quinn, D.B. (ed.) (1941b), 'The bills and statutes of the Irish parliaments of Henry VII and Henry VIII' in *Analecta Hibernica*, x.

Quinn, D.B. (1943), 'Government printing and the publication of the Irish statutes' in *PRIA*, xlix C.

Quinn, D.B. (1945), 'Sir Thomas Smith (1513–1577) and the beginnings of English colonial theory' in *Proceedings of the American Philosophical Society*, lxxxix.

Quinn, D.B. (1946–7), 'Edward Walshes's "Conjectures" concerning the state of Ireland [1552]' in *IHS*, v.

Quinn, D.B. (1958), 'Ireland and sixteenth century European expansion' in *Historical Studies*, i.

Quinn, D.B. (1960–1), 'Henry VIII and Ireland, 1509–34' in *IHS*, xii.

Quinn, D.B. (1966a), *The Elizabethans and the Irish* (Ithaca, NY).

Quinn, D.B. (1966b), 'The Munster plantation: problems and opportunities' in *Cork Historical and Archaeological Society Journal*, lxxi.

Quinn, D.B. (ed.) (1967), 'Calendar of the Irish council book, 1581–1586' in *Analecta Hibernica*, xxiv.

Quinn, D.B. (1976a), 'Renaissance influences in English colonization' in *Transactions of the Royal Historical Society*, 5th ser., xxvi.

Quinn, D.B. (1976b), 'Edward Walshe's *The office and duety in fighting for our countrey* (1545)' in *Irish Book Lore*, iii.

Rae, T.I. (1966), *The administration of the Scottish frontier, 1513–1603* (Edinburgh).

Ranger, T.O. (1956–7), 'Richard Boyle and the making of an Irish fortune, 1588–1614' in *IHS*, x.

Read, C. (1959), *Bibliography of British History: the Tudor period, 1485–1603* (2nd edn) (Oxford).

Reid, R.R. (1921), *The king's council in the north* (London).

Report of the Deputy Keeper of the Public Records in Ireland (Dublin, 1869–).

Richardson, H.G. (1962), 'Irish revenue, 1278–1384' in *PRIA*, lxii C.

Richardson, H.G. and Sayles, G.O. (1952), *The Irish parliament in the middle ages* (Philadelphia).

Ronan, M.V. (1930), *The Reformation in Ireland under Elizabeth, 1558–80* (London).

Ross, C. (1974), *Edward IV* (London).

Ross, N. (ed.) (1939), *Heroic poetry from the Book of the Dean of Lismore* (Edinburgh).

Sayles, G.O. (1951), 'The vindication of the earl of Kildare from treason in 1496' in *IHS*, vii.

Scarisbrick, J.J. (1968), *Henry VIII* (London).

Seymour, St J.D. (1929), *Anglo-Irish literature, 1200–1582* (Cambridge).

Sheehan, A.J. (1982), 'The population of the plantation of Munster: Quinn reconsidered' in *Cork Historical and Archaeological Society Journal*, lxxxvii.

Sheehan, A.J. (1982–3a), 'Official reaction to native land claims in the plantation of Munster' in *IHS*, xxiii.

Sheehan, A.J. (1982–3b), 'The overthrow of the plantation of Munster in October 1598' in *Irish Sword*, xv.

Sheehan, A.J. (1983a), 'The recusancy revolt of 1603: a reinterpretation' in *Archivium Hibernicum*, xxxviii.

Sheehan, A.J. (1983b), 'The killing of the earl of Desmond, November 1583' in *Cork Historical and Archaeological Society Journal*, lxxxviii.

Sheehan, A. (1986), 'Irish towns in a period of change, 1558–1625' in Brady & Gillespie (eds) (1986).

Sheehan, A. (1990), 'Irish revenues and English subventions, 1559–1622' in *PRIA*, xc C, pp. 35–65.

Silke, J.J. (1959), 'The Irish appeal of 1593 to Spain' in *Irish Ecclesiastical Record*, 5th ser., xcii.

Silke, J.J. (1966), *Ireland and Europe, 1559–1607* (Dublin).

Silke, J.J. (1970), *Kinsale: the Spanish intervention in Ireland at the end of the Elizabethan wars* (Liverpool).

Simms, K. (1975–6), 'Warfare in the medieval Gaelic lordships' in *Irish Sword*, xii.

Simms, K. (1981), ' "The king's friend": O'Neill, the crown and the earldom of Ulster' in Lydon.

Simms, K. (1987a), *From kings to warlords: the changing political structure of Gaelic Ireland in the later middle ages* (Woodbridge).

Simms, K. (1987b), 'Bardic poetry as a historical source' in Dunne (ed.) (1987), pp. 58–75.

Simms, K. (1996), 'Gaelic warfare in the middle ages' in Bartlett and Jeffery (eds) (1996), pp. 99–115.

Smith, A.G.R. (1984), *The emergence of a nation state: the commonwealth of England, 1529–1660* (London).

Smout, T.C. (1972), *A history of the Scottish people, 1560–1830* (London).

Spenser, E. (1970), *A view of the present state of Ireland*, ed. W.L. Renwick (Oxford).

State papers, Henry VIII (11 vols) (London, 1830–52) (= *StP*).

Stevenson, D. (1980), *Alasdair MacColla and the Highland Problem in the seventeenth century* (Edinburgh).

Storey, R.L. (1957), 'The Wardens of the Marches of England towards Scotland, 1377–1489' in *English Historical Review*, lxxii.

The statutes at large passed in the parliaments held in Ireland (20 vols) (Dublin, 1786–1801).

Thompson, M.W. (1987), *The decline of the castle* (Cambridge).

Thomson, R.L. (ed.) (1970), *Foirm na n-Urrnuidheadh: John Carswell's Gaelic translation of the Book of Common Order* (Edinburgh).

Tout, T.F. and Tait J. (eds) (1902), *Historical essays* (London).

Treadwell, V. (1966), 'The Irish parliament of 1569–71' in *PRIA*, lxv C.

Treadwell, V. (1976–7), 'The Irish customs administration in the sixteenth century' in *IHS*, xx.

Treadwell, V. (1985), 'Sir John Perrot and the Irish parliament of 1585–6' in *PRIA*, lxxxv C, pp. 259–308.

Vale, M.G.A. (1970), *English Gascony, 1399–1453* (Oxford).

Valor (1741), *Valor beneficiorum ecclesiasticorum in Hibernia*, printed for Edward Exshaw (Dublin).

Vergil, P. (1950), *Anglica Historia*, ed. D. Hay (London).

Walsh, K. (1993), 'In the wake of Reformation and Counter-Reformation: Ireland's belated reception of Renaissance humanism?' in Otto Harrassowitz (ed.), *Die Renaissance im Blick der Nationen Europas* (Wiesbaden), pp. 33–50.

Walshe, H.C. (1988–9), 'Enforcing the Elizabethan settlement: the vicissitudes of Hugh Brady, bishop of Meath, 1563–84' in *IHS*, xxvi, pp. 352–76.

Walshe, H.C. (1990), 'The rebellion of William Nugent, 1581' in Comerford *et al.* (eds) (1990), pp. 26–52.

Watson W.J. (ed.) (1937), *Scottish verse from the Book of the Dean of Lismore* (Edinburgh).

Watt, J. (1972), *The church in medieval Ireland* (Dublin).

Weiss, M. (1976), 'A power in the north? The Percies in the fifteenth century' in *Historical Journal*, xix.

Wernham, R.B. (1966), *Before the Armada: the growth of English foreign policy, 1485–1588* (London).

Whelan, K. (1990), 'Clio agus Caitlín Ní Uallacháin' in *Oghma 2* (Dublin), pp. 9–19.

White, D.G. (1957–8), 'Henry VIII's Irish kerne in France and Scotland, 1544–1545' in *Irish Sword*, iii.

White, D.G. (1964–5), 'The reign of Edward VI in Ireland: some political, social and economic aspects' in *IHS*, xiv.

White, N.B. (ed.) (1943), *Extents of Irish monastic possessions, 1540–41* (Dublin).

Wilkie, W.E. (1974), *The Cardinal Protectors of England: Rome and the Tudors before the Reformation* (Cambridge).

Williams, G. (1967), *Welsh Reformation essays* (Cardiff).

Williams, P. (1958), *The council in the marches of Wales under Elizabeth I* (Cardiff).

Williams, P. (1979), *The Tudor regime* (Oxford).

Williams, P. (1995), *The later Tudors: England, 1547–1603* (Oxford).

Wolffe, B.P. (1972), 'The personal rule of Henry VI' in Chrimes, Ross & Griffiths.

Wood, H. (1928), 'Two chief governors of Ireland at the same time' in *Journal of the Royal Society of Antiquaries of Ireland*, lviii, pp. 156–7.

Woodward, D. (1970), *The trade of Elizabethan Chester* (Hull).

Youings, J. (1971), *The dissolution of the monasteries* (London).

INDEX

(The index excludes persons who appear only in the Tables.)

417